CONTENTS

Section

In addition to providing a wide ranging bank of real past exam questions, we have also included in this edition:

- An analysis of all of the recent new syllabus examination papers.
- Paper specific information and advice on exam technique.
- Our recommended approach to make your revision for this particular subject as effective as possible.

  This includes step by step guidance on how best to use our Kaplan material (Complete text, pocket notes and exam kit) at this stage in your studies.
- Enhanced tutorial answers packed with specific key answer tips, technical tutorial notes and exam technique tips from our experienced tutors.
- Complementary online resources including full tutor debriefs and question assistance to point you in the right direction when you get stuck.

June and December 2011, June and December 2012 – Real examination questions

The real June 2011, December 2011, June 2012 and December 2012 exam papers are available on Kaplan EN-gage at:

www.MyKaplan.co.uk

You will find a wealth of other resources to help you with your studies on the following sites:
www.MyKaplan.co.uk
www.accaglobal.com/students/

Quality and accuracy are of the utmost importance to us so if you spot an error in any of our products, please send an email to mykaplanreporting@kaplan.com with full details, or follow the link to the feedback form in MyKaplan.

Our Quality Co-ordinator will work with our technical team to verify the error and take action to ensure it is corrected in future editions.

INDEX TO QUESTIONS AND ANSWERS

INTRODUCTION

Paper P1: Governance, Risk and Ethics was first tested in December 2007 under its previous name Professional Accountant. At that time it was a new paper, added to the syllabus to place ethics and governance prominently within the qualification.

Recent research and feedback from employers on ACCA's 2010 syllabus indicates risk is an important issue, especially in the current economic climate. It is therefore essential that this topic is adequately covered by the syllabus.

In the ACCA Qualification, introduced in 2007, ACCA increased the coverage of risk. However, based on employer feedback, ACCA has increased this even further in the revised syllabuses, first examined in June 2011.

To reflect this increased coverage of risk, ACCA considered it appropriate to change the name of Paper P1 from *Professional Accountant* to *Governance, Risk and Ethics*. This is a more accurate description of the syllabus content and will give employers the assurance that risk is adequately covered by the ACCA Qualification.

The paper name change came into effect June 2011.

Note that this kit contains past ACCA exam questions for this paper, which are labelled as such in the index.

KEY TO THE INDEX

PAPER ENHANCEMENTS

We have added the following enhancements to the answers in this exam kit:

Key answer tips

All answers include key answer tips to help your understanding of each question.

Tutorial note

All answers include more tutorial notes to explain some of the technical points in more detail.

Top tutor tips

For selected questions, we "walk through the answer" giving guidance on how to approach the questions with helpful 'tips from a top tutor', together with technical tutor notes.

These answers are indicated with the "footsteps" icon in the index.

ONLINE ENHANCEMENTS

 Timed question with Online tutor debrief

For selected questions, we recommend that they are to be completed in full exam conditions (i.e. properly timed in a closed book environment).

In addition to the examiner's technical answer, enhanced with key answer tips and tutorial notes in this exam kit, online you can find an answer debrief by a top tutor that:

- works through the question in full

- points out how to approach the question

- how to ensure that the easy marks are obtained as quickly as possible, and

- emphasises how to tackle exam questions and exam technique.

These questions are indicated with the "clock" icon in the index.

> ## Online question assistance

Have you ever looked at a question and not know where to start, or got stuck part way through?

For selected questions, we have produced "Online question assistance" offering different levels of guidance, such as:

- ensuring that you understand the question requirements fully, highlighting key terms and the meaning of the verbs used

- how to read the question proactively, with knowledge of the requirements, to identify the topic areas covered

- assessing the detail content of the question body, pointing out key information and explaining why it is important

- help in devising a plan of attack

With this assistance, you should then be able to attempt your answer confident that you know what is expected of you.

These questions are indicated with the "signpost" icon in the index.

Online question enhancements and answer debriefs will be available on MyKaplan:

www.MyKaplan.co.uk

SECTION A TYPE QUESTIONS

SECTION B TYPE QUESTIONS

KAPLAN PUBLISHING

ANALYSIS OF PAST PAPERS

The table below summarises the key topics that have been tested in the examinations to date.

	D07	J08	D08	J09	D09	J10	D10	J11	D11	J12	D12	J13	D13
Governance and responsibility													
The scope of governance	✓	✓				✓	✓	✓		✓	✓	✓	
Agency relationships and theories	✓			✓		✓				✓			✓
The board of directors	✓	✓	✓	✓	✓		✓	✓	✓	✓			✓
Board committees		✓	✓			✓						✓	✓
Directors' remuneration	✓			✓		✓			✓				
Different approaches	✓	✓				✓			✓	✓	✓		✓
Corporate governance and CSR	✓	✓		✓		✓							✓
Reporting and disclosure			✓	✓			✓		✓				
Internal control and review													
Management control systems	✓	✓	✓	✓	✓	✓	✓					✓	
Internal control, audit and compliance	✓	✓	✓	✓		✓		✓		✓	✓	✓	✓
Internal control and reporting		✓						✓	✓			✓	
Management information in audit and internal control					✓			✓		✓			✓
Identifying and assessing risk													
Risk and risk management process			✓	✓		✓	✓	✓		✓		✓	
Categories of risk			✓						✓	✓	✓		✓
Identification, assessment and measurement of risk		✓		✓			✓		✓			✓	

	D07	J08	D08	J09	D09	J10	D10	J11	D11	J12	D12	J13	D13
Controlling risk													
Targeting and monitoring risk			✓	✓	✓			✓		✓		✓	
Controlling and reducing risk	✓		✓	✓	✓			✓	✓				✓
Risk avoidance, retention and modelling	✓		✓								✓		
Professional values and ethics													
Ethical theories	✓	✓	✓	✓	✓		✓	✓		✓		✓	
Different approaches to ethics and social responsibility	✓		✓	✓			✓		✓		✓	✓	✓
Professions and the public interest		✓		✓		✓			✓			✓	
Professional practice and codes of ethics		✓	✓		✓	✓		✓	✓	✓			✓
Conflicts of interest and the consequences of unethical behaviour				✓	✓					✓		✓	
Ethical characteristics of professionalism						✓		✓					✓
Social and environmental issues		✓				✓			✓		✓	✓	

EXAM TECHNIQUE

- Use the allocated **15 minutes reading and planning time** at the beginning of the exam:
  - read the questions and examination requirements carefully, and
  - begin planning your answers.

  See the Paper Specific Information for advice on how to use this time for this paper.

- **Divide the time** you spend on questions in proportion to the marks on offer:
  - there are 1.8 minutes available per mark in the examination
  - within that, try to allow time at the end of each question to review your answer and address any obvious issues

  Whatever happens, always keep your eye on the clock and **do not over run on any part of any question!**

- Spend the last **five minutes** of the examination:
  - reading through your answers, and
  - **making any additions or corrections**.

- If you **get completely stuck** with a question:
  - leave space in your answer book, and
  - **return to it later.**

- Stick to the question and **tailor your answer** to what you are asked.
  - pay particular attention to the verbs in the question.

- If you do not understand what a question is asking, **state your assumptions**.

  Even if you do not answer in precisely the way the examiner hoped, you should be given some credit, if your assumptions are reasonable.

- You should do everything you can to make things easy for the marker.

  The marker will find it easier to identify the points you have made if your **answers are legible**.

- **Written questions**:

  Your answer should have:
  - a clear structure
  - a brief introduction, a main section and a conclusion.

  Be concise.

  It is better to write a little about a lot of different points than a great deal about one or two points.

- **Reports, memos and other documents**:

  Some questions ask you to present your answer in the form of a report, memo, letter, press statement, briefing notes, management reporting narrative, presentation or other document.

  Make sure that you use the correct format – there are usually professional marks awarded for these styles, and they could be easy marks to gain here.

PAPER SPECIFIC INFORMATION

THE EXAM

FORMAT OF THE EXAM

		Number of marks
Section A:	One compulsory question of 50 marks, based on a case study scenario of several hundred words. Requirements will include several distinct tasks and will sample the syllabus broadly.	50
Section B:	Two questions from a choice of three, each worth 25 marks. Short scenarios will be given, to which all questions relate, with each question likely to contain several tasks.	50
		———
		100
		———

Total time allowed: 3 hours plus 15 minutes reading and planning time.

Note that:

- Question 1 may contain requirements on any aspect of the syllabus. It will, however, *always* contain some aspects of ethics.

- From June 2011 onwards the examiner said "I am also introducing the possibility of introducing some simple arithmetic calculations into Paper P1 exam paper"

- Professional marks totalling 4–6 marks will usually be awarded in Section A (Question 1).

- Section B questions are likely to explore one part of the syllabus in a little more depth than Question 1. They will not, necessarily, examine only one part of the syllabus.

- Generally, at least one Section B question will be heavily focused on governance and at least one on ethics.

PASS MARK

The pass mark for all ACCA Qualification examination papers is 50%.

READING AND PLANNING TIME

Remember that all three hour paper based examinations have an additional 15 minutes reading and planning time.

ACCA GUIDANCE

ACCA guidance on the use of this time is as follows:

This additional time is allowed at the beginning of the examination to allow candidates to read the questions and to begin planning their answers before they start to write in their answer books.

This time should be used to ensure that all the information and, in particular, the exam requirements are properly read and understood.

During this time, candidates may only annotate their question paper. They may not write anything in their answer booklets until told to do so by the invigilator.

KAPLAN GUIDANCE

Since there is a choice of questions in Section B, you must decide which questions to attempt, and in which order.

During the 15 minutes of reading time you should be able to review the questions in Section B and decide which ones are most appealing. All students have different strengths and preferred topics, so it is impossible to give general advice on which questions should be chosen. When making this choice ensure that you are comfortable with **all** parts of the questions.

In relation to paper P1, we recommend that you take the following approach with your reading time:

- **Skim through Section B**, assessing the level of difficulty of each question. Try to decide if there is one question that looks very unappealing and ignore it straight away.

- If you haven't managed to eliminate one question immediately, **have a detailed look at the requirements for each of the Section B questions**. Go through each part slowly and assess how well you could score, hence enabling you to make the choice as to which two questions you will be attempting. Ignore the other question from now on.

- **Now focus on the Section B questions you will be attempting**. For each of the questions, review the requirements for all parts (there are often two elements to one part) and decide if there is any theory or model that will help you tackle them.

- **Turn to Section A requirements**. Work carefully through the requirements, ensuring that you are clear on the headings you will be using and what the verb requires you to do.

- **Write down** on the question paper next to the mark allocation **the amount of time you should spend on each part.** Do this for each part of every question.

- **Read through the scenario** in Section A, noting any key issues in the given information.

- **Decide the order** in which you think you will attempt each question:

  This is a personal choice and you have time on the revision phase to try out different approaches, for example, if you sit mock exams.

A common approach is to tackle the question you think is the easiest and you are most comfortable with first.

Others may prefer to tackle the longest question first, or conversely leave them to the last.

It is usual, however, that students tackle their least favourite topic and/or the most difficult question in their opinion last.

Whatever you approach, you must make sure that you leave enough time to attempt all questions fully and be very strict with yourself in timing each question.

- **Now, for each question** in turn, read the requirements and then the detail of the question carefully.

  Always read the requirement first as this enables you to **focus on the detail of the question with the specific task in mind**.

  Take notice of the format required (e.g. letter, memo, report, presentation – particularly since you will be awarded professional marks for these) and identify the recipient of the answer.

  Plan your beginning, middle and end and the key areas to be addressed and your use of titles and sub-titles to enhance your answer.

  Spot the easy marks to be gained in a question and parts which can be performed independently of the rest of the question. Make sure that you do these parts first when you tackle the question.

  Don't go overboard in terms of planning time on any one question – you need a good measure of the whole paper and an outline plan for all of the questions at the end of the 15 minutes.

  With your plan of attack in mind, **start answering your chosen question** with your plan to hand, as soon as you are allowed to start.

 Always keep your eye on the clock and do not over run on any part of any question!

DETAILED SYLLABUS

The detailed syllabus and study guide written by the ACCA can be found at:

www.accaglobal.com/students/

KAPLAN'S RECOMMENDED REVISION APPROACH

QUESTION PRACTICE IS THE KEY TO SUCCESS

Success in professional examinations relies upon you acquiring a firm grasp of the required knowledge at the tuition phase. In order to be able to do the questions, knowledge is essential.

However, the difference between success and failure often hinges on your exam technique on the day and making the most of the revision phase of your studies.

The **Kaplan complete text** is the starting point, designed to provide the underpinning knowledge to tackle all questions. However, in the revision phase, pouring over text books is not the answer.

Kaplan Online fixed tests help you consolidate your knowledge and understanding and are a useful tool to check whether you can remember key topic areas.

Kaplan pocket notes are designed to help you quickly revise a topic area, however you then need to practise questions. There is a need to progress to full exam standard questions as soon as possible, and to tie your exam technique and technical knowledge together.

The importance of question practice cannot be over-emphasised.

The recommended approach below is designed by expert tutors in the field, in conjunction with their knowledge of the examiner and their recent real exams.

The approach taken for the fundamental papers is to revise by topic area. However, with the professional stage papers, a multi topic approach is required to answer the scenario based questions.

You need to practise as many questions as possible in the time you have left.

OUR AIM

Our aim is to get you to the stage where you can attempt exam standard questions confidently, to time, in a closed book environment, with no supplementary help (i.e. to simulate the real examination experience).

Practising your exam technique on real past examination questions, in timed conditions, is also vitally important for you to assess your progress and identify areas of weakness that may need more attention in the final run up to the examination.

In order to achieve this we recognise that initially you may feel the need to practise some questions with open book help and exceed the required time.

The approach below shows you which questions you should use to build up to coping with exam standard question practice, and references to the sources of information available should you need to revisit a topic area in more detail.

Remember that in the real examination, all you have to do is:

- attempt all questions required by the exam
- only spend the allotted time on each question, and
- get them at least 50% right!

Try and practise this approach on every question you attempt from now to the real exam.

EXAMINER COMMENTS

We have included the examiner's comments to specific examination questions in this kit for you to see the main pitfalls that students fall into with regard to technical content.

However, too many times in the general section of the report, the examiner comments that students had failed due to:

- "failure to read the question carefully enough"

- "failure to answer at the level of the verbs used in the questions"

- "expecting to be able to answer the exam using 'book work' or 'rote learning'" and

- not appreciating that "marks will not be awarded for non-case based answers if this was the requirement of the question".

Good exam technique is vital.

THE KAPLAN PAPER P1 REVISION PLAN

Stage 1: Assess areas of strengths and weaknesses

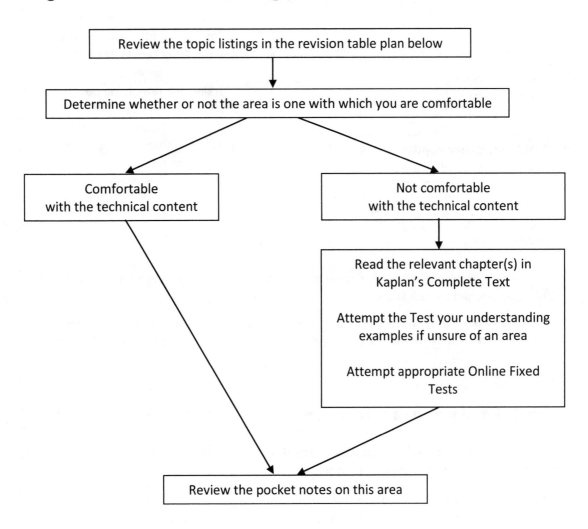

Review the topic listings in the revision table plan below

↓

Determine whether or not the area is one with which you are comfortable

Comfortable
with the technical content

Not comfortable
with the technical content

Read the relevant chapter(s) in Kaplan's Complete Text

Attempt the Test your understanding examples if unsure of an area

Attempt appropriate Online Fixed Tests

Review the pocket notes on this area

Stage 2: Practice questions

Follow the order of revision of topics as recommended in the revision table plan below and attempt the questions in the order suggested.

Try to avoid referring to text books and notes and the model answer until you have completed your attempt.

Try to answer the question in the allotted time.

Review your attempt with the model answer and assess how much of the answer you achieved in the allocated exam time.

Fill in the self-assessment box below and decide on your best course of action.

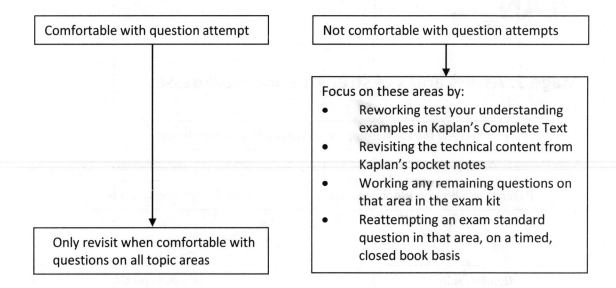

| Comfortable with question attempt | | Not comfortable with question attempts |

Focus on these areas by:

- Reworking test your understanding examples in Kaplan's Complete Text
- Revisiting the technical content from Kaplan's pocket notes
- Working any remaining questions on that area in the exam kit
- Reattempting an exam standard question in that area, on a timed, closed book basis

Only revisit when comfortable with questions on all topic areas

Note that:

 The "footsteps questions" give guidance on exam techniques and how you should have approached the question.

 The "clock questions" have an online debrief where a tutor talks you through the exam technique and approach to that question and works the question in full.

Stage 3: Final pre-exam revision

We recommend that you **attempt at least one three hour mock examination** containing a set of previously unseen exam standard questions.

It is important that you get a feel for the breadth of coverage of a real exam without advanced knowledge of the topic areas covered – just as you will expect to see on the real exam day.

Ideally this mock should be sat in timed, closed book, real exam conditions and could be:

- a mock examination offered by your tuition provider, and/or

- the pilot paper in the back of this exam kit, and/or

- the last real examination paper (available shortly afterwards on Kaplan EN-gage with "enhanced walk through answers" and a full "tutor debrief").

THE DETAILED REVISION PLAN

Topic	Complete Text Chapter	Pocket note Chapter	Questions to attempt	Tutor guidance	Date attempted	Self assessment
Corporate governance						
– what is it and why	1 – 2	1 – 2	Q2(a) Q9(d)(iii)	Review the introductory sections about corporate governance, including revision of the key concepts in governance. These concepts are often tested as a small part of question, such as in Q2 (a) and Q9 (d)(iii).		
– theories of governance	1	1	Q29(a) Q26(a) Q27(a)	Agency theory is another popular topic, but again rarely forms an entire question on its own. Q23 (a) allows you to start with a straightforward theory question. Once you are happy with the theory, move onto tackle Q26 (a) and Q27 (a) which requires application to a scenario. It would be good to try these questions in full to ensure you can explain the concepts clearly.		
– corporate governance approaches	7	7	Q18	Q18 covers a range of questions on the varying approaches to corporate governance.		

Topic	Complete Text Chapter	Pocket note Chapter	Questions to attempt	Tutor guidance	Date attempted	Self assessment
– board of directors	3	3	Q11(a), (c)&(d) Q17 Q23	This is the biggest topic in the area of corporate governance and appears, in some form or another, on every exam. Q11 (a),(c)&(d) provides good practice on board composition and structures. Q17 allows you to look at the chairman/CEO roles more closely, and it is a good question to try in full. Q27 moves onto the areas of nominations and removal of directors. Q23 also provides coverage of the induction process.		
– directors' remuneration	4	4	Q31 Q34	This is a highly topical area and hence is examined fairly frequently. Q31 covers both the topics of the remuneration package and the committee that sets it. Q34 proves to be a challenging question on a number of topics relating to directors and their remuneration. Try this one in full, to time, and review the solution carefully.		
– relations with shareholders and disclosure	5	5	Q4(d) Q19	This is a small area of the syllabus, and appears occasionally in exam questions. When asked, it is only for a few marks. Q4 (d) looks at the subject of disclosure for 10 marks. Q19 provides coverage of shareholder intervention and some other governance topics – a good recap question.		

KAPLAN PUBLISHING

Topic	Complete Text Chapter	Pocket note Chapter	Questions to attempt	Tutor guidance	Date attempted	Self assessment
Internal control and review						
– internal control systems	9	9	Q42 Q44 Q46	Internal controls has been examined frequently; sometimes in a theory question, often requiring application. It is generally part of a question with either audit or risk. Q42 (a) is good practice of the theory in the area (try it later – once you have revised audit) with Q44 and Q46 moving onto an application type question.		
– information requirements	9	9	Q47	The topic is rarely examined, focussing on the information needs of management in control, risk management and review. Q45 provides practice in this area.		
– audit and compliance	10 (and part of 6)	10 (and part of 6)	Q43 Q42	Q43 covers a range of topics within this area. Note the overlap with ethical threats in part (d). Q42 (c) provides practical application to a given scenario. Try Q42 in full and practise your time management.		
Identifying and assessing risk						
– identifying risk	11	11	Q11(b) Q4(b)	Risk identification is usually asked in a broad question requiring you to look within a scenario for examples of risks – this can be seen in Q11 (b). Risk classifications are an alternative way of addressing the subject, as seen in Q4 (b).		

Topic	Complete Text Chapter	Pocket note Chapter	Questions to attempt	Tutor guidance	Date attempted	Self assessment
– risk assessment	11	11	Q9(b)&(c)	Q9 (b)&(c) looks at the next stages of the risk management process, risk assessment, requiring a theoretical discussion and then application of the method. This is a good question to practise in full. It is useful to be aware of the overall risk management process, but be prepared for questions to focus on just one aspect or stage.		
– controlling risk	12 (and part of 6)	12 (and part of 6)	Q54 Q55 Q57 Q58 Q59 Q60	The topics in this area tend to be examined together in a single question. Question 54 looks at risk management strategies (a popular question). In addition Q55(c) looks as the concept of embedding risk. Q58 is additional practice on risk management strategies. Q59 and Q60 provide practice on the overall risk management process along with a couple of other specific topics – try these questions in full, to time.		
Professional values and ethics						
– CSR	8	8	Q35	CSR pulls on the governance and ethics syllabus areas. It has rarely been examined directly, but is forming a significant part of the reality of the business environment. Q37(c) provides practice in this area.		

KAPLAN PUBLISHING

Topic	Complete Text Chapter	Pocket note Chapter	Questions to attempt	Tutor guidance	Date attempted	Self assessment
– Stakeholder theory	8	8	Q9(a) Q8(d)	Stakeholders are an important part of this exam, and have been tested frequently. Generally questions require you to identify, or classify stakeholders in a scenario, and consider their claims in some manner. Q9(a) is a good question to start practising on. Once you are happy with that, move on and look at Q8(d) and attempt this in full.		
– Ethical theories	13	13	Q67(c) Q78(c) Q8(a) Q21 Q4(c)	There are a number of ethical theories and at least one pairing or model is examined in every diet, hence there are many questions to practise on. – relativism/absolutism: Q67(c) – deontological/teleological: Q70(c) and Q78(c) – Kohlberg's CMD: Q8(a) – Gray, Owens and Adams: Q21. The latter has appeared a couple of times requiring you to view something from the perspective of a particular social stance. This is more challenging, so practise Q4(c) to time and review the solution carefully.		

Topic	Complete Text Chapter	Pocket note Chapter	Questions to attempt	Tutor guidance	Date attempted	Self assessment
– Professional and corporate ethics	14	14	Q67 Q68 Q69(b) Q70 Q71(a)	An underpinning concept to the role of a professional is that of public interest. See Q71 (a) for an example of a recent question on this. The role of the professional is covered well in Q67. This is an excellent broad question and worth attempting in full to practise many areas. Q69 (b) is another example of question in this area. Professional codes of ethics can be seen in Q70, and corporate codes in Q75.		
– Ethical decision making	15	15	Q4(a)	The two key models here: AAA and Tucker were the subject of an article by the examiner. Tucker was subsequently examined in Q4 (a) – a good question to practise your understanding of the model.		
– Social and environmental issues	16	16	Q10	Many scenarios, especially in Section A, contain some environmental reference, so it often forms part of a question. Q10 (e) is a good example of this. The topic of environmental audit can be reviewed in Q80(b), along with some revision of other audit types.		

For many questions the above programme covers just some part, or parts, of the requirements. You should complete all questions that you have started as a good basis for further practice.

Note: not all of the questions are referred to in the programme above. The remaining questions are available in the kit and should be attempted for extra practice for those who require more questions on some areas.

Section 1

PRACTICE QUESTIONS – SECTION A

1 MANAGE LTD

Background information

Manage Ltd is a large family-owned private company operating in the UK in the contract services sector. The principle business that Manage undertakes is project management on large, long-term building projects in the UK. Manage Ltd has no overseas customers. The company provides a complete project management service, enabling the customers to deal just with Manage Ltd. Manage deal with all sub-contractors. The business has been very successful in recent years and as a result has become a potential acquisition target for a major international company, Utopia Inc, based in the US. Utopia Inc is listed on the New York Stock Exchange and is interested in furthering its businesses in Europe.

Some of the members of the family that own Manage Ltd (the Inglesons) are keen to dispose of their shares and it is therefore expected they will sell to Utopia if a suitable price can be agreed. The managing director of Manage, Jean Smith (not in the Ingleson family), is currently negotiating with the directors of Utopia over a price for the shares. Following the negotiation Jean will make a proposal to the Ingleson family. Jean and other selected staff have already been offered positions in Utopia if the acquisition proceeds.

Financing the acquisition

Utopia Inc have a corporate policy of financing their acquisitions through loans. In previous foreign acquisitions, they have used either US or foreign loans depending on their views on economic and political factors in the US and in the foreign markets. They have no strong views on where to raise finance. They expect to need to borrow in 4 months' time to finance the acquisition.

One factor that the directors of Utopia Inc do feel needs to be considered however is that they are considering selling an existing UK division within a year and the proceeds are expected to be in the region of the acquisition price for Manage Ltd. The disposal will definitely occur after the acquisition of Manage Ltd, probably six months later.

Corporate governance

In anticipation of Manage Ltd becoming part of the Utopia Group the group CFO, Bert Bailey, has forwarded to Jean Smith a memo he sent last year to all divisional CEOs on corporate governance. He told Jean that the same process would operate for Manage Ltd, but with the dates about a year on.

MEMO

To:	Divisional CFOs and CEOs
From:	Bert Bailey
Subject:	SOX compliance
Date:	15 January 20X4

As you are all no doubt aware, we are implementing Sarbanes-Oxley (SOX) this year. This memo summarises the timetable; more detail on the processes and procedures required will follow later.

Feb – May	Document key financial reporting systems and controls. Decide key controls and report any material design weaknesses in systems;
Jun – July	Divisional management to test key controls to confirm compliance and the effectiveness of the systems;
Aug – Sept	Group internal audit to review documentation and testing, and report on each division to the audit committee;
Oct – Nov	External audit to conduct the majority of their attestation work;
Dec	Management certification and assertions as required by sections 302 and 404.

The control framework the US companies will be using is the COSO framework. Overseas companies can use a local framework, if desired, provided it is approved in advance by the group SOX project team. Documentation must be standard across the group.

Required:

(a)   Explain the difference between strategic and operational risks.   **(10 marks)**

(b)   Explain the risks that could exist for Utopia in making the investment in Manage Ltd and discuss how Utopia could assess their likely impact on the company.
                                                                                (15 marks)

Jean Smith does not understand the memo she has been sent. She knows that Sarbanes-Oxley is the American corporate governance requirements but has not heard of any 'control frameworks'.

(c)   (i)   List some of the typical requirements for corporate governance in the areas of:

            directors and the board

            accountability and audit.   **(10 marks)**

      (ii) Explain the elements of an effective internal control system (such as in the COSO framework or Turnbull report) giving practical examples of how Manage Ltd could demonstrate they have met all elements.   **(15 marks)**

                                                                        (Total: 50 marks)

---

2   WORLDWIDE MINERALS (DEC 07) *Walk in the footsteps of a top tutor*

The board of Worldwide Minerals (WM) was meeting for the last monthly meeting before the publication of the yearend results. There were two points of discussion on the agenda. First was the discussion of the year-end results; second was the crucial latest minerals reserves report.

WM is a large listed multinational company that deals with natural minerals that are extracted from the ground, processed and sold to a wide range of industrial and construction companies. In order to maintain a consistent supply of minerals into its principal markets, an essential part of WM's business strategy is the seeking out of new sources and the measurement of known reserves. Investment analysts have often pointed out that WM's value rests principally upon the accuracy of its reserve reports as these are the best indicators of future cash flows and earnings. In order to support this key part of its strategy, WM has a large and well-funded geological survey department which, according to the company website, contains 'some of the world's best geologists and minerals scientists'. In its investor relations literature, the company claims that:

'our experts search the earth for mineral reserves and once located, they are carefully measured so that the company can always report on known reserves. This knowledge underpins market confidence and keeps our customers supplied with the inventory they need. You can trust our reserve reports – our reputation depends on it!'

At the board meeting, the head of the geological survey department, Ranjana Tyler, reported that there was a problem with the latest report because one of the major reserve figures had recently been found to be wrong. The mineral in question, mallerite, was WM's largest mineral in volume terms and Ranjana explained that the mallerite reserves in a deep mine in a certain part of the world had been significantly overestimated. She explained that, based on the interim minerals report, the stock market analysts were expecting WM to announce known mallerite reserves of 4.8 billion tonnes. The actual figure was closer to 2.4 billion tonnes. It was agreed that this difference was sufficient to affect WM's market value, despite the otherwise good results for the past year. Vanda Monroe, the finance director, said that the share price reflects market confidence in future earnings. She said that an announcement of an incorrect estimation like that for mallerite would cause a reduction in share value. More importantly for WM itself, however, it could undermine confidence in the geological survey department. All agreed that as this was strategically important for the company, it was a top priority to deal with this problem.

Ranjana explained how the situation had arisen. The major mallerite mine was in a country new to WM's operations. The WM engineer at the mine said it was difficult to deal with some local people because, according to the engineer, 'they didn't like to give us bad news'. The engineer explained that when the mine was found to be smaller than originally thought, he was not told until it was too late to reduce the price paid for the mine. This was embarrassing and it was agreed that it would affect market confidence in WM if it was made public.

The board discussed the options open to it. The chairman, who was also a qualified accountant, was Tim Blake. He began by expressing serious concern about the overestimation and then invited the board to express views freely. Gary Howells, the operations director, said that because disclosing the error to the market would be so damaging, it might be best to keep it a secret and hope that new reserves can be found in the near future that will make up for the shortfall. He said that it was unlikely that this concealment would be found out as shareholders trusted WM and they had many years of good investor relations to draw on. Vanda Monroe, the finance director, reminded the board that the company was bound to certain standards of truthfulness and transparency by its stock market listing. She pointed out that they were constrained by codes of governance and ethics by the stock market and that colleagues should be aware that WM would be in technical breach of these if the incorrect estimation was concealed from investors. Finally, Martin Chan, the human resources director, said that the error should be disclosed to the investors because he would not want to be deceived if he were an outside investor in the company. He argued that whatever the governance codes said and whatever the cost in terms of reputation and market value, WM should admit its error and cope with whatever consequences arose. The WM board contains three non-executive directors and their views were also invited.

At the preliminary results presentation some time later, one analyst, Christina Gonzales, who had become aware of the mallerite problem, asked about internal audit and control systems, and whether they were adequate in such a reserve-sensitive industry. WM's chairman, Tim Blake, said that he intended to write a letter to all investors and analysts in the light of the mallerite problem which he hoped would address some of the issues that Miss Gonzales had raised.

Required:

(a)   Define 'transparency' and evaluate its importance as an underlying principle in corporate governance and in relevant and reliable financial reporting. Your answer should refer to the case as appropriate.   **(10 marks)**

(b)   Explain Kohlberg's three levels of moral development and identify the levels of moral development demonstrated by the contributions of Gary Howells, Vanda Monroe and Martin Chan.   **(12 marks)**

(c)   Critically discuss FOUR principal roles of non-executive directors and explain the potential tensions between these roles that WM's non-executive directors may experience in advising on the disclosure of the overestimation of the mallerite reserve.   **(12 marks)**

(d)   Draft a letter for Tim Blake to send to WM's investors to include the following:

(i)   why you believe robust internal controls to be important; and

(ii)   proposals on how internal systems might be improved in the light of the overestimation of mallerite at WM.

Note: Four professional marks are available within the marks allocated to requirement (d) for the structure, content, style and layout of the letter.

(16 marks)

(Total: 50 marks)

3 HAYHO (JUN 12)

Hayho is a large international company with direct investments in 65 countries. It is a manufacturer of high technology products, with each Hayho factory typically employing over 3,000 people. Hayho factories also support local supply chains employing many more people so each Hayho plant is considered a vital part of the regional economy in which it is located.

Several years ago, Hayho was widely criticised for its operations in Arrland, a developing country with an oppressive and undemocratic government. Investigative journalists produced material showing the poor conditions of workers, and pollution around the Hayho factories in Arrland. They also showed evidence suggesting that Hayho had paid bribes to the Arrland government so that local opposition to the Hayho operation could be forcefully stopped. After this episode, the company became very sensitive to criticism of its operations in developing countries. A press statement at the time said that Hayho, in future, would always uphold the highest standards of integrity, human rights and environmental protection whilst at the same time 'responsibly' supporting developing countries by providing jobs and opportunities to enable greater social and economic development.

The board of Hayho is now deciding between two possible large new investments, both directly employing about 3,000 people. Both options have a number of advantages and disadvantages and Mr Woo, Hayho's finance director, has recently made clear that only one can be chosen at this stage. The two options are of similar investment value and are referred to as the 'Jayland option' and the 'Pealand option'.

The 'Jayland option' is to build a new large factory in Jayland and to recruit a completely new local workforce to work in it. Jayland is a developing country with few environmental and labour regulations. It has a poorly developed education and training system, and is generally considered to be undemocratic. Its president, Mr Popo, has been in office since he seized power in a military coup 30 years ago. Human rights organisations say that he maintains order by abusing the rights of the people and cruelly suppressing any dissent against him. In early exploratory talks between Hayho and the Jayland government, Hayho was given assurances that it could pursue its activities with little regulation from the government as long as the Jayland president, Mr Popo, received a personal annual 'royalty' (effectively a bribe) for allowing Hayho to operate in his country.

Finance director Mr Woo said that some stakeholders would probably criticise Hayho, perhaps in the international media, for investing in Jayland. Hayho may be accused of supporting the dictatorship of Mr Popo in that country, especially if the 'royalty' was ever discovered. Mr Woo calculated that the NPV (net present value) of projected pretax returns of the Jayland option over a ten-year period was $2 billion but that there was also a risk of potential political instability in Jayland during the lifetime of the investment.

The 'Pealand option' is to buy an existing plant in Pealand which would then be refurbished to facilitate the manufacture of Hayho products. This would involve 'inheriting' the workforce of the previous owners. Pealand is a 'new democracy', and a transitional economy, having gained its independence ten years ago. In an attempt to purge the corrupt business practices associated with its past, the Pealand government has become very thorough in ensuring that all inward investments, including Hayho's factory purchase, meet exacting and demanding standards of environmental protection and work conditions. Mr Woo, the finance director, said that the NPV of projected pre-tax returns over a ten-year period was $1 billion for the Pealand option but that the risk of political instability in Pealand was negligible. Both of the returns, the forecast $2 billion for Jayland and the $1 billion for Pealand, were considered to be acceptable in principle.

Mr Woo also said that there were issues with the two options relating to the effectiveness of necessary internal controls. Whichever option was chosen (Jayland or Pealand), it would be necessary to establish internal controls to enable accurate and timely reporting of production and cost data back to head office. So a number of systems would need to be put in place to support the production itself. One staff member, Emily Baa, who had previously worked in Jayland for another company, gave her opinion to the board about some of the issues that Hayho might encounter if it chose the Jayland option. She said that Jayland was very under developed until relatively recently and explained how the national culture was unfamiliar with modern business practice and behaviour. She said that property security may be a problem and that there was a potential risk to assets there. She also said that, in her opinion, there was a lack of some key job skills among the potential workforce in Jayland such as quality control and accounting skills. She explained that quality control skills would be necessary to ensure product specifications were met and that accounting skills would be necessary for the provision of internal and external reporting. As a manufacturer of very technologically advanced products, a number of stringent international product standards applied to Hayho products wherever in the world they were produced.

Meanwhile, news that Hayho was considering a large investment in Jayland leaked out to the press. In response, Hayho's chief executive, Helen Duomo received two letters. The first was from a prominent international human rights lobbying organisation called 'Watching Business' (WB). In the letter, the lobby group said that because of its 'terrible track record' in Arrland and elsewhere, Hayho was being carefully monitored for its 'unethical business practices'. WB said its interest in Hayho's activities had been rekindled since it had received intelligence about the possible investment in Jayland and warned Mrs Duomo not to make the investment because it would provide credibility for the 'brutal dictatorship' of Mr Popo.

Whilst Mrs Duomo, known for her forthright manner, would normally dismiss threats from groups of this type, she knew that WB had a lot of support among senior politicians and legislators in many parts of the world. She believed that WB could achieve some power through mobilising public opinion through effective use of mass media, such as newspapers and television. WB was also respected as a research organisation and its advice was often sought by politicians and trade organisations.

Mrs Duomo said she was frustrated whenever anybody got in the way of her accountability to the Hayho shareholders, but that some interests could not be ignored because of their potential to influence. WB fell into this category.

The second letter she received was from the head of Quark Investments, Hayho's single biggest institutional shareholder. The letter sought to remind Mrs Duomo that the Hayho board was employed by its shareholders and that Mrs Duomo should be determined and resolute in maximising shareholder returns. The letter encouraged the board not to be diverted by 'well meaning but misinformed outsiders concerned with things that were actually none of their business'.

Aware that she had to manage two competing demands placed on her, Mrs Duomo sought advice from Emily Baa, who had experience of life in Jayland. So she asked Emily Baa to prepare some notes for the next board meeting to clarify whom the board of Hayho was actually accountable to and how it might respond to the letter from WB.

Required:

(a) Explain 'risk appetite' and demonstrate how different risk appetites might affect the selection of investments between Jayland and Pealand. (6 marks)

(b) Use the AAA (American Accounting Association) seven-step model to examine the ethical decision whether to select the Jayland option or the Pealand option.

(14 marks)

(c) Describe the general purposes of an internal control system and, based on Emily Baa's views, assess the main internal control challenges that Hayho might encounter if it chose the Jayland option. (12 marks)

(d) Prepare briefing notes from Emily Baa to prepare chief executive of Hayho, Helen Duomo, for the board meeting as requested in the case. The notes should cover the following:

(i) A discussion of the meaning of accountability at Hayho and of how the Mendelow framework can be used to predict the influence of the Watching Business pressure group (7 marks)

(ii) A brief explanation of the agency relationship between the board of Hayho and Quark Investments, and advice on why the demands from Watching Business should be carefully considered. (7 marks)

Professional marks will be awarded in part (d) for the clarity, flow, persuasiveness and structure of the briefing notes. (4 marks)

(Total: 50 marks)

4 SWAN HILL COMPANY (DEC 08)

The scientists in the research laboratories of Swan Hill Company (SHC, a public listed company) recently made a very important discovery about the process that manufactured its major product. The scientific director, Dr Sonja Rainbow, informed the board that the breakthrough was called the 'sink method'. She explained that the sink method would enable SHC to produce its major product at a lower unit cost and in much higher volumes than the current process. It would also produce lower unit environmental emissions and would substantially improve product quality compared to its current process and indeed compared to all of the other competitors in the industry.

SHC currently has 30% of the global market with its nearest competitor having 25% and the other twelve producers sharing the remainder. The company, based in the town of Swan Hill, has a paternalistic management approach and has always valued its relationship with the local community. Its website says that SHC has always sought to maximise the benefit to the workforce and community in all of its business decisions and feels a great sense of loyalty to the Swan Hill locality which is where it started in 1900 and has been based ever since.

As the board considered the implications of the discovery of the sink method, chief executive Nelson Cobar asked whether Sonja Rainbow was certain that SHC was the only company in the industry that had made the discovery and she said that she was. She also said that she was certain that the competitors were 'some years' behind SHC in their research.

It quickly became clear that the discovery of the sink method was so important and far reaching that it had the potential to give SHC an unassailable competitive advantage in its industry. Chief executive Nelson Cobar told board colleagues that they should clearly understand that the discovery had the potential to put all of SHC's competitors out of business and make SHC the single global supplier. He said that as the board considered the options, members should bear in mind the seriousness of the implications upon the rest of the industry.

Mr Cobar said there were two strategic options. Option one was to press ahead with the huge investment of new plant necessary to introduce the sink method into the factory whilst, as far as possible, keeping the nature of the sink technology secret from competitors (the 'secrecy option'). A patent disclosing the nature of the technology would not be filed so as to keep the technology secret within SHC. Option two was to file a patent and then offer the use of the discovery to competitors under a licensing arrangement where SHC would receive substantial royalties for the twenty-year legal lifetime of the patent (the 'licensing option'). This would also involve new investment but at a slower pace in line with competitors. The licence contract would, Mr Cobar explained, include an 'improvement sharing' requirement where licensees would be required to inform SHC of any improvements discovered that made the sink method more efficient or effective.

The sales director, Edwin Kiama, argued strongly in favour of the secrecy option. He said that the board owed it to SHC's shareholders to take the option that would maximise shareholder value. He argued that business strategy was all about gaining competitive advantage and this was a chance to do exactly that. Accordingly, he argued, the sink method should not be licensed to competitors and should be pursued as fast as possible. The operations director said that to gain the full benefits of the sink method with either option would require a complete refitting of the factory and the largest capital investment that SHC had ever undertaken.

The financial director, Sean Nyngan, advised the board that pressing ahead with investment under the secrecy option was not without risks. First, he said, he would have to finance the investment, probably initially through debt, and second, there were risks associated with any large investment. He also informed the board that the licensing option would, over many years, involve the inflow of 'massive' funds in royalty payments from competitors using the SHC's patented sink method. By pursuing the licensing option, Sean Nyngan said that they could retain their market leadership in the short term without incurring risk, whilst increasing their industry dominance in the future through careful investment of the royalty payments.

The non-executive chairman, Alison Manilla, said that she was looking at the issue from an ethical perspective. She asked whether SHC had the right, even if it had the ability, to put competitors out of business.

Required:

(a)   **Assess the secrecy option using Tucker's model for decision-making.**   **(10 marks)**

(b)   **Distinguish between strategic and operational risks, and explain why the secrecy option would be a source of strategic risk.**   **(10 marks)**

(c)   Mr Cobar, the chief executive of SHC, has decided to draft two alternative statements to explain both possible outcomes of the secrecy/licensing decision to shareholders. Once the board has decided which one to pursue, the relevant draft will be included in a voluntary section of the next corporate annual report.

Required:

(i) Draft a statement in the event that the board chooses the secrecy option. It should make a convincing business case and put forward ethical arguments for the secrecy option. The ethical arguments should be made from the stockholder (or pristine capitalist) perspective. **(8 marks)**

(ii) Draft a statement in the event that the board chooses the licensing option. It should make a convincing business case and put forward ethical arguments for the licensing option. The ethical arguments should be made from the wider stakeholder perspective. **(8 marks)**

(iii) Professional marks for the persuasiveness and logical flow of arguments: two marks per statement. **(4 marks)**

(d) Corporate annual reports contain both mandatory and voluntary disclosures.

Required:

(i) Distinguish, using examples, between mandatory and voluntary disclosures in the annual reports of public listed companies. **(6 marks)**

(ii) Explain why the disclosure of voluntary information in annual reports can enhance the company's accountability to equity investors. **(4 marks)**

(Total: 50 marks)

5 COASTAL OIL (DEC 11)

Coastal Oil is one of the world's largest petrochemical companies. It is based in Deeland and is responsible alone for 10% of Deeland's total stock market value. It employs 120,000 people in many countries and has an especially strong presence in Effland because of Effland's very large consumption of oil and gas products and its large oil reserves. Coastal Oil is organised, like most petrochemical companies, into three vertically integrated business units: the exploration and extraction division; the processing and refining division; and the distribution and retailing division.

Because of the risks and the capital investment demands, Coastal Oil has joint venture (JV) agreements in place for many of its extraction operations (i.e. its oil and gas rigs), especially those in the deep-water seas. A joint venture is a shared equity arrangement for a particular project where control is shared between the JV partners. In each of its JVs, Coastal Oil is the largest partner, although operations on each rig are divided between the JV member companies and the benefits are distributed according to the share of the JV.

As a highly visible company, Coastal Oil has long prided itself on its safety record and its ethical reputation. It believes both to be essential in supporting shareholder value. Its corporate code of ethics, published some years ago, pledges its commitment to the 'highest standards' of ethical performance in the following areas: full compliance with regulation in all jurisdictions; safety and care of employees; transparency and communication with stakeholders; social contribution; and environmental responsibility. In addition, Coastal Oil has usually provided a lot of voluntary disclosure in its annual report and on its website. It says that it has a wide range of stakeholders and so needs to provide a great deal of information.

One of the consequences of dividing up the different responsibilities and operations on an oil or gas rig is that Coastal Oil does not have direct influence over some important operational controls. The contractual arrangements on any given oil rig can be very complex and there have often been disagreements between JV partners on some individual legal agreements and responsibilities for health and safety controls. Given that Coastal Oil has JV interests in hundreds of deep-water oil and gas rigs all over the world, some observers have said that this could be a problem should an accident ever occur.

This issue was tragically highlighted when one of its deep-water rigs, the Effland Coastal Deep Rig, had an explosion earlier this year. It was caused by the failure of a valve at the 'well-head' on the sea floor. The valve was the responsibility of Well Services, a minor partner in the JV. Eight workers were killed on the rig from the high pressure released after the valve failure, and oil gushed into the sea from the well-head, a situation that should have been prevented had the valve been fully operational. It was soon established that Well Services' staff failed to inspect the valve before placing it at the well-head at the time of installation, as was required by the company's normal control systems. In addition, the valve was attached to a connecting part that did not meet the required technical specification for the water depth at which it was operating. The sea bed was 1,000 metres deep and the connecting part was intended for use to a depth of up to 300 metres. There was a suggestion that the need to keep costs down was a key reason for the use of the connecting part with the inferior specification.

Reports in the media on the following day said that the accident had happened on a rig 'belonging to Coastal Oil' when in fact, Coastal Oil was technically only a major partner in the joint venture. Furthermore, there was no mention that the accident had been caused by a part belonging to Well Services. A journalist did discover, however, that both companies had operated a more lax safety culture on the deep-water rigs than was the case at facilities on land (the 'land-side'). He said there was a culture of 'out of sight, out of mind' on some offshore facilities and that this meant that several other controls were inoperative in addition to the ones that led to the accident. Information systems reporting back to the 'land-side' were in place but it was the responsibility of management on each individual rig to enforce all internal controls and the 'land-side' would only be informed of a problem if it was judged to be 'an exceptional risk' by the rig's manager.

The accident triggered a large internal argument between Coastal Oil and Well Services about liability and this meant that there was no public statement from Coastal Oil for seven days while the arguments continued. Lawyers on both sides pointed out that liability was contractually ambiguous because the documentation on responsibilities was far too complex and unclear. And in any case, nobody expected anything to go wrong. In the absence of any official statement from Coastal Oil for those seven days, the media had no doubts who was to blame: Coastal Oil was strongly criticised in Effland with the criticism growing stronger as oil from the ruptured valve was shown spilling directly into the sea off the Effland coast. With no contingency plan for a deep-water well-head rupture in place, the ruptured valve took several months to repair, meaning that many thousands of tonnes of crude oil polluted the sea off Effland. Images of seabirds covered in crude oil were frequently broadcast on television and thousands of businesses on the coast reported that the polluted water would disrupt their business over the vital tourist season. Public statements from Coastal Oil that it was not responsible for the ruptured valve were seemingly not believed by the Effland public. Senior legislators in Effland said that the accident happened on 'a rig belonging to Coastal Oil' so it must be Coastal Oil's fault.

A review by the Coastal Oil board highlighted several areas where risk management systems might be tightened to reduce the possibility of a similar accident happening again. Finance director, Tanya Tun, suggested that the company should disclose this new information to shareholders as it would be value-relevant to them. In particular, she said that a far more detailed voluntary statement on environmental risk would be material to the shareholders. The annual report would, she believed, be a suitable vehicle for this disclosure.

Because of the high media profile of the event, politicians from Effland involved themselves in the situation. Senator Jones's constituency on the coast nearest the rig was badly affected by the oil spill and many of his constituents suffered economic loss as a result. He angrily retorted in a newspaper interview that Coastal Oil's CEO, Susan Ahmed, 'should have known this was going to happen', such was the poor state of some of the internal controls on the Effland Coastal Deep Rig.

As the oil spill continued and the media interest in the events intensified, CEO Mrs Ahmed was summoned to appear before a special committee of the Effland national legislature 'to explain herself to the citizens of Effland'. The Coastal Oil board agreed that this would be a good opportunity for Mrs Ahmed to address a number of issues in detail and attempt to repair some of the company's damaged reputation. The board agreed that Mrs Ahmed should provide as full a statement as possible on the internal control failures to the special committee.

Required:

(a) **Describe the general purposes of a corporate code of ethics and evaluate Coastal Oil's performance against its own stated ethical aims as set out in its code of ethics.**

(10 marks)

(b) **Explain, using examples, the difference between voluntary and mandatory disclosure, and assess Tanya Tun's proposition that additional voluntary disclosure on environmental risk management would be material to the shareholders.**

(10 marks)

(c) In preparing to appear before the special committee of the Effland national legislature, CEO Mrs Ahmed has been informed that she will be asked to explain the causes of the accident and to establish whether she can give assurances that an accident of this type will not re-occur.

Required:

Prepare a statement for Mrs Ahmed to present before the committee that explains the following:

(i) **The internal control failures that gave rise to the accident** (10 marks)

(ii) **The difference between subjective and objective risk assessment (using examples). Argue against Senator Jones's view that Mrs Ahmed 'should have known this was going to happen'** (8 marks)

(iii) **'Health and safety' risk and the factors that can increase this risk in an organisation** (4 marks)

(iv) **Why Coastal Oil cannot guarantee the prevention of further health and safety failures, using the ALARP (as low as reasonably practicable) principle** (4 marks)

Professional marks will be awarded in part (c) for logical flow, persuasiveness, format and tone of the answers. (4 marks)

(Total: 50 marks)

6 FUEL SURCHARGES

TY and JK are two airline companies providing scheduled flights between a number of major cities on two continents. Both companies are respected and have policies of providing full and detailed information in their financial statements as well as providing excellent customer service. TY and JK maintain some element of rivalry, and frequently produce adverts explaining how, for example, their seats have the most distance between them or their in-flight menus and entertainments are 'better' than the other company's.

As part of their pricing policy, both companies charge a basic price for each seat purchased. The basic price is then supplemented by an excess to travel at weekends, airport taxes and a fuel surcharge. The latter varies during the year depending on the price of oil and is designed to allow the airline companies to pass on increases in fuel price to their customers. Over the past 20 months, the fuel surcharges of TY and JK have changed on six occasions, with both airlines' surcharges changing at the same time and by the same amount.

One week ago, the legal department of the JK airline discovered that both airlines had colluded to set identical surcharges and that this collusion was illegal under the Anti-Competition laws of most jurisdictions. The matter was brought to the attention of the board of JK and a full disclosure statement was made to the airline industry regulator and the relevant governmental departments. JK stated that this action was being taken 'in the public interest'. As a result of the disclosure JK escaped any liability for damages, but TY was fined €250 million for entering into a price fixing agreement.

The chairman of JK promised to provide additional disclosure on this and other matters in the company's new Corporate and Social Responsibility (CSR) report. The board of TY were obviously annoyed with the decision by JK to disclose, and even more annoyed when it was discovered that the surcharges had been agreed by senior managers below board level without board approval. Those managers were immediately suspended.

The remuneration policy for directors in each company is slightly different.

- In TY, remuneration is determined 40% as a fixed salary, 40% based on a proportion of profit for the year and 20% on long-term incentives by granting share options.

- In JK, remuneration is determined 30% as a fixed salary, 30% based on the movement in share price over the last 12 months and 40% on share options.

Board remuneration in TY fell as a result of the fine and the board are now considering amending their remuneration to include a higher fixed element to overcome this shortfall.

Required:

(a) (i) **Explain Kohlberg's levels of moral development.**

(ii) **Discuss the price fixing agreement for fuel surcharges in terms of Kohlberg's theory and evaluate whether the action of JK to disclose the agreement was morally correct.**
(20 marks)

(b) (i) **Define and explain the term 'public interest'.**

    (ii) **Evaluate whether the decision to disclose the fuel surcharge by JK was in the 'public interest' as the directors maintain.** **(8 marks)**

(c) **With respect to the elements of remuneration in TY and JK, discuss whether the elements are correctly implemented according to codes of corporate governance and evaluate the effectiveness of each element.** **(15 marks)**

(d) **Explain the reasons for JK providing a CSR report.** **(7 marks)**

(Total: 50 marks)

7 AEI

You are the audit manager in charge of the field work of the AEI Co; it is the first year you have been involved with this client, although your audit firm has carried out the audit for the last eight years. AEI is a general manufacturing company which is listed on the stock exchange of the country it is based in. The company manufactures and distributes household products including kitchen equipment, chairs, tables, and bedroom furniture.

The audit work for the year to 30 June has been in progress for the last three weeks, and there is one week to go before it is completed. The audit team of five staff comprises two juniors, two seniors and yourself.

Ethical issues

P, one of the audit juniors, has been working exclusively on checking the existence and valuation of the inventory in the kitchen equipment division of AEI. The work is not particularly difficult, but it is quite time-consuming and means checking many items of inventory in a large warehouse. A lot of the inventory is old and dirty and P normally brings old clothes each day to wear around the warehouse. The warehouse manager recently approached P and offered a free re-fitting of P's kitchen as a 'thank you' for carrying out the inventory work. The warehouse manager stated this was a normal activity each year, in recognition of P's difficult working conditions. During the audit P has identified that the inventory is over-valued, particularly in respect of many old kitchen units being maintained at full cost price, even though those units have had no sales in the last 18 months. The extent of the over-valuation appears to be material to the financial statements.

Q, an audit senior, has been working on the disclosure elements of directors' remuneration for the financial statements and the directors' remuneration regulations disclosure for that jurisdiction. Q has discovered that disclosure in the financial statements and remuneration regulations is different from the information provided by and checked by the audit committee. When queried, the newly appointed chair of the audit committee stated that share options were not considered part of disclosable remuneration as the value was uncertain, being based on future share price, which could not be determined. This element of remuneration was therefore omitted from the financial statements and remuneration regulations disclosure. The chair informed Q that due to the confidential nature of directors' remuneration, no further disclosure of this situation was to be made. The chair also noted that recent review of shareholdings indicated that Q had a 2.5% share of the company and again this would not be disclosed due to the confidential nature of the information. Finally, the chair noted that the facts that the chair of the remuneration committee was also a director of IEA and that the chair of the remuneration committee of IEA was also a director of AEI should not be disclosed in the financial statements; again citing confidentiality issues.

R, the second audit junior, has been auditing the bank reconciliations on AEI's 26 different bank accounts. The work is considered suitable for a junior member as it mainly entails checking that cheques issued prior to the year end were presented to the bank for payment after the end of the year. R has completed work on the reconciliations, and stated correctly that all cheques were presented to AEI's bank for payment after the end of the year. However, R failed to state that a number of cheques, material in amount, were only presented two months after the year end. In other words the financial statements were 'window dressed' to show a lower creditors' amount than was actually the case at the year end. When queried about this omission during final review of the audit files, R correctly stated that he was never informed that timing of presentation of cheques was part of the audit procedures.

Governance issues

Recently, under pressure from the governing body of the stock exchange where AEI is listed, all four NEDs were urged to resign. Four new NEDs have recently been appointed; the NEDs have the knowledge and experience to be able to assist the board in their strategic and scrutinising roles, the NEDs have backgrounds in production, operations and HR roles. The term of the NED contracts of employment is the same as executive directors; that is three years between renewals. One minor concern is that the NEDs were appointed in a hurry and they have not worked with the executive directors on the board of AEI before.

Required:

(a)   Discuss the extent to which provision of an ethical code assists in resolving ethical dilemmas.   **(11 marks)**

(b)   (i)   Explain the terms 'ethical threat' and 'ethical safeguard'.   **(2 marks)**

      (ii)   From the information above, identify any ethical threats and recommend appropriate ethical safeguards explaining why that safeguard is appropriate.
(20 marks)

(c)   Explain the advantages and disadvantages of having NEDs on the board of a listed company.   **(7 marks)**

(d)   Explain the key functions of NEDs and evaluate whether those functions are being carried out effectively on the board of AEI.   **(10 marks)**

(Total: 50 marks)

8   **GLOBAL-BANK (JUN 09)**

 Timed question with Online tutor debrief

Global-bank is a prominent European bank with branches throughout Europe and investment arms in many locations throughout the world. It is regarded as one of the world's major international banks. Through its network of investment offices throughout the world, fund managers trade in local investment markets and equities. Futures and derivative traders also operate. Its primary listing is in London although it is also listed in most of the other global stock markets including New York, Hong Kong, Frankfurt and Singapore. As with similar banks in its position, Global-bank's structure is complicated and the complexity of its operations makes the strategic management of the company a demanding and highly technical process. Up until the autumn of 2008, investors had a high degree of confidence in the Global-bank board as it had delivered healthy profits for many years.

In the autumn of 2008, it came to light that Jack Mineta, a Global-bank derivatives trader in the large city office in Philos, had made a very large loss dealing in derivatives over a three-month period. It emerged that the losses arose from Mr Mineta's practice of ignoring the company trading rules which placed limits on, and also restricted, the type of financial instruments and derivatives that could be traded.

The loss, estimated to be approximately US$7 billion, was described by one analyst as 'a huge amount of money and enough to threaten the survival of the whole company'. As soon as the loss was uncovered, Mr Mineta was suspended from his job and the police were called in to check for evidence of fraud. The newspapers quickly reported the story, referring to Mr Mineta as a 'rogue trader' and asking how so much money could be lost without the bank's senior management being aware of it. It turned out that Mr Mineta's line manager at the Philos office had ignored the trading rules in the past in pursuit of higher profits through more risky transactions. Mr Mineta had considerably exceeded his trading limit and this had resulted in the huge loss. It later emerged that Mr Mineta had been dealing in unauthorised products which were one of the riskiest forms of derivatives.

At a press conference after Mr Mineta's arrest, Global-bank's chief executive, Mrs Barbara Keefer, said that her first priority would be to ask the Philos office why the normal internal controls had not been effective in monitoring Mr Mineta's activities. It emerged that Mr Mineta had in the past been one of Global-bank's most profitable derivatives traders. Some journalists suggested to Mrs Keefer that the company was happy to ignore normal trading rules when Mr Mineta was making profits because it suited them to do so.

Another derivatives trader in the Philos office, Emma Hubu, spoke to the media informally. She said that Mr Mineta was brilliant and highly motivated but that he often said that he didn't care about the trading rules. Miss Hubu explained that Mr Mineta didn't believe in right and wrong and once told her that 'I'm in this job for what I can get for myself – big risks bring big returns and big bonuses for me.' She also explained that the culture of the Philos office was driven by Mr Mineta's line manager, Juan Evora. She said that Mr Evora knew that Mr Mineta was breaking trading rules but was also very profits driven and kept compliance information from head office so that the nature of Mr Mineta's trading was not uncovered. The compliance information was required by head office but several failures to return the information had not been acted upon by head office. Mr Evora's bonus was directly linked to the size of the Philos office's profits and all of the derivatives traders, including Mr Mineta, were regularly reminded about the importance of taking risks to make big returns. Miss Hubu said that trading rules were not enforced and that head office never got involved in what went on in Philos as long as the annual profits from the Philos derivative traders were at or above expectations.

It emerged that the lack of correct information from Philos and elsewhere meant that Global-bank's annual report statement of internal control effectiveness was not accurate and gave an unduly favourable impression of the company's internal controls. In addition, the company's audit committee had been recently criticised by the external auditors for a lack of thoroughness. Also, the audit committee had recently lost two non-executive members that had not been replaced.

The amount lost by Mr Mineta made it necessary to refinance the Global-bank business and when the board recommended a US$5 billion rights issue, some of the institutional investors demanded an extraordinary general meeting (EGM). Global-bank's largest single shareholder, the Shalala Pension Fund, that held 12% of the shares, was furious about the losses and wanted an explanation from Mrs Keefer on why internal controls were so ineffective. When the Shalala trustees met after the losses had been reported, it was decided to write an urgent letter to Mrs Keefer expressing the trustees' disappointment at her role in the internal control failures at Global-bank. The letter would be signed by Millau Haber, the chairman of the Shalala trustees.

At the EGM, Mrs Keefer made a statement on behalf of the Global-bank board. In it she said that Mineta had been a rogue trader who had wilfully disregarded the company's internal controls and was, in breaking the company's trading rules, criminally responsible for the theft of company assets. She denied that the main Global-bank board had any responsibility for the loss and said that it was a 'genuinely unforeseeable' situation.

(a)   Kohlberg's theory of the development of moral reasoning contains three levels, with each level containing two stages or 'planes'. It is a useful framework for understanding the ways in which people think about ethical issues.

Required:

(i)   **Explain the three levels of Kohlberg's theory.**   **(6 marks)**

(ii)   **Identify the level that Mr Mineta operated at and justify your choice using evidence from the case.**   **(4 marks)**

(iii) **Identify, with reasons, the stage (or 'plane') of Kohlberg's moral development most appropriate for a professional bank employee such as Mr Mineta as he undertakes his trading duties.**   **(2 marks)**

(b)   **Explain FIVE typical causes of internal control failure and assess the internal control performance of Global-bank in the case scenario.**   **(10 marks)**

(c)   Analyse the agency relationship that exists between the board of Global-bank and the trustees of the Shalala Pension Fund.   **(4 marks)**

(d)   Distinguish between narrow and wide stakeholders and identify three narrow stakeholders in Global-bank (based on Evan & Freeman's definition) from information in the case. Assess the potential impact of the events described on each narrow stakeholder identified.   **(10 marks)**

(e)   You have been asked to draft a letter from Millau Haber, chairman of the Shalala trustees, to Mrs Keefer as a result of concerns over the events described in the case. The letter should explain the roles and responsibilities of the chief executive in internal control, and criticise Mrs Keefer's performance in that role.   **(10 marks)**

Professional marks are available in part (e) for the structure, content, style and layout of the letter.   **(4 marks)**

(Total: 50 marks)

9   ROWLANDS & MEDELEEV (JUN 08)

Rowlands & Medeleev (R&M), a major listed European civil engineering company, was successful in its bid to become principal (lead) contractor to build the Giant Dam Project in an East Asian country. The board of R&M prided itself in observing the highest standards of corporate governance. R&M's client, the government of the East Asian country, had taken into account several factors in appointing the principal contractor including each bidder's track record in large civil engineering projects, the value of the bid and a statement, required from each bidder, on how it would deal with the 'sensitive issues' and publicity that might arise as a result of the project.

The Giant Dam Project was seen as vital to the East Asian country's economic development as it would provide a large amount of hydroelectric power. This was seen as a 'clean energy' driver of future economic growth. The government was keen to point out that because hydroelectric power did not involve the burning of fossil fuels, the power would be environmentally clean and would contribute to the East Asian country's ability to meet its internationally agreed carbon emission targets. This, in turn, would contribute to the reduction of greenhouse gases in the environment. Critics, such as the environmental pressure group 'Stop-the-dam', however, argued that the project was far too large and the cost to the local environment would be unacceptable. Stop-the-dam was highly organised and, according to press reports in Europe, was capable of disrupting progress on the dam by measures such as creating 'human barriers' to the site and hiding people in tunnels who would have to be physically removed before proceeding. A spokesman for Stop-the-dam said it would definitely be attempting to resist the Giant Dam Project when construction started.

The project was intended to dam one of the region's largest rivers, thus creating a massive lake behind it. The lake would, the critics claimed, not only displace an estimated 100,000 people from their homes, but would also flood productive farmland and destroy several rare plant and animal habitats. A number of important archaeological sites would also be lost. The largest community to be relocated was the indigenous First Nation people who had lived on and farmed the land for an estimated thousand years. A spokesman for the First Nation community said that the 'true price' of hydroelectric power was 'misery and cruelty'. A press report said that whilst the First Nation would be unlikely to disrupt the building of the dam, it was highly likely that they would protest and also attempt to mobilise opinion in other parts of the world against the Giant Dam Project.

The board of R&M was fully aware of the controversy when it submitted its tender to build the dam. The finance director, Sally Grignard, had insisted on putting an amount into the tender for the management of 'local risks'. Sally was also responsible for the financing of the project for R&M. Although the client was expected to release money in several 'interim payments' as the various parts of the project were completed to strict time deadlines, she anticipated a number of working capital challenges for R&M, especially near the beginning where a number of early stage costs would need to be incurred. There would, she explained, also be financing issues in managing the cash flows to R&M's many subcontractors. Although the major banks financed the client through a lending syndicate, R&M's usual bank said it was wary of lending directly to R&M for the Giant Dam Project because of the potential negative publicity that might result. Another bank said it would provide R&M with its early stage working capital needs on the understanding that its involvement in financing R&M to undertake the Giant Dam Project was not disclosed. A press statement from Stop-the-dam said that it would do all it could to discover R&M's financial lenders and publicly expose them. Sally told the R&M board that some debt financing would be essential until the first interim payments from the client became available.

When it was announced that R&M had won the contract to build the Giant Dam Project, some of its institutional shareholders contacted Richard Markovnikoff, the chairman. They wanted reassurance that the company had fully taken the environmental issues and other risks into account. One fund manager asked if Mr Markovnikoff could explain the sustainability implications of the project to assess whether R&M shares were still suitable for his environmentally sensitive clients. Mr Markovnikoff said, through the company's investor relations department, that he intended to give a statement at the next annual general meeting (AGM) that he hoped would address these environmental concerns. He would also, he said, make a statement on the importance of confidentiality in the financing of the early stage working capital needs.

(a)   Any large project such as the Giant Dam Project has a number of stakeholders.

   Required:

   (i)   **Define the terms 'stakeholder' and 'stakeholder claim', and identify from the case FOUR of R&M's external stakeholders as it carries out the Giant Dam Project**   **(6 marks)**

   (ii)   **Describe the claim of each of the four identified stakeholders.**   **(4 marks)**

(b)   **Describe a framework to assess the risks to the progress of the Giant Dam Project. Your answer should include a diagram to represent the framework.**   **(6 marks)**

(c)   **Using information from the case, assess THREE risks to the Giant Dam Project.**

                                                                                          (9 marks)

(d)   **Prepare the statement for Mr Markovnikoff to read out at the AGM. The statement you construct should contain the following.**

   (i)   **A definition and brief explanation of 'sustainable development'**   **(3 marks)**

(ii) An evaluation of the environmental and sustainability implications of the Giant Dam Project (8 marks)

(iii) A statement on the importance of confidentiality in the financing of the early stage working capital needs and an explanation of how this conflicts with the duty of transparency in matters of corporate governance. (6 marks)

Professional marks for layout, logical flow and persuasiveness of the statement.

(4 marks)

(e) Internal controls are very important in a complex civil engineering project such as the Giant Dam Project.

Required:

Describe the difficulties of maintaining sound internal controls in the Giant Dam Project created by working through sub-contractors. (4 marks)

(Total: 50 marks)

10 CHEMCO (PILOT 07)

Chemco is a well-established listed European chemical company involved in research into, and the production of, a range of chemicals used in industries such as agrochemicals, oil and gas, paint, plastics and building materials. A strategic priority recognised by the Chemco board some time ago was to increase its international presence as a means of gaining international market share and servicing its increasingly geographically dispersed customer base. The Chemco board, which operated as a unitary structure, identified JPX as a possible acquisition target because of its good product 'fit' with Chemco and the fact that its geographical coverage would significantly strengthen Chemco's internationalisation strategy. Based outside Europe in a region of growth in the chemical industry, JPX was seen by analysts as a good opportunity for Chemco, especially as JPX's recent flotation had provided potential access to a controlling shareholding through the regional stock market where JPX operated.

When the board of Chemco met to discuss the proposed acquisition of JPX, a number of issues were tabled for discussion. Bill White, Chemco's chief executive, had overseen the research process that had identified JPX as a potential acquisition target. He was driving the process and wanted the Chemco board of directors to approve the next move, which was to begin the valuation process with a view to making an offer to JPX's shareholders. Bill said that the strategic benefits of this acquisition was in increasing overseas market share and gaining economies of scale.

While Chemco was a public company, JPX had been family owned and operated for most of its 35 year history. Seventy-five percent of the share capital was floated on its own country's stock exchange two years ago, but Leena Sharif, Chemco's company secretary suggested that the corporate governance requirements in JPX's country were not as rigorous as in many parts of the world. She also suggested that the family business culture was still present in JPX and pointed out that it operated a two-tier board with members of the family on the upper tier. At the last annual general meeting, observers noticed that the JPX board, mainly consisting of family members, had 'dominated discussions' and had discouraged the expression of views from the company's external shareholders. JPX had no non-executive directors and none of the board committee structure that many listed companies like Chemco had in place. Bill reported that although JPX's department heads were all directors, they were not invited to attend board meetings when strategy and management monitoring issues were being discussed. They were, he said, treated more like middle management by the upper tier of the JPX board and that important views may not be being heard when devising strategy. Leena suggested that these features made the JPX board's upper tier less externally accountable and less likely to take advice when making decisions. She said that board accountability was fundamental to public trust and that JPX's board might do well to recognise this, especially if the acquisition were to go ahead.

Chemco's finance director, Susan Brown advised caution over the whole acquisition proposal. She saw the proposal as being very risky. In addition to the uncertainties over exposure to foreign markets, she believed that Chemco would also have difficulties with integrating JPX into the Chemco culture and structure. While Chemco was fully compliant with corporate governance best practice, the country in which JPX was based had few corporate governance requirements. Manprit Randhawa, Chemco's operations director, asked Bill if he knew anything about JPX's risk exposure. Manprit suggested that the acquisition of JPX might expose Chemco to a number of risks that could not only affect the success of the proposed acquisition but also, potentially, Chemco itself. Bill replied that he would look at the risks in more detail if the Chemco board agreed to take the proposal forward to its next stage.

Finance director Susan Brown, had obtained the most recent annual report for JPX and highlighted what she considered to be an interesting, but unexplained, comment about 'negative local environmental impact' in its accounts. She asked chief executive Bill White if he could find out what the comment meant and whether JPX had any plans to make provision for any environmental impact. Bill White was able to report, based on his previous dealings with JPX, that it did not produce any voluntary environmental reporting. The Chemco board broadly supported the idea of environmental reporting although company secretary Leena Sharif recently told Bill White that she was unaware of the meaning of the terms 'environmental footprint' and 'environmental reporting' and so couldn't say whether she was supportive or not. It was agreed, however, that relevant information on JPX's environmental performance and risk would be necessary if the acquisition went ahead.

Required:

(a)   Evaluate JPX's current corporate governance arrangements and explain why they are likely to be considered inadequate by the Chemco board.   **(10 marks)**

(b)   Manprit suggested that the acquisition of JPX might expose Chemco to a number of risks. Illustrating from the case as required, identify the risks that Chemco might incur in acquiring JPX and explain how risk can be assessed.   **(15 marks)**

(c)   Construct the case for JPX adopting a unitary board structure after the proposed acquisition. Your answer should include an explanation of the advantages of unitary boards and a convincing case FOR the JPX board changing to a unitary structure.   **(10 marks)**

(Including 2 professional marks)

(d)   Explain FOUR roles of non-executive directors (NEDs) and assess the specific contributions that NEDs could make to improve the governance of the JPX board.   **(7 marks)**

(e)   Write a memo to Leena Sharif defining 'environmental footprint' and briefly explaining the importance of environmental reporting for JPX.   **(8 marks)**

(Including 2 professional marks)

(Total: 50 marks)

11 MARY JANE (DEC 09)

The Mary Jane was a large passenger and vehicle ferry operating between the two major ports of Eastport and Northport across a busy section of ocean known as the 'Northport route'. Prior to this, the Mary Jane had operated for many years in the much calmer waters of the 'Southsea route' but she had been transferred to the Northport route because her large size meant that more profit could be made by carrying more passengers and vehicles per journey. She was capable of carrying up to 1,000 passengers, 300 cars and 100 lorries per trip. The Mary Jane belonged to Sea Ships Company, a long established international company with a fleet of five ships operating on routes in other parts of the world. The Mary Jane had large doors at both the front and rear. Vehicles would drive in through the rear doors in Eastport and when she arrived in Northport, the Mary Jane would dock the other way round so that the vehicles could drive straight out using the forward doors. There were two doors at each end, upper and lower, and it was important that all four doors were securely closed before setting out to sea.

As with all marine operations, the safety procedures aboard the Mary Jane were subject to regulation, but her design left one weakness which was eventually to prove a disaster. From the main control bridge of the ship, it was not possible to see the front or rear doors, which meant that it wasn't possible to check from the main control bridge that they were closed upon departure from a port. On the night of 7 November, the Mary Jane was leaving Eastport in a storm for a crossing to Northport, a journey which should have taken five hours. It was dark and the weather was very poor. When she was only a few kilometres out from the Eastport harbour, water entered the car decks through the upper rear doors that had been left open after the Mary Jane had left port. The stormy conditions meant that the waves were very high and on this occasion, high enough so that when a large wave hit, the water entered through the open rear doors. Once enough water had entered her car decks, the Mary Jane began to lean to 30 degrees before completely falling over onto her side. The speed of the event, less than two minutes, meant that escape via lifeboats wasn't possible and the Mary Jane sank with the loss of many lives.

Among the survivors was first officer Ned Prop. Mr Prop later told how a recent change to staff reporting procedures had produced a situation in which the responsibility for checking that the rear doors were closed before sailing had changed. He said that, under the new system, two people were responsible for safety on the car deck but each person assumed that the other had checked that the upper rear doors had been closed. A reporting system in which each department head (car deck, navigation, etc.) on the ship separately reported readiness for sea to the captain at the beginning of each journey had been abandoned because it was too inconvenient to operate. Mr Prop said that the normal procedure was that if they didn't hear anything to the contrary by the departure time, he and Captain Mullett assumed that all was well throughout the ship and they could put to sea.

Mr Prop told how procedures on board ship often relied on 'human teamwork' rather than 'following paperwork systems'. It also emerged that, on the day of the disaster, a mistake in loading vehicles onto the wrong decks had delayed the ship's departure and created pressure to leave as soon as possible after all the vehicles were loaded. Mr Prop said that this too may have been a contributory factor to the confusion over who should have checked that the rear doors were closed. Mr Prop's superior officer, Captain Mullet, was drowned in the disaster.

Sea Ships Company, the Mary Jane's owner, was one of the longest established and most respected companies listed on the stock exchange. Although best known for its ferry operations, it had diversified into other activities in recent years. It was considered by investment analysts to be a 'steady and reliable' investment and the company chief executive, Wim Bock, had often said that Sea Ships Company employed 'the highest standards of corporate ethics'. It also valued its reputation as a well-run company and believed that the company's value was primarily due to its reputation for 'outstanding customer care'. The board often claimed that Sea Ships was a socially responsible company.

When Sea Ships' board met to discuss how to proceed after the disaster, Wim Bock said that the company could expect to receive substantial claims from victims' relatives. He also reported that, because of a regrettable oversight in the company's legal department, only a proportion of that liability would be covered by the company's insurance. There would also be punitive fines from the courts, the size of which would, a legal advisor said, reflect the scale of Sea Ship's negligence in contributing to the disaster. The finance director, Jill Wha, reported that if the company met the expected uninsured liabilities in full, even if reduced on appeal, it would severely threaten future cash flows as it would most likely have to sell non-current assets (most of its ships) to settle the claims. If large punitive fines were also imposed after the legal process, Mr Bock said that the company may not survive.

The government ordered an enquiry and a senior official was appointed to investigate the disaster. In her conclusions, enquiry chairman Caroline Chan said that in addition to the human error in not ensuring that the upper rear doors had been closed, it had also emerged that the Mary Jane had been travelling above the local shipping speed limit out of Eastport harbour. The excess speed had caused increased turbulence in the water and this was made much worse by the storm on the night in question. The combination of these factors meant that water gradually entered the open upper rear doors and this eventually caused the ship to lean and then capsize. Mrs Chan said that contrary to the board's perception of itself as a well-run company, she had encountered a 'culture of carelessness' at Sea Ships and that the internal control systems were inadequate for safely operating a fleet of ships. She reserved particular criticism for the board of Sea Ships saying that it was unbalanced, lacked independent scrutiny and, because none of the existing directors had ever served on board a ship, lacked representation from technically qualified nautical officers.

After the enquiry was concluded, but before the level of claims and punitive damages had been set by the courts, a document emerged within the company confirming that certain independent advice had been received from an external consultant. The advice was received at the time of the Mary Jane's transfer from the Southsea route to the Northport route. Because the Northport route is a much rougher area of sea, the advice concerned structural changes to the Mary Jane that would make her safer in rougher seas. Had the advice been followed, the Mary Jane would have had additional doors inserted inside the car deck to act as a second internal bulkhead to prevent water flooding the whole deck. Water would still have entered through the open rear doors on the night of 7 November, but would have been kept sealed in that rear section of the car deck and the Mary Jane would not have sunk. The company had received the advice but had not acted upon it as it would have required an expensive refit for the Mary Jane. This advice was then 'lost' in the company and only emerged later on.

Required:

(a) The independent consultant's advice was that the Mary Jane should have received structural work to make her safe for operating in the rougher seas of the Northport route. Sea Ships Company did not act on the advice.

Using the seven-step American Accounting Association (AAA) model for ethical decision-making, examine the company's dilemma on whether or not to disclose this information publicly. **(14 marks)**

(b) Using information from the case, identify and analyse the internal control failures at Sea Ships Company and on the Mary Jane. **(12 marks)**

(c) Assess the contribution that non-executive directors might have made in improving the corporate governance at Sea Ships Company. **(8 marks)**

(d) Draft a memo from chief executive Wim Bock to the senior officers on the other ships in the Sea Ships fleet informing them of vital internal control and risk issues following the loss of the Mary Jane. The memo should include the following, all placed in the context of the case.

   (i) An assessment, based on information in the case, of the importance for the board of Sea Ships to have all the information relating to key operational internal controls and risks **(6 marks)**

   (ii) An explanation of the qualitative characteristics of information needed by the Sea Ships' board for the assessment of internal controls and risks. **(6 marks)**

Professional marks will additionally be awarded in part (d) for drafting a memo that is clear, has a logical flow, is persuasive and is appropriately structured. **(4 marks)**

(Total: 50 marks)

12 HESKET NUCLEAR (JUN 10)

Hesket Nuclear (HN) is a nuclear power station in Ayland, a large European country. The HN plant is operated by Hesket Power Company (HPC), which in turn is wholly owned by the government of Ayland. Initially opened in the late 1950s, the power station grew in subsequent decades by the addition of several other facilities on the same site. HN now has the ability to generate 5% of Ayland's entire electricity demand and is one of the largest nuclear stations in Europe. At each stage of its development from the 1950s to the present day, development on the site was welcomed by the relevant local government authorities, by the businesses that have supported it, by the trade union that represents the majority of employees (called Forward Together or FT for short) and also by the national Ayland government. A nuclear reprocessing facility was added in the 1980s. This is a valuable source of overseas income as nuclear power producers in many other parts of the world send material by sea to HN to be reprocessed. This includes nuclear producers in several developing countries that rely on the cheaper reprocessed fuel (compared to 'virgin' fuel) that HN produces.

HPC is loss-making and receives a substantial subsidy each year from the government of Ayland. HPC has proven itself uneconomic but is deemed politically and environmentally necessary as far as the government is concerned. The government of Ayland has reluctantly accepted that large subsidies to HPC will be necessary for many years but considers nuclear power to be a vital component of its energy portfolio (along with other energy sources such as oil, gas, coal, renewables and hydroelectric) and also as a key part of its 'clean' energy strategy. Unlike energy from fossil fuels (such as coal, gas and oil), nuclear power generates a negligible amount of polluting greenhouse gas. HN also provides much needed employment in an otherwise deprived part of the country. The HN power station underpins and dominates the economy of its local area and local government authorities say that the HN plant is vital to the regional economy.

Since it opened, however, the HN power station has been controversial. Whilst being welcomed by those who benefit from it in terms of jobs, trade, reprocessing capacity and energy, a coalition has gradually built up against it comprising those sceptical about the safety and environmental impact of nuclear power. Some neighbouring countries believe themselves to be vulnerable to radioactive contamination from the HN plant. In particular, two countries, both of whom say their concerns about HN arise because of their geographical positions, are vocal opponents. They say that their geographical proximity forced them to be concerned as they are affected by the location of the HN plant which was not of their choosing.

The government of Beeland, whose capital city is 70 km across the sea from HN (which is situated on the coast), has consistently opposed HN and has frequently asked the government of Ayland to close HN down. The Beeland government claims that not only does 'low-level' emission from the site already contaminate the waters separating the two countries but it also claims that any future major nuclear 'incident' would have serious implications for the citizens of Beeland. There is some scientific support for this view although opinion is divided over whether Beeland is being irrational in its general opposition to HN.

The government of Ceeland is also a vocal opponent of HN. Ceeland is located to the north of Beeland and approximately 500 km away from Ayland. Some nuclear scientists have said that with such a large stretch of water between the HN plant and Ceeland, even a much-feared incident would be unlikely to seriously impact on Ceeland. Some commentators have gone further and said that Ceeland's concerns are unfounded and 'borne of ignorance'. FT, the trade union for HN employees, issued a statement saying that Ceeland had no reason to fear HN and that its fears were 'entirely groundless'.

HN's other vocal and persistent opponent is No Nuclear Now (NNN), a well-organised and well-funded campaigning group. Describing itself on its website as 'passionate about the environment', it describes HN's social and environmental footprint as 'very negative'. NNN has often pointed to an environmentally important colony of rare seals living near the HN plant. It says that the seals are dependent on a local natural ecosystem around the plant and are unable to move, arguing that the animals are at significant risk from low-level contamination and would have 'no chance' of survival if a more serious radioactive leak ever occurred. NNN points to such a leak that occurred in the 1970s, saying that such a leak proves that HN has a poor safety record and that a leak could easily recur.

Each time an objection to the HN power station is raised, FT, the trade union, robustly defends the HN site in the media, and argues for further investment, based on the need to protect the jobs at the site. Furthermore, the radiation leak in the 1970s led to FT uniting with the HPC board to argue against those stakeholders that wanted to use the leak as a reason to close the HN site. The combination of union and HPC management was able to counter the arguments of those asking for closure.

HN places a great deal of emphasis on its risk management and often publicises the fact that it conducts continual risk assessments and is in full compliance with all relevant regulatory frameworks. Similarly, FT recently pointed out that HN has had an 'impeccable' safety record since the incident in the 1970s and says on its website that it is 'proud' that its members are involved in ensuring that the company is continually in full compliance with all of the regulatory requirements placed upon it.

The board of HPC, led by chairman Paul Gog, is under continual pressure from the government of Ayland to minimise the amount of government subsidy. Each year, the government places challenging targets on the HPC board requiring stringent cost controls at the HN power station. In seeking to reduce maintenance costs on the expiry of a prior maintenance contract last year, the board awarded the new contract to an overseas company that brought its own workers in from abroad rather than employing local people. The previous contract company was outraged to have lost the contract and the move also triggered an angry response from the local workforce and from FT, the representative trade union.

FT said that it was deplorable that HPC had awarded the contract to an overseas company when a domestic company in Ayland could have been awarded the work. The union convenor, Kate Allujah, said that especially in the nuclear industry where safety was so important, domestic workers were 'more reliable' than foreign workers who were brought in purely on the basis of cost and in whose countries safety standards in similar industries might not be so stringent. HPC said that it had done nothing illegal as the foreign workers were allowed to work in Ayland under international legal treaties. Furthermore, it argued that pressure by FT to raise wages over recent years had created, with the government's subsidy targets, the cost pressure to re-tender the maintenance contract.

On HN's 50th anniversary last year, NNN published what it called a 'risk assessment' for the HN power station. It said it had calculated the probabilities (P) and impacts (I) of three prominent risks.

Risk of major radioactive leak over the next 10 years: P = 10%, I = 20

Risk of nuclear explosion over the next 50 years: P = 20%, I = 100

Risk of major terrorist attack over next 10 years: P = 10%, I = 80

Impacts were on an arbitrary scale of 1–100 where 100 was defined by NNN as 'total nuclear annihilation of the area and thousands of deaths'.

The governments of Beeland and Ceeland seized upon the report, saying that it proved that HN is a genuine threat to their security and should be immediately closed and decommissioned. HN's risk manager, Keith Wan, vigorously disagreed with this assessment saying that the probabilities and the impacts were 'ridiculous', massively overstated and intended to unnecessarily alarm people. HN's public relations office was also angry about it and said it would issue a rebuttal statement.

Required:

(a) Distinguish between voluntary and involuntary stakeholders, identifying both types of stakeholders in Hesket Nuclear. Assess the claims of THREE of the involuntary 'affected' stakeholders identified. **(12 marks)**

(b) The trade union, Forward Together, has had a long relationship with HN and represents not only the main workforce but also the employees of the maintenance company replaced by the foreign workers.

Required:

Explain the roles of employee representatives such as trade unions in corporate governance and critically evaluate, from the perspective of HPC's board, the contribution of Forward Together in the governance of HPC. **(10 marks)**

(c) Explain what an agency relationship is and examine the board of HPC's current agency relationship and objectives. Briefly explain how these would differ if HPC was a company with private shareholders. **(10 marks)**

(d) As a part of HPC's public relations effort, it has been proposed that a response statement should be prepared for the company's website to help address two major challenges to their reputation.

Required:

Draft this statement to include the following:

(i) Referring to the NNN report, explain why accurate risk assessment is necessary at Hesket Nuclear. **(8 marks)**

(ii) Explain what a social and environmental 'footprint' is and construct the argument that HN's overall social and environmental footprint is positive. **(6 marks)**

Professional marks will additionally be awarded in part (d) for drafting a statement that is clear, has a logical flow, is persuasive and is appropriately structured. **(4 marks)**

(Total: 50 marks)

13 ZPT (DEC 10)

In the 2009 results presentation to analysts, the chief executive of ZPT, a global internet communications company, announced an excellent set of results to the waiting audience. Chief executive Clive Xu announced that, compared to 2008, sales had increased by 50%, profits by 100% and total assets by 80%. The dividend was to be doubled from the previous year. He also announced that based on their outstanding performance, the executive directors would be paid large bonuses in line with their contracts. His own bonus as chief executive would be $20 million. When one of the analysts asked if the bonus was excessive, Mr Xu reminded the audience that the share price had risen 45% over the course of the year because of his efforts in skilfully guiding the company. He said that he expected the share price to rise further on the results announcement, which it duly did. Because the results exceeded market expectation, the share price rose another 25% to $52.

Three months later, Clive Xu called a press conference to announce a restatement of the 2009 results. This was necessary, he said, because of some 'regrettable accounting errors'. This followed a meeting between ZPT and the legal authorities who were investigating a possible fraud at ZPT. He disclosed that in fact the figures for 2009 were increases of 10% for sales, 20% for profits and 15% for total assets which were all significantly below market expectations. The proposed dividend would now only be a modest 10% more than last year. He said that he expected a market reaction to the restatement but hoped that it would only be a short-term effect.

The first questioner from the audience asked why the auditors had not spotted and corrected the fundamental accounting errors and the second questioner asked whether such a disparity between initial and restated results was due to fraud rather than 'accounting errors'. When a journalist asked Clive Xu if he intended to pay back the $20 million bonus that had been based on the previous results, Mr Xu said he did not. The share price fell dramatically upon the restatement announcement and, because ZPT was such a large company, it made headlines in the business pages in many countries.

Later that month, the company announced that following an internal investigation, there would be further restatements, all dramatically downwards, for the years 2006 and 2007. This caused another mass selling of ZPT shares resulting in a final share value the following day of $1. This represented a loss of shareholder value of $12 billion from the peak share price. Clive Xu resigned and the government regulator for business ordered an investigation into what had happened at ZPT. The shares were suspended by the stock exchange. A month later, having failed to gain protection from its creditors in the courts, ZPT was declared bankrupt. Nothing was paid out to shareholders whilst suppliers received a fraction of the amounts due to them. Some non-current assets were acquired by competitors but all of ZPT's 54,000 employees lost their jobs, mostly with little or no termination payment. Because the ZPT employees' pension fund was not protected from creditors, the value of that was also severely reduced to pay debts which meant that employees with many years of service would have a greatly reduced pension to rely on in old age.

The government investigation found that ZPT had been maintaining false accounting records for several years. This was done by developing an overly-complicated company structure that contained a network of international branches and a business model that was difficult to understand. Whereas ZPT had begun as a simple telecommunications company, Clive Xu had increased the complexity of the company so that he could 'hide' losses and mis-report profits. In the company's reporting, he also substantially overestimated the value of future customer supply contracts. The investigation also found a number of significant internal control deficiencies including no effective management oversight of the external reporting process and a disregard of the relevant accounting standards.

In addition to Mr Xu, several other directors were complicit in the activities although Shazia Lo, a senior qualified accountant working for the financial director, had been unhappy about the situation for some time. She had approached the finance director with her concerns but having failed to get the answers she felt she needed, had threatened to tell the press that future customer supply contract values had been intentionally and materially overstated (the change in fair value would have had a profit impact). When her threat came to the attention of the board, she was intimidated in the hope that she would keep quiet. She finally accepted a large personal bonus in exchange for her silence in late 2008.

The investigation later found that Shazia Lo had been continually instructed, against her judgement, to report figures she knew to be grossly optimistic. When she was offered the large personal bonus in exchange for her silence, she accepted it because she needed the money to meet several expenses related to her mother who was suffering a long-term illness and for whom no state health care was available. The money was used to pay for a lifesaving operation for her mother and also to rehouse her in a more healthy environment. Shazia Lo made no personal financial gain from the bonus at all (the money was all used to help her mother) but her behaviour was widely reported and criticised in the press after

The investigation found that the auditor, JJC partnership (one of the largest in the country), had had its independence compromised by a large audit fee but also through receiving consultancy income from ZPT worth several times the audit fee. Because ZPT was such an important client for JJC, it had many resources and jobs entirely committed to the ZPT account. JJC had, it was found, knowingly signed off inaccurate accounts in order to protect the management of ZPT and their own senior partners engaged with the ZPT account. After the investigation, JJC's other clients gradually changed auditor, not wanting to be seen to have any connection with JJC. Accordingly, JJC's audit business has since closed down. This caused significant disturbance and upheaval in the audit industry.

Because ZPT was regarded for many years as a high performing company in a growing market, many institutional investors had increased the number of ZPT shares in their investment portfolios. When the share price lost its value, it meant that the overall value of their funds was reduced and some individual shareholders demanded to know why the institutional investors had not intervened sooner to either find out what was really going on in ZPT or divest ZPT shares. Some were especially angry that even after the first restatement was announced, the institutional investors did not make any attempt to intervene. One small investor said he wanted to see more 'shareholder activism', especially among the large institutional investors.

Sometime later, Mr Xu argued that one of the reasons for the development of the complex ZPT business model was that it was thought to be necessary to manage the many risks that ZPT faced in its complex and turbulent business environment. He said that a multiplicity of overseas offices was necessary to address exchange rate risks, a belief challenged by some observers who said it was just to enable the ZPT board to make their internal controls and risk management less transparent.

(a)   Because of their large shareholdings, institutional investors are sometimes able to intervene directly in the companies they hold shares in.

Required:

(i)   **Explain the factors that might lead institutional investors to attempt to intervene directly in the management of a company**   **(6 marks)**

(ii) **Construct the case for institutional investors attempting to intervene in ZPT after the first results restatement was announced.**   **(6 marks)**

(b)   **Distinguish between absolutist and relativist approaches to ethics and critically evaluate the behaviour of Shazia Lo (the accountant who accepted a bonus for her silence) using both of these ethical perspectives.**   **(10 marks)**

(c) The ZPT case came to the attention of Robert Nie, a senior national legislator in the country where ZPT had its head office. The country did not have any statutory corporate governance legislation and Mr Nie was furious at the ZPT situation because many of his voters had been badly financially affected by it. He believed that legislation was needed to ensure that a similar situation could not happen again. Mr Nie intends to make a brief speech in the national legislative assembly outlining the case for his proposed legislation and some of its proposed provisions.

Required:

Draft sections of the speech to cover the following areas:

(i) **Explain the importance of sound corporate governance by assessing the consequences of the corporate governance failures at ZPT** **(10 marks)**

(ii) **Construct the case for the mandatory external reporting of internal financial controls and risks** **(8 marks)**

(iii) **Explain the broad areas that the proposed external report on internal controls should include, drawing on the case content as appropriate.**

(6 marks)

Professional marks will be awarded in part (c) for the structure, flow, persuasiveness and tone of the answer. **(4 marks)**

(Total: 50 marks)

14 BOBO CAR COMPANY (JUN 11)

The Bobo car company decided to launch a new model of car to compete in the highly competitive 'economy' market. Although Bobo was a long-established and profitable car manufacturer with a wide range of vehicles in other markets (such as family cars, four-wheel drives, etc), it had not entered the economy market because it believed profit margins would be too low. Company research showed that this was the car market segment with the smallest unit profits. The appointment of James Tsakos as chief executive changed that, however, as he believed that Bobo should offer a model in every category of car. It was announced that the new economy car, when launched, would be called the 'Bobo Foo'. The key concepts in the new model were conveyed to the design team led by executive director and head of design, Kathy Yao: cheap to buy, economical to run, cheap to repair, easy to park, fun to drive.

At the outset, James Tsakos met to discuss the new model with Kathy Yao. Because it was to enter the economy market, the minimisation of unit costs would be absolutely paramount. Mr Tsakos had some posters printed to hang in the design offices that read: 'The Bobo Foo – keep it cheap!' They were all signed personally by Mr Tsakos to emphasise the message to the design team as they were designing the car.

As well as repeating the 'Keep it cheap' message as often as possible, Mr Tsakos also instructed Kathy Yao that rather than the usual 43 months it took to develop a new model of car 'from the drawing board to the road', he wanted the Bobo Foo ready in 25 months. This, again, was about saving on costs to increase the eventual unit profits once the Bobo Foo was on sale. The design team was placed under a lot of pressure by Mr Tsakos, and Kathy Yao became stressed with the demand to complete the project in such a short time period. She privately told colleagues that the period was too short to ensure that all design features were safety tested. (This case took place before rigid safety regulations were imposed by governments so legal issues can be ignored.)

Kathy Yao's team worked out that one way of reducing manufacturing costs would be to position the car's fuel tank slightly differently from usual. She calculated that a small amount could be saved on producing each unit of production if the fuel tank was placed behind the rear axle rather than on top of the axle as was the normal practice. Along with other cost saving measures, this was incorporated into the finished prototype. In order to shorten the time to market, the factory started to be prepared for production of the Bobo Foo (called 'tooling up') as soon as the completed design was available but before the prototype was fully tested.

When the prototype Bobo Foo went through a range of crash tests, the positioning of the fuel tank was shown to be a potential fire risk in the event of a rear collision. No action was taken in the light of this observation because, as part of the low-cost strategy for the Bobo Foo, the factory had already been tooled up and was ready to begin production. The board decided that it would have been too expensive to retool the production line to a modified design and so it went into production as it was.

The Bobo Foo quickly became a big seller and sold half a million units of the model a year, making it appear that the Bobo Foo was another successful product for the Bobo Company. Sometime later, however, a lorry crashed into the back of a Bobo Foo containing three young women. Upon impact, the fuel tank was ruptured causing a fire in which all three passengers in the car were killed. The company then began to receive other claims from lawyers acting for people killed or injured by fires started by several rear-end collisions and fuel tank damage. Bobo accepted legal advice to pay compensation for each injury or loss of life caused by the fuel tank design fault.

The board then met to discuss the options for the Bobo Foo. Kathy Yao said her team had worked out that the cars could be made safe by adding some reinforcing metalwork around the tank area. Vernon Vim, the finance director, said that there were two options in the light of what Kathy had said. First was the 'universal recall' option. The company could recall, at its own expense, all Bobo Foos to make the modifications suggested by Kathy Yao and retool the production line to ensure safe positioning of the fuel tank on all future cars. The second option, the 'compensation option', was not to recall the existing cars nor to make changes to the production line but to continue to pay full compensation to victims or their families if, or when, a serious or fatal liability arose as a result of fuel tank damage from rear collisions.

Vernon Vim produced some calculations to illustrate the dilemma. They showed that, assuming that the Bobo Foo will be produced for ten years, the universal recall option would amount to $750 million over those ten years whilst the compensation option was likely to amount to approximately $200 million in total.

Vernon Vim said that even allowing for substantial errors in the calculation, there was still at least a three-fold difference in cost between the two options. Because the board's bonuses were partly based on the company's annual profits, he said that the board should simply continue to pay compensation claims and not issue the universal recall. He reminded the board that the difference between the two options was half a billion dollars over ten years.

Kathy Yao said that the company should consider the universal recall option and think about retooling the production line to ensure the safe repositioning of the fuel tank on future production. It was important, she believed, for customers to know they could trust Bobo cars for their safety and that customers associated the brand with social responsibility. She said this was an important part of the company's strategic positioning and that the company should comply with the expectations that society has of a large company like Bobo.

Chief executive James Tsakos was concerned about complying with the expectations of shareholders and with how events might affect the company's share price and longer term prospects. The company's reputation as a strong investment was very important and any long-term damage to the brand would be very unfortunate. He said that issuing a universal recall would send out a terrible signal to the financial markets and would damage confidence.

After a lengthy and heated discussion of the two options, it was decided that the 'compensation option' would be adopted. This was for financial reasons and it was decided that any discussion of the decision in public should be avoided because of the potential risk to reputation that may arise.

An unknown member of the board, outraged by the decision, informed the media about the choice the board had made and about the design process that led to the Bobo Foo (thereby acting as a 'whistleblower'). With a great deal of resulting negative publicity for Bobo on TV, radio and in the press, the institutional shareholders demanded an extraordinary general meeting to discuss the relevant issues with the board. In particular, the shareholders wanted to hear the chief executive explain why the board took the decision it did. In particular, they wanted to hold James Tsakos accountable for the decision: to establish how he understood his role as chief executive and how he arrived at the decision not to issue a universal recall on the Bobo Foo.

(a)   The fuel tank risk with the Bobo Foo was subsequently classified by an insurance company as a product and a safety risk.

Required:

Explore the circumstances leading to the fuel tank problem. Identify and explain internal control measures capable of mitigating the risk in future car development projects.

Note: Ignore any possible legal or regulatory issues that may arise.   (12 marks)

(b)   **Explain Kohlberg's three levels of moral development and identify, with reasons, the levels of development exhibited by James Tsakos, Kathy Yao and Vernon Vim.**

(12 marks)

(c)   **Distinguish between annual general meetings (AGMs) and extraordinary general meetings (EGMs). Explain the purpose of each and the advantages of holding an EGM to discuss the issues raised by the whistleblower.   (8 marks)**

(d)   **Prepare a statement for Mr Tsakos, the chief executive, to read at the EGM to address the following areas.**

(i)   **An explanation of the roles of the chief executive in managing the issues described in the case at Bobo Company   (8 marks)**

(ii)   **A defence of the company's decisions on the Bobo Foo from a 'pristine capitalist' ethical perspective (using Gray, Owen & Adams's framework).**

(6 marks)

Professional marks will additionally be awarded in part (d) for drafting a statement that is clear, has a logical flow, is persuasive and is appropriately structured.

(4 marks)

(Total: 50 marks)

15 P&J (DEC 12)

P&J is a long established listed company based in Emmland, a highly developed and relatively prosperous country. For the past 60 years, P&J has been Emmland's largest importer and processor of a product named X32, a compound used in a wide variety of building materials, protective fabrics and automotive applications. X32 is a material much valued for its heat resistance, strength and adaptability, but perhaps most of all because it is flexible and also totally fireproof. It is this last property that led to the growth of X32 use and made P&J a historically successful company and a major exporter.

X32 is mined in some of the poorest developing countries where large local communities depend heavily on X32 mining for their incomes. The incomes from the mining activities are used to support community development, including education, sanitation and health facilities in those developing countries. The X32 is then processed in dedicated X32 facilities near to the mining communities, supporting many more jobs. It is then exported to Emmland for final manufacture into finished products and distribution.

Each stage of the supply chain for X32 is dedicated only to X32 and cannot be adapted to other materials. In Emmland, P&J is the major employer in several medium-sized towns. In Aytown, for example, P&J employs 45% of the workforce and in Betown, P&J employs 3,000 people and also supports a number of local causes including a children's nursery, an amateur football club and a number of adult education classes. In total, the company employs 15,000 people in Emmland and another 30,000 people in the various parts of the supply chain (mining and processing) in developing countries. Unlike in Emmland, where health and safety regulations are strong, there are no such regulations in most of the developing countries in which P&J operates.

Recently, some independent academic research discovered that X32 was very harmful to human health, particularly in the processing stages, causing a wide range of fatal respiratory diseases, including some that remain inactive in the body for many decades. Doctors had suspected for a while that X32 was the cause of a number of conditions that P&J employees and those working with the material had died from, but it was only when Professor Harry Kroll discovered how X32 actually attacked the body that the link was known for certain. The discovery caused a great deal of distress at P&J, and also in the industries which used X32.

The company was faced with a very difficult situation. Given that 60% of P&J's business was concerned with X32, Professor Kroll's findings could not be ignored. Although demand for X32 remained unaffected by Kroll's findings in the short to medium term, the company had to consider a new legal risk from a stream of potential litigation actions against the company from employees who worked in environments containing high levels of X32 fibre, and workers in industries which used X32 in their own processes.

In order to gain some understanding of the potential value of future compensation losses, P&J took legal advice and produced two sets of figures, both describing the present value of cumulative future compensation payments through litigation against the company. These forecasts were based on financial modelling using another product of which the company was aware, which had also been found to be hazardous to health.

	In 5 years $(M)	In 15 years $(M)	In 25 years $(M)	In 35 years $(M)
Best case	5	30	150	400
Worst case	20	80	350	1,000

The finance director (FD), Hannah Yin, informed the P&J board that the company could not survive if the worst-case scenario was realised. She said that the actual outcome depended upon the proportion of people affected, the period that the illness lay undetected in the body, the control measures which were put in place to reduce the exposure of employees and users to X32, and society's perception of X32 as a material. She estimated that losses at least the size of the best case scenario were very likely to occur and would cause a manageable but highly damaging level of losses.

The worst case scenario was far less likely but would make it impossible for the company to survive. Although profitable, P&J had been highly geared for several years and it was thought unlikely that its banks would lend it any further funds. Hannah Yin explained that this would limit the company's options when dealing with the risk. She also said that the company had little by way of retained earnings.

Chief executive officer, Laszlo Ho, commissioned a study to see whether the health risk to P&J workers could be managed with extra internal controls relating to safety measures to eliminate or reduce exposure to X32 dust. The confidential report said that it would be very difficult to manage X32 dust in the three stages of the supply chain unless the facilities were redesigned and rebuilt completely, and unless independent breathing apparatus was issued to all people coming into contact with X32 at any stage. FD Hannah Yin calculated that a full refit of all of the company's mines, processing and manufacturing plants (which Mr Ho called 'Plan A') was simply not affordable given the current market price of X32 and the current costs of production. Laszlo Ho then proposed the idea of a partial refit of the Aytown and Betown plants because, being in Emmland, they were more visible to investors and most other stakeholders.

Mr Ho reasoned that this partial refit (which he called 'Plan B') would enable the company to claim it was making progress on improving internal controls relating to safety measures whilst managing current costs and 'waiting to see' how the market for X32 fared in the longer term. Under Plan B, no changes would be made to limit exposure to X32 in the company's operations in developing countries.

Hannah Yin, a qualified accountant, was trusted by shareholders because of her performance in the role of FD over several years. Because she would be believed by shareholders, Mr Ho offered to substantially increase her share options if she would report only the 'best case' scenario to shareholders and report 'Plan B' as evidence of the company's social responsibility. She accepted Mr Ho's offer and reported to shareholders as he had suggested. She also said that the company was aware of Professor Kroll's research but argued that the findings were not conclusive and also not considered a serious risk to P&J's future success.

Eventually, through speaking to an anonymous company source, a financial journalist discovered the whole story and felt that the public, and P&J's shareholders in particular, would want to know about the events and the decisions that had been taken in P&J. He decided to write an article for his magazine, Investors in Companies, on what he had discovered.

Required:

(a) Define 'social footprint' and describe, from the case, four potential social implications of Professor Kroll's discovery about the health risks of X32. **(10 marks)**

(b) Describe what 'risk diversification' means and explain why diversifying the risk related to the potential claims against the use of X32 would be very difficult for P&J. **(10 marks)**

(c) As an accountant, Hannah Yin is bound by the IFAC fundamental principles of professionalism.

Required:

Criticise the professional and ethical behaviour of Hannah Yin, clearly identifying the fundamental principles of professionalism she has failed to meet. **(9 marks)**

(d) Writing as the journalist who discovered the story, draft a short article for the magazine *Investors in Companies*. You may assume the magazine has an educated readership. Your article should achieve the following:

(i) Distinguish between strategic and operational risk and explain why Professor Kroll's findings are a strategic risk to P&J **(8 marks)**

(ii) Discuss the board's responsibilities for internal control in P&J and criticise Mr Ho's decision to choose Plan B. **(9 marks)**

Professional marks will be awarded in part (d) for the structure, logical flow, persuasiveness and tone of the article. **(4 marks)**

(Total: 50 marks)

16 HOPPO (JUN 13)

A report was recently published by an international accounting organisation on the future of certain rare chemicals used in industrial processes. The report said that some of these chemicals, crucial to many industrial processes, were now so scarce that there was a threat to supply chains for items such as computer circuitry and the rechargeable batteries used in electronic goods. One of these scarce and rare chemicals, the highly toxic trans-Y13 (TY13), has become increasingly rare and, therefore, very expensive. It requires careful processing and, although used in small quantities in each product, its high cost means that even small inefficiencies in its treatment can disproportionately affect final product costs.

The report's conclusions included this statement: 'Put simply, we are living beyond the planet's means. Businesses that use these materials will experience new risks. It may even become seen as socially unacceptable to use some of these materials. Finally, if supply stops, then manufacturing stops.'

One company which depends on a continuous and reliable supply of TY13 is Hoppo Company. Hoppo is a listed company based in the highly developed country of Essland. It has, for several years, designed and developed its products in Essland and then outsourced manufacturing to another company, Red Co, which is based in the developing country of Teeland. This means that Red Co manufactures Hoppo's products for an agreed price and to Hoppo's designs and technical specifications.

Because Red Co is based in Teeland (a developing country with lower land and labour costs than Essland), working with Red Co has offered Hoppo cost advantages over manufacturing its products in its home country. As a company which outsources many of its functions, Hoppo tries to ensure that in each case of outsourcing, working conditions and environmental responsibility are the same at each outsourcing company as they would be if carried out in its highly-regulated home country of Essland.

Hoppo itself is one of the most valuable companies on the Essland stock exchange and has strategically positioned itself as a company that is seen as a trustworthy and responsible producer, that is also responsible in its social and environmental behaviour. In its press statements and annual reports, it has frequently highlighted the high value it places on integrity and transparency as fundamental values in its corporate governance. It has recently considered producing an annual environmental report, as it believes its shareholders would value the information it contains.

Red Co is an experienced producer of electronic circuits and has a long history of working with TY13. It has relationships with the main TY13 suppliers going back many years, and these relationships ensure that it can normally obtain supplies even during periods when world supply is short. Because the supply quality of TY13 varies widely, Red Co has developed finely-tuned methods of ensuring that the TY13 received is of suitable quality. The performance of the finished product is very sensitive to the quality of the TY13 and so this pre-production testing is considered vital. In addition, TY13's toxicity and high cost mean that other systems are put in place at Red Co to ensure that it is safely stored until needed for manufacture.

Earlier this year, however, two issues arose at Red Co which caused Hoppo to reconsider its outsourcing relationship. The first one was the publication of an international media report showing evidence that, despite Hoppo's claims about having the same working conditions at all of its outsourcing clients, labour conditions were unacceptably poor at Red Co. Because labour regulations were less stringent in Teeland, Red Co had been forcing employees to work excessively long hours without breaks, and other measures that would not have been permitted in Essland. It was reported that workers were being bullied, and threatened with dismissal if they complained about their working conditions.

The second problem was a leakage of unprocessed TY13 from the Red Co factory. Not only was this seen as wasteful and careless, it also poisoned a local river, killing many fish and contaminating local farmland. The community living nearby said that it would be unable to use the contaminated land for many years and that this would affect local food supply.

When a journalist, Bob Hob, discovered information about these two issues, the media interpreted the story as a problem for Hoppo, partly because of its reputation as a responsible company. Hoppo's own research had shown that many of its customers valued its environmental reputation and that some of its key employees were attracted to Hoppo for the same reason.

Some important customers began to associate Hoppo directly with the problems at Red Co, even though it was Red Co which had actually been responsible for the employee issues and also the TY13 leak. Hoppo's share price fell when some investors considered the problems to be important enough to undermine future confidence in Hoppo's management and brand value.

In an effort to protect its reputation in future, Hoppo began to review its outsource arrangement with Red Co. The board considered the options for taking manufacturing under its own direct control by building a new factory in another low-cost country, which would be owned and operated by Hoppo. It quickly realised that stopping the outsourcing relationship with Red Co would mean the loss of about 1,000 jobs there and could also raise the likelihood of legal action by Red Co against Hoppo for loss of contract. As Hoppo's manufacturing contract is so valuable to Red Co, some people thought it likely that Red Co would sue Hoppo for loss of future earnings, despite the terms of the contract being legally ambiguous. This lack of clarity in the contract arose because of differences in Essland and Teeland law and as a consequence of poor legal advice that Hoppo received when drawing up the contract. It was believed that any legal action would be widely reported because of Hoppo's international profile and that this may result in some unfavourable publicity.

When considering its options for a directly-owned factory, Hoppo's plan was to build a modern and efficient plant with 'state of the art' environmental controls. Yuland was chosen as a suitable country and Hoppo narrowed the choice down to two possible sites in Yuland for its new factory: Ootown and Aatown. The mayors of both towns wrote to Hoppo's chief executive saying that they would welcome any potential investment from Hoppo. In addition, the mayor of Ootown asked for a 'personal gift' (relatively immaterial although not a trivial amount to Hoppo but a large amount of money locally) to facilitate a trouble-free passage of the necessary planning permission for a new Hoppo factory in the town.

When deciding between Ootown and Aatown in Yuland, the general view was that, all other things being equal, Ootown was a better location. But there was some discussion about whether the 'personal gift' requested by the mayor of Ootown was ethical. The board thought that the decision was an important one and so took some time to reflect before reaching a decision on whether to continue with Red Co or to build a new factory in either Ootown or Aatown.

Having become aware that investing in Ootown and paying the money to its mayor was being considered by Hoppo, a member of the chief executive's office staff informed the journalist, Bob Hob, and a story appeared in an Essland national newspaper saying, 'Hoppo considers paying a bribe to get preferred site in Yuland.' Bob Hob made remarks challenging Hoppo's claims about integrity and transparency, and suggested that recent events had shown that it had demonstrated neither. Public discussion then took place on the internet saying that Hoppo, previously considered a highly ethical company, had been corrupt and incompetent, both in allowing Red Co to breach employment and environmental best practice, and then to consider paying a bribe to the mayor of Ootown.

It was decided that, in seeking to restore its reputation, the company needed to publish a detailed press statement responding to the issues raised in the media. Because Hoppo's reputation for integrity and transparency were considered to be strategically important and had been questioned, it was decided that the statement should also contain reassurances about these important themes.

Required:

(a) Briefly explain 'related' and 'correlated' risks. Explore the correlation between legal risk and reputation risk for Hoppo if it were to cancel its contract with Red Co.

(10 marks)

(b) Describe an environmental report, including its purpose and contents, and discuss the potential advantages of an environmental report for Hoppo and its shareholders.

(10 marks)

(c) Briefly explain how internal controls can be strategic in nature. Explain, using detailed examples from the case, why developing sound internal controls over the supply and processing of TY13 would be important if Hoppo opted to build its own factory in Yuland.

(10 marks)

(d) Draft the press release as discussed in the case. It should:

(i) Define and explain the importance of 'integrity' and 'transparency' in the context of the case.

(6 marks)

(ii) Construct an argument against paying the bribe to the mayor of Ootown from both business and ethical perspectives. Your ethical arguments should include both deontological and consequentialist perspectives.

(10 marks)

Professional marks will be awarded in part (d) for the format, tone, logical flow and persuasiveness of the press release.

(4 marks)

(Total: 50 marks)

Section 2

PRACTICE QUESTIONS – SECTION B

GOVERNANCE AND RESPONSIBILITY

17 CORPORATE GOVERNANCE GUIDELINES

The following are extracts from the corporate governance guidelines issued by a large, publicly-quoted company:

(i) All auditors' fees, including fees for services other than audit, should be fully disclosed in the annual report. In order to ensure continuity of standards the same audit partner, wherever possible, should be responsible for a period of at least three years.

(ii) The board shall establish a remuneration committee comprising 50% executive directors, and 50% non-executive directors. A non-executive director shall chair the committee.

(iii) The Chairman of the company may also hold the position of Chief Executive, although this shall not normally be for a period of more than three years.

(iv) The annual report shall fully disclose whether principles of good corporate governance have been applied.

(v) No director shall hold directorships in more than 20 companies.

(vi) Directors should report regularly on the effectiveness of the company's system of internal control.

Required:

(a) Discuss the extent to which each of points (i) – (vi) is likely to comply with a principles-based corporate governance system. Use examples from a system with which you are familiar to illustrate your answer. **(12 marks)**

(b) Prepare a brief report advising senior managers of your company who are going to work in subsidiaries in:

   (i) A country with a rules-based corporate governance system which is similar to that in the USA and which applies to subsidiaries of overseas companies.
   (8 marks)

   (ii) A country where companies have two-tier boards. **(5 marks)**

   (Total: 25 marks)

18   GEELAND (DEC 11)

There has been a debate in the country of Geeland for some years about the most appropriate way to regulate corporate governance. Several years ago, there were a number of major corporate failures and 'scandals' caused in part by a number of single powerful individuals dominating their boards. Business leaders and policy-makers were sceptical about a rules-based approach, and this led the Geeland stock exchange to issue guidance in the 'Geeland Code' as follows:

'Good corporate governance is not just a matter of prescribing particular corporate structures and complying with a number of rules. There is a need for broad principles. All stakeholders should then apply these flexibly to the varying circumstances of individual companies.'

Given the causes of the Geeland corporate governance failures, there was a debate about whether the separation of the roles of chairman and chief executive should be made a legal requirement. This resulted in the stock exchange issuing guidance that whilst a rules-based or 'box ticking' approach would specify that 'the roles of chairman and chief executive officer should never be combined... We do not think that there are universally valid answers on such points.'

One company to take advantage of the flexibility in Geeland's principles-based approach was Anson Company. In July 2010, Anson Company announced that it had combined its roles of chairman and chief executive in a single role carried out by one individual. In accordance with the Geeland listing rules, it made the following 'comply or explain' statement in its 2011 annual report:

'Throughout the year the company complied with all Geeland Code provisions with the exception that from 1 July 2010 the roles of chairman and chief executive have been exercised by the same individual, William Klunker. We recognise that this has been out of line with best practice. We understand the concerns of shareholders but believe that we have maintained robust governance while at the same time benefiting from having Mr Klunker in control. On 31 July 2012 Mr Klunker will step down as executive chairman, remaining as chairman until we conclude our search for a non-executive chairman to succeed him, no later than March 2013.'

Required:

(a)   Briefly distinguish between rules and principles-based approaches to corporate governance. Critically evaluate the Geeland stock exchange's guidance that 'all stakeholders should then apply these flexibly to the varying circumstances of individual companies.'   **(12 marks)**

(b)   Explain why a separation of the roles of chairman and chief executive is considered best practice in most jurisdictions.   **(8 marks)**

(c)   Assess the 'comply or explain' statement made by Anson Company in its 2011 annual report.   **(5 marks)**

(Total: 25 marks)

19 KK (DEC 10)

KK is a large listed company. When a non-executive directorship of KK Limited became available, John Soria was nominated to fill the vacancy. John is the brother-in-law of KK's chief executive Ken Kava. John is also the CEO of Soria Supplies Ltd, KK's largest single supplier and is, therefore, very familiar with KK and its industry. He has sold goods to KK for over 20 years and is on friendly terms with all of the senior officers in the company. In fact last year, Soria Supplies appointed KK's finance director, Susan Schwab, to a non-executive directorship on its board. The executive directors of KK all know and like John and so plan to ask the nominations committee to appoint him before the next AGM.

KK has recently undergone a period of rapid growth and has recently entered several new overseas markets, some of which, according to the finance director, are riskier than the domestic market. Ken Kava, being the dominant person on the KK board, has increased the risk exposure of the company according to some investors. They say that because most of the executive directors are less experienced, they rarely question his overseas expansion strategy. This expansion has also created a growth in employee numbers and an increase in the number of executive directors, mainly to manage the increasingly complex operations of the company. It was thought by some that the company lacked experience and knowledge of international markets as it expanded and that this increased the risk of the strategy's failure. Some shareholders believed that the aggressive strategy, led by Ken Kava, has been careless as it has exposed KK Limited to some losses on overseas direct investments made before all necessary information on the investment was obtained.

As a large listed company, the governance of KK is important to its shareholders. Fin Brun is one of KK's largest shareholders and holds a large portfolio of shares including 8% of the shares in KK. At the last AGM he complained to KK's chief executive, Ken Kava, that he needed more information on directors' performance. Fin said that he didn't know how to vote on board reappointments because he had no information on how they had performed in their jobs. Mr Kava said that the board intended to include a corporate governance section in future annual reports to address this and to provide other information that shareholders had asked for. He added, however, that he would not be able to publish information on the performance of individual executive directors as this was too complicated and actually not the concern of shareholders. It was, he said, the performance of the board as a whole that was important and he (Mr Kava) would manage the performance targets of individual directors.

Required:

(a) Explain the term 'conflict of interest' in the context of non-executive directors and discuss the potential conflicts of interest relating to KK and Soria Supplies if John Soria were to become a non-executive director of KK Limited. **(8 marks)**

(b) Assess the advantages of appointing experienced and effective non-executive directors to the KK board during the period in which the company was growing rapidly. **(7 marks)**

(c) Explain the typical contents of a 'best practice' corporate governance report within an annual report and how its contents could help meet the information needs of Fin Brun. **(10 marks)**

(Total: 25 marks)

20 MULTI-JURISDICTIONAL GOVERNANCE (DEC 07)

At a recent international meeting of business leaders, Seamus O'Brien said that multi-jurisdictional attempts to regulate corporate governance were futile because of differences in national culture. He drew particular attention to the Organisation for Economic Co-operation and Development (OECD) and International Corporate Governance Network (ICGN) codes, saying that they were, 'silly attempts to harmonise practice'. He said that in some countries, for example, there were 'family reasons' for making the chairman and chief executive the same person. In other countries, he said, the separation of these roles seemed to work. Another delegate, Alliya Yongvanich, said that the roles of chief executive and chairman should always be separated because of what she called 'accountability to shareholders'.

One delegate, Vincent Viola, said that the right approach was to allow each country to set up its own corporate governance provisions. He said that it was suitable for some countries to produce and abide by their own 'very structured' corporate governance provisions, but in some other parts of the world, the local culture was to allow what he called, 'local interpretation of the rules'. He said that some cultures valued highly structured governance systems while others do not care as much.

Required:

(a)   Explain the roles of the chairman in corporate governance.   **(5 marks)**

(b)   Assess the benefits of the separation of the roles of chief executive and chairman that Alliya Yongvanich argued for and explain her belief that 'accountability to shareholders' is increased by the separation of these roles.   **(12 marks)**

(c)   Critically evaluate Vincent Viola's view that corporate governance provisions should vary by country.   **(8 marks)**

(Total: 25 marks)

21 FOOTBALL CLUB (DEC 07)

When a prominent football club, whose shares were listed, announced that it was to build a new stadium on land near to its old stadium, opinion was divided. Many of the club's fans thought it a good idea because it would be more comfortable for them when watching games. A number of problems arose, however, when it was pointed out that the construction of the new stadium and its car parking would have a number of local implications. The local government authority said that building the stadium would involve diverting roads and changing local traffic flow, but that it would grant permission to build the stadium if those issues could be successfully addressed. A number of nearby residents complained that the new stadium would be too near their homes and that it would destroy the view from their gardens. Helen Yusri, who spoke on behalf of the local residents, said that the residents would fight the planning application through legal means if necessary. A nearby local inner-city wildlife reservation centre said that the stadium's construction might impact on local water levels and therefore upset the delicate balance of animals and plants in the wildlife centre. A local school, whose pupils often visited the wildlife centre, joined in the opposition, saying that whilst the school supported the building of a new stadium in principle, it had concerns about disruption to the wildlife centre.

The football club's board was alarmed by the opposition to its planned new stadium as it had assumed that it would be welcomed because the club had always considered itself a part of the local community. The club chairman said that he wanted to maintain good relations with all local people if possible, but at the same time he owed it to the fans and the club's investors to proceed with the building of the new stadium despite local concerns.

Required:

(a) Define 'stakeholder' and explain the importance of identifying all the stakeholders in the stadium project. **(10 marks)**

(b) Compare and contrast Gray, Owen and Adams's 'pristine capitalist' position with the 'social contractarian' position. Explain how these positions would affect responses to stakeholder concerns in the new stadium project. **(8 marks)**

(c) Explain what 'fiduciary responsibility' means and construct the case for broadening the football club board's fiduciary responsibility in this case. **(7 marks)**

(Total: 25 marks)

22 DELCOM

Jason Kumas is the CEO and majority shareholder of Delcom, a large conglomerate listed on a European stock exchange. Mr Kumas created the company less than ten years ago and during this time has successfully acquired a portfolio of manufacturing businesses across the region. The company was listed three years ago in order to gain access to the large amounts of capital needed to continue growth through acquisition. Since his decision to float the company institutional investors have begun to take an increasingly active role in the governance of Delcom.

Investors are concerned about the risk profile of the organisation. In particular, they point to two recent takeovers of production companies where, in his haste to close the deal, Mr Kumas failed to adequately carry out due diligence, relying instead on his own intuitive feelings as to the value of the going concerns. This insight was subsequently found to be impaired as it is generally agreed that much of the companies' technologies are poor and the price paid was therefore far too high. Acquisitive transactions such as this are common and although Delcom has a board of directors it is evident that such decision making authority rests solely with the CEO.

Disclosure through the annual report is also considered to be inadequate. Mr Kumas has repeatedly failed to address this issue, privately viewing disclosure as little more than a paper exercise since he is the majority shareholder and has an insider's perspective on the success of the business.

Concerns have been voiced at the AGM calling for Mr Kumas to recognise the need to adhere to global governance standards such as those published by the OECD and ICGN. In response, Mr Kumas insists that local stock exchange regulation, although far below these global standards, provides an adequate basis upon which to operate, and that if change is necessary, it is for regulators to enforce such measures.

Required:

(a) Define 'insider governance' structure and evaluate the worth of such structures.

(8 marks)

(b) Describe the application of transaction cost theory to corporate governance.

(6 marks)

(c) Recommend improvements to disclosure that would be applicable in the situation of Delcom.

(6 marks)

(d) Discuss the focus for action within global governance standards.

(5 marks)

(Total: 25 marks)

23 VESTEL *Online question assistance*

Vestel is a drinks manufacturer that specialises in producing wine and spirit products for consumption in its home markets and abroad. The company has been very successful in recent years culminating in its ability to gain listing on the local stock exchange.

Acceptance as a member of the stock exchange has placed pressure on the board of directors to ensure the company is fully compliant with the principles-based governance regime currently in operation. This compliance includes the need for appropriate committee structures and support for all board members in ensuring appropriate skills and expertise are developed over time.

As a relatively small public company Vestel has needed to be innovative and adaptive in order to compete against global competitors that operate in its markets. In addition, it has recently been faced with a number of market challenges that threaten shareholder prospects over the next period. These include the rising price of grapes, molasses and grain due to a series of harsh winters and poor harvests as well as rising costs in energy and transport. At the retail end, government taxation on alcoholic drinks has dramatically increased following public outcry over levels of alcohol abuse amongst the country's citizens.

Ethics, environmentalism, skills in government lobbying and operational infrastructure are all seen as key areas for improvement following a recent review of board performance. In response a nomination committee is being created for the first time in the company's history in order to recruit a number of non-executive directors onto the board. Finding suitable candidates may be difficult in a country where the size of the economy and number of large companies is relatively small.

The need to ensure such individuals' take an active role as soon as possible has highlighted the importance of induction as part of the recruitment process.

Required:

(a)   Explain why a nomination committee is suggested to be essential for effective board operations.   **(6 marks)**

(b)   Describe how the committee might tackle the recruitment process.   **(7 marks)**

(c)   Briefly discuss the business case for induction and consider the content of such a process.   **(12 marks)**

                                                                                  (Total: 25 marks)

 Online question assistance

---

24   CORPORATE GOVERNANCE *Walk in the footsteps of a top tutor*

Required:

(a)   Identify the key reasons for the emergence of corporate governance regulations around the world.   **(5 marks)**

(b)   Explain the key areas and principles of corporate governance regulations.

                                                                                  (10 marks)

(c)   Discuss the role and responsibilities of audit committees as laid down in a major principles-based corporate governance code of your choice.   **(10 marks)**

                                                                                  (Total: 25 marks)

25   LALAND (JUN 11)

In the country of Laland, aid organisations registered as charities are not subject to the same financial reporting requirements as limited companies (this is not the case in many other countries where they are treated equally in law). One person to take advantage of this is Horace Hoi who has led his vigorous campaign in favour of animal protection for the past 25 years. As a highly competent self-publicist for his charity and an engaging media performer, he has raised the public profile of his charity substantially. He can and does raise large amounts of money for his charity through his personal charm and passionate appeals on television and in large meetings of supporters. His charity is called the 'Horace Hoi Organisation' (HHO) and its stated aim is to 'stop animals suffering'.

Mr Hoi has recently become the subject of criticism by the media because of allegations that he lived a lavish lifestyle and personally owned a large mansion and a number of classic cars. The HHO recently bought a private jet to support Mr Hoi in his travels around the world for speaking engagements and for his work for the HHO charity. One journalist reported that most of the donors to HHO are well-meaning individuals, mainly of modest means, that care greatly about animal suffering and who would be 'horrified' if they knew of the luxury in which Mr Hoi lived.

Despite the fact that Mr Hoi had claimed that he personally takes only a modest salary from the organisation for his work, a journalist recently estimated Mr Hoi's personal wealth, thought to be gained from the HHO, to be around $10 million. When challenged to disclose the financial details of the HHO and Mr Hoi's own personal earnings, a HHO spokesman simply replied that this was not required under the law in Laland and that the HHO was therefore fully compliant with the law. The HHO has refused to join a group of other charities that have undertaken to make full financial disclosures despite it not being mandatory in law. The HHO says that although it does produce financial information for the charity and tax authorities, it has no intention of making this information public. The HHO also makes no disclosures about its governance structures and was once criticised as being 'intentionally opaque in order to hide bad practice'.

In yielding to the media pressure to provide some information on its financial affairs, HHO eventually published a pie chart on its website saying that its expenditure was divided between animal shelters (57%), field work helping animals (32%), administration (6%) and other causes (5%). This was the totality of its public financial disclosure.

Required:

(a) **Discuss the ways in which charities differ from public listed companies and explain how these differences affect their respective governance structures.** **(9 marks)**

(b) **Define 'transparency' and construct the case for greater transparency in the governance of the Horace Hoi Organisation.** **(8 marks)**

(c) Audit committees can have a role in reviewing internal controls and addressing areas of deficiency.

Required:

Explain how an audit committee might assist in addressing the apparent internal control deficiencies at HHO. **(8 marks)**

(Total: 25 marks)

26 OLAND (DEC 12)

After a recent financial crisis in the country of Oland, there had been a number of high profile company failures and a general loss of confidence in business. As a result, an updated corporate governance code was proposed, with changes to address these concerns.

Before the new code was published, there was a debate in Oland society about whether corporate governance provisions should be made rules-based, or remain principles-based as had been the case in the past. One elected legislator, Martin Mung, whose constituency contained a number of the companies that had failed with resulting rises in unemployment, argued strongly that many of the corporate governance failures would not have happened if directors were legally accountable for compliance with corporate governance provisions. He said that 'you can't trust the markets to punish bad practice', saying that this was what had caused the problems in the first place. He said that Oland should become a rules-based jurisdiction because the current 'comply or explain' was ineffective as a means of controlling corporate governance.

Mr Mung was angered by the company failures in his constituency and believed that a lack of sound corporate governance contributed to the failure of important companies and the jobs they supported. He said that he wanted the new code to make it more difficult for companies to fail.

The new code was then issued, under a principles-based approach. One added provision in the new Oland code was to recommend a reduction in the re-election period of all directors from three years to one year. The code also required that when seeking re-election, there should be 'sufficient biographical details on each director to enable shareholders to take an informed decision'. The code explained that these measures were 'in the interests of greater accountability'.

Required:

(a)   **Examine how sound corporate governance can make it more difficult for companies to fail, clearly explaining what 'corporate governance' means in your answer.**

(10 marks)

(b)   Martin Mung believes that Oland should become a rules-based jurisdiction because the current 'comply or explain' approach is ineffective as a means of controlling corporate governance.

Required:

Explain the difference between rules-based and principles-based approaches to corporate governance regulation, and argue against Martin Mung's belief that 'comply or explain' is ineffective.   (8 marks)

(c)   **Explain what 'accountability' means, and discuss how the proposed new provisions for shorter re-election periods and biographical details might result in 'greater accountability' as the code suggests.**   (7 marks)

(Total: 25 marks)

27   LUM CO

Lum Co is a family business that has been wholly-owned and controlled by the Lum family since 1920. The current chief executive, Mr Gustav Lum, is the great grandson of the company's founder and has himself been in post as CEO since 1998. Because the Lum family wanted to maintain a high degree of control, they operated a two-tier board structure: four members of the Lum family comprised the supervisory board and the other eight non-family directors comprised the operating board.

Despite being quite a large company with 5,000 employees, Lum Co never had any non-executive directors because they were not required in privately-owned companies in the country in which Lum Co was situated.

The four members of the Lum family valued the control of the supervisory board to ensure that the full Lum family's wishes (being the only shareholders) were carried out. This also enabled decisions to be made quickly, without the need to take everything before a meeting of the full board.

Starting in 2008, the two tiers of the board met in joint sessions to discuss a flotation (issuing public shares on the stock market) of 80% of the company. The issue of the family losing control was raised by the CEO's brother, Mr Crispin Lum. He said that if the company became listed, the Lum family would lose the freedom to manage the company as they wished, including supporting their own long-held values and beliefs. These values, he said, were managing for the long term and adopting a paternalistic management style. Other directors said that the new listing rules that would apply to the board, including compliance with the stock market's corporate governance codes of practice, would be expensive and difficult to introduce.

The flotation went ahead in 2011. In order to comply with the new listing rules, Lum Co took on a number of non-executive directors (NEDs) and formed a unitary board. A number of problems arose around this time with NEDs feeling frustrated at the culture and management style in Lum Co, whilst the Lum family members found it difficult to make the transition to managing a public company with a unitary board. Gustav Lum said that it was very different from managing the company when it was privately owned by the Lum family. The human resources manager said that an effective induction programme for NEDs and some relevant continuing professional development (CPD) for existing executives might help to address the problems.

Required:

(a)   Compare the typical governance arrangements between a family business and a listed company, and assess Crispin's view that the Lum family will 'lose the freedom to manage the company as they wish' after the flotation.   **(10 marks)**

(b)   Assess the benefits of introducing an induction programme for the new NEDs, and requiring continual professional development (CPD) for the existing executives at Lum Co after its flotation.   **(8 marks)**

(c)   Distinguish between unitary and two-tier boards, and discuss the difficulties that the Lum family might encounter when introducing a unitary board.   **(7 marks)**

(Total: 25 marks)

28   ZOGS (JUN 12)

John Louse, the recently retired chief executive of Zogs Company, a major listed company, was giving a speech reflecting on his career and some of the aspects of governance he supported and others of which he was critical. In particular, he believed that board committees were mainly ineffective. A lot of the ineffectiveness, he said, was due to the lack of independence of many non-executive directors (NEDs). He believed that it was not enough just to have the required number of non-executive directors; they must also be 'truly independent' of the executive board. It was his opinion that it was not enough to have no material financial connection with a company for independence: he believed that in order to be truly independent, NEDs should come from outside the industry and have no previous contact with any of the current executive directors.

In relation to risk committees, he said that in his experience, the company's risk committee had never stopped any risk affecting the company and because of this, he questioned its value. He said that the risk committee was 'always asking for more information, which was inconvenient' and had such a 'gloomy and pessimistic' approach to its task. He asked, 'why can't risk committees just get on with stopping risk, and also stop making inconvenient demands on company management? Do they think middle managers have nothing else to do?' He viewed all material risks as external risks and so the risk committee should be looking outwards and not inwards.

Since retiring from Zogs, Mr Louse had taken up a non-executive directorship of SmallCo, a smaller private company in his town. In a meeting with Alan Ng, the new chief executive of Zogs, Mr Ng said that whilst risk management systems were vital in large companies like Zogs, fewer risk controls were needed in smaller companies like SmallCo.

Required:

(a) Define 'independence' in the context of corporate governance and critically evaluate Mr Louse's comment that greater independence of non-executive directors is important in increasing the effectiveness of board committees.

(8 marks)

(b) Describe the roles of a risk committee and criticise Mr Louse's understanding of the risk committee in Zogs Company. (9 marks)

(c) Assess whether risk committees and risk mitigation systems are more important in larger companies, like Zogs, than in smaller companies like SmallCo. (8 marks)

(Total: 25 marks)

29 ROSH AND COMPANY (JUN 08)

Mary Hobbes joined the board of Rosh and Company, a large retailer, as finance director earlier this year. Whilst she was glad to have finally been given the chance to become finance director after several years as a financial accountant, she also quickly realised that the new appointment would offer her a lot of challenges. In the first board meeting, she realised that not only was she the only woman but she was also the youngest by many years.

Rosh was established almost 100 years ago. Members of the Rosh family have occupied senior board positions since the outset and even after the company's flotation 20 years ago a member of the Rosh family has either been executive chairman or chief executive. The current longstanding chairman, Timothy Rosh, has already prepared his slightly younger brother, Geoffrey (also a longstanding member of the board) to succeed him in two years' time when he plans to retire. The Rosh family, who still own 40% of the shares, consider it their right to occupy the most senior positions in the company so have never been very active in external recruitment. They only appointed Mary because they felt they needed a qualified accountant on the board to deal with changes in international financial reporting standards.

Several former executive members have been recruited as non-executives immediately after they retired from full-time service. A recent death, however, has reduced the number of non-executive directors to two. These sit alongside an executive board of seven that, apart from Mary, have all been in post for over ten years.

Mary noted that board meetings very rarely contain any significant discussion of strategy and never involve any debate or disagreement. When she asked why this was, she was told that the directors had all known each other for so long that they knew how each other thought. All of the other directors came from similar backgrounds, she was told, and had worked for the company for so long that they all knew what was 'best' for the company in any given situation. Mary observed that notes on strategy were not presented at board meetings and she asked Timothy Rosh whether the existing board was fully equipped to formulate strategy in the changing world of retailing. She did not receive a reply.

Required:

(a) Explain 'agency' in the context of corporate governance and criticise the governance arrangements of Rosh and Company. **(12 marks)**

(b) Explain the roles of a nominations committee and assess the potential usefulness of a nominations committee to the board of Rosh and Company. **(8 marks)**

(c) Define 'retirement by rotation' and explain its importance in the context of Rosh and Company. **(5 marks)**

(Total: 25 marks)

30 CORPORATE GOVERNANCE DEBATE (JUN 08)

At an academic conference, a debate took place on the implementation of corporate governance practices in developing countries. Professor James West from North America argued that one of the key needs for developing countries was to implement rigorous systems of corporate governance to underpin investor confidence in businesses in those countries. If they did not, he warned, there would be no lasting economic growth as potential foreign inward investors would be discouraged from investing.

In reply, Professor Amy Leroi, herself from a developing country, reported that many developing countries are discussing these issues at governmental level. One issue, she said, was about whether to adopt a rules-based or a principles-based approach. She pointed to evidence highlighting a reduced number of small and medium sized initial public offerings in New York compared to significant growth in London. She suggested that this change could be attributed to the costs of complying with Sarbanes-Oxley in the United States and that over-regulation would be the last thing that a developing country would need. She concluded that a principles-based approach, such as in the United Kingdom, was preferable for developing countries.

Professor Leroi drew attention to an important section of the Sarbanes-Oxley Act to illustrate her point. The key requirement of that section was to externally report on – and have attested (verified) – internal controls. This was, she argued, far too ambitious for small and medium companies that tended to dominate the economies of developing countries.

Professor West countered by saying that whilst Sarbanes-Oxley may have had some problems, it remained the case that it regulated corporate governance in the 'largest and most successful economy in the world'. He said that rules will sometimes be hard to follow but that is no reason to abandon them in favour of what he referred to as 'softer' approaches.

(a) There are arguments for both rules and principles-based approaches to corporate governance.

Required:

(i) Describe the essential features of a rules-based approach to corporate governance **(3 marks)**

(ii) Construct the argument against Professor West's (and in favour of Professor Leroi's) opinion that a principles-based approach would be preferable in developing countries. Your answer should consider the particular situations of developing countries. **(10 marks)**

(b)   The Sarbanes-Oxley Act contains provisions for the attestation (verification) and reporting to shareholders of internal controls over financial reporting.

Required:

Describe the typical contents of an external report on internal controls.   **(8 marks)**

(c)   **Construct the arguments in favour of Professor Leroi's remark that external reporting requirements on internal controls were 'too ambitious' for small and medium companies.**   **(4 marks)**

(Total: 25 marks)

31   BOOM

In early 2013, the remuneration committee of Boom Co (a listed company) met to determine the rewards for the executive directors. It was the practice of the committee to meet annually to decide on executive rewards for the forthcoming financial year. In line with best practice, the committee was made up entirely of non-executive directors.

When the remuneration committee met, its chairman, Sarah Umm, reminded those present that the committee should comply with the guidance of the relevant code of corporate governance. She read out the section that she believed was most relevant to their discussions.

'A significant proportion of executive directors' remuneration should be structured so as to link rewards to corporate and individual performance. The remuneration committee should judge where to position their company relative to other companies. But they should use such comparisons with caution in view of the risk of an upward movement of remuneration levels with no corresponding improvement in performance. Remuneration for non-executive directors should not include share options or other performance-related elements.'

She explained that the committee should balance several concerns when setting rewards: the link with performance, market rates and the company's overall strategy. The strategic priority in the next few years, she explained, was to incentivise medium to long-term growth whilst retaining the existing executive board in place as long as possible.

At the end of the meeting, a new member of the committee, Sam South, asked whether there were any performance-related elements of non-executive directors' rewards. Sarah Umm explained that these were only available to executive members of the board in line with the terms of the corporate governance code.

Required:

(a)   **Explain what is meant by a 'code of corporate governance' and discuss the general purposes of such a code in listed companies such as Boom Co.**   **(7 marks)**

(b)   **Propose how the components of a reward package might be balanced to 'incentivise medium to long-term growth whilst retaining the existing executive board in place as long as possible.'**   **(8 marks)**

(c)   **Briefly explain the general roles of non-executive directors in a listed company such as Boom Co, and discuss why non-executive directors should not receive performance-related elements in their rewards as Sam South enquired.**   **(10 marks)**

(Total: 25 marks)

32   EASTERN PRODUCTS (PILOT 07)

Sonia Tan, a fund manager at institutional investor Sentosa House, was reviewing the annual report of one of the major companies in her portfolio. The company, Eastern Products, had recently undergone a number of board changes as a result of a lack of confidence in its management from its major institutional investors of which Sentosa House was one.

The problems started two years ago when a new chairman at Eastern Products (Thomas Hoo) started to pursue what the institutional investors regarded as very risky strategies whilst at the same time failing to comply with a stock market requirement on the number of non-executive directors on the board.

Sonia rang Eastern's investor relations department to ask why it still was not in compliance with the requirements relating to non-executive directors. She was told that because Eastern was listed in a principles-based jurisdiction, the requirement was not compulsory. It was simply that Eastern chose not to comply with that particular requirement. When Sonia asked how its board committees could be made up with an insufficient number of non-executive directors, the investor relations manager said he didn't know and that Sonia should contact the chairman directly. She was also told that there was no longer a risk committee because the chairman saw no need for one.

Sonia telephoned Thomas Hoo, the chairman of Eastern Products. She began by reminding him that Sentosa House was one of Eastern's main shareholders and currently owned 13% of the company. She went on to explain that she had concerns over the governance of Eastern Products and that she would like Thomas to explain his non-compliance with some of the stock market's requirements and also why he was pursuing strategies viewed by many investors as very risky. Thomas reminded Sonia that Eastern had outperformed its sector in terms of earnings per share in both years since he had become chairman and that rather than question him, she should trust him to run the company as he saw fit. He thanked Sentosa House for its support and hung up the phone.

Required:

(a)   Explain what an 'agency cost' is and discuss the problems that might increase agency costs for Sentosa House in the case of Eastern Products.   **(7 marks)**

(b)   Describe, with reference to the case, the conditions under which it might be appropriate for an institutional investor to intervene in a company whose shares it holds.   **(10 marks)**

(c)   Evaluate the contribution that a risk committee made up of non-executive directors could make to Sonia's confidence in the management of Eastern Products.

     (4 marks)

(d)   Assess the opinion given to Sonia that because Eastern Products was listed in a principles-based jurisdiction, compliance with the stock market's rules was 'not compulsory'.   **(4 marks)**

     (Total: 25 marks)

33   TQ COMPANY (JUN 09)

 Timed question with Online tutor debrief

TQ Company, a listed company, recently went into administration (it had become insolvent and was being managed by a firm of insolvency practitioners). A group of shareholders expressed the belief that it was the chairman, Miss Heike Hoiku, who was primarily to blame. Although the company's management had made a number of strategic errors that brought about the company failure, the shareholders blamed the chairman for failing to hold senior management to account. In particular, they were angry that Miss Hoiku had not challenged chief executive Rupert Smith who was regarded by some as arrogant and domineering. Some said that Miss Hoiku was scared of Mr Smith.

Some shareholders wrote a letter to Miss Hoiku last year demanding that she hold Mr Smith to account for a number of previous strategic errors. They also asked her to explain why she had not warned of the strategic problems in her chairman's statement in the annual report earlier in the year. In particular, they asked if she could remove Mr Smith from office for incompetence. Miss Hoiku replied saying that whilst she understood their concerns, it was difficult to remove a serving chief executive from office.

Some of the shareholders believed that Mr Smith may have performed better in his role had his reward package been better designed in the first place. There was previously a remuneration committee at TQ but when two of its four non-executive members left the company, they were not replaced and so the committee effectively collapsed. Mr Smith was then able to propose his own remuneration package and Miss Hoiku did not feel able to refuse him. He massively increased the proportion of the package that was basic salary and also awarded himself a new and much more expensive company car. Some shareholders regarded the car as 'excessively' expensive. In addition, suspecting that the company's performance might deteriorate this year, he exercised all of his share options last year and immediately sold all of his shares in TQ Company.

It was noted that Mr Smith spent long periods of time travelling away on company business whilst less experienced directors struggled with implementing strategy at the company headquarters. This meant that operational procedures were often uncoordinated and this was one of the causes of the eventual strategic failure.

(a)   Miss Hoiku stated that it was difficult to remove a serving chief executive from office.

   Required:

   (i)   **Explain the ways in which a company director can leave the service of a board.**   **(4 marks)**

   (ii)   **Discuss Miss Hoiku's statement that it is difficult to remove a serving chief executive from a board.**   **(4 marks)**

(b)   **Assess, in the context of the case, the importance of the chairman's statement to shareholders in TQ Company's annual report.**   **(5 marks)**

(c)   **Criticise the structure of the reward package that Mr Smith awarded himself.**   **(4 marks)**

(d)   **Criticise Miss Hoiku's performance as chairman of TQ Company.**   **(8 marks)**

                                                                          (Total: 25 marks)

34 ROLES AND RELEVANCE

Many countries have developed best practice guidelines for corporate governance, although the details of what constitutes best practice vary from one country to another. There are also differences between statutory and regulatory corporate governance, as in the US, and voluntary codes of practice, as in Europe.

In all countries with a corporate governance regime, the composition of the board of directors is a key issue. In some countries, the remuneration of directors is another important aspect of corporate governance.

Required:

(a) Explain why it is considered appropriate for the positions of chairman and chief executive officer of a company to be held by different individuals. **(5 marks)**

(b) Describe the roles of non-executive directors, and suggest why there might be tension in these roles between contributing to strategy development and monitoring executive activity. **(8 marks)**

(c) Explain the reasons why directors' remuneration might be regarded as an important issue in corporate governance, and explain the principles that should be applied by a remuneration committee when negotiating a remuneration package with an executive director. **(12 marks)**

(Total: 25 marks)

35 METTO MINING

There have been articles in the media recently regarding Metto Mining's operations around the world. In one 'whistleblower' documentary carried out by an investigative journalist, a hidden camera revealed a scandalous disregard for safety at three mines, with employees working in conditions far below legal standards set by the host country.

Local activist groups and citizens have been demonstrating outside one of the facilities for the past two months, ever since an underground explosion killed a number of employees. The company's response has been to pay local police to keep the crowds away from the gates of the mine. It has also issued a statement referring to the incident as 'regrettable but unavoidable'. Most impartial observers believe improved safety standards could have prevented the disaster.

At its European head quarters, Professor Lee, Metto's ethics manager has been handling questions from reporters all week. Due to the gravity of the situation he is now blaming local explosives suppliers for providing faulty products to the mines whilst also pointing out that the company contributes financially to the health and schooling of the local population through payments for mining rights paid to the local government. This government refuses to comment on any issues involving the mines.

Professor Lee's words have done little to appease institutional investors such as Julie Walker, head of Walker investments. She believes that share ownership is coupled with an obligation to act responsibly and is now threatening to divest unless Metto takes positive action to improve its ethical positioning. This includes making large charitable donations direct to families and communities affected by its operations. Professor Lee and the board of directors have so far failed to respond to her written request.

Required:

(a) Examine the Corporate Social Responsibility issues at Metto and discuss possible responses to ethical conflict. **(12 marks)**

(b) Discuss Metto's rights and responsibilities with regard to its position of corporate citizenship. **(6 marks)**

(c) Briefly explain FOUR classifications of stakeholders that may assist in determining a response to the ethical conflict at Metto. **(4 marks)**

(d) Assess the responsibilities of ownership and property as identified by Julie Walker.

(3 marks)

(Total: 25 marks)

36 SARBANES-OXLEY (DEC 13)

The Sarbanes-Oxley legislation in the United States was introduced in 2002, partly in response to the earlier failure of the American energy company, Enron. It was decided by United States legislators that compliance should be enforceable under law rather than under listing rules. At the time it was being debated, some said that the legal enforceability of Sarbanes-Oxley would be unfair to smaller companies without the infrastructure needed to generate internal control data and to report on it. One example of this was the debate over s.404 of Sarbanes-Oxley, which mandated external reporting on the adequacy of internal controls. Before a size criterion was later introduced, this applied equally to all companies but now smaller companies are partly exempted from this requirement.

In its advice on this requirement, the United States Securities and Exchange Commission (SEC) published the following comments:

The rules we adopted in June 2003 to implement s.404 of the Sarbanes-Oxley Act of 2002 ('Sarbanes-Oxley') require management to annually evaluate whether internal control over financial reporting (ICFR) is effective at providing reasonable assurance and to disclose its assessment to investors. Management is responsible for maintaining evidential matter, including documentation, to provide reasonable support for its assessment. This evidence will also allow a third party, such as the company's external auditor, to consider the work performed by management.

Required:

(a) Distinguish between rules and principles-based approaches to the regulation of corporate governance, and explain the disadvantages of a rules-based system such as Sarbanes-Oxley in the United States. **(7 marks)**

(b) Define 'agency' in the context of corporate governance and discuss the benefits to shareholders of 'maintaining a system of internal control over financial reporting' in a rules-based jurisdiction. **(10 marks)**

(c) Construct the case to exempt smaller companies from the full reporting requirements of s.404 of the Sarbanes-Oxley Act 2002. **(8 marks)**

(Total: 25 marks)

37 HWL (DEC 13)

'Help-with-life' (HWL) is a charitable organisation established ten years ago. Its stated purpose is, 'to help individuals and families with social problems and related issues.' Its work, in a large city with people from many countries and backgrounds, involves advising, counselling, giving practical support to service users (the people who come for help). Over the years it has been operating, HWL has realised that the best outcomes are achieved when the staff member understands and sympathises with the service users' social norms, ethical and cultural beliefs.

40% of HWL's funding comes from local government. This means that HWL has to account for its use of that portion of its funding and comply with several rules imposed by local government. One of these rules concerns demonstrating appropriate diversity amongst the managers of services such as those delivered by HWL. It requires the charity management team to involve the widest feasible range of people and to reflect the demographic make-up of the community.

HWL has recently had to replace a number of executive and non-executive members of its board. The external auditor suggested that setting up a nominations committee would help in these board appointments. The CEO, Marian Ngogo, has always stressed that all directors should share the ethical values of HWL and agree to take reduced rewards because, 'every dollar we pay a director is a dollar less we are spending on service delivery.' She stressed that the culture in a charity was very different from a commercial ('for profit') business and that staff and directors must share the ethical stance of HWL and had to accept a different approach to social responsibility if they joined.

Required:

(a) **Explain the roles of a nominations committee and describe how the Help-with-life (HWL) nominations committee might approach the task of nominating and appointing new directors.** **(8 marks)**

(b) **Explain the advantages of diversity on the board of HWL.** **(8 marks)**

(c) **Explain 'corporate social responsibility' (CSR) and discuss the ways in which CSR and the ethical stance might differ between HWL and a commercial 'for profit' business.** **(9 marks)**

(Total: 25 marks)

38 BADISON

For some time there has been some significant confusion within the population of the suburban town of Badison as to the obligations that a public sector body has toward those people or organisations affected by their actions. At a recent meeting of the resident involvement focus group, these questions again arose clearly indicating a lack of understanding on behalf of the attendees who were felt to be an accurate representation of the local community.

Of particular concern was how the local council were held to account for actions taken. One member of the residents in attendance suggested that the public sector had no clearly published objective setting process or accountability for actions taken. Another attendee, a retired lawyer, echoed these concerns and questioned the chairman of the group to explain that given the employees were all acting on behalf of the wider resident group, how they were accountable for actions taken.

Another member commented that she had heard the term "stakeholder" being used and whilst familiar with the concept in the context of the private sector was concerned as to how it applied to the council's treatment of local residents. She added that that if there was no accountability for public sector actions, then how did the public sector add any value at all – " surely we would be better off with using the funds allocated to the public sector elsewhere" she was heard to say.

The focus group chairman, a member of the council, was embarrassed by the lack of response from the council members attending. She stated that this lack of understanding must be resolved and a motion was passed that a formal presentation be scheduled to be delivered at the next meeting to clear this confusion once and for all. The following day she has asked you, her assistant to prepare explanatory notes for her attention to be used as the basis for the forthcoming presentation.

Required:

(a)   **Explain the term public sector.**   **(5 marks)**

(b)   **Describe an approach to the creation of objectives in the public sector.**   **(6 marks)**

(c)   **Distinguish between the concepts of agency in the private and public sector and identify how accountability is monitored in public sector organisations.**   **(8 marks)**

(d)   **Explain the term stakeholder in the context of the public sector and describe how accountability maybe achieved.**   **(6 marks)**

(Total: 25 marks)

INTERNAL CONTROL AND REVIEW

39   DING (DEC 09)

Sam Mesentery was appointed a director of Ding Company in October this year taking on the role of financial controller. He had moved himself and his family to a new country to take up the post and was looking forward to the new challenges. When he arrived he learned that he was on the 'operating board' of Ding Company and that there was a 'corporate board' above the operating board that was senior to it. This surprised him as in the companies he had worked for in his own country, all directors in the company were equal. The corporate board at Ding was small, with five directors in total, while the operating board was larger, with ten members.

After a few days in the job he received an e-mail requiring him to report to Annette Hora, the managing director. She said that she had regretfully received two complaints from another senior colleague about Sam's behaviour. First, Sam had apparently made a highly inappropriate remark to a young female colleague and second, his office was laid out in the wrong way. Not only was his desk positioned in breach of fire regulations but also, he was told that it was normal to have the desk facing towards the door so that colleagues felt more welcomed when they went in. 'It's company policy' she said abruptly. Sam remembered the conversation with the young female colleague but was unaware of anything inappropriate in what he had said to her. He said that he positioned his desk so he could get the best view out of the window when he was working.

The following day he arrived at work to find that the corporate board was in an emergency meeting. There had been a sudden and dramatic change in the circumstances of one of Ding's major suppliers and the corporate board later said that they needed to meet to agree a way forward and a strategy to cope with the change. Annette said that because of the competitive nature of its resource markets, Ding had to act fast and preferably before its competitors. Hence the necessity of a two-tier board structure. She said there was no time for lengthy discussions which was why the operating board was excluded. Sam was told that Ding operated in a 'complex and turbulent' environment and when strategic factors in the environment changed, the company often had to respond quickly and decisively.

It was a month later that Sam first met with Arif Zaman, Ding's non-executive chairman. After Arif asked Sam how he was settling in, Sam asked Arif why he preferred a two-tier board structure and Arif replied that actually it was Annette's idea. He said that she prefers it that way and because he is a non-executive member doesn't feel able to challenge her opinion on it. Because 'it seems to work' he had no plans to discuss it with her. He went on to say that he was an old friend of Annette's and was only in post to satisfy the corporate governance requirements to have a non-executive chairman. He said that he saw his role as mainly ceremonial and saw no need to take any direct interest in the company's activities. He said that he chaired some board meetings when he was available and he sometimes wrote the chairman's statement in the annual report.

Required:

(a) Explain the content of a director's induction programme and assess the advantages of such a programme for Sam. (8 marks)

(b) Using information from the case, critically evaluate Annette's belief that two-tier boards are preferable in complex and turbulent environments such as at Ding Company. (8 marks)

(c) Assess Arif Zaman's understanding of his role as non-executive chairman. (9 marks)

(Total: 25 marks)

40 TOMATO BANK (JUN 10)

Five years ago, George Woof was appointed chief executive officer (CEO) of Tomato Bank, one of the largest global banks. Mr Woof had a successful track record in senior management in America and his appointment was considered very fortunate for the company. Analysts rated him as one of the world's best bankers and the other directors of Tomato Bank looked forward to his appointment and a significant strengthening of the business.

One of the factors needed to secure Mr Woof's services was his reward package. Prior to his acceptance of the position, Tomato Bank's remuneration committee (comprised entirely of non-executives) received a letter from Mr Woof saying that because his track record was so strong, they could be assured of many years of sustained growth under his leadership. In discussions concerning his pension, however, he asked for a generous non-performance related pension settlement to be written into his contract so that it would be payable whenever he decided to leave the company (subject to a minimum term of two years) and regardless of his performance as CEO. Such was the euphoria about his appointment that his request was approved. Furthermore in the hasty manner in which Mr Woof's reward package was agreed, the split of his package between basic and performance-related components was not carefully scrutinised. Everybody on the remuneration committee was so certain that he would bring success to Tomato Bank that the individual details of his reward package were not considered important.

In addition, the remuneration committee received several letters from Tomato Bank's finance director, John Temba, saying, in direct terms, that they should offer Mr Woof 'whatever he wants' to ensure that he joins the company and that the balance of benefits was not important as long as he joined. Two of the non-executive directors on the remuneration committee were former colleagues of Mr Woof and told the finance director they would take his advice and make sure they put a package together that would ensure Mr Woof joined the company.

Once in post, Mr Woof led an excessively aggressive strategy that involved high growth in the loan and mortgage books financed from a range of sources, some of which proved unreliable. In the fifth year of his appointment, the failure of some of the sources of funds upon which the growth of the bank was based led to severe financing difficulties at Tomato Bank. Shareholders voted to replace George Woof as CEO. They said he had been reckless in exposing the company to so much risk in growing the loan book without adequately covering it with reliable sources of funds.

When he left, the press reported that despite his failure in the job, he would be leaving with what the newspapers referred to as an 'obscenely large' pension. Some shareholders were angry and said that Mr Woof was being 'rewarded for failure'. When Mr Woof was asked if he might voluntarily forego some of his pension in recognition of his failure in the job, he refused, saying that he was contractually entitled to it and so would be keeping it all.

Required:

(a) Criticise the performance of Tomato Bank's remuneration committee in agreeing Mr Woof's reward package. **(10 marks)**

(b) Describe the components of an appropriately designed executive reward package and explain why a more balanced package of benefits should have been used to reward Mr Woof. **(10 marks)**

(c) Construct an ethical case for Mr Woof to voluntarily accept a reduction in his pension value in recognition of his failure as chief executive of Tomato Bank.

(5 marks)

(Total: 25 marks)

41   ABC CO (PILOT 07) *Walk in the footsteps of a top tutor*

In a recent case, it emerged that Frank Finn, a sales director at ABC Co, had been awarded a substantial over-inflation annual basic pay award with no apparent link to performance. When a major institutional shareholder, Swanland Investments, looked into the issue, it emerged that Mr Finn had a cross directorship with Joe Ng, an executive director of DEF Co. Mr Ng was a non-executive director of ABC and chairman of its remunerations committee. Swanland Investments argued at the annual general meeting that there was 'a problem with the independence' of Mr Ng and further, that Mr Finn's remuneration package as a sales director was considered to be poorly aligned to Swanland's interests because it was too much weighted by basic pay and contained inadequate levels of incentive.

Swanland Investments proposed that the composition of Mr Finn's remuneration package be reconsidered by the remunerations committee and that Mr Ng should not be present during the discussion. Another of the larger institutional shareholders, Hanoi House, objected to this, proposing instead that Mr Ng and Mr Finn both resign from their respective non-executive directorships as there was 'clear evidence of malpractice'. Swanland considered this too radical a step, as Mr Ng's input was, in its opinion, valuable on ABC's board.

Required:

(a) **Explain FOUR roles of a remunerations committee and how the cross directorship undermines these roles at ABC Co.** **(12 marks)**

(b) **Swanland Investments believed Mr Finn's remunerations package to be 'poorly aligned' to its interests. With reference to the different components of a director's remunerations package, explain how Mr Finn's remuneration might be more aligned to shareholders' interests at ABC Co.** **(8 marks)**

(c) **Evaluate the proposal from Hanoi House that both Mr Ng and Mr Finn be required to resign from their respective non-executive positions.** **(5 marks)**

(Total: 25 marks)

42 YAYA (DEC 12)

In Yaya Company, operations director Ben Janoon recently realised there had been an increase in products failing the final quality checks. These checks were carried out in the QC (quality control) laboratory, which tested finished goods products before being released for sale. The product failure rate had risen from 1% of items two years ago to 4% now, and this meant an increase of hundreds of items of output a month which were not sold on to Yaya's customers. The failed products had no value to the company once they had failed QC as the rework costs were not economic. Because the increase was gradual, it took a while for Mr Janoon to realise that the failure rate had risen.

A thorough review of the main production operation revealed nothing that might explain the increased failure and so attention was focused instead on the QC laboratory. For some years, the QC laboratory at Yaya, managed by Jane Goo, had been marginalised in the company, with its two staff working in a remote laboratory well away from other employees. Operations director Ben Janoon, who designed the internal control systems in Yaya, rarely visited the QC lab because of its remote location. He never asked for information on product failure rates to be reported to him and did not understand the science involved in the QC process. He relied on the two QC staff, Jane Goo and her assistant John Zong, both of whom did have relevant scientific qualifications.

The two QC staff considered themselves low paid. Whilst in theory they reported to Mr Janoon, in practice, they conducted their work with little contact with colleagues. The work was routine and involved testing products against a set of compliance standards. A single signature on a product compliance report was required to pass or fail in QC and these reports were then filed away with no-one else seeing them.

It was eventually established that Jane Goo had found a local buyer to pay her directly for any of Yaya's products which had failed the QC tests. The increased failure rate had resulted from her signing products as having 'failed QC' when, in fact, they had passed. She kept the proceeds from the sales for herself, and also paid her assistant, John Zong, a proportion of the proceeds from the sale of the failed products.

Required:

(a) **Explain typical reasons why an internal control system might be ineffective.**

(5 marks)

(b) **Explain the internal control deficiencies that led to the increased product failures at Yaya.** **(10 marks)**

(c) **Discuss the general qualities of useful information, stating clearly how they would be of benefit to Mr Janoon, and recommend specific measures which would improve information flow from the QC lab to Mr Janoon.** **(10 marks)**

(Total: 25 marks)

43 SPQ

As an ACCA member, you have recently been appointed as the head of internal audit for SPQ, a multinational listed company that carries out a large volume of Internet sales to customers who place their orders using their home or work computers. You report to the chief executive, although you work closely with the finance director. You have direct access to the chair of the audit committee whenever you consider it necessary.

One of your internal audit teams has been conducting a review of IT security for a system which has been in operation for 18 months and which is integral to Internet sales. The audit was included in the internal audit plan following a request by the chief accountant. Sample testing by the internal audit team has revealed several transactions over the last three months which have raised concerns about possible hacking or fraudulent access to the customer/order database. Each of these transactions has disappeared from the database after deliveries have been made, but without sales being recorded or funds collected from the customer. Each of the identified transactions was for a different customer and there seems to be no relationship between any of the transactions.

You have received the draft report from the internal audit manager responsible for this audit which suggests serious weaknesses in the design of the system. You have discussed this informally with senior managers who have told you that such a report will be politically very unpopular with the chief executive as he was significantly involved in the design and approval of the new system and insisted it be implemented earlier than the IT department considered was advisable. No post-implementation review of the system has taken place.

You have been informally advised by several senior managers to lessen the criticism and work with the IT department to correct any deficiencies within the system and to produce a report to the audit committee that is less critical and merely identifies the need for some improvement. They suggest that these actions would avoid criticism of the Chief Executive by the board of SPQ.

Required:

(a) Explain the role of internal audit in internal control and risk management. (5 marks)

(b) Analyse the potential risks faced by SPQ that have been exposed by the review of IT security and recommend controls that should be implemented to reduce them.

(8 marks)

(c) Discuss the issues that need to be considered when planning an audit of activities and systems such as the one undertaken at SPQ. (5 marks)

(d) Explain the ethical principles you should apply as the head of internal audit for SPQ when reporting the results of this internal review and how any ethical conflicts should be resolved. (7 marks)

(Total: 25 marks)

44 GLUCK AND GOODMAN (DEC 08)

Susan Paullaos was recently appointed as a non-executive member of the internal audit committee of Gluck and Goodman, a public listed company producing complex engineering products. Barney Chester, the executive finance director who chairs the committee, has always viewed the purpose of internal audit as primarily financial in nature and as long as financial controls are seen to be fully in place, he is less concerned with other aspects of internal control. When Susan asked about operational controls in the production facility Barney said that these were not the concern of the internal audit committee. This, he said, was because as long as the accounting systems and financial controls were fully functional, all other systems may be assumed to be working correctly.

Susan, however, was concerned with the operational and quality controls in the production facility. She spoke to production director Aaron Hardanger, and asked if he would be prepared to produce regular reports for the internal audit committee on levels of specification compliance and other control issues. Mr Hardanger said that the internal audit committee had always trusted him because his reputation as a manager was very good. He said that he had never been asked to provide compliance evidence to the internal audit committee and saw no reason as to why he should start doing so now.

At board level, the non-executive chairman, George Allejandra, said that he only instituted the internal audit committee in the first place in order to be seen to be in compliance with the stock market's requirement that Gluck and Goodman should have one. He believed that internal audit committees didn't add materially to the company. They were, he believed, one of those 'outrageous demands' that regulatory authorities made without considering the consequences in smaller companies nor the individual needs of different companies. He also complained about the need to have an internal auditor. He said that Gluck and Goodman used to have a full time internal auditor but when he left a year ago, he wasn't replaced. The audit committee didn't feel it needed an internal auditor because Barney Chester believed that only financial control information was important and he could get that information from his management accountant.

Susan asked Mr Allejandra if he recognised that the company was exposing itself to increased market risks by failing to have an effective audit committee. Mr Allejandra said he didn't know what a market risk was.

Required:

(a) Internal control and audit are considered to be important parts of sound corporate governance.

    (i) Describe FIVE general objectives of internal control. **(5 marks)**

    (ii) Explain the organisational factors that determine the need for internal audit in public listed companies. **(5 marks)**

(b) Criticise the internal control and internal audit arrangements at Gluck and Goodman as described in the case scenario. **(10 marks)**

(c) Define 'market risk' for Mr Allejandra and explain why Gluck and Goodman's market risk exposure is increased by failing to have an effective audit committee.

(5 marks)

(Total: 25 marks)

45 YAHTY *Walk in the footsteps of a top tutor*

The YAHTY organisation provides investment services to individuals living away from their country of residence. For example, a person may be required to work in a foreign country for two or three years, but will retain an investment portfolio of shares, bank account deposits, pension contributions, etc in their home country. The YAHTY organisation manages this portfolio for the individual until they return to their country.

YAHTY employs 35 investment accountants to provide the investment services. Each accountant controls the portfolio of up to 200 clients, with an average fund value of €500,000. Decisions regarding the companies to invest in, the pension scheme funds to use, etc are made by the individual financial accountant. The accountant retains a computer record for each client which shows the funds invested in, the values and recent transfers. As long as the individual requirements of the client are met, then the YAHTY organisation is deemed to have been successful in managing that client. A senior accountant provides additional investment advice should the need arise.

For each client, the investment accountant is the authorised signatory on the client accounts, enabling funds transfers to be made by that individual. Any payment over €100,000 has to be authorised by the senior accountant. Most transfers are between €10,000 and €50,000 – the senior accountant only checking material transactions. At any time, the list of investments on the computer must agree to share certificates, etc retained by the accountant. The list of investments is not, however, linked to the payments systems in YAHTY.

Documentation for each transfer has to be retained by each investment accountant. Documents regarding fund transfers are retained in date order within a central filing system. This procedure provides YAHTY with significant savings in storage costs while ensuring that documentation can be obtained when necessary.

When a client returns to their home country, the investment manager transfers all funds back into the client's name. A list of the investments is printed off from the accountant's computer system and this is given to the client along with share certificates, pension scheme reports, etc. Full transaction histories are not available due to the time required for obtaining detailed historical documentation from the filing system already mentioned above. To ensure completeness and accuracy of transfer, the senior accountant reviews all funds with a value of more than €750,000 by checking the list of investments to the supporting documentation.

Required:

Prepare a report for the directors of YAHTY which:

(a) Explains the principles of a sound system of internal control within the context of corporate governance. You should include examples based on guidance with which you are familiar. **(6 marks)**

(b) Identifies and describes the directors' responsibilities in relation to internal controls. **(6 marks)**

(c) Evaluates the YAHTY organisation's internal control systems, identifying any weaknesses; assesses the effectiveness of any controls over those weaknesses; and recommends improvements to the system of internal controls. **(13 marks)**

(Total: 25 marks)

46 BLUP (JUN 13)

When Blup Co (a listed company involved in water supply) decided to establish an internal audit function, in line with new listing rules, the board approached Karen Huyer, an external consultant. She explained that internal audit is especially important in highly regulated industries but that it could also offer benefits to companies regardless of the industry context.

Karen was particularly keen to talk to John Xu, the head of the audit committee. John explained that because Blup Co was a water supply company and was thus highly regulated, he considered it important that all of the members of the audit committee were professional water engineers so that they fully understood the industry and its technical challenges. All three members of the audit committee were non-executive directors and all were recently retired members of the Blup executive board. When Karen asked about the relationship with external auditors, John said that they had an 'excellent' relationship, saying that this was because the external audit practice was run by the chairman's son-in-law.

Karen said that one of the essential functions of internal audit is to provide assurance that the internal controls which underpinned financial reporting are effective. She said that effective internal controls are necessary for maintaining the integrity of financial reporting and that the new internal audit function could help with that.

Required:

(a) Discuss the importance of internal audit in a highly regulated industry such as the water industry that Blup Co operates in. **(7 marks)**

(b) (i) Criticise the ways in which Blup Co's audit committee has failed to meet best practice.

    (ii) Explain why the audit committee is responsible for overseeing the internal audit function.

The total marks will be split equally between each part. **(12 marks)**

(c) Discuss how effective internal controls can provide assurance on the integrity of financial reporting. **(6 marks)**

(Total: 25 marks)

47   FIS

FIS Ltd is located in the capital of a large country. Its main business is investing money from a variety of clients in stocks, shares, government bonds and other similar products. The investment portfolio managed by FIS runs into hundreds of millions of dollars across several hundred different investments.

Three fund managers are responsible for investing client money, and transferring funds between different investments, depending on their view of the risk of each investment and expected return from that investment. Funds can be moved between investments in a matter of minutes, if required.

To help the managers assess the risk of each investment, FIS maintains a management information system, linked to the Internet, which provide the managers with an hourly update on the value of the investments and current news stories which may affect the value of those investments. Detailed information on the value of each fund, the investment history, number of stocks and shares held, location of the appropriate certificates etc. is also provided automatically by the MIS. However, the system is relatively old (being installed four years ago) and has to be supplemented with information from other sources including:

- newspapers, and

- Internet news services (available on a separate computer system).

Information may also be available from an in-house information system maintained in the new business department. The new business department is responsible for contacting potential clients and offering investment services to those clients. This MIS provides information to assist with the initial investment decision for client funds. However, fund managers do not have access to this system.

The board of FIS has proposed a new system for the fund managers, because the old system is old and fund managers have made some poor investment decisions in the last few months. However, the cost appears to outweigh the tangible benefits of installing the system.

Required:

Identify and explain the inefficiencies in the knowledge management information system for the fund managers in FIS Ltd. Recommend processes for removing these inefficiencies.

(25 marks)

48 **RG** *Online question assistance*

RG manufactures industrial glues and solvents in a single large factory. Approximately 400 different inputs are used to produce the 35 specialist outputs, which range from ultra-strong glues used in aircraft manufacture to high-impact adhesives that are required on construction sites.

Two years ago, with the company only just breaking even, the directors recognised the need for more information to control the business. To assist them with their strategic control of the business, they decided to establish a MIS. This is now operational but provides only the following limited range of information to the directors via their networked computer system:

- A summary business plan for this and the next two years. The plan includes details of the expected future incomes and expenditure on existing product lines. It was produced by a new member of the accounting department without reference to past production data.

- Stock balances on individual items of raw materials, finished goods etc. This report is at a very detailed level and comprises 80% of the output from the MIS itself.

- A summary of changes in total demand for glues and solvents in the market place for the last five years. This information is presented as a numerical summary in six different sections. Each section takes up one computer screen so only one section can be viewed at a time.

Required:

(a) (i) Comment on the weaknesses in the information currently being provided to the directors of the company. **(11 marks)**

(ii) Suggest how the information may be improved, with particular reference to other outputs which the MIS might usefully provide to the directors. **(8 marks)**

(b) Explain what strategic information any MIS is unlikely to be able to provide. **(6 marks)**

(Total: 25 marks)

 Online question assistance

49   SUPERMARKET

In pursuit of ever greater profits to satisfy the shareholders, the supermarket chain had searched overseas for cheaper suppliers. Unfortunately this strategy failed when the following headline appeared in the newspapers:

'Supermarket poisons customers'

Government inspections of farming facilities in the chosen countries were almost non-existent so the supermarket had employed a local inspector to work closely with factory managers and to carry out food hygiene audits. When the news of the disaster was first reported to the board six months after problems begun the inspector simply disappeared and still cannot be traced.

In their defence, the suppliers say they were forced to cut veterinary attention to their herds because of the low rate paid by the supermarket for their meat. The result was that large amounts of infected foodstuffs were exported to the supermarket's home country.

When interviewed as part of a review of the failure in control supermarket store managers said that they had known for some time that there was something wrong with the meat. As part of their routine goods inward inspection they examined the cellophane wrapped cuts and threw out any that seemed discoloured. Most say that they had not received any complaints from customers regarding ill effects following consumption of the product.

The Chief Executive (CEO) of the supermarket chain, Jon Cooper, fears that the repercussions of this event will have a serious effect on this year's profit. Some customers have defected to competitors whilst an environmental group is protesting at some of the larger stores. There are rumours of a government audit of the company's supplier systems and they have, of course, needed to commence a search for a new and hopefully cheaper supplier in another country.

Required:

(a)   **Examine failures in internal control and recommend improvements.**   **(16 marks)**

(b)   **Describe a process through which the board of directors can carry out a formal review of internal control in this company.**   **(9 marks)**

(Total: 25 marks)

50   TREADWAY (JUN 10)

The Committee of Sponsoring Organisations (COSO) of the Treadway Commission is an American voluntary, private sector organisation and is unconnected to government or any other regulatory authority. It was established in 1985 to help companies identify the causes of fraudulent reporting and to create internal control environments able to support full and accurate reporting. It is named after its first chairman, James Treadway, and has issued several guidance reports over the years including important reports in 1987, 1992 and 2006.

In 2009, COSO issued new 'Guidance on monitoring internal control systems' to help companies tighten internal controls and thereby enjoy greater internal productivity and produce higher quality reporting. The report, written principally by a leading global professional services firm but adopted by all of the COSO members, noted that 'unmonitored controls tend to deteriorate over time' and encouraged organisations to adopt wide ranging internal controls. It went on to say that, the 'assessment of internal controls [can] ... involve a significant amount of ... internal audit testing.'

After its publication, the business journalist, Mark Rogalski, said that the latest report contained 'yet more guidance from COSO on how to make your company less productive by burdening it even more with non-productive things to do' referring to the internal control guidance the 2009 report contains. He said that there was no industry sector-specific advice and that a 'one-size-fits-all' approach to internal control was 'ridiculous'. He further argued that there was no link between internal controls and external reporting, and that internal controls are unnecessary for effective external reporting.

Another commentator, Claire Mahmood, wrote a reply to Rogalski's column pointing to the views expressed in the 2009 COSO report that, 'over time effective monitoring can lead to organisational efficiencies and reduced costs associated with public reporting on internal control because problems are identified and addressed in a proactive, rather than reactive, manner.' She said that these benefits were not industry sector specific and that Rogalski was incorrect in his dismissal of the report's value. She also said that although primarily concerned with governance in the USA, the best practice guidance from COSO could be applied by companies anywhere in the world. She said that although the USA, where COSO is based, is concerned with the 'rigid rules' of compliance, the advice ought to be followed by companies in countries with principles-based approaches to corporate governance because it was best practice.

Required:

(a) **Distinguish between rules-based and principles-based approaches to internal control system compliance as described by Claire Mahmood and discuss the benefits to an organisation of a principles-based approach.** **(7 marks)**

(b) Mr Rogalski is sceptical over the value of internal control and believes that controls must be industry-specific to be effective.

Required:

Describe the advantages of internal control that apply regardless of industry sector and briefly explain the meaning of the statement, 'unmonitored controls tend to deteriorate over time'. Your answer should refer to the case scenario as appropriate. **(10 marks)**

(c) The COSO report explains that 'assessment of internal controls [can] ... involve a significant amount of ... internal audit testing.'

Required:

Define 'internal audit testing' and explain the roles of internal audit in helping ensure the effectiveness of internal control systems. **(8 marks)**

(Total: 25 marks)

51   FF CO (PILOT 07)

As part of a review of its internal control systems, the board of FF Co, a large textiles company, has sought your advice as a senior accountant in the company.

FF's stated objective has always been to adopt the highest standards of internal control because it believes that by doing so it will not only provide shareholders with confidence in its governance but also enhance its overall reputation with all stakeholders. In recent years, however, FF's reputation for internal control has been damaged somewhat by a qualified audit statement last year (over issues of compliance with financial standards) and an unfortunate internal incident the year prior to that. This incident concerned an employee, Miss Osula, expressing concern about the compliance of one of the company's products with an international standard on fire safety. She raised the issue with her immediate manager but he said, according to Miss Osula, that it wasn't his job to report her concerns to senior management. When she failed to obtain a response herself from senior management, she decided to report the lack of compliance to the press. This significantly embarrassed the company and led to a substantial deterioration in FF's reputation.

The specifics of the above case concerned a fabric produced by FF Co, which, in order to comply with an international fire safety standard, was required to resist fire for ten minutes when in contact with a direct flame. According to Miss Osula, who was a member of the quality control staff, FF was allowing material rated at only five minutes fire resistance to be sold labelled as ten minute rated. In her statement to the press, Miss Osula said that there was a culture of carelessness in FF and that this was only one example of the way the company approached issues such as international fire safety standards.

Required:

(a)   **Describe how the internal control systems at FF Co differ from a 'sound' system of internal control, such as that set out in the Turnbull guidance, for example.**

(10 marks)

(b)   **Define 'reputation risk' and evaluate the potential effects of FF's poor reputation on its financial situation.** (8 marks)

(c)   **Explain, with reference to FF as appropriate, the ethical responsibilities of a professional accountant both as an employee and as a professional.** (7 marks)

(Total: 25 marks)

52   FRANKS AND FISHER (PILOT 07)

The board of Franks & Fisher, a large manufacturing company, decided to set up an internal control and audit function. The proposal was to appoint an internal auditor at mid-management level and also to establish a board level internal audit committee made up mainly of non-executive directors.

The initiative to do so was driven by a recent period of rapid growth. The company had taken on many more activities as a result of growth in its product range. The board decided that the increased size and complexity of its operations created the need for greater control over internal activities and that an internal audit function was a good way forward. The need was highlighted by a recent event where internal quality standards were not enforced, resulting in the stoppage of a production line for several hours. The production director angrily described the stoppage as 'entirely avoidable' and the finance director, Jason Kumas, said that the stoppage had been very costly.

Mr Kumas said that there were problems with internal control in a number of areas of the company's operations and that there was a great need for internal audit. He said that as the head of the company's accounting and finance function, the new internal auditor should report to him. The reasons for this, he said, were because as an accountant, he was already familiar with auditing procedure and the fact that he already had information on budgets and other 'control' information that the internal auditor would need.

It was decided that the new internal auditor needed to be a person of some experience and with enough personality not to be intimidated nor diverted by other department heads who might find the internal audits an inconvenience. One debate the board had was whether it would be better to recruit to the position from inside or outside the company. A second argument was over the limits of authority that the internal auditor might be given. It was pointed out that while the board considered the role of internal audit to be very important, it didn't want it to interfere with the activities of other departments to the point where their operational effectiveness was reduced.

Required:

(a) **Explain, with reference to the case, the factors that are typically considered when deciding to establish internal audit in an organisation.** **(10 marks)**

(b) **Construct the argument in favour of appointing the new internal auditor from outside the company rather than promoting internally.** **(6 marks)**

(c) **Critically evaluate Mr Kumas's belief that the internal auditor should report to him as finance director.** **(4 marks)**

(d) **Define 'objectivity' and describe characteristics that might demonstrate an internal auditor's professional objectivity.** **(5 marks)**

(Total: 25 marks)

53 CC & J

Audit firm CC & J had worked extensively with the global banking organisation Banco for many years. Senior audit partner, Andrezej Puczynski, had built up a close working and personal relationship with the Chief Finance Officer (CFO), often attending private family barbeques. In return for his diligent support and low fee audit work he had been rewarded with hugely lucrative management consultancy contracts that made his local office profits the envy of senior CC&J partners around the world.

The closeness of the relationship could be seen in the automatic selection of CC & J by the CFO, operating as chair of the audit committee of Banco, despite the existence of cut price tenders from audit firm competitors. Andrezej had only met the other two members of the committee once on a shooting trip organised by the CFO. The other members of the committee had no financial expertise and little, if any, involvement in Banco outside of an annual meeting with the committee chairman.

Last week significant financial impropriety was uncovered at Banco leading to the collapse of the firm and its suspension on the stock exchange. Andrezej knew that many of the accounting treatments he had personally signed off were, at the least, stretching the interpretation of accounting standards to their breaking point.

Required:

(a)   Discuss the nature of threats to auditor independence and identify a measure to reduce each threat.   **(10 marks)**

(b)   Assess an appropriate composition of an audit committee using evidence within the scenario.   **(5 marks)**

(c)   Describe how an audit committee operates as an interface within an organisation.   **(5 marks)**

(d)   Identify the characteristics of good quality information required by an audit committee.   **(5 marks)**

(Total: 25 marks)

IDENTIFYING AND ASSESSING RISK

54   LANDMASS

Landmass is a property company that is planning to obtain a listing for its shares on the stock market of the country in which it is based. The directors are aware, however, that the company will be required to comply with the corporate governance requirements including an annual review by the directors of the adequacy of its risk management systems. This country has a principles-based system of corporate governance which covers all companies with a listing on the stock market.

At the moment, the company does not have any formal risk management system, and the directors need advice on how such a system might be established. They have been informed that the risks of the business should be categorised, but they do not know how this might be done.

The company operates in three different areas:

1   It manages business property which it rents to business customers under short-term and medium-term lease arrangements.

2   It buys and re-sells office property and property used by retail businesses (such as shopping arcades).

3   It has a subsidiary that specialises in building high-quality residential property.

Required:

(a)   Explain how risks might be categorised by companies, and suggest the risk categories that might be used by Landmass.   **(9 marks)**

(b)   Recommend how Landmass might establish a risk management system prior to its listing and the introduction of its shares to trading on the stock exchange.   **(16 marks)**

(Total: 25 marks)

55 DUBLAND (JUN 13)

Because of a general lack of business confidence in Dubland, its major banks had severely restricted new lending. This lack of lending extended to small and large businesses, and also to individuals in society. Press statements from the banks often referred to the need to mitigate financial risks and the need to maintain capital adequacy. Over time, the lower lending produced some negative consequences in the wider Dubland economy.

Responding to these problems, the Dubland finance minister remarked that, 'financial risks may not only cause companies to fail but they can also cause problems in wider society. Banks, in particular, need to be more aware of their financial risks than most other sectors of the economy. They have to manage a unique set of risks and I strongly urge the directors of banks to institute robust risk management systems as part of their corporate governance.

'As finance minister, however, I also believe that banks have a vital role in supporting the economic strength of this country. They hold cash deposits and make short and long-term loans, which are vital to other businesses. Taking risks is a normal part of all business operations and our banks need to accept this risk when it comes to lending.'

Ron Ng, the chief executive of BigBank, Dubland's largest bank, said that continuous and ongoing risk assessment was necessary. He said that despite the finance minister's call for higher lending, his only duty was to BigBank's shareholders and it was this duty that guided BigBank's reduced lending.

Required:

(a) **Explain the meaning of 'risk assessment' as used by Ron Ng and discuss, in the context of the case, the need for risk assessment to be 'continuous and ongoing'.**

(8 marks)

(b) Ron Ng believed that his 'only duty' as BigBank's CEO was to the BigBank shareholders.

Required:

Describe 'fiduciary duty' in the context of the case and critically evaluate the issues raised by Ron Ng's belief. (7 marks)

(c) **Explain the term 'financial risk' and discuss how management of these risks can be embedded in a large organisation such as BigBank.** (10 marks)

(Total: 25 marks)

56 ULTRA UBER (DEC 10)

During the global economic recession that began in mid 2008, many companies found it difficult to gain enough credit in the form of short-term loans from their banks and other lenders. In some cases, this caused working capital problems as short-term cash flow deficits could not be funded.

Ultra-Uber Limited (UU), a large manufacturer based in an economically depressed region, had traditionally operated a voluntary supplier payment policy in which it was announced that all trade payables would be paid at or before 20 days and there would be no late payment. This was operated despite the normal payment terms being 30 days. The company gave the reason for this as 'a desire to publicly demonstrate our social responsibility and support our valued suppliers, most of whom, like UU, also provide employment in this region'. In the 20 years the policy had been in place, the UU website proudly boasted that it had never been broken. Brian Mills, the chief executive often mentioned this as the basis of the company's social responsibility. 'Rather than trying to delay our payments to suppliers,' he often said, 'we support them and their cash flow. It's the right thing to do.' Most of the other directors, however, especially the finance director, think that the voluntary supplier payment policy is a mistake. Some say that it is a means of Brian Mills exercising his own ethical beliefs in a way that is not supported by others at UU Limited.

When UU itself came under severe cash flow pressure in the summer of 2009 as a result of its bank's failure to extend credit, the finance director told Brian Mills that UU's liquidity problems would be greatly relieved if they took an average of 30 rather than the 20 days to pay suppliers.

In addition, the manufacturing director said that he could offer another reason why the short-term liquidity at UU was a problem. He said that the credit control department was poor, taking approximately 50 days to receive payment from each customer. He also said that his own inventory control could be improved and he said he would look into that. It was pointed out to the manufacturing director that cost of goods sold was 65% of turnover and this proportion was continuously rising, driving down gross and profit margins. Due to poor inventory controls, excessively high levels of inventory were held in store at all stages of production. The long-serving sales manager wanted to keep high levels of finished goods so that customers could buy from existing inventory and the manufacturing director wanted to keep high levels of raw materials and work-in-progress to give him minimum response times when a new order came in.

One of the non-executive directors (NEDs) of UU Limited, Bob Ndumo, said that he could not work out why UU was in such a situation as no other company in which he was a NED was having liquidity problems. Bob Ndumo held a number of other NED positions but these were mainly in service-based companies.

Required:

(a) Define 'liquidity risk' and explain why it might be a significant risk to UU Limited.

(5 marks)

(b) Define 'risk embeddedness' and explain the methods by which risk awareness and management can be embedded in organisations. (7 marks)

(c) Examine the obstacles to embedding liquidity risk management at UU Limited.

(8 marks)

(d) Criticise the voluntary supplier payment policy as a means of demonstrating UU's social responsibility. (5 marks)

(Total: 25 marks)

57 REGIONAL POLICE FORCE

A regional police force has the following corporate objectives:

- to reduce crime and disorder
- to promote community safety
- to contribute to delivering justice and maintaining public confidence in the law.

The force aims to achieve these objectives by continuously improving its resources management to meet the needs of its stakeholders. It has no stated financial objective other than to stay within its funding limits.

The force is mainly public-funded but, like other regional forces, it has some commercial operations, for example policing football matches when the football clubs pay a fee to the police force for its officers working overtime. The police force uses this money to supplement the funding it receives from the government.

Required:

(a) **Discuss the risks to the achievement of the corporate objectives of the regional police force.** **(12 marks)**

(b) **Discuss the risks associated with a regional structure for the national police force.** **(7 marks)**

(c) **Describe the types of internal controls that might be applied by the police force in order to assist with the achievement of its objectives.** **(6 marks)**

(Total: 25 marks)

58 GHI GROUP

The GHI Group is a major listed travel company based in northern Europe, with a market capitalisation of €200 million. GHI specialises in the provision of budget-priced short and long haul package holidays targeted at the family market. The term 'package holiday' means that all flights, accommodation and overseas transfers are organised and booked by the tour operator on behalf of the customer.

The GHI Group encompasses a number of separate companies that include a charter airline, a chain of retail travel outlets, and several specialist tour operators who provide package holidays. Each subsidiary is expected to be profit generating, and each company's performance is measured by its residual income. The capital charges for each company are risk adjusted, and new investments are required to achieve a base hurdle rate of 10% before adjustment for risk.

The package holiday market is highly competitive, with fewer than five main players all trying to gain market share in an environment in which margins are continually threatened. The key threats include rising fuel prices, last minute discounting and the growth of the 'self managed' holiday, where individuals by-pass the travel retailers and use the Internet to book low cost flights and hotel rooms directly with the service providers. Also, customer requirements regarding product design and quality are continuously changing, thereby increasing the pressure on travel companies to devise appropriate strategies to maintain profitability.

Sales of long haul packages to North America are relatively static, but the number of people travelling to South East Asian destinations has fallen substantially following the 2004 tsunami disaster. Africa, New Zealand, Australia and certain parts of the Caribbean are the only long haul growth areas, but such growth is from a small base. Sales within the European region are shifting in favour of Eastern Mediterranean destinations such as Cyprus and Turkey as the traditional resorts of Spain and the Balearic Islands fall out of favour. Short 'city breaks' are also growing rapidly in popularity, reflecting higher spending power particularly amongst the over 50s.

The shift in patterns of demand has created some problems for GHI in a number of Eastern Mediterranean resorts over the last two summer seasons. There are not many hotels that meet the specified quality standards, and consequently there is fierce competition amongst travel operators to reserve rooms in them. In addition GHI customers have experienced very poor service from hotels, which has resulted in adverse publicity and high compensation payments.

GHI has recently invested €8 million in purchasing two new hotels in the affected resorts. Sales forecasts indicate demand will grow at approximately 15% per year in the relevant resorts over the next five years. It is anticipated that the hotels will supply 70% of the group's accommodation requirements for the next season. The package holidays to the GHI owned hotels will be sold as premium all-inclusive deals that include all food, soft drinks and local beers, wines and spirits. Such all-inclusive deals are not currently offered by other hotels in the target resorts.

GHI's local currency is the Euro.

Required:

(a) **Identify and briefly discuss two risks that are likely to be faced by the GHI Group under each of the following categories:**

- **Financial**
- **Political**
- **Environmental**
- **Economic.** **(12 marks)**

(b) **Identify and comment upon the changes in risks to GHI Group that might arise from the decision to sell premium all-inclusive deals, and suggest methods by which these risks might be monitored and controlled.** **(8 marks)**

(c) **List the tasks that the internal audit department of GHI should have performed to ensure that the risks associated with the new hotel purchases are managed effectively. You should assume that its involvement commenced immediately the strategic decision was made to purchase overseas property – in other words, prior to identification of target sites.** **(5 marks)**

(Total: 25 marks)

CONTROLLING RISK

59 CHEN PRODUCTS (DEC 08)

Chen Products produces four manufactured products: Products 1, 2, 3 and 4. The company's risk committee recently met to discuss how the company might respond to a number of problems that have arisen with Product 2. After a number of incidents in which Product 2 had failed whilst being used by customers, Chen Products had been presented with compensation claims from customers injured and inconvenienced by the product failure. It was decided that the risk committee should meet to discuss the options.

When the discussion of Product 2 began, committee chairman Anne Ricardo reminded her colleagues that, apart from the compensation claims, Product 2 was a highly profitable product.

Chen's risk management committee comprised four non-executive directors who each had different backgrounds and areas of expertise. None of them had direct experience of Chen's industry or products. It was noted that it was common for them to disagree among themselves as to how risks should be managed and that in some situations, each member proposed a quite different strategy to manage a given risk. This was the case when they discussed which risk management strategy to adopt with regard to Product 2.

Required:

(a) Describe the typical roles of a risk management committee. **(6 marks)**

(b) Using the TARA framework, construct four possible strategies for managing the risk presented by Product 2. Your answer should describe each strategy and explain how each might be applied in the case. **(10 marks)**

(c) Risk committee members can be either executive or non-executive.

Required:

(i) Distinguish between executive and non-executive directors. **(2 marks)**

(ii) Evaluate the relative advantages and disadvantages of Chen's risk management committee being non-executive rather than executive in nature. **(7 marks)**

(Total: 25 marks)

60 H&Z COMPANY (JUN 09)

 Timed question with Online tutor debrief

John Pentanol was appointed as risk manager at H&Z Company a year ago and he decided that his first task was to examine the risks that faced the company. He concluded that the company faced three major risks, which he assessed by examining the impact that would occur if the risk were to materialise. He assessed Risk 1 as being of low potential impact as even if it materialised it would have little effect on the company's strategy. Risk 2 was assessed as being of medium potential impact whilst a third risk, Risk 3, was assessed as being of very high potential impact.

When John realised the potential impact of Risk 3 materialising, he issued urgent advice to the board to withdraw from the activity that gave rise to Risk 3 being incurred. In the advice he said that the impact of Risk 3 was potentially enormous and it would be irresponsible for H&Z to continue to bear that risk.

The company commercial director, Jane Xylene, said that John Pentanol and his job at H&Z were unnecessary and that risk management was 'very expensive for the benefits achieved'. She said that all risk managers do is to tell people what can't be done and that they are pessimists by nature. She said she wanted to see entrepreneurial risk takers in H&Z and not risk managers who, she believed, tended to discourage enterprise.

John replied that it was his job to eliminate all of the highest risks at H&Z Company. He said that all risk was bad and needed to be eliminated if possible. If it couldn't be eliminated, he said that it should be minimised.

(a)   The risk manager has an important role to play in an organisation's risk management.

Required:

(i)   **Describe the roles of a risk manager.**   **(4 marks)**

(ii)   **Assess John Pentanol's understanding of his role.**   **(4 marks)**

(b)   **With reference to a risk assessment framework as appropriate, criticise John's advice that H&Z should withdraw from the activity that incurs Risk 3.**   **(6 marks)**

(c)   Jane Xylene expressed a particular view about the value of risk management in H&Z Company. She also said that she wanted to see 'entrepreneurial risk takers'.

Required:

(i)   **Define 'entrepreneurial risk' and explain why it is important to accept entrepreneurial risk in business organisations**   **(4 marks)**

(ii)   **Critically evaluate Jane Xylene's view of risk management.**   **(7 marks)**

(Total: 25 marks)

61   SALTOC (DEC 09)

After a major fire had destroyed an office block belonging to Saltoc Company, the fire assessment reported that the most likely cause was an electrical problem. It emerged that the electrical system had suffered from a lack of maintenance in recent years due to cost pressures. Meanwhile in the same week, it was reported that a laptop computer containing confidential details of all of Saltoc's customers was stolen from the front seat of a car belonging to one of the company's information technology (IT) mid-managers. This caused outrage and distress to many of the affected customers as the information on the laptop included their bank details and credit card numbers. Some customers wrote to the company to say that they would be withdrawing their business from Saltoc as a result.

When the board met to review and consider the two incidents, it was agreed that the company had been lax in its risk management in the past and that systems should be tightened. However, the financial director, Peter Osbida, said that he knew perfectly well where systems should be tightened. He said that the fire was due to the incompetence of Harry Ho the operations manager and that the stolen laptop was because of a lack of security in the IT department led by Laura Hertz. Peter said that both colleagues were 'useless' and should be sacked. Neither Harry nor Laura liked or trusted Peter and they felt that in disputes, chief executive Ken Tonno usually took Peter's side.

Both Harry and Laura said that their departments had come under severe pressure because of the tight cost budgets imposed by Peter. Ken Tonno said that the last few years had been 'terrible' for Saltoc Company and that it was difficult enough keeping cash flows high enough to pay the wage bill without having to worry about 'even more' administration on risks and controls. Peter said that Harry and Laura both suffered in their roles by not having the respect of their subordinates and pointed to the high staff turnover in both of their departments as evidence of this.

Mr Tonno asked whether having a complete risk audit (or risk review) might be a good idea. He shared some of Peter's concerns about the management skills of both Harry and Laura, and so proposed that perhaps an external person should perform the risk audit and that would be preferable to one conducted by a colleague from within the company.

Required:

(a) **Describe what 'embedding' risk means with reference to Saltoc Company.**

(6 marks)

(b) **Assess the ability of Saltoc's management culture to implement embedded risk systems.** (8 marks)

(c) **Explain what external risk auditing contains and construct the case for an external risk audit at Saltoc Company.** (11 marks)

(Total: 25 marks)

62 BTS COMPANY

Required:

(a) **Explain the importance of monitoring risks at the strategic, tactical and operational levels in an organisation, discussing any problems that may occur from not doing this effectively.** (13 marks)

(b) The BTS company manufactures and sells chairs and sofas for use in the 'sitting' or 'living' rooms of houses. The company's products are displayed on an internet site and orders received via this site only. Order processing takes place on the company's in-house computer systems along with inventory control and payment to suppliers. The computer systems are managed in-house with no external links other than the Internet for selling.

Production is carried out in BTS's factory. There is little automation and production is dependent on the knowledge of Mr Smith and Mr Jones, the production controllers. Similarly, BTS rely on the Woody company for the supply of 80% of the wood used in the manufacture of BTS products. BTS's supplier policy is to pay as late as possible, providing little information on future production requirements.

Other raw materials purchased include fabrics for chair and sofa covers. However, a minority of sales orders are lost because the correct fabric is not available for the customer. The main reason for these stock-outs appears to be that the procurement manager forgets to order the fabric when inventory levels are low.

BTS's products are distributed by FastCour – a nationwide courier firm. However, due to the size of the chairs and sofas it is essential that the customer is available to take delivery of the goods when the courier arrives at their house. FastCour offer a 2-hour 'window' for delivery although only 55% of deliveries are actually meeting this criteria providing poor publicity for BTS and an increasing number of customer complaints. The board of BTS do not believe a strategic review of courier services is required at this time.

Required:

Identify and explain any strategic, tactical and operational risks affecting the BTS company. For each risk, discuss method(s) of alleviating this risk.   (12 marks)

(Total: 25 marks)

63   SOUTHERN CONTINENTS COMPANY (DEC 07)

 Walk in the footsteps of a top tutor

The risk committee at Southern Continents Company (SCC) met to discuss a report by its risk manager, Stephanie Field. The report focused on a number of risks that applied to a chemicals factory recently acquired by SCC in another country, Southland. She explained that the new risks related to the security of the factory in Southland in respect of burglary, to the supply of one of the key raw materials that experienced fluctuations in world supply and also an environmental risk. The environmental risk, Stephanie explained, was to do with the possibility of poisonous emissions from the Southland factory.

The SCC chief executive, Choo Wang, who chaired the risk committee, said that the Southland factory was important to him for two reasons. First, he said it was strategically important to the company. Second, it was important because his own bonuses depended upon it. He said that because he had personally negotiated the purchase of the Southland factory, the remunerations committee had included a performance bonus on his salary based on the success of the Southland investment. He told Stephanie that a performance-related bonus was payable when and if the factory achieved a certain level of output that Choo considered to be ambitious. 'I don't get any bonus at all until we reach a high level of output from the factory,' he said. 'So I don't care what the risks are, we will have to manage them.'

Stephanie explained that one of her main concerns arose because the employees at the factory in Southland were not aware of the importance of risk management to SCC. She said that the former owner of the factory paid less attention to risk issues and so the staff were not as aware of risk as Stephanie would like them to be. 'I would like to get risk awareness embedded in the culture at the Southland factory,' she said.

Choo Wang said that he knew from Stephanie's report what the risks were, but that he wanted somebody to explain to him what strategies SCC could use to manage the risks.

Required:

(a) Describe four strategies that can be used to manage risk and identify, with reasons, an appropriate strategy for each of the three risks mentioned in the case.

(12 marks)

(b) Explain the meaning of Stephanie's comment: 'I would like to get risk awareness embedded in the culture at the Southland factory.' (5 marks)

(c) Explain the benefits of performance-related pay in rewarding directors and critically evaluate the implications of the package offered to Choo Wang. (8 marks)

(Total: 25 marks)

64 TASS *Online question assistance*

The grocery business is heavily dominated by four major players, between them accounting for approximately 80% of householder purchases. The cost of competing for the dwindling additional market share in the home country makes the substantial returns available from opening stores in new countries seem very attractive.

The Chief Executive of TASS, one of the major players, knows that this strategy is not without its risks. Capital from existing operations is available to finance the investment, but each targeted country has a distinct culture and appetites that might not match the supermarket's high volume, limited choice offering. TASS knows that one of its competitors has already tried to breach this cultural divide but is finding it hard to attract customers, whilst dealing with local trading difficulties and a highly bureaucratic government.

TASS's risk auditor has raised a number of concerns. She stated that existing supply chain challenges were creating problems in ensuring continued supply of fresh vegetable and fruit products to its stores and these issues are likely to be exacerbated by the poor road infrastructure in some of the target countries and the need to import many more exotic products from abroad. Those sourced from local markets would need to be rigorously quality controlled, and competition from a network of well known local brands was likely to be fierce.

The Chief Executive, with thirty years experience in the industry, has absolute faith in the retail model that has created the stores' success over the last decades. He knows that the company's buying power, possibly assisted by the existence of some of its main competitors in the new markets, will, over time, drive out local competition and create trading conditions similar to those in its home markets.

His is acutely aware of the need for sustained profits in order to meet the expectations of the market. Talk of recession in the company's home market makes him even more determined to spread the risk of fluctuating profits through a number of different markets rather than remain reliant on one.

Required:

(a)   Describe a risk management process that could assist the company in determining strategy.   **(14 marks)**

(b)   Explain the role of a risk auditor.   **(6 marks)**

(c)   Discuss how risk can be embedded into the systems of an organisation.   **(5 marks)**

(Total: 25 marks)

 Online question assistance

65   YGT (JUN 11)

The board of YGT discussed its need for timely risk information. The consensus of the meeting was that risk consultants should be engaged to review the risks facing the company. One director, Raz Dutta, said that she felt that this would be a waste of money as the company needed to concentrate its resources on improving organisational efficiency rather than on gathering risk information. She said that many risks 'didn't change much' and 'hardly ever materialised' and so can mostly be ignored. The rest of the board, however, believed that a number of risks had recently emerged whilst others had become less important and so the board wanted a current assessment as it believed previous assessments might now be outdated.

The team of risk consultants completed the risk audit. They identified and assessed six potential risks (A, B, C, D, E and F) and the following information was discussed when the findings were presented to the YGT board: Avoid .

Risk A was assessed as unlikely and low impact whilst Risk B was assessed as highly likely to occur and with a high impact. The activities giving rise to both A and B, however, are seen as marginal in that whilst the activities do have value and are capable of making good returns, neither is strategically vital.   *Accept*

Risk C was assessed as low probability but with a high potential impact and also arises from an activity that must not be discontinued although alternative arrangements for bearing the risks are possible. The activity giving rise to Risk C was recently introduced by YGT as a result of a new product launch.   *Transfer*

Risk D was assessed as highly likely but with a low potential impact, and arose as a result of a recent change in legislation. It cannot be insured against nor can it be outsourced. It is strategically important that the company continues to engage in the activity that gives rise to Risk D although not necessarily at the same level as is currently the case.   *Reduce.*

In addition, Risks E and F were identified. Risk E was an environmental risk and Risk F was classed as a reputation risk. The risk consultants said that risks E and F could be related risks. In the formal feedback to the board of YGT, the consultants said that the company had to develop a culture of risk awareness and that this should permeate all levels of the company.

Required:

(a) Criticise Raz Dutta's beliefs about the need for risk assessment. Explain why risks are dynamic and therefore need to be assessed regularly. **(8 marks)**

(b) Using the TARA framework, select and explain the appropriate strategy for managing each risk (A, B, C and D). Justify your selection in each case. **(6 marks)**

(c) Explain what 'related risks' are and describe how Risks E and F might be positively correlated. **(5 marks)**

(d) The risk consultants reported that YGT needed to cultivate a culture of risk awareness and that this should permeate all levels of the company.

Required:

Explain and assess this advice. **(6 marks)**

(Total: 25 marks)

66 DOCTORS' PRACTICE

A large doctors' practice, with six partners and two practice nurses, has decided to increase its income by providing day surgery facilities. The existing building would be extended to provide room for the surgical unit and storage facilities for equipment and drugs. The aim is to offer patients the opportunity to have minor surgical procedures conducted by a doctor at their local practice, thus avoiding any unfamiliarity and possible delays to treatment that might result from referral to a hospital. Blood and samples taken during the surgery will be sent away to the local hospital for testing but the patient will get the results from their doctor at the practice. It is anticipated that the introduction of the day surgery facility will increase practice income by approximately 20%.

Required:

(a) Identify the additional risks that the doctors' practice may expect to face as a consequence of the introduction of the new facility. **(12 marks)**

(b) A partner in another practice has suggested that in order to improve the way in which the practice manages its risks, risk management should be embedded in the organisation. Explain what is meant by 'embedding' risk and what steps need to be taken to ensure that this happens. **(13 marks)**

(Total: 25 marks)

PROFESSIONAL VALUES AND ETHICS

67 VAN BUREN (JUN 08)

It was the final day of a two-week-long audit of Van Buren Company, a longstanding client of Fillmore Pierce Auditors. In the afternoon, Anne Hayes, a recently qualified accountant and member of the audit team, was following an audit trail on some cash payments when she discovered what she described to the audit partner, Zachary Lincoln, as an 'irregularity'. A large and material cash payment had been recorded with no recipient named. The corresponding invoice was handwritten on a scrap of paper and the signature was illegible.

Zachary, the audit partner, was under pressure to finish the audit that afternoon. He advised Anne to seek an explanation from Frank Monroe, the client's finance director. Zachary told her that Van Buren was a longstanding client of Fillmore Pierce and he would be surprised if there was anything unethical or illegal about the payment. He said that he had personally been involved in the Van Buren audit for the last eight years and that it had always been without incident. He also said that Frank Monroe was an old friend of his from university days and that he was certain that he wouldn't approve anything unethical or illegal. Zachary said that Fillmore Pierce had also done some consultancy for Van Buren so it was a very important client that he didn't want Anne to upset with unwelcome and uncomfortable questioning.

When Anne sought an explanation from Mr Monroe, she was told that nobody could remember what the payment was for but that she had to recognise that 'real' audits were sometimes a bit messy and that not all audit trails would end as she might like them to. He also reminded her that it was the final day and both he and the audit firm were under time pressure to conclude business and get the audit signed off.

When Anne told Zachary what Frank had said, Zachary agreed not to get the audit signed off without Anne's support, but warned her that she should be very certain that the irregularity was worth delaying the signoff for. It was therefore now Anne's decision whether to extend the audit or have it signed off by the end of Friday afternoon.

Required:

(a) **Explain why 'auditor independence' is necessary in auditor-client relationships and describe THREE threats to auditor independence in the case.**   **(9 marks)**

(b) Anne is experiencing some tension due to the conflict between her duties and responsibilities as an employee of Fillmore Pierce and as a qualified professional accountant.

   Required:

   (i) **Compare and contrast her duties and responsibilities in the two roles of employee and professional accountant.**   **(6 marks)**

   (ii) **Explain the ethical tensions between these roles that Anne is now experiencing.**   **(4 marks)**

(c) **Explain how absolutist (dogmatic) and relativist (pragmatic) ethical assumptions would affect the outcome of Anne's decision.**   **(6 marks)**

(Total: 25 marks)

68 DUNDAS (DEC 09)

John Wang is a junior partner and training manager at Miller Dundas, a medium sized firm of auditors. He oversees the progress of the firm's student accountants. One of those under John's supervision, Lisa Xu, recently wrote in her progress and achievement log about a situation in an audit that had disturbed her.

On the recent audit of Mbabo Company, a medium sized, family-run business and longstanding client of Miller Dundas, Lisa was checking non-current asset purchases when she noticed what she thought might be an irregularity. There was an entry of $100,000 for a security system for an address in a well-known holiday resort with no obvious link to the company. On questioning this with Ellen Tan, the financial controller, Lisa was told that the system was for Mr Martin Mbabo's holiday cottage (Martin Mbabo is managing director and a minority shareholder in the Mbabo Company). She was told that Martin Mbabo often took confidential company documents with him to his holiday home and so needed the security system on the property to protect them. It was because of this, Ellen said, that it was reasonable to charge the security system to the company.

Ellen Tan expressed surprise at Lisa's concerns and said that auditors had not previously been concerned about the company being charged for non-current assets and operational expenses for Mr Mbabo's personal properties.

Lisa told the engagement partner, Potto Sinter, what she had found and Potto simply said that the charge could probably be ignored. He did agree, however, to ask for a formal explanation from Martin Mbabo before he signed off the audit. Lisa wasn't at the final clearance meeting but later read the following in the notes from the clearance meeting: 'discussed other matter with client, happy with explanation'. When Lisa discussed the matter with Potto afterwards she was told that the matter was now closed and that she should concentrate on her next audit and her important accounting studies.

When John Wang read about Lisa's concerns and spoke to her directly, he realised he was in an ethical dilemma. Not only should there be a disclosure requirement of Mr Mbabo's transaction, but the situation was made more complicated by the fact that Potto Sinter was senior to John Wang in Miller Dundas and also by the fact that the two men were good friends.

Required:

(a) Explain the meaning of 'integrity' and its importance in professional relationships such as those described in the case. **(5 marks)**

(b) Criticise Potto Sinter's ethical and professional behaviour in the case. **(10 marks)**

(c) Critically evaluate the alternatives that John Wang has in his ethical dilemma.

(10 marks)

(Total: 25 marks)

69   HAPPY AND HEALTHY (JUN 10)

'Happy and Healthy' is a traditional independent health food business that has been run as a family company for 40 years by Ken and Steffi Potter. As a couple they have always been passionate campaigners for healthy foods and are more concerned about the quality of the foods they sell than the financial detail of their business. Since the company started in 1970, it has been audited by Watson Shreeves, a local audit firm. Mr Shreeves has overseen the Potters' audit for all of the 40 year history (rotating the engagement partner) and has always taken the opportunity to meet with Ken and Steffi informally at the end of each audit to sign off the financial statements and to offer a briefing and some free financial advice in his role as what he calls, 'auditor and friend'. In these briefings, Mr Shreeves, who has become a close family friend of the Potters over the years, always points out that the business is profitable (which the Potters already knew without knowing the actual figures) and how they might increase their margins. But the Potters have never been too concerned about financial performance as long as they can provide a good service to their customers, make enough to keep the business going and provide continued employment for themselves and their son, Ivan. Whilst Ken and Steffi still retain a majority shareholding in 'Happy and healthy' they have gradually increased Ivan's proportion over the years. They currently own 60% to Ivan's 40%. Ivan was appointed a director, alongside Ken and Steffi, in 2008.

Ivan grew up in the business and has helped his parents out since he was a young boy. As he grew up, Ken and Steffi gave him more and more responsibility in the hope that he would one day take the business over. By the end of 2009, Ken made sure that Ivan drew more salary than Ken and Steffi combined as they sought to ensure that Ivan was happy to continue in the business after they retired.

During the audit for the year ended 31 March 2010, a member of Watson Shreeves was performing the audit as usual when he noticed a dramatic drop in the profitability of the business as a whole. He noticed that whilst food sales continued to be profitable, a large amount of inventory had been sold below cost to Barong Company with no further explanation and it was this that had caused the reduction in the company's operating margin. Each transaction with Barong Company had, the invoices showed, been authorised by Ivan.

Mr Shreeves was certain Ken and Steffi would not know anything about this and he prepared to tell them about it as a part of his annual end of audit meeting. Before the meeting, however, he carried out some checks on Barong Company and found that it was a separate business owned by Ivan and his wife. Mr Shreeves's conclusion was that Ivan was effectively stealing from 'Happy and healthy' to provide inventory for Barong Company at a highly discounted cost price. Although Mr Shreeves now had to recommend certain disclosures to the financial statements in this meeting, his main fear was that Ken and Steffi would be devastated if they found out that Ivan was stealing and that it would have long-term implications for their family relationships and the future of 'Happy and healthy'.

Required:

(a)   Explain how a family (or insider-dominated) business differs from a public listed company and, using evidence from the case, explore the governance issues of a family or insider-dominated business.   **(10 marks)**

(b)   Mr Shreeves is a professional accountant and auditor. Explain why he is considered a professional by society and describe the fundamental principles (or responsibilities) of professionalism that society expects from him and all other accountants.   **(7 marks)**

(c)   Discuss the professional and ethical dilemma facing Mr Shreeves in deciding whether or not to tell Ken and Steffi about Ivan's activity. Advise Mr Shreeves of the most appropriate course of action.   **(8 marks)**

(Total: 25 marks)

70   PROFESSIONAL CODES OF ETHICS (PILOT 07)

At a recent conference on corporate social responsibility, one speaker (Professor Cheung) argued that professional codes of ethics for accountants were not as useful as some have claimed because:

'they assume professional accountants to be rules-driven, when in fact most professionals are more driven by principles that guide and underpin all aspects of professional behaviour, including professional ethics.'

When quizzed from the audience about his views on the usefulness of professional codes of ethics, Professor Cheung suggested that the costs of writing, implementing, disseminating and monitoring ethical codes outweighed their usefulness. He said that as long as professional accountants personally observe the highest values of probity and integrity then there is no need for detailed codes of ethics.

Required:

(a)   Critically evaluate Professor Cheung's views on codes of professional ethics. Use examples of ethical codes, where appropriate, to illustrate your answer.

(11 marks)

(b)   With reference to Professor Cheung's comments, explain what is meant by 'integrity' and assess its importance as an underlying principle in corporate governance.   **(7 marks)**

(c)   Explain and contrast a deontological with a consequentialist based approach to business ethics.   **(7 marks)**

(Total: 25 marks)

71   PHARMA   *Online question assistance*

Pharma is a global pharmaceutical company producing many of the world's leading over-the-counter and prescription drugs. Many of these brands are household names sold through major retail chains in over 100 countries or direct to governments for use through public sector health services. Recently, the company has funded a research project into the effectiveness of one of its new products designed to combat a particular childhood disease. The project is designed to evaluate effectiveness in comparison with a competitor brand as a foundation for a future marketing campaign. The drug was released into markets around the world two years ago.

All trials of the new drug have been carried out by Professor Zac Jones at the Massachusetts State University who receive a multi-million dollar support grant for their assistance in projects of this nature. The contract with Pharma insists on no publicity being given to projects and that all findings are kept strictly confidential.

Professor Jones has just returned from a meeting with Chief Executive and Chief Finance Officer (CFO) of Pharma. He has told them that, in his view, although the new product is effective, its side effects can be damaging to children in some cases and possibly even fatal. Although the probability of loss of life is small he is recommending removing the product from the shelves immediately. Professor Jones also states that he is ethically bound to publish his findings so that governments and health services around the world may take appropriate action.

The CFO has reminded him of the considerable revenue loss involved in such a move and of the size of the grant given to the University. He insists the findings remain confidential, pointing out a clause in the contract between Pharma and the University that forbids the disclosure of 'trade secrets' to third parties. Professor Jones is appalled and has openly questioned the CFO's integrity as a member of an esteemed profession.

Required:

(a)   Define 'profession' and evaluate the role of the accountant in support of the public interest.   **(10 marks)**

(b)   Discuss how an accountant might support a wider, value laden role in society.
                                                                                                               (6 marks)

(c)   Define 'confidentiality' and assess its importance as an underlying ethical principle.
                                                                                                               (5 marks)

(d)   Advise Professor Jones as to possible courses of action given the ethical dispute with Pharma.   **(4 marks)**

                                                                                                          (Total: 25 marks)

   Online question assistance

72 DEONTOLOGICAL ETHICS

Required:

(a) **Explain the deontological approach to ethics and the application of this approach by Kant in his three maxims.** **(12 marks)**

(b) A recent newspaper report explained that a toy re-seller was recalling over 500,000 toys because they were unsafe. Following use of the toys, it was discovered that small magnets attached to each toy could become dislodged and accidentally swallowed by children. Swallowing a number of magnets could produce digestion problems and in extreme cases death. Subsequent investigation by the Trading Standards Authority (TSA) identified that these toys were produced in a country where the use of child labour is common – this was not the case in the country of sale. Also the manufacturer did not always provide safe conditions for the workers. Workers were also paid on a piece-rate which meant they hurried to complete each toy, and the magnets were not always properly attached to the toy. The reason for the lack of safety and poor working conditions was ascribed to pressure from the toy re-seller to provide toys at a low price. The toy re-seller indicated that low prices were expected by its customers, and that the use of child labour had not been publicised.

Required:

Apply Kant's deontological maxims to the above situation evaluating whether the use of child labour is acceptable. **(13 marks)**

(Total: 25 marks)

73 RDC (DEC 12)

Railway Development Company (RDC) was considering two options for a new railway line connecting two towns. Route A involved cutting a channel through an area designated as being of special scientific importance because it was one of a very few suitable feeding grounds for a colony of endangered birds. The birds were considered to be an important part of the local environment with some potential influences on local ecosystems.

The alternative was Route B which would involve the compulsory purchase and destruction of Eddie Krul's farm. Mr Krul was a vocal opponent of the Route B plan. He said that he had a right to stay on the land which had been owned by his family for four generations and which he had developed into a profitable farm. The farm employed a number of local people whose jobs would be lost if Route B went through the house and land. Mr Krul threatened legal action against RDC if Route B was chosen.

An independent legal authority has determined that the compulsory purchase price of Mr Krul's farm would be $1 million if Route B was chosen. RDC considered this a material cost, over and above other land costs, because the projected net present value (NPV) of cash flows over a ten-year period would be $5 million without buying the farm. This would reduce the NPV by $1 million if Route B was chosen.

The local government authority had given both routes provisional planning permission and offered no opinion of which it preferred. It supported infrastructure projects such as the new railway line, believing that either route would attract new income and prosperity to the region. It took the view that as an experienced railway builder, RDC would know best which to choose and how to evaluate the two options. Because it was very keen to attract the investment, it left the decision entirely to RDC. RDC selected Route A as the route to build the new line.

A local environmental pressure group, 'Save the Birds', was outraged at the decision to choose Route A. It criticised RDC and also the local authority for ignoring the sustainability implications of the decision. It accused the company of profiting at the expense of the environment and threatened to use 'direct action' to disrupt the building of the line through the birds' feeding ground if Route A went ahead.

Required:

(a)   Use Tucker's 'five question' model to assess the decision to choose Route A.

(10 marks)

(b)   Discuss the importance to RDC of recognising all of the stakeholders in a decision such as deciding between Route A and Route B. (8 marks)

(c)   Explain what a stakeholder 'claim' is, and critically assess the stakeholder claims of Mr Krul, the local government authority and the colony of endangered birds.

(7 marks)

(Total: 25 marks)

74   POLICY SPEECH (JUN 09)

 Timed question with Online tutor debrief

In a major policy speech, Government finance minister Mrs Wei Yttria said that the audit and assurance industry's work should always be judged by the effect it has on public confidence in business. She said that it was crucial that professional services such as audit and assurance should always be performed in the public interest and that there should be no material threats to the assurer's independence. Enron and other corporate failures happened, she said, because some accountants didn't understand what it was to act in the public interest. She stressed that it was important that firms should not provide more than one service to individual clients. If a firm audited a client then, she said, it shouldn't provide any other services to that client.

Mr Oggon Mordue, a financial journalist who had worked in audit and assurance for many years, was in the audience. He suggested that the normal advice on threats to independence was wrong. On the contrary in fact, the more services that a professional services firm can provide to a client the better, as it enables the firm to better understand the client and its commercial and accounting needs. Mrs Yttria disagreed, saying that his views were a good example of professional services firms not acting in the public interest.

Mr Mordue said that when he was a partner at a major professional services firm, he got to know his clients very well through the multiple links that his firm had with them. He said that he knew all about their finances from providing audit and assurance services, all about their tax affairs through tax consulting and was always in a good position to provide any other advice as he had acted as a consultant on other matters for many years including advising on mergers, acquisitions, compliance and legal issues. He became very good friends with the directors of client companies, he said. The clients, he explained, also found the relationship very helpful and the accounting firms did well financially out of it.

Another reporter in the audience argued with Mr Mordue. Ivor Nahum said that Mr Mordue represented the 'very worst' of the accounting profession. He said that accounting was a 'biased and value laden' profession that served minority interests, was complicit in environmental degradation and could not serve the public interest as long as it primarily served the interests of unfettered capitalism. He said that the public interest was badly served by accounting, as it did not address poverty, animal rights or other social injustices.

Required:

(a) Explain, using accounting as an example, what 'the public interest' means as used by Mrs Yttria in her speech. **(5 marks)**

(b) This requirement concerns ethical threats. It is very important for professional accountants to be aware of ethical threats and to avoid these where possible.

Required:

(i) With reference to the case as appropriate, describe five types of ethical threat. **(5 marks)**

(ii) Assess the ethical threats implied by Mr Mordue's beliefs. **(8 marks)**

(c) Assess Ivor Nahum's remarks about the accounting profession in the light of Gray, Owen & Adams' deep green (or deep ecologist) position on social responsibility.

(7 marks)

(Total: 25 marks)

75 INO COMPANY *Walk in the footsteps of a top tutor*

Required:

(a) Explain the term 'corporate ethics', discussing the extent to which organisations must have corporate ethics and how those ethics are reported. **(6 marks)**

(b) The INO Company produces a range of motor vehicles in a central European country. INO currently produces nine different models, and it has a good reputation for safety and has build up customer trust in its products in this respect.

One model produced by INO, the N920, has been identified as having a potential failure. There is a remote chance that the engine will overheat during use, causing the vehicle to stop. The INO R&D department estimates that this error will affect one car in 125,000 (or five cars overall). The board considers that the costs of rectification are excessive and far outweigh the potential costs of rectifying faults as and when they occur.

INO obtains tyres for its vehicles from the UIN Company. UIN is part of INO's preferred supplier scheme and enjoy close working relations with INO as well as prompt payment of invoices for goods supplied. However, INO has recently learnt that UIN are employing children as young as nine in an overseas production facility, although this is not against the law in that particular country.

As part of its perceived duty to society, the board of INO does promote charitable giving and support of community projects such as sponsorship of local schools and colleges. Employees are also providing with 'fair' wages and additional facilities such as a sports hall providing fitness training. However, INO does not produce any CSR report and the board prefers to invest in ethical activities as and when it chooses to rather than having any formal structure or systems in place.

INO has a range of shareholders from large corporate investors to smaller personal investments. Shareholders are generally pleased with the way in which directors run their business; growth in turnover and profits has been steady in recent years while dividends have consistently exceeded competitors by 25% or more.

The board of INO also recognises that motor vehicles are potentially damaging to the environment. An R&D budget of €25 million has therefore been targeted at reducing emissions from INO's vehicles.

Required:

Identify and explain any issues relevant to the ethical stance of INO and discuss the potential impact of those issues on the company and its stakeholders. Where appropriate, recommend amendments to the corporate ethics of INO. (19 marks)

(Total: 25 marks)

76 IFAC

The IFAC code of professional ethics (2009), adopted as being relevant to ACCA members and students, contains the following advice.

'A professional accountant in business or an immediate or close family member may be offered an inducement. Inducements may take various forms, including gifts, hospitality, preferential treatment, and inappropriate appeals to friendship or loyalty. Offers of inducements may create threats to compliance with the fundamental principles [of professionalism].'

Executive director and qualified accountant Ann Koo was in charge of awarding large outsourcing contracts for a large public listed company. When her family fell into debt, she looked for a way to make some additional income. When her company was seeking to place a contract for a large outsourced service, without inviting other tenders from which to select, she accepted a bid from one supplier who said it would pay her $50,000 as a 'thank you' once the contract was awarded. She justified her behaviour by reminding herself that she obtained her job partly because she was an accountant and that she had worked extremely hard to obtain her accounting qualification. She believed she was entitled to make a 'higher personal return' on her investment of time and effort in her accountancy training and through successful qualification as a professional accountant.

Required:

(a) Briefly describe the five types of ethical threats in the IFAC code of professional ethics (2009) and discuss how accepting excessive 'gifts' or 'hospitality' can give rise to some of these threats within this case. **(9 marks)**

(b) Criticise Ann Koo's beliefs and behaviour, and explain why accepting the $50,000 conflicts with her duty to uphold the public interest. **(10 marks)**

(c) The IFAC code also highlights the need for:

'up-to-date education [for directors] on ethical issues and the legal restrictions and other regulations around potential insider trading.'

Required:

Explain what 'insider dealing/trading' is and why it is an unethical and often illegal practice. **(6 marks)**

(Total: 25 marks)

77 FIVE ETHICAL SITUATIONS

In all of the ethical situations below, the people involved are qualified members of ACCA.

1 A applies for a job and enhances his CV by indicating he obtained first time passes in all his examinations, although he actually failed three exams at the first attempt.

2 B is the management accountant in C Ltd. B is paid a bonus based on the profits of C Ltd. During accounts preparation B notices an error in the inventory calculation which has the effect of overstating profits. B decides to take no action as this would decrease the bonus payable.

3 D is responsible for the purchase of computer equipment in E Ltd. Quotes from three suppliers have been received for installation of new hardware; one supplier, F Co, has promised a 10% discount payable to D if their quote is accepted.

4 G is preparing the management accounts in H Ltd. Part of the information presented to him indicates that H Ltd entered into an illegal agreement with I Ltd to fix price increases in the goods H and I supply. H and I together supply 90% of the total market. The price setting enabled H and I to obtain higher than expected profits for their sales.

5 J is preparing the management accounts for K Ltd. L, the senior management accountant, has instructed J to omit the negative overhead variance from the accounts on the grounds that they show an 'unacceptable loss' with the inclusion of the variance.

Required:

(a) Explain how professional codes of ethics address possible conflicts of interest facing accountants. **(5 marks)**

(b) For each of the situations above:

(i) Identify and explain the ethical threat to the accountant. **(10 marks)**

(ii) Discuss the ethical safeguards available to overcome that threat. **(10 marks)**

NB: Each situation is worth four marks – two for part (i) and two for part (ii).

(Total: 25 marks)

78   HOGG PRODUCTS COMPANY (DEC 08)

Hogg Products Company (HPC), based in a developing country, was recently wholly acquired by American Overseas Investments (AOI), a North American holding company. The new owners took the opportunity to completely review HPC's management, culture and systems. One of the first things that AOI questioned was HPC's longstanding corporate code of ethics.

The board of AOI said that it had a general code of ethics that HPC, as an AOI subsidiary, should adopt. Simon Hogg, the chief executive of HPC, disagreed however, and explained why HPC should retain its existing code. He said that HPC had adopted its code of ethics in its home country which was often criticised for its unethical business behaviour. Some other companies in the country were criticised for their 'sweat shop' conditions. HPC's adoption of its code of ethics, however, meant that it could always obtain orders from European customers on the guarantee that products were made ethically and in compliance with its own highly regarded code of ethics. Mr Hogg explained that HPC had an outstanding ethical reputation both locally and internationally and that reputation could be threatened if it was forced to replace its existing code of ethics with AOI's more general code.

When Ed Tanner, a senior director from AOI's head office, visited Mr Hogg after the acquisition, he was shown HPC's operation in action. Mr Hogg pointed out that unlike some other employers in the industry, HPC didn't employ child labour. Mr Hogg explained that although it was allowed by law in the country, it was forbidden by HPC's code of ethics. Mr Hogg also explained that in his view, employing child labour was always ethically wrong. Mr Tanner asked whether the money that children earned by working in the relatively safe conditions at HPC was an important source of income for their families. Mr Hogg said that the money was important to them but even so, it was still wrong to employ children, as it was exploitative and interfered with their education. He also said that it would alienate the European customers who bought from HPC partly on the basis of the terms of its code of ethics.

Required:

(a)   **Describe the purposes and typical contents of a corporate code of ethics.**

(9 marks)

(b)   **'Strategic positioning' is about the way that a company as a whole is placed in its environment and concerns its 'fit' with the factors in its environment.**

With reference to the case as appropriate, explain how a code of ethics can be used as part of a company's overall strategic positioning.   **(7 marks)**

(c)   **Assess Mr Hogg's belief that employing child labour is 'always ethically wrong' from deontological and teleological (consequentialist) ethical perspectives.**   **(9 marks)**

(Total: 25 marks)

79 JH GRAPHICS (PILOT 07)

The board of JH Graphics, a design and artwork company, was debating an agenda item on the possible adoption of a corporate code of ethics. Jenny Harris, the chief executive and majority shareholder, was a leading supporter of the idea. She said that many of the large companies in the industry had adopted codes of ethics and that she thought it would signal the importance that JH Graphics placed on ethics. She also said that she was personally driven by high ethical values and that she wanted to express these through her work and through the company's activities and policies.

Alan Leroy, the creative director, explained that he would support the adoption of the code of ethics as long as it helped to support the company's long-term strategic objectives. He said that he could see no other reason as the company was 'not a charity' and had to maximise shareholder value above all other objectives. In particular, he was keen, as a shareholder himself, to know what the code would cost to draw up and how much it would cost to comply with it over and above existing costs.

Jenny argued that having a code would help to resolve some ethical issues, one of which, she suggested, was a problem the company was having over a particular image it had recently produced for a newspaper advertisement. The image was produced for an advertising client and although the client was pleased, it had offended a particular religious group because of its content and design.

When it was discovered who had produced the 'offending' image, some religious leaders criticised JH Graphics for being insensitive and offensive to their religion. For a brief time, the events were a major news story. As politicians, journalists and others debated the issues in the media, the board of JH Graphics was involved in intense discussions and faced with a dilemma as to whether or not to issue a public apology for the offence caused by the image and to ask the client to withdraw it.

Alan argued that having a code of ethics would not have helped in that situation, as the issue was so complicated. His view was that the company should not apologise for the image and that he didn't care very much that the image offended people. He said it was bringing the company free publicity and that was good for the business. Jenny said that she had sympathy for the viewpoint of the offended religious leaders. Although she disagreed with them, she understood the importance to some people of firmly-held beliefs. The board agreed that as there seemed to be arguments both ways, the decision on how the company should deal with the image should be Jenny's as chief executive.

Required:

(a) Analyse Jenny's and Alan's motivations for adopting the code of ethics using the normative-instrumental forms of stakeholder theory.   (8 marks)

(b) Assess Jenny's decision on the possible apology for the 'offending' image from conventional and pre-conventional moral development perspectives.   (4 marks)

(c) Explain and assess the factors that the board of JH Graphics might consider in deciding how to respond to the controversy over the offending image.   (10 marks)

(d) Comment on the legitimacy of the religious group's claims on JH Graphics' activities.   (3 marks)

(Total: 25 marks)

80   CARPETS AND FLOOR COVERINGS

BK is a company specialising in the sale of carpets and floor coverings to sports clubs, sports halls and social centres around the country. It obtains its carpeting and other materials directly from suppliers in Eastern Asia.

When it provides new carpeting to a customer, BK also undertakes to remove and dispose of the old carpeting or floor covering, but charges a fee for the service. The old carpets are taken to waste disposal sites or occasionally burned.

You have recently been appointed as an internal auditor to the company, and you are discussing your plan of work for the next 12 months with the finance director. The following points arise in your discussion.

The work of the internal audit section has so far been largely restricted to audits of elements of the financial accounting system, although there have been occasional management audits. You suggest that it might be appropriate to carry out some value for money audits.

The board of directors has come under pressure from its major shareholders to publish an annual Social and Environmental Report for inclusion in the annual report and accounts. You suggest that it might be appropriate to check and verify the contents of this report before publication.

There has been considerable publicity in the national press recently about the use of child labour and slave labour in certain parts of the country from which BK purchases its carpets. The finance director expresses the view that BK benefited from low purchase costs for carpets and floor coverings, but he would be disappointed if BK's suppliers were associated with these labour practices.

The finance director informs you that your predecessor as internal auditor resigned from the company after a dispute with the executive director concerning a department where the auditor had carried out a management audit. Apparently, the internal auditor had criticised the director and his department severely for lax controls and inefficiency. The director had argued that the internal auditor had not discussed any of the criticisms before preparing the report, had been deceitful in asking questions and was probably not qualified to do the audit work. On being told that the auditor was a ACCA member, you express the view that this seemed to be a matter where the Institute's Ethical Guidelines should have been followed.

Required:

(a)   Explain the difference between a value for money audit of the accounts department and an audit of the accounting system.   **(7 marks)**

(b)   Suggest how you might plan a social and environmental audit of the company and what you would consider to be the main social and environmental risks facing BK.
                                                                                   (8 marks)

(c)   From the information available about the dispute between the previous internal auditor and the executive director, suggest how ACCA's Code of Ethics and Conduct might have been relevant to the way in which the auditor acted, or ought to have acted.   **(10 marks)**

                                                                          (Total: 25 marks)

81 JOJO AUDITORS

Jojo Auditors is an audit practice with five partners. The five partners have worked together for several years and, as well as being work colleagues, are personal friends with each other. At Jojo it is customary for the performance of all student accountants to be appraised after their first year of a training contract using a range of criteria including examination success, technical ability and professionalism. Three levels of outcome are possible:

(1)   'Good', allowing students to continue with no issues

(2)   'Some concerns', meaning students are counselled and then allowed to continue; and,

(3)   'Poor', where students are dismissed from the audit practice.

The appraisal committee is comprised of three people: managing partner Jack Hu, the training manager (both of whom are professional accountants) and the person responsible for human resources. The committee receives confidential reports on each student and makes decisions based on the views of relevant engagement partners and also exam results. It is normally the training manager who makes the recommendation and in most cases his appraisal is agreed and then acted upon accordingly. Because the appraisals are confidential between the student and the firm, the list of students and their appraisal categories are not publicised within the firm.

When the 2010 intake was being appraised last year, one student was appraised by the training manager as 'poor' but was not dismissed. Polly Shah was unpopular among other students because she was considered lazy and technically weak. She also failed a number of her exams. Other students who were appraised as 'poor' were dismissed, but Polly received a brief counselling session from Jack Hu and then returned to her duties. Polly stayed for another year and then, having failed more exams, left Jojo to pursue other career interests outside accounting.

Polly's departure triggered some discussion amongst Jojo's partners as to why she had been retained when other poor performers had not. It later emerged that Jack Hu was a close friend of Polly's parents and had enjoyed free holidays in the Shah family's villa for several years. Because he was the managing partner, Mr Hu was able to insist on retaining Polly, despite the objections of the training manager and the human resources representative, although the training manager was reported to be furious at the decision to retain Polly.

Required:

(a)   **Define 'conflict of interest' and assess the consequences of Jack Hu's behaviour after Polly Shah's appraisal.   (10 marks)**

(b)   **Describe four ethical safeguards that could be used in Jojo to prevent a recurrence of the events like those described in the case.   (8 marks)**

(c) The case raises issues of the importance of senior management performance measurement. In a public company, this refers to directors, and in a privately-owned partnership like Jojo, it refers to partners. The managing partner (Mr Hu's position) is equivalent to the role of chief executive.

Required:

Explain the typical criteria used in the performance measurement of individual directors and discuss the reasons why individual performance measurement of partners may be difficult to implement at Jojo. **(7 marks)**

(Total: 25 marks)

82 MATTI

(a) As a newly-qualified certified accountant, you are assisting in the preparation of the accounts of MATTI. Part of your duties involves calculating the provision for inventory. Part way through this calculation, the senior accountant notices that you are providing against inventory lines which have not sold any units for the last six months. 'That provision will adversely affect profit by €520,000' he notes. 'The company cannot afford that additional fall in profit and anyway, provision for those items has not been made in this way before; we normally wait and see what the scrap value will be in 12 months time.' The senior accountant states that the provision must not be entered into the accounting system.

Required:

Explain each of Kohlberg's levels of Cognitive Mental Development (6 levels in total) and using the above example, provide an example of a decision and the rationale behind it for each level of development. **(18 marks)**

(b) Z's son needs a drug costing €40,000 to improve the quality of his son's life, and potentially stop him from dying. Z lives in a state where healthcare requirements are provided almost exclusively by the state.

Z has a discussion with M, a doctor. M informs Z that the hospital budget (which is set by the state) cannot afford this amount of expenditure on one individual. M advises Z to try and obtain the money privately – Z informs M this is not possible.

Z takes a job as a hospital cleaner and one night breaks into the hospital storeroom and steals the drug. Z's son recovers from his illness.

Required:

Using Kohlberg's model of CMD, explain the actions of Z and M. **(7 marks)**

(Total: 25 marks)

83 BIGGO MANUFACTURING

When Biggo Manufacturing (a public listed company) needed to build an extension to its factory, it obtained planning permission to build it on an adjacent field. The local government authority was keen to attract the new jobs that would go with the expansion and so granted the permission despite the objections of a number of residents, who were concerned that the new factory extension would mean the loss of a children's play area.

When the board of Biggo met after the building approval had been given, the chief executive read out a letter from Albert Doo, leader of the local government authority, saying that although permission to build had been given, the company should consider making a sizeable contribution towards creating a new children's play area in a nearby location. Mr Doo said that Biggo 'should recognise its social responsibility'. He said that the company should consider itself a citizen of society and should, accordingly, 'recognise its responsibilities as well as its legal rights'.

One of Biggo's directors, Robert Tens, said he thought the request was entirely reasonable given the displacement of the play area. He also said that they could use the donation strategically to help cultivate the company's reputation locally to help in future recruitment. It might also, he said, help to reduce resistance to any future expansion the company might need to make.

Margaret Heggs, in contrast, argued that the company should not make the donation as it was likely that company profits would be low in the current year. She said that the acquisition of the land and the gaining of planning permission were done through the normal legal channels and so the company had no further contractual or ethical duties to the local government, nor to the local community. She said that Biggo provided local employment and produced excellent products and so it was unreasonable for the request for a donation to have been made. 'This board is accountable to the shareholders of Biggo and not to the local community or the local government authority', she said.

Required:

(a) Explain the meaning of 'rights' and 'responsibilities' in the context of Biggo and describe how these terms are interpreted at the two ends of the Gray, Owen & Adams 'continuum'. **(10 marks)**

(b) Justify, using evidence from the case, which of Gray, Owen & Adams's positions are best described by the comments made by Robert Tens and also Margaret Heggs. **(6 marks)**

(c) Define 'social responsibility' as used by Albert Doo. Contrast how short and long-term shareholder interest perspectives may affect Biggo's attitude to the requested contribution for the children's play area. **(9 marks)**

(Total: 25 marks)

84   JGP LTD (DEC 10)

At a board meeting of JGP Chemicals Limited, the directors were discussing some recent negative publicity arising from the accidental emission of a chemical pollutant into the local river. As well as it resulting in a large fine from the courts, the leak had created a great deal of controversy in the local community that relied on the polluted river for its normal use (including drinking). A prominent community leader spoke for those affected when she said that a leak of this type must never happen again or JGP would suffer the loss of support from the community. She also reminded JGP that it attracts 65% of its labour from the local community.

As a response to the problems that arose after the leak, the JGP board decided to consult an expert on whether the publication of a full annual environmental report might help to mitigate future environmental risks. The expert, Professor Appo (a prominent academic), said that the company would need to establish an annual environmental audit before they could issue a report. He said that the environmental audit should include, in addition to a review and evaluation of JGP's safety controls, a full audit of the environmental impact of JGP's supply chain. He said that these components would be very important in addressing the concerns of a growing group of investors who are worried about such things. Professor Appo said that all chemical companies had a structural environmental risk and JGP was no exception to this. As major consumers of natural chemical resources and producers of potentially hazardous outputs, Professor Appo said that chemical companies should be aware of the wide range of ways in which they can affect the environment. CEO Keith Miasma agreed with Professor Appo and added that because JGP was in chemicals, any environmental issue had the potential to affect JGP's overall reputation among a wide range of stakeholders.

When the board was discussing the issue of sustainability in connection with the environmental audit, the finance director said that sustainability reporting would not be necessary as the company was already sustainable because it had no 'going concern' issues. He said that JGP had been in business for over 50 years, should be able to continue for many years to come and was therefore sustainable. As far as he was concerned, this was all that was meant by sustainability.

In the discussion that followed, the board noted that in order to signal its seriousness to the local community and to investors, the environmental audit should be as thorough as possible and that as much information should be made available to the public 'in the interests of transparency'. It was agreed that contents of the audit (the agreed metrics) should be robust and with little room left for interpretation – they wanted to be able to demonstrate that they had complied with their agreed metrics for the environmental audit.

Required:

(a)   Explain 'sustainability' in the context of environmental auditing and criticise the finance director's understanding of sustainability.   **(6 marks)**

(b)   Explain the three stages in an environmental audit and explore, using information from the case, the issues that JGP will have in developing these stages.   **(9 marks)**

(c)   Define 'environmental risk'. Distinguish between strategic and operational risks and explain why the environmental risks at JGP are strategic.   **(10 marks)**

(Total: 25 marks)

85 BRIBERY

ZZM is a multinational company which buys agricultural products for use in its manufacturing process. ZZM has committed to observe all guidelines and codes of conduct for multinationals. This policy was prompted by ZZM's desire to be a good corporate citizen.

ZZM has been trading profitably for ten years with farmers' co-operatives in Agriland, an agricultural country. ZZM's business is an important part of Agriland's economy. ZZM has made efforts to improve both the production techniques of the farmers and the living conditions of farm workers and their families. ZZM has built a number of schools and also a district hospital in Agriland.

The farmers' co-operatives have freedom to trade with anyone but have chosen to deal exclusively with ZZM. ZZM has enjoyed an excellent relationships within Agriland but this now seems threatened by a number of factors.

The Government of Agriland has been under the control of the same political party for the previous 15 years. Recently there have been allegations of corruption made against the Government and its popularity has decreased: some analysts think it might lose the next general election. The main opposition party is very nationalistic and opposed to free trade. It has stated that if it is elected it will nationalise all foreign owned businesses without compensation.

The farm workers' union in Agriland has asked for an immediate 10% pay rise as farm workers' pay has not increased for two years although prices have increased by 20%. The farm workers have never been militant but this is changing. In some areas of Agriland, farm workers have gone on strike.

At a recent meeting between the President of Agriland and ZZM, the President said there was a common interest in preventing the main opposition party from winning the next general election. The President suggested a number of strategies which could be followed:

1 ZZM could give a substantial donation to the President's party for its election funds.

2 ZZM could agree to an extra tax on its Agriland operations. This could be used to increase the national minimum wage for farm workers.

3 ZZM could open an agricultural processes factory within Agriland to assist economic development.

The President stated his strategies were not mutually exclusive. He added that if ZZM was not able to help him, then he would seriously consider nationalising ZZM's operations without any compensation.

Required:

(a) **Advise how stakeholder mapping could assist ZZM in deciding which of the options it should pursue with respect to Agriland.**

Note: You are not required to draw Mendelow's matrix **(4 marks)**

(b) **Define 'Social Responsibility'. Contrast how short- and long-term shareholder interest perspectives may affect ZZM's attitude to the requested political donation (strategy option 1).** **(9 marks)**

(c) **Evaluate the other two options suggested by the President – option 2 and option 3 – and one other option which you have identified.** **(8 marks)**

(d) **Recommend the option which you consider ZZM should follow. Explain the reason(s) for your recommendation.** **(4 marks)**

(Total: 25 marks)

86 GRINDLE

The directors of Grindle plc, a listed company with a reputation for ensuring the transparency of company information, have discussed a recent study which indicates that over 35% of the world's 250 largest corporations are voluntarily complying with new initiatives in the constantly changing world of corporate reporting. They see being innovative in the context of providing information to stakeholders as critical objective to promote performance and to retain and attract customers and investors.

In addition they have heard that their main competitors are applying the new principles of integrated reporting <IR>. However, the directors are unsure as to what this initiative actually means. The Non executive directors were questioning the purpose of <IR> being specifically concerned that it was just another in a long line of dubious initiatives which would result in additional costs with little perceived benefit. They were also having specific concerns about the different definitions of capital which are reputedly a key part of this new initiative. In particular they are concerned as to the definitions of natural and social capital.

At a recent meeting one of the board was very critical of <IR> commenting that he couldn't identify with this new terminology commenting "why call them capitals when they actually relate to resources" The Finance Director had some sympathy with this view bearing in mind that almost any definition of capital makes the connection between capital and money and was unclear as to whether or not "it may be just a case of changing the words we use to refer to creating money?"

Additionally they require advice as to the nature of any suggested standards over the collation and inclusion of information relating to integrated reporting. They are worried that any report produced by the company may not be of sufficient quality requiring additional informational needs and additional costs. In this context they argue that <IR> may detract rather than enhance their image if the end report does not comply with recognised standards.

Required:

(a) Explain integrated reporting and explain the meaning of the terms natural and social capital. **(6 marks)**

(b) Construct a case for the incorporation of the principles of integrated reporting into Grindle. **(9 marks)**

(c) Advise the board of Grindle of the suggested reporting requirements and guidelines relating to the compilation of an integrated report. **(6 marks)**

(d) Recommend the course of action Grindle should follow. Explain the reason(s) for your recommendation. **(4 marks)**

(Total: 25 marks)

Section 3

ANSWERS TO PRACTICE QUESTIONS – SECTION A

1 MANAGE LTD

Key answer tips

This question is typical of the scenario questions for this exam in that it covers many syllabus areas. You must use the marks to guide you as to the depth of your answer. Part (a) requires plenty of detail to earn five marks about each risk categorisation – you will need to be very explicit as to what is meant by strategic and operational.

In part (b) make sure that you explain your risks precisely and clearly, don't just stop at things like 'interest rate risk'. Note the careful wording of the second part of the requirement: you are asked to discuss how they could assess impact on the company. As such you are not required to formulate a view on the impact or likelihood, but discuss how Utopia could assess these. Be careful that you answer this precise question.

Part (c) is a much more theoretical part on corporate governance.

(a) Strategic risks

Strategic risks are those which have a direct impact on the overall mission of the company. The first group of strategic risks is those which arise from the possible consequences of strategic decisions taken by the company. For example, one company might pursue a strategy of growth by acquisitions, whilst another might seek slower, organic growth. Growth by acquisition is likely to be much more high-risk than organic growth, although the potential returns might also be much higher.

A second group of strategic risks arises from the way in which an organisation is strategically positioned within its environment. A company may decide to expand into higher or lower risk areas, for example by manufacturing new products or simply enhancing older products

Adverse consequences can also result from failings in the strategic management of an organisation. A company may have the right strategy but fail to monitor or implement it effectively, or identify and follow the wrong strategy.

Strategic risks should be identified and assessed at senior management and board or director level.

Operational risks

Operational risks affect the day-to-day activities of the company. These risks are potential losses which may arise from the people or processes or the structure of the organisation. Operational risks can be defined as 'the risk of losses resulting from inadequate or failed internal processes, people and systems, or external events' (Basel Committee on Banking Supervision). Operational risks include risks of fraud or employee malfeasance as well as risks from production (such as poor quality) or lack of production (not having inputs available at the correct time).

Other examples include:

- business interruption
- product design failures
- loss of key people
- termination of contracts by suppliers.

Operational risks can be most effectively identified, assessed and managed at the level in the organisation at which they arise. Most can be managed by internal control systems.

(b) A number of risks exist for Utopia Inc in making the acquisition of Manage Ltd. The following explains some of the main risks.

Strategic risks – understanding market

The investment in Manage Ltd is a strategic investment and there is the chance that the investment will not generate the returns expected. The reason for this could be that Utopia has not understood the market in which Manage Ltd operates and therefore predicts growth that may not actually arise. There is perhaps a danger of this in the scenario as Manage Ltd has been very successful in recent years and Utopia could be paying a price based on the growth continuing, which it may not.

Carrying out market research will enable Utopia to assess the likelihood of the sales revenue failing to grow as expected. The use of scenario planning to assess the outcome of different levels of sales would enable the company to quantify the impact on the business.

Loss of staff

There is a danger that key staff in Manage Ltd will leave after the acquisition and as a result there will be a loss of goodwill and customer support. If the staff leave they may join competitors or set up in competition with Manage. It appears that Utopia Inc is attempting to reduce this risk by offering positions to Jean Smith and other selected staff.

Utopia may be able to assess the probability of staff leaving based on the experience from previous acquisitions. Feedback from discussions with selected staff could also give an indication of the likelihood that staff will leave. The company will also be able to estimate the cost of replacing staff who leave.

Culture

There is a serious risk of a cultural issue in Utopia investing in Manage. It is possible that Utopia's management style will not fit with the style of Manage. This could result in the existing Manage staff being demotivated and therefore either leaving or not putting their full effort into making Utopia a successful business.

There is also a risk that Utopia will not understand the UK culture and therefore as a result they might operate in a way which is unacceptable to UK customers.

It may be possible for Utopia to gain an understanding of the culture of Manage and assess how different it is and the likely problems from the conversations it is having with staff. Utopia should also be able to draw on the company's experience of previous acquisitions of UK companies to make an assessment of the risk of losing customers due to differences between the cultures in the US and the UK.

Financial risk

There are distinct financial risks for Utopia in different areas. One area is interest rate risk. As Utopia is planning to finance the acquisition of Manage through loans, there is the chance that interest rates will increase meaning that the loans become more expensive.

In addition there is currency risk. Even though Manage does not have any foreign suppliers or customers and therefore is not exposed to currency risk in the Manage business, Utopia will be exposed to translation risk as they will have a foreign asset and economic risk as they are now exposed to the UK economy affecting exchange rates. The final area to consider with currency risk is the issue of remitting funds to the US. If sterling weakens in the future against the dollar, the value of the dollar profits made by Manage Ltd will fall, as will the level of dividends Manage Ltd could remit to the US.

If Utopia is planning to use the proceeds from the sale of an existing UK division to finance this acquisition or repay any loan, then there is a risk that if the sale does not achieve the price expected or takes place later than anticipated. This will affect the amount of finance required and the level of interest paid.

To assess the risks arising from the disposal of the division, Utopia needs to ensure that sufficient research has been carried out to give as much information as possible about the likely timing and proceeds. The company should then evaluate the different financial options, varying the level of factors such as interest and exchange rates.

Political and regulatory risks

There is an increased political and regulatory risk if operations are conducted in overseas countries as it is unlikely Utopia will understand the political and regulatory environment in the UK as well as the environment in the US. This may not be a significant extra risk because Utopia is continuing to employ key staff of Manage and it already has operations in the UK.

Tutorial note

*The requirement is quite precise here, and so you will only be rewarded if you are answering **this** question. The risks to discuss need to be as a result of the investment in Manage Ltd, not just general risks facing this business.*

(c) (i) **Directors and the board**

- There should be a significant number of independent non-executive directors on the board.

- The board should take responsibility for controlling the activities of a business and devising long-term strategy.

- There should be separate people in the positions of chairman and chief executive.

- There should be full transparency of directors' pay with disclosure of the levels of directors' pay and policies for setting pay in the annual report.

- Directors should be allowed to seek independent advice if they feel it necessary at the expense of the company.

- There should be biographical details of all proposed directors sent to the shareholders prior to the directors' appointment.

- Directors should have service contracts of relatively short duration (e.g. one or two years) and they should have to be re-elected by shareholders regularly (for example every three years).

Accountability and audit

- Directors should be responsible for maintaining an adequate system of internal control and have to report on its effectiveness annually.

- All listed companies should have an audit committee of independent non-executive directors (including financial experts) that appoints external auditors and receives internal audit reports.

- There should be restrictions on the non-audit work performed by the company's external auditors.

- Directors should review the need for internal audit and ensure an internal audit function is maintained if necessary.

(ii) The five main elements of an effective internal control framework are as follows:

Control environment

A company must have a strong control environment which means that the senior management must have a good attitude towards internal controls, awareness of the need for controls and take action to improve and monitor controls.

For Manage Ltd, senior management could demonstrate this by, for example:

- Employing people who have the appropriate experience and qualification for a position and having a good training regime.

- Acting on recommendations for control improvements that are sent to them.

- Establishing internal audit as an important function with independence from operational departments.

- Establishing good segregation of duties between different parts of systems and also establishing good supervisory and authorisation controls.

Risk assessment

An integral part of good control is an assessment of risk. It should only be acceptable for management to accept low risks in significant and material areas of the business and therefore risks must be assessed. Greater internal control will be needed over areas with high risks.

Manage Ltd could do the following to improve risk assessment:

- Establish risk management committees that set up processes for the review of risk and suggest policies to reduce it.

- Management of operational departments could be asked to prepare risk assessments in their areas of operation.

- If it was felt serious enough, or there were inadequate skills within Manage Ltd, risk consultants could be employed.

Control activities

These are the detailed internal controls that operate over business processes to ensure that those processes remain low risk. Every business will have many controls, some of which will be key (i.e. they will have to work if overall risk is to be low) and some of which will be non-key.

To understand and improve its control activities Manage Ltd could:

- Document fully the key business processes and controls that should operate over them. This may well lead to the identification of areas where there are deficiencies in the controls and improvements are necessary.

- Identify key controls as these will require more management time and effort to ensure they are operating effectively.

- Ensure that any material weaknesses in the design or operation of the controls are reported to the audit committee.

Information and communication

Manage Ltd must have good information systems that supply high quality control information to the people that need it at the time that they need it. In addition there must be communication lines established within the organisation that communicate control actions and recommendations swiftly both vertically and horizontally.

Actions that Manage Ltd could take are:

- A review of control information that is used by managers (such as budgets and variance analysis) to ensure that it is presented in an efficient and user-friendly way.

- Asking Jean Smith and the other directors to set procedures for communication of control issues so that all staff are clear about the reporting lines.

- Appointing or nominating a person to be responsible for communication of control suggestions around the organisation.

Monitoring

The final element of an effective internal control system is good monitoring. The internal controls need to be reviewed regularly to ensure they are working properly and also to ensure that they develop as the business develops. Internal audit is often a key function in effective monitoring.

To demonstrate effective monitoring, Manage Ltd could:

- Establish an effective, relatively independent internal audit department (if they currently do not have one) that has the right to investigate and report on all aspects of internal control.

- Set up, possibly through internal audit, a regular control testing regime that would identify if controls are being followed and what improvements in the control system are necessary.

Overall

If all of these elements work together then Manage Ltd should have an effective system of internal control.

2 WORLDWIDE MINERALS (DEC 07) *Walk in the footsteps of a top tutor*

Key answer tips

This question, in line with most of the Section A questions, covers a number of areas of the syllabus including governance, ethics and internal control. There are many parts to the question, and some of the requirements are broken down into sub-sections, so it is essential that you manage your time carefully to ensure you tackle all areas.

The highlighted words are key phrases that markers are looking for.

Tutor's top tips

Within the 15 minutes reading time, you should have managed a detailed read of the requirement and perhaps a quick skim read of the scenario. From reading the first two paragraphs only the following can be determined:

- *this is a large listed multinational company*

- *this is a mineral extraction company*

- *new sources of reserves and measurement of known reserves are critical to business success*

- *highly respected geological survey department.*

Tutor's top tips

Part (a) starts with a definition, which is a common question style for your exam. To help you to evaluate the importance of transparency it is sometimes easier to consider it in reverse, i.e. what would happen if there wasn't any transparency? The things that would go wrong will provide ideas for your answer as to the importance.

(a) **Transparency and its importance at WM**

Define transparency

Transparency is one of the underlying principles of corporate governance. As such, it is one of the 'building blocks' that underpin a sound system of governance. In particular, transparency is required in the agency relationship. In terms of definition, transparency means openness (say, of discussions), clarity, lack of withholding of relevant information unless necessary and a default position of information provision rather than concealment. This is particularly important in financial reporting, as this is the primary source of information that investors have for making effective investment decisions.

Evaluation of importance of transparency

There are a number of benefits of transparency. For instance, it is part of gaining trust with investors and state authorities (e.g. tax people). Transparency provides access for investors and other stakeholders to company information thereby dispelling suspicion and underpinning market confidence in the company through truthful and fair reporting. It also helps to manage stakeholder claims and reduces the stresses caused by stakeholders (e.g. trade unions) for whom information provision is important. Reasons for secrecy/confidentiality include the fact that it may be necessary to keep strategy discussions secret from competitors. Internal issues may be private to individuals, thus justifying confidentiality. Finally, free (secret or confidential) discussion often has to take place before an agreed position is announced (cabinet government approach).

Reference to case

At Worldwide Minerals, transparency as a principle is needed to deal with the discussion of concealment. Should a discussion of possible concealment even be taking place? Truthful, accurate and timely reporting underpins investor confidence in all capital-funded companies including WM. The issue of the overestimation of the mallerite reserve is clearly a matter of concern to shareholders and so is an example of where a default assumption of transparency would be appropriate.

Tutor's top tips

Part (b) is a straightforward application of Kohlberg's Cognitive Moral Development model. It is essential that you explain why, citing examples from the scenario, you have selected the level for each of the directors mentioned.

(b) **Kohlberg's levels of moral development**

Description of levels

Kohlberg described human moral development in terms of three consecutive levels.

Preconventional moral responses view morality in terms of rewards, punishments and whether or not the act will be penalised, found out or rewarded.

Conventional moral responses view morality in terms of compliance with the agreed legal and regulatory frameworks relevant at the time and place in which the decision is taking place.

Postconventional responses go beyond the other two and frame morality in terms of the effects of the action on oneself and others, on how it will affect one's own moral approach and how it will accord with wider systems of ethics and social norms.

Three people in the case

The three people mentioned in the case exhibit different levels of moral development.

Gary Howells is demonstrating the *preconventional* in that he sees the decision to disclose or not in terms of whether WM can get away with it. He was inclined to conceal the information because of the potential impact on the company's share price on the stock market. His suggestion was underpinned by his belief that the concealment of the incorrect valuation would not be 'found out'.

Vanda Monroe demonstrates *conventional* behaviour, reminding the WM board of its legal and regulatory obligations under the rules of its stock market listing. In particular, she reminded the board about the importance of the company's compliance with corporate governance and ethics codes by the stock market. To fail to disclose would, in Vanda's view, be a breach of those stock market expectations. Rather than rewards and punishments, Vanda was more concerned with compliance with rules and regulations.

Martin Chan is demonstrating *postconventional* morality by referring to consistency of treatment and the notion of 'do as you would be done by'. He said that he wouldn't want to be deceived if he were an outside investor in the company. His response was underpinned neither by rewards or punishments, nor by compliance with regulations, but rather than a persuasion that moral behaviour is about doing what one believes to be right, regardless of any other factors.

Tutor's top tips

Part (c) starts with a theoretical element about roles of non-executive directors. The second part of the requirement is very precise in referring to tensions in advising on the disclosure point. Ensure that your answer only focuses on this matter; general tensions between the roles would not earn marks.

(c)   **Non-executive directors**

Roles of NEDs

Non-executive directors have four principal roles.

The *strategy* role recognises that NEDs are full members of the board and thus have the right and responsibility to contribute to the strategic success of the organisation for the benefit of shareholders. The enterprise must have a clear strategic direction and NEDs should be able to bring considerable experience from their lives and business experience to bear on ensuring that chosen strategies are sound. In this role they may challenge any aspect of strategy they see fit and offer advice or input to help to develop successful strategy.

In the *scrutinising* or performance role, NEDs are required to hold executive colleagues to account for decisions taken and company performance. In this respect they are required to represent the shareholders' interests against the possibility that agency issues arise to reduce shareholder value.

The *risk* role involves NEDs ensuring the company has an adequate system of internal controls and systems of risk management in place. This is often informed by prescribed codes (such as Turnbull in the UK) but some industries, such as chemicals, have other systems in place, some of which fall under ISO standards. In this role, NEDs should satisfy themselves on the integrity of financial information and that financial controls and systems of risk management are robust and defensible.

Finally, the *'people'* role involves NEDs overseeing a range of responsibilities with regard to the management of the executive members of the board. This typically involves issues on appointments and remuneration, but might also involve contractual or disciplinary issues and succession planning.

Tensions in NED roles in the case

This refers to a potential tension in the loyalties of the NEDs. Although the NED is accountable, through the chairman to the shareholders and thus must always act in the economic best interests of the shareholders, he or she is also a part of the board of the company and they may, in some situations, advise discretion. Withholding information might be judged correct because of strategic considerations or longer-term shareholder interests. In most situations, NEDs will argue for greater transparency, less concealment and more clarity of how and why a given action will be in the interests of shareholders.

The case of mallerite overestimation places the WM NEDs in a position of some tension. Any instinct to conceal the full extent of the overestimate of the reserve for the possible protection of the company's short-term value must be balanced against the duty to serve longer-term strategic interests and the public interest. Whilst concealment would protect the company's reputation and share price in the short term, it would be a duty of the NEDs to point out that WM should observe transparency as far as possible in its dealing with the shareholders and other capital market participants.

Tutorial note

These four roles are as described in the UK Higgs Report and are also contained in the UK Corporate Governance code. Hence, they are a useful basis to any question about roles of NEDs.

Tutor's top tips

There is no specific theory that is required to answer part (d). In fact, your answer to part (ii) needs to be very specific to the situation in WM. To gain the full professional marks ensure that you correctly focus your letter, addressing the investors at all stages. References to 'your company' and 'we, on the board' will keep this targeted as is necessary.

(d)   **Letter for Tim Blake to send to WM's investors**

> Worldwide Minerals plc
> Address line 1
> Address line 2
> Address line 3

Date

Dear Shareholders,

Estimation of mallerite reserves

You will be aware of the importance of accurate resource valuation to Worldwide Minerals (WM). Unfortunately, I have to inform you that the reserve of mallerite, one of our key minerals in a new area of exploration, was found to have been overestimated after the purchase of a mine. It has been suggested that this information may have an effect on shareholder value and so I thought it appropriate to write to inform you of how the board intends to respond to the situation.

In particular, I would like to address two issues. It has been suggested that the overestimation arose because of issues with the internal control systems at WM. I would firstly like to reassure you of the importance that your board places on sound internal control systems and then I would like to highlight improvements to internal controls that we shall be implementing to ensure that the problem should not recur.

(i)   **Importance of internal control**

Internal control systems are essential in all public companies and Worldwide Minerals (WM) is no exception. If anything, WM's strategic position makes internal control even more important, operating as it does in many international situations and dealing with minerals that must be guaranteed in terms of volume, grade and quality. Accordingly, your board recognises that internal control *underpins investor confidence*. Investors have traditionally trusted WM's management because they have assumed it capable of managing its internal operations. This has, specifically, meant *becoming aware of and controlling known risks*. Risks would not be known about and managed without adequate internal control systems.

Internal control, furthermore, *helps to manage quality throughout the organisa*tion and it provides management with *information on internal operations and compliance*. These features are important in ensuring quality at all stages in the WM value chain from the extraction of minerals to the delivery of product to our customers. Linked to this is the importance of internal control in helping to *expose and improve underperforming internal operations.* Finally, internal control systems are essential in providing *information for internal and external reporting* upon which, in turn, investor confidence rests.

(ii) **Proposals to improve internal systems at WM**

As you may be aware, mineral estimation and measurement can be problematic, particularly in some regions. Indeed, there are several factors that can lead to under or overestimation of reserves valuations as a result of geological survey techniques and regional cultural/social factors. In the case of mallerite, however, the issues that have been brought to the board's attention are matters of internal control and it is to these that I would now like to turn.

In first instance, it is clear from the fact that the overestimate was made that we will need to audit geological reports at an appropriate (and probably lower) level in the organisation in future.

Once a claim has been made about a given mineral resource level, especially one upon which investor returns might depend, appropriate systems will be instituted to ask for and obtain evidence that such reserves have been correctly and accurately quantified.

We will recognise that single and verbal source reports of reserve quantities may not necessarily be accurate. This was one of the apparent causes of the overestimation of mallerite. A system of auditing actual reserves rather than relying on verbal evidence will rectify this.

The purchase of any going concern business, such as the mallerite mine, is subject to due diligence. WM will be examining its procedures in this area to ensure that they are fit for purpose in the way that they may not have been in respect of the purchase of the mallerite mine. I will be taking all appropriate steps to ensure that all of these internal control issues can be addressed in future.

Thank you for your continued support of Worldwide Minerals and I hope the foregoing goes some way to reassure you that the company places the highest value on its investors and their loyalty.

Yours faithfully,

Tim Blake

Chairman

	Marking scheme		Marks
(a)	Up to 2 marks for definition of transparency.		2
	1 mark per relevant point on advantages of transparency		Up to 3
	1 mark per relevant point on reasons for confidentiality or concealment		Up to 3
	Relevance to case		Up to 2
		Maximum	10
(b)	Up to 2 marks for each Kohlberg level identified and described		Up to 6
	Up to 2 marks for each person's position identified with reasons/evidence from the case. 1 mark for identification only		Up to 6
		Maximum	12
(c)	2 marks for each NED role identified and briefly explained		Up to 8
	Discussion of tension in advising on reserve overestimate.		4
		Maximum	12
(d)	(i) 1 mark for each relevant point made on importance of internal control		Up to 6
	(ii) Up to 2 marks for each relevant point identified and examined		Up to 6
	Up to 4 professional marks for structure, content, style and layout of letter		4
		Maximum	16
Total			**50**

Examiner's comments

Introduction

The case scenario for Question 1 was based around a company (Worldwide Minerals) faced with a difficult situation arising from an inaccurate estimate of a crucial mineral inventory in a recently purchased mine. The length and complexity of the scenario is typical of what candidates can expect in future P1 section A cases.

In the December 2007 paper, Question 1 consisted of four parts. **Part (a)** asked about one of the key underlying concepts in corporate governance and 10 marks were available for a definition of the term 'transparency' followed by an evaluation. Candidates were asked to evaluate the importance of transparency in financial reporting with reference to the case. The case was about the board of Worldwide Minerals (WM) considering how it should behave having discovered a value-material overestimate of a key mineral inventory in a mine. Most candidates were able to define the term and explain its relevance to the case of

WM but fewer were able to perform the evaluation, which, in this case, involved a consideration of the issues surrounding fully reporting the error to shareholders. Many candidates made the case as to why WM should disclose the error but very few candidates went as far as explaining the opposite argument. There are times when full disclosure is not appropriate and a full evaluation would have brought that out. It is very important that the verb used in the question is used as the basis for the answer.

Part (b) was answered well overall. The first part was of part (b) was an explanation of Kohlberg's three levels of moral development and this was done well by most well-prepared candidates. The second part about identifying the levels of the three people in the case was answered less well with some candidates failing to interpret the evidence in the case scenario correctly.

Part (c) was a near-repeat of a question in the pilot paper on the principal roles of non-executive directors (NEDs) and candidates should therefore have been familiar with how to address the question. Most of the marks were awarded for a description of the roles with some also being available for the more challenging task of an explanation of the tensions that WM's NEDs might experience in the case scenario. This second part was not answered well overall with many answers containing descriptive content rather than serious efforts to consider the difficult situation that the NEDs were in at WM.

Part (d) was the most ambitious component of Question 1. A question requiring the demonstration of professional presentation skills will be a part of future P1 papers and in the case of this first paper, the question required writing a letter from Tim Blake, the chairman of WM, to its shareholders. Most candidates made some attempt to present the answer in the form of a letter but many didn't pick up as many professional marks as they might have because:

The answer did not read like a letter (perhaps more like a memo).

It was not in the form of a formal letter to shareholders which would typically have a beginning and an end with a logical flow of content in the 'middle'.

It was addressed to the wrong audience ('Dear Mr Blake')

It used bullet points and short, unconnected paragraphs with no sense of 'flow' between them.

There were four professional marks available. In terms of marks allocation, one professional mark was available for the basic form of a letter meaning it was correctly headed, finished, addressed and physically laid out. The other three were awarded for the composition, flow and persuasiveness of the narrative itself. The letter was from a company chairman to the company's shareholders and those gaining all four professional marks were those that read most like a letter of its type would read in 'real life'. A good answer contained an explanatory introduction, a discussion in the form of narrative (rather than bullet points) of the content of parts (i) and (ii) of the question finished off with a brief paragraph drawing the threads together. Future P1 papers will ask candidates to 'draft' or 'write' content in the form of various types of written communication. Candidates are advised to pay attention to the professional marks as the four marks available could make the difference between a pass and a fail. Four marks are worth approximately seven minutes in time (4% of 180 minutes), which should give candidates some idea of how much investment to make in the professional marks.

In terms of the content of Q1 (d), part (i) asked candidates to explain why they believed internal controls to be important. This was intended to convey Mr Blake's competence to WM's shareholders and to reassure them that despite the recent problem with the mallerite measurement, they should continue having full confidence in him as chairman. Part (ii) invited candidates to put themselves in Mr Blake's position and suggest the types of measures that WM might introduce to improve things. Part (i) was not done well overall despite it being, in cognitive level terms, 'lower' than the task in part (ii). Some candidates introduced the letter and then misinterpreted the 'importance of' internal controls to mean 'components of' and such answers obviously were not well rewarded. The marking team allowed for a range of reasonable interpretations of part (ii) and answers making a serious attempt to address the types of changes that WM might make were rewarded to some extent.

3   HAYHO (JUN 12)

Key answer tips

This was a question, requiring a significant degree of application.

For part (a) there is a need to understand the theory to earn three marks for risk appetite definition and each preference. Then two marks to demonstrate the application of risk and return to each option

For part (b) this is application of a key syllabus to model to the facts of the case. Requires planning and clarity of presentation.

Part (c) in the first instance is pure syllabus knowledge requiring a statement of the purposes of internal control. Perhaps the most challenging part of the question came next, requiring you to identify and say how important the internal control challenges would be if the Jayland option were taken. Close attention to the use of verbs was needed.

Part (d) is a familiar requirement, though you will need to be careful in how you apply the theories tested. In particular part (ii) which required the application of case evidence to the reasons why a key stakeholder (WB) should deserve careful treatment. Ensure that your answer is in the correct format, so as not to lose the professional marks that are available.

(a)   **Risk appetite**

Explanation

Risk appetite describes the willingness of an entity to become exposed to an unrealised loss (risk). It is usually understood to mean the position taken with regard to two notional preferences: risk aversion and risk seeking. Both preferences are associated with different levels of returns: those that are risk-seeking favour higher risks and higher returns with the converse being true for the risk averse.

Risk-averse entities will tend to be cautious about accepting risk, preferring to avoid risk, to share it or to reduce it. In exchange, they are willing to accept a lower level of return. Those with an appetite for risk will tend to accept and seek out risk, recognising risk to be associated with higher net returns.

Risk appetite and selection

The Jayland option has a higher political risk, a threat to the integrity of the company (by paying the bribe) and an element of reputation risk. There is also a risk arising from the lack of business culture in Jayland and a possibility that it will be more difficult to maintain normal operations there than in Pealand. Offset against these risks is the potential return of $2 billion over ten years, which is twice that of the Pealand option.

The Pealand option has negligible political risk but a slightly higher risk that internal controls will be difficult to implement. It has a much lower likelihood of reputation risk and there is no risk connected with bribery. The return is half that of the Jayland option (for an approximately equal investment value).

The two options offer two different risk and return profiles: the Jayland option offers a higher return but a higher risk profile and the Pealand option offers a lower return but also a lower risk profile. If the company has a higher risk appetite it is more likely to choose Jayland and if it has a lower risk appetite it is likely to select the Pealand option.

(b)   **AAA seven-step model**

(1)   **What are the facts of the case?**

The facts of the case are that there are two investment options and each has a different ethical and risk profile although the AAA model is mainly concerned with the ethical aspects. The ability to operate the necessary internal controls for Hayho manufacturing also differs between the two options. Only one option can be pursued and both are capable of making an acceptable level of return.

(2)   **What are the ethical issues?**

The ethical issues are over the potential complicity of Hayho in supporting a corrupt regime in Jayland, in paying what appears to be a bribe to Mr Popo under the Jayland option and in operating under less stringent regulatory conditions in Jayland compared to Pealand. Another issue to consider is that it is alleged the president of Jayland maintains order by abusing the rights of the people. The company is very sensitive to allegations of human rights abuses after criticisms of Hayho were made in Arrland recently and it is reluctant to expose itself to similar criticisms again.

A further ethical issue is whether there is a corporate social obligation for companies to invest in developing or transitional economies to help stimulate these economies. However, these disadvantages have to be weighed against the likelihood of making twice the return for shareholders in Jayland against the option of operating sustainably in a more stable Pealand. In Pealand, there may be ethical issues concerning taking over an existing workforce and changing working terms and conditions, perhaps in terms of changed expectations, contractual issues and redundancies.

(3)   **What are the norms and principles that apply?**

The norms and principles that apply in this situation are that business investment decisions should be taken on a sound commercial basis with risk, return and ethical considerations fully taken into account.

The case says that the company seeks to 'always uphold the highest standards of integrity, human rights and environmental protection whilst at the same time 'responsibly' supporting developing countries by providing jobs and opportunities to enable greater social and economic development.'

This would tend to favour decisions that do not involve bribery (against integrity), human rights abuses (perhaps through supporting corrupt governments), but at the same time seeking, where possible, to use investments to support local economic development (perhaps by investing in developing countries, all other things being equal).

(4)   **What are the alternatives?**

The first alternative is to invest in Jayland, where a 'new-build' factory would enable Hayho to implant its culture and systems but where there is a poorly developed education system, a potentially unstable political environment and an absence of internal control and corporate governance regulations.

The other alternative is the Pealand option, to take over an existing plant and an inherited workforce in a more highly regulated business environment.

(5)   **Which option is most consistent with norms and principles?**

Both options have strengths and weaknesses, depending upon how the different factors are evaluated. The Jayland option would meet the criteria for financial acceptability and would be favourable through supporting economic growth and by providing net additional employment in a developing country.

The option most consistent with stated norms and principles is the Pealand option. This option has the benefit of inheriting a trained and competent workforce and avoids the reputation risk of providing credibility for the Popo regime and of being exposed, perhaps by a whistleblower, for paying the 'royalty' (which is effectively a bribe to Mr Popo). The Jayland option would provide a greater financial return and provide net additional employment in a developing country. But it also would violate the principle of sound risk management because investing in an unstable and potentially hostile political environment could expose Hayho to unacceptable levels of long-term operational, financial and reputational risk.

(6)   **What are the consequences of each option?**

In Jayland, as opposed to Pealand, a completely new factory would be built providing new additional employment, although there could be an issue with sourcing the appropriate staff, given the poor levels of education and training. The Jayland option would provide a higher potential return to shareholders, but at a greater risk. It would make implementing the internal controls potentially easier but would risk reputation-damaging allegations of supporting Mr Popo's regime. Were the 'royalty' to be made public, it would have severe consequences for the trustworthiness of the Hayho board, having given the reassurances it did after the Arrland incident.

The Pealand option would make a smaller return and involve lower risk, but could introduce potential problems with implementing the necessary internal controls. This option would be more ethically acceptable. Hayho would be severely criticised for supporting a corrupt regime if it invested in Jayland. But if it invested in Pealand, no bribery would be necessary and it could publicise the fact that it chose to invest in Pealand over Jayland because it is seeking to honour its commitments made after the previous Arrland incident.

(7)   **What is the decision?**

The decision most aligned to the company's stated norms and principles is the Pealand option. Other powerful countervailing factors would also have an influence, however, as risk and internal control considerations would also be taken into account.

Tutorial note

Reward answers arguing for Jayland if shown to be based on reasoning from step 6.

(c)   **General purposes of internal control systems and main challenges**

General purposes

The first general purpose of internal control is to achieve the *orderly conduct of business by facilitating effective and efficient operation* of an organisation's activities. In doing this, it must be able to respond appropriately to relevant risks and to configure activities to be able to achieve the organisation's strategic objectives. This includes *safeguarding the assets* of the organisation from external and internal threats and to ensure that all actual and potential liabilities and sources of loss are identified and controlled. The protection of value is important in underpinning confidence in internal controls and in providing the capacity for future value adding.

Internal controls are essential in *ensuring the robustness, quality and timeliness of both internal and external financial reporting.* The provision of this information is important in managing internal systems (e.g. budgetary controls) and in maintaining and cultivating confidence among shareholders and capital markets. This involves maintaining accurate records and processes capable of generating and processing the relevant information.

Internal control is necessary to *ensure compliance* with any external laws, standards or regulations that apply. These could arise from companies' legislation, listing rules or, in some industries, regulations imposed by sector-specific regulators.

Main challenges

Jayland was *very under developed until relatively recently and the national culture is, according to Emily Baa, unfamiliar with modern business practice and behaviour. Achieving effective and efficient operation of the business* would be an early priority for the Hayho investment and this limitation would necessitate substantial initial training and cultural-familiarisation. If these cultural values (e.g. time-keeping, work commitment, honesty of workers, etc) cannot be taken for granted in a national culture then it represents a major obstacle in achieving normal plant operation.

Emily reported an *unknown security situation in the region with regard to the safeguarding of assets.* Being able to ensure that non-current assets owned by Hayho are secure and being used for the intended purpose is an essential element of internal control. The value of Hayho belongs to its shareholders and it would be irresponsible of the board (as agents) to invest in assets in Jayland unless reasonable assurances could be given that they will be safe from sabotage, damage, theft, deterioration or inefficient utilisation.

Emily's third point was about the level of *necessary skills in the local labour pool.* She mentioned the state of *quality control and accounting skills* and both of these are necessary for a sound system of internal control.

Appropriate quality control staff are necessary to ensure that the product *complies with the stringent international product standards* that apply to Hayho's products. Where technical skills such as these are difficult to obtain in local labour markets, unskilled people may need to undergo training, or expatriates may need to be persuaded to move to the Jayland facility. Guaranteeing that outputs from the Jayland plant were fully compliant with all applicable standards would be an important early priority for customers and investors and so this issue is likely to be of great importance.

Accounting skills are necessary for guaranteeing *accurate and complete accounting records and for reliable financial information.* Gathering required data and reporting to management at head office is required, for example on metrics such as variance against agreed targets. For a new investment such as those being considered by the Hayho board, the provision of accurate and timely information is essential in controlling activities under either of the options.

(d)   (i)   **Meaning of accountability and Mendelow**

Briefing notes for board meeting.

Prepared for Helen Duomo, chief executive.

By Emily Baa, company accountant.

Wednesday 20 June, 2012.

Accountability of the Hayho board

The two letters received raise important issues of accountability, and specifically, the issue of to whom the board of Hayho is accountable. In reflecting on how to deal with this and how to frame our response, it may be helpful to consider the accountability situation we face as a board.

Accountability is a key relationship between two or more parties. It implies that one party is accountable to, or answerable to, another. This means that the accountable entity can reasonably be called upon to explain his, her or its actions and policies.

This means that the accountable party can be held to account and may be required to actually give an account. This has the potential to influence the behaviour of the accountable party, in this case Hayho, because of the knowledge that they will have to answer for it when they give that account.

Whilst it is clear that the board is accountable to the shareholders as stewards of their investment, it may be the case, nevertheless, that the board may need to account to WB because of its influence among politicians and in wider society, as outlined below.

Influence of Watching Business

The Mendelow framework is a way of mapping stakeholders with regard to the two variables of interest and power. The combination of these is a measure of any given stakeholder's likely influence over an entity such as Hayho. The framework is dynamic in that stakeholders move around the map as their power and interest rise and fall with events. WB has a moderate degree of power and a variable degree of interest. Because its interest (in Hayho) has recently increased, its overall influence has risen. Our response to WB must be responsive to this.

WB's power derives from its ability to conduct research and mobilise opinion, including among policymakers and trade organisations, against businesses like Hayho. We do not need to agree with its agenda to appreciate its power. Its power is expressed as influence when its interest is also increased.

It was news of our possible investment in Jayland that increased WB's interest in Hayho. This, combined with its evident power, increases its net influence over Hayho. This makes WB difficult to ignore in our decision over whether to invest in Jayland or Pealand.

(ii)   **Agency and demands from WB**

Responsibilities to shareholders

The board of Hayho exists in an agency relationship with its shareholders, who collectively own the company and have the legal and moral right to determine objectives. As agents of our shareholders and appointed by them, we have a fiduciary duty to seek to manage the company's resources for their overall economic benefit. In the case of Hayho, as with most business organisations, this involves maximising returns consistent with our complying with relevant laws, regulations and norms. Quark Investments, as one of our major shareholders, has every right to remind us of this duty and we should take its reminder very seriously.

Lobby group demands

Whilst being well-meaning, the lobby group WB is against one of the investment options we have at this time. It claims that an investment in Jayland would be damaging to human rights in that country. Without commenting on the accuracy or validity of that claim, we should remind colleagues why we might think carefully about the investment, as it would bring us into conflict with WB.

First, WB is respected and its views are trusted by many people. In terms of reputation, it has highlighted our problems in Arrland and, as a result of that, has been monitoring our activities. We may need to consider public opinion before going ahead with a potential Jayland investment as we need the general support of society to operate.

Second, WB has influence among politicians and policymakers both in this country and abroad. We risk the censure of influential people and increase the pressure for increased regulation if we disregard or act against the lobby group's demands. Our reputation in international markets is one of our strategic assets and it may compromise our commitment, given the Arrland incident, if we were not to uphold the highest standards of integrity, human rights and environmental protection from now on.

Third, WB is very adept at mobilising public opinion through the media. This means that it can stimulate interest in conditions in Jayland and we would be likely to be heavily scrutinised on an ongoing basis were this investment to be made. This could attract public anger and risk disruptions, such as boycotts of our products.

Because of these issues, it would seem prudent to consider these issues as a part of our investment appraisal between the Jayland and Pealand options.

	ACCA marking scheme		Marks
(a)	3 marks for explanation of risk appetite. 1 mark for definition, 1 mark for evidence of understanding of each preference. 2 marks for demonstrating risk and return of each option with correct risk appetite preference to a maximum of 4 marks. Maximum		6
(b)	1 mark for each relevant point, wherever made in the answer. Half a mark for identification only.		14
(c)	1 mark for each purpose of IC to a maximum of 4 marks. 2 marks for each challenge identified and assessed to a maximum of 8 marks. Maximum		12
(d)	(i)	1 mark for each relevant point on accountability to a maximum of 3 marks. 2 marks for evidence of understanding of Mendelow framework 2 marks for discussion of WB's power, interest and influence. Maximum	7
	(ii)	1 mark for each relevant point on agency to a maximum of 2 marks. 2 marks for each argument on WB's demands to a maximum of 6 marks.	7
		Professional marks for clarity, flow, persuasiveness and structure.	4
Total			**50**

Tutorial note

Other relevant controls, well explained, would be awarded marks.

Examiners comments

The case in section A concerned Hayho Company. In the scenario, Hayho is considering two possible foreign investments and both options have particular issues associated with them. These issues include different risk and internal control problems, and the fact that the projected returns on the two options are significantly different. The Jayland option would also involve dealing with its president, Mr Popo, who, as well as having a questionable record on human rights, also demanded a personal royalty from Hayho (effectively a bribe) if the company chose to invest in his country. A further complicating factor was the presence of a human rights lobbying organisation called 'Watching Business' (WB) that was already monitoring Hayho because of its past behaviour in another country (Arrland).

WB was influential and was warning Hayho not to invest in Jayland because of the record of Mr Popo's government.

Part (a) asked about the risk profiles of the two options (Jayland and Pealand). Drawing upon the idea of risk appetite, candidates were required to explain risk appetite and then to demonstrate how different risk appetites might affect which option may be chosen. This task was done well by most candidates although some failed to explain risk appetite as a continuum, saying instead that risk appetite meant risk seeking. In fact, companies and individuals can have either a high, low or medium risk appetite. In the scenario, the Jayland option was the higher risk (with a higher potential return) of the two and so would have been attractive to companies with a higher risk appetite or which were more risk-seeking.

Part (b) asked candidates to use the seven step AAA model to examine the choice between Jayland and Pealand. A minority chose the wrong framework for this (employing, for example, the Tucker framework or the Gray, Owen and Adams continuum) but most were able to correctly identify the seven AAA questions. Not all of these were presented in the correct and logical order.

There were a range of approaches taken. The AAA framework is used to establish the ethical norms of the company and/or culture in which it operates, and to weigh the consequences of the two options, before finally selecting the option most in line with those norms and with the more favourable consequences. Some candidates failed to achieve higher marks here by producing only a shallow analysis of each stage or by confusing the things to consider under each question. But overall, this question was done quite well by the majority of candidates.

There were two tasks in part (c). The first, for 4 marks, was to describe the general purposes of an internal control system. This was bookwork and should have been straightforward to any well-prepared P1 candidate. It was frustrating that many candidates failed to take into account the verb, 'describe'. It was not enough to 'list' or produce a short bullet list. To get full marks for this first task, markers were looking for a brief description of each general purpose as asked for in the question.

4   SWAN HILL COMPANY (DEC 08)

Key answer tips

This was a heavily 'ethics-based' question, requiring a significant degree of application of ethical theories.

In tackling part (a) there is plenty of information in the scenario to draw on to earn two marks per question within the Tucker model. There are some straightforward marks to be earned in part (b) for definitions, so make sure you tackle these quickly.

Part (c) is the most challenging part of the question, requiring you to view the situation from two differing ethical stances. This level of ethical application can be difficult, but with practice on more questions like this you will improve your skills. Ensure that your answer is in the correct format, so as not to lose the professional marks that are available.

Part (d) is a simpler requirement, though you will need to provide several examples of the different disclosure types.

(a) **Tucker's framework**

Is the decision:

Profitable? For SHC, the answer to this question is yes. Profits would potentially be substantially increased by the loss of all of its competitors and the emergence of SHC, in the short to medium term at least, as a near monopolist.

Legal? The secrecy option poses no legal problems as it is a part of normal competitive behaviour in industries. In some jurisdictions, legislation forbids monopolies existing in some industries but there is no indication from the case that this restriction applies to Swan Hill Company.

Fair? The fairness of the secrecy option is a moral judgment. It is probably fair when judged from the perspective of SHC's shareholders but the question is the extent to which it is fair to the employees and shareholders of SHC's competitors.

Right? Again, a question of ethical perspective. Is it right to pursue the subjugation of competitors and the domination of an industry regardless of the consequences to competitors? The secrecy option may be of the most benefit to the local community of Swan Hill that the company has traditionally valued.

Sustainable or environmentally sound? The case says that the sink method emits at a lower rate per unit of output than the existing process but this has little to do with the secrecy option as the rates of emissions would apply if SHC licensed the process. This is also an argument for the licensing option; however, as environmental emissions would be lower if other competitors switched to the sink method as well. There may be environmental implications in decommissioning the old plant to make way for the new sink method investment.

Tutorial note

The last of Tucker's questions is sometimes mistakenly interpreted. Sustainable is referring to the environmental impact of the decision in question, not the continuing existence of the business.

(b) **Strategic and operational risks**

Strategic risks

These arise from the overall strategic positioning of the company in its environment. Some strategic positions give rise to greater risk exposures than others. Because strategic issues typically affect the whole of an organisation and not just one or more of its parts, strategic risks can potentially concern very high stakes – they can have very high hazards and high returns. Because of this, they are managed at board level in an organisation and form a key part of strategic management.

Operational risks

Operational risks refer to potential losses arising from the normal business operations. Accordingly, they affect the day-to-day running of operations and business systems in contrast to strategic risks that arise from the organisation's strategic positioning. Operational risks are managed at risk management level (not necessarily board level) and can be managed and mitigated by internal control systems.

The secrecy option would be a strategic risk for the following reasons.

It would radically change the environment that SHC is in by reducing competition. This would radically change SHC's strategic fit with its competitive environment. In particular, it would change its 'five forces' positioning which would change its risk profile.

It would involve the largest investment programme in the company's history with new debt substantially changing the company's financial structure and making it more vulnerable to short term liquidity problems and monetary pressure (interest rates).

It would change the way that stakeholders view SHC, for better or worse. It is a 'crisis issue', certain to polarise opinion either way.

It will change the economics of the industry thereby radically affecting future cost, revenue and profit forecasts.

There may be retaliatory behaviour by SHC's close competitor on 25% of the market.

Tutorial note

Similar reasons, if relevant and well argued, will attract marks.

(c) (i) **For the secrecy option**

Important developments at SHC

This is an exciting time for the management and shareholders of Swan Hill Company. The research and development staff at SHC have made a groundbreaking discovery (called the 'sink method') that will enable your company to produce its major product at lower cost, in higher volumes and at a much higher quality than our competitors will be able to using, as they do, the existing production technology. The sink process also produces at a lower rate of environmental emissions which, as I'm sure shareholders will agree, is a very welcome development.

When considering the options following the discovery, your board decided that we should press ahead with the investment needed to transform the production facilities without offering the use of the technology to competitors under a licensing arrangement. This means that once the new sink production comes on stream, SHC shareholders can, your board believes, look forward to a significant strengthening of our competitive position.

The business case for this option is overwhelming. By pushing ahead with the investment needed to implement the sink method, the possibility exists to gain a substantial competitive advantage over all of SHC's competitors. It will place SHC in a near monopolist position in the short term and in a dominant position long term. This will, in turn, give the company pricing power in the industry and the likelihood of superior profits for many years to come. We would expect SHC to experience substantial 'overnight' growth and the returns from this will reward shareholders' loyalty and significantly increase the value of the company. Existing shareholders can reasonably expect a significant increase in the value of their holdings over the very short term and also over the longer term.

Ethical implications of the secrecy option

In addition to the overwhelming business case, however, there is a strong ethical case for the secrecy option. SHC recognises that it is the moral purpose of SHC to make profits in order to reward those who have risked their own money to support it over many years. Whilst some companies pursue costly programmes intended to serve multiple stakeholder interests, SHC recognises that it is required to comply with the demands of its legal owners, its shareholders, and not to dilute those demands with other concerns that will reduce shareholder returns. This is an important part of the agency relationship: the SHC board will always serve the best economic interests of its shareholders: its legal owners. The SHC board believes that any action taken that renders shareholder returns suboptimal is a threat to shareholder value and an abuse of the agency position. Your board will always seek to maximise shareholder wealth; hence our decision to pursue the secrecy option in this case. The secrecy option offers the possibility of optimal shareholder value and because shareholders invest in SHC to maximise returns, that is the only ethical action for the board to pursue. Happily, this option will also protect the employees' welfare in SHC's hometown of Swan Hill and demonstrate its commitment to the locality. This, in turn, will help to manage two of the key value-adding resources in the company, its employees and its reputation. This will help in local recruitment and staff retention in future years.

(ii) **For the licensing option**

Important developments at SHC

Your board was recently faced with a very difficult business and ethical decision. After the discovery by SHC scientists of the groundbreaking sink production method, we had a choice of keeping the new production technology secret or sharing the breakthrough under a licensing arrangement with our competitors. After a lengthy discussion, your board decided that we should pursue the licensing option and I would like to explain our reasons for this on both business and ethical grounds.

In terms of the business case for licensing, I would like shareholders to understand that although the secrecy option may have offered SHC the possibility of an unassailable competitive advantage, in reality, it would have incurred a number of risks. Because of the speed with which we would have needed to have acted, it would have necessitated a large increase in our borrowing, bringing about a substantial change in our financial structure. This would, in turn, increase liquidity pressures and make us more vulnerable to rising interest rates. A second risk with the secrecy option would involve the security of the sink technology 'secret'. If the sink process was leaked or discovered by competitors and subsequently copied, our lack of a legally binding patent would mean we would have no legal way to stop them proceeding with their own version of the sink process.

As well as avoiding the risks, however, the licensing option offers a number of specific business advantages. The royalties from the licences granted to competitors are expected to be very large indeed. These will be used over the coming years to extend our existing competitive advantage in the future. Finally, the 'improvement sharing' clause in the licensing contract will ensure that the sink process will be improved and perfected with several manufacturers using the technology at the same time. SHC's sink production may, in consequence, improve at a faster rate than would have been the case were we to have pursued the secrecy option.

Ethical implications of the secrecy option

In addition to the business case, there is also a powerful ethical case for the decision we have taken. As a good, responsible corporate citizen, Swan Hill Company acknowledges its many stakeholders and recognises the impacts that a business decision has on others. Your board recognises that in addition to external stakeholders having influence over our operations, our decisions can also affect others. In this case, we have carefully considered the likelihood that keeping the new technology a secret from our competitors would radically reshape the industry. The superior environmental performance of the sink process over existing methods will also mean that when fully adopted, the environmental emissions of the entire industry will be reduced. SHC is very proud of this contribution to this reduction in overall environmental impact.

There seems little doubt that the secrecy option would have had far-reaching and unfortunate effects upon our industry and our competitors. The licensing option will allow competitors, and their employees and shareholders, to survive. It is a compassionate act on our part and shows mercy to the other competitors in the industry. It recognises the number of impacts that a business decision has and would be the fairest (and most just) option given the number of people affected.

(d)   (i)   **Mandatory and voluntary disclosures**

Mandatory disclosures

These are components of the annual report mandated by law, regulation or accounting standard.

Examples include (in most jurisdictions) statement of comprehensive income (income or profit and loss statement), statement of financial position (balance sheet), cash flow statement, operating segmental information, auditors' report, corporate governance disclosure such as remuneration report and some items in the directors' report (e.g. summary of operating position). In the UK, the business review is compulsory.

Voluntary disclosures

These are components of the annual report not mandated in law or regulation but disclosed nevertheless. They are typically mainly narrative rather than numerical in nature.

Examples include (in most jurisdictions) risk information, operating review, social and environmental information, and the chief executive's review.

(ii) **Accountability to equity investors**

Voluntary disclosures are an effective way of redressing the information asymmetry that exists between management and investors. In adding to mandatory content, voluntary disclosures give a fuller picture of the state of the company.

More information helps investors decide whether the company matches their risk, strategic and ethical criteria, and expectations.

Makes the annual report more forward looking (predictive) whereas the majority of the numerical content is backward facing on what has been.

Helps transparency in communicating more fully thereby better meeting the agency accountability to investors, particularly shareholders.

There is a considerable amount of qualitative information that cannot be conveyed using statutory numbers (such as strategy, ethical content, social reporting, etc).

Voluntary disclosure gives a more rounded and more complete view of the company, its activities, strategies, purposes and values.

Voluntary disclosure enables the company to address specific shareholder concerns as they arise (such as responding to negative publicity).

Tutorial note

Other valid points will attract marks.

			Marks
		Marking scheme	*Marks*
(a)		1 mark for evidence of understanding of each of Tucker's criteria	
		1 mark for application of each to case	10
		Maximum	10
(b)		1 mark for each relevant point demonstrating understanding of operational risk	Up to 3
		1 mark for each relevant point demonstrating understanding of strategic risk	Up to 3
		1 mark for each reason explaining why the secrecy option is a strategic risk	Up to 4
		Maximum	10
(c)	(i)	1 mark for each relevant point making the business case up to a maximum of 4	
		1 mark for each relevant point making the stockholder (shareholder) moral case up to a maximum of 5	
		Maximum	8
	(ii)	1 mark for each relevant point making the business case up to a maximum of 4	
		1 mark for each relevant point making the stakeholder moral case up to a maximum of 5	
		Maximum	8
		Professional marks: up to 2 marks per part	4
		Maximum	20
(d)	(i)	1 mark for definition of each (mandatory and voluntary)	
		Half mark for each example up to a max of 2 marks per category (allow latitude for jurisdictional differences)	6
	(ii)	1 mark for each relevant point made and briefly explained (half mark for mention only)	4
		Maximum	10
Total			**50**

Examiner's comments

Introduction

The scenario for this question was based on a company whose research scientists had made a potentially industry-changing discovery. The discovery concerned a change to a production process that was capable of providing the company (SHC) with an unassailable competitive advantage but at the same time placing the management in an ethical quandary. The dilemma was over whether to pursue an option involving licensing the technology to competitors thereby gaining a flow of royalties and allowing competitors to survive, or a 'secrecy option' denying use by competitors and probably putting them all out of business. Each option had its own risks and benefits.

Part (a) asked candidates to evaluate the secrecy option using Tucker's framework. This involved interrogating the option using five criteria with each one requiring reference back to the case study as well as a sound knowledge of the Tucker framework itself. This was the question that candidates did the best on with many achieving all ten marks. I included an article on this framework in Student Accountant early in 2008 and it is gratifying that many performed well on this part. Some candidates failed to gain high marks because of a failure to relate the answer to the case or by misunderstanding one or more of the criteria. Some, for example, wrongly construed 'sustainable' as referring to the continuance of the SHC business rather than the environmental implications of the option.

Part (b) asked candidates to distinguish between strategic and operational risks and then explain why the secrecy option would be a source of strategic risk. The marking scheme allowed a maximum of six marks for the theoretical component of this question with the remaining four being reserved for explaining the 'why' question with reference to the case. There was a recent article in student accountant on this issue by Nick Weller so it was good to see many candidates achieving good marks on understanding strategic and operational risks. It was disappointing to see that many candidates were less able to use their theoretical knowledge of strategic risk by relating it back to the case. In order to attract maximum marks, candidates had to show how the secrecy option would be a strategic risk and not just general risk. Some candidates discussed the general risks associated with the option without distinguishing between the strategic and the operational and those answers were not well rewarded.

Part (c) was the most ambitious component of question 1. In it, candidates had to not only construct arguments in favour of both options, but they also had to write their answers in the manner of a management narrative in an annual report. Each part (i and ii) asked for a convincing business case for one of the options and also an ethical case. The question specified that the ethical case should be made from the pristine capitalist perspective in favour of the secrecy option and from the wider stakeholder perspective for the licensing option. Candidates therefore had to be aware of what each ethical perspective was 'about' and also to apply it to the case.

This application of ethical theory to the case proved difficult for many candidates. A common approach was to attempt to make the business case for the two options and then to include a paragraph briefly providing the candidate's understanding of the two ethical stances but failing to develop those by referring to the case. Again, it is the application of theory to the case that was the reason why many candidates did not perform well in part (c).

The application of ethical theory was not well done overall. It is not enough to understand ethical perspectives. Candidates will usually be required to apply them in some way to get the majority of marks in P1 ethics questions.

Part (c) also contained 4 professional marks. Professional marks are a part of all professional level ACCA papers and examiners can choose a range of ways to examine these. In each case, however, candidates must present their answers in the manner prescribed and it follows that candidates must know how to write in the prescribed manner to gain the 4 professional marks. Accordingly, I strongly advise tutors to ensure that candidates are familiar with the common types of presentation format. Similarly, candidates studying the subject alone would ensure they are familiar with formats including letters, presentations, briefing notes, management reporting narratives (such as was asked for in this diet), press statements, memos and the like. Some candidates, for example, wrote a letter from chief executive Nelson Cobar while in other cases the answer was more like a memo. Neither of these incorrect approaches was rewarded with professional marks.

Issues concerning the contents of annual reports continued in **part (d)** of question 1. Reporting is a crucial part of corporate governance and business accountability. Part (d) sought to explore issues in that regard. Part (d)(i) asked candidates to distinguish between mandatory and voluntary disclosures with examples and it wasn't surprising that most candidates were able to do that to some extent. Part (d)(ii) was a little more challenging as many candidates were unsure as to the link between voluntary disclosure and accountability. The link between disclosure and accountability is an important one and addresses one of the key themes of the whole P1 study guide. Once an item is disclosed it means that stakeholders gain information on which to hold the business to account. Again, a sound understanding of accountability was helpful to candidates who scored highly in this part of question 1.

5   COASTAL OIL (DEC 11)

Key answer tips

This was question, requiring a detailed reading of the case scenario reflecting a real life situation and application to corporate ethical standpoints.

For part (a) it was important to describe the purpose of a corporate code of ethics. This should have presented few problems. In the second part of (a) the key was to reflect the verb used and "evaluate" not describe the performance of the company against its own ethical aims.

Part (b) proved challenging for some candidates. The key was to be sure to explain the terms (voluntary and mandatory) and then provide illustrations to make the differences clear.

Part (c) a multi part requirement of the question, referred to a speech made to a key stakeholder explaining the company's stance on internal control and risk as well as failure to achieve the standards set. It was best to adopt a systematic approach, particularly in the answer to part (c) (i) explaining the internal control failures, one by one. Part (c) (ii) and (iv) were questions drawn from new syllabus content and reflected the need to be able to apply rather than list knowledge for success in P1.

Part (c) (iii) on health and safety risk, by comparison, should have been straightforward Ensure that your answer is in the correct format, so as not to lose the professional marks that are available.

(a)   **Corporate code of ethics.**

Purposes

A corporate code of ethics (sometimes contrasted with a professional code) has five general purposes.

The first is communicating the organisation's values into a succinct and sometimes memorable form. This might involve defining the strategic purposes of the organisation and how this might affect ethical attitudes and policies.

Second, the code serves to identify the key stakeholders and the promotion of stakeholder rights and responsibilities. This may involve deciding on the legitimacy of the claims of certain stakeholders and how the company will behave towards them.

Third, a code of ethics is a means of conveying these values to stakeholders. It is important for internal and external stakeholders to understand the ethical positions of a company so they know what to expect in a given situation and to know how the company will behave. This is especially important with powerful stakeholders, perhaps including customers, suppliers and employees.

Fourth, a code of ethics serves to influence and control individuals' behaviour, especially internal stakeholders such as management and employees. The values conveyed by the code are intended to provide for an agreed outcome whenever a given situation arises and to underpin a way of conducting organisational life in accordance with those values.

Fifth, a code of ethics can be an important part of an organisation's strategic positioning. In the same way that an organisation's reputation as an employer, supplier, etc. can be a part of strategic positioning, so can its ethical reputation in society. Its code of ethics is a prominent way of articulating and underpinning that.

Evaluate Coastal Oil's performance

In the case of Coastal Oil, the company appears to have failed its own code of ethics in terms of its pledges on full compliance with regulation in all jurisdictions: safety and care of employees, transparency and communication with stakeholders, social contribution and environmental responsibility.

Coastal Oil stated its aim to achieve full compliance with regulation in all jurisdictions. The contract with Well Services was clearly contestable in terms of who was liable, partly due to the complexity of the documentation. There is no evidence from the case that the company was criminally negligent but health and safety or environmental controls, relevant to companies operating in Effland waters, may have been breached.

In terms of the safety and care of employees, the company also did not perform well against its own standards. The deaths of eight employees on the Effland Coastal Oil Rig resulted from health and safety failures because of a number of internal control failures. If Coastal Oil saw the protection of employees as an ethical issue, it might have adopted, or ensured that its JV partners adopted, the 'highest standards' of performance in ensuring their safety.

The company gave the appearance of a lack of transparency and communication failure. Because of the internal arguments between Coastal Oil and Well Services, it took seven days to make a public statement about the event. Clearly, there would be many stakeholders eager to hear Coastal Oil's view on what had happened, including the families of those killed and injured, and the delay caused by the internal arguments was a breach of its own code of ethics on this issue.

In terms of social contribution, the oil spill had a number of negative social consequences. The oil spill caused a number of problems to the communities along the Effland coast. Business was damaged during the important tourist season meaning that communities were less supported, in terms of income, over those important months.

The valve failure caused an oil leak on the sea floor which took several months to stop. This is an environmental failure and, given that Coastal Oil stated that environmental responsibility was a key heading in its code of ethics, stakeholders will be reasonably entitled to conclude that it has failed against its own ethical standards. Given that the company operates in such an environmentally sensitive industry, it would clearly require a high level of commitment to internal controls to maintain this, whether directly by Coastal Oil employees or through the partners in the JV such as Well Services.

(b)   **Voluntary disclosure and environmental risk**

Difference between

Company reporting, usually in annual reports, interim reports or on websites, contains both mandatory and voluntary disclosures. Mandatory disclosures are those statements that are compulsory under relevant company laws or stock market listing rules. In most jurisdictions, mandatory items are the main financial statements such as income statement, statement of financial position and statement of cash flows. Listing rules in many jurisdictions, such as in the UK, also mandate some corporate governance disclosures such as directors' shareholdings and emoluments, and details of directors' contracts.

Voluntary disclosures are not required by any mandate but are provided, usually in narrative rather than quantitative form. There is a belief that some information of interest or relevance to shareholders or other stakeholders cannot be conveyed numerically and so additional information is needed. The chairman's statement, chief executive's review, social and environmental disclosure, intellectual capital reporting and risk reporting are all examples of voluntary disclosure in most jurisdictions.

Tutorial note

Mandatory and voluntary disclosures vary slightly between jurisdictions.

Material to shareholders

Voluntary disclosure is of interest to shareholders because it provides information that cannot be easily conveyed in statutory statements or in numerical form. In the case of environmental risk reporting at Coastal Oil, it is likely that shareholders will welcome the environmental risk measures put in place after the accident as reported in the annual report.

First, in the case of Coastal Oil, the fact that there has been a recent and expensive environmental accident means that environmental risk is clearly material to shareholder value and is likely to remain so while the company continues to extract and process oil. This is a 'structural' risk resulting from the company's core activity. This makes environmental disclosure potentially highly material and capable of affecting the value of the company. The extent of potential exposure (total impacts), and hence the potential losses, would be a key piece of information needed, and also the previous environmental accident statistics.

Second, it will allow the shareholders to understand the extent and nature of the risk which clearly wasn't fully known before the accident. By knowing this, shareholders can assess whether the risk profile of the business matches their own attitudes to or appetite for risk. In a portfolio of shares, some investors will want to blend certain risks and returns, and knowing about a company's risks is important in making these judgements.

Third, the additional environmental risk information will allow the shareholders to judge how the risk might affect company value and hence the potential volatility and attractiveness of the share. The case says that the disclosure would contain 'value relevant' information meaning that the risks described will be capable of affecting returns, costs or both. The materiality of environmental risk reporting is potentially quite high: shareholders were unaware of the poor internal controls on the Effland Coastal Oil Rig and, had they been more aware, may have discounted the share price accordingly.

Fourth, risk reporting can explain the new risk controls put in place. After a confidence-threatening event such as the valve rupture and oil spill on the Effland Coastal Oil Rig, the explanation of these measures could be vital in restoring investor confidence. In particular, they should reassure shareholders that the accident should not re-occur, or that if it were to re-occur, further controls would be in place to offset the worst of the damage. It is likely that more detailed and granulated environmental reporting would be valued by shareholders, especially those specialist institutional shareholders made cautious by the Effland accident.

(c)   (i)   **Internal control failures**

In keeping with Coastal Oil's stated commitment in its code of ethics to transparency, I have been authorised by my board to provide a full and frank statement on the internal control failures that led to the accident on the Effland Coastal Oil Rig. I will be happy to explain any particular point in more detail if required, but if you will allow me I will outline where I believe our internal controls were below standard.

I should inform the committee that the ownership and management of the oil rig was complicated by the fact that Coastal Oil was part of a joint venture in which, despite being the major partner, we did not have complete control. This means that other partners had responsibilities, including control of some operations crucial to the safety of staff and the oil supply.

The complexities of ownership may have led to the first of the failures which was a lack of clarity on individual and collective legal responsibilities. Accordingly, liability for the valve failure was ambiguous even though it was another company, Well Services, who directly caused the problem. We work very closely with joint venture partners on projects such as the Effland Coastal Oil Rig and rely on each other's controls. In this case, the situation was made worse for Coastal Oil by a lack of clarity on these agreements and this is salutary for future projects.

It is my understanding that the engineers belonging to Well Services failed in regard to two operational controls. The valve that was the site of the pipeline's rupture was not tested in accordance with their normal procedures. Also, a connecting part was deployed at a depth beyond that at which it was designed to operate (i.e. beyond its safety tolerance). I was troubled by the suggestion that cost may have been a partial explanation for this. In both of these cases, a failure of operational controls contributed to the failure of the valve.

I sadly have no reason to doubt reports suggesting that the culture on the rig was less rigorous than it should have been. It is important that stringent controls are operated throughout Coastal Oil and it is especially important at the sites of operation where hazardous work takes place. There are issues with the reporting of exceptions to the land-side and hence the management style of a rig's individual manager becomes the defining issue on whether a certain internal control problem is reported to us. On reflection, this could have been more robust and it relied more on objective measures and less on human judgement.

Finally, we had no effective contingency plan in place for sealing the well-head or stopping the flow of oil from the well after the valve ruptured. This was the cause of the leakage of oil into the sea over several months. Contingency plans or system backups may have helped in this regard but we were unable to respond with the speed necessary and this resulted in such environmental and economic damage.

(ii) **Subjective and objective risk assessment**

I would like to respond directly to Senator Jones's remark in the media that I as the company's CEO 'should have known this was going to happen'. Whilst I understand the senator's anger at the events that have so badly affected his constituency, I owe it to Coastal Oil's shareholders to respond to him for the purposes of clarity.

Risk assessment is an important but complicated process and involves establishing both the probability of a particular risk event happening and also the impact or hazard that would arise if it was realised. A key point is that some of these calculations can be made with some degree of objectivity whilst others rely more on subjective assessment. There is an important distinction, then, between objective and subjective assessments. A risk can be objectively assessed if we can 'scientifically' measure the probability of a given outcome or predict, with some certainty, the impact. I can predict with some confidence, for example, based on past data, the number of working days likely to be lost in a given year through absenteeism of employees. I can predict with much less certainty, the probability that the stock market will rise or fall on a given day. In such a situation, I must use more subjective judgement.

Similarly with regard to impact, I might be able to assess the impact of my loss should my car get stolen but I could much less accurately predict the number of people hurt or injured in an accident. Again, I would use a more subjective figure for assessing that risk. The probability of having my car stolen would increase if I were to leave it unlocked and this underlines the importance of controls to help reduce the probabilities of adverse events happening.

Argue against Senator Jones

This brings me to Senator Jones's remark that I 'should have known' the accident was going to occur. I'm afraid that his remark does not recognise the complexities of risk management and risk assessment. I have outlined the reasons for uncertainty in both assessing the probabilities and impacts of risk events.

Accidents do occur in many industries including in the petrochemicals industry. Given that Coastal Oil operates hundreds of similar deep sea rigs in waters all over the world, I could not, with any degree of certainty, predict the probability of a fatal accident on a given oil rig and much less could I have known about the probability of an accident on the Effland Coastal Oil Rig. Similarly, there is no information that I could have received that could have predicted the scale of death or injury in the event of a given incident.

I concede that there were a number of internal control failures on the rig in question, but would point out to the senator that I was unaware of those failures because of the nature of the information systems linking rigs to our land-side operations. It is the responsibility of each rig's management to enforce safety controls on that rig and no such information would have reached me except by exception. He may be justified in criticising these, and I have explained already that I view these information failures as an internal control issue that we must resolve.

(iii) **Health and safety risk**

The board of Coastal Oil was deeply saddened to hear of the loss of life on the Effland Coastal Oil Rig. As a petrochemical company involved in each stage of the extraction, processing and distribution of oil products, we are naturally very aware of the health and safety risks that we face. These are risks to individuals, employees or others, arising from any failure in our operations giving rise to compromised human welfare.

Health and safety risk, and particularly the probability of a given health and safety risk materialising, is generally increased by a number of factors. The first is a lack of a health and safety policy. In some industries, including petrochemicals, large parts of this policy are underpinned by legislation, depending on jurisdiction, but it is also in the interests of a business to ensure that robust policies are in place covering all aspects of health and safety and indeed this was the case on the oil platform in question. The second is a lack of emergency procedures or a failure to deal with hazards that arise. Once identified, a new hazard or impact must be addressed with a policy or a way of dealing with it. Ineffective operational controls, such as was the case on the Effland Coastal Oil Deep Rig, contribute to this failure. Third, a poor health and safety culture can undermine an otherwise good policy if management and staff are lax towards health and safety, or believe it to be unimportant. There is some evidence that this was sadly the case on the rig.

(iv) **ALARP**

I understand and share the committee's desire to ensure that an accident of this type does not happen again. However, risk management is partly a trade-off between the cost of control and level of perceived risk. We operate to a principle known as ALARP or that risks should be 'as low as reasonably practicable'. There is an inverse relationship between a risk and the acceptability of that risk or, in other words, a risk is more acceptable when it is low and less acceptable when it is high. Accordingly, risks assessed as 'high' in terms of probability and/or impact, must have credible and affordable strategies put in place for their management. The extent and cost of that risk strategy is a matter of judgement and you will appreciate that as the chief executive of Coastal Oil, I owe it to our shareholders and customers to control costs. This means that risks cannot be completely eliminated, much as I might wish that they could.

Accordingly, then, each risk is managed so as to be as low as is reasonably practicable because we can never say that a risk has a zero value. It would be financially and operationally impracticable to completely eliminate health and safety risks, and so we must live with the ever-present possibility that they can happen. This does not mean we would ever become complacent, of course, but merely that I should be honest in saying that the probability of occurrence cannot be zero. Because of this, we maintain a number of controls that should reduce the probability of the risks materialising, such as by having a policy in place and enforcing it. We also have protections in place, such as the compulsory wearing of safety equipment, to reduce the impact of an event should it occur.

Thank you for listening to this statement. I am now happy to take questions.

		ACCA marking scheme	
			Marks
(a)		1 mark for each purpose of a code of ethics to a maximum of 5 marks. 1 mark for evaluation of each point.	
		Maximum	10
(b)		2 marks for distinguishing between voluntary and mandatory disclosure. Half a mark for each example of mandatory and voluntary to a maximum of 2 marks. 2 marks for each benefit to shareholders identified and assessed to a maximum of 8 marks. Half a mark for identification only.	
			10
(c)	(i)	2 marks for each internal control failure identified and explained. Half a mark for identification only.	10
	(ii)	2 marks for distinguishing between objective and subjective risk. Half a mark for explanation of each and/or evidence of understanding to a maximum of 2 marks. 2 marks for each argument developed against the senator's statement to a maximum of 4 marks.	8
	(iii)	1 mark for explanation of health and safety risk. 1 mark for explanation of each factor to a maximum of 3. Half a mark for identification only.	4
	(iv)	2 marks for evidence of understanding of ALARP.	4
		2 marks for explanation of why health and safety risks cannot be completely eliminated under the ALARP principle.	4
		Professional marks for logical flow, persuasiveness, format and tone of the answers.	4
Total			50

Examiners comments

The case for the compulsory (50 mark) question 1 was on Coastal Oil, a petrochemical company that had experienced difficulties with an explosion on a deep sea oil extraction rig. It was similar to a real-life case that arose with a company that had suffered an explosion on a rig with a resultant loss of life and a number of other negative consequences.

As in previous exams, I used the longer case in question 1 to examine several areas of the study guide including content from the ethics component (study guide section E). Also as before, a careful and detailed analysis of the case itself was essential to achieve good marks.

Part (a) asked about corporate codes of ethics for ten marks. For five of the marks, candidates were asked to describe the general purposes of a corporate (not to be confused with a professional) code of ethics. These should have been relatively straightforward for most well-prepared candidates and indeed, most candidates were able to collect some marks here. Many achieved all five marks.

For the second 5 marks of the 10, the requirement was to evaluate Coastal Oil's performance against its own stated ethical aims. These were clearly set out in the third paragraph in the case and many candidates were able to correctly identify these. Marks were awarded where candidates were able to show, from the case, how the company had failed to meet its own ethical standards. A common mistake was to list the five areas (full compliance with regulation, etc.) but then to describe what the terms meant rather than searching the case for evidence to evaluate the company's performance.

Part (b) was about mandatory and voluntary disclosure and in particular, the potential materiality of environmental risk disclosure at Coastal Oil. The first task was to explain what the two terms meant (voluntary and mandatory) and then to give some examples to demonstrate understanding. Most candidates were able to gain some marks here although quite a lot were not able to say any more than that mandatory was required by law and that voluntary was not. This missed the point about how listing rules also place disclosure requirements on companies, including, in many jurisdictions, details of the company's corporate governance, executive remuneration, etc.

Part (c) was the multi-part requirement. Candidates were asked to answer each part, sequentially, in the form of a speech by Susan Ahmed, CEO of Coastal Oil. She was asked to appear before a special committee of the national legislature and wanted to use the speech to explain several things to the committee about the company's internal controls and risk management. In particular, she wanted to explain the IC failures and to respond to points made against the company in the controversy that had followed the explosion of the oil rig.

Questions involving the examination of a case to pick out and explain internal control failures have been used before on P1 papers on several occasions. Part (c) (i) required Mrs Ahmed to explain to the committee where IC failures had occurred. The case itself, as in previous questions of this type, was seeded with the information required to provide a comprehensive answer. Because (in the last paragraph of the case) the Coastal Oil board agreed that she should provide a full and uncensored statement to the legislative committee, there was no reason for Mrs Ahmed to conceal or play down particular failures. Accordingly, the best answers were those that carefully and systematically explained (i.e. did more than just identify) each of the five major IC failures in the case. Those that explained internal controls in general terms, perhaps explaining the importance of ICs, received low or no marks because they failed to adequately analyse the case.

Part (c) requirements (ii) and (iv) were both from the new content on risk that I mentioned in the introduction to this report. Both were done with variable degrees of success. In part (ii), most candidates were able to distinguish between subjective and objective risk assessment but fewer were able to gain the marks for arguing against Senator Jones's view. The point here was to explain to the committee that Senator Jones did not appreciate the subjective nature of risk measurements and that probabilities of risk events happening are often very difficult to estimate. Subjective assessments, importantly, are not invented or fabricated, but are based on less-than-scientific assessments which are sometimes difficult for some stakeholders to understand.

Part (iv) seemed to be difficult for many candidates. I covered the ALARP principle in a technical article in 2010 and whilst many candidates were able to show some evidence of knowing what it was (sometimes with the help of a simple graph), fewer were able to weave it into the speech as required.

Part (iii) on health and safety risk required candidates to explain what it means, and then to explain what can increase this risk in an organisation. This should have been straightforward because it was mainly bookwork. Some candidates defined the term and then did not do so well on explaining the factors.

There was a full spread of marks awarded for the presentation itself. As usual there were four professional marks available. Some made no attempt to frame their answers in the form of a speech. Others (wrongly) began their answer with 'Dear committee' and ended with 'Yours faithfully'. Another error was to frame it as a memo with 'To: Committee, From: Mrs Ahmed' or similar. It is important to be able to judge the tone of an answer based on what the question asks in terms of format. I have raised this before in my examiner's reports and I would again encourage candidates and their tutors to work on these formats as a part of preparing for future P1 exams.

6 FUEL SURCHARGES

Key answer tips

Parts (a) and (b) of this question have a similar style, allowing you a theoretical starting point for a few marks, and then moving onto the application of the theory. Take advantage of these questions and ensure that you earn full marks for your knowledge of the theories, and at least you have a basis for your answer to the second part of the question!

Part (c) will require you to look at the separate elements of a directors' remuneration package, describe what would be required under good corporate governance principles and then assess whether this has occurred. Again, a starting point of theory before moving onto the application.

Any valid points made in part (d) will earn marks.

(a) (i) **Kohlberg's theory**

Kohlberg's theory relates to cognitive moral development (CMD) – that is theories that attempt to explain cognitive processes and the decisions taken by individuals. Kohlberg's theory of CMD attempts to show the reasoning processes used by individuals, and how those processes change as the individual matured from a 'child' to be an 'adult'.

CMD therefore relates to the different levels of reasoning that an individual can apply to ethical issues and problems.

Kohlberg identified three levels of moral development, with two sub-stages within each level – giving six stages in total.

Level one: Pre-conventional

The individual is focused on self-interest, external rewards and punishment. Decisions are likely to be unethical because the person makes decisions entirely in accordance with expected rewards and punishment protecting their own interests.

The two sub-levels are:

1.1   Right and wrong are defined according to expected rewards and/or punishment from figures of authority.

1.2   Right is defined according to whether there is fairness in exchanges – individuals are concerned therefore with their own immediate interests.

Level two: Conventional

The individual tends to do what is expected of them by others. 'Others' in this situation relates to work colleagues initially but is broadened to society in general in the second sub-stage of this level. In other words the person is starting to think about their actions and society as a whole rather than focusing on just their immediate peers.

The two sub-levels are:

2.1   Actions are defined by what is expected of individuals by their peers and those close to them.

2.2   The consideration of the expectations of others is broadened to social accord in general terms rather than immediate peers.

Level three: Post-conventional

The individual starts to develop autonomous decision making which is based on internal perspectives of right/wrong ethics etc. rather than based on any external influences.

The two sub-levels are:

3.1   Right and wrong are determined by reference to basic rights, values and contracts of society.

3.2   Individuals make decisions based on self-chosen ethical principles which they believe everyone should follow. Individuals therefore have a strong ethical stance, meaning that ethical decisions are made, even when they mean harm is incurred to the individual from making those decisions.

As individuals move through the stages then they are moving onto higher levels of moral reasoning – with higher levels in general terms providing more 'ethical' methods of reasoning. Most individuals operate at level two reasoning – so decisions are made in accordance with what an individual perceives others to believe and in accordance with what is therefore expected of that individual by others.

(ii) The initial decision by TY and JK to collude on the fuel surcharge appears to meet the interests of both companies to maximise profits. In this sense, it appears they were acting at level 1.2 – there was fairness in the exchange in that both companies benefited from the increased prices being charged. The collusion meant that there was fairness in the exchanges – both airlines benefited.

It is unlikely that the price fixing could be explained as level two of Kohlberg. While airline customers would expect TY and JK to make some profit (else they would go out of business) that profit would not be 'excessive'. It is possibly reasonable to expect an airline to charge a fuel surcharge, placing the decision at level 2.1. However, the fact that there was collusion means there was an attempt to raise prices artificially, which would not be expected by customers. Level 2.1 action is therefore not appropriate.

Regarding the decision by JK to disclose that there had been a price fixing agreement, it appears that the directors are attempting to justify the company's initial lack of disclosure. The argument that disclosure is now 'in the public interest' appears to be focused on Kohlberg stage 3.1. In other words, disclosure was expected by society and therefore disclosure was made. This reasoning obviously ignores the initial issue of collusion and lack of disclosure. The disclosure could therefore simply be stated as being at level 2.1; disclosure would be expected by their customers.

Given the rivalry between TY and JK another aspect of disclosure can be considered. Given that either company could have disclosed the price fixing, there could be an element of JK attempting to gain moral superiority over TY; disclosure could also be explained as JK being 'better' morally than TY. In this case JK was therefore attempting again to achieve level 2.2 or even 3.1 by acting in the interests of society. However, disclosure could also have been prompted by level 1.1 – if disclosure was not made then JK would have been punished by the imposition of a fine as TY was.

In conclusion, disclosure was probably prompted by the necessity of avoiding a large fine – but with the intention of making JK appear to be more morally superior to TY.

(b) (i) **Public interest**

There is no overall definition or agreement on the term 'public interest'. However, the public interest is normally seen to refer to the 'common well-being' or 'general welfare.'

An action is usually thought to be in the public interest where it benefits society in some way. It is unclear though how many members of society must benefit before the action can be declared to be in the public interest. Some people would argue an action has to benefit every single member of society in order to be truly in the public interest. At the other extreme, any action can be in the public interest as long as it benefits some of the population and harms no one.

The extent to which an individual will make a disclosure 'in the public interest' depends on their moral stance. In terms of Kohlberg this means that the individual will be at level three and is prepared to 'blow the whistle' on unethical conduct.

(ii) In terms of the disclosure, JK is attempting to show a better moral stance than TY. In other words, disclosure was in the public interest because customers of TY and JK were being overcharged. However, only a limited number of 'members of society' would benefit from the disclosure – that is customers of TY and JK. If public interest disclosure means that all members of society must benefit, this argument cannot be used by JK. However, the argument that disclosure has benefited some members of society and has not harmed anyone else would mean disclosure was in the public interest.

(c) **Evaluation of remuneration**

Remuneration for directors is normally based on two elements:

- Firstly a basic annual salary 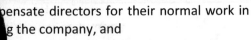 compensate directors for their normal work in attending board meetings a   r   g the company, and

- Secondly, a performance   mponent to provide compensation for good decision making in   g that the company is successful and profitable.

Tutorial note

There are generally considered to be four elements of a directors' remuneration package: basic salary, performance related element, pension contributions and benefits in kind. The focus here is on the first two since these are the most significant, and the only ones that are discussed in the case.

This means that whatever remuneration package is determined, it is essential to ensure that the directors have a stake in doing a good job for the shareholder. Each element of a remuneration package should therefore be designed to ensure that the director remains focused on the company and motivated to improve performance.

A balance must be struck between offering a package:

- that is too small and hence demotivating and leading to potential underachievement, and

- that is too easily earned.

This implies that there is a mix of salary and performance related pay as noted above. Corporate governance guidelines do not provide a precise 'mix' but indicate that the performance related element should be substantial.

In terms of TY and JK, there is a performance related element of remuneration. At 40% and 30% it could be argued that the fixed salary percentage is too low – there is a risk that directors will not be sufficiently well compensated if their company does not perform well. A company needs to attract and retain directors with sufficient knowledge and skill to run the company and 30% specifically may be too low an amount to meet this objective. Marks & Spencer, for example, have 55% of remuneration from fixed salary etc.

Role of remuneration committee

Remuneration will be set by the remuneration committee taking into account the amount of compensation being paid by comparable companies. No information is provided in the scenario regarding other companies; however, it is not clear whether the board of TY are actually meeting governance regulations in this area. The directors appear to be discussing methods of increasing their remuneration following the fall in profits with the fine. This decision should be taken by the remuneration committee, ensuring that no director is also responsible for setting their own remuneration. The committee removes any conflict of interest in this area.

Performance-related elements of remuneration

Performance related remuneration is defined as those elements of remuneration dependent on the achievement of some form of performance-measurement criteria. Care must be taken in determining the elements of performance related remuneration. For example, if the market goes down as a whole, then this could potentially penalise directors for an outcome that has nothing to do with their performance. In other words, the performance related element should be linked to the performance of the company and not to the stock markets as a whole.

TY and JK have chosen different methods of doing this.

TY Company – proportion of profit

Part of remuneration is based on the profit for the year. At 40%, this is a relatively high amount as it tends to focus the directors on achieving a high profit in absolute terms, and could lead to attempts to amend the financial statements to increase profit. The imposition of the fine on TY has had the immediate effect of making the directors try to amend their remuneration package, again indicating that reliance on profit may be too high.

TY and JK Companies – share options

The granting of share options means that the directors have the right to buy shares at the current price in a number of years' time. If the price of shares has increased, then the directors will make a profit based on the difference between the two share prices (current and the future price). Options appear to be a good method of rewarding long term performance as they are normally granted for periods in excess of three years. However, there remains the issue that directors may attempt to increase share price near the option date.

Having 20% of remuneration as options is probably acceptable. Many companies even require directors to purchase company shares to show their long-term commitment to the company. Forty per cent may be excessive as this does focus longer-term remuneration on one measure. If there is a declining market overall, then the value of JK's shares may also be falling through no fault of the directors. Use of share options in this situation is unlikely to be particularly motivating.

JK Company – change in share price

Basing incentive on movement in share price again forces directors to look to improvement in the company as part of their compensation package. However, as the movement is based on the price at two specific points in time, then again there is the incentive to try and maximise the share price at these times to provide the highest possible level of remuneration. The only benefit of using the share price is that 'inflating' the value in one year means that next year's bonus is likely to be reduced as it will be difficult to obtain a similar increase in price.

(d) **Reasons for providing a CSR report**

Accountability:

Disclosure is the dominant philosophy of the modern system and the essential aspect of corporate accountability. Providing appropriate disclosure shows the company to be a good 'corporate citizen'.

Information asymmetry:

Disclosure provides an attempt to deal with information asymmetry between managers and owners in terms of agency theory. The managers or directors have more information about the company than the owners – the shareholders. Provision of a CSR helps to minimise this information imbalance.

Attracts investment:

Institutional investors are likely to be attracted by increased disclosure and transparency provided by the CSR.

Compliance:

Although not a precise listing requirement, it is possible that non-compliance would threaten listing in the future. Provision of information now helps to ensure that JK will be able to meet any future requirements regarding CSR. For example, Marks & Spencer and other UK listed companies already provide information over and above statutory and listing requirements as a sign of good governance and to show that information can be provided should listing rules change.

Stakeholders:

The amount of voluntary disclosure helps in discharging the multiple accountabilities of various stakeholder groups. For example, shareholders obtain a better picture of the company (as noted above) but other interested parties such as pressure groups can see progress being made on the ethical stance of the company, for example.

7   AEI

Key answer tips

This question combines corporate governance with professional values and ethics topics – a frequent combination in the Section A questions in this exam. The question contains a mixture of theoretical parts (including part (b) (i), part (c) and part of part (d)) with application of this knowledge.

When tackling a question such as this it is essential to ensure that you manage your time effectively, and allow yourself the opportunity to score well on the knowledge areas since these are the easier marks.

(a)   **Ethical codes and ethical dilemmas**

Ethical codes may assist in resolving ethical dilemmas for the following reasons:

Provision of a framework

Ethical codes provide a framework within which ethical dilemmas can be resolved. The codes set the basic standards of ethics as well as the structures that can be applied. For example, most codes provide a general sequence of steps to be taken to resolve dilemmas. That sequence can then be applied to any specific dilemma.

Provision of example methods of resolution

Ethical codes also provide examples of ethical situations and how those example situations were expected to be resolved. Specific ethical dilemmas can be compared to those situations for guidance on how to resolve them.

Establishes boundaries

Ethical codes provide boundaries which ethically it will be incorrect to cross. For example, many accountants prepare personal taxation returns for their clients. However, it is also known that ethically, it is incorrect to suggest illegal methods of saving tax or to knowingly prepare incorrect tax returns. Maintenance of ethical conduct in this situation ensures that the accountant continues to be trusted by both his clients and by the taxation authorities.

Ethical codes do not always assist in resolving ethical dilemmas for the following reasons:

Codes only

Ethical codes are literally what they say – they are 'only' a code. As a general code it may not fit the precise ethical dilemma and therefore the code will be limited in use.

Interpretation of code

As a code, it is subject to interpretation. This means that two different people could form two entirely different but potentially correct views on the same element of the code. For example, terms such as 'incorrect' will mean that an action should not be attempted at all by some people, while others will interpret this as a warning that the action may be attempted, as long as good reasons are given for the attempt.

Lack of enforcement provisions

Many codes have limited or inadequate penalties and/or enforcement provisions. Breach of the code may result in fines, or simply a warning not to breach the code again. Again, a code is subject to interpretation making a 'breach' of the code difficult to identify anyway.

(b)   (i)   **Ethical threats and safeguards**

An *ethical threat* is a situation where a person or corporation is tempted not to follow their code of ethics.

An *ethical safeguard* provides guidance or a course of action which attempts to remove the ethical threat.

(ii) **Attempting 'bribery' of P**

P, an audit junior, has been offered a free re-fitting of his kitchen with AEI goods. The manager in charge of the department mentioned that this was standard practice each year as a 'thank you' to the member assigned to carry out the inventory checking and subsequent valuation of that inventory. P has also discovered that the inventory is materially overvalued.

There appears to be a threat to P's objectivity. P needs to ensure that audit work is being carried out correctly, while at the same time ensuring there are no factors influencing judgment in this respect. The offer of a free kitchen could influence that judgment as P may be being asked to ignore the over-valuation of inventory and consequent over-statement of profits in AEI. However, it is also concerning that this situation appears to be 'normal' and has therefore been the practice for some years.

To remove the threat P needs to:

- Inform you, the audit manager, of the situation and ask for advice. As a junior member of staff P would be expected to refer the issue to senior management for advice.

Actions that the audit manager should then take include:

- Ascertaining the situation from previous years, including contacting the previous audit manager and juniors to determine action taken in previous years.

- Inform the manager of the warehouse that P is concerned about the situation and ask the manager to confirm this is standard practice.

- Inform the audit partner and ask for his or her advice.

- Inform P not to accept any free goods until the situation has been resolved.

It is possible, albeit unlikely, that this is standard practice. However, this does not assist in resolving the objectivity issue. It is more likely that P will have to decline the offer and also recommend the inventory valuation adjustment. At this stage, actions will include:

- The audit partner explaining the need for the adjustment to AEI's directors.

- Where the adjustment is carried out, no further action will be required.

- Where the adjustment is refused, then there will be the requirement for further discussion with the possibility of the audit report being modified, even if this leads to the loss of the audit client.

Q and disclosure requirements, holding of shares in AEI

Q has two ethical issues to resolve:

- Firstly, to determine whether or not disclosure of directors' remuneration is complete

- Secondly, the issue of holding shares in the audit client.

Regarding disclosure of remuneration, statute requires the disclosure of the different elements of remuneration, including share options. The fact that the total remuneration payable cannot be determined when options are granted is not a reason for non-disclosure. In this situation Q appears to be being pressured into disclosing incorrect information. The ethical threat is therefore not behaving with integrity – Q understands what should be disclosed and integrity would be threatened if this disclosure was not made.

The argument from the chair of the audit committee is not valid. While disclosure of information between an audit client and the auditor attracts confidential status, this confidentiality cannot hold where statutory requirements have not been fulfilled. To maintain integrity, Q must recommend that share option information is disclosed.

However, the situation is made more complicated by the fact that Q holds shares in AEI. The ethical threat here is that Q's objectivity may be compromised. Q may overlook issues which would adversely affect the profit of AEI as this would also affect the share price and dividend that would be obtained as a shareholder.

Furthermore, it is not clear whether Q has disclosed this information to his employer. The 2.5% holding is below the disclosure limit (currently 3% in the UK) for the financial statements, so it is also possible the audit firm is unaware of this conflict. To resolve the conflict, Q should dispose of the audit shares and inform his employer.

The situation is made more complex by the fact that the share price of Q is likely to fall when the results for the year are announced. It could therefore be argued that Q is using inside information and in breach of insider trading rules if shares were sold now. It therefore appears that Q must resign from the audit immediately and make full disclosure of the shareholding and the lack of information in the directors' remuneration statement.

Finally, by resigning now, Q may well face disciplinary action from the employer and/or from the institute for not disclosing the conflict of interest earlier. There is therefore still the temptation to 'keep quiet' about the directors' remuneration disclosure and trust that the chair of the audit committee will not disclose information about Q's shareholding to any third party.

Cross-directorships

The ethical threat here appears to be a lack of independence and self-interest regarding the setting of remuneration for these directors. The chair of the remuneration committee of AEI will be voting on the remuneration of directors in AEI; similarly, one of those directors as chair of the remuneration committee of IEA would be voting on remuneration of that executive director in IEA. There would be a temptation to vote for high remuneration levels in AEI in the knowledge that reciprocal high levels of remuneration would be voted for in IEA.

In corporate governance terms, one ethical safeguard is to ban these cross-directorships. The ban would be enforceable as the directors of companies must be stated in annual accounts; hence it would be easy to identify cross-directorships. The ban would also be effective as the conflict of interest would be removed. However, in principles based jurisdictions, the fact that the rule had been broken would only lead to disclosure of this fact; the actual directorships could continue. It is only by making corporate governance regulations enforceable by statute (as in the USA) that the situation could be removed.

In professional terms, the directors clearly have a conflict of interest. While their professional code of ethics may mention this precisely as an ethical threat. Both directors should follow the spirit of the code and resign their non-executive directorships. This again would remove the threat.

Bank reconciliation

R has not carried out work on the bank reconciliation correctly. Ethically accountants must have the correct level of knowledge to perform their duties, otherwise audit and other clients will not receive the standard of service they are paying for. It would be unethical therefore to imply knowledge was available when this was not the case.

However, in this situation, it appears that R has simply followed the instructions given; there was no indication that the timing of clearance of cheques was an issue to be identified as an error. The problem, if anything, is therefore lack of appropriate training of R and/or supervision of R by the audit manager. The 'real' ethical threat is that the audit firm are not training their staff correctly decreasing the standard of service provided to their clients.

Actions to be taken to resolve the situation include:

- Ensuring that training within the audit firm does include appropriate knowledge on audit procedures for all levels of staff.

- Contacting the client to determine why the cheques were presented for payment late. If 'window dressing' has taken place then ask the client to amend the financial statements. Lack of amendment may again result in a modification of the audit report.

Tutorial note

In making your recommendations of ethical safeguards it is essential that your suggestions are practical and relate to the business situation provided. If your answer contains points other than those mentioned above, that you have explained clearly and related to the case of AEI, you will be awarded marks.

(c) **Advantages of NEDs**

Monitoring

They offer a clear monitoring role on the executive directors of a company. For example, on the remuneration committees they provide a check on the level of remuneration to prevent adverse publicity that executives are being paid excessive amounts.

Expertise

They provide external expertise in general terms of managing companies or specific skills such as finance and audit to complement and expand the knowledge and skills of executive directors.

Perception

The presence of NEDs provides evidence to third parties that executive directors are being monitored. NEDs also provide 'whistle-blowing' opportunities to employees and third parties, again providing the perception of good corporate governance.

Communication

There is an implied improvement in communication between shareholders' interests and the company. The senior non-independent director, for example, will normally try and maintain a dialogue with major institutional investors.

Disadvantages of NEDS

Unity

There is a risk that the presence of NEDs on a board will undermine the working of the board. There can be a lack of trust as the executives and NEDs may not know each other and find it different to work together. Similarly, there may be resentment against the NEDs if they provide needless input during board meetings.

Quality

There may be a poor gene pool for NEDs willing to serve on boards. This issue is particularly relevant as the liability for NEDs for default is the same as that for executive directors, although NED time and commitment is a lot less than for executive directors. Few potential NEDs may be willing to take this risk.

Remuneration

NED remuneration is basic salary only, there is no reward linked to company performance. While this does help ensure independence, the lack of significant remuneration may again deter potential NEDs from accepting the position.

(d) **Roles of NEDs in AEI Co**

Strategy role

NEDs have the right and responsibility to contribute to strategic success of AEI, challenging strategy and offering advice on direction to the executive directors.

The NEDs should be able to offer this advice, as they have the appropriate qualifications and experience to provide this input. However, the potential to provide input will be limited by the fact that all NEDs were appointed this year and they have not had any contact with the executive directors before. There is a danger of the board becoming focused on conflict between the executives and non-executives rather than working together.

Scrutinising role

NEDs are required to hold executive colleagues to account for decisions taken and results obtained.

Again, the NEDs have the ability to provide this checking role. Whether this will be accepted by the executive directors is another matter. Previous NEDs did not appear to be carrying out a particularly good job, hence their removal and appointment of the new NEDs. It is possible that the executives will resent their actions being queried, limiting the effectiveness of the NEDs.

Risk role

NEDs ensure the company has an adequate system of internal controls and system of risk management in place.

The new NEDs may find this role difficult. There is no indication that any NED has experience in this area – many companies appoint a senior NED with relevant financial and or audit experience (e.g. member of ACCA or similar institution). There is a risk that controls in AEI will not be sufficiently well monitored.

People role

NEDs oversee a range of responsibilities with regard to the appointment and remuneration of executives and will be involved in contractual and disciplinary issues.

The NEDs will be able to provide this role, although again effectiveness will be limited by their relative 'newness' to AEI. The NEDs need to discuss their roles with the executive directors initially, and then ensure that appropriate amendments are made within AEI. One area for consideration is the contracts of executive directors which are currently the same in length as NEDs. Listing requirements normally provide for a one year contract length.

8 GLOBAL-BANK (JUN 09)

Key answer tips

This question covered a full range of syllabus areas, and was helpfully broken down into several sub-sections, making the requirements very clear and precise.

Part (a) focuses on the popular exam topic of Kohlberg's theory of cognitive moral development. Be careful of the distinction between levels and stages that is required here.

If you could remember the 'text-book' causes of internal control failure that would have helped in part (b). Alternatively you could focus on problems evident in the case, and draw some general causes out from these.

Part (c) does not require you to discuss whether the agency relationship is good or bad, it merely requires you to identify the *aspects* of an agency relationship in this scenario. Part (d) starts with the shareholder classification distinctions, and then moves onto use these in the case.

Part (e) is the most challenging section, though the format of a letter provided easy access to the professional marks. To score well in this part your answer would need to avoid generalisations.

(a) (i) **Three Kohlberg levels**

At the *preconventional* level of moral reasoning, morality is conceived of in terms of rewards, punishments and instrumental motivations. Those demonstrating intolerance of regulations in preference for self-serving motives are typical preconventionalists.

At the *conventional* level, morality is understood in terms of compliance with either or both of peer pressure/social expectations or regulations, laws and guidelines. A high degree of compliance is assumed to be a highly moral position.

At the *postconventional* level, morality is understood in terms of conformance with 'higher' or 'universal' ethical principles. Postconventional assumptions often challenge existing regulatory regimes and social norms and so postconventional behaviour is often costly in personal terms.

Level 1: Preconventional level   Stage/Plane 1: Punishment-obedience orientation   Stage/Plane 2: Instrumental relativist orientation
Level 2: Conventional level   Stage/Plane 3: Good boy-nice girl orientation   Stage/Plane 4: Law and order orientation
Level 3: Postconventional level   Stage/Plane 5: Social contract orientation   Stage/Plane 6: Universal ethical principle orientation

(ii) **The level that Jack Mineta operated at**

The evidence from the case suggests that Mr Mineta operated at the *preconventional* level. Although he seemed less concerned with punishment, his actions were *strongly driven by the incentives of financial rewards* suggesting a rewards orientation consistent with preconventional thinking. He seemed prepared to *ignore internal control systems* ('I'm in this job for what I can get for myself – big risks bring big returns and big bonuses for me.'). The internal control systems at Global-bank placed clear limits on traders' behaviour in terms of limits and exposure to the highest risk derivative instruments. Mr Mineta was unconcerned about compliance with controls and prevailing rules would have suggested conventional thinking. Had he complied with the internal control constraints, he would not have lost the large amount of money. Nor would he have made the large prior profits but these were manifestly not sustainable. Miss Hubu's comment that he *'didn't believe in right and wrong'* excludes any suggestion that his ignoring of rules was driven by postconventional assumptions.

(iii)   **Stage most appropriate for a professional bank employee**

The most appropriate level of moral development for Mr Mineta in his work is stage 4 within the conventional level (level 2). This level stresses compliance with laws and regulations rather than the 3rd stage which is about compliance with norms to gain social acceptance.

Stage 4 is concerned with legal and regulatory compliance and the moral right is that which is the most compliant with prevailing regulatory systems.

Tutorial note

It is possible to argue for other stages. Credit would be given for this only when robustly defended with evidence. Unsupported assertions would not be rewarded.

(b)   **FIVE typical causes of internal control failure and the performance of Global-bank**

There are several possible causes of internal control failure. The UK Turnbull report (in paragraph 22) gives examples of causes of failure but this list is not exhaustive.

Poor judgement in decision-making. Internal control failures can sometimes arise from individual decisions being made based on inadequate information provision or by inexperienced staff.

Human error can cause failures although a well-designed internal control environment can help control this to a certain extent.

Control processes being *deliberately circumvented* by employees and others. It is very difficult to completely prevent deliberate circumvention, especially if an employee has a particular reason (in his or her opinion) to do so, such as the belief that higher bonuses will be earned.

Management overriding controls, presumably in the belief that the controls put in place are inconvenient or inappropriate and should not apply to them.

The occurrence of *unforeseeable circumstances* is the final cause referred to in the Turnbull Report. Control systems are designed to cope with a given range of variables and when an event happens outside that range, the system may be unable to cope.

Tutorial note

Other equivalent explanations or references to other governance codes would be accepted, if valid. The above points can be expressed in different ways.

In assessing the performance of Global-bank, there is evidence of a widespread failure of internal control systems and a weak internal control environment. It is possible to highlight five specific failures.

- Poor judgement by Mr Mineta as he breached trading rules (exceeding his trading limit and trading in unauthorised instruments).

- Poor judgement and management over-rides by Mr Evora and an inability or unwillingness to enforce trading rules at the Philos office.

- Mr Evora's withholding of compliance information. He seems to view the Philos office as his own personal fiefdom in which head office directives on trading rules and internal controls do not apply.

- Failure of the head office system to insist on full compliance by acting upon failure by Mr Evora to return the required compliance information.

- Mrs Keefer/head office's attitude does not inspire confidence that the incident could not recur. She has failed to enforce controls throughout the company including at its remote offices. Her denial that the board had any responsibility for the loss would only apply if they had ensured that all internal controls had applied throughout the company including at the Philos office. This was not the case.

(c) **Agency relationship in the case**

Any agency relationship involves two parties: a principal and an agent. The agent is accountable to the principal. The relationship arises from the separation of management and ownership in public companies (and in other situations in society).

In the case scenario, the principal is the Shalala Pension Fund. Its purpose is to manage a fund of many different shares and investments with the explicit aim of maximising the fund's value for the benefit of its members' pension values. Accordingly, it is unable and unwilling to take part in directly controlling the organisation itself and indeed, this would be outside the area of expertise of the fund's management. Shalala therefore entrusts the agents – the directors of Global-bank – with the task of acting in its interests and it holds the directors (agents) to account for their performance.

The agent in the scenario is Mrs Keefer and the board of Global-bank. As CEO, Mrs Keefer is entrusted with running the company and ensuring strategies and controls are in place to achieve the objectives set by the principal. She is therefore, accountable to the principal for all of her actions and she has an unambiguous fiduciary duty to act in the sole interests of the principal. Because the principal (in this case the Shalala Pension Fund) invests for maximum capital growth, this should be Mrs Keefer's primary concern. Anything that means that capital growth is less than it otherwise might be is a failure of her agency responsibility (such as failing to enforce internal controls resulting in Mr Mineta's aberrant behaviour).

(d) **Narrow and wide stakeholders**

According to the technical article in Student Accountant in February 2008, 'Narrow stakeholders are those that are *the most affected by the organisation's policies* and will usually include shareholders, management, employees, suppliers, and customers that *are dependent on the organisation's* output. Wider stakeholders are those *less affected* and may typically include government, less-dependent customers, the wider community (as opposed to local communities) and other peripheral groups.'

The three narrow stakeholders identified in the case are investors, employees and the directors.

Investors such as the Shalala Pension Fund have experienced a real reduction in the value of their Global-bank holding and the publicity associated with the loss means that the share price will suffer in the short to medium term. These investors are being asked to re-finance the capital base of Global-bank to make good the losses, via the rights issue. The investors would look for some reassurance that their further investment would not be squandered before committing. If the rights issue goes ahead and Shalala chooses not to increase its investment, Shalala's 12% holding could be diluted, thereby reducing its influence over the company. In the worst case scenario, should the re-financing fail, Shalala would be unlikely to recover much value from its holding if Global-bank was consequently forced into administration.

Employees such as Miss Hubu and Mr Evora are likely to experience some concerns about their job security in the aftermath of the loss with those at the Philos office perhaps being the most likely to be affected. Mr Evora may be the subject of disciplinary action for his repeated failures of internal control compliance.

Directors such as Mrs Keefer are likely to experience a much higher level of investor scrutiny for some time to come and Mrs Keefer herself may not survive in her post. The apparent failure of the Global-bank board in its agency responsibilities is likely to increase the amount of intervention by investors and this will be an inconvenience for the board until such time as investor confidence is fully restored. Benefits such as bonuses may be subject to revisions at general meetings and other directors, seen as complicit in Mr Mineta's losses, may not survive their next retirement by rotation election.

Tutorial note

Some parts of the assessment may be assumed to apply to more than one stakeholder. Individual employees listed as separate stakeholders would attract marks for one stakeholder in total.

(e) **Letter to Mrs Keefer**

Shalala Pension Fund
Spanner Street
Big City
8 June 2009

Global-bank
16 St Thomas's Doubt London
WC2T 8XX

Dear Mrs Keefer,

Internal control issues within Global-bank

I have been asked by the trustees of the Shalala Pension Fund to convey our expectations of you in respect of your roles and responsibilities in internal controls. We very much regret the circumstances that have made this reminder necessary. In line with the COSO recommendations, the trustees of the Shalala Pension Fund expect you to adopt four major responsibilities in respect of overseeing internal controls in Global-bank.

At the outset, the trustees of the Shalala Pension Fund would like to express their disappointment that you should suggest, as you did at the recent EGM, that the loss incurred by Mr Mineta was 'genuinely unforeseeable'. From our reading of the situation, you are highly complicit in the loss through your failure in respect of the company's internal controls.

Ultimately, it is the chief executive of any organisation who *must assume final responsibility for all internal controls*. It is you as CEO who must assume 'ownership' of the systems and this ownership must be a part of the manner in which you lead the company. In particular, this means that you must set the tone from the top in both *establishing and enforcing the control environment*. We understand that a number of *failures to return compliance information* from Philos were not acted upon and this is a clear failure on head office's part to enforce the internal control environment throughout the company. The control environment is enforced through having internal control compliance *embedded within the culture* of the company and it was, in our view, clearly your responsibility to facilitate this. From what we can gather, the *culture in the Philos office was more driven by Mr Evora's personality* than by your imposition of norms from head office and this was clearly one of the causes of Mr Mineta's behaviour.

This setting of the tone should express itself in terms of the way that managers are treated and the way that the *tone is cascaded down through the company* including to individual branch offices such as Philos and other subsidiary companies if relevant. It seems self-evident, in hindsight, that the *Philos office felt they could act in breach of the relevant internal controls with impunity* and this most certainly should not have been allowed. Finally, as major shareholders in Global-bank, the Shalala trustees expect you to *pay particular attention to those areas most vulnerable or open to damaging breaches*. The financial products being traded at Philos clearly fit into this in our view as the *company has demonstrated its vulnerability to losses on derivatives* trading when inadequately controlled.

In addition, I have been asked in particular to draw your attention to the *failure of the company to operate an effective internal audit function*. We understand that the audit committee has been compromised by a shortage of members to the point that its reporting was *criticised by the external auditors*. The Shalala Pension Fund considers the internal audit function to be an imperative part of the governance structure and we are disappointed that *you have seemingly failed to give it the priority it clearly deserves*. We trust that recent events have reinforced this importance to yourself and other members of the Global-bank board.

I would emphasise again the seriousness with which the trustees of the Shalala Pension Fund view your management failures in this unhappy episode and we look forward to hearing your considered responses to the points made.

Yours sincerely,

M. Haber.

On behalf of Shalala Pension Fund.

Tutorial note

Underlined points are the CEO's responsibilities; italicised points are the criticisms of Mrs Keefer. Marks would be awarded to allow for a range of ways of expressing these points.

Marking scheme

				Marks
(a)	(i)	2 marks for each Kohlberg level identified and explained. Half mark for identification only		Up to 6
	(ii)	Half mark for correct identification of Mineta's level. One mark for each relevant justifying point		Up to 4
	(iii)	1 mark for correct identification of stage 4 in conventional level with brief explanation		1
		Half mark for identification of conventional only		
		1 mark for explanation of why it is most appropriate level		1
			Maximum	12
(b)		1 mark for each cause of failure identified and briefly explained (half mark for identification only)		Up to 5
		1 mark for each internal control failure at Global-bank identified and briefly explained (half mark for identification only)		Up to 5
			Maximum	10
(c)		1 mark for evidence of understanding the principal-agency relationship		1
		1 mark for explanation of principal side		Up to 2
		1 mark for explanation of agency side		Up to 2
			Maximum	4
(d)		3 marks for distinguishing between narrow and wide stakeholders		3
		Half mark for each narrow stakeholder identified		Up to 1.5
		2 marks for assessment of the loss and refinancing on each identified narrow stakeholder		Up to 6
			Maximum	10
(e)		1 mark for each CEO role identified and briefly explained		Up to 4
		1 mark for each relevant criticism of Mrs Keefer's performance (linked to case)		Up to 6
			Maximum	10
		Professional marks		
		1 mark for the physical layout of the letter, address and signoff.		
		3 marks for flow, persuasiveness and tone.		
			Maximum	4
Total				**50**

Examiner's comments

Introduction

Question 1, the compulsory 50 mark question on P1, was based on a case about the behaviour of a 'rogue' trader in a bank. The case raised a number of issues concerning the governance of the bank, the relationship with one of its major shareholders (the Shalala pension fund) and the individual ethics of the 'rogue trader', Jack Mineta.

Accordingly, the requirements probed themes in those areas. The requirements began **part (a)** with what should have been a straightforward explanation of the three levels of Kohlberg's theory of moral development. It was when looking at some candidates' answers to this task that I realised one of the issues I highlighted above, namely the notion that some had 'guessed' that Kohlberg wouldn't come up on this paper. Q1(a)(i) should, then, have been 6 relatively straightforward marks for the well-prepared candidate.

In the other two parts of Q1(a), candidates were invited to identify and justify the Kohlberg level at which Mr Mineta operated. The answer, based on evidence from the case, was the preconventional level. Most candidates that got part (i) right also got some marks on part (ii). In part (iii), candidates had to identify the stage or plane most appropriate for a bank employee. This raised two issues.

Firstly, many candidates failed to recognise the difference between a level and a stage or plane. The Kohlberg framework has three levels, each of which is divided into two stages/planes (stages and planes mean the same thing). Second, some candidates, perhaps less well versed in the meanings of Kohlberg's levels, assumed that the highest level (post-conventional) was the best one to say in an exam answer. This missed the point of the question which was to highlight the importance of compliance in organisations (plane 4 or level 2.2).

I was generally more pleased with the answers to **part (b)** on internal control failures. Through a mix of book work and case analysis, many candidates were able to get some marks on pointing out the internal control problems at Global-bank, even if they couldn't remember the five main causes of internal control failure from the study texts.

Part (c) on agency theory was probably the part of question 1 that was the most competently answered overall. Although only worth 4 marks, most answers correctly identified the principals and agents in the case and analysed (this being the verb used in the question) some of the issues raised by the agency relationship.

Part (d) was worth 10 marks and examined stakeholder issues in the case. I wrote an article for Student Accountant on the different ways of categorising stakeholders last year and so was disappointed that so many candidates failed to either know the difference between narrow and wide stakeholders or to identify the narrow stakeholders in the case. The stakeholder debate is an important part of the P1 study guide and so I would encourage candidates and their tutors to ensure that stakeholders are well understood. The case contained three obvious narrow stakeholders (those most affected by the actions of Global-bank) but few candidates failed to identify all three and explain how they are affected by the events in the case.

Part (e) was where candidates could gain the four professional marks. Following on from the agency problem referred to in part (c), candidates were invited to draft a letter from the chairman of the Shalala pension fund trustees to Mrs Keefer, CEO of Global-bank. The letter was to contain two sections, and, of course, it had to be written as a letter.

A common mistake in the letter itself was to misread the question. The first task in the question was not to explain the roles and responsibilities of the CEO, but rather to explain the roles and responsibilities of the CEO in *internal control.* Lists of general roles of the CEO were not well rewarded.

The second part of the task was to criticise Mrs Keefer's performance. The verb 'criticise' also appeared twice in question 3. When candidates see this verb, the task is to show how the performance falls below that which would be expected or that which conforms to best practice. Of course candidates need to know what good or best practice is before they can criticise it which is why sound theoretical knowledge underpins case analysis.

The professional marks were awarded for the structure, content, style and layout of the letter. I was disappointed to see that many candidates struggled to lay out a business letter correctly whilst others could lay out the letter but failed to use the type of language typical of a business letter. I would encourage candidates to read Sarah Condon's article in a recent edition of Student Accountant on P1 professional marks. It explains how to get the professional marks and how these can often make the difference between a pass and a marginal fail.

9 ROWLANDS & MEDELEEV (JUN 08)

Key answer tips

This question has been broken down into many small sections to assist you in structuring your answer. A couple of sections ((a)(i) and (c)) ask for a specific number of points – do not exceed this number, since you will gain no additional marks.

Part (a) commences with some definitions, so it is always useful to ensure you have practiced these in your revision. It goes on to ask you to identify four stakeholders and their claims – ensure that you only refer to external stakeholders.

In drawing the diagram of a risk map in part (b) use a ruler and pencil, labelling the diagram in pen. This will ensure you gain all marks available. The assessment of risks in (c) is highly subjective, so marks will be awarded for any well justified assessment that you make.

In Part (d) it is critical to ensure that your answer is a statement that can be read out. Focus on the audience and insert some opening and closing phrases to assist you in gaining the four professional marks.

Part (e) requires a common sense approach to the difficulties of working with external sub-contractors, and why this enhances the need for sound internal controls. Do not take this as an opportunity to write all you know about sound internal control systems.

(a)   (i)   **Stakeholders**

A stakeholder can be defined as any person or group that can affect or be affected by an entity. In this case, stakeholders are those that can affect or be affected by the building of the Giant Dam Project. Stakeholding is thus bi-directional. Stakeholders can be those (voluntarily or involuntarily) affected by the activities of an organisation or the stakeholder may be seeking to influence the organisation in some way.

All stakeholding is characterised by the making of 'claims' upon an organisation. Put simply, stakeholders 'want something' although in some cases, the 'want' may not be known by the stakeholder (such as future generations). It is the task of management to decide on the strengths of each stakeholder's claim in formulating strategy and in making decisions. In most situations it is likely that some stakeholder claims will be privileged over others.

R&M's external stakeholders include:

The client (the government of the East Asian country)

Stop-the-dam pressure group

First Nation (the indigenous people group)

The banks that will be financing R&M's initial working capital

Shareholders

(ii)   **Stakeholder claims**

Four external stakeholders in the case and their claims are as follows.

The client, i.e. the government of the East Asian country. This stakeholder wants the project completed to budget and on time. It may also be concerned to minimise negative publicity in respect of the construction of the dam and the possible negative environmental consequences.

Stop-the-dam, the vocal and well organised pressure group. This stakeholder wants the project stopped completely, seemingly and slightly paradoxically, for environmental and social footprint reasons.

First Nation, the indigenous people group currently resident on the land behind the dam that would be flooded after its construction. This stakeholder also wants the project stopped so they can continue to live on and farm the land.

The banks (identified as a single group). These seem happy to lend to the project and will want it to proceed so they make a return on their loans commensurate with the risk of the loan. They do not want to be publicly identified as being associated with the Giant Dam Project.

Shareholders. The shareholders have the right to have their investment in the company managed in such a way as to maximise the value of their shareholding. The shareholders seek projects providing positive NPVs within the normal constraints of sound risk management.

Tutorial note

Only four stakeholders need to be identified. Marks will be given for up to four relevant stakeholders only.

(b) **Framework for assessing risk**

Risk is assessed by considering each identified risk in terms of two variables:

its hazard (or consequences or impact) and,

its probability of happening (or being realised or 'crystallising').

The most material risks are those identified as having high impact/hazard and the highest probability of happening. Risks with low hazard and low probability will have low priority whilst between these two extremes are situations where judgement is required on how to manage the risk.

In practice, it is difficult to measure both variables with any degree of certainty and so if is often sufficient to consider each in terms of relative crude metrics such as 'high/medium/low' or even 'high/low'. The framework can be represented as a 'map' of two intersecting continuums with each variable being plotted along a continuum.

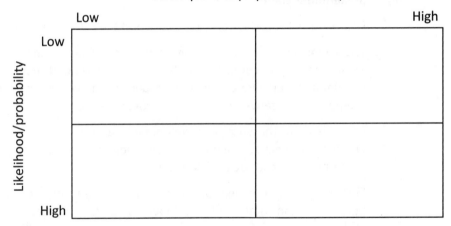

Tutorial note

Other relevant risk assessment frameworks are valid.

(c)   **Assessment of three risks**

Disruption and resistance by Stop-the-dam. Stop-the-dam seems very determined to delay and disrupt progress as much as possible. The impact of its activity can be seen on two levels. It is likely that the tunnelling and other 'human' disruption will cause a short-term delay but the more significant impact is that of exposing the lenders. In terms of probability, the case says that it 'would definitely be attempting to resist the Giant Dam Project when it started' but the probability of exposing the lenders is a much lower probability event if the syndicate membership is not disclosed.

Impact/hazard: low

Probability/likelihood: high

The *risk to progress offered by First Nation* can probably be considered to be low impact/hazard but high probability. The case says that it 'would be unlikely to disrupt the building of the dam', meaning low impact/hazard, but that 'it was highly likely that they would protest', meaning a high level of probability that the risk event would occur.

Impact: low

Probability: high

There are *financing risks* as banks seem to be hesitant when it comes to lending to R&M for the project. Such a risk event, if realised, would have a high potential for disruption to progress as it may leave R&M with working capital financing difficulties. The impact would be high because the bank may refuse to grant or extend loans if exposed (subject to existing contractual terms). It is difficult to estimate the probability. Perhaps there will be a range of attitudes by the lending banks with some more reticent than others (perhaps making it a 'medium' probability event).

Impact: medium to high (depending on the reaction of the bank)

Probability: low to medium (depending on how easy it would be to discover the lender)

(d)   **Chairman's statement at AGM**

Thank you for coming to the annual general meeting of Rowlands & Medeleev. I would like to make a statement in response to the concerns that a number of our investors have made in respect to our appointment as the principal contractor for the prestigious and internationally important Giant Dam Project. We are very pleased and honoured to have won the contract but as several have observed, this does leave us in a position of having a number of issues and risks to manage.

As a project with obvious environmental implications, the board and I wish to reassure investors that we are aware of these implications and have taken them into account in our overall assessment of risks associated with the project.

(i)   **A definition of 'sustainable development'**

One investor asked if we could explain the sustainability issues and I begin with addressing that issue. According to the well-established Brundtland definition, sustainable development is development that meets the needs of the present without compromising the ability of future generations to meet their own needs.

This definition has implications for energy, land use, natural resources and waste emissions. In a sustainable development, all of these should be consumed or produced at the same rate they can be renewed or absorbed so as to prevent leaving future generations with an unwanted legacy of today's economic activity. We believe that our involvement in the Giant Dam Project has implications for environmental sustainability and it is to these matters that I now turn.

Tutorial note

Other relevant definitions of sustainability will be equally acceptable.

(ii)   **Environmental and sustainability implications of the Giant Dam Project**

In our preparation for the bid to act as principal contractor for the Giant Dam Project, we established that there were two prominent negative implications of the project but these are, in our view, more than offset by two major environmental positives.

The environmental arguments against the Giant Dam Project both concern the flooding of the valley behind the dam. Regrettably, it seems that there will be some loss of important habitats. This, in turn, may mean the removal of balanced environmental conditions for certain animal and plant species. In addition, the flooding of the valley will result in the loss of productive farmland. This will mean reduced capacity for the host country to grow food and thus support citizens such as the members of First Nation. From our point of view, as the board of R&M, however, we would remind shareholders and other observers that the decisions involving the size and positioning of the Giant Dam were taken by the client, the government. It is R&M's job, having won the contract as principal contractor, to now carry out the plans, regardless of our own views.

Happily, however, there are two very powerful environmental arguments in favour of the Giant Dam Project. It will create a large source of clean energy for economic development that will be sustainable, as it will create no carbon emissions nor will it consume any non-renewable resources as it does so (compared to, for example, fossil fuels).

At a time when people are becoming very concerned about greenhouse gases produced from conventional power generation, the Giant Dam Project will contribute to the East Asian country's internationally agreed carbon reduction targets. This, in turn, will contribute to the reduction of greenhouse gases in the environment.

It is clear that the construction of the Giant Dam Project is an environmental conundrum with strong arguments on both sides. The deciding factor may be the opinion that we each have of the desirability of economic growth in the East Asian country (which the energy from the dam is intended to support). It seems that Stop-the-dam values the preservation of the original environment more than the economic growth that the energy from the dam would support. The client does not agree with this assessment and we are happy to be involved with a project that will create such a useful source of renewable and non-polluting energy.

(iii) **Importance of confidentiality in the financing of the project and the normal duty of transparency.**

I have been asked to include a statement in my remarks on the balance between our duty to be transparent whenever possible and the need for discretion and confidentiality in some situations. In the case of our initial working capital needs for the Giant Dam Project, the importance of confidentiality in financing is due to the potential for adverse publicity that may arise for the lender. It is important that R&M have the project adequately financed, especially in the early stages before the interim payments from the client become fully effective.

In general, of course, we at R&M attempt to observe the highest standards of corporate governance and this involves adopting a default position of transparency rather than concealment wherever possible. We recognise that transparency is important to underpin investor confidence and to provide investors with the information they need to make fund allocation decisions.

Whilst it is normal to disclose the amount of debt we carry at any given point (on the statement of financial position), it is rarely normal practice to disclose the exact sources of those loans. In the case of the financing of initial working capital for the Giant Dam Project, I'm sure you will realise that in this unique situation, disclosure of the lender's identity could threaten the progress of the project. For this reason we must resist any attempts to release this into the public domain. We are aware of one pressure group that is actively seeking to discover this information in order to disrupt the project's progress and we shall be taking all internal measures necessary to ensure they do not obtain the information.

Thank you for listening.

(e) **Control and sub-contractors**

Specifically in regard to the maintenance of internal controls when working with sub-contractors, the prominent difficulties are likely to be in the following areas:

- Configuring and co-ordinating the many activities of sub-contractors so as to keep progress on track. This may involve taking the different cultures of sub-contractor organisations into account.

- Loss of direct control over activities as tasks are performed by people outside R&M's direct employment and hence its management structure.

- Monitoring the quality of work produced by the sub-contractors. Monitoring costs will be incurred and any quality problems will be potentially costly.

- Budget 'creep' and cost control. Keeping control of budgets can be a problem in any large civil engineering project (such the construction of the new Wembley Stadium in the UK) and problems are likely to be made worse when the principal contractor does not have direct control over all activities.

- Time limit over-runs. Many projects (again, such as the new Wembley Stadium, but others also) over-run significantly on time.

Tutorial note

Only four difficulties need to be described.

		Marking scheme		*Marks*
(a)	(i)	1 mark for each relevant point made on definition of stakeholder		Up to 2
		1 mark for each relevant point made on definition of stakeholder claim		Up to 2
		0.5 marks for each stakeholder correctly identified		Up to 2
	(ii)	1 mark for a brief description of each claim		Up to 4
			Maximum	10
(b)		1 mark each for recognition of impact and probability as the two variables (alternative terms may be used to mean the same thing)		Up to 2
		1 mark each for explanation of each variable in context		Up to 2
		2 marks for a correct diagram (axis labelling may vary)		2
			Maximum	6
(c)		1 mark for identification of each risk		Up to 3
		2 marks for assessment of each risk (1 for impact, 1 for probability)		Up to 6
			Maximum	9
(d)	(i)	1 mark for each relevant point made		Up to 3
	(ii)	1 mark for each environmental impact identified up to a maximum of 4 (2 positive, 2 negative factors)		
		1 mark for description of each up to a maximum of 4		
			Maximum	8
	(iii)	1 mark for each relevant point on the 'normal duty of transparency' up to a maximum of 3		
		1 mark for each relevant point on the importance of confidentiality in the case up to a maximum of 4		
			Maximum	6
		Professional marks for layout, logical flow and persuasiveness of the answer (i.e. the professionalism of the statement)		4
			Maximum	21
(e)		1 mark for each difficulty briefly identified and explained (half mark for mention only)		4
			Maximum	4
Total				**50**

Examiner's comments

Introduction

The rubric for the P1 paper was the same as for the pilot paper and for the December 07 paper. Section A thus contained a case study of about a page followed a number of requirements that sampled the syllabus so as to draw content from several areas of the study guide. The case study described a large civil engineering project ('the Giant Dam Project') that had a large environmental impact and also finance issues associated with the fact that some banks wanted to remain confidential as lenders. The case was designed to underpin several questions from across the P1 study guide.

Part (a) was about the stakeholders in R&M, the principal contractor building the Giant Dam. Part (a)(i) required candidates to define the terms 'stakeholder' and 'stakeholder claim' and then to identify four external stakeholders in R&M. Most candidates performed well on this although there was some confusion over internal and external (R&M's employees are not 'external' stakeholders). Part (a)(ii) was a little more ambitious as candidates were required to analyse the case to establish what each of the four identified stakeholders' claims were on R&M. What this meant was what each of the stakeholders wanted R&M to do in respect of the project. Candidates who performed well on this were able to point to what each stakeholder's objectives were for the project. This meant, for example, that First Nation's claim was not that hydroelectric power represented 'misery and cruelty' but that they wanted to project to be discontinued.

Part (b) asked candidates to describe a framework to assess risks and to include a diagram as part of the answer. The correct answer was, of course, the intersecting continua of probability and impact. Markers allowed for a latitude of ways of expressing these variables, allowing, for example for terms such as 'likelihood' and 'hazard', both of which are completely correct terms. Some candidates incorrectly thought that this question might be referring to the Mendelow framework. The Mendelow map is a way of understanding the sources of influence of various stakeholders, not necessarily of risk assessment, although understanding the extent of influence and power of particular stakeholders may in some circumstances have some use in mitigating or avoiding some potential risks.

Part (c) invited candidates to use the risk assessment framework they had just described to actually assess three risks. The question specifically asked candidates to use 'information from the case' and to assess 'three risks to the Giant Dam Project'. Some candidates failed to address the specific risks in the case and described risks in more general terms, perhaps describing risks such as 'exchange rate risk', 'environmental risk' and 'reputation risk', which were not necessarily related to the case. The case contained three specific risks to the project with enough information to make an assessment of each. In order to gain maximum marks, therefore, candidates had to identify those three specific risks and, using information from the case, describe each one's impact and probability. Any other risks the candidates mentioned in their answers could not be assessed as there was no information in the case to do so.

It was thus crucial to adequately analyse the case. If a requirement asks candidates specifically to use information from the case as this one did, then they will not be awarded the best marks unless they do what the question requires.

Part (d) was a multi-part question containing professional marks for the drafting of a statement for Mr Markivnikoff to read out at the annual general meeting. All P1 papers will contain between 4 and 6 professional marks and candidates are well-advised to note that these can make the difference between a marginal fail and a pass. The time budget for 4 marks in a three hour paper is about 7 minutes and some of this time should have been spent on planning how to draft answers in line with the requirements of the question. In December 2007, professional marks were awarded for the drafting of a letter and in this paper, they were for the drafting of a formal statement.

If a senior company director were to address shareholders in a formal meeting, how would it sound? It would begin with a formal introduction, provide an overview of what he was going to cover and, as he spoke, the sections would be connected with narrative designed to make the speech sound convincing, logical and persuasive. It would, obviously, not contain bullet points (how would they be delivered in a speech?).

The actual content of Mr Markovnikoff's statement should have contained three elements, as set out in the three requirements of Q1(d). The majority of candidates were able to define and briefly explain what 'sustainable development' is although (incorrectly) some seemed to think that 'sustainability' referred to the continuance of R&M as a going concern!

Part (d) (ii) required an evaluation of the environmental and sustainability implication of the project. In one sense, the whole point of using a big civil engineering project as the basis for Q1 in this paper was to probe the environmental implication of such a project. In an evaluation, candidates are required to present both sides of the argument – explaining the environmental negatives and also the positives. Importantly, this question was about environmental and sustainability implications and therefore was not concerned with 'social' matters such as neither the fate of First Nation nor the unfortunate fate of the important archaeological sites.

Part (d) (iii), for 6 marks, invited candidates to wrestle with one of the conundrums raised by the situation of R&M in the case. Again, this involved applying prior learning to the case. It concerned two seemingly conflicting themes with relevance to the case: the duty of transparency and the importance of confidentiality in respect of the lenders.

In **part (e)**, for 4 marks, candidates were invited to bring in prior learning on internal controls and to apply this to a particular situation when a sub-contractor carries out activities over which R&M would not have direct control. Whereas R&M could manage its own internal controls directly, sub-contractors may compromise the project's progress through having inadequate internal controls. Many candidates correctly picked up on issues such as the sub-contractors having different corporate cultures, structures and control regimes to R&M whilst others struggled to make any coherent points.

10 CHEMCO (PILOT 07)

Key answer tips

This requirement shows just how broad a range of syllabus your examiner can cover in a 50 mark question. It ranges from Corporate Governance to risk to environmental issues.

(a)   Ensure you explain why the governance arrangements of JPX are inadequate to the Chemco board and not just list the inadequacies of the arrangement.

(b)   There are two parts to this requirement: (1) Identify risks – try to find approx. 5 distinct risks. (2) Explain how risk can be assessed. Make sure you clearly answer both parts.

(c)   The requirement asks you to construct a case: this means you need to argue for a change to unitary; only positive points for change will receive credit – your examiner is looking for a persuasive argument in order to award the two professional marks available here.

(d)   This is firstly straight forward book work marks for the four roles of NEDs. Then it is necessary to apply to the scenario and answer the question 'what difference would NEDs make here to JPX'.

(e)   There are two marks here for correct format, so ensure you are aware of a standard Memo format and also that a memo to Leena would be an internal document. Finally, when writing the memo, make clear that the 'environmental footprint' of JPX is large.

(a)   **JPX's current corporate governance arrangements**

Inadequacy of JPX's current corporate governance arrangements

The case highlights a number of ways in which the corporate governance at JPX is inadequate. JPX's history as a privately run family business may partly explain its apparent slowness to develop the corporate governance structures and systems expected in many parts of the world. There are five ways, from the case, that JPX can be said to be inadequate in its corporate governance although these are linked. There is overlap between the points made.

In the first instance, the case mentions that there were no non-executive directors (NEDs) on the JPX board. It follows that JPX would be without the necessary balance and external expertise that NEDs can provide. Second, there is evidence of a corporate culture at JPX dominated by the members of the family. The case study notes that they dominate the upper tier of the board. This may have been acceptable when JPX was a family owned company, but as a public company floated on a stock exchange and hence accountable to external shareholders, a wider participation in board membership is necessary. Third, the two-tier board, whilst not necessarily being a problem in itself (two-tier boards work well in many circumstances), raises concern because the department heads, who are on the lower tier of the board, are excluded from strategic discussions at board level. It is likely that as line managers in the business, the departmental heads would have vital inputs to make into such discussions, especially on such issues as the implementation of strategies. It is also likely that their opinions on the viabilities of different strategic options would be of value. Fourth, it could be argued that JPX's reporting is less than ideal with, for example, its oblique reference to a 'negative local environmental impact'. However, it might be noted that ambiguity in reporting is also evident in European and American reporting. Finally, having been subject to its own country's less rigorous corporate governance requirements for all of its previous history, it is likely that adjusting to the requirements of complying with the European-centred demands of Chemco will present a challenge.

(b)   **Risks of the proposed acquisition**

Risks that Chemco might incur in acquiring JPX

The case describes a number of risks that Chemco could become exposed to if the acquisition was successful. Explicitly, the case highlights a possible environmental risk (the 'negative local environmental impact') that may or may not be eventually valued as a provision (depending on whether or not it is likely to result in a liability). Other risks are likely to emerge as the proposed acquisition develops. Exchange rate risks apply to any business dealing with revenue or capital flows between two or more currency zones. The case explicitly describes Chemco and JPX existing in different regions of the world. Whilst exchange rate volatility can undermine confidence in cash flow projections, it should also be borne in mind that medium term increases or decreases in exchange values can materially affect the returns on an investment (in this case, Chemco's investment in JPX). There is some market risk in Chemco's valuation of JPX stock. This could be a substantial risk because of JPX's relatively recent flotation where the market price of JPX may not have yet found its intrinsic level. In addition, it is not certain that Chemco has full knowledge of the fair price to pay for each JPX share given the issues of dealing across national borders and in valuing stock in JPX's country. All mergers and acquisitions ('integrations') are exposed to synergy risks. Whilst it is expected and hoped that every merger or acquisition will result in synergies (perhaps from scale economies as the case mentions), in practice, many integrations fail to realise any. In extreme cases, the costs arising from integration can threaten the very survival of the companies involved. Finally, there are risks associated with the bringing-together of the two board structures. Specifically, structural and cultural changes will be required at JPX to bring it in line with Chemco's. The creation of a unitary board and the increased involvement of NEDs and departmental heads may be problematic, for example, Chemco's board is likely to insist on such changes post-acquisition.

Assessment of risk

The assessment of the risk exposure of any organisation has five components. Firstly, the identity (nature and extent) of the risks facing the company should be identified (such as considering the risks involved in acquiring JPX). This may involve consulting with relevant senior managers, consultants and other stakeholders. Second, the company should decide on the categories of risk that are regarded as acceptable for the company to bear. Of course any decision to discontinue exposure to a given risk will have implications for the activities of the company and this cost will need to be considered against the benefit of the reduced risk. Third, the assessment of risk should quantify, as far as possible, the likelihood (probability) of the identified risks materialising. Risks with a high probability of occurring will attract higher levels of management attention than those with lower probabilities. Fourth, an assessment of risk will entail an examination of the company's ability to reduce the impact on the business of risks that do materialise. Consultation with affected parties (e.g. departmental heads, stakeholders, etc.) is likely to be beneficial, as information on minimising negative impact may sometimes be a matter of technical detail. Fifth and finally, risk assessment involves an understanding of the costs of operating particular controls to review and manage the related risks. These costs will include information gathering costs, management overhead, external consultancy where appropriate, etc.

Tutorial note

When discussing risk assessment, link to the language of a 'Risk Map' i.e. likelihood and probability. In the June 2008 Rowland exam paper question, your examiner asks you to draw a diagram to assess risk – it is the 'Risk map'.

(c) **Unitary and two-tier board structures**

Advantages of unitary board structure in general

There are arguments for and against unitary and two-tier boards. Both have their 'place' depending on business cultures, size of business and a range of other factors. In general, however, the following arguments can be put for unitary boards.

One of the main features of a unitary board is that all directors, including managing directors, departmental (or divisional) directors and NEDs all have equal legal and executive status in law. This does not mean that all are equal in terms of the organisational hierarchy, but that all are responsible and can be held accountable for board decisions. This has a number of benefits. Firstly, NEDs are empowered, being accorded equal status to executive directors. NEDs can bring not only independent scrutiny to the board, but also experience and expertise that may be of invaluable help in devising strategy and the assessment of risk. Second, board accountability is enhanced by providing a greater protection against fraud and malpractice and by holding all directors equally accountable under a 'cabinet government' arrangement. These first two benefits provide a major underpinning to the confidence that markets have in listed companies. Third, unitary board arrangements reduce the likelihood of abuse of (self-serving) power by a small number of senior directors. Small 'exclusivist' boards such as have been evident in some corporate 'scandals' are discouraged by unitary board arrangements. Fourth, the fact that the board is likely to be larger than a given tier of a two-tier board means that more viewpoints are likely to be expressed in board deliberations and discussions. In addition to enriching the intellectual strength of the board, the inclusivity of the board should mean that strategies are more robustly scrutinised before being implemented.

Relevance to JPX in particular

If the JPX acquisition was to proceed, there would be a unitary board at Chemco overseeing a two-tier board at JPX. The first specific argument for JPX adopting a unitary board would be to bring it into line with Chemco's. Chemco clearly believes in unitary board arrangements and would presumably prefer to have the benefits of unitary boards in place so as to have as much confidence as possible in JPX's governance. This may be especially important if JPX is to remain an 'arms length' or decentralised part of Chemco's international operation. Second, there is an argument for making changes at JPX in order to signal a departure from the 'old' systems when

JPX was independent of the 'new' systems under Chemco's ownership. A strong way of helping to 'unfreeze' previous ways of working is to make important symbolic changes and a rearrangement of the board structure would be a good example of this. Third, it is clear that the family members who currently run JPX have a disproportionate influence on the company and its strategy (the 'family business culture'). Widening the board would, over time, change the culture of the board and reduce that influence. Fourth, a unitary board structure would empower the departmental heads at JPX whose opinions and support are likely to be important in the transition period following the acquisition.

(d) **Non executive directors**

Tutorial note

The four roles of a non-executive director were asked by your examiner in the December 2007 50-mark question, 'Worldwide Minerals'.

Four roles of non-executive directors

The Higgs Report (2003) in the United Kingdom helpfully described the function of non-executive directors (NEDs) in terms of four distinct roles. These were the strategy role, the scrutinising role, the risk advising role and the 'people' role. These roles may be undertaken as part of the general discussion occurring at board meetings or more formally, through the corporate governance committee structure.

The strategy role recognises that NEDs are full members of a unitary board and thus have the right and responsibility to contribute to the strategic success of the organisation for the benefit of shareholders. In this role they may challenge any aspect of strategy they see fit, and offer advice or input to help to develop successful strategy.

In the scrutinising role, NEDs are required to hold executive colleagues to account for decisions taken and results obtained. In this respect they are required to represent the shareholders' interests against the possibility that agency issues arise to reduce shareholder value.

The risk role involves NEDs ensuring the company has an adequate system of internal controls and systems of risk management in place. This is often informed by prescribed codes (such as Turnbull) but some industries, such as chemicals, have other systems in place, some of which fall under International Organisation for Standardisation (ISO) standards.

Finally, the 'people' role involves NEDs overseeing a range of responsibilities with regard to the management of the executive members of the board. This typically involves issues on appointments and remuneration, but might also involve contractual or disciplinary issues.

Specific benefits for JPX of having NEDs

The specific benefits that NEDs could bring to JPX concern the need for a balance against excessive family influence and the prior domination of the 'family business culture'. Chemco, as JPX's new majority shareholder, is unlikely to want to retain a 'cabal' of an upper tier at JPX and the recruitment of a number of NEDs will clearly help in that regard. Second, NEDs will perform an important role in representing external shareholders' interests (as well as internal shareholders). Specifically, shareholders will include Chemco. Third, Chemco's own board discussion included Bill White's view that the exclusion of departmental heads was resulting in important views not being heard when devising strategy. This is a major potential danger to JPX and NEDs could be appointed to the board in order to ensure that future board discussions include all affected parties including the previously disenfranchised department heads.

(e)   **Environmental reporting**

Memorandum

From: Professional Accountant

To: Leena Sharif

Date: DD/MM/YYYY

Subject: Environmental issues at Chemco and JPX

(1)   **Introduction**

I have been asked to write to you on two matters of potential importance to Chemco in respect of environmental issues. The first of these is to consider the meaning of the term, 'environmental footprint' and the second is to briefly review the arguments for inviting JPX (should the acquisition proceed) to introduce environmental reporting.

(2)   **'Environmental footprint'**

Explanation of 'environmental footprint'

The use of the term 'footprint' with regard to the environment is intended to convey a meaning similar to its use in everyday language. In the same way that humans and animals leave physical footprints that show where they have been, so organisations such as Chemco leave evidence of their operations in the environment. They operate at a net cost to the environment. The environmental footprint is an attempt to evaluate the size of Chemco's impact on the environment in three respects. Firstly, concerning the company's resource consumption where resources are defined in terms of inputs such as energy, feedstock, water, land use, etc. Second, concerning any harm to the environment brought about by pollution emissions. These include emissions of carbon and other chemicals, local emissions, spillages, etc. It is likely that as a chemical manufacturer, both of these impacts will be larger for Chemco than for some other types of business. Thirdly, the environmental footprint includes a measurement of the resource consumption and pollution emissions in terms of harm to the environment in either qualitative, quantitative or replacement terms.

(3)   **Environmental reporting at JPX**

Arguments for environmental reporting at JPX

There are number of arguments for environmental reporting in general and others that may be specifically relevant to JPX. In general terms and firstly, I'm sure as company secretary you will recognise the importance of observing the corporate governance and reporting principles of transparency, openness, responsibility and fairness wherever possible. We should invite JPX to adopt these values should the acquisition proceed. Any deliberate concealment would clearly be counter to these principles and so 'more' rather than 'less' reporting is always beneficial. Second, it is important to present a balanced and understandable assessment of the company's position and prospects to external stakeholders. Third, it is important that JPX recognises the existence and size of its environmental footprint, and reporting is a useful means if doing this. Fourth, and specifically with regard to JPX and other companies with a substantial potential environmental footprint, there is a need to explain environmental strategy to investors and other interested stakeholders (e.g. Chemco). Finally, there is a need to explain in more detail the 'negative local environmental impact' and an environmental report would be an ideal place for such an explanation.

Summary:

As JPX's 'environmental footprint' is potentially quite large, it is important that Chemco ensures as far as possible, that any such footprint left by JPX is known and measured. Additionally, in the interests of transparency, openness, responsibility and fairness, it is important that it is also fully reported upon for the information of both investors and other interested stakeholders.

	Marking scheme		Marks
(a)	Up to two marks per valid point made on the inadequacy of JPX's governance		*Up to 10*
		Maximum	10
(b)	One mark for identifying and describing each risk to Chemco in the JPX acquisition		Up to 6
	Up to one mark per relevant point on assessing each risk and a further one mark for development of relevant points		Up to 10
		Maximum	15
(c)	One mark for each relevant point made.		
	(i) Explanation of the advantages of unitary boards		Up to 4
	(ii) Case concerning the advantages of a unitary board at JPX		Up to 5
	(iii) Clarity and persuasiveness of the argument for change in the JPX board		Up to 2
		Maximum	10
(d)	One mark for each explanation of the four roles of non-executive directors.		Up to 4
	One mark for each specific benefit of NEDs to JPX		Up to 4
		Maximum	7
(e)	Memo to Leena Sharif explaining environmental footprint – one mark for each relevant point made		Up to 2
	Explain importance of environmental reporting – one mark for each relevant point made		Up to 4
	Up to two marks for the form of the answer (memo in which content is laid out in an orderly and informative manner).		2
		Maximum	8
Total			50

11   MARY JANE (DEC 09)

Key answer tips

This question covers ethical decision making, internal controls, governance and also includes syllabus areas such as characteristics of information, an area never previously examined!

(a)   A nice clear approach to this requirement was necessary. Each step needed to be fully explored, maximum 3 marks for each. Only ½ a mark for knowing the step. So book work only would not be enough.

(b)   This is an application-based requirement: each failure identified needs to be analysed to ensure 2 marks per point raised.

(c)   This requirement is reminiscent of the pilot paper Chemco requirement – part d. Again each point needs to be applied – but the four roles of non-executive directors i.e. Strategy, Scrutiny, People and Risk is a good starting point.

(d)   (i)   Important here to stress just how severe the situation is, how appalling the loss of life and how the very a survival of the company is threatened.

(ii)   A nice mnemonic to use here is ACCURATE – Accurate, Complete, Cost-Beneficial, User focused, Relevant, Authoritative, Timely and Easy to use. ½ a mark for identifying characteristics and 1½ for applying to the case.

(a)   **Seven-Step (AAA) Model**

Step 1: What are the facts of the case?

The facts are that the Mary Jane, one of the company's ships, has sunk and that one contributory cause of the disaster was that the ship had not received the necessary modifications for operating in the rougher seas between Eastport and Northport. Had the recommended structural changes been made, the Mary Jane would not have sunk.

Step 2: What are the ethical issues in the case?

The ethical issues are whether to disclose the information publicly, thereby providing bereaved families with a better explanation of why their loved ones died (and potentially opening the company up to greater liability), or to conceal the information, thereby limiting the value of any punitive damages and protecting shareholder value, at least in the short term.

Step 3: What are the norms, principles and values relevant to the case?

The company is bound by the norms and expectations of its stock exchange and it has voluntarily claimed to have 'the highest standards of corporate ethics', particularly valuing its reputation for 'outstanding customer care'. This means that it owes an implicit and explicit duty of care to both its customers and its shareholders. As a company that seemingly values its reputation as a well-governed organisation, it is also bound by the underlying principles of corporate governance that include integrity, probity and transparency. Health and safety issues are also very important in all shipping operations and Sea Ships should ensure that all of its ferries are compliant with the highest health and safety standards.

Step 4: What are the alternative courses of action?

Alternative 1 is to disclose the information about the advice on structural work to the Mary Jane to the media, the government and the bereaved families. Alternative 2 is to seek to suppress the information within the company and hope that there is no leak.

Step 5: What course of action is most consistent with the norms, values and principles identified in step 3?

The information is material to a number of parties' better understanding of why the Mary Jane sank. The bereaved families, maritime accident investigators, the government, the ship's insurers and other shipping companies would all benefit from having the information. Disclosure would seem to be the most appropriate course of action notwithstanding the potentially unfortunate consequences for Sea Ships Company of this information leaking out. However, disclosure may result in greater penalties which will be harmful to shareholder value.

Step 6: What are the consequences of each possible course of action?

If the company makes the disclosure, there is a risk that the punitive damages (not yet agreed by the court) would be higher. The case says that 'the size of [the punitive damages] would ... reflect the scale of Sea Ships' negligence in contributing to the disaster'. A large enough fine would threaten future cash flows and hence future shareholder value. It would also threaten employees' jobs and the ability of the company to continue to provide the existing level of service to customers. Disclosure would potentially invalidate any insurance policy they had to deal with such a disaster, further harming shareholder value.

If the company were to suppress the information, then each person in possession of the knowledge would not only have to examine his or her own responsibilities in the matter but each would also have potentially damaging information if they were to leave Sea Ships or become disillusioned with it. The consultant who recommended the upgrade will also be a potentially major risk in the leaking of the information.

Step 7: What is the decision?

Alternative 1 is that the company should make a full and detailed disclosure, probably with an acceptance of full responsibility for the failure to make the necessary amendments to the ship. This would be a very costly choice but would be consistent with the company's claimed ethical values and also with the important core values of corporate governance (integrity, transparency, etc).

Alternative 2 is to suppress the information and take all necessary measures to ensure that it is not revealed. This would be a very risky option as the cost to the company and to the directors personally, if the information was ever to emerge, would be very serious. It would also be against the letter and spirit of the core values of corporate governance. It would be unlikely to protect shareholder value in the longer term, is the least ethical of the options and so should be avoided.

Tutorial note

It is possible to argue for suppression of the report in the short term protection of shareholder value. Allow some marks for logic of reasoning process if coherently argued but alignment with the stated values of the company does not allow for suppression as a final decision.

(b) **Identify and analyse the internal control failures at Sea Ships Company and on the Mary Jane**

The case describes internal control failures both on the Mary Jane herself and also at Sea Ships' head office.

The company *ignored important advice about necessary structural changes needed to the Mary Jane* to make her seaworthy for the Northport route. If there was an internal procedure for processing advice, presumably as a part of an economic evaluation of transferring the Mary Jane to the Northport route, then it was clearly ineffective. The document identified a major risk, but had been suppressed within the company and not brought to the attention of any party who could have authorised this to go ahead.

At head office, an *'oversight in the company's legal department' resulted in the full value of the Mary Jane's liabilities not being insured*. Presumably a human error, this created uninsured liabilities for Sea Ships after the Mary Jane sank. All insurance policies should be reviewed annually and major changes in cover or changes of terms be recommended to the board so that issues like this do not arise. All insurance policies should be reviewed annually and major changes in cover or changes of terms be recommended to the board so that issues like this do not arise.

On the Mary Jane herself, lax internal controls produced four internal control problems. There should be a 'safety first' culture on board all ships in which safety considerations outweigh all commercial issues such as meeting schedules.

First, *a system put in place to ensure that each department head signalled readiness for sea departure was abandoned*. This is an example of a 'reporting by exception' system being wrongly assumed to be appropriate. Internal control reporting systems are there because they are important and the fact that they may be inconvenient should not be a reason for abandoning them.

Second, there was a *'mistake' in loading vehicles onto the car deck*. A sound internal control system would have ensured that such a mistake could not have happened, possibly using physical 'fit' issues of loading ramps, appropriate signage, staff training, or similar mechanisms to ensure compliance. The result of the 'mistake' was that it created time pressure to leave the port and this contributed to the oversight of the rear doors not being secured and, possibly, the excess speed after leaving port.

The third internal control problem on the Mary Jane was the *confusion over responsibility for ensuring that the rear doors were closed* – a key safety procedure for any ferry. It is baffling that two people were, seemingly simultaneously, responsible for this and is a problem created by the poor design of internal reporting systems. According to the case, both had assumed that the other person was checking the doors.

The fourth problem was that the Mary Jane was *going too fast* and exceeding the maritime rules about speed in that section of sea. This created swell and caused turbulence at the back of the ship. This, in turn, caused water to enter the ship that wouldn't have been the case at lower speed. This was a failure to observe regulatory speed restrictions on the part of senior ship officers.

(c) **Contribution that NEDs might make**

The board of Sea Ships appears to be in need of help on a number of issues, some of which may be addressed by the use of non-executive directors.

Mrs Chan's conclusions noted that the board *lacked independent scrutiny*. One of the most important purposes of any non-executive appointment is to bring an outside perspective (sometimes acting as a 'corporate conscience') on what can at times be an insular executive culture. In the case of Sea Ships, *a number of important internal control issues went unchallenged* and a strong non-executive presence could have helped that.

Also mentioned by Mrs Chan was the fact that the board *lacked nautical and technical expertise*. This is a disturbing finding as some detailed knowledge of a company's products or operations is very important in guiding discussions about those parts of the business. *The non-executive appointment of serving or retired senior ferry operating personnel from other companies would rectify this* and bring the requisite level of expertise.

The Corporate Governance Code in the UK (based on the Smith Report) and other statutory and advisory codes of corporate governance, specify that every listed company should have an audit committee made up entirely of non-executive directors. The functions of the committee, according to the UK's Corporate Governance Code, include reviewing *'the company's internal control and risk management systems'* and monitoring and reviewing *'the effectiveness of the company's internal audit function'. Both of these are deficient at Sea Ships* and so an effective audit committee would be a major contribution. We are not told if the company currently has one but we can assume that if it has, it is ineffective.

There are *legal compliance issues at Sea Ships*, including a failure to enforce the observation of maritime speed limits among its senior ships' officers. One of the advantages of any independent non-executive presence is the enforcement of regulatory and legal rules on company boards with the knowledge that all directors, including *non-executives, can be held legally accountable for non-compliance*.

(d) **Memo**

(i) **Importance of information on operational internal controls and risks**

From: Wim Bock (CEO)

To: All Sea Ships senior officers

Date: 14 December 2009

Re: information on internal control and risks following the loss of the Mary Jane

Colleagues,

I know you all share with me and the other directors our heartfelt sorrow at the sinking of the Mary Jane with so many lives being lost. Our deepest sympathies go out to the families and friends of all those involved. In the light of the tragic loss, the board felt it vital to write to you all at this time to remind you all of a number of crucial aspects of internal control and risk.

First, I wanted to make clear to you all why the flow of information upwards to the board on matters of internal control and risk is so important. We feel that one contributory factor in the loss of the Mary Jane was a lack of information flow on relevant issues hence my writing to you about this at this time.

In the first instance, the information provided enables the board to *monitor the performance* of the company on the crucial issues in question. This includes compliance, performance against targets and the effectiveness of existing controls. We, the board, need to know, for example, if there are issues with internal controls on board our ships, in ports or in any other area of ships' operations. By being made aware of the key risks and internal control issues at the operational level, we can work with you to address them in the most appropriate way.

We also need to be aware of the business impact of operational controls and risks to enable us at board level to *make informed business decisions* at the strategic level. If we are receiving incomplete, defective or partial information then we will not be in full possession of the necessary facts to allocate resources in the most effective and efficient way possible.

You will be aware that at board level we have the responsibility *to provide information about risks and internal controls to external audiences*. Best practice reporting means that we have to provide information to shareholders and others, about our systems, controls, targets, levels of compliance and improvement measures and we need quality information to enable us to do this. This brings me to the second purpose of this memo.

(ii) **Qualitative characteristics of information needed**

Secondly, I want to write to you about the most helpful ways in which to convey this crucial information to us. The information we receive on risks and internal controls should be high quality information. This means that it enables the full information content to be conveyed to the board in a manner that is clear and has nothing in it that would make any part of it difficult to understand. In particular I would ask that you consider that your communications should be reliable, relevant and understandable. They should also be complete.

By *reliable* I refer to the trustworthiness of the information: the assumption that it is 'hard' information, that it is correct, that it is impartial, unbiased and accurate. In the event that you must convey bad news such as some of the issues raised by the loss of the Mary Jane, we expect you to do so with as much truthfulness and clarity as if you were conveying good news.

By *relevant* I mean not only that due reports should be complete and delivered promptly, but also that anything that you feel should be brought to the board's attention, such as maritime safety issues, emergent risks, issues with ports, etc. should be brought to our attention while there is still time for us to do something about it. In the case of the Mary Jane there were technical issues with the fit of the ship with her berth at Eastport that were important and we should be made aware of such problems as soon as possible.

Not all directors of Sea Ships possess the technical and nautical knowledge of senior operating personnel on board the ferries. It is therefore particularly important that information you convey to us is *understandable*. This means that it should contain a minimum of technical terms that have obvious meaning to you on board ships, but may not be understandable to a non-marine specialist. All communication should therefore be as plain as possible within the constraints of reliability and completeness. This brings me to my final point.

By *complete*, I mean that all information that we need to know and which you have access to, should be included. Particularly with relevance to on-board accidents or risks, you must convey all relevant information to us regardless of the inconvenience that it may cause to one or more colleagues.

As we have learned at the highest cost to those involved in the loss of the Mary Jane and to ourselves commercially, the flow of information on controls and risks is of vital importance to us. Timely receipt of, and appropriate response to, high quality information is not only important to the safe operation of the ships but also to the company itself.

Thank you very much for your understanding and full co-operation on behalf of Sea Ships.

Wim Bock

Chief executive

Tutorial note

Candidates may express similar information qualities in different ways in part (ii). Using the ACCURATE mnemonic as a thought process might help.

	Marking scheme	Marks
(a)	1 mark for recognition and evidence of understanding of each question (half mark for identification only). Allow maximum of 3 marks for step 6 (evaluation of consequences). 1 mark for correct application of each point to case.	14
(b)	1 mark for identification of each internal control failing. 1 mark for analysis of the point.	12
(c)	1 mark for recognition of the areas where NEDs could improve. 1 mark for application to case.	8
(d) (i)	1 mark for each point on importance. 1 mark for application to case.	6
(ii)	Half mark for recognition of each quality of information: 1 for development of the quality based on the content of the case. Maximum of 1.5 marks per quality recognised and developed. Maximum of 2 marks for recognition of points.	6
	An additional 4 professional marks are available for the layout, logical flow, persuasiveness and tone of the memo.	4
Total		**50**

Examiner's comments

As in previous diets, the compulsory question was based on an extended case. In the December 2009 exam, the case concerned the sinking of a ship (the Mary Jane) and its owner, Sea Ships Company. The central event of the case was the loss of a ship, the Mary Jane, in a storm but the case explains that the ship sank because of a series of internal control failures both on board the ship itself whilst the company's future was threatened because of other internal control failures at the Sea Ships head office. Because of the loss of life on the Mary Jane, the government held an inquiry which identified and highlighted a range of failures leading to the loss. It was a scenario, drawn from a range of real maritime disasters, which shows the importance of risk management and internal controls in business operations. Lives can and do depend upon them and internal control failures can result in the loss of lives and threaten the viability of companies.

As in some earlier P1 exams, Question 1 contained an ethical reasoning task, this time using the 7-step American Accounting Association model (in Q1(a)). The company had evidence from an independent consultant that a range of structural changes to the Mary Jane would have prevented it from sinking but that the changes had not been carried out due to cost constraints. The task in **Q1(a)** was to use the AAA model to consider the ethical dilemma of whether or not to publicly disclose the fact that the report had been received but not acted upon. All of the information needed to conduct the analysis was in the case scenario. Candidates that could only recall some of the 7 steps did receive some recognition but it was disappointing to see some candidates reproduce the seven steps but then to either ignore or misinterpret the ethical dilemma. A careful reading of the question should have indicated exactly what the requirement was to consider 'whether or not to disclose this information [about the independent consultant's report on structural changes] publicly' but some failed to recognise that this was the dilemma to be considered and thereby did not achieve high marks for this part.

Part (b) was an 'identify and analyse' task where candidates had to study the case and draw out the internal control failure both at Sea Ships Company and on the Mary Jane itself. This required a careful reading of the case but the internal control failures were relatively clear to many candidates. Some candidates missed out on some of the internal control failures at the Sea Ships Company itself (such as the failure to ensure adequate insurance cover). This type of question, involving a careful analysis of case material to draw out relevant content, is one that tests both understanding (being able to identify the internal control failures) and analysis (being able to say why the identified issues are important IC failures and their implications) is a useful way to test candidates on a range of topics on the P1 study guide. A similar approach was taken, using different verbs, in this paper in Q2(c) and Q3 (b). It is not possible to perform well on these questions without a careful scrutiny of the case scenario.

Part (c) asked how non-executive directors (NEDs) might have helped in improving the governance at Sea Ships Company. The issues highlighted by the government inquiry were useful starting points for this question. I was disappointed that many candidates automatically wrote about the four general roles of NEDs in this question as though this were an automatic response to all NED questions! Candidates that based their answers on the unique governance situation at Sea Ships were rewarded whilst those that reproduced an auto-response ('strategy, scrutiny, risk and people') tended to achieve few or no marks on this question. Again, it was important to analyse the case and read the question carefully. The question was not asking about the roles of NEDs but rather the contribution they (rather than executive directors) could make given the governance failures at Sea Ships Company.

Part (d) contained two requirements which were linked and were required to be answered within the same 'flow' of narrative. As in previous P1 papers, four professional marks were available for the correct presentation of the answer. These two requirements (part (b) (i) and ii) were poorly done overall with some candidates refusing to attempt them at all. Both areas asked about were well covered in the study texts so I was surprised and disappointed that some candidates did so poorly. Again, in both cases, I suspect that a reason for poor performance was an inadequate reading of what the question was actually asking for.

Part (d)(i) asked candidates to assess the importance of information on controls and risks. The range of answers I saw on this suggested that some candidates misinterpreted its meaning. The key words in the question were 'importance of information' or, in other words, why does the board of Sea Ships need information on controls and risks? The importance of information is covered in the P1 study guide section B4a but this subject is also covered in other ACCA papers so candidates should have been aware of this area.

Part (d)(ii) was also done poorly overall but was also relatively straightforward in what it was asking. Following on from the importance of information, this part asked about the nature of the information itself. A good answer explained that good information was reliable, relevant, understandable and complete although markers accepted other relevant qualitative characteristics as equally valid. The six marks in Q1(d)(ii) should have been relatively straightforward to achieve so it was disappointing that many candidates failed to see what the question was asking them to write about. Again, I would reiterate and emphasise the point that a careful reading of each question is crucial.

One of the most disappointing things to report on Question 1 was the poor attempts to gain the professional parks in Q1(d). I have highlighted this as an issue in past exam reports and there was a useful article on professional marks for P1 in a recent edition of Student Accountant. The question required the answers to Q1(d) (i) and (ii) to be in the form of a memo. This was worth 4 marks and it was disappointing that so few managed to gain high professional marks. I have made the point before that the various forms of narrative communication should be taught to and learned by P1 candidates and I repeat this point in this report. It was evident that many candidates were unsure of how to frame and draft a memo to management and this was reflected in the professional marks awarded. A common error was to write the answer in the form of a letter.

12   HESKET NUCLEAR (JUN 10)

Key answer tips

This question covers a broad range of topic areas:

(a)   For the prepared student a requirement such as part (a) requiring you to distinguish between stakeholders group should not be seen as problem. This category of stakeholder classifications was discussed by the examiner in the 'Who's Who' article.

(b)   Again an area of discussion 'employee representatives' that has been discussed in the 'Internal and External Actors' article.

(c)   Agency is an important area in the P1 syllabus and will therefore be examined frequently.

(d)   The examiner here uses an interesting reporting structure. He asks you to prepare a statement for the company's website. Again the examiner noted that very few students managed to gain the full four professional marks and many students seem to insist on either writing in report or letter format.

(a)   **Distinguish and identify**

Voluntary stakeholders are those that engage with an organisation of their own choice and free will. They are ultimately (in the long term) able to detach and discontinue their stakeholding if they choose. Involuntary stakeholders have their stakeholding imposed and are unable to detach or withdraw of their own volition.

The voluntary stakeholders identified in the case are: Forward Together (the trade union), Hesket Nuclear employees, the Ayland government, the board of HPC, local authorities, No Nuclear Now and other nuclear producers who use the reprocessing facility.

The involuntary stakeholders – those whose stakeholding is placed upon them by virtue of their physical position – are the governments of Beeland and Ceeland, the local community and the seal colony.

Tutorial note

Membership of these categories is contestable if time perspectives are introduced. In the short term, some voluntary stakeholders are involuntary in that their involvement cannot be quickly withdrawn. The case clearly identifies the involuntary stakeholders.

Assess the claims

The case identifies three 'affected' stakeholders that are clearly involuntary. Both Beeland and Ceeland say that they are stakeholders because of their geographical position and the seals are unable to move because of local environmental conditions. Beeland government's claim is based on its position near to the Hesket plant. With the capital 70 km from the plant, it claims that it is already the 'victim' of low level radiation in the sea between the two countries. The case does not give the radius of damage if a major incident were to occur but it does say that there is 'scientific support' for the view that it could affect the capital of Beeland. Assuming that both of these statements are accurate then the Beeland government would appear to have a legitimate and reasonable claim that they are affected by the Hesket Nuclear plant and could be further affected in the future.

The government of Ceeland claims to be a potential 'victim' of nuclear contamination from the HN plant and has sought to have the plant closed as a result. The weakness of its claim rests upon the physical distance away from HN (500 km). If the threats to Ceeland are, as scientists have suggested, 'unfounded and borne of ignorance' then clearly Ceeland has a weak claim over Hesket Nuclear. It may have political reasons of its own to make protestations, perhaps to appease opinion in Ceeland or to be populist to manage dissent at home.

The case says that the local seal colony is unable to move away from the HN plant because of the local environmental conditions there and so it is unable to discontinue its stakeholding. It is thus involuntary. Low level emissions could potentially affect the seals and their food sources and any major incident would obviously impact it significantly. Whilst their affectedness is therefore indisputable, the value of the colony's claim rests in part upon the value placed upon sea life value against human and economic value. This assessment is therefore contestable.

The local community is another involuntary stakeholder albeit with a weaker involuntary element than the above three described. Whilst not structurally involuntary (they are able to move away if they do not like it), many local citizens may have lived near the HN plant for many years before it was built and may therefore have simply had to accept its development regardless of their views. The impacts on local communities can be positive or negative in that HN supports them through the provision of jobs but they would also be the first and most affected if there ever was a major incident at the HN plant.

Tutorial note

Allow for other 'affected' stakeholders if coherently argued. It is possible to argue that the taxpayers of Ayland are affected involuntary stakeholders, for example.

(b)   **Roles of employee representatives**

Trade unions are the most usual example of employee representation in corporate governance. Trade unions represent employees in a work facility such as an office or a plant. Membership is voluntary and the influence of the union is usually proportional to its proportion of membership.

Although a trade union is by default assumed to have an adversarial role with management, its ability to 'deliver' the compliance of a workforce can help significantly in corporate governance. When an external threat is faced, such as with the reputation losses following the 1970s leak, then the coalition of workforce (via Forward Together) and management meant that it was more difficult for external critics to gain support.

A trade union is an actor in the checks and balances of power within a corporate governance structure. Where management abuses occur, it is often the trade union that is the first and most effective reaction against it and this can often work to the advantage of shareholders or other owners, especially when the abuse has the ability to affect productivity.

Trade unions help to maintain and control one of the most valuable assets in an organisation (employees). Where a helpful and mutually constructive relationship is cultivated between union and employer then an optimally efficient industrial relations climate exists, thus reinforcing the productivity of human resources in the organisation. In defending members' interests and negotiating terms and conditions, the union helps to ensure that the workforce is content and able to work with maximum efficiency and effectiveness.

Critically evaluate the contribution of Forward Together from HPC's perspective

Helpful roles

The case describes Forward Together's (FT) role as *generally supportive of the development of the Hesket Nuclear site.* Clearly, with a primary loyalty to its members, FT will always pursue causes that are going to maximise members' job security. When the primary external stakeholder pressure is for the reduction of the HN site, the union and board are aligned in their objectives for the continuation of the facility.

FT's statement over *Ceeland's concern was very helpful to the HPC board.* FT has a clear interest in diffusing unfounded concern where it exists and its statement that Ceeland's fears were 'entirely groundless' would reinforce the power of any similar such statement made by others. Similarly, FT provided support after the leakage incident in the 1970s. The helpful reinforcement was evident when FT pointed to the impeccable safety record and compliance. This may have meant more as a public relations exercise coming from the trade union rather than the HPC board as FT is independent of the company.

Unhelpful roles

FT's wage pressure, over time, put a pressure on the company's costs that had, according to the HPC board, created the need to bring in cheaper foreign workers to fulfil the maintenance contract. From the board of HPC's viewpoint, such pressure was ultimately self-defeating for the union and effectively meant that the previous maintenance contractor was priced out. The union had been short-sighted in its year-on-year wage demands.

We are not told whether the board agrees with Kate Allujah that workers from Ayland were 'more reliable' in such a risk sensitive industry, but her comment was possibly based on prejudice against foreign workers entering the country. She seemed to be *unconcerned with the legal implications* of her outrage. Given that the company was legally entitled to employ foreign workers in Ayland, she had no valid legal argument for her position. From an economic perspective, it is also unhelpful, from HPC's perspective to have the union making high wage demands and then complaining about legitimate measures that the company takes to stay within its government subsidy such as cutting costs, including labour costs.

Conclusion

HPC's relationship with FT has been *positive and mutually beneficial* for the majority of the company's history. Clearly seeing their destinies to be linked, *FT has supported the company against external threats but has, at the same time, used its good relations to make wage demands* that ultimately led to the award of a maintenance contract to the foreign workers. This would have broken an important relationship with experienced maintenance personnel and the foreign workers may or may not have had the same level of expertise as the previous workers.

(c) **Explain agency relationship**

An agency relationship is one of trust between an agent and a principal which obliges the agent to meet the objectives placed upon it by the principal. As one appointed by a principal to manage, oversee or further the principal's specific interests, the primary purpose of agency is to discharge its fiduciary duty to the principal. In this case, there is an agency relationship between the government and the board of HPC.

Examine existing agency relationship

Although HPC is run by a conventional board, the company is wholly owned by the government of Ayland. This means that the company's strategic objectives are determined by the government and these are likely to be different from purely commercial concerns. The nuclear operation is clearly not economic in terms of profit and so the government's objectives for the company must be other than that. The case describes this in terms of broadening its energy portfolio and meeting environmental objectives. The board's objectives are likely to be predominantly financial, due to the control by subsidy placed upon it, but the principal's political and environmental concerns may also affect the objectives placed upon the HPC board (such as employment objectives in what is a deprived region of Ayland).

The principal is the government of Ayland and ultimately the board is accountable to the taxpayers of Ayland. This means that the development and even the existence of HN is ultimately under democratic control. The agency relationship means that the board of HPC has subsidy targets and also sees its role as fulfilling an important role in Ayland's energy portfolio.

HPC as a 'conventional' company owned by private shareholders

If HPC was a private company, its principals would be shareholders with very different objectives. Shareholders would be predominantly concerned with the economic performance of HP and the economies of the nuclear power industry. It would insist that the board pursued only those parts of the business that were profitable. This would necessitate a radical redesign of HPC's business as we are told that in its present form it is loss-making.

(d) (i) **Statement**

Hesket Power Company's response to the report produced by NNN

Importance of risk assessment at Hesket Power Company

Hesket Power Company was recently dismayed to have been made aware of a report conducted by an anti-nuclear pressure group purporting to be a risk assessment of selected risks to the Hesket Nuclear plant. The company would like to take this opportunity to inform the public about the irresponsibility of the pressure group's activity whilst comprehensively rejecting its arguments.

In all industries it is important to assess risks as accurately as possible but in the nuclear power industry, it is critical. It is because the pressure group misrepresented our risks that we feel it necessary to remind stakeholders about the importance of a correct risk assessment based on valid measurements.

In observing best practice, Hesket Nuclear carries out thorough and continual risk assessments in compliance with our regulatory frameworks. The information going into the process must be as accurate as possible because resources are allocated in part on the *basis of our risk assessments*. Clearly, a risk assessed as probable and of high impact would attract a significant resource allocation and to have incorrect information could conceivably lead to the misallocation of company resources. This, in turn, would be a failure of our duty to the HPC company and ultimately to our owners, the government of Ayland and its taxpayers. The fact that there has not been a serious incident since the 1970s highlights the efforts that we take with risk assessment.

The *ways in which we manage risk also depend upon the assessment.* Once a risk, such as the risk of a nuclear leakage, is identified and assessed, the company pursues a strategy for managing that risk, typically to transfer or share the risk, avoid the risk, reduce it or accept it. This has implications for the entire strategy of the organisation, especially where the assessed risks are strategic in nature. Inaccurate assessment might, for example, mean accepting a risk that should have been avoided or vice versa.

Our stakeholders expect us to be a responsible company in all matters but especially in matters of safety and the environment. *We owe it to our local community, employees and others to ensure that all risks are fully but accurately understood.* In addition to ensuring that we are fully compliant with all regulatory regimes applicable to us, we believe that accurate risk assessment is necessary to our valued reputation as an ethical and responsible employer and neighbour.

Finally, as we have seen in the case of this misguided report by the pressure group, inaccurate assessments can breed fear, distrust and unnecessary panic. HPC was disappointed to hear the report being used by critics when the information it contained was inaccurate and this leads us to the second matter.

(ii) **HN's social and environmental 'footprint'**

HPC is aware of some critics that have asserted that our overall footprint is negative. In responding to this, we feel it necessary to remind readers that the footprint of any organisation includes the *sum total of its positive and negative interactions* with the environment. Whilst this sometimes involves negative impacts such as carbon emissions and accidental pollution, it also takes into account the positive impacts such as social benefit, through such things as job creation, and positive environmental impacts. Both 'sides' need to be taken into account before an overall evaluation of the social and environmental footprint can be established. To focus on only a small number of measures, as some of our critics have done, is to provide an unfair and biased account of our genuine overall footprint.

Social arguments

It is our belief that Hesket Nuclear makes a substantial positive contribution on both social and environmental measures. In terms of social contribution, HN makes a positive impact for several reasons. Whilst accepting that Hesket Nuclear has its critics, the company would like to remind the public both in Ayland and Beeland that the plant is a very large employer and *vital to the economic well-being of the region*, a fact recognised by a wide range of local and national stakeholders. Others have noted the importance of the jobs provided at Hesket Nuclear to the social and economic well-being of the region and HPC fully agrees with this analysis.

In addition to the jobs provided in Ayland, Hesket Nuclear also provides reprocessed fuel that is cheaper than virgin fuel. This provides support for *nuclear power, and hence clean energy, in several developing countries* that are our valued customers. Hesket Nuclear therefore indirectly *supports employment and social development in those countries*. Were our reprocessed fuel unavailable to them, rates of economic and social development growth may be slowed in those countries. We are therefore determined to continue to supply this vital input into those countries and to continue to support them.

Environmental arguments

In addition, as a non-fossil fuel industry, nuclear is *relatively non-polluting and is an essential component of the government of Ayland's clean energy strategy*. Hesket Nuclear is proud to be a part of that strategy and will continue to be a dependable producer of nuclear power and reprocessing services. In so doing we will continue to carefully manage the risks of nuclear power supply whilst providing the jobs and clean energy for which Hesket Nuclear is corporately responsible. A likely alternative to nuclear is the burning of more polluting fossil fuels which would presumably be as unacceptable to our critics as it is to us.

Whilst conceding that all nuclear operations require a high level of safety and regulatory observance, we are pleased to be able to remind our stakeholders, including the governments of Beeland and Ceeland, of our very high performance in this area. As our colleagues in the Forward Together trade union recently said, Hesket Nuclear has had an impeccable safety record since the 1970s and is fully compliant with all relevant safety regulations. We fully intend to maintain this high level of performance.

Tutorial note

The examiner allowed latitude here in responding to part (ii), especially rewarding answers referring to the specific case of nuclear.

		Marking scheme	Marks
(a)		2 marks for distinguishing between the two types of stakeholders ½ mark for each voluntary stakeholder identified up to a maximum of 2 ½ mark for each involuntary stakeholder identified up to a maximum of 2 2 marks for each assessment of the three involuntary stakeholders (which may include explanation of why they are involuntary)	
		Maximum	12
(b)		2 marks for each relevant role identified and explained up to a maximum of 6 marks Critical evaluation 2 marks for each helpful/positive role identified and discussed 2 marks for each unhelpful/negative role identified and discussed 2 marks for conclusion/summary	
		Maximum	10
(c)		1 mark for each relevant point on explaining agency relationship to a maximum of 2 1 mark for each relevant point in the exploration of HPC's agency with the government of Ayland to a maximum of 6 1 mark for each relevant point on HPC as a 'conventional' company to a maximum of 2	
		Maximum	10
(d)	(i)	1 mark for each relevant point identified and 1 for explanation in the context of the case	8
	(ii)	2 marks for evidence of understanding of 'footprint' in context 1 mark for each relevant positive social and environmental impact convincingly argued for, to a maximum of 4 marks	6
		Professional marks	4
Total			**50**

Examiner's comments

Part (a) was about stakeholders. It contained three distinct tasks: to distinguish between voluntary and involuntary stakeholders, to identify the voluntary and involuntary stakeholders in Hesket Nuclear and finally to assess the claims of three of the involuntary stakeholders previously identified. The first task (distinguish) was done quite well in the majority of cases but after that, candidates often became confused over which stakeholders were in which 'camp'. The most prominent involuntary stakeholders were the governments of Beeland, Ceeland and the rare seals near the HN facility. A common mistake was to nominate the anti-nuclear group NNN as an involuntary stakeholder when it is obviously voluntary: it chose to engage with HN of its own free will.

Part (b) covered the roles of a trade union in corporate governance for the first time on a P1 paper. The question contained two tasks: to explain the roles and then to evaluate the contribution of FT, the trade union in the case, to the governance of HPC. This was one of the better questions in terms of candidate answers but the highest marks went to those able to show how FT had helped and challenged HPC using the evidence from the case. It was important to recognise that the union had been helpful to HPC in some respects but unhelpful in others.

Part (c) examined agency but introduced the important idea that agency relationships need not just be between directors and shareholders. In the case of HPC, the agency relationship was between the board of HPC and the government of Ayland. This meant that HPC had objectives other than profit maximisation because of the political objectives of its principal, the government. Most successful candidates achieved a pass mark on this part although others failed to see the difference between a government being the principal rather than shareholders.

Part (d) was the 'professional marks' component of question 1. It contained two tasks: the first about the importance of accurate risk assessment and the second about HN's social and environmental footprint. Common errors in (d)(i) were to explain what risk assessment is rather than its importance or to fail to link the answer strongly enough with the case. Those achieving the highest marks were able to show, as the model answer shows, the links with the NNN assessment and the effects that this flawed assessment might have. In particular, this task was asking about the importance of accurate (as opposed to inaccurate and spurious) risk assessment.

Part (d)(ii) contained two tasks. Many candidates were able to explain 'social and environmental footprint' but fewer were able to do well on the second task which was a level 3 intellectual outcome: to construct a case. In this task, candidates were required to construct the argument in favour of the proposition that HN's social and environmental footprint is positive (i.e. to argue that it made a favourable social and environmental contribution). In order to be able to do this, candidates needed to know what such a footprint was and what it involved, and then to study the case for evidence to support the argument. The case study contained evidence on both the social footprint (about local jobs, energy and development abroad) and the environmental footprint (clean energy and very good safety/leakage record).

Despite my highlighting a poor 'professional marks' performance in previous examiner's reports, many candidates failed to approach the answer as required in order to gain all of these marks. In this case, the required format for the answer was a response statement for a website. This means it was NOT a letter or a report.

13   ZPT (DEC 10)

Key answer tips

All of the key syllabus areas are tackled in this question, requiring a significant degree of application of ethical theories.

In tackling part (a) there is plenty of information in the scenario to draw on to earn two marks per reason. There are some straightforward marks to be earned in part (b) for definitions, so make sure you tackle these quickly.

Part (c) is the most challenging part of the question Ensure that your answer is in the correct format, so as not to lose the professional marks that are available.

Part (c) (iii) is a simple requirement. Just apply a 'common sense' approach to reporting the material issues

(a)   (i)   **Institutional investor intervention**

Six reasons are typically cited as potential grounds for investor intervention. Whilst it would be rare to act on the basis of one factor (unless it was particularly unfavourable), an accumulation of factors may have such an effect. Furthermore, institutional investors have a moral duty to use their power to monitor the companies they invest in for the good of all investors, as recognised in most codes of corporate governance. Institutional investors have the expertise at their disposal to understand the complexities of managing large corporations. As such, they can take a slightly detached view of the business and offer advice where appropriate. The typical reasons for intervention are cited below.

Concerns about strategy, especially when, in terms of long-term investor value, the strategy is likely to be excessively risky or, conversely, unambitious in terms of return on investment. The strategy determines the long-term value of an investment and so is very important to shareholders.

Poor or deteriorating performance, usually over a period of time, although a severe deterioration over a shorter period might also trigger intervention, especially if the reasons for the poor performance have not been adequately explained in the company's reporting.

Poor non-executive performance. It is particularly concerning when non-executives do not, for whatever reason, balance the executive board and provide the input necessary to reassure markets. Their contributions should always be seen to be effective. This is especially important when investors feel that the executive board needs to be carefully monitored or constrained, perhaps because one or another of the factors mentioned in this answer has become an issue.

Major *internal control failures.* These are a clear sign of the loss of control by senior management over the operation of the business. These might refer, for example, to health and safety, quality, budgetary control or IT projects. In the case of ZPT, there were clear issues over the control of IC systems for generating financial reporting data.

Compliance failures, especially with statutory regulations or corporate governance codes. Legal non-compliance is always a serious matter and under comply-or-explain, all matters of code non-compliance must also be explained. Such explanations may or may not be acceptable to shareholders.

Excessive directors' remuneration or defective remuneration policy. Often an indicator of executive greed, excessive board salaries are also likely to be an indicator of an ineffective remunerations committee which is usually a non-executive issue. Whilst the absolute monetary value of executive rewards are important, it is usually more important to ensure that they are highly aligned with shareholder interests (to minimise agency costs).

Poor CSR or *ethical performance,* or lack of social responsibility. Showing a lack of CSR can be important in terms of the company's long-term reputation and also its vulnerability to certain social and environmental risks.

Tutorial note

The study texts approach this slightly differently.

(ii) **Case for intervention**

After the first restatement, it was evident that three of the reasons for interventions were already present. Whilst one of these perhaps need not have triggered an intervention alone, the number of factors makes a strong case for an urgent meeting between the major investors and the ZPT board, especially Mr Xu.

Poor performance. The restated results were 'all significantly below market expectations'. Whilst this need not in itself have triggered an institutional investor intervention, the fact that the real results were only made public after an initial results announcement is unfortunate. The obvious question to ask the ZPT board is why the initial results were mis-stated and why they had to be corrected as this points to a complete lack of controls within the business. A set of results well below market expectations always needs to be explained to shareholders.

Internal control and potential compliance failures. There is ample evidence to suggest that internal controls in ZPT were very deficient, especially (and crucially) those internal controls over external financial reporting. The case mentions, 'no effective management oversight of the external reporting process and a disregard of the relevant accounting standards', both of which are very serious allegations. Linked to this, the investors need an urgent clarification of the legal allegations of fraud, especially in the light of the downward restatement of the results. Any suggestion of compliance failure is concerning but fraud (down to intent rather than incompetence) is always serious as far as investors are concerned.

Excessive remuneration in the form of the $20 million bonus. It is likely that this bonus was excessive even had the initial results been accurate, but after the restatement, the scale of the bonus was evidently indefensible as it was based on false figures. The fact that the chief executive is refusing to repay the bonus implies a lack of integrity, adding weight to the belief that there may be some underlying dishonesty. Furthermore, although the investors thought it excessive, the case describes this as within the terms of Mr Xu's contract. A closer scrutiny of remunerations policy (and therefore non-executive effectiveness) would be appropriate.

(b) **Absolutist and relativist perspectives**

Absolutism and relativism

An absolutist ethical stance is when it is assumed that there is an unchanging set of ethical principles which should always be obeyed regardless of the situation or any other pressures or factors that may be present. Typically described in universalist ways, absolutist ethics tends to be expressed in terms such as 'it is always right to...', 'it is never right to...' or 'it is always wrong to...'

Relativist ethical assumptions are those that assume that real ethical situations are more complicated than absolutists allow for. It is the view that there are a variety of acceptable ethical beliefs and practices and that the right and most appropriate belief depends on the situation. The best outcome is arrived at by examining the situation and making ethical assessments based on the best outcomes in that situation.

Evaluation of Shazia Lo's behaviour – absolutist ethics

Firstly, Shazia Lo was correct to be concerned about the over-valuation of contracts at ZPT. As a qualified accountant, she should never be complicit in the knowing mis-statement of accounts or the misrepresentation of contract values. For a qualified accountant bound by very high ethical and professional standards, she was right to be absolutist in her instincts even if not in her eventual behaviour.

Secondly, she was also right to raise the issue with the finance director. This was her only legitimate course of action in the first instance and it would have been wrong, in an absolutist sense, to remain silent. Given that she was intimidated and threatened upon raising the issue, she was being absolutist in threatening to take the issue to the press (i.e. whistle blowing). It would be incompatible with her status as a professional accountant to be complicit in false accounting as she owed it to the ZPT shareholders, to her professional body and to the general public (the public interest) never to process accounting data she knows to be inaccurate. An effective internal audit process would be a source of information for this action.

Evaluation of Shazia Lo's behaviour – relativist ethics

It is clear from Shazia Lo's behaviour that despite having absolutist instincts, other factors caused her to assume a relativist ethic in practice.

Her mother's serious illness was evidently the major factor in overriding her absolutist principles with regard to complicity in the fraudulent accounting figures. It is likely she weighed her mother's painful suffering against the need to be absolutist with regard to the mis-statement of contract values. In relativist situations, it is usually the case that *one 'good' is weighed against another* 'good'. Clearly it is good (an absolute) to show compassion and sympathy toward her mother but this *should not have caused her to accept the payment* (effectively a bribe to keep silent). She may have *reasoned that the continued suffering of her mother was a worse ethical outcome than the mis-statement of ZPT accounts* and the fact that she received no personal income from the money (it all went to support her mother) would suggest that she acted with reasonable motives even though her decision as a professional accountant was definitely inappropriate. Given that accepting bribes is a clear breach of professional codes of ethics for accountants and other professionals, there is no legitimate defence of her decision and her behaviour was therefore wrong.

(c)   (i)   **Speech on importance of good corporate governance and consequences of failure**

Introduction

Ladies and Gentlemen, I begin my remarks today by noting that we meet at an unfortunate time for business in this country. In the wake of the catastrophic collapse of ZPT, one of the largest telecommunications companies, we have also had to suffer the loss of one of our larger audit firms, JJC. This series of events has heightened in all of us an awareness of the vulnerability of business organisations to management incompetence and corruption.

The consequences of corporate governance failures at ZPT

I would therefore like to remind you all why corporate governance is important and I will do this by referring to the failures in this unfortunate case. Corporate governance failures affect many groups and individuals and as legislators, we owe it to all of them to ensure that the highest standards of corporate governance are observed.

Firstly and probably most obviously, effective corporate governance *protects the value of shareholders' investment in a company.* We should not forget that the majority of shareholders are not 'fat cats' who may be able to afford large losses. Rather, they are individual pension fund members, small investors and members of mutual funds. The hard-working voters who save for the future have their efforts undermined by selfish and arrogant executives who deplete the value of those investments. This unfairness is allowed to happen because of a lack of regulation of corporate governance in this country.

The second group of people to lose out after the collapse of ZPT were *the employees.* It is no fault of theirs that their directors were so misguided and yet it is they who bear a great deal of the cost. I should stress, of course, that jobs were lost at JJC as well as at ZPT. Unemployment, even when temporary and frictional, is a personal misery for the families affected and it can also increase costs to the taxpayer when state benefits are considered.

Thirdly, because of the collapse of ZPT, *creditors have gone unpaid and customers have remained unserviced.* Again, we should not assume that suppliers can afford to lose their receivables in ZPT and for many smaller suppliers, their exposure to ZPT could well threaten their own survival. Where the value of net assets is inadequate to repay the full value of payables, let alone share capital, there has been a failure in company direction and in corporate governance so I hope you will agree with me that effective management and sound corporate governance are vital.

The loss of two such important businesses, ZPT and JJC, has *caused great disturbance in the telecommunications and audit industries.* As JJC lost its legitimacy to provide audit services and its clients moved to other auditors, the structure of the industry changed. Other auditors will eventually be able to absorb the work previously undertaken by JJC but clearly this will cause short-to-medium term capacity issues for those firms as they redeploy resources to make good on those new contracts. This was, I should remind you, both unnecessary and entirely avoidable.

Linked to this point, I would remind colleagues that it is important for *business in general and auditing in particular to be respected in society.* The *loss of* auditors' *reputation* caused by these events is very unfortunate as *auditing underpins our collective confidence in business reporting.* It would be wholly inappropriate for other auditors to be affected by the behaviour of JJC or for businesses in general to be less trusted because of the events at ZPT. I very much hope that such losses of reputation and in public confidence will not occur.

Finally, we have all been dismayed by the case of Shazia Lo that was reported in the press. A lack of sound corporate governance practice *places employees such* as Ms *Lo in impossible positions.* Were she to act as whistleblower she would, by all accounts, have been victimised by her employers. Her acceptance of what was effectively a bribe to remain silent brings shame both on Ms Lo and on those who offered the money. An effective audit committee at ZPT would have offered a potential outlet for Ms Lo's concerns and also provided a means of reviewing external audit and other professional services at ZPT. This whole situation could, and would have been, avoided had the directors of ZPT managed the company under an effective framework of corporate governance.

(ii)   **The case for the mandatory external reporting of internal controls and risks**

I now turn to the issue of the mandatory external reporting of internal controls and risks. My reason for raising this as an issue is because this was one of the key causes of ZPT's failure.

My first point in this regard is that *disclosure allows for accountability.* Had investors been aware of the internal control failures and business probity risks earlier, it may have been possible to replace the existing board before events deteriorated to the extent that they sadly did. In addition, however, the need to generate a report on internal controls annually will *bring very welcome increased scrutiny from shareholders* and others. It is only when things are made more transparent that effective scrutiny is possible.

Secondly, I am firmly of the belief that more information on internal controls would *enhance shareholder confidence and satisfaction.* It is vital that investors have confidence in the internal controls of companies they invest in and increased knowledge will encourage this. It was, I would remind you, a *lack of confidence in* ZPT's *internal controls* and the strong suspicion of fraud that caused the share price to collapse and the company to ultimately fail.

Furthermore, compulsory external reporting on internal controls will *encourage good practice inside the company.* The knowledge that their work will be externally reported upon and scrutinised by investors will *encourage greater rigour in the IC function* and in the audit committee. This will further increase investor confidence.

To those who might suggest that we should opt for a comply-or-explain approach to this issue, I would argue that this is simply *too important an issue to allow companies to decide for themselves* or to interpret non-mandatory guidelines. It must be legislated for because otherwise *those with poor internal controls will be able to avoid reporting* on them. By specifying what should be disclosed on an annual basis, companies will need to make the audit of internal controls an integral and ongoing part of their operations. It is to the contents of an internal control report that I now turn.

(iii)   **Content of external report on internal controls**

I am unable, in a speech such as this, to go into the detail of what I would like to see in an external report on internal controls, but in common with corporate governance codes elsewhere, there are four broad themes that such a report should contain.

Firstly, the report should contain *a statement of acknowledgement by the board* that it is responsible for the company's system of internal control and for reviewing its effectiveness. This might seem obvious but it has been shown to be an important starting point in *recognising responsibility*. It is only when the board accepts and acknowledges this responsibility that the impetus for the collection of data and the authority for changing internal systems is provided. The 'tone from the top' is very important in the development of my proposed reporting changes and so this is a very necessary component of the report.

Secondly, the report should summarise the *processes the board (or where applicable, through its committees) has applied* in reviewing the effectiveness of the system of internal control. These may or may not satisfy shareholders, of course, and weak systems and processes would be a matter of discussion at AGMs for non-executives to strengthen.

Thirdly, the report should *provide meaningful, high level information* that does not give a misleading impression. Clearly, internal auditing would greatly increase the reliability of this information but a robust and effective audit committee would also be very helpful.

Finally, the report should contain *information about any weaknesses in internal control* that have resulted in error or material losses. This would have been a highly material disclosure in the case of ZPT and the costs of non-disclosure of this was a major cause of the eventual collapse of the company

I very much hope that these brief remarks have been helpful in persuading colleagues to consider the need for increased corporate governance legislation. Thank you for listening.

Marking scheme			Marks
(a)	(i)	1 mark for each reason identified and explained (half for identification only).	6
	(ii)	2 marks for each point identified and argued in context. (half mark for identification only).	6
(b)		4 marks for distinguishing between absolutism and relativism (2 marks for each). 3 marks for evaluation of Shazia Lo's behaviour from an absolutist perspective. 3 marks for evaluation of Shazia Lo's behaviour from a relativist perspective.	10
(c)	(i)	2 marks for assessment of each consequence of ZPT's governance failures (1 mark for brief explanation only).	10
	(ii)	2 marks for each argument identified and made.	8
	(iii)	2 marks for each broad theme identified and explained.	6
		Professional marks for the structure, flow, persuasiveness and tone of the answer to (c) parts (i), (ii) and (iii).	4
Total			**50**

14   BOBO CAR COMPANY (JUN 11)

Key answer tips

This scenario and question cover a broad range of topic areas:

For part (a) a new verb "explore" was used which allowed a degree of flexibility when raising salient points. The second part of the question required students to "identify and explain" The prepared student would have noted that the answer to the question lay in the scenario not simply noting a pre learned list of appropriate actions.

For part (b) was the familiar topic of Kohlberg. The well rehearsed student would be aware of the popularity of this topic and should have done well. It was important to recognise however that not all three levels were tested.

Part (c) required "distinguish" and "explain" advantages of one of the forms of general meetings. It was important to recognise the difference between the two.

Part (d) in two parts contained the professional marks. The method of communication was a speech. One needed to be aware of the roles of the CEO to do well – emphasising the practical nature of this paper. Part (d) (ii) required a n understanding but not listing of the seven positions of Gray, Own and Adams.

Again the examiner noted the need to follow the guidance when constructing the appropriate form of communication with a range of approaches being adopted. Question practice is key in this respect.

(a)   **Internal controls**

Circumstances leading to the problem

The case describes four clear causes of the fuel tank problems with the Bobo Foo.

The first one was the brief given by the board in which *cost reduction was emphasised above all other considerations.* This was underpinned in the design team by a 'tone from the top' conveyed on posters that said 'keep it cheap'. The key concepts for the car also conveyed the message of cost and Mr Tsakos's seniority in the company had the effect of cementing the cost message into the design team including Kathy Yao.

This was exacerbated by the second cause which was a radical *reduction in the normal development time.* Whereas the design team were used to working with timetables of 43 months, Mr Tsakos imposed a 25-month time limit on the project. This in itself conveys a powerful message that the board wants the project completed as quickly and cheaply as possible.

Third, the board *ignored the crash test result* for reasons of cost. In order to hasten the product launch, presumably to make a return on investment as early as possible, the company tooled up the factory as early as possible. This meant that it was too late to make changes to the fuel tank positioning without incurring excessive cost.

Fourth, *Kathy did not speak out when pressured by Mr* Tsakos to reduce the development time. She, and other directors involved in the project, should have stood up to Mr Tsakos, but they failed to do so. She was also complicit in ignoring the crash test and allowing the Bobo Foo to go into production before all the tests were completed. Had she felt able to challenge Mr Tsakos, the problems with the car could have been avoided. An effective non-executive presence on the board would also have been a way of countering Mr Tsakos's persistence in 'forcing' the development time for the car.

Internal control measures

Establishing a standard development time sufficient to meet a range of agreed metrics on all new car models. Kathy Yao's private comments to colleagues about her fears for the safety of the car given such a short development time are relevant. If the company places a minimum time to market for a new model (say 40 months or thereabouts), it would ensure that there was sufficient time or all proposed features of any product feature could be fully safety tested. Being so rushed was presumably a factor in the incorrect and unsafe positioning of the fuel tank.

Embed safety metrics into all design briefs in future. None of the key concepts underpinning the Bobo Foo were concerned with safety and none of the messages conveyed in the key design concepts ('cheap to buy, economical to run', etc) included a reference to product safety. Risk mitigation is most effective when it is placed as a normal part of any role. For a car design team such as that led by Kathy Yao, the introduction of a safety metric into the brief could have prevented such an unsafe feature as the badly positioned fuel tank being allowed to happen.

Procedures to sign off each stage of the development process based on safety criteria. Without an effective 'sign off' for each identified stage, the next stage cannot continue. This would involve establishing an agreed set of stages in a development process at which safety criteria should be applied. The crash test would be an obvious such stage. Once the crash test had taken place, it should be made a mandatory procedure that any failings in the vehicle should be addressed before it can be 'signed off' to go into production (unlike at Bobo where the factory was tooled up regardless of the crash test failure).

Tutorial note

Allow latitude in candidate's answers. Reward points that address the causes of the risks.

(b) **Kohlberg**

Explain Kohlberg's levels

Kohlberg's theory of moral development is a framework for classifying a range of responses to ethical situations. Kohlberg argued that these were indicative of the moral development of the individual. Kohlberg identified three levels that people can operate at.

At the preconventional level of moral reasoning, morality is conceived of in terms of rewards, punishments and instrumental motivations. Those demonstrating intolerance of norms and regulations in preference for self-serving motives are typically preconventional.

At the conventional level, morality is understood in terms of compliance with either or both of peer pressure/social expectations or regulations, laws and guidelines. A high degree of compliance is assumed to be a highly moral position.

At the postconventional level, morality is understood in terms of conformance with perceived 'higher' or 'universal' ethical principles. Postconventional assumptions often challenge existing regulatory regimes and social norms and so postconventional behaviour can often be costly in personal terms.

Levels of people in the question

James Tsakos is exhibiting a *conventional level* of moral development. His main concern is with compliance with the expectations of shareholders. The 'good boy-nice girl' orientation component of the conventional level is that which is concerned with how society sees the company and with shareholders being a prominent stakeholder, Mr Tsakos's expressed concerns are about placating and managing their concerns. He is against the universal recall option because of the signal it would send to markets.

Kathy Yao is also exhibiting a *conventional level* of moral development. Although her concern was driven by a personal concern arising from her part in the design of the Bobo Foo's fuel tank, her motivations were concerned with compliance and strategic interests. Whereas Mr Tsakos was more concerned with the expectations of shareholders, Kathy Yao was more concerned with the expectation of customers. Her concern was rooted in what customers thought of the company. She framed her concerns in terms of product safety whilst also pointing to the importance of a reputation for social responsibility and compliance with the interests of society.

Vernon Vim is exhibiting *a preconventional level* of moral development. He pointed to his personal loss of bonus if the recall option was taken and quantified the choice in purely financial terms. It was 'because the board's bonuses were partly based on the company's annual profits' that he opposed the recall option. He was unconcerned with any compliance or higher ethical purpose.

Tutorial note

Allow James Tsakos to be described as preconventional if his motivations are seen as self-serving with the loss of shareholder value.

(c)   **AGMs and EGMs**

Distinguish between

Annual general meetings (AGMs) are a part of the normal financial calendar for all limited companies and take place on the occasion of the year-end results presentation and the publication of the annual report. Extraordinary general meetings are called to discuss strategic and other issues with shareholders outside the normal financial calendar.

Purposes of each

Both types of meetings are formal meetings between company directors and the shareholders of the company. They typically involve presentations by the board (typically the chairman and/or CEO) and a chance for shareholders to question the board.

AGMs

The AGM is a formal part of a company financial year. Its purpose is to allow the board to present the year's results, discuss the outlook for the coming year, present the formal, audited accounts and to have the final dividend and directors' emoluments approved by shareholders. Shareholder approval is signalled by the passing of resolutions in which shareholders vote in proportion to their holdings. It is usual for the board to make a recommendation and then seek approval of that recommendation by shareholders. The dividend per share, for example, is recommended by the board but only paid after approval by the shareholders at the AGM. Institutional shareholders may employ proxy voting if they are unable to attend in person.

EGMs

Extraordinary meetings are called when issues need to be discussed and approved that cannot wait until the next AGM. A full year can be a very long time. In some business environments when events necessitate substantial change or a major threat, an EGM is sometimes called. Management may want a shareholder mandate for a particular strategic move, such as for a merger or acquisition. Other major issues that might threaten shareholder value may also lead to an EGM such as a 'whistleblower' disclosing information that might undermine shareholders' confidence in the board of directors. In this case, given the nature of the disclosure, there is a case for James Tsakos to answer in terms of shareholders continuing to have confidence in him as CEO.

Advantages

In the case of Bobo, the *shareholders will be able to gain reassurance* that the public disclosure of important safety concerns being ignored will not threaten shareholder value because of lost sales or damaged reputation. There is a clear risk to the reputation of the company as a whole if it is associated in the public mind with unsafe product designs.

The shareholders can *hold James Tsakos accountable* for his actions and demand explanations. There is *a prima facie* case to answer that he presided over the development of a car with a safety risk to its occupants and then opted to resist suggestions to recall the vehicles to have the safety problems addressed.

Mr Tsakos, in return, will be able to *speak directly to shareholders* rather than through written communication and this may be a more convincing way of explaining his position. Given that the shareholders 'wanted to hold James Tsakos accountable for the decision' and wanted to hear from him directly, the EGM will enable him to address these demands.

Resolutions of confidence or no confidence can be passed if proposed and this would 'clear the air' one way or the other to enable the company to resolve its issues quickly. Shareholders have the right to remove Mr Tsakos if they are not satisfied with his explanations and this could be resolved quickly at an EGM rather than having it drift on to the next AGM, which could be many months away.

(d)   (i)   **Role of CEO**

Thank you for attending this EGM. I know that you will have questions in the light of recent media reports about our economy car model, the Bobo Foo, and I hope to address some of these questions in my remarks.

As your chief executive, you will understand that it is my job to lead the company and to protect shareholder interests above all others. These are responsibilities I take very seriously.

In particular, and in explaining how your board arrived at the decision it did, I would like to briefly outline my roles. It is my role to develop and implement policies and strategies capable of delivering superior shareholder value and to assume full responsibility for all aspects of the company's operations. It was I who commissioned the Foo in the first place in pursuit of the strategy that Bobo should be represented in all of the main car segments. The correctness of that decision is shown by the outstanding sales of the model at half a million units a year in what is a very competitive part of the market.

I must also manage the financial and physical resources of the company, monitor results, and ensure that effective operational and risk controls are in place. Bobo is a profitable company and in designing and developing the Foo, I personally took a direct interest in maintaining its low cost ethos. I assigned our expert design team to create the product and we then submitted it to the crash test to gain information on its safety vulnerabilities.

My role also involves overseeing the management team, co-ordinating the interface between the board and the other employees in the company, and assisting in the appointment of directors to the board. In a large company such as Bobo, it is obviously vital that we have the best people at all levels and I am pleased to be able to have Kathy Yao on the board. She leads our talented team of car designers and the excellent design of the Foo is testimony to their talents.

Finally, it is my role to relate to a range of external parties including the company's shareholders, suppliers, customers and state authorities. The legal issues that have confronted us with regard to compensation claims against the Foo's design are mainly my responsibility and it is to these matters that I now turn.

Tutorial note

These paragraphs contain two roles in each. Allow for different ways of expressing the roles.

(ii)   **Defence of company decision**

I am very aware of the reason we meet today in this EGM and I want to explain to you why the board took the decision it did, resisting the idea to issue a universal recall of the Foo.

As your chief executive, it is my responsibility to *take a wide range of opinions and viewpoints into account,* some of which are conflicting. The protection and maximisation of shareholder value is, however, my highest and most important duty in all contestable cases. I have many potential accountabilities, but *my primary accountability is to you, the shareholders.*

Accordingly, the decision I took was that which I thought would provide the *best value to shareholders.* This was only my view of course and others will disagree, but given the calculations made available to me, the choice was clear. It would have been an abdication of my fiduciary duty to allow an option to be adopted that reduced shareholder value as significantly as the recall option would have. In making this judgement I took into account the very small number of incidents that have occurred with this product as a proportion of all the Bobo Foo cars sold to date.

The *margin between the two options was not close* with the choice of resisting the recall outweighing the other option by a factor of three in terms of costs to the company. If it were a more finely balanced financial calculation, I may have opted for the recall option but given the projected difference of half a billion dollars over 10 years, I really had no choice because I had no right to erode shareholder value to that extent. I do not necessarily expect you all to agree with me, especially those who may have alternative ethical perspectives on these issues, but I do hope you can accept that the decision was taken in good faith as the most financially prudent and commercially responsible of the two stark options available to us.

Tutorial note

Allow different ways of expressing these thoughts within the pristine capitalist perspective.

		ACCA marking scheme	
			Marks
(a)		2 marks for each cause identified and described to a maximum of	8
		2 marks for each IC measure identified and described to a maximum of	6
		Total	12
(b)		2 marks for each Kohlberg level explained to a maximum of	6
		2 marks for each level correctly assigned to a person with evidence (½ for correct recognition only).	
		Total	12
(c)		2 marks for distinguish between.	
		1 mark for purpose of AGMs.	
		1 mark for purpose of EGMs.	
		1 mark for each relevant point for advantages to a maximum of 4 marks.	
		Total	8
(d)	(i)	1 for each role identified and 1 for placing in context, to a maximum of	8
		Or	
		1 for each role identified and briefly explained, in context, to a maximum of	8
	(ii)	2 marks for each point of defence identified and developed.	6
		Professional marks for clarity, logical flow, persuasiveness and appropriate structure.	4
Total			**50**

Examiner's comments

The case scenario in question 1, as previously, was a detailed case to enable a number of areas of the study guide to be examined. The scenario concerned a number of issues associated with the development of a new model of car, the Bobo Foo, and it was a story loosely based in a real-life story of some years ago. In an attempt to produce a new car model quickly and cheaply, a design flaw was introduced that was potentially dangerous to users. When confronted with a choice of what to do about it, the Bobo company chose to pay out compensation to affected users rather than retool the plant because, over the lifetime of the car's production, it was by far the cheaper option even although the company knew the car to be unsafe.

As usual, I used the scenario to examine a number of outcomes which not only sampled the study guide and also required candidates to answer at more than one level intellectual level. Also as previously, the requirements were based heavily upon the case meaning that candidates had to study the case in some detail to gain marks.

Part (a) was an 'internal controls' question and contained two tasks. The first task was to explore the circumstances that led to the fuel tank problem on the Bobo Foo. The verb 'explore' was used here to enable candidates to have latitude in responding to this task. Many candidates were able to correctly pick out and explore the causes of the problem. These included cost pressures, a shortening of the usual development time, ignoring the outcome of a crash test and failure to challenge senior management on the issues associated with these problems. A careful study of the case enabled stronger candidates to gain the majority of the marks for this task.

The second task in part (a) was to propose ('identify and explain') internal control measures capable of mitigating the fuel tank risk in future car development projects. This was less well done than the first task in part (a). Again, a careful consideration of the specific problems at Bobo was the secret to gaining marks. Candidates that attempted to answer this using a memorised list of points from a study text or other notes were less well rewarded.

Part (b) was a Kohlberg question. This was the third time I have examined this and on each occasion, I have used people in the case to illustrate the different levels. In December 2007, the issue concerned a decision on how to react to the overestimation of a mineral and in June 2009, it concerned the level of moral development of the 'rogue trader' Jack Mineta. In December 2007, the three levels were represented by the three people in the case but in this paper, two were conventional and one was pre conventional. There was nobody at the post conventional level. I think some candidates assumed there must have been a post conventional person and Kathy Yao was the person most often, but incorrectly, associated with this level. Many candidates were able to get most of the first six marks for the 'explain' requirement but others became confused when allocating James Tsakos, Kathy Yao and Vernon Vim to the appropriate levels.

Part (c) was about annual and extraordinary general meetings, and asked about the value of an EGM for Bobo and its shareholders. Candidates were required to distinguish between AGMs and EGMs, and then explain the advantages of an EGM for Bobo in the case. The first part was done better than the second. To get marks on the 'advantages' part, candidates had to analyse the case to see why it was important for Mr Tsakos, Bobo's CEO, to face the shareholders in person.

Part (d) contained two parts and also had the four professional marks. The professional marks were allocated for the construction of a speech that Mr Tsakos was to give to the shareholders at the EGM. As usual, there was a full range of approaches to this including candidates who (wrongly) wrote their answers in the form of a letter, a memo or with no apparent structure at all. In terms of the substance of part (d)(i), the chief executive was required to explain his roles as CEO in managing the issues described in the case. Some candidates did poorly on this, perhaps confused by the 'in managing the issues described in the case', but a well-prepared candidate familiar with the usual roles of a chief executive was able to do quite well if the roles were discussed in context.

Part (d)(ii) was about defending the company's decision to pursue the 'compensation option' over the 'universal recall' option but to do so from a 'pristine capitalist' perspective. This means that candidates had to argue from a particular ethical perspective. Lists of Gray, Owen & Adams's seven positions were not rewarded at all and those with the highest marks were usually those able to argue using the information in the case, for example arguing that the financial cost of the 'compensation option' was much less than the alternative and was thus greatly to the benefit of shareholder value.

15   P&J (DEC 12)

(a)   **Social footprint and potential social implications.**

Social footprint

The term 'footprint' is used to refer to the impact or effect that an entity (such as an organisation) can have on a given set of concerns or stakeholder interests. A 'social footprint' is the impact on people, society and the wellbeing of communities. Impacts can be positive (such as the provision of jobs and community benefits) or negative, such as when a plant closure increases unemployment or when people become sick from emissions from a plant or the use of a product. Professor Kroll's findings have both positive and negative impacts upon society and communities in the case of P&J.

Potential implications

The discovery by Professor Kroll will lead, whether by a tightening of controls or by a reduction in P&J's activities, to lower exposures to X32 in Aytown and Betown, and hence there will, over time, be *less X32-related disease.* There will, in consequence, be fewer people suffering, and, accordingly, less misery for the affected families and friends of sufferers. *A lower mortality* from X32-related disease will benefit communities and families as well as those individuals directly affected. However, as they are continuing to manufacture the product, if Professor Kroll's findings prove correct, larger numbers of people using the product will ultimately be affected worldwide.

Loss of jobs in the various stages of the P&J supply chain. The forecast losses, even in the best case scenario, would be likely to involve the loss of jobs and employment levels at P&J plants and its suppliers. The worst case scenario, in which the company itself would be lost, would involve the loss of the 45,000 P&J jobs plus many more among suppliers and in the communities supported by the P&J plants (such as in local businesses in Aytown and Betown).

Loss of, or serious damage to, communities in which the operations are located. This includes the economic and social benefits in the developing countries and a very high level of social loss in Aytown and Betown (in Emmland), where both towns are highly dependent on a single employer. It is likely that Aytown, effectively a 'company town' with 45% of the jobs at P&J, will be very badly affected and the good causes in Betown, such as the nursery and adult education classes, will no longer be able to be supported. The loss of a major employer from a town can lead to a loss of community cohesion, net outward migration and a loss of, or deterioration in, community facilities.

There will be a loss *of economic value for shareholders,* and a reduction in the standards of living for those depending upon the company's value for income or capital growth. This might result in a reduction in pension benefits or endowment values, where P&J shares are a part of the value of such funds. Individuals holding P&J shares may lose a substantial proportion of their personal wealth.

Tutorial note

Allow other relevant impacts such as loss of taxes to fund states services, increases in state funding to support unemployed/sick workers, etc.

(b) **Risk diversification**

Diversification of risk means adjusting the balance of activities so that the company is less exposed to the risky activities and has a wider range of activities over which to spread risk and return. Risks can be diversified by discontinuing risky activities or reducing exposure by, for example, disposing of assets or selling shares associated with the risk exposure.

Problems with diversification of risks

In the case of P&J, the case highlights a number of issues that make P&J particularly vulnerable and which would place constraints on its ability to diversify the X32 legal risk.

A key risk is that the company's portfolio of activities is heavily skewed towards X32 with *60% of its business in* X32 when Kroll's findings were published. This is a very unbalanced portfolio and makes the company structurally vulnerable to any health threat that X32 poses. It means that a majority of its assets and expertise will be dedicated to a single material and anything that might be a risk relating to sales of that material would be a risk to the whole company.

The case says that the *plant cannot be adapted to produce other materials.* A mine, for example, cannot suddenly be 'adapted' to produce a safer alternative. The case also says that processing plants are dedicated exclusively to X32 and cannot be modified to process other materials. This means that they either continue to process X32 or they must be completely refitted to work on alternative materials.

As a result of that, P&J is *unlikely to be able to dispose of X32 assets profitably* now that Kroll's findings are known about and the reasons for the health concerns have been identified. The reaction of society to X32 was highlighted by Hannah Yin as a key factor in determining the likelihood of the risk and this might make it difficult to sell the assets on to others.

Finally, the obvious way to diversify the risk is to expand the remaining 40% of the portfolio to become more prominent. However, the company has *little by way of retained earnings and is already highly geared* with little prospect of further borrowing. This is likely to limit its options for developing new products as a means of diversification. Share issues would be a possible way of re-financing, but with such a high exposure to X32 losses, this would be problematic.

Tutorial note

Some candidates may attempt to interpret the data in the case numerically. Allow marks if relevant points are made.

(c) **Criticisms of Hannah Yin's behaviour related to fundamental principles**

There are five fundamental principles that apply to all professionals including professional accountants. They are integrity, objectivity, professional competence and due care, confidentiality and professional behaviour. In this case, the fundamental principles that Hannah Yin has breached are integrity, objectivity and professional behaviour.

Criticise Hannah Yin

Hannah *betrayed the trust of shareholders,* making a disclosure in her name precisely because she knew she would be believed. This shows *a lack of integrity* and is also very *unprofessional behaviour.* Her status as a professional and her performance over recent years had built up a stock of trust in her. It was her responsibility to maintain and cultivate this trust and to continue to give shareholders good reason to trust her as a professional accountant. To make biased and partial disclosures precisely because she was trusted is cynical and a betrayal of her duty as a company director and as a professional. As a professional with integrity, Hannah Yin should have the highest levels of probity in all personal and professional dealings. Professionals should be straightforward and honest in all relationships, and never take part in anything that might undermine, or appear to undermine, the trust which society has placed in them.

Furthermore, she *accepted inducements* to comply with Mr Ho's wishes. A significant increase in share options made her disproportionately concerned with the short-term maintenance of the company share price, and this helped to cloud her judgement and *reduced her objectivity* as a professional. She may have reasoned that it would have been against her own economic self interest to disclose the worst case scenario because it would reduce the value of her share options in the short term. Hannah Yin should not have allowed bias, conflicts of interest or undue influence to cloud her judgements on professional decisions. This means, for example, that she must not allow the possibility of particular personal gains to over-ride the imperative to always uphold the public interest and represent the best interests of shareholders.

Finally, she *knowingly and intentionally misled shareholders* by only reporting the most optimistic risk forecasts. This is a clear breach of the integrity and *professional behaviour* required of a person in her position. The principles of transparency and fairness require companies to be truthful and complete in their disclosures to shareholders, especially when price-sensitive information (such as the health risks of X32) is involved. Professionals such as Hannah Yin should comply fully with all relevant laws and regulations, whilst at the same time avoiding anything that might discredit the profession or bring it into disrepute. This involves complying with the spirit as well as the letter of whichever regulations apply.

(d) **Article for *Investors in Companies*.**

(i) **Strategic and operational risk and explain why findings are strategic**

Trouble at P&J

These must be difficult times to be a director at P&J, Emmland's largest producer of X32. What does a board do when it is faced with having caused a large number of terrible health problems for employees and users of X32, whilst at the same time having no strategic alternative but to carry on and try to manage what are sure to be enormous long-term liabilities?

Strategic and operational risks

The company is facing a highly strategic risk since the publication of Professor Kroll's findings. Whereas operational threats are those affecting a part of a company, perhaps a risk to a raw material or the loss of a product market, a strategic risk is one that has the possibility, if realised, to affect the company as a whole and its future strategic success. We have seen similar risks before to important industries where, for example, entire industries have disappeared from some developed countries because of changes in international labour market costs and political changes. These are examples of strategic risks materialising, and the effects can be disastrous for those affected.

Strategic risk to P&J

P&J shareholders will appreciate knowing that Kroll's report has the effect of being a strategic risk for P&J for at least three reasons. To begin with, his findings potentially *affect the whole company* rather than just parts of it, such is the extent of P&J's exposure to this commodity through vertical integration. Presumably this strategy had previously been thought a good idea, with the company directly owning all three stages in the supply chain, from mining, to processing, to the manufacturing operations in Emmland. All stages are threatened by Kroll's findings. Plus, if product sales eventually slow down and stop, its sources of cash flow will also disappear.

Second, this is bound to *affect* P&J's *strategic positioning* and the way that it is viewed by investors, suppliers, employees and a range of other stakeholders. It has a weaker offering to potential skilled employees than before Kroll's findings were published, it will be harder to raise capital and also to sell its products. Its reputation as a sound company will be reduced as a result, and these things matter in a highly developed country such as Emmland.

Third, and perhaps most importantly, this could eventually be a *threat to the company itself.* This depends upon how large the liabilities eventually become and how well the company handles the issue in the coming years, but this is a real possibility if the worst-case projections turn out to be accurate. Its heavy reliance on X32 over many years has left it with a 60% dependence on X32, which was fine when the material was in high demand, but it leaves the company very vulnerable when and if that market falls away.

Given these risks facing P&J, this is not a share that will be attractive to investors for the foreseeable future.

(ii)   **Board responsibilities for IC and criticise Mr Ho**

Responsibilities for internal controls

Readers will also be alarmed to hear of the decision by CEO Laszlo Ho to impose a limited tightening of X32 process controls that only involved doing so where the company was visible to the Emmland public, a compromise he called 'Plan B'. The board's responsibilities for internal control are detailed in the COSO guidance on this subject and are very clear. Mr Ho's, and the P&J board's, responsibilities for effective internal controls include, in this case, control over X32 fibres in the working environments of each stage in the whole X32 supply chain.

The responsibilities include *establishing a control environment* capable of supporting the internal control arrangements necessary. This includes a suitable 'tone from the top' and a high level commitment to effective controls. It also involves *conducting risk assessments* to establish which risks need to be controlled by the internal control processes (health risks, perhaps?). The introduction of relevant control activities is especially important when a hazardous material like X32 is being considered. This, of course, applies to all of the company's employees and not just those based in Emmland. It is also the board's responsibility to provide *information and maintain relevant communications* with those affected by the control measures, and to ensure that important measures are fully implemented and understood. Finally, the COSO guidelines specify that all controls should be *monitored* for the degree of compliance and for their effectiveness. This should be a continuous, ongoing process, capable of immediately highlighting any weaknesses or breaches in the implemented controls.

Criticisms of Mr Ho's 'Plan B'

In the case of P&J, Mr Ho has taken a deliberate and premeditated decision to *ignore the health needs* of some of the company's employees on the basis of cost. X32 has been clearly shown to be a health risk and Mr Ho is knowingly allowing employees to be exposed to the material in the course of their normal jobs. The people in the mines and processing facilities will still be exposed to X32, and will presumably continue to get ill and die in the full knowledge of the company management. This is a failure of the fiduciary duty that the P&J board owes to its employees.

Mr Ho is implementing an upgrade to internal control, *not on the basis of need but on the basis of how visible the changes will be* to investors, most of whom will be based in the developed world. So residents of Aytown and Betown can look forward to a tightening of controls to limit their X32 exposure whilst those in countries with no health and safety legislation cannot. This could be seen as a cynical move to manage the company's image in Emmland. They are taking advantage of the relative weakness of their developing countries' host governments and being selective in whom they extend the necessary X32 process controls to.

Recent events have raised a number of very serious issues for P&J. It is difficult to know what the future will hold for the company, with such a substantial external threat and with management so determined to act unethically in managing that threat. I do not predict an easy time ahead for P&J shareholders.

	ACCA marking scheme	Marks
(a)	2 marks for definition of social footprint. 2 marks for each implication identified and discussed.	10
(b)	2 marks for description of risk diversification. 2 marks for each problem with diversification.	10
(c)	1 mark for identification of the fundamental principles breached by Hannah. Up to 2 further marks for explanation of how each principle is breached. Maximum	9
(d) (i)	2 marks for distinguishing between operational and strategic risk. 2 marks for each reason why risk is strategic.	8
(ii)	1 mark for each control responsibility. 2 marks for each relevant criticism to a maximum of 4 marks.	9
	Professional marks for structure, logical flow, persuasiveness and tone of the article.	4
Total		50

Examiner's comments

The case in section A (question 1) was about a company called P&J that made a product (X32) that was discovered to be toxic and hazardous to health. With so much investment in the X32 supply chain, P&J had to face several strategic problems, not least of which was a likely long-term liability from litigation claims from employees and others that had been exposed to X32. The requirements examined a range of issues concerned with P&J and its difficult situation.

Part (a) asked about P&J's social footprint. Most candidates were able to define what it means (the first requirement) and the question then asked for four particular social implications of Professor Kroll's findings. The case described these and this showed the importance of carefully studying the case to gather this information.

The emphasis here was on exploring how people and communities can be affected by business issues. In the case of X32, these issues concerned health, employment and the loss of company value.

Part (b) asked about the diversification of risk. Overall, this requirement was done poorly. A minority was able to describe well what the term means. The requirement was to explain why diversification of its risks would be very difficult for P&J. Again, it was necessary to study the case in some detail to answer this well as all the reasons for the difficulties were there. Weaker answers attempted to fit the TARA framework into the answer although this was an inappropriate and incorrect approach.

Part (c) was about the unethical and unprofessional behaviour of Hannah Yin, who was a qualified accountant and therefore subject to the fundamental principles of professionalism contained in the IFAC code of ethics. The case contained evidence that her behaviour breached three specific fundamental principles (integrity, objectivity and professional behaviour). Weak answers listed all of the IFAC principles with some attempting to show either their importance (which was not required) or to show how Hannah had somehow breached all of them. In understanding ethical behaviour for professionals, it is important to be able to criticise poor ethical behaviour and this was the main purpose of this question.

I was disappointed that neither requirement in part (d) was done well by many candidates. The first part of (d) (i) was to distinguish between strategic and operational risk and this was done quite well by many candidates. It was the second requirement in (d) (i) that was done less well: to show how the findings in the Kroll report are a strategic risk to P&J. This involved being able to apply the idea of strategic risk and to analyse the case to show why these risks are strategic (as opposed to operational). This second requirement was less well done. It is important, then, not only to know what terms like 'strategic risk' mean, but also to be able to apply them in the context of information from a case study.

I was surprised that part (d) (ii) was not so well done because five of the nine marks available were effectively testing theoretical knowledge (the board's responsibilities for internal control). A thorough and systematic revision schedule should have provided candidates with a full knowledge of the board's responsibilities in respect of internal controls and the COSO guidelines were a helpful framework around which to base a good answer.

The second task in (d) (ii) was to criticise Mr Ho's decision to choose Plan B. This was poorly done overall even although there were clear criticisms to be made of Plan B (in the case) from an ethical perspective: Plan B knowingly overlooked the health needs of some employees and acted based on how visible the changes would be, thereby ignoring the need to upgrade the facilities in the developing countries.

The four professional marks were awarded for writing the answer in the form of an article in a magazine called Investors in Companies. There were some excellent attempts from some candidates whilst others seem to have made no attempt at all to frame their answers according to this requirement. As is previous reports, I would remind candidates, that making an attempt to gain the professional marks is very worthwhile and in some cases, can be the difference between a pass and a fail.

16   HOPPO (JUN 13)

Key answer tips

This scenario and question covered a report from a major accounting firm on the future supply of a rare material, essential for some modern electronic products. As is often the case this was based on a real life situation. The questions covered several aspect of the study guide. Key to success was the application of knowledge to the material in the scenario. Somewhat unusually parts (a) – (c) were each for 10 marks.

Part (a) required candidates to "briefly explain" different aspects of risk focussing in the correlation between legal and reputational risk.

Part (b) used two verbs the use of which was critical to success in the context of environmental reporting. The first to "describe" the purpose and content; the second to "discuss" advantages for the company and its stakeholders. It was important to address these tasks individually.

Part (c) required students to complete two tasks in the context of internal control. Firstly, to explain how internal control could be strategic; secondly to use examples from the case to illustrate. This approach provides further evidence that detailed reading of the case scenario is vital to success in P1.

Part (d) in two parts contained the professional marks. The method of communication was a press release. Defining the theory in part i) should have presented few problems but this needed to be applied to the case. Part ii) was a good opportunity to develop the case against paying a bribe applying deontological and teleological perspectives. Again the examiner noted the need to follow the guidance when constructing the appropriate form of communication requested as heavy use of theoretical terms would be detrimental to understanding.

(a)   **Related and correlated risks**

Related risks are risks that vary because of the presence of another risk or where two risks have a common cause. This means when one risk increases, it has an effect on another risk and it is said that the two are related. Risk correlation is a particular example of related risk. Risks are positively correlated if the two risks are positively related in that one will fall with the reduction of the other, and increase with the rise of the other. They would be negatively correlated if one rose as the other fell.

Legal risk and reputation risk

At Hoppo, legal risk and reputation risk are likely to be positively correlated because it is likely that as legal risk rises, then, for the reasons explored below, so will reputation risk. Were the legal risk to recede, then risk of reputational damage would also recede. In the case of legal and reputation risks at Hoppo, legal risk is the independent variable and reputation risk is the dependent variable. This is because the reputation risk incurred will largely depend on the legal risk.

The legal risk in this case is the possibility that, if Red Co's outsourced manufacturing contract is cancelled, Red Co will pursue a legal case against Hoppo. Because so many jobs (about 1,000) and a lot of future earnings for Red Co are at stake, Red Co may vigorously pursue the case and seek to gain damages for the loss of a valuable contract and employee termination costs. It is not certain that Red Co would take this option, though, and so the probability of this occurring is not known.

The reputation risk is the loss to Hoppo if issues were to be raised in the public consciousness that might cast the company in a negative light. It is hard to know in advance how a legal challenge would be reported but Hoppo could be accused, justly or unjustly, of several things. Legal cases sometimes raise issues in the public consciousness that the company would have otherwise not had exposed. Some of these may be perfectly legitimate in business terms but may offend one or more stakeholders.

In the case of Hoppo, they may be accused of incompetence in drawing up the outsourcing contract with Red Co. The fact that the *legal agreement is considered by some to be ambiguous* suggests incompetence and this may erode Hoppo's reputation for competence. The *loss of about 1,000 jobs at Red Co*, arising from the loss of the Hoppo contract, is likely to be widely reported, particularly in Teeland. Although jobs are likely to be created in Yuland if the new facility is built there, some may interpret this re-location as a breach of good faith with Red Co and demonstrating a lack of business integrity on Hoppo's part. The effect of any loss of reputation for Hoppo could be serious.

Hoppo may also be portrayed as an *unreliable business partner* and this may affect future outsource opportunities, especially where the other company is in another jurisdiction and legal complications may consequently arise. In addition, any loss of reputation is probably quite important for Hoppo, as the case makes clear that both *customers and some key employees interact* with the company partly based on its favourable social and environmental reputation. In that case, an eroded reputation may affect product sales and also recruitment.

(b)   **Description of environmental report**

In most jurisdictions, the production of environmental information is voluntary in that it is not required by any accounting standard or legal statute. In some cases, environmental information is included in the regular annual report and in other cases, 'stand alone' environmental and/or sustainability reports are published, usually annually. Although these are often published as hard copy documents, they are also often made available on company websites.

In each case, however, the purpose of an environmental report is to report on some of the details of the company's environmental impact or 'footprint'. Because some of this information is technical in nature, systems need to be put in place to generate and internally assure the data, similar to those systems necessary for generating accurate financial data.

The contents of an environmental report typically include information on the company's direct environmental impact (through its own manufacturing and distribution) and also its indirect impacts (through its forward and backward supply chains). It involves recording, measuring, analysing and reporting on the environmental impact, usually in respect of two aspects: consumption (of energy and other resources) and production. This latter impact (production) involves the measurement and reporting of the environmental impact of products and also any other emissions, such as by-products and any pollutants.

Advantages for Hoppo and its shareholders

The first advantage of environmental reporting would be to provide information to investors on the *sources and ways of mitigating environmental risk*, and of those risks correlated with environmental risk. The events at Red Co have the potential to damage Hoppo's reputation and potentially turn some customers away from buying Hoppo products because of the implication that Hoppo has poor environmental controls in its supply chain.

Second, an environmental report would enable Hoppo to *demonstrate its responsiveness to major issues* such as the leakage of TY13 at Red Co. Likewise, it would be a suitable place to inform shareholders on the 'state of the art' environmental performance of its new factory in Yuland. Some customers are known to buy from Hoppo partly because of its environmental reputation, and some employees, similarly, are attracted for the same reason. These factors make this responsiveness potentially very important.

Third, the regular production of an environmental report would necessitate the *establishment of measurement systems* able to generate the information for the report. This would mean that the company would have greater knowledge of, and control over, its resource consumption, environmental efficiency and emissions. This knowledge could then, in turn, save costs and improve internal controls in the company. In the case of a new-build facility in Yuland, systems for gathering this data can be 'designed-in' to ensure that information is meaningful, accurate and timely. These measures may help convince investors that Hoppo is a sound long-term and sustainable source of shareholder value.

Fourth, *reporting strengthens the accountability to the shareholders* and encourages better environmental performance as a result. Once a company reports on a policy, a measure or a target (for example), it provides something against which it can be later held to account. For shareholders, the publication of environmental information means that the company can be required to respond to queries on underperformance against agreed standards. This could serve, over time, to make the board more answerable to shareholders and reduce the agency gap.

(c) **Strategic internal controls**

Internal controls can be at the strategic or operational level. At the strategic level, controls are aimed at ensuring that the organisation 'does the right things'; at the operational level, controls are aimed at ensuring that the organisation 'does things right'. Those controls that operate at the strategic level are capable of influencing activities over a longer period. This concerns issues capable of affecting the strategic positioning of the organisation. In the case of Hoppo, the shortage of the supply of TY13 is capable of affecting its output and hence its ability to meet its strategic objectives in terms of the TY13-containing products. The overall objective of internal control is to ensure the orderly conduct of business and this requires effective controls from the top to the bottom of the organisation.

Internal controls in the Yuland factory

Internal controls apply to all processes and procedures within an organisation. For controls in an internal value chain for a manufacturer, effective internal controls are necessary to ensure the efficient adding of value to inputs and the minimisation of waste. In the case of working with TY13, however, the case describes several specific reasons that need to be taken into account. Red Co, having worked with TY13 for many years, has developed some competence in this, but evidently not entirely so, as evidenced by the leakage of TY13 from its plant in Teeland.

The first issue that makes internal controls over TY13 so important is its *high cost* and the fact that *small inefficiencies can disproportionately affect final product costs* and hence profitability. As a highly specialised material, TY13 is used in small quantities but any inaccuracies in application, or losses in the process, can affect the economics of the production process. This may affect the profitability of production in extreme cases.

Second, TY13 is *highly toxic* and so should be controlled internally (to prevent exposure to employees) and externally, to prevent leakage such as happened at Red Co. This is likely to be controlled by regulation in Essland but the situation is unclear in Yuland. It is likely that stringent controls will be needed to minimise the chances of leakage or loss and this is not only an economic issue (protecting value) but also a social and environmental issue.

Third, there are *general supply problems*. TY13 is a rare material as highlighted by the report. This means that relationships with suppliers may become strategically important. The case indicates that Red Co had cultivated strong relationships with suppliers and a challenge for Hoppo would be to build up similar relationships, so that supply would be safeguarded if world shortages occur.

Fourth, because supply quality varies, the *testing of TY13* at the 'factory gate' can be important in ensuring that the delivered material is fit for purpose. Because the performance of the finished product depends heavily on obtaining the required grade of TY13, control over this test is likely to be very important. Hoppo would need to have stringent material tests if this variability of supply quality is not to undermine the quality of its finished goods.

(d) (i) **Press release**

Hoppo Co is pleased to respond to allegations made in the media about the events surrounding recent discussions concerning its outsourcing activities. In seeking to protect Hoppo's business and ethical reputation, it is true that we are considering the future of our links with one of our outsourcing partners. Hoppo was very disappointed to learn of the poor employee conditions at Red Co and also the leakage of TY13 into a local river. The company is considering options for the future to prevent such events from happening again. This includes the option of taking manufacturing under direct control.

We take this opportunity to inform the public and our shareholders about the importance we place upon the highest levels of integrity and transparency, and why we believe these to be of the utmost importance in corporate governance. We also wish to explain the circumstances around the demand for an irregular payment from an individual in Ootown and why Hoppo considers it wrong to consider paying this in pursuit of its business objectives.

Integrity at Hoppo

For the avoidance of doubt, Hoppo accepts and agrees with the IFAC definition of integrity as that which, *'imposes an obligation... to be straightforward and honest in professional and business relationships. Integrity also implies fair dealing and truthfulness.'*

Hoppo believes that integrity is steadfast adherence to strict ethical standards despite any other pressures to act otherwise. Integrity describes an ethical position of the highest standards of professionalism and probity. It is an underlying and underpinning principle of corporate governance and requires anybody representing shareholders to possess and exercise absolute integrity at all times. Hoppo unreservedly and unambiguously accepts this and the duty it places on the board of directors.

Transparency and Hoppo

Hoppo regrets the perception that it lacked transparency in considering issues concerning its investment in Yuland. The company also wishes to re-emphasise its belief in the importance of transparency in matters of corporate governance. To Hoppo, transparency means *providing open and clear disclosure* of relevant information to shareholders and other stakeholders. Hoppo believes that it should *not conceal information when it may materially affect others*. It means open discussions and a *default position of information provision rather than concealment*. This means that when there is no good and legitimate reason to conceal discussions or other information, it should be disclosed as a matter of course. This has been, and remains, Hoppo's position.

(ii) ### The issue of the 'personal gift' (bribe)

Hoppo would like to publicly explain, to reassure our stakeholders and again for the avoidance of any doubt, why it believes that paying a bribe to the mayor of Ootown is wrong. This is despite the fact that, all other things being equal, Ootown was and remains an attractive location for the construction of the new factory. The board accepts that this is a serious issue relating directly to the integrity of the board and so a direct and detailed response is merited. As a company that believes in the highest standards of conduct in all business matters, Hoppo always seeks to apply best practice and, accordingly, believes it is never appropriate to consider paying bribes, whatever the circumstances.

First, there is a strong business case for rejecting this demand. It is very important that *Hoppo is trusted by its shareholders* and others. It is equally important that employees find Hoppo a *good and ethical company to work for*, and to invest their working lives with. In both cases, any suggestion of a lack of probity would be potentially very damaging and this may *harm Hoppo's goodwill* and the quality of the relationship with its employees. Even though, all other things being equal, we believe that Ootown may be a very good option for the new factory, being exposed for paying a bribe would do *long-term damage to the business*.

More importantly, though, there is an overwhelming ethical case to reject the option to pay the bribe and to investigate the feasibility of using Ootown without doing this, or choosing Aatown.

Tutorial note

This is the deontological perspective.

From one perspective, Hoppo believes that principles and duties are important in business. Businesses and individuals have an ethical duty to act with integrity and the highest standards of professionalism at all times. We believe that the *world would be a poorer place and that business would be very badly affected* if bribery became an acceptable and a normal part of business life. If everybody practised bribery in making business transactions, then this would *undermine trust in business* and make international business investments, like that in Yuland, almost impossible. Because it would, *if generalised, have a negative set of outcomes*, Hoppo believes it is unethical in principle. *If it is wrong in general, then it cannot be right in specific cases.*

Tutorial note

This is the consequentialist perspective.

Hoppo also believes that paying the bribe is *wrong in terms of achieving the outcomes that the company seeks*. Were the company to pay the mayor of Ootown in order to facilitate the planning permission needed, a number of very unfortunate consequences might arise. First, Hoppo might *gain a very unhelpful reputation in the region as a company that can be bribed*, and this, in turn, would increase the possibility of repeat occurrences. Second, even if the payment were not discovered, it would mean that the *threat of public disclosure* would make Hoppo vulnerable to other demands from the mayor of Ootown.

We hope that this statement has addressed the concerns of all of our stakeholders.

			Marks
	ACCA marking scheme		
(a)	1 mark for explaining related risks. 1 mark for explaining correlated risks. 1 mark each for evidence of understanding of legal and reputation risk. 1·5 marks for each issue explored from case exploring link between legal and reputation risk. Half mark for identification only.		
		Maximum	10
(b)	Up to 4 marks for description. 2 marks for each advantage.		
		Maximum	10
(c)	2 marks for explaining strategic. 2 marks each for each IC explanation in context.		
		Maximum	10
(d) (i)	1 mark for each relevant point explaining integrity in context to a maximum of 3 marks. 1 mark for each relevant point explaining transparency in context to a maximum of 3 marks.		
		Maximum	6
(ii)	1 mark for each relevant point on the business case. 1 mark for each relevant point on deontological arguments (of which 1 for evidence of understanding). 1 mark for each relevant point on the consequentialist case (of which 1 for evidence of understanding). Points may be made anywhere in the answer.		
		Maximum	10
	Professional marks for the format, tone, logical flow and persuasiveness of the press release.		4
Total			**50**

Examiner's comments

The scenario in section A was about a report produced by a major accounting firm on a rare material (TY13) that was essential for use in some modern electronic products. As with many previous cases, this scenario was based on a real-life situation.

As in the past, the requirements for question one covered several areas of the study guide and, as mentioned above, most required answers related to details in the case in order to attract the highest marks.

Parts (a), (b) and (c) were worth ten marks each. Part (a) asked about related and correlated risk, with the particular example of the correlation between legal risk and reputation risk given the situation in the case. Many candidates were able to explain the two terms although some candidates confused positive and negative correlation of risks in their explanations. The better answers were able to see and explore the reputational difficulties of legal cases especially if details of Hoppo's own behaviour was made public in a legal case.

Part (b) was about environmental reporting. The wording of the requirement showed that it is important to determine how many tasks there are in the requirement. The first was to describe the purpose and contents of an environmental report, and the second was to discuss the advantages of an environmental report for the company and its shareholders. The best answers divided up these two tasks and approached them separately. Candidates who had read the technical article on this would have been better prepared for this requirement than others. There were some very good answers to the first part (on purpose and content) but the highest marks were awarded for those also able to meaningfully approach the second part, on the advantages to Hoppo and its shareholders. This involved examining the specific environmental challenges faced by Hoppo and then showing how producing and environmental report could help with these. General answers on the generic advantages of environmental reporting were less well-rewarded.

Part (c) was about internal controls and, again, the requirement contained two tasks. The first task was to explain how internal controls can be strategic in nature. In order to answer this well, it was necessary to know what 'strategic' meant and this is usually contrasted with the operational. Each level has its own objectives, activities, timescales and areas of responsibility. In addition though, risks can also be strategic or operational in nature, and the internal controls at the two levels are also different. Many candidates had a good idea about this and were able to gain at least one of the two marks available, with many achieving both marks.

The more ambitious task in part (c) was to 'explain, using detailed examples from the case, why developing sound internal controls over the supply and processing of TY13 would be important if Hoppo opted to build its own factory in Yuland'. This obviously necessitated a detailed analysis of the case in order to gather the reasons why such internal controls would be necessary. The case mentioned a number of features about TY13 that meant that sound controls would be necessary were Hoppo to process it in its Yuland factory. These included its high cost, its toxicity, the general supply problems and the variable quality of the raw material. All of these would be essential in any processing facility. It is clear from this example that it would not be possible to gain marks in this task without a detailed examination of the case.

The professional marks in part (d) were for presenting the answers in the form of a press release. As with previous exams, there was a full range of attempts with varying degrees of success in framing the answers in the requested manner. Many made a good attempt, gaining three or four of the professional marks, whilst others made no obvious attempt at all. It was frustrating to see some candidates setting out their answer as a memo or a letter when this was clearly not what was being asked in the requirement. It was also important to present the answer as a press release and not just as an exam answer. In a press release, for example, it would be unusual to see terms like deontological or consequentialist in part (d)(ii). The model answers present the contents of these two positions but do not use the actual terms except as a commentary. The content of the press release was intended to address concerns over the request for a bribe by the mayor of Ootown. For six marks in part (d)(i), candidates were required to define and explain integrity and transparency in the context of the case. The marking scheme allowed three marks for each but answering it 'in the context of case', i.e. relating to Hoppo's situation, was important to get full marks. A common approach was to define the two terms (essentially bookwork) but then fail to adequately develop the connection to the case. It was disappointing to see this because it didn't take very much extra analysis to attract the extra 'case related' or applied marks.

There was a wide range of answers to part (d)(ii). The requirement examined the content on bribery in the P1 study guide and asked candidates to construct the argument against paying the bribe to the mayor of Ootown. The requirement asked that this argument should include both business and ethical perspectives against paying the bribe. For ten marks, candidates should have been alerted to the need for a fairly detailed consideration of these issues. A typical poor answer briefly discussed the essential features of both deontological and consequentialist ethical approaches, but did not then adequately relate these to the case. This requirement was done poorly on average. Perhaps the verb 'construct' was difficult for some candidates but in addition, the business case for not paying the bribe was often poorly developed.

Section 4

ANSWERS TO PRACTICE QUESTIONS – SECTION B

GOVERNANCE AND RESPONSIBILITY

17 CORPORATE GOVERNANCE GUIDELINES

Key answer tips

The suggested answer focuses on the UK Corporate Governance Code. However, the question does not specifically ask about corporate governance in the UK, and a well-prepared answer can refer to the governance rules in any other country. Answers which included comments on how points (i) – (vi) might comply with other corporate governance systems are equally acceptable.

(a) Many aspects of the extracts in the question would not comply with corporate governance systems such as the UK Corporate Governance Code guidelines.

   (i) Audit fees and auditor independence. In the UK, it is a requirement of company law that all audit fees and fees for other services provided by auditors should be fully disclosed. Non-audit fees include fees for tax advice, management consultancy and general accountancy services.

   It has been argued that the partner(s) responsible for the audit should be changed regularly so that the audit is perceived to be more objective, and there is less chance of missing important anomalies in the audit process. However, there are no provisions about audit partner rotation in the Corporate Governance Code. It should be the responsibility of the audit committee to ensure the independence of the auditors, and to review the appointment/re-appointment and make suitable recommendations to the full board.

   (ii) The UK Corporate Governance Code states that the remuneration committee should consist of at least three (or two, in the case of smaller companies) members, and these should all be independent non-executive directors. The committee should objectively determine the remuneration and individual packages for each executive director and also the chairman and 'senior management' (but consult with the chairman and/or CEO about the remuneration of the other executive directors).

(iii)   The UK Corporate Governance Code states that the roles of chairman and chief executive should not be exercised by the same individual. The division of responsibilities between the chairman and chief executive should also be clearly established, agreed by the board and set out in writing. The chairman should be independent, and the CEO should not go on to become chairman in the same company.

(iv)   The disclosure of whether principles of good corporate governance have been applied is not normally enough; companies should also fully explain how such principles have been applied. The requirements for preparing a corporate governance report (and 'comply or explain' in this report) are contained in the UK Listing Rules for listed companies.

(v)   There is a requirement for directors to meet regularly and to retain full and effective control over the company. In practice, it is doubtful if anyone holding so many directorships, whether executive or non-executive, could devote sufficient time to each company to effectively fulfil their responsibilities. However, the Corporate Governance Code makes no specific reference to the number of directorships any individual may hold. The Code merely states that the letter of appointment of a NED should set out the expected time commitment, and the individual should also make a disclosure to the board, before his or her appointment, of his or her other time commitments. There is also a requirement in the Code for individual directors to undergo a performance appraisal annually. Presumably, any director who does not have the time to perform his or her duties properly will be identified and asked either to commit more time or to resign.

(vi)   This is likely to comply with the Corporate Governance Code, although the board should also review risk management generally, not just the system of internal controls. The Corporate Governance Code states that the directors should maintain a sound system of internal control and, at least annually, conduct a review of the effectiveness of the group's system of internal controls and they should report to the shareholders that they have done so. The review should cover all material controls. These include not just financial controls, but also operational controls, compliance controls and the risk management system.

Tutorial note

This question – and solution – does not cover every aspect of the UK Corporate Governance Code. Similarly, corporate governance codes in other countries will address other issues, in addition to those covered by this question.

Perhaps a significant item to remember in the UK is that it is recommended that at least one half of the board of directors in large listed companies (and at least two directors in smaller companies) should be independent non-executive directors. A further item to note for the UK is the introduction of the Directors' Remuneration Disclosure Regulations in 2002, amending the Companies Act 1985 and requiring detailed disclosures about directors' remuneration and remuneration policy.

(b) (i) **Report on Corporate Governance in a rules-based system**

The broad principles of corporate governance are similar in the UK and the USA, but there are significant differences in how they are applied. In particular, whereas the UK has a voluntary corporate governance code, the US system is based on legislation which sets statutory requirements for publicly-traded companies which are imposed through the Sarbanes-Oxley Act (SOX). The Act is relevant to directors of subsidiaries of US-listed businesses and auditors who are working on US-listed businesses.

Advantages are that there is clarity in terms of the requirements for companies and standardisation for all companies. However, this also means that there is no room for flexibility or to improve governance beyond the level set by the law. Non-compliance with the law is a criminal offence.

These requirements include the certification of published financial statements by the CEO and the chief financial officer (finance director), faster public disclosures by companies, legal protection for whistleblowers, a requirement for an annual report on internal controls, and requirements relating to the audit committee, auditor conduct and avoiding 'improper' influence of auditors.

The Act also requires the Securities and Exchange Commission and the main stock exchanges to introduce further rules, relating to matters such as the disclosure of critical accounting policies, the composition of the board and the number of independent directors. The Act has also established an independent body to oversee the accounting firms. (This is called the Public company Accounting Oversight Board, or 'Peek-a-Boo'). Managers must be careful to comply with regulations to avoid possible legal action against the company or themselves individually.

(ii) **Two-tier boards**

Germany is an example of a country with two-tier boards for companies. This contrasts with the UK where the board structure is a unitary board (consisting of executive and non-executive directors together).

The supervisory board of non-executives (Aufsichrat) has responsibility for corporate policy and strategy, and the management board of executive directors (Vorstand) has responsibility primarily for the day to day operations of the company. The supervisory board typically includes representatives from major banks that have historically been large providers of long-term finance to German companies (and are often major shareholders). The supervisory board does not have full access to financial information, is meant to take an unbiased overview of the company, and is the main body responsible for safeguarding the external stakeholders' interests. The presence on the supervisory board of representatives from banks and employees (trade unions) may introduce perspectives that are not present in some UK boards. In particular, many members of the supervisory board would not meet the criteria under UK Corporate Governance Code guidelines for being considered independent.

18   GEELAND (DEC 11)

Key answer tips

This is a question based real life quotes as to how corporate governance should be regulated in a fictitious country. Part (a)–(c) cover fundamental and central parts of the P1 syllabus so should have been straightforward.

(a)   **Rules and principles**

Distinguish between

There are two broad approaches to the regulation of corporate governance provisions: rules-based and principles-based. In a rules-based country (jurisdiction), all provisions are legal rules, underpinned by law, transgression against which is punishable in law. Often characterised as a 'box ticking' approach, full compliance is required by all companies at all times (excepting where dispensations are granted, again, under the provisions of the law).

In a principles-based jurisdiction, legal force applies to the provisions of company laws but additional listing rules are enforced on a 'comply or explain' basis. It is important to note that compliance is not voluntary in that the provisions can be ignored, but that provisions may not be complied with in full, usually for a limited period if the full reason for non-compliance is explained to the shareholders. This allows for the market to judge the seriousness of the non-compliance and to potentially re-appraise or revalue the company as a result.

Critical evaluation of remark

The remark in the Geeland Code strongly argues in favour of a principles-based approach to corporate governance. In particular, it is critical of rules-based codes that would, for example, place a blanket ban on combining the roles of chairman and chief executive. In order to allow for differences between circumstances, it is arguing for flexibility and 'common sense'.

The arguments in favour of the remark.

In most cases, compliance with general principles is cheaper than compliance with a detailed 'box ticking' regime. A common criticism of rules-based approaches is the expense of compliance including the establishment of information systems to meet reporting requirements (for example on internal controls), consultancy costs, increased management costs and reporting costs. Where some flexibility is possible, the principles-based approach allows some 'common sense' to be employed in the extent of detailed compliance.

A principles-based approach is flexible and allows companies to develop their own approach, perhaps with regard to the demands of their own industry or shareholder preferences. This places the emphasis on investor needs rather than legal demands. There may be no reason, for example, why companies in lower risk industries should be constrained by the same internal control reporting requirements as companies in higher risk industries. As long as shareholders recognise and are satisfied with this, the cost advantages can be enjoyed.

An example of the flexibility afforded by a principles-based approach is that it allows for transitional arrangements and unusual circumstances. Details such as the contract terms of directors may need to be varied to meet individual needs or the notice periods might similarly be varied. In the event of a sudden, unexpected change such as a death in service, a company can enter a phase of technical non-compliance but, with suitable explanation of the reason for non-compliance, most shareholders will nevertheless be satisfied.

It avoids the need for expensive and inconvenient monitoring and support structures, the costs of which are ultimately borne by the companies themselves (through stock market or regulatory bodies) or by the taxpayer. The costs and inconvenience of policing compliance with rules has been shown to be material in some situations, especially in smaller companies. Similarly, the costs of a large national 'watchdog' to monitor and enforce detailed compliance is considerable.

Arguments against

There may be confusion over what is compulsory under law and what is principles-driven under listing rules. A lack of clarity might be present, especially where compliance expertise is not available to management (such as in some smaller companies) between legally-required compliance and listing rules which are subject to comply or explain. This may confuse some management teams and cause non-compliance borne of lack of advice and information.

A principles-based approach assumes that markets are capable of understanding the seriousness of any temporary or more lengthy periods of non-compliance and of revaluing the shares as a result. Non-specialist shareholders may not understand why a given provision is not complied with nor appreciate the potential consequences of the non-compliance. Cleverly-worded comply or explain statements might mislead shareholders.

A 'box ticking' approach offers the advantage of gaining full compliance at all times (i.e. all boxes are actually ticked) whereas a principles-based approach allows some bad practice to continue. A full compliance regime is likely to provide a greater overall confidence in regulation and this, in turn, will further support long-term shareholder value.

A rules-based approach provides standardisation and prevents any individual companies gaining competitive or cost advantages with lower levels of compliance. This creates a 'level playing field' in which all competitors in an industry understand what is required.

Tutorial note

Critically evaluate requires candidates to examine both sides of the debate.

(b) **Separation of roles**

The strongest and most common reason for the separation of these roles is to avoid the dangers of unfettered power that may arise when power is concentrated in a single, powerful individual. The original proposition for the separation of roles was in the UK's Cadbury Report in 1992 which was itself a response to a number of corporate 'scandals', similar to those in Geeland, involving unfettered power and the abuse of shareholder wealth as a result.

Accountability is better served by the separation of roles because the chief executive has a named person, in addition to the non-executive directors, to whom he or she must account for the company's performance and his or her own behaviour. This serves to protect against conflicts of interest where chief executives may be tempted to act in their own self-interest rather than to serve the best interests of the shareholders.

Third, both roles are complex and demanding. In large companies, it is likely that the two roles cannot be carried out effectively by one person. By gaining the advantages of a separation of duties (and hence a division of labour), the performance of the company's management in total will be enhanced. The two roles are materially different in terms of their skills, and it enhances organisational effectiveness for one to chair the board (chairman) and another, with different skills, to manage the strategy of the company. It is usual for the chairman role to be undertaken by a non-executive director, whilst the chief executive is an executive director. Having this distinction at the top of the company allows the chief executive to be hands on and directly involved in the management of the company, whilst the chairman can adopt a more supervisory position.

Finally, it is considered best practice because it provides a reassurance to investors and ensures compliance with relevant codes. Investor confidence in company management is very important and this is enhanced by having a transparent and clear separation of roles. Where codes specify separation and this can be demonstrated, unlike at Anson Company, unqualified comply or explain statements can be issued thereby promoting investor confidence.

(c)   **Comply or explain**

The statement clearly identifies the one area of non-compliance and represents a full discharge of the company's reporting obligation to comply or explain. In a principles-based jurisdiction, this statement is required under listing rules and involves informing shareholders of the level of compliance and also specifying any areas of non-compliance, which the company has done in this case.

It is clear and free of ambiguity in what it says. Clearly though, one area of non-compliance is explained. The area of non-compliance is identified and the individual is named. The naming of William Klunker may be material because if he is known and trusted by shareholders, the breach may be less important than if he were less known and less trusted.

It does not provide a good reason for the non-compliance other than saying that it was 'benefiting from having Mr Klunker in control' which might be seen as weak by some investors. The reasons for combining the roles in July 2009 are not given and so it could probably be argued that this is not a full explanation.

It does, however, provide a date for returning to full compliance against which management can be held accountable for failure. This will reassure investors that its period of non-compliance is temporary and the default position of the company is to remain in full compliance with the relevant code.

ACCA marking scheme		
		Marks
(a)	4 marks for distinguishing between rules and principles based approaches. Up to 2 marks for each argument for or against, to a maximum of 10 marks.	
	Maximum	10
(b)	2 marks for definition of market risk. 2 marks for each relevant point of justification made to a maximum of 8 marks.	
	Maximum	10
(c)	1½ marks for each relevant point of assessment. Half a mark for identification only.	
	Maximum	5
Total		**25**

Examiner's comments

The case in question 2 was about a debate in Geeland over how corporate governance should be regulated. It contained a quotation on how a principles-based system might be applied and also one from Anson Company, which had a temporary compliance failure in respect of its executive chairman. Both of these quotations were based on real-life examples, slightly modified for the purposes of making them fit the exam paper. Most candidates attempted this question.

Part (a) first asked candidates to distinguish between rules and principles-based approaches to corporate governance. This has been examined before and is a central part of the P1 study guide and so I was pleased to see that most who attempted the question did quite well on that task. The more ambitious task followed, which was to critically evaluate the quotation in the case about the application of principles in corporate governance.

The task was to explore the two sides of the debate which some candidates did very well indeed whilst others seemed not to understand the task at all. This should have been a straightforward task for a candidate who had studied the debate over rules and principles but there was evidence that some candidates appeared not to grasp this important area of the P1 study guide.

Part (b) also examined a central part of the corporate governance debate: the separation of the roles of chief executive and chairman. The case study described a situation at Anson Company in which Mr Klunker had temporarily adopted the role of executive chairman. In line with best practice in a principles-based jurisdiction, the company had made a 'comply or explain' statement in its annual report and this was the subject of part (c).

Part (b) was done quite well overall but some candidates struggled to actually assess the 'comply or explain' statement in part (c). The task in part (c) was not to explain what 'comply or explain' meant (this was a common mistake) but to take an informed view on the statement provided by Anson on explaining why it had an executive chairman and was thus in breach of the relevant code provisions.

19   KK (DEC 10)

Key answer tips

Use the requirement to form a structured answer using appropriate headings.

(a)   **Conflict of interest**

A conflict of interest is a situation in which an individual has compromised independence because of another countervailing interest which may or may not be declared. In the case of non-executive directors, shareholders have the right to expect each NED to act wholly in the shareholders' interests whilst serving with the company. Any other factors that might challenge this sole fiduciary duty is likely to give rise to a conflict of interest. Does the director pursue policies and actions to benefit the shareholders or to benefit himself in some other way?

Conflicts of interest in the case

John has a longstanding and current *material business relationship with KK Limited* as CEO of its largest supplier. This creates an obvious incentive to influence future purchases from Soria Supplies over and above other competitor suppliers, even if the other suppliers are offering more attractive supply contracts as far as KK is concerned. It is in the interests of KK shareholders for inputs to be purchased from whichever supplier is offering the best in terms of quality, price and supply. This may or may not be offered by Soria Supplies. Similarly, a conflict of interest already exists in that Susan Schwab, KK's finance director, is a NED on the board of Soria Supplies. Soria has a material business relationship with KK and Susan Schwab has a conflict of interest with regard to her duty to the shareholders of KK and the shareholders of Soria Supplies.

His appointment, if approved, would create a cross *directorship with Susan Schwab.* As she was appointed to the board of Soria Supplies, any appointment from Soria's board to KK's board would be a cross directorship. Such arrangements have the ability to create a disproportionately close relationship between two people and two companies that may undermine objectivity and impartiality in both cases. In this case, the cross directorship would create too strong a link between one supplier (Soria Supplies) and a buyer (KK) to the detriment of other suppliers and thus potentially lower unit costs.

John's brother-in-law is Ken Kava, the chief executive of KK. Such a close *family relationship* may result in John supporting Ken when it would be more in the interests of the KK shareholders for John to exercise greater objectivity. There should be no relationships between board members that prevent all directors serving the best interests of shareholders and a family relationship is capable of undermining this objectivity. This is especially important in public listed companies such as KK Limited.

(b)   **Advantages of appointing non-executives to the KK board**

The case discusses a number of issues that were raised as a result of the rapid expansion. An effective NED presence during this period would expect to bring several benefits.

In the case of KK, the NEDs could provide essential input into two related areas: monitoring the strategies for suitability and for excessive risk. In *monitoring the strategies for suitability,* NEDs could have an important scrutinising and advising role to fulfil on the 'aggressive' strategies pursued by KK. All strategy selection is a trade-off between risk and return and so experience of strategy, especially in risky situations, can be very valuable.

NEDs could also *monitor the strategies for excessive risk.* The strategy role of NEDs is important partly because of increasing the collective experience of the board to a wide range of risks. With KK pursuing an 'aggressive' strategy that involved the 'increasingly complex operations', risk monitoring is potentially of great importance for shareholders. There is always a balance between aggression in a growth strategy and caution for the sake of risk management. The fact that some of the other executive directors are both new to the company (resulting from the expansion) and less experienced means, according to the case, that they may be less able and willing to question Mr Kava. Clearly, an effective non-executive presence would be able to bring such scrutiny to the board. They may also place a necessary restraint on the strategic ambitions of Mr Kava.

They could *provide expertise on the foreign investments including,* in some cases, country-specific knowledge. It is careless and irresponsible to make overseas investments based on incomplete intelligence. Experienced NEDs, some of whom may have done business in or with the countries in question, could be very valuable. Experienced NEDs capable of offering specific risk advice, possibly through the company's committee structure (especially the risk committee) would be particularly helpful.

Investors are reassured by an effective non-executive presence on a board. The fact that investors have expressed concerns over the strategy and risk makes this factor all the more important in this case. An experienced and effective NED presence would provide shareholders with a higher degree of confidence in the KK board so that when large overseas investments were made, they would be more assured that such investments were necessary and beneficial.

Finally, through an effective nominations committee, the NEDs could have *involvement in the recruitment and appointment of executive and non-executive directors* through the nominations committee structure. Specifically when the business is growing the need for new people is at its height and the *appointment of specialists at board level in such periods is strategically important.* Through the use of contacts and through the experience of recruiting directors for many years, experienced NEDs could make a worthwhile contribution.

Tutorial note

This is a case analysis task. Do not reward the four roles: people, strategy, risk, scrutiny unless clearly used to analyse the case.

(c)   **Corporate governance report**

Best practice CG report

Several corporate governance codes of practice prescribe the content for a report as part of an annual report. Although these vary slightly, the following are prominent in all cases.

Information on the *board and its functioning*. Usually seen as the most important corporate governance disclosure, this concerns the details of all directors including brief biographies and the career information that makes them suitable for their appointment. Information on how the board operates, such as frequency of meetings and how performance evaluation is undertaken is also included in this section. This section is particularly important whenever unexpected or unanticipated changes have taken place on the board. Investors, valuing transparency in reporting, would always expect a clear explanation of any sudden departures of senior management or any significant changes in personnel at the top of the company. Providing investor confidence in the board is always important and this extends to a high level of disclosure in board roles and changes in those roles.

The *committee reports* provide the important non-executive input into the report. Specifically, a 'best practice' disclosure includes reports from the non-executive-led remuneration, audit, risk and nominations committees. In normal circumstances, greatest interest is shown in the remuneration committee report because this gives the rewards awarded to each director including pension and bonuses. The report on the effectiveness of internal controls is provided based in part on evidence from the audit committee and provides important information for investors.

There is a section on *accounting and audit issues* with specific content on who is responsible for the accounts and any issues that arose in their preparation. Again, usually a matter of routine reporting, this section can be of interest if there have been issues of accounting or auditor failure in the recent past. It is often necessary to signal changes in accounting standards that may cause changes in reporting, or other changes such as a change in a year-end date or the cause of a restatement of the previous accounts. These are all necessary to provide maximum transparency for the users of the accounts.

Finally there is usually a section containing *other papers and related matters* which, whilst appearing to be trivial, can be a vital part of the accountability of directors to the shareholders. This section typically contains committee terms of reference, AGM matters, NED contract issues, etc.

Fin Brun's information needs

Fin Brun is voicing a reasonable and realistic concern to Mr Kava because it is usually difficult to determine the contributions of individual directors (unless there has been some other publicity, positive or negative, throughout the year). The *bonuses awarded to each director* are, however, disclosed in the report of the remuneration committee and this gives an indication of the committee's view on each director's performance. The biographies of all directors, including NEDs, is *included in a best practice disclosure and that can also provide information* on the type of person the director is and an indication of his or her fitness for the job.

Tutorial note

The study texts approach this content in slightly different ways (different headings). Allow for variations in expression of ideas].

Marking scheme		Marks
(a)	2 marks for an explanation of conflict of interest. 2 marks for each potential conflict of interest identified and explained.	8
(b)	2 marks for each advantage assessed. Maximum	7
(c)	2 marks for each section explained (allow for cross marking between points) to a maximum of 8 marks. 2 marks for explanation of information needs of Fin Brun.	10
Total		**25**

20 MULTI-JURISDICTIONAL GOVERNANCE (DEC 07)

Key answer tips

This question focuses in parts (a) & (b) on one of the key concepts of corporate governance: the separation of roles of chairman and chief executive. For part (a) you will need to find five separate roles to earn full marks, so make sure you don't put two roles into one sentence.

To earn the marks for 'assess' in part (b) you will need to describe each benefit, then go on to say something additional about it – how big is the benefit or what problem can it help with. Ensure that you separate your answer into two parts, and focus on the idea of accountability to shareholders in the second part of the answer. Planning your answer before writing up will ensure that you don't talk about accountability as a benefit in the first part of (b).

Part (c) requires you to critically evaluate. To answer this requirement you will need to consider arguments for and against the idea, but giving more emphasis to the points against this statement, i.e. in favour of a single set of governance provisions. There is no need to go into the detail of the OECD or ICGN codes since the question requires you to consider the overall concept of a single set of governance codes.

(a) **Roles of the chairman in corporate governance**

The chairman is the leader of the board of directors in a private or public company although other organisations are often run on similar governance lines.

In this role, he or she is responsible for *ensuring the board's effectiveness* as a unit, in the service of the shareholders. This means agreeing and, if necessary, *setting the board's agenda* and ensuring that board meetings take place on a regular basis.

The chairman represents the *company to investors* and other outside stakeholders/constituents. He or she is often the 'public face' of the organisation, especially if the organisation must account for itself in a public manner. Linked to this, the chairman's roles include *communication with shareholders*. This occurs in a statutory sense in the annual report (where, in many jurisdictions, the chairman must write to shareholders each year in the form of a chairman's statement) and at annual and extraordinary general meetings.

Internally, the chairman ensures that directors receive relevant information in advance of board meetings so that all discussions and decisions are made by directors fully apprised of the situation under discussion. Finally, his or her role extends to *co-ordinating the contributions of non-executive directors* (NEDs) and *facilitating good relationships between executive and non-executive directors.*

(b)   **Separation of the roles of CEO and chairman**

Benefits of separation of roles

The separation of the roles of chief executive and chairman was first provided for in the UK by the 1992 Cadbury provisions although it has been included in all codes since. Most relevant to the case is the terms of the ICGN clause s.11 and OECD VI (E) both of which provide for the separation of these roles. In the UK it is covered in the Corporate Governance Code.

The separation of roles offers the benefit that it frees up the chief executive to *fully concentrate on the management of the organisation* without the necessity to report to shareholders or otherwise become distracted from his or her executive responsibilities. The arrangement provides a position (that of chairman) that is *expected to represent shareholders' interests* and that is the point of contact into the company for shareholders. Some codes also require the chairman to represent the interests of other stakeholders such as employees.

Having two people rather than one at the head of a large organisation *removes the risks of 'unfettered powers'* being concentrated in a single individual and this is an important safeguard for investors concerned with excessive secrecy or lack of transparency and accountability. The case of Robert Maxwell is a good illustration of a single dominating executive chairman operating unchallenged and, in so doing, acting illegally. Having the two roles separated *reduces the risk of a conflict of interest* in a single person being responsible for company performance whilst also reporting on that performance to markets. Finally, the chairman provides a *conduit for the concerns of non-executive directors* who, in turn, provide an important external representation of external concerns on boards of directors.

Tutorial note

Reference to codes other than the UK is also acceptable. In all cases, detailed (clause number) knowledge of code provisions is not required.

Accountability and separation of roles

In terms of the separation of roles assisting in the accountability to shareholders, four points can be made.

The chairman scrutinises the chief executive's management performance on behalf of the shareholders and will be involved in approving the design of the chief executive's reward package. It is the responsibility of the chairman to hold the chief executive to account on shareholders' behalf.

Shareholders have an identified person (chairman) to hold accountable for the performance of their investment. Whilst day-to-day contact will normally be with the investor relations department (or its equivalent) they can ultimately hold the chairman to account.

The presence of a separate chairman ensures that a system is in place to ensure NEDs have a person to report to outside the executive structure. This encourages the freedom of expression of NEDs to the chairman and this, in turn, enables issues to be raised and acted upon when necessary.

The chairman is legally accountable and, in most cases, an experienced person. He/she can be independent and more dispassionate because he or she is not intimately involved with day-to-day management issues.

(c) **Corporate governance provisions varying by country**

There is a debate about the extent to which corporate governance provisions (in the form of written codes, laws or general acceptances) should be global or whether they should vary to account for local differences. In this answer, Vincent Viola's view is critically evaluated.

In general terms, corporate governance provisions vary depending on such factors as local business culture, businesses' capital structures, the extent of development of capital funding of businesses and the openness of stock markets. In Germany, for example, companies have traditionally drawn much of their funding from banks thereby reducing their dependence on shareholders' equity. Stock markets in the Soviet Union are less open and less liquid than those in the West. In many developing countries, business activity is concentrated among family-owned enterprises.

Against Vincent's view

Although business cultures vary around the world, all business financed by private capital have private shareholders. Any dilution of the robustness of provisions may *ignore the needs of local investors* to have their interests adequately represented. This dilution, in turn, may *allow bad practice*, when present, to exist and proliferate.

Some countries suffer from a poor reputation in terms of endemic corruption and fraud and any reduction in the rigour with which corporate governance provisions are implemented fail to address these shortcomings, notwithstanding the fact that they might be culturally unexpected or difficult to implement.

In terms of the effects of macroeconomic systems, Vincent's views *ignore the need for sound governance systems to underpin confidence in economic systems*. This is especially important when inward investment needs are considered as the economic wealth of affected countries are partly underpinned by the robustness, or not, of their corporate governance systems.

Supporting Vincent's view

In favour of Vincent's view are a number of arguments. Where local economies are driven more by small family businesses and less by public companies, *accountability relationships are quite different* (perhaps the 'family reasons' referred to in the case) and require a different type of accounting and governance.

There is a high *compliance and monitoring cost* to highly structured governance regimes that some developing countries may deem unnecessary to incur.

There is, to some extent, a link between the stage of economic development and the adoption of formal governance codes. It is generally accepted that developing countries need not necessarily observe the same levels of formality in governance as more mature, developed economies.

Some countries' governments may feel that they can use the laxity of their corporate governance regimes as a *source of international comparative advantage*. In a 'race to the bottom', some international companies seeking to minimise the effects of structured governance regimes on some parts of their operations may seek countries with less tight structures for some operations.

	Marking scheme		Marks
(a)	1 mark for each relevant role clearly identified		5
		Maximum	5
(b)	'Cross mark' points made in these answers		
	Benefits of separation of roles: Up to 2 marks for each point identified and assessed as an argument		Up to 10
	Accountability and separation of roles: 1 mark for each point made explaining the comment		Up to 4
		Maximum	12
(c)	'Cross mark' points made/issues raised in the two parts of this answer		
	1 mark for each relevant point made on why corporate governance provisions should not vary by country		Up to 5
	1 mark for each relevant point made on why corporate governance provisions might vary by country		Up to 5
		Maximum	8
Total		**Maximum**	**25**

Examiner's comments

Introduction

This question drew from the main corporate governance sections of the study guide. The answers to the question showed that whilst most had a basic knowledge of the content area in question, the less-prepared candidates struggled when it came to responding to the higher level verbs used in parts (b) and (c).

Part (a) was, at first sight, a fairly simple task to explain the roles of a chairman in corporate governance. It is when answering questions like this one that candidates have to pay special attention to the cognitive level of the verb in the question. The question specifically asked candidates to 'explain' the roles. Accordingly, answers that merely 'identified' the roles did not receive good marks. Short bullet lists of 'identified' roles received less than a pass (i.e. less than 3 out of 5) because they did not answer at the required cognitive level. An 'explanation' differs from an 'identification' in that it offers some evidence of understanding of the role over and above a mere identification. This need not be a long explanation but something rather more than a brief bullet list.

Part (b) was the most substantive part in Question 3 and asked two questions about the separation of the roles of chairman and chief executive. The first task was to assess the benefits of separating the roles. The idea of separating the roles was formally proposed in the UK by the Cadbury code back in 1992. Although there are other reasons for the separation of roles, Cadbury's proposals took place in the wake of a number of 'scandals' in which the abuse of power at the top of a company was a major cause. The report said (s. 4.9):

'If the two roles are combined in one person, it represents a considerable concentration of power. We recommend, therefore, that there should be a clearly accepted division of responsibilities at the head of a company, which will ensure a balance of power and authority, such that no one individual has unfettered powers of decision.'

Good answers usually contained a clear statement on the increased accountability arising from the separation of roles reducing the 'unfettered power' of a single, powerful individual. In order to score highly on part (b), however, a second task was to explain how the separation of roles led to increased accountability to shareholders. Fewer candidates did as well on this as on the first task, perhaps because it was a little unexpected. Candidates should be aware, though, the questions on Paper P1 will often ask candidates to think about something in the exam that they may not have read directly in the study guides or been taught in class. The structure of Q3 (b) is one that candidates should expect in future P1 papers.

21   FOOTBALL CLUB (DEC 07)

Key answer tips

This question focuses on the areas of stakeholders and Corporate Social Responsibility which are important topics for this paper.

Part (a) begins with a definition of a stakeholder, which is something that you need to ensure you can produce in two sentences. It goes onto discuss why it is important to identify all stakeholders. This is **not** asking you to identify the stakeholders in this scenario, but to discuss **why** a business would need to carry out such an exercise. Think of what would happen if they ignored all stakeholders – this may give you some thoughts as to why it is important to identify them.

The first part of the requirement for part (b) is to compare and contrast. This can be done either by highlighting similarities and differences between the two positions, or simply by describing them in a couple of sentences each. There is no need to describe the other five positions that Gray, Owens and Adams discussed.

A simple structure for your answer would be to describe the position and then go onto the second part of the question and explain how a company operating from this perspective would respond to stakeholder concerns. Then repeat for the other position.

Fiduciary responsibility (part (c)) is generally discussed in the context of agency theory. 'Construct the case' requires you to highlight the benefits of broadening the responsibility in this situation. There is no need to bring any problems with doing this into your answer.

(a)   **Stakeholders**

Definition

There are a number of definitions of a stakeholder. Freeman (1984), for example, defined a stakeholder in terms of any organisation or person that can affect or be affected by the policies or activities of an entity. Hence stakeholding can result from one of two directions: being able to affect and possibly influence an organisation or, conversely, being influenced by it. Any engagement with an organisation in which a stake is held may be voluntary or involuntary in nature.

Tutorial note

Any definition of a stakeholder that identifies bi-directional influence will be equally valid.

Importance of identifying all stakeholders

Knowledge of the stakeholders in the stadium project is important for a number of reasons. This will involve surveying stakeholders that can either affect or be affected by the building of the stadium. In some cases, stakeholders will be bi-directional in their stakeholding (claim) upon the stadium project. Stakeholders in the stadium project include the local government authority, the local residents, the wildlife centre, the local school and the football club's fans.

Stakeholder identification is necessary to gain an understanding of the sources of risks and disruption. Some external stakeholders, such as the local government authority, offer a risk to the project and knowledge of the nature of the claim made upon the football club by the stakeholder will be important in risk assessment.

Stakeholder identification is important in terms of assessing the *sources of influence* over the objectives and outcomes for the project (such as identified in the Mendelow model). In strategic analysis, stakeholder influence is assessed in terms of each stakeholder's power and interest, with higher power and higher interest combining to generate the highest influence. In the case, it is likely that the fans are more influential on the club's objectives than, say, the local wildlife centre, as they have more economic power over the club.

It is necessary in order to identify *areas of conflict and tension* between stakeholders, especially relevant when it is likely that stakeholders of influence will be in disagreement over the outcomes for the project. In this case, for example, the claims of the football club board and the local residents are in conflict.

There is a *moral case* for knowledge of how decisions affect people both inside the organisation or (as is the case with the stadium project) externally.

(b)   **Pristine capitalist and social contract approaches**

Definitions

The *pristine capitalist* position sees economic performance as the primary and only legitimate goal of all business organisations, especially those publicly owned by private shareholders. The *agency relationship is viewed as monofiduciary.* Any claim upon the organisation that would threaten the optimal profitability of the organisation is viewed as morally unacceptable as it would be an *effective theft of shareholder wealth.* It would also introduce economic inefficiencies that lead to the misallocation of capital resources. All such claims are therefore dismissed. The position is sometimes put as 'the business of business is business'.

The *social contractarian* position sees a business organisation as a citizen of society bound by society's norms and beliefs. Accordingly, organisations exist and thrive *only with a societal 'licence' to operate* in the same way that democratic governments only exist with the explicit consent of the governed. Discordance between organisational and societal values can result in the *withdrawal of support by society.* Accordingly, organisations seek to align themselves with social values, norms and expectations so as to maximise their social legitimacy. This sometimes necessitates modifying business objectives to take account of certain stakeholders' concerns.

Application to case

The pristine capitalist position *would recommend proceeding with the stadium project* notwithstanding local concerns. The reason is that the building of the stadium *offered the club the best way of maximising its primary strategic goals* by gaining larger crowds and thereby increasing revenues and obtaining more funds for players and other improvements.

Conversely, the social contractarian position would suggest that *the club only exists with the permission of its local stakeholders* (that could, collectively, harm the club) and accordingly, the *club needs to align its values with those of its key stakeholders* to continue to enjoy its 'licence' to exist. It may, therefore, need to amend its plans to continue to enjoy ongoing social support. It would be against the interests of the club to be seen to harm the interests of the school or the wildlife centre, for example, and so stadium plans may need to be amended accordingly to take their concerns into account.

(c) **Fiduciary responsibility**

Definition of 'fiduciary responsibility'

A fiduciary responsibility is a duty of trust and care towards one or more constituencies. It describes direction of accountability in that one party has a fiduciary duty to another. In terms of the case, the question refers to whose interests the directors of the football club should act in. Traditionally, the fiduciary duty of directors in public companies is to act in the economic interests of shareholders who invest in the company but are unable to manage the company directly. The case raises a number of issues concerning broadening the fiduciary duties of the directors of the football club with regard to the building of the new stadium, to other stakeholder groups.

The case for extending fiduciary responsibility

Although the primary fiduciary duty of directors in large public companies will be to shareholders, directors in businesses such as the football club described in the case may have good reason to broaden their views on fiduciary responsibility. This would involve taking into account, and acting in the interests of, the local wildlife centre, the residents, the school, the local government authority and the fans. The stakeholders in the case are not in agreement on the outcome for the new stadium and the club will need to privilege some stakeholders over others, which is a common situation whenever a proposal involving multiple impacts is considered. The specific arguments for broadening the fiduciary duties in this case include the following:

Such an acceptance of claims made on the football club would clearly demonstrate that the *club values the community* of which it considers itself a part.

It would help to maintain and manage its *local reputation*, which is important in progressing the stadium project.

To broaden the fiduciary responsibility in this case would be to an important part of the *risk management strategy*, especially with regard to risks that could arise from the actions of local stakeholders.

It could be argued that there is a moral case for all organisations to include other stakeholders' claims in their strategies as it *enfranchises and captures the views* of those affected by an organisation's policies and actions.

	Marking scheme		
			Marks
(a)	1 mark for each relevant point made on definition of 'stakeholder'		Up to 2
	Up to 2 marks for each relevant point on the importance of stakeholder identification		Up to 8
			────
		Maximum	10
			────
(b)	2 marks for description of pristine capitalist position		2
	2 marks for description of social contractarian position		2
	1 mark for each relevant point made applying the theories to the case		Up to 4
			────
		Maximum	8
			────
(c)	1 mark for each relevant point made defining 'fiduciary responsibility'		Up to 3
	1 mark for each relevant point made in favour of extending fiduciarity		Up to 4
			────
		Maximum	7
			────
Total			25
			────

Examiner's comments

Introduction

This was the section B question that caused candidates the most problems. The content of the question was drawn from parts of the study guide concerned with stakeholders, ethical perspectives and the arguments about extending corporate responsibility beyond the duties to shareholders. In each case, the reason why candidates underperformed was, again, because they failed to answer the question as it was actually set. It may be tempting to answer the question you wish was being set but unfortunately that will sometimes not achieve very many marks.

Part (a) asked candidates to define stakeholder (which most candidates got right) and then to 'explain the importance of identifying stakeholders...' It was the second task that confused many candidates. It might be worth noting what this part did NOT ask candidates to do. It did NOT ask candidates to:

Identify the stakeholders (so lists of stakeholders did not attract marks)

Describe the Mendelow framework

Describe each stakeholder's position on the Mendelow matrix

Explain each stakeholder's claim on the stadium project.

Most poor answers followed one or more of these paths.

Some marks would have been available for stating that one of the main purposes of identifying all stakeholders is to take into account the relative power and influence of stakeholder groups when planning for and communicating about the stadium project. However this was not specifically a 'Mendelow' question. The correct approach required candidates to 'take a step back' and place themselves in the position of the board of the football club, considering all the benefits of knowing who the stakeholders and their different claims were? That is what the question was probing.

Part (b) invited candidates to apply an important area of ethical theory to the case. Gray et al.'s 'seven positions' describe the possible perspectives that people can adopt in respect of the ethical role of business. The question specifically mentioned two of these – the pristine capitalist position and the social contractarian position. Again, it is worth noting that the question did not ask candidates to list the seven positions nor to explain any of the other five.

There were two tasks in part (b). The first was to compare and contrast the two positions. This involved recognising that the pristine capitalist position recognised only a responsibility to shareholders whilst the social contractarian position sees a 'deal' being done between an organisation and the society in which it operates. In the 'social contract', the organisation agrees to act in line with the norms of the society in which it operates in exchange for the support of that society in allowing it to survive and prosper. The second part was to explain how adopting each position as an ethical stance would affect how the football club responded to the stakeholder concerns. The way that many candidates answered this question was to correctly describe the two ethical positions but then to fail to adequately apply them to the situation facing the football club. It was this failure to apply, both in this question and elsewhere in the paper, that explains why many candidates did not achieve higher marks than they did. Again, it is not enough to rely on the 'book knowledge' learned from the study texts or classes. An ability to apply that knowledge to the case is essential in achieving higher marks.

The final part of question 4, **part (c)**, also asked for some evidence of understanding and then some application. In addition to explaining what 'fiduciary responsibility' meant, candidates were also invited to 'construct' a case for something. To 'construct', or 'synthesise', is a level 3 verb alongside others like assess or evaluate. It requires candidates to prepare an argument in favour of a particular position or course of action (or against, of course, depending on the question). Candidates do not need to personally believe in that position, of course, but to prepare the main points of a convincing case in support of the position stated.

In this case, the task was to prepare a case in favour of extending the fiduciary responsibility toward stakeholders other than the club's shareholders. The limit of accountability of a business organisation is one of the key arguments in the debate over the social responsibility of business and this case probed some of the issues involved in that debate. This part was not done well overall. For many candidates it was the final part of the examination itself and there was evidence in some exam papers of time pressure compromising the quality of the answers but it was also true that many candidates struggled with the task of constructing an argument. This should represent a challenge to candidates sitting the P1 paper in future.

22   DELCOM

Key answer tips

This question tackles a number of the less popular parts of the governance section of the syllabus. Ensure that you try all sections, and use the solution as a learning tool to recap these topics.

(a)   **Insider governance**

Insider structure refers to a company that is majority owned by individuals who have substantial influence over the executive operations at the organisation. This means that major shareholders are also directors. In this instance, Mr Kumas is both a majority shareholder and the CEO of the enterprise. Further, he effectively runs the company since the rest of the directors do not seem to have input to major strategy decision making.

Insider structures are very common as a global form of governance, being associated with the German and Asian model. Governments and financial institutions may be insiders although family structures are the most common form of insider model. Mr Kumas's involvement could be generalised as a family form of insider governance since it is run in his interests and therefore presumably those of his siblings and dependents.

Evaluation of insider governance structure

An evaluation should consider positive and negative aspects to this form of governance.

As identified in the scenario by Mr Kumas, there are potentially less agency costs in the form of directorial salaries and substantial disclosure since, as the majority shareholder, the major owner is well aware of how the company is performing and has little need for high paid executives to act for him.

The negative side of this is the lack of independence between decisions in the best interests of the company and his own individual shareholder needs. These may be at odds with other shareholders. There is clearly a lack of transparency in disclosure and this has been the cause of complaint by other shareholders at the AGM.

A lack of minority protection is often associated with insider structures and, through the above, can been seen to be at least a potential problem here. The poor local stock exchange regulatory regime may not highlight the importance of not disadvantaging the minority, and legal systems may offer little recourse. This subsequently becomes the focus for action in global governance standards discussed below.

Mr Kumas demonstrates that he has a tight control over company operations. This can be seen through taking sole responsibility for many decisions. Tight control can however lead to a lack of scope of skills in decision making. This insider failing can also be associated with governance theory and considered as a problem in transaction cost theory.

The personal nature of ownership and executive control coupled with the potential lack of transparency and threat to minority protection often restrict the flow of capital into such companies.

(b) **Transaction cost theory**

Transaction cost theory is a framework for managerial decision making. It has its roots in management accounting but can be adapted to consider governance and strategic control.

Strategic transactions are often complex and risky involving large scale resources. The growth of this organisation highlights the importance of acquisitive decisions in order to build the company portfolio. Such decisions require close consideration of the costs involved in the transaction and its outcomes.

Transaction cost theory identifies potential problems in such decisions arising from the bounded rationality of the decision maker and problems in opportunistic behaviour. Mr Kumas's failure to adequately consider due diligence in recent acquisitions and his reliance on intuition is an example of the former. The lack of any other board members involvement simply reinforces the problem of bounded rationality.

Opportunism is essential for growth and Mr Kumas has shown great skill in this area. The problem within opportunism is the personal nature of the perception of gain and thus consideration as to whether the decision maker is acting in the company's or his/her best interests. This issue is of concern to shareholders who require better information in order to understand the reasoning behind decisions made.

The greater the extent to which these two problems exist, the greater the need for change through improvements in the governance of the enterprise. This can be seen in shareholders requests for improvements in disclosure and accountability of Mr Kumas.

Governance measures taken are however about balancing increased governance measures with the potential to restrict entrepreneurial flair. The greater the external control the weaker the innovative response and motivation within. This can have a detrimental effect on shareholders returns.

Ultimately, through transaction cost theory, we see governance as a balance between the need to control and monitor whilst allowing a degree of professional freedom that is the very basis for the investment decision in the first place.

Tutorial note

The key concepts in transaction cost theory are the costs that occur in dealings with other parties, the limitations on the analysis of these costs (bounded rationality and opportunism) and the factors that affect the decisions (frequency, uncertainty and asset specificity). Try to bear these in mind when tackling this part of the question, and see how many of them can be related to the situation of Delcom.

(c) **Disclosure improvements**

There are a wide range of measures that can be taken in order to improve the level of disclosure made by the organisation in its annual report in order to appease the shareholders.

More information regarding strategic rationale would seem an obvious and immediate area where improvement is required. This should be accompanied by information regarding objectives and performance measures for future strategies. In general shareholders would like to see more information concerning future rather than current operations since the latter only provides comfort in previous performance and no real information relating to the security of their investment or the need to increase their investment in the company.

Stakeholder information is considered a prerequisite in order to satisfy the growing ethical standpoint of investors. They would like, especially under ICGN regulation, to see the company taking its responsibilities as a corporate citizen seriously. Stakeholder information may relate to direct and indirect stakeholders, narrow and wide, national and global. This does not seen from the scenario to be an area that Mr Kumas is likely to dramatically improve in the short term but may be a long term aspiration.

Specific rather than general information is a final important consideration. Annual accounts can be plagued with meaningless management speak and rhetoric rather than attempt to communicate anything meaningful to shareholders. There has recently been a backlash against this marketing fuelled use of jargon, hence the greater emphasis on such issues in governance such as Corporate Governance Code reference C1 in the UK.

(d) **Focus for action within global governance standards**

The focus for action should relate to the major issues raised in previous sections of the question. Shareholder rights and protection of the minority is the most important concern in stimulating global investment. This should be enshrined in law as well as in governance standards.

Directorial responsibility to act in shareholder interests or more specifically to develop and monitor strategy is also important as is the need to improve disclosure in order to communicate the nature of decision made and their reasons. This should be coupled with the need to consider the need for control and risk management with governance structures in place to address these issues or at least the need to report on them.

Finally, as mentioned, corporate citizenship or stakeholder analysis and consideration in strategy is often considered a facilitator to attracting investment in organisations.

23   VESTEL *Online question assistance*

Key answer tips

Your answer to parts (b) and (c) of this question can pull upon your own experience and business knowledge. The recruitment of a board member will have many similarities to the process that you will have been through to get your current job. And, similarly, to earn marks for the content of an induction process consider the things that you do, or are shown, in the first few days in a new job.

(a)   **Nomination committee**

Committees form an important part of board operations and, as stated, are generally included within principles laid down by regulatory bodies in order to advise as to appropriate governance structures. In the UK the role of nomination committees is outlined in the Corporate Governance Code.

Committees allow the expertise and skills of a focused group of individuals to be used in order to form advisory opinion for the board of directors. They usually consist of non-executive directors who have specialist skills in areas such as environmentalism or ethics. The non-executive nature of membership creates a degree of independence from executive management and this in turn suggests that no undue influence has been placed upon them in relation to conclusions drawn.

Skill provision, appropriate balance to membership and the independence of thought suggested will be important for a nomination committee. Their decisions will affect board composition and the independence of non-executives selected will be vital to ensure that shareholder needs are paramount in the decision making process of the board.

The committee structure offers a channel of communication for both executives and external consultants to ensure all relevant views are canvassed. At the same time they allow the board to off load responsibility for some key areas of decision making so allowing them to focus on other considerations such as strategy definition.

Nomination committees are essential for effective board operations because of the results they produce. The provision of new directors refreshes the board and ensures succession into roles, promoting stability and loyalty of senior management given a route through which promotion on merit can be achieved.

(b)   **Director recruitment**

There is no set approach to recruitment of new non-executive directors although certain issues in the case highlight the need for thoughtful and exacting methodology in order to subsequently ensure quality in the outcome.

The scenario suggests there may be a shortage of suitable local candidates for the job. It draws this conclusion through an analysis of the size of the corporate skill base available locally. This raises a number of issues.

Firstly, candidates will need to be carefully sought out and selected possibly through the use of search firms to act as intermediaries, approaching those in senior roles within other companies with a degree of confidentiality.

Secondly, candidates from outside the private sector should be considered, particularly in areas such as ethics and environmentalism. Academics and activists may be a part of the gene pool trawled in this respect.

Thirdly, overseas or foreign candidates should not be excluded, particularly when a large part of the company's business is in the export market. This will require a benchmarking exercise in order to ensure the company can afford the costs of drawing individuals from their home country in order to serve.

The Chairman's and CEO's view should be canvassed as part of the process. It may be the case that the Chairman takes overall responsibility for the committee. Since it has such a vital role to perform this is likely to be the case.

Standard background checks and interviews should be used as part of the selection process prior to selection of the best candidate and the negotiation over terms and contracts. Critically, the most important aspect of committee operations takes place following selection. The committee must ensure that their operations are appropriately disclosed to shareholders in the form of a separate section within the annual report. This ensures a degree of transparency exists in order to deal with the agency issue.

Performance appraisal is a final aspect to any board operation. The nomination committee must critically appraise the success and failures within the recruitment process used and ensure it continually evolves and improves over time.

(c)   **Business case for induction**

Induction for UK governance is included in the Corporate Governance Code. This highlights the need for the process to occur, managed by the Company Secretary, as well as the need for ongoing CPD arrangements to be available to all board members.

The business case for induction is partially discussed in the scenario as to the need to ensure individuals are able to be active members of board decision making as quickly as possible. This rapid assimilation assists in ensuring the board continues to be effective and able to deal with the operational and market challenges detailed in the scenario.

A high quality induction process also ensure individuals feel they have been given the right knowledge and support to ensure they are effective. This has ramifications in terms of ensuring retention of non-executives over time.

The business case can be considered in terms of what is delivered through induction. In this way the process ensures individuals are knowledgeable concerning the vision, objectives, customer base, operational value chain and ethics at the centre of board decision deliberations. Induction gives individuals the skills to do their job.

This can be extended to information concerning the legal and procedural framework within which the board operates so ensuring shareholders needs are continually met and risks reduced coupled with improved efficiency and effectiveness of board meetings.

Induction is an accepted part of human resource management for all employees and so there is no reason why it should not be a part of operations at the highest level. In fact, the gravity and consequence of decisions made suggests a greater need to ensure skills exist at this level and that individuals are fully aware of their roles and responsibilities.

Induction process

The content of induction should vary according to need and ability, especially at this level when dealing with executive status management. Information provision concerning legal duties may include provision of standard text on responsibilities such as that provided by the Institute of Directors in the UK. Company specific information would embrace data on markets and competitors, key customers, product portfolio and strategy.

Induction must include introducing the new non-executive to shareholders. This may be restricted initially to a meeting with key institutional shareholders and a pseudo induction meeting at the AGM when the candidate is introduced to shareholders in general meeting as they are given the opportunity to vote the person onto the board or reject them.

Visits to key corporate sites and even suppliers would be very useful as well as the need to meet key personnel below the board level as part of familiarisation or to open communication channels for future use by the non-executive.

Induction is really the start of a continuous learning process that occurs at each board meeting and which should be formalised through CPD. The induction process itself offers an opportunity to identify future training needs for non-executives.

Tutorial note

Any practical suggestions drawn from your own experience would be relevant here. Make sure they are well explained to earn the available marks.

24   CORPORATE GOVERNANCE *Walk in the footsteps of a top tutor*

Key answer tips

Overall, this is a factual question – if you know the material you can score high marks, otherwise it is a question to avoid as there is no scenario or other hints as to the content required in your answer.

The highlighted words are key phrases that markers are looking for.

Tutor's top tips

Look at the requirements carefully and from these you can establish the headings for your plan, and also your answer. Ensure that you are clear with the verb in the question, and what is required for that verb.

Tutor's top tips

For part (a) you will need to find five reasons for the emergence of governance regulations to earn the five marks. The verb 'identify' does not require you to go into much detail about each reason – one or two sentences explanation will suffice.

Your answer will need to do more than just refer to major corporate collapses and scandals. If you think of the various aspects of governance regulations that exist you should be able to establish what 'issue' these were introduced to avoid/prevent. This 'issue' would be the answer to the question that is being asked here.

(a) **Key reasons for the emergence of corporate governance regulations** include:

- Concern in the ways in which organisations are run, with particular focus on corporate scandals such as Maxwell (UK), Holtzman (Germany), Enron (USA) and OneTel (Australia).

- The need to provide some form of enforcement mechanism to try to stop company failures such as those noted above, occurring again in the future.

- The desire of many institutional investors to become more involved with the companies in which they have invested.

- The need for stability and security in the equities markets as investment from areas such as pension schemes expands. Private individuals as well as corporate investors are looking for similar stability in equities as in, say, government stocks to protect their investments and eventually their financial security in old age.

- The need to raise the standard of corporate reporting, particularly when auditors appear to 'miss' important control failures or window dressing of financial statements.

Tutorial note

Other points may also be relevant here, such as to avoid unfettered power of a single individual, or to reduce the tendency towards 'rewards for failure' in directors' remuneration.

Tutor's top tips

*There is a lot to cover for the 10 marks available in part (b). You could choose to use the framework provided by the UK Corporate Governance Code of corporate governance, or any other code of your choice to provide a structure to your answer. Be aware of the mark allocation here – you will not have time to describe **all** the aspects of the principles.*

(b)   The **main areas of corporate governance** included in typical requirements such as the UK's Corporate Governance Code are:

- Directors
- Remuneration of directors
- Accountability and audit
- Relations with shareholders
- Institutional investors
- Disclosure.

Core principles underpin each of these areas.

Directors

A company should be led by an effective board which is also responsible for the success of the company.

To limit the power of any one individual, there should be a division of responsibilities between the person running the board (the chair) and the person running the company (the CEO). One person should not therefore hold both posts at the same time.

To ensure that the board focuses attention on the best interests of the company, and no group of directors can exert too much power, the board should comprise of a mix of executive and non-executive directors.

So shareholders and other interested parties have confidence in the abilities of board members, the appointment procedure for directors should be transparent.

To ensure that directors can carry out decision making effectively, they should be provided with information in a timely manner.

To check that the board is working effectively and efficiently, an annual evaluation should take place of the performance of the board against agreed standards and targets.

To ensure that board members do not become too blinkered in their decision making, new board members should be introduced on a regular basis to question the decisions and philosophy of the board.

Remuneration

To attract directors with the necessary skills, remuneration levels should be adequate but not excessive compared to other companies. Some elements of the reward systems should also be linked to company performance so as not to reward 'failure'.

The way in which remuneration is decided should be transparent so that third parties can see clearly how much remuneration each director is receiving.

Accountability and audit

So investors and other interested parties can check on how their investment is being managed, the directors are charged with presenting an understandable assessment of the company's financial position.

Similarly, the board has to maintain a sound system of internal control to protect the assets of the company and therefore the investment of the shareholders.

To provide confidence in the financial statements, the method of preparation of those statements should be transparent and understandable.

Relations with shareholders

Shareholders, particularly institutional shareholders, require input into how their investment in the company is being managed; the board has the responsibility of ensuring that this input is received.

Additional input should also be obtained from investors at the Annual General Meeting.

Institutional investors

Institutional investors are recommended to use their votes carefully. They should also ensure that the objectives of the company fit their objectives (e.g. perhaps regarding ethical trading) to ensure there is no conflict of interest between their objectives and the company.

Disclosure

The core principle here relates to the information which should be provided in the annual report. In overview, the report should provide investors with all the information that they need to confirm that the directors are managing their company effectively without any conflicts of interest. The reports will therefore include information such as:

- a statement of how the board operates
- details of all board members
- details of board sub-committees and their work (e.g. remuneration and audit committees)
- details of remuneration
- how the board conducts its activities.

Tutor's top tips

Role and responsibilities are separate components in this question and both must be addressed in order to gain maximum marks. Role refers to the overall reason for the audit committee existing and the purposes of its formation. Responsibilities are concerned with the detail of the specific activities that the audit committee carries out.

(c)   This answer has been based on the UK's Corporate Governance Code.

Audit committees

According to the UK's Corporate Governance Code, the board of a company should establish an audit committee of at least three or, in the case of smaller companies, two members who should all be independent non-executive directors. The board should satisfy itself that at least one member of the audit committee has recent and relevant financial experience.

The audit committee is therefore a formal sub-committee of the board of a company. Its main role is to assist the board in fulfilling its stewardship responsibilities by reviewing the system of internal control, the external audit process, the work of internal audit and the financial information that is provided to shareholders. The overall role is therefore supporting the board by providing an independent check on the process of production and review of financial information in the company.

At a more detailed level, specific responsibilities of the audit committee include:

- Checking the integrity of the company's financial statements. The committee will review the judgments made by the board in preparing the financial statements, ensuring these are appropriate to the company. The committee will also check stock exchange announcements to confirm those announcements accurately reflect the situation of the company.

- Reviewing the company's internal control and risk management systems (unless the latter is undertaken by a separate risk management committee). The committee will ensure that the directors establish suitable systems of internal control including internal audit. Reports from internal audit will also be received by the committee which will then ensure that appropriate action is taken on those reports.

- Reviewing the work of the external auditor, with specific responsibility to recommend to the board the re-appointment of existing auditors, or their removal and appointment of a different firm. Making this decision helps maintain the external auditor's independence from the board of directors, improving the effectiveness of the external audit function. The audit committee will also recommend the remuneration level of the external auditor.

- Producing and implementing a policy regarding the provision of non-audit services to be provided by the external auditor (where specific country legislation or corporate governance guidance allows this). Again, this process helps to protect the independence of the external auditor while demonstrating that the company itself does not automatically appoint the same external audit firm to provide all financial services.

- Finally, the audit committee has the responsibility of reporting to the board regarding matters such as recommending amendments to internal control systems. The committee may also be available to receive confidential reports from staff regarding financial irregularities in the company.

25   LALAND (JUN 11)

> **Key answer tips**
>
> In your answer to part (a)-(c) ensure that you allocate your time carefully as the marks are more or less the same for each section. The question, at least in part, related to a technical article written by the examiner further indication to be sure your include all of these in your preparation.

(a)   **Charities and public listed companies**

Differences

Firstly, the two types of organisation are different in terms of regulation. Listed companies are subject to all the provisions of company law plus any listing rules that apply. Listing rules, such as the need to adopt the Combined Code in the UK, impose a number of obligations upon listed companies such as non-executive directors, committee structures, a range of reporting requirements, etc. Charities, in contrast, must receive recognition by a country's charity authority to operate and they then receive the concessions that charitable status confers. This often involves favourable tax treatment and different reporting requirements. Because charities are not public companies they are not subject to listing rules although, depending upon the country's rules, they may be subject to audit and have some reporting requirements.

The second difference is in the strategic purpose of the organisation. Listed companies exist primarily to make a financial return for their investors (shareholders). This means that they employ and incentivise people, including directors, to maximise long-term cash flows. Value is added by the creation of shareholder wealth and this is measured in terms of profits, cash flows, share price movements and price/earnings. For a charity, the strategic purpose is to support the charitable cause for which the organisation was set up. It is likely to be a social or benevolent cause and funds are donated specifically to support that cause and this expectation places a different emphasis on the purpose of governance.

Thirdly, the two are different in terms of stakeholders and societal expectations. Society typically expects a business to be efficient in order to be profitable so that, in turn, it can create jobs, wealth and value for shareholders. Society expresses its support for a business by participating in its resource or product markets, i.e. by supplying its inputs (including working for it) or buying its products. A charity's social legitimacy is tied up with the charity's achievement of benevolent aims. Stakeholders in a business often have an economic incentive to engage with the organisation whereas most stakeholders in a charity have claims more concerned with its benevolent aims.

Governance arrangements

There can be a number of substantive differences between the governance structures of public companies and charities. In a public company, a board consisting of executive and non-executive directors is accountable to the shareholders of the company. The principals are able to hold the board accountable through AGMs (annual general meetings) and EGMs (extraordinary general meetings) at which they can vote on resolutions and other issues to convey their collective will to the board.

In a charity, the operating board is usually accountable to a board of trustees. It is the trustees who act as the interpreters and guarantors of the fiduciary duty of the charity (because the beneficiaries of the charity may be unable to speak for themselves). The trustees ensure that the board is acting according to the charity's stated purposes and that all management policy, including salaries and benefits, are consistent with those purposes.

Tutorial note

Be careful with your answer to part b) particularly the emphasis on using the case scenario to construct the case for greater transparency..

(b)   **Transparency**

Define transparency

Transparency is usually defined in terms of openness and adopting a default position of information provision rather than concealment. This means that unless there is an overwhelming reason not to disclose information of any kind (perhaps for reasons of commercial sensitivity) then information should be disclosed or made available upon request to any interested stakeholder.

The case for greater transparency at HHO

Transparency is an important principle in corporate governance, including at HHO, for a number of reasons.

In general, transparency has the effect of *reassuring investors* that their funds are being responsibly stewarded and used for worthwhile investments. In the case of a charity, such as HHO, without shareholders in the conventional sense, donors give money to support the charity's stated aims and purposes. With the relief of suffering to animals being a prominent reason any donors give to HHO, the amount of money diverted for other purposes, such as salaries, would be information of considerable interest.

Transparency would *inform and placate HHO's critics,* including the journalists who are investigating it. Public commentators like journalists are capable of causing damage to HHO's reputation and this in turn can affect donations and support for the organisation.

There are a number of potentially *damaging allegations* made against Mr Hoi including the likelihood of large payments to himself and some profligacy in the purchase of the private jet. These allegations could be rebutted if the organisation were to make the accounts public and explain the case for the purchase of the jet. For a charity receiving money from 'well-meaning individuals that care greatly about animal suffering', the allegations have the potential to do much reputational damage to the charity.

The *publication of the financial data is an inadequate expression of transparency* and appears to be a poor attempt to give the appearance of providing information whilst providing no useful detail at all. This would not meet any stakeholder's information needs and fails to address any of the concerns raised about HHO. It does not give any absolute financial figures, for example, in terms of income and costs. Such a truncated summary actually gives the impression, to any informed observer, of an attempt at concealment and this provides a strong reason to provide a full financial statement.

(c)   **Audit committee and internal controls**

There are a number of apparent internal control deficiencies, although the case does not permit definite and specific allegations of IC deficiencies to be made or to conclude that a complete lack of governance structure exists at HHO. However, any such organisation would benefit from having an audit committee with wide-ranging powers and responsibilities when reviewing internal controls. With regard to the situation at HHO, the most important areas for audit committee attention are monitoring the adequacy of internal controls, checks for compliance with relevant regulation and codes, checking for fraud and reviewing existing IC statements for accuracy.

Monitoring the adequacy of internal controls involves analysing the controls already in place to establish whether they are capable of mitigating risks. In the case of HHO, there are internal risks that the controls need to be capable of controlling. The risk of fraud and the risk of compliance failure are relevant internal risks.

To check for compliance with relevant regulation and codes refers to HHO's compliance with its legal and other regulatory constraints. It is likely that HHO has a number of regulatory constraints as a result of its charitable status. It may also have voluntary codes it seeks to abide by, perhaps made public through its marketing or reporting literature, and the audit committee could also test for compliance with these.

Checking for fraud is also within the remit of an audit committee and this would, at first glance, be a priority at HHO. There are grounds for believing that inadequate remuneration policies exist at HHO and grounds for suspecting some financial dishonesty. There also seems to be a lack of accountability for the behaviour and actions of Horace Hoi, especially if the claims about his lavish lifestyle are accurate. The misuse of donations for personal enrichment would be outside of what is allowed under his charitable status and this could be reviewed by the audit committee.

Finally, an audit committee could play a more supervisory role if necessary, for example reviewing major expenses and transactions for reasonableness. This might include measuring transactions against its regulatory regime and the reasonable expectations of its trustees and donors.

Tutorial note

Part (c) needed careful thought to determine the deficiencies in internal control with the scenario and then how the audit committee might assist when addressing them. It did not require listing the roles of the audit or risk committee.

ACCA marking scheme		
		Marks
(a)	2 marks for each area of difference identified and explained to a maximum of 6 marks. Half mark for identification only. 3 marks for differences in governance structures.	
	Total	9
(b)	2 marks for definition of transparency. 2 marks for each point made for greater transparency.	
	Total	8
(c)	2 marks for each relevant area of internal control explained	
	Total	8
Total		**25**

Examiner's comments

The case in question 3 was about a charity, HHO, registered in Laland. Horace Hoi was clearly a difficult character, living a lavish lifestyle on charitable proceeds gained from the charity, and at the same time reporting very misleading and highly selective financial information. The content drew partly upon a technical article I wrote in October 2010 (which is on the ACCA website).

Part (a) drew partly upon the content of the October 2010 technical article (which itself was an expansion on content in study guide section A1f). There were two tasks in part (a) and both were knowledge based, so should have been straightforward to candidates that were familiar with the relevant part of the study guide and who had studied the relevant technical article. This part was done quite well by many of those who attempted question 3. Part (b) offered more of a challenge because after a relatively straightforward opening (to define transparency), a higher level verb ('construct') invited candidates to examine the case in detail and to pick out those things that were wrong at HHO and to use those issues to argue in favour of greater transparency. HHO had clearly used the legal framework in Laland to conceal transactions and to provide no effective external reporting. The result of the lax legal constraints in Laland was that Mr Hoi had accumulated substantial personal wealth, almost certainly from the donations of well-meaning donors concerned about animal suffering. There was plenty of ammunition in the case to construct an argument for greater transparency at HHO.

Part (c) brought together study guide content on audit committees and internal controls. There were clearly a number of internal control deficiencies at HHO and the question asked candidates to consider the roles of an audit committee (assuming they knew what these roles were) and how these might be applied to HHO's failings.

A typical poor response to this was to list the roles of a risk committee without applying them meaningfully to the case.

26 OLAND (DEC 12)

Key answer tips

Thorough rehearsal of previous exam questions would have made this question very achievable. Further evidence of the need for lots of question practice as the themes in this question had been asked several times before.

Nonetheless careful reading of the requirement was needed, particularly in part (a) which was concerned with sound governance making it hard for companies to fail, rather than listing facts about good governance practice.

(a) **How sound corporate governance addresses company failure**

Corporate governance is the system by which organisations are directed and controlled. A sound system of corporate governance, whether rules or principles-based, is capable of reducing company failures in a number of ways.

First, it *addresses issues of management,* management succession and *alignment of board interests* with those of shareholders. This reduces the agency problem and makes it less likely that management will promote their own self-interests above those of shareholders. By promoting longer-term shareholder interests over personal or short-term interests, companies are less likely to come under the types of pressures that might lead to failure.

Second, a sound system of corporate governance helps to *identify and manage the wide range of risks* that a company can face, some of which will be capable of causing the company to fail. These might arise from changes in the internal or external environments, and most codes specify a strict set of management procedures for identifying and controlling such risks.

Third, an effective code will *specify a range of effective internal controls* that will ensure the effective use of resources and the minimisation of waste, fraud, and the misuse of company assets. Internal controls are necessary for maintaining the efficient and effective operation of a business, whereas weak or absent controls are more likely to lead to the conditions that could threaten its survival.

Fourth, effective codes *encourage reliable and complete external reporting* of financial data and a range of other voluntary disclosures. By using this information, investors can establish what is going on in the company and will have advanced warning of any problems. This need to report creates an accountability of management to shareholders and restricts the types of actions and behaviours likely to threaten company survival.

Fifth, *compliance with a code underpins investor confidence* and gives shareholders a belief that their investments are being responsibly managed. This confidence extends to other stakeholders such as tax authorities, industry regulators and others, some of whom can cause a great deal of trouble for the company if they believe the company is being poorly managed.

Finally, sound corporate governance will *encourage and attract new investment* of share capital and also make it more likely that lenders will extend credit and provide increased loan capital if needed. This could help some companies survive in difficult times in terms of cash flow and capital requirements when companies with poorer corporate governance reputations may receive less of such support.

(b) **Rules and principles, and why 'comply or explain' is effective**

Rules and principles

In a rules-based approach to corporate governance, provisions are made in law and a breach of any applicable provision is therefore a legal offence. This means that companies become legally accountable for compliance and are liable for prosecution in law for failing to comply with the detail of a corporate governance code or other provision.

A principles-based approach works by (usually) a stock market making compliance with a detailed code a condition of listing. Shareholders are then encouraged to insist on a high level of compliance in the belief that higher compliance is more robust than lower compliance. When, for whatever reason, a company is unable to comply in detail with every provision of a code, the listing rules state that the company must explain, usually in its annual report, exactly where it fails to comply and the reason why it is unable to comply. The shareholders, and not the law, then judge for themselves the seriousness of the breach. This is what Martin Mung meant by markets punishing bad practice.

Comply or explain

Comply or explain is intended to allow latitude in compliance with details of corporate governance provision, but is not 'optional' in the usual meaning of the term. Listing rules insist on compliance with codes in many countries with 'comply or explain' allowed when compliance with detail is not possible or desirable, usually in the short to medium term. If the shareholders are not satisfied with the explanation for lack of compliance, they can punish the board by several means including holding them directly accountable at general meetings, by selling shares (thereby reducing the value of the company) or by direct intervention if a large enough shareholder.

Comply or explain is seen as an alternative to a rigid 'rules-based' approach and is effective for the following reasons:

It enables the policing of compliance by those who own the entity and have *a stronger vested interest* in compliance than state regulators who monitor compliance in a legal sense. This places the responsibility for compliance upon the investors who are collectively the legal owners of the company. It makes the company accountable directly to shareholders who can decide for themselves on the materiality of any given non-compliance.

It *reduces the costs of compliance* and recognises that 'one size' does not fit all. There may be legitimate reasons for temporary or semi-permanent non-compliance with the detail of a corporate governance code, perhaps because of size or the company adopting its own unique approach for highly specific and context-dependent reasons.

It *avoids the need for inflexible legislation,* which, itself, is sometimes also ineffective. Whereas the effectiveness of a 'comply or explain' principles-based approach relies on the ability and willingness of shareholders and capital markets to enforce compliance, rules-based approaches rely on the effectiveness of law enforcement officials.

(c) **Accountability and provisions resulting in 'greater accountability'**

Accountability

Boards of directors are accountable to the shareholders of the company. This means they are answerable to them in that they can be called to give an account for their behaviour and actions as agents of the shareholders. In the context of the code, it is recognised that boards do not always fully reflect the wishes and needs of shareholders and this can represent a failure of accounting from the board to the shareholders. The measures proposed aim to close that gap and make it less likely that unqualified or ill-equipped people will be appointed to, or remain on, the board.

Resulting in greater accountability

Corporate governance codes have had provisions for the retirement of directors by rotation for some time. This is when a fixed period of time is set for directorships, after which the default position is that the director retires or leaves the service of the company unless actively re-elected by the shareholders to serve another term in office. Enhancing accountability to shareholders is a key objective of any corporate governance code. The shortening of service contracts from three years to one year may result in greater accountability for the following reasons:

It will enable shareholders to *remove underperforming directors* much more quickly and to impose their will upon a board with less delay than previously. Rather than paying for underperforming directors to remain in post, with possible damage to the company as a result, or by paying out severance costs, they can simply decide not to re-elect them at the end of the one-year service contract.

It will enable shareholders to *rebalance or refresh a* board in the light of environmental changes or changes in strategy, rather than waiting for a period of time for the three-year terms of previously re-elected directors to elapse. This would make the company more responsive to the wishes of shareholders and reduce the feeling that any director has a 'right' to be on the board at any point. However, a shorter period may leave the board under greater pressure to demonstrate short term success and that could be at the expense of longer term prosperity.

The availability of biographical details will enable shareholders to *clearly see the experience of a candidate* and decide for themselves whether they are likely to add value at a given point. The effect of this will be to act as a 'check and balance' against vested interests that may exist between and among directors. It also places a responsibility upon candidates seeking election or re-election to a board to actively demonstrate their suitability rather than just expecting it as an entitlement.

ACCA marking scheme		
		Marks
(a)	2 mark for each point examined on CG and failure. 2 marks for explanation of corporate governance somewhere in answer. Maximum	— 10 —
(b)	2 marks for distinguishing between rules and principles. 2 marks for each argument supporting comply or explain to a maximum of 6 marks.	8
(c)	2 marks for an explanation of accountability. 2 marks for each relevant discussion point on greater accountability. Maximum	— 7
Total		25 —

Examiner's comments

The case in question 2 was about corporate governance in the country of Oland. All of the themes raised in the requirements had been on previous P1 papers (some on more than one) and so well-prepared candidates who had worked through the past papers would have seen similar requirements before.

Part (a) appeared to be straightforward at first glance but the emphasis here was on how sound corporate governance can make it more difficult for companies to fail. This, after all, is one of the most important purposes of corporate governance (protecting the value of shareholders' investment) and so the emphasis here was on showing how the measures in sound corporate governance make a company more robust and more able to cope with threats to its ongoing existence.

Weaker answers listed the key underpinning concepts from study guide section A1d). It wasn't clear how this approach was attempting to answer the requirement about making it more difficult for companies to fail and so these answers were not well-rewarded. Good answers reflected upon the essential features of good governance and then, importantly, considered how each of these made a company more robust and less likely to get into financial difficulty.

Part (b) was quite well done overall. The distinction between rules and principles-based approaches to corporate governance was well understood by most candidates but the second task was less well done by some. In the case, Martin Mung had insisted that 'comply or explain' was ineffective, thereby arguing for a more rules-based approach in Oland. The task was to argue against his position, thereby arguing in favour of 'comply or explain'.

Some tagged this onto their discussion of the principles-based approach whilst others added it as a separate section after distinguishing between the two. Either was acceptable as long as the appropriate content was included in the answer.

Part (c) began by asking for an explanation of 'accountability', which most candidates could do successfully. The tasks asking about how shorter re-election periods and the provision of biographical detail might result in greater accountability were less well done by candidates. It was important to understand the link between accountability as a concept and the mechanisms of calling to account (such as those described in the case). Again, the ability to apply a piece of knowledge (knowing what accountability means) to a case was key to gaining good marks.

27   LUM CO

Key answer tips

The question requires candidates to consider the change of legal form of companies and the effect on key aspects of corporate governance. The issues to be considered are common themes in the P1 syllabus.

Part (a) required candidates to recognise the difference in governance arrangements and the importance of those changes – the effect of listing and the involvement of institutional investors at the forefront.

Part (b) of the question is not asking content of induction programmes or CPD. It required an assessment of the benefits of both for "new" NED's and executives in situ

Part (c) has been included in previous P1 papers and should be core syllabus knowledge.

(a)   **Family business and a listed company**

Compare family and listed

There are a number of differences between the governance arrangements for a privately-owned family business like Lum Co and a public company which Lum Co became after its flotation.

In general, governance arrangements are much *more formal* for public companies than for family businesses. This is because of the need to be accountable to external shareholders who have no direct involvement in the business. In a family business that is privately owned, shareholders are likely to be members of the extended family and there is usually less need for formal external accountability because there is less of an agency issue.

Linked to this, it is generally the case that larger companies, and public companies in particular, are *more highly regulated* and have many more stakeholders to manage than privately-owned, smaller or family businesses. The higher public visibility that these businesses have makes them more concerned with maintaining public confidence in their governance and to seek to reassure their shareholders. They use a number of ways of doing this.

For example, public companies must comply with regulations that apply to their stock market listing *(listing rules)*. Whilst not a legal constraint in a principles-based jurisdiction, listing rules require listed companies to meet certain standard of behaviour and to meet specific conditions. These sometimes include using a unitary board structure and thus, in the case, would require a change in the governance arrangements at Lum Co.

The more formal governance structures that apply to public companies include the requirement to *establish a committee structure* and other measures to ensure transparency and a stronger accountability to the shareholders. Such measures include additional reporting requirements that do not apply to family firms.

Assess Crispin's view

It is likely that the flotation will bring about a change in the management culture and style in Lum Co. Flotations often cause the loss of the family or entrepreneurial culture and this contains both favourable and unfavourable aspects. Whether the company loses the freedom to manage as they wish will depend upon a number of factors.

Firstly, *whether Gustav* Lum's 'wishes' *(such as the values and beliefs) are known and trusted by the shareholders.* The need for returns to meet shareholder expectations each year often places cost pressures on boards and this, in turn, sometimes challenges a paternalistic management style (such as at Lum Co) which some investors see as self-indulgent and costly.

Second, the company will become *subject to listing rules* such as the governance code, and, because of its higher visibility on the stock market, a range of *other societal expectations* may be placed upon the company. This will have an effect on all aspects of the company's internal systems and norms, including its prior management style. Because of these things, the family will no longer be able to choose how to act in a number of ways, which supports Crispin's view.

Third, the board of Lum Co will be subject to *influence from institutional investors.* They will demand an effective investor relations department, information on a number of issues throughout the year, briefings on final year and interim results and sound explanations whenever performance or behaviour is below expectation. This places the management of Lum Co in a very different environment to when it was privately owned.

Fourth, the board will be under pressure to produce *profits against targets* each year, which may militate against the company's previous long-term and sustainable commercial approach. If, for example, the long-term approach may have meant taking less profit from a particular operation in one year to leave liquidity or cash in place for a future period, this may become more difficult for a listed company, which can sometimes be under pressure to achieve short-term financial targets such as a dividend payment.

(b) **Induction and CPD**

Induction for the new NEDs

Induction is a process of orientation and familiarisation that new members of an organisation undergo upon joining. It is designed to make the experience as smooth as possible and to avoid culture or personality clashes, unexpected surprises or other misunderstandings. In the case of the problems with NEDs at Lum, an effective induction programme will enable the new NEDs to gain *familiarisation with the norms and culture* of Lum. This might be more important for Lum, being at flotation stage and having a deep-seated family culture.

They will be able to gain an understanding of the *nature of the company and its business model.* This will, as with the culture and norms, be especially relevant for a company like Lum emerging from a long period as a private company with little need to explain its business model to outside parties.

Induction will help NEDs in *building a link with people* in Lum Co and other directors. The building of good quality interpersonal links is important in NEDs working effectively. This applies to their relationships with other executive and non-executive directors, and also with relevant people in the company itself. This is especially important in NEDs populating the board committees.

Induction will enable the new NEDs to gain an *understanding of key stakeholders* and relationships including those with auditors, regulators, key competitors and suppliers. In order to understand the business model operated by Lum Co, NEDs need to understand its external relationships and how these support the company's operation.

CPD for the existing executives

The purpose of any programme of CPD is to *update skills and knowledge* as relevant to the professional situation. This will typically involve content on regulation and law, best practice, new developments, etc. Directors should undergo CPD regularly to keep these areas up to date and to ensure they do not 'fall behind' on key skills.

In the case of the changes at Lum Co, another specific benefit of CPD will be *learning about working with NEDs and the new board procedures* that apply to listed companies. For Lum Co this involved creating a new unitary board, employing NEDs and generally taking a more consultative approach to decision-making.

They would also benefit from *learning about compliance requirements* as a listed company. Legal and regulatory frameworks differ between private and public companies. The listing rules that will be imposed by the stock exchange may be seen as an imposition, especially the need to comply with the corporate governance code. This is likely to necessitate a lot of internal change in governance and reporting behaviour and the CPD will help to provide the directors with this support.

After the flotation, the board of Lum Co gained a number of shareholders other than the Lum family. This would have created a new governance environment and so *learning about coping with the expectations of shareholders* would also be a benefit of the CPD. This would include, for example, learning about investor relations, dealing with shareholders at an AGM and similar.

(c)   **Unitary and two-tier boards**

Distinguish between

In a unitary board, all directors, including all executive and non-executive directors, are members. All directors are of equal 'rank' in terms of their ability to influence strategy and they also all share the collective responsibility in terms of legal and regulatory liability. There is no distinction in constitution or law between strategic oversight and operational management.

In a two-tier board, responsibilities are split between a supervisory or oversight board (chaired by the company chairman), and an operational board (usually chaired by the chief executive). The supervisory board decides on strategic issues and the operational board becomes responsible for executing the strategy determined by the supervisory board. Responsibilities between the boards are clearly demarcated with the supervisory board responsible for many legal and regulatory compliance issues (such as financial reporting). Directors on the lower tier (operational board) do not have the same levels of responsibility or power as those on the supervisory board.

Difficulties for the Lum family

The first difficulty for the Lum family is the *loss of the tight control* they enjoyed prior to the flotation. In a unitary board, all strategic decisions need to be taken by a full board including the NEDs. It is precisely to prevent small groups of powerful executives from making decisions on their own that the counterweight of the non-executive board was introduced. This may lead to frustration in the Lum family members, which may affect the objectivity of some decisions.

The company will *lose the capacity for fast decision-making* in the family supervisory board because of the need to involve everybody. Large boards generally meet regularly but on fixed dates. NEDs and other executive directors are likely to seek explanations for decisions taken outside the main board discussions and can act against any members, including family members as the Lum family only controls 20% of the shares.

The *change in culture* brought about by the governance changes are difficult for the family to manage and the movement to a unitary board is likely to add to the difficulty of this adjustment. The need to consult widely (on a larger board) and to seek consensus are likely to be significant changes for the Lum family. For those used to the family way of managing the company, these changes are likely to be difficult to deal with.

Tutorial note

The 'difficulties' part of this answer would have presented some candidates with their own issues. Please review the answer carefully as there is no one right solution.

	ACCA marking scheme		
			Marks
(a)	4 marks for contrasting family and listed.		
	2 marks for each relevant point of assessment to a maximum of 6 marks.		
		Maximum	10
(b)	1 mark for each contribution of induction to a maximum of 4 marks.		
	1 mark for each contribution of CPD to a maximum of 4 marks.		
		Maximum	8
(c)	4 marks for distinguishing between (2 marks for each).		
	1 mark for each difficulty discussed.		
		Maximum	7
Total			**25**

Examiner's comments

This was a question about a family business that decided to convert to a public company and it examined a number of issues around that theme. Part (a) asked about the differences in governance arrangement between a family business and a listed company, and then asked about how the family's ability to manage as they wished would change after the flotation. The first task was done quite well overall but candidates sometimes failed to recognise the importance of listing rules in the second task. In order to comply with listing rules and to fit in with the expectations of institutional investors, the management would have to change quite radically from that of a family business. These changes were what Gustav Lum was concerned about when he feared that the Lum family would 'lose the freedom' they had previously enjoyed.

Part (b) asked about induction programmes and continuing professional development for directors. A common error was to discuss the contents of an induction programme when the question specifically asked for an assessment of the benefits.

A common error was to treat the two under the same heading when in fact the two (induction and CPD) are quite different and serve different needs within a company.

I was surprised to see that many candidates struggled to achieve high marks in part (c) on unitary and two-tier boards, despite this topic having been on previous P1 papers. There was evidence that some candidates did not understand the roles of NEDs on the two types of boards nor how the two approaches might affect the control that the Lum family might have over the company after flotation.

Question 4 was about a common issue in corporate governance. Businesses do occasionally change their legal form and such changes are almost always associated with governance changes.

28 ZOGS (JUN 12)

Key answer tips

The scenario is based on a retiring CEO reflecting on his career and expressing his views on aspects of corporate governance.

Parts (a) required careful reading. It was not about listing roles of NED's but rather more about evaluating the need for fully independent NED's or those with more industry knowledge.

The remaining parts also needed close attention to be paid to the verb. Part (b) asked candidates to describe not list. Part (c) to assess the importance of risk in different size companies, with the obvious need therefore to look at strategic and regulatory issues.

(a) **Independence and NEDs**

Define independence

Independence is a quality possessed by individuals and refers to the avoidance of being unduly influenced by a vested interest. This freedom enables a more objective position to be taken on issues compared to those who consider vested interests or other loyalties.

Independence can be threatened by over-familiarity with the executive board, which is why many corporate governance codes have measures in place to prevent this. These include restrictions on share option schemes for NEDs, time-limited appointments and bans on cross-directorships. Other restrictions, depending on jurisdiction and code, include salaries being set at an appropriate level for NEDs, a compulsory number of years after retirement from a company before being eligible for a NED role (if ever), and no close personal relationships between executives and non-executives.

Benefits of greater independence

In the case of the independence of non-executive directors, Mr Louse is arguing that those with no previous contact with the other members of the board and who come from outside the industry that Zogs is in, will be more independent than those who may have some form of vested interest. In this he is only partly accurate: whilst succession to a NED role from an executive position in the same company is likely to threaten independence, appointments to NED positions from other companies within the same sector are quite common and still provide industry knowledge to a board.

The first benefit of greater independence is that independent people brought in as NEDs are *less likely to have prior vested interests* in terms of material business relationships that might influence judgments or opinions. Such vested interests may involve friendships with other board members or past professional relationships. Past or current equity holdings in companies within the industry may encourage unhelpful loyalties (many CG codes restrict NEDs from holding shares or share options in companies they are on the boards of).

Second, they are *likely to have fewer prejudices* for or against certain policies or individuals as working relationships will not have been built up over a number of years. Accordingly, they are likely to start from the 'ground up' in seeking clarifications and explanations for each area of discussion. Previous rivalries, alliances or embedded ideas would not frustrate discussions and this may allow for more objective discussions.

Third, independent non-executive directors are more likely to *challenge the established beliefs of less independent people* (such as executive directors). This is a more effective way of scrutinising the work of board committees and of increasing their effectiveness. This has the advantage of challenging orthodoxy and bringing fresh perspectives to committee discussions.

Disadvantages of greater independence

Some NEDs are appointed because of their connections with the existing board, either through prior industry involvement, prior executive membership or prior service on another board with one or more other directors. These are considered by Mr Louse to be less independent.

There are, however, a number of advantages when NEDs have some familiarity with a company and board they are joining. A key non-executive role, including in board committees, is providing strategic advice. This can often arise from *a thorough knowledge of the strategic issues in a company or industry.* Retired executive directors, like Mr Louse, sometimes serve as NEDs in the same company and are thus able to bring their experience of that industry and company to bear on committee discussions (although in some countries, there are time restrictions on executives becoming NEDs in the same company).

Some level of prior connection is advantageous when *some level of technical knowledge is required.* Therefore, Mr Louse's comments about independence depending upon NEDs' needing to be from a different industry background or sector is not quite appropriate. When serving on an appointments committee, for example, knowledge of the industry and the technical aspects of a company's operations will increase effectiveness. This might apply in electronics, chemicals, accounting services and financial services, for example. When serving on a risk committee in, for example, a bank, a technical knowledge of key risks specific to that particular industry can be very important.

The *contacts and personal networks* that a NED with industry experience can bring may be of advantage, especially for informal discussions when serving on a nominations committee, for example.

(b) **Risk committee and criticise Mr Louse's understanding**

Roles

There are five general roles of a risk committee. The first is *agreeing and approving the* organisation's *risk management strategy,* including strategies for strategic risks. This is likely to be drawn up in discussion with other parts of the organisation, including the main board.

Second, the risk committee *reviews reports on key risks* prepared by departments on operational risks. These might be reports from operations (e.g. production), finance or technical departments on risks that specifically may affect them.

Third, it *monitors overall risk exposure* and ensures it remains within the limits established by the main board. Exposure is generally defined as the totality of losses that could occur and the acceptable exposure will vary according to the risk strategy. Some organisations accept a higher exposure than others because of their varying risk appetites.

Fourth, the risk committee assesses *the effectiveness of risk management systems and policies.* This is usually based on past data, where a risk has materialised, or 'stress testing' of systems where the risk has not yet materialised.

Fifth, the risk committee *approves and agrees any statements or disclosures* made to internal or external audiences, such as risk reporting to analysts or in the annual report. Shareholders have the right to expect accurate and relevant reports on the risks in their investments, and so any reports issued outside the company need to be approved by the risk committee.

Criticise Mr Louse's understanding

Mr Louse has a weak understanding of the roles and purposes of a risk committee.

First, 'stopping *risks* affecting' *companies is not within the remit of a risk committee.* Some risks affect everybody including businesses; others apply because of industry membership, geographical location, business activity, strategic positioning or business strategy. The role of a risk committee is to identify, review and construct a strategy for managing those risks.

Second, he complained that the risk committee was 'always asking for more information, which was inconvenient'. *Gathering information is a crucial part* of a risk committee's role and it is in the company's overall interest to ensure that information supplied to the risk committee is accurate, current and complete.

Third, *he misunderstands the nature of the* committee's *role if he perceives it to be* 'gloomy *and* pessimistic'. This is an understandable but unfair criticism. Risks are, by their nature, things that might go wrong or potential liabilities, but the reason why risks need to be understood is to ensure the ongoing success and prosperity of Zogs Company, and that is a very positive thing.

Finally, he *wrongly believed that all material risks were external* risks and so the risk committee should be looking outwards and not inwards. Risks can be internal or external to the company and many internal risks can be highly material such as financial risks, liquidity risks, operational risks, etc.

(c) **Risk monitoring more important in larger companies than in smaller companies?**

Small companies exist in different strategic environments to large companies and because of this, a number of differences apply when it comes to corporate governance systems. There are a number of compliance issues, for example, where large companies are required to comply with provisions that smaller companies are not. Some of the differences in regulation and shareholder expectations are driven by differences in the legal status of the organisation (e.g. whether incorporated, whether listed, where domiciled, etc.).

In the case of risk management systems in smaller companies, there will be *a lower overall (aggregate) loss to shareholders* than in a large company in the event of a major risk being realised. In larger companies, especially listed companies, a major event can affect markets around the world and this can affect the value of many funds including pension funds, etc. This is unlikely to be the case in any given smaller company.

Many smaller companies, including SmallCo, are privately owned and they are therefore *not subject to listing rules and, in some cases, other legal regulations.* In many smaller companies, any loss of value when a risk is realised is a personal loss to owners and does not affect a high number of relatively 'disconnected' shareholders as would be the case in a large public company.

Risk probability and impact is often correlated with size. Smaller companies have fewer risks because of their lower profiles, fewer stakeholders and less complex systems than larger organisations. Accordingly, the elaborate risk management systems are less necessary in smaller companies and could be a disproportionate use of funds. This is not to say that smaller companies do not face risks, of course, but that the impacts, say to shareholders or society, are less with a smaller rather than a larger company because of the totality of the losses incurred.

The costs of *risk monitoring and control may often outweigh the impacts of losses* being incurred from risks, if not in a single financial period then maybe over a period of years. There are substantial set-up fixed costs in establishing some risk management systems and, in some cases, variable costs also (e.g. linked to production output). With fewer total risks, there could be less value for money in having risk controls.

In summary, risk committees and risk mitigation systems are more important in larger companies than in smaller companies. However it is good practice for all companies, however small, to carry out some form of risk monitoring in order to remain competitive in their environment.

ACCA marking scheme		
		Marks
(a)	2 marks for definition of independence. 1 mark for each argument for or against (allow cross marking) to a maximum of 6 marks.	
	Maximum	8
(b)	1 mark for each role described to a maximum of 5 marks. 1 mark for each point of criticism to a maximum of 4 marks.	
	Maximum	9
(c)	2 marks for each explanation of Mr Louse's belief.	
	Maximum	8
Total		25

Examiner's comments

The scenario in question 2 was about a recently retired chief executive, Mr Louse, who was giving a speech on various aspects of corporate governance. Having enjoyed a long and successful career in business, he had a number of views that he presented in his speech.

He expressed views on the actual independence of non-executive committees and on risk committees. These subjects were asked about in parts (a) and (b). Part (c) was about differences in risk management between large and small companies.

Part (a), about the independence of non-executive directors (NEDs), touched on a debate about whether NEDs should be fully independent of executives in order to bring more scrutiny, or familiar with the industry, in order to bring more relevant strategic expertise. It was disappointing to see that some candidates answered a question that was not set. Some produced the list of the roles of NEDs (strategic, risk, people and scrutiny) and some discussed regulation. Neither of these were correct approaches.

The first task in part (a) was to define 'independence'. Because this is such an important concept in corporate governance, and one of the underpinning concepts in A1(d) of the study guide, I was pleased to see that most candidates were able to attempt this task. The second was about the debate on independence and this was less well done with a wide range of approaches being taken.

There were two tasks in part (b). Candidates were firstly asked to describe the roles of a risk committee. The most common error with this was, as with question 1, part (c), to disobey the verb (which was 'describe'). It was clear that many candidates knew these roles but a short bullet list is not a description. The best way to answer a question such as this is to start with the single short sentence and then to expand that with a description to show the marker that the thing being described is fully understood. Where bookwork marks like these are available on a professional paper like P1, it is essential that they are gained if a high mark overall is to be attained. Other common errors in this task (as well as just producing a bullet list) included discussing the factors that determine whether the company should establish a risk committee, and also regulatory and listing rule issues with risk committees. Neither of these was asked for in the requirement.

The second task in part (b) was to criticise (to say what is wrong) with some comments that Mr Louse made in the case about the roles of risk committees in Zogs Company. This involved picking out the various comments and then showing how Mr Louse misunderstood risk committees. This involved discussing the true roles of risk committees and showing how risk committees were not in fact an inconvenience but rather an essential part of sound corporate governance. Some candidates were able to extract the quotations from the case but were then unable to enter into a meaningful criticism of the views expressed. These answers received fewer marks than those able to include the criticisms.

Part (c) asked about whether risk mitigation systems were more important in larger companies than in small companies. The answer should have included points including strategic and regulatory issues but this part was the weakest for many candidates who attempted question 2. Some sought to explain, often without using a meaningful argument, that large and small companies were the same with regard to risk systems and such answers were not well rewarded.

29 ROSH AND COMPANY (JUN 08)

Key answer tips

All parts of this question can be separated into two sections, so ensure that your answer reflects this (use headings for each section).

The second half of part (a) only requires criticisms of the situation at Rosh and Company – so do not waste time commenting on anything that it is doing well.

Careful planning should ensure that you can separate out the theory of the roles of the nominations committee in (b) from the application in the case given.

The definition in part (c) should be of a couple of sentences, with your emphasis going on how this may assist in this situation. There are some clear hints in the scenario about longstanding directors and family members. Ensure that your answer states these points clearly.

The highlighted words are key phrases that markers are looking for.

(a) **Defining and explaining agency**

Agency is defined in relation to a principal. A principal appoints an agent to act on his or her behalf. In the case of corporate governance, the principal is a shareholder in a joint stock company and the agents (that have an agency relationship with principals) are the directors. The directors remain accountable to the principals for the stewardship of their investment in the company. In the case of Rosh, 60% of the shares are owned by shareholders external to the Rosh family and the board has agency responsibility to those shareholders.

Criticisms of Rosh's CG arrangements

The corporate governance arrangements at Rosh and Company are far from ideal. Five points can be made based on the evidence in the case.

There are several issues associated with the non-executive directors (NEDs) at Rosh. It is doubtful whether two NEDs are enough to bring sufficient scrutiny to the executive board. Some corporate governance codes require half of the board of larger companies to be non-executive and Rosh would clearly be in breach of such a requirement. Perhaps of equal concern, there is significant doubt over the independence of the current NEDs as they were recruited from retired executive members of the board and presumably have relationships with existing executives going back many years. Some corporate governance codes (such as the UK Corporate Governance Code) specify that NEDs should not have worked for the company within the last five years. Again, Rosh would be in breach of this provision.

Succession planning for senior positions in the company seems to be based on Rosh family membership rather than any meritocratic approach to appointments (there doesn't appear to be a nominations committee). Whilst this may have been acceptable before the flotation when the Rosh family owned all of the shares, the flotation introduced an important need for external scrutiny of this arrangement. The lack of NED independence makes this difficult.

There is a poor (very narrow) diversity of backgrounds among board members. Whilst diversity can bring increased conflict, it is generally assumed that it can also stimulate discussion and debate that is often helpful.

There is a somewhat entrenched executive board and Mary is the first new appointment to the board in many years (and is the first woman). Whilst experience is very important on a board, the appointment of new members, in addition to seeding the board with talent for the future, can also bring fresh ideas and helpful scrutiny of existing policies.

There is no discussion of strategy and there is evidence of a lack of preparation of strategic notes to the board. The assumption seems to be that the 'best' option is obvious and so there is no need for discussion and debate. Procedures for preparing briefing notes on strategy for board meetings appear to be absent. Most corporate governance codes place the discussion and setting of strategy as a high priority for boards and Rosh would be in breach of such a provision.

There is no evidence of training for Mary to facilitate her introduction into the organisation and its systems. Thorough training of new members and ongoing professional development of existing members is an important component of good governance.

(b) **Nominations committees**

General roles of a nominations committee

It advises on the balance between executives and independent non-executive directors and establishes the appropriate number and type of NEDs on the board. The nominations committee is usually made up of NEDs.

It establishes the skills, knowledge and experience possessed by current board and notes any gaps that will need to be filled.

It acts to meet the needs for continuity and succession planning, especially among the most senior members of the board.

It establishes the desirable and optimal size of the board, bearing in mind the current size and complexity of existing and planned activities and strategies.

It seeks to ensure that the board is balanced in terms of it having board members from a diversity of backgrounds so as to reflect its main constituencies and ensure a flow of new ideas and the scrutiny of existing strategies.

Tutorial note

Don't confuse the work of the nominations committee with the roles of the HR department in looking at matters such appraisals and induction.

In the case of Rosh, the needs that a nominations committee could address are:

To recommend how many directors would be needed to run the business and plan for recruitment accordingly. The perceived similarity of skills and interests of existing directors is also likely to be an issue.

To resolve the issues over numbers of NEDs. It seems likely that the current number is inadequate and would put Rosh in a position of non-compliance with many of the corporate governance guidelines pertaining to NEDs.

To resolve the issues over the independence of NEDs. The closeness that the NEDs have to existing executive board members potentially undermines their independence and a nominations committee should be able to identify this as an issue and make recommendations to rectify it.

To make recommendations over the succession of the chairmanship. It may not be in the interests of Rosh for family members to always occupy senior positions in the business.

(c) **Retirement by rotation**

Definition

Retirement by rotation is an arrangement in a director's contract that specifies his or her contract to be limited to a specific period (typically three years) after which he or she must retire from the board or offer himself (being eligible) for re-election. The director must be actively re-elected back onto the board to serve another term. The default is that the director retires unless re-elected.

Importance of

Retirement by rotation reduces the cost of contract termination for underperforming directors. They can simply not be re-elected after their term of office expires and they will be required to leave the service of the board as a retiree (depending on contract terms).

It encourages directors' performance (they know they are assessed by shareholders and reconsidered every three years) and focuses their minds upon the importance of meeting objectives in line with shareholders' aims.

It is an opportunity, over time, to replace the board membership whilst maintaining medium term stability of membership (one or two at a time).

Applied to Rosh

Retirement by rotation would enable the board of Rosh to be changed over time. There is evidence that some directors may have stayed longer than is ideal because of links with other board members going back many years.

Marking scheme			
			Marks
(a)	1 mark for each relevant point made		Up to 4
	1 mark for identification of each criticism		Up to 5
	1 mark for brief discussion of each criticism		Up to 5
		Maximum	12
(b)	1 mark for each relevant role of the nominations committee		Up to 5
	1 mark for each relevant point on the usefulness of a nominations committee to Rosh		Up to 4
		Maximum	8
(c)	1 mark for each relevant point made for definition		Up to 2
	1 mark for each relevant point made on importance		Up to 3
	1 mark for each relevant point made on applying to Rosh		Up to 2
		Maximum	5
Total			**25**

Examiner's comments

Introduction

This was the most popular question in section B with most candidates attempting it. The case describes a company with a number of poor practices in its corporate governance.

In the first task, **(part a)**, candidates were required to explain one of the key themes in corporate governance, agency, and then, using their knowledge of best practice, to criticise the company in the case. 'Criticise' is a level 3 verb (along with assess, evaluate, construct, etc.) because a certain amount of understanding is necessary before the criticism can be undertaken. There was plenty to criticise in the case and most candidates did well in this task.

> **Part (b)** was done well by some but poorly by others. Where candidates weren't sure they often wrote what they thought might be the roles of a nominations committee. These were sometimes right but sometimes they confused the nominations committee with the roles of the HR department (appraisals, induction, etc.). The second part, typical of a P1 task, was to apply the knowledge to the case. This involved an assessment of how a nominations committee would be useful to the company in the case which does, of course, require a close study of the case.
>
> There was some confusion over the meaning of the term 'retirement by rotation' which was asked for in **part (c)**. Again, there was some evidence that candidates had not fully revised the whole syllabus for P1. The form of this question again shows the importance of not only knowing the whole of the P1 syllabus but also being prepared to apply the knowledge to the case.

30 CORPORATE GOVERNANCE DEBATE (JUN 08)

Key answer tips

Be very careful with the requirements for part (a) (ii) and ensure that your answer keeps to this point. When you have a long requirement like this one you may find it helpful to paraphrase it and write out the simple version on your question paper to avoid confusion. Ensure that all points you make are applied to developing countries since this will be key to earning the marks.

Part (b) requires details of a report to be published by the company about internal controls. This is a not a request to write all you know about internal controls, nor internal control systems, but to provide details of the requirements under Sarbanes-Oxley for reporting on such controls. You will need to have the relevant knowledge at hand to score well in this part.

(a)   (i)   **Describe rules-based**

In a rules-based jurisdiction, corporate governance provisions are legally binding and enforceable in law. Non-compliance is punishable by fines or ultimately (*in extremis*) by delisting and director prosecutions.

There is limited latitude for interpretation of the provisions to match individual circumstances ('one size fits all'). Some have described this as a 'box ticking' exercise as companies seek to comply despite some provisions applying to their individual circumstances more than others.

Investor confidence is underpinned by the quality of the legislation rather than the degree of compliance (which will be total for the most part).

(ii)   **Principles-based approach**

Advantages of a principles-based approach

The rigour with which governance systems are applied can be varied according to size, situation, stage of development of business, etc. Organisations (in legal terms) have a choice to the extent to which they wish to comply, although they will usually have to 'comply or explain'. Explanations are more accepted by shareholders and stock markets for smaller companies.

Obeying the spirit of the law is better than 'box ticking' ('sort of business you are' rather than 'obeying rules'). Being aware of overall responsibilities is more important than going through a compliance exercise merely to demonstrate conformance.

Avoids the 'regulation overload' of rules based (and associated increased business costs). The costs of compliance have been a cause of considerable concern in the United States.

Self-regulation (e.g. by Financial Services Authority in the UK) rather than legal control has proven itself to underpin investor confidence in several jurisdictions and the mechanisms are self-tightening (quicker and cheaper than legislation) if initial public offering (IPO) volumes fall or capital flows elsewhere.

Context of developing countries

Developing countries' economies tend to be dominated by small and medium sized organisations (SMEs). It would be very costly and probably futile, to attempt to burden small businesses with regulatory requirements comparable to larger concerns.

Having the flexibility to 'comply or explain' allows for those seeking foreign equity to increase compliance whilst those with different priorities can delay full compliance. In low-liquidity stock markets (such as those in some developing countries) where share prices are not seen as strategically important for businesses, adopting a more flexible approach might be a better use of management talent rather than 'jumping through hoops' to comply with legally-binding constraints.

The state needs to have an enforcement mechanism in place to deal with non-compliance and this itself represents a cost to taxpayers and the corporate sector. Developing countries may not have the full infrastructure in place to enable compliance (auditors, pool of NEDs, professional accountants, internal auditors, etc) and a principles-based approach goes some way to recognise this.

(b)   **Internal control statement**

The United States Securities and Exchange Commission (SEC) guidelines are to disclose in the annual report as follows:

* A statement of management's responsibility for establishing and maintaining adequate internal control over financial reporting for the company. This will always include the nature and extent of involvement by the chairman and chief executive, but may also specify the other members of the board involved in the internal controls over financial reporting. The purpose is for shareholders to be clear about who is accountable for the controls.

* A statement identifying the framework used by management to evaluate the effectiveness of this internal control. This will usually involve a description of the key metrics, measurement methods (e.g. rates of compliance, fair value measures, etc) and tolerances allowed within these. Within a rules-based environment, these are likely to be underpinned by law.

- Management's assessment of the effectiveness of this internal control as at the end of the company's most recent fiscal year. This may involve reporting on rates of compliance, failures, costs, resources committed and outputs (if measurable) achieved.

- A statement that its auditor has issued an attestation report on management's assessment. Any qualification to the attestation should be reported in this statement.

Tutorial note

Guidance from other corporate governance codes is also acceptable.

(c) **The external reporting requirements (from the Sarbanes-Oxley section 404) being 'too ambitious' for small and medium companies**

There are several arguments to support Professor Leroi's remark.

- Fewer spare resources to carry out internal control. SMEs tend to operate with lower levels of spare resource than larger businesses and conducting internal reviews would be more of a challenge for them.

- The extra attestation fee (over and above normal audit fee) for the attestation of the internal control report could be a constraint for many SMEs.

- Lack of expertise from within existing employees (to internally audit/police as well as carry out internal activities) would be a likely constraint.

- SMEs will have fewer activities and less complexity, hence less need for shareholders to require the information (less to go wrong).

Marking scheme			
			Marks
(a)	(i)	1 mark for each essential feature briefly described	3
	(ii)	1 mark for each relevant point made on the advantages of principles-based	Up to 4
		2 marks for each relevant point on developing countries	Up to 6
		Maximum	13
(b)		2 marks for each relevant area of content identified and briefly described	8
		Maximum	8
(c)		1 mark for each relevant valid argument put forward	4
		Maximum	4
Total			25

Examiner's comments

Introduction

This was the least well done question in section B. Although the case scenario mentioned Sarbanes Oxley, none of the tasks actually required a knowledge of Sarbanes Oxley.

The first part **(part (a)(i))** was well done on the whole, asking as it did for the essential features of a rules-based approach to corporate governance.

Part (a)(ii) was not so well done overall. The question required candidates to construct an argument in favour of applying a principles-based approach to developing countries. The question assumed that candidates were aware of the features of, and argument for, principles rather than rules. If candidates were not aware of these, then obviously it would be very hard to get a good mark. Then, candidates were required to consider these advantages in the specific context of developing economies and to construct an argument accordingly.

Similarly, many candidates were confused in answering **part (c)**. The question asked candidates to 'describe the typical contents of an external report on internal controls' this being the nature of the content of section 404 of Sarbanes Oxley. This is not a uniquely Sarbanes Oxley issue, however as other codes have similar provisions. The question tended to be misinterpreted in two ways: that it was about external reporting in general (it wasn't) and it was about internal controls in general (it wasn't). This question highlights the importance of knowledge of the whole syllabus (this is from section B3b and C3d) and not just hoping that what has been revised will come up in the exam.

Part (c) was about external reporting requirements rather than about (as some candidates wrongly believed) principles based approaches in developing countries. One of the criticisms of rigid reporting requirements is that they are burdensome for smaller companies and this question sought to explore some of those issues.

31   BOOM

Key answer tips

This scenario considers the situation of a listed company and its deliberations surrounding its remuneration committee. It was again critical to read the requirement carefully as the development of the second part of the requirement, where relevant, was essential to score well.

Part (b) in particular required some thought as the word "propose" does not mean produce a list of the components but more how they could be combined to achieve the purpose of incentivising senior management.

(a)   **Codes of corporate governance**

A code (of corporate governance) is a document that specifies certain standards, principles, norms of behaviour or specific instructions over matters of corporate governance. Some have evolved over time as different previous reports were written for different aspects of governance, which were then brought together in combined codes. Others have borrowed from existing codes, perhaps amended slightly to account for national differences.

Codes of corporate governance are issued by regulatory authorities (such as stock exchanges, governments or semi-autonomous government bodies) and are statements of general principles and detailed guidelines on many matters of corporate governance. They can be implemented either as listing rules (in principles-based jurisdictions) or in law (in rules-based jurisdictions). They typically cover all relevant aspects of corporate governance including the roles of the board, risk management, internal controls, executive remuneration and contracts, reporting issues and similar relevant themes. The purpose is to ensure that companies are well-run and in line with shareholders' interests.

The purposes of such codes are as follows. First, they guide and *specify behaviour* in matters of governance, internal control and risk management with the objective that by complying with the code, corporate governance will be improved and enhanced. Second, they aim to *encourage best practice* and to *improve management performance* by preventing practice that might reduce value added or shareholder value.

Third, codes aim to *underpin investor confidence* in that high levels of compliance tend to be appreciated by shareholders and poor levels of compliance are sometimes punished. It enables boards to demonstrate the value they place upon the agency relationship and to more adequately discharge the agency responsibilities placed upon them. Fourth, codes aim to *reduce fraud, waste or inefficiency*. One of the main causes of the development of codes (for example in the UK and in the USA) was in response to high profile frauds, and it was hoped at the time that codes would address this.

Fifth, in principles-based jurisdictions, the implementation of codes is thought to be a way of *reducing the chances of governmental legislation* being implemented. Governments are more likely to legislate where other regulatory failure is evident and so an effective code applied as listing rules should (many hope and believe) reduce the likelihood of having inflexible laws applied.

(b) **Components of reward package**

Sarah Umm told the remuneration committee that the rewards should be linked strongly with the company's strategy and that these strategic priorities were to 'incentivise medium to long-term growth whilst retaining the existing executive board as long as possible.'

The *retention* of the existing board will be aided by providing a *basic salary that meets market rate* with in-kind benefits commensurate with the role. This is to ensure that the director is satisfied, and believes himself or herself to be fairly rewarded, regardless of performance in the role. Retention can be helped by the payment of one or more *loyalty bonuses* for staying more than an agreed time period. Again, these would be regardless of performance and intended solely to reward loyalty. These may not necessarily be monetary rewards. It may be, for example, that a director receives a car upgrade or additional days paid holiday after the agreed time period.

The incentivisation of medium to long-term performance will require the use of reward components such as performance bonuses and share options. Performance *bonuses* can be included for achieving certain targets in alignment with strategy. The dates on which these are paid can reflect the time-element of the incentivisation. Sarah Umm wants to incentivise medium to long-term performance, so this is likely to refer to years rather than months. In addition, the package could include *share options* which can be exercised after a number of years. These enable directors to benefit directly from increases in share value and because this is often a longer-term effect, share options may be designed to come into effect after, say, three years.

(c) **General roles of non-executive directors (NEDs)**

The four general roles of NEDs are: the strategy role, scrutinising role, risk role and the people role. In the *strategy role*, NEDs may challenge any aspect of strategy they see fit and offer advice or input to help to develop successful strategy. The *scrutinising* or performance role is where the NEDs' independence is perhaps the most important. NEDs are required to hold executive colleagues to account for decisions taken and company performance. In this respect, they are required to represent the shareholders' interests against any vested interests or short-term executive pressures.

The *risk* role involves NEDs ensuring the company has an adequate system of internal controls and systems of risk management in place. Finally, in the *people* role, NEDs oversee a range of responsibilities with regard to the management of the executive members of the board. This typically involves issues concerning appointments and remuneration, but might also involve contractual or disciplinary issues, and succession planning.

NEDs and performance-related elements

The main reason why NEDs are usually not allowed to receive share options or other performance-related elements as part of their reward packages (as Sam South asked) is because it could *threaten their independence* and hence their usefulness to the company's shareholders. Whereas executive directors may, for example, be incentivised to take excessive risks to maximise their own rewards, a non-executive, without the performance-related element, will have no such incentive and will be likely to take a more objective view of the strategy being discussed.

In order to be effective in their roles, NEDs need to be motivated in different ways to their executive colleagues and too much similarity can mean that the *scrutiny role is weakened*. If both executive and non-executive directors are similarly motivated, there will be less scrutiny of proposed strategies for wider impacts, risks, complications and stakeholder impacts, because there will be no-one incentivised to exercise effective scrutiny.

If they received a similar mix of rewards to executives, they would be motivated to act in similar ways and this might involve favouring *short-term measures* at variance with longer-term strategic perspectives. A concern over short-term share price movements, for example, might take the NEDs' focus away from longer-term strategic issues and make them more concerned with maximising market value in the short term.

Because non-executives comprise the remuneration committee, it would be *inappropriate for them to decide on their own rewards.* It would be an abuse of the responsibility and trust invested in them by shareholders were NEDs to reward themselves too much or incentivise themselves in an inappropriate way. Accordingly, it is usual for NEDs to be paid a fair rate based on external comparison figures (often a daily rate or similar), so that there is no question of it being seen as excessive. A NED's pay is usually a small fraction of that for executive colleagues.

ACCA marking scheme		Marks
(a)	2 marks for explanation (wherever made). 1 mark for each purpose discussed. Half mark for identification only.	
	Maximum	7
(b)	2 marks for each relevant component discussed.	
	Maximum	8
(c)	1 mark for each general NED role to a maximum of 4 marks. 2 marks for each problem with NEDs to a maximum of 6 marks.	
	Maximum	10
Total		**25**

Examiner's comments

This question was about Boom Co and the deliberations of its remuneration committee in meeting to agree the rewards of its executive directors. In the committee's discussions, its chairman, Sarah Umm, read out the relevant part of the corporate governance code on the subject (this was drawn from a real code of corporate governance). The requirements were on the purposes of corporate governance codes, how reward packages can be balanced to achieve a particular outcome (in this case, to incentivise medium to long-term growth) and finally on the roles of non-executive directors.

Many candidates performed poorly on parts (a) and (c) and in most cases, this was due to a failure to develop answers to the second task in each requirement. The first task in part (a) asked for an explanation of a code of corporate governance and whilst most candidates were able to offer a fair answer to this, a minority seemed to be confused over the word 'code', and instead offered a definition of corporate governance itself. The second task in part (a) was about the general purposes of a CG code for listed companies such as Boom Co and I was surprised that many answers failed to address this very well, especially as it was substantially bookwork and could have been answered by a well-prepared candidate.

A frustration with part (b) was candidates, seeing the term 'components of a reward package', automatically reproduced the list of such components (basic pay, performance bonuses, etc.). This was not what the question was asking for. The requirement specifically asked about incentivising medium to long term growth whilst retaining the existing board in place. So candidates needed to think about how these components could be blended and offered to achieve these outcomes. There were no marks for a list of the components of a reward package on its own.

Part (c) contained two tasks. The first was a relatively straightforward task about the general roles of non executive directors. The second was poorly done overall requiring the candidate to discuss a specific restriction on the rewards of non executive directors.

Tutorial note

You do not need to write much here if your points are appropriate and well-explained.

32 EASTERN PRODUCTS (PILOT 07)

Key answer tips

Make sure you read the scenario and apply carefully to this case. Sentosa house is an institutional investor and must therefore ensure they protect their own shareholders first.

(a) An agency cost is a cost incurred by the shareholder in monitoring the activities of company agents (i.e. directors). Agency costs are normally considered as 'over and above' existing analysis costs and are the costs that arise because of compromised trust in agents (directors). In this case, the increased agency costs that arise are the increased monitoring and 'policing' costs that Sentosa House (Sonia) will incur because of the irregular behaviour described in the case.

The first problem identified is Eastern's non-compliance with relevant codes/ requirements in respect of non-executive directors and committee structure. There are an insufficient number of NEDs to form the normal committee structure for a public company which means that Sentosa may consider itself to have to monitor some of the risks to Eastern that otherwise the risk committee would undertake. The investor relations department shows evidence of being unhelpful and uninformed – an unfortunate combination of failings. The chairman appears to be arrogant and potentially untrustworthy (he saw no need for risk committee and dealt very abruptly with Sonia when she called). Finally, the company is pursuing risky strategies with no obvious explanation as to why such strategies are necessary.

In this situation, then, Sentosa House has the choice of selling its holding in Eastern or incurring increased monitoring costs to ensure that its own investors' interests, in turn, are adequately represented.

(b)   Intervention by an institutional investor in a company whose stock it holds is usually considered to be radical step and normally represents a step change in agency costs for the investor. This caveat notwithstanding, it is an important 'last resort' for institutional investors to have available to them as they seek to adequately represent the interests of their own investors.

There are a number of conditions under which it would be appropriate for institutional investors to intervene in a company whose shares it is holding.

The first condition is concerns about strategy in terms of products sold, markets serviced, expansions pursued or any other aspect of the company's overall strategic positioning.

Its operational performance may give rise, especially if there are one or more segments that have consistently underperformed without adequate explanation.

The third condition is when non-executive directors do not hold executive management to account. There may, for example, be evidence of unaccountable 'kitchen cabinets' or curious executive decisions that are not adequately challenged by non-executive directors.

Fourth, consistent or serious failure in internal controls would justify intervention, although this, in turn, may become evident through operational underperformance. Ongoing or unaddressed failures in, for example, quality assurance, health and safety, environmental emissions, budgetary control or information systems might justify intervention.

Failing to comply with the relevant code, laws or stock market rules is the next situation. If the company is listed in a rules-based jurisdiction, it is a matter of law but in a principles-based country, compliance is only 'optional' under the stock market's 'comply or explain' rules. Consistent or unexplained non-compliance is like to be penalised by the market

Sixth, inappropriate remuneration policies, if extreme or obviously self-serving, might attract intervention. Such a situation would normally also signify a failure of the remunerations committee which would make it a double cause for concern.

Finally, a poor approach to social responsibility is a condition for possible intervention, especially if there is publicly-available evidence that might adversely affect the reputation of the company.

With reference to the case, Eastern Products fails on several counts that might encourage institutional shareholder intervention. Firstly, its failure to comply with relevant code (particularly on number of non-executive directors and lack of risk committee). Second, the non-executive directors are not holding executives to account because there is an insufficient number of them. Third, there are concerns about strategy (which is considered to be very risky).

(c)   Risk committees are considered best practice by most corporate governance regimes around the world for a number of reasons. Sonia has, for good reason, doubts over the competence and good faith of the management of Eastern Products and a risk committee made up of non-executive directors could help her confidence in a number of ways.

In the first instance, the information systems put in place to provide information for the risk committee. This would generate awareness of and facilitate review of all relevant risks for discussion by the risk committee, including those arising from the 'very risky' strategy.

It would review and assess the effectiveness of internal controls on risk. A committee made up of independent, non-executive directors would bring scrutiny to Thomas on two fronts. There is evidence that Thomas may be relatively inexperienced, having been in post for only two years, and the way that he dealt with Sonia's entirely legitimate enquiry shows some evidence of immaturity and/or impatience. Non executive presence would be able to challenge and act as a counterweight to this failing. Non-executive directors would also bring scrutiny of Thomas's leadership over strategy, especially (in the context of the risk committee) the wisdom of his 'very risky' strategies.

Tutorial note

The important point here is to note that the best practice solution is to have a risk committee with a majority not wholly-Non Executive Director composition.

(d) The opinion shows confusion over the meaning of the term 'compulsory'. Whilst in a principles-based jurisdiction, compliance is not legally compulsory, it is required for the stock market listing. Accordingly, compliance is effectively compulsory if the company wishes to enjoy the benefits of its listing. Companies in principles-based jurisdictions are subject to 'comply or explain' in that non-compliance needs to be explained in terms of specific areas of non-compliance and the reason for noncompliance. Compliance is also necessary for market confidence in the Eastern Products stock in that the market would be likely to devalue a stock that was a consistent non-complier. Finally, shareholders and stock markets are entitled to challenge the explanation for non-compliance if they aren't satisfied with the explanation given in the annual report.

Tutorial note

This requirement is a commonly assessed topic area: please ensure you fully revise this topic. For further guidance read the Examiner's article 'Corporate Governance Codes' published in April 2008.

Marking scheme			Marks
(a)	Definition of agency costs		2
	1 mark for each problem identified and briefly discussed		Up to 5
		Maximum	7
(b)	1 mark for each relevant point identified and briefly described on conditions for intervention		Up to 7
	1 mark for each relevant point made on Eastern House		Up to 3
		Maximum	10
(c)	1 mark for each relevant point made		Up to 4
		Maximum	4
(d)	1 mark for each relevant point made		Up to 4
		Maximum	4
Total			25

33 TQ COMPANY (JUN 09)

Key answer tips

This question covers corporate governance topics, though extends to some of the more minor areas of the syllabus.

Part (a) starts with some text-book knowledge of removal of directors, but then moves onto a difficult section of application to the given scenario. Fortunately, only for four marks!

No theoretical knowledge would assist with part (b) with marks being awarded for relevant suggestions. Part (c) returns to a much more familiar area of governance, looking at the popular topic of directors' remuneration.

Part (d) (as with part (c)) had a requirement to 'criticise'. It is not sufficient to simply state the roles of the chairman and you would certainly not be expected to conclude that Miss Hoiku was an effective chairman. Applying the roles, and your knowledge of what a chairman should do to the given scenario would enable you to identify shortcomings in her actions.

(a) (i) **Leaving the service of a board**

Resignation with or without notice. Any director is free to withdraw his or her labour at any time but there is normally a notice period required to facilitate an orderly transition from the outgoing chief executive to the incoming one.

Not offering himself/herself for re-election. Terms of office, which are typically three years, are renewable if the director offers him or herself for re-election and the shareholders support the renewal. Retirement usually takes place at the end of a three-year term when the director decides not to seek re-election.

Death in service when, obviously, the director is unable to either provide notice or seek retirement.

Failure of the company. When a company fails, all directors' contracts are cancelled although this need not signal the end of the directors' involvement with company affairs as there may be ongoing legal issues to be resolved.

Being removed e.g. by being dismissed for disciplinary offences. It is relatively easy to 'prove' a disciplinary offence but much more difficult to 'prove' incompetence. The nature of disciplinary offences is usually made clear in the terms and conditions of employment and company policy.

Prolonged absence. Directors unable to perform their duties owing to protracted absence, for any reason, may be removed. The length of qualifying absence period varies by jurisdiction.

Being disqualified from being a company director by a court. Directors can be banned from holding directorships by a court for a number of reasons including personal bankruptcy and other legal issues.

Failing to be re-elected if, having offered him or herself for re-election, shareholders elect not to re-appoint. An 'agreed departure' such as by providing compensation to a director to leave.

Tutorial note

For each point that has been explained in full, one mark was awarded. So, you would have only needed to come up with FOUR of the above points on this section.

(ii) **Discuss Miss Hoiku's statement**

The way that directors' contracts and company law are written (in most countries) makes it difficult to remove a director such as Mr Smith from office during an elected term of office so in that respect, *Miss Hoiku is correct*. Unless his contract has highly specific performance targets built in to it, it is *difficult to remove Mr Smith for incompetence* in the short-term as it is sometimes *difficult to* assess *the success of strategies* until some time has passed. If the alleged incompetence is within Mr Smith's term of office (typically three years) then it will usually be necessary to *wait until the director offers himself for re-election.* The shareholders can then simply not re-elect the incompetent director (in this case, Mr Smith). The most likely way to achieve the departure of Mr Smith within his term of office will be to 'encourage' *him to resign* by other directors failing to support him or by shareholders issuing a vote of no confidence at an AGM or EGM. This would probably involve offering him a suitable financial package to depart at a time chosen by the other members of the board or company shareholders.

(b) **Importance of the chairman's statement**

The chairman's statement (or president's letter in some countries) is an important and usually *voluntary item,* typically carried at the very beginning of an annual report. In general terms, it is intended to *convey important* messages *to shareholders in general, strategic terms.* As *a separate section from other narrative reporting* sections of an annual report, it offers the chairman the opportunity to inform shareholders about issues that he or she feels it would be beneficial for them to be aware of. This *independent communication* is an important part of the separation of the roles of CEO and chairman.

In the case of TQ Company, the role of the chairman is of particular importance *because of the dominance of Mr Smith.* Miss Hoiku had a particular responsibility to use her most recent statement *to inform shareholders about going concern issues* notwithstanding the difficulties that might cause in her relationship with Mr Smith.

Miss Hoiku has an ethical as well as an agency responsibility to *express her independence in the* chairman's *statement and convey issues relevant to company value* to the company's shareholders. She can use her chairman's statement for this purpose.

(c) **Criticise the structure of the reward package that Mr Smith awarded himself**

The balance between *basic to performance related pay was very poor.* Mr Smith, perhaps being aware that the prospect of gaining much performance related income was low, took the opportunity to increase the fixed element of his income to compensate. This was not only unprofessional and unethical on Mr Smith's part, but it also represented very bad value for shareholders. Having exercised his share options and sold the resulting shares, there was now *no element of alignment of his package with shareholder interests* at all. His award to himself of an *'excessively' expensive company car was also not in the shareholders' interests.* The fact that he *exercised and sold all of his share options* means that he will now have no personal financial motivation to take strategic decisions intended to increase TQ Company's share value. This represents a poor degree of alignment between Mr Smith's package and the interests of TQ's shareholders.

(d) **Criticise Miss Hoiku's performance as chairman of TQ Company**

The case describes a particularly poor performance by a company chairman. It is a key function of the chairman to represent the shareholders' interests in the company and Miss Hoiku has *clearly failed in this duty.*

A key reason for her poor performance was her reported inability or *unwillingness to face up to Mr Smith* who was clearly a domineering personality. A key quality of a company chairman is his or her ability and willingness to personally challenge the chief executive if necessary.

She *failed to ensure that a committee structure was in place,* allowing as she did, the remunerations committee to atrophy when two members left the company.

Linked to this, it appears from the case that the *two non-executive directors that left were not replaced* and again, it is a part of the chairman's responsibility to ensure that an adequate number of non-executives are in place on the board.

She inexplicably allowed Mr Smith to *design his own rewards package* and presided over him reducing the performance related element of his package which was clearly misaligned with the shareholders' interests.

When Mr Smith failed to co-ordinate the other directors because of his unspecified business travel, *she failed to hold him to account* thereby allowing the company's strategy to fail.

There seems to have been some *under-reporting of potential strategic problems in the most recent annual report.* A 'future prospects' or 'continuing business' statement is often a required disclosure in an annual report (in many countries) and there is evidence that this *statement may have been missing or misleading* in the most recent annual report.

		Marking scheme		Marks
(a)	(i)	1 mark for each way identified and explained. Half for identification only		4
	(ii)	1 mark for each relevant discussion point made		4
			Maximum	8
(b)		1 mark for each relevant comment made		Up to 5
			Maximum	5
(c)		1 mark for each relevant point of criticism clearly made		Up to 4
			Maximum	4
(d)		1 mark for each relevant point of criticism clearly made		Up to 8
			Maximum	8
Total				25

Examiner's comments

Question 3 discussed a company that had recently failed. A prominent reason for the failure was a corporate governance arrangement in which there was an 'arrogant and domineering' chief executive and an ineffective chairman. The chairman was unable to check the activities of the CEO and accordingly, the CEO was able to abuse his power in various ways.

The requirements were about directors leaving service, the chairman's statement and then two tasks on criticising a reward package structure and the chairman's performance.

Part (a)(i) on the ways in which a director can leave a company was well done in most cases although as elsewhere, bullet lists were not well-rewarded. In **part (a)(ii)**, poorer answers said that it was easy to remove a serving chief executive from service. Better answers were able to draw out some of the issues surrounding the costs of removal, difficulties in proving incompetence and so on.

A common problem on **part (b)** was failing to see that the task was specific to the company in the case. The question was specifically asking candidates to assess the importance of the chairman's statement in the context of the case. The point was that the chairman had a particular duty to report truthfully to shareholders. The chairman's duty to shareholders (this was the way the question was phrased) was to exercise her duty of transparency and truthfulness, and not to conceal information on executive performance that was material to shareholders. The question was not asking about the general purposes of a general chairman's statement in an annual report.

Part (c) and (d) were both pitched at level 3 outcomes in which candidates had to show how the situations in question fell short of expectations or best practice. Overall, part (c), on criticising the CEO's reward package, was done better than part (d) on criticising the chairman's performance. Good performance in 'criticise' questions relies on two things: a sound knowledge of the expectation or best practice against which to measure, and careful study of the text of the case scenario.

34   ROLES AND RELEVANCE

Key answer tips

This question requires a good knowledge of corporate governance principles relating to the board of directors. Although there is little scenario to apply your answers to, do not take this as an opportunity to simply write all you know on a given topic in each section. To earn good marks you will need to carefully identify the separate requirements of each part of the question and ensure all are covered.

(a)   It is generally regarded as best practice in corporate governance that the roles of chairman of the board and chief executive officer should be held by different individuals. The chairman of the board has the responsibility for managing the board of directors, and ensuring that the board functions effectively. The Chief Executive Officer (CEO) is head of the executive management team, and all executive management, including the executive directors, are accountable to the CEO.

Best practice in corporate governance is therefore for the chairman to control the board and the CEO to control the company. However, if the same individual combines these two roles, there would be a high risk of the company being dominated by one individual.

The scale of this risk, and the potential consequences for the company, are possibly difficult to assess. However, there have been reported cases of companies coming under the control of an over-powerful chairman/CEO, with harmful consequences for shareholders.

In the UK, the Corporate Governance Code also recommends that the chairman of the board should not be a former CEO, because this would create a risk that the new CEO would be subject to the chairman's influence on executive matters, and that the chairman would try to persuade the new CEO to run the company in the same way as the chairman did in the past.

(b) A Non-Executive Director (NED) has several roles

(i) NEDs are expected to bring a variety of skills and experience to the board of directors from outside the company to complement the experience and skills of the executive directors. They should therefore bring greater balance and a broader outlook to the discussions of the board. In general terms, the NEDs should help to prevent the domination of the board by a single individual chairman or CEO.

(ii) They should contribute to the decisions of the board of directors. The board should reserve certain decisions to itself, and should not delegate the decision-making authority to only executive management. NEDs should contribute fully to the decision-making processes of the board, for example making decisions about the company's strategy.

(iii) NEDs also perform a policing and monitoring role. Under the leadership of the senior independent director, NEDs in UK listed companies are expected to monitor the performance of the chairman. The NEDs are also expected to meet at least once each year, with no executive directors present.

(iv) The audit committee, consisting entirely of independent NEDs, is required to monitor the integrity of the financial statements and the independence of the external auditors.

(v) The remuneration committee, also consisting entirely of independent NEDs, is responsible for negotiating the remuneration of their executive director colleagues.

(vi) Independent NEDs should make up a majority of the members of the nominations committee, which is responsible for recommending board appointments to the main board.

(vii) There should be a senior independent director, whose functions include acting as an alternative channel of communication for the shareholders in the event that their communications with the chairman are ineffective and unsatisfactory.

(viii) Some NEDs are not independent, and represent the interests of a major shareholder. These NEDs are therefore expected to express the views of the major shareholder at board meetings. However, all directors are expected to carry out their fiduciary duties, and consider the interests of the company when expressing their views.

Tutorial note

A NED can be thought of as having four main roles relating to strategy, scrutinising, risk and people. You could have used these as a basis for your answer for this part of the question, though you would have needed to explain clearly what is entailed in each role.

In their role as contributors to decision-making about the company's strategy, NEDs work together with their executive director colleagues. All directors, executive and NED, have fiduciary duties to the company and a duty of skill and care. All directors are in principle equally liable for the consequences of decisions taken by the board.

However, in their roles on the audit committee and the remunerations committee, and in their role as monitor of the chairman's performance, and in the potential role of the senior independent director as a channel for shareholders to express complaints, NEDs act as a policeman or monitor of the executive management and the chairman.

These two broad roles of colleague and policeman might be difficult to reconcile, and this can create a tension for the NEDs in carrying out their responsibilities.

(c) There is a risk that the directors of a company will run the company in their own personal interests, without sufficient regard to the interests of the shareholders.

It is generally accepted that executive directors will respond to incentives in their remuneration package to improve the company's performance. In theory, a remuneration package should therefore be structured in such a way that directors are suitably rewarded for company performance that benefits shareholders. With a well-structured package, there should be shared interests of shareholders and directors in improving performance in both the long-term and short-term.

On the other hand there is a risk that the remuneration package of an executive director will provide an incentive to the director to achieve performance targets that are not in the company's best interests.

The principles that should be applied by a remuneration committee in negotiating a remuneration package for an executive director are as follows:

(i) The remuneration package should consist of a combination of basic salary and incentive payments. A good basic salary is considered necessary to attract individuals of a suitable calibre.

(ii) The proportion of a remuneration package that is basic salary and the proportion that consists of incentives and rewards is a matter for negotiation, but the incentives element should be significant.

(iii) There should be a combination of long-term and short-term incentives. Executive directors should be rewarded for achieving performance levels that benefit the company both in the long-term and the short term. It is usual to reward directors with cash bonuses for achieving annual performance targets, and with shares or share options that reward the director over time for growth in the company's share price.

(iv) The remuneration package will probably also contain a pension element, with the company making contributions into a personal pension scheme for the director, or guaranteeing a minimum pension on retirement. An attractive pension package is often regarded as a necessary feature of remuneration to attract suitable talent, but it can also be a means of persuading a talented executive to remain with the company.

(v)   The remuneration committee should also consider the possibility that the executive director will perform badly, and might be asked to resign from the company. In these circumstances, there is a risk that the 'dismissed' director will receive a high payment on leaving the company, in settlement of the company's contractual obligations. Such settlements, if excessive, might be criticised as 'rewards for failure' and damage the company's reputation with investors. The remuneration committee should therefore negotiate terms with a director that seek to limit any such payments in the event of dismissal: for example, the director should have a right in his or her contract to a notice period not exceeding one year (or even less) – as recommended in most cases by the UK Corporate Governance Code. In addition, the remuneration committee should seek to negotiate terms such as the payment in lieu of notice to be made in instalments over a one-year period, and to be forfeited if the individual finds similar new employment with another company during the notice period.

The NEDs on the remuneration committee are faced with the problem that they are not remuneration experts, and many remuneration committees in the UK hire the services of external remuneration consultants. The committee should be aware, however, that remuneration consultants might recommend comparatively high remuneration packages with complex conditions and terms. A principle for the committee should therefore be to consider the advice of remuneration consultants, but to make decisions on remuneration that appear to be in the company's best interests – which might be something different.

35 METTO MINING

Key answer tips

You might find it useful to use Carroll's work will provide structure to part (a) of the question, both in terms of social responsibility issues and responses to the conflict.

In part (c) you are only asked to briefly explain, so not much detail is required for the four marks available.

(a)   **Corporate social responsibility**

Carroll identifies four ascending levels of corporate social responsibility. Lower levels should generally be addressed first although true responsibility can only be demonstrated with reference to all four.

Since an organisation exists in order to meet the *economic* needs of its shareholders this provides the foundation to the model. These economic needs can be seen in the need to generate profits and through them dividends and share price growth over time. It might also be the case that economically the company should produce products of worth to society in a cost effective manner. In the scenario institutional investors' needs for an adequate return would be associated with this level of responsibility.

Legal responsibility relates to the need to operate within national and international frameworks and standards. The company has a legal responsibility to act in shareholders' interests creating a cross over between this and the foundation level. More importantly to the scenario the company is failing to adhere to the legal standard within the host country for health and safety. This should have serious repercussions although the willingness of the state to act in this matter is called into question.

Ethical requirements call for the company to operate with a level of integrity. This would include showing due concern for stakeholders, honesty and integrity in dealings and a level of social and environmental concern. The company is failing to meet these obligations. The changing position of the ethics manager suggests the company could have taken action to better protect its workforce. This disregard as to the needs of others is both an ethical and a legal issue. Further, action taken to silence protests does not suggest openness and fairness in dealings with stakeholders. Finally, their lack of support for the changes proposed by the Institutional shareholder cannot be considered an appropriate ethical response.

Philanthropic needs relate to charitable work and so could be associated with the recommendations put forward by Julie Walker. Although this might demonstrate social responsibility at an ethical level it does not really satisfy the demands of Carroll's model since the action is taken under duress and not in a way that would not directly benefit the company. Charitable acts should not be self serving and here they probably would.

Responses to ethical conflict

The company's initial stance is a reactive denial of responsibility. This is one of a number of positions it may take.

Once it appears that a *reactive* stance is not sufficient it shifts to a *defensive* stance by attempting to blame the problem on suppliers. This externalisation of blame is very common and is a slight improvement on simply saying the explosions were unavoidable, at least someone is responsible.

Internalisation of responsibility has not occurred here. If it does then the company might attempt to *accommodate* stakeholders' wishes by making charitable donations and improving safety standards in line with legal requirements.

The final stance sees the organisation move a more *proactive* approach to social responsibility. This would involve identifying stakeholder needs in a formal risk management process and seeking to meet needs as part of a structured strategy, acting in a positive way to promote corporate citizenship.

Tutorial note

Your answer to this second part of the question did not need to refer to the terms reactive, defensive, accommodate and proactive. Answers would have been rewarded if they had simply explained four clear responses to ethical conflict, using the situation of Metto as an example.

(b)   **Corporate citizenship**

Corporate citizenship identifies a number of rights associated with a person's position as a member of society. These rights relate to a social right to basic levels of education and health, civil rights including the right to freedom of speech and movement and political rights to vote or attain political office.

Accompanying the bestowing of benefit through these rights is a responsibility to uphold rights of others in society. In this way the person has a responsibility to pay taxes in order to support a public education system, responsibility to allow others freedom to speak and responsibility to support democracy, possibly by ensuring the individual exercises their voting prerogative when required.

In as much as companies are artificial people they too have rights and responsibilities. It is in the latter area that the company has failed to meet its obligation. It denies the right of others to protest against its action, does not do what it can to provide them with social wellbeing through a safe work environment and possibly places undue pressure on the local government so circumventing the democratic wishes of the people for fair government.

These are serious allegations and should be known and answered by the ethics manager. Unfortunately the board has remained silent on these issues, again calling into question their belief in supporting a basic level of morality in their business activities.

(c)   **Stakeholder classifications**

There are a number of ways in which stakeholders can be classified:

Primary and secondary

This could relate to the perceived level of importance of stakeholders. In this respect shareholders would be narrow and suppliers would be wide or more distant in the thinking of directors. Classifications such as this do not necessarily suggest a disregard for given groups but do suggest a level of investment in supporting a fruitful relationship. The company's accusations against its suppliers follow as a result of classifications such as this.

Narrow and wide

This could be interpreted in the same way as primary and secondary or considered in terms of the impact of stakeholders on the organisation. This might mean that the government is a narrow target being able to stop mining operations if it desires. Wider classifications include a replaceable low paid work force who have little individual power to force change.

Active and passive

The collective will of activists and employees protesting together is a much more potent force rather than the passive acceptance by those not demonstrating for change. The government is at present passive since it does not comment on any mining activities carried out by the company.

Voluntary and involuntary

The Institutional Shareholder has a voluntary relationship and may withdraw from that relationship at any time. The workforce to a degree might be considered involuntary given that employment opportunities are likely to be few forcing people to consider dangerous and difficult work in mines.

(d) **Responsibilities of property and ownership**

Julie Walker identifies the need for share ownership to be coupled with a responsibility to act. This statement attempts to convey that share ownership is asset ownership no different from owning a motor car or house. This being the case the owner must take responsibility for the upkeep, use and disposal of the asset. In the same way shareholders cannot deny their responsibilities simply because the agency relationship creates distance and intangibility in assessing the degree to which true ownership exists.

Many shareholders believe that share ownership does not convey any responsibility on the share holder to act in a responsible way for the actions of the company. In turn directors state that the company is not theirs to use as they will since it belongs to shareholders. The vacuum that this thinking creates leads to a general lack of care and ethical behaviour that leads to disasters such as those identified in the scenario.

36 SARBANES-OXLEY (DEC 13)

Key answer tips

This question and in particular part a) was mainly bookwork and should have presented few problems for the well prepared candidate.

Part (c) was a little more challenging with the question requiring you to "construct a case" for exempting smaller companies. With some thought around costs and time this should have been very achievable..

(a) **Distinguish between rules and principles**

Rules and principles are the two general approaches taken to the regulation of corporate governance practice. The United States and Sarbanes-Oxley is the only major example of a rules-based approach, with most countries preferring to regulate governance behaviour through the observation of general principles.

In a rules-based approach such as Sarbanes-Oxley ('Sarbox' or 'Sox'), the legal enforceability of the Act requires total compliance in all details. This places a substantial compliance cost upon affected companies and creates a large number of compliance advice consultancies to help companies ensure compliance. It is the judiciary rather than investors which monitors and punishes transgression and this means that there is no theoretical distinction drawn between major or minor compliance failures. This is sometimes seen, therefore, to be clumsy or un-nuanced as a means of enforcement.

In a principles-based jurisdiction, listed companies are required by the stock exchange (rather than the law) to meet certain standards of compliance. These standards are usually expressed in a corporate governance code. Companies are required, by the stock exchange's listing rules, to comply in detail with all provisions in the code but may, if unable to do so, report to the shareholders the ways in which compliance is not fully achieved, the reasons for the lack of compliance and when the company expects to be back in full compliance. The shareholders may then assess the transgression and take appropriate action themselves. Such action can be in the form of direct complaints to management or investor relations, or reducing their holdings of those shares, thereby reducing company value. In other words, the market rather than the state enforces and regulates compliance and this is thought by some to be a more efficient enforcement mechanism.

Disadvantages of Sarbanes-Oxley and rules-based approaches

The first disadvantage is that costs are incurred in ensuring and demonstrating compliance. It can be convincingly argued that a *substantial proportion of this cost adds very little value to shareholders*, especially in small companies, and resources are diverted to demonstrating minor areas of compliance which could be used more effectively elsewhere (such as in company operations). Because compliance on the 'big' issues is accorded equal weight in law to compliance with 'small' issues, costs are disproportionately incurred in demonstrating compliance in some non-critical areas.

Second, compliance is seen to be an *inflexible 'box ticking' exercise* and this can sometimes mean that companies lose perspective of what are the most important aspects of governance and what can sometimes be a less important provision to comply with. Disproportionate amounts of management time can be used in ensuring compliance in an area which may be less important to shareholders, but which is nevertheless an important 'box' to have ticked.

Third, infringements and transgressions are punished by the state through its judiciary and *not by those most directly affected by such transgressions*: the shareholders. Those in favour of principles-based approaches argue that there is a greater economic efficiency in having governance monitored by those with the strongest stake in gains and losses (the shareholders), rather than the (in comparison) inefficient and undiscerning agents of the state. In many cases, agents of the state are unable to distinguish between major and minor infringements, merely noticing that a 'box' is 'unticked' and pursuing punishment as a result.

(b) **Agency**

In the context of corporate governance, agency refers to the relationship between the principal and an agent. The principal appoints an agent to act on his or her behalf in order to maximise the outcome sought by the principal. In the case of a business organisation with a separation of ownership and control, this relationship comprises shareholders (principals) and directors (agents). As agents, directors' responsibilities should be primarily concerned with maximising the long-term returns to shareholders and providing timely, accurate and truthful information to shareholders in terms of reporting. The production of reports on internal controls is an important part of this reporting.

Benefits of '*maintaining a system of internal control over financial reporting*'

First, the system is important for *ensuring that information can be accessed* as necessary for management decision-making purposes, for reporting, or as part of an audit trail. Information needs to be reliable whenever it is used, either for internal management purposes or for shareholders, and a robust system to produce reporting information is necessary for that. This includes the benefit of the timely delivery of reports.

Second, the case describes the importance of accurate 'evidential matter' in the preparation of reports. This may be important in providing an audit trail and to *demonstrate that the systems and reporting are compliant* with GAAP or other relevant systems of accounting rules (such as IFRS). These make it more likely that the reports will be truthful and reliable, both of which are important information qualities for shareholders. The evidential matter is likely to be able to demonstrate that the contents of the external report have been arrived at by using outputs from measurement systems compliant with relevant standards and this will satisfy external auditors, and, in turn, shareholders.

Third, the report on internal control (IC) is capable of providing *assurance to investors that the company is being well run and that it has effective internal controls* capable of supporting a strategy which can maximise the long-term returns needed. As agents of the shareholders' interests, directors must demonstrate they are responsible stewards of shareholder value. A report on the adequacy of internal controls in place in the company is a convincing way of achieving this.

Fourth, because code compliance is mandatory in a rules-based jurisdiction (Sarbanes-Oxley in the case scenario), the maintenance of an effective system of internal control allows management to *clearly demonstrate its compliance* with the effective laws governing corporate governance. Because there are legal and reputational penalties for any compliance failures (even small ones), the clear and unambiguous signalling of compliance is important to shareholders and the availability of legal sanctions for non-compliance provides greater deterrents and provides greater assurance about the effectiveness of internal controls to shareholders.

(c) **Arguments for the exemption**

First, smaller companies generally exist in *less complicated environments* than larger companies (i.e. with fewer potential risks and less dynamic risks) and are consequently less exposed than larger companies to some losses. Size confers political visibility and a wider range of stakeholder claims upon the organisation. Furthermore, there is less risk to society and to investors from individual smaller company losses. Whereas a large company with inadequate internal controls and/or poor IC reporting may cause thousands of job losses, large losses to share portfolios and individual investors, there is likely to be less overall risk to society and to general investors if a small company slightly misreports the adequacy of its internal controls. It is also likely that small companies *do not have widely distributed share ownership*, in many cases having the owners being managers. This may mean that shareholders may not need or want the full levels of disclosure of such monitoring compared to larger companies with more distributed share ownership and a greater 'distance' between ownership and management.

Second, there are also likely to be disproportionate costs (compared to output volumes) of putting systems in place for *gathering the necessary 'evidential matter'*. Even when infrastructure is installed, management time is required to prepare evidence of compliance. The preparation and publication of the s.404 report itself can also be *disproportionately expensive* for a small company because of the fixed costs of report preparation which apply regardless of the variable costs of volumes actually produced.

The third reason for exempting smaller companies is that the *fixed costs of the infrastructure systems which need to be put into place are disproportionately high for a small company*. For a larger company which can allocate the overheads of this investment over a high number of outputs, such costs are manageable or even negligible. For a smaller company with fewer outputs, fixed cost allocation per unit may be seen as unfairly high, especially when cash flow is already very tight and the scope for investment in systems for compliance are very limited.

Fourth, the costs of compliance could be a *barrier to growth* for smaller companies and a *disincentive to entrepreneurship*. Many believe that any regulation seen as unnecessarily bureaucratic or which does not enjoy the broad support of those affected by it can discourage value creation. This might mean, for example, that affected companies do not grow as quickly as they might, that they may make lower profits and thereby create fewer jobs.

ACCA marking scheme		
		Marks
(a)	4 marks for distinguishing between rules and principles. 1.5 marks for each disadvantage explained (half for identification only).	
	Maximum	7
(b)	2 marks for defining agency. 2 marks for each relevant discussion point to a maximum of 8 marks.	
	Maximum	10
(c)	2 marks for each relevant point convincingly made in support of the case.	
	Maximum	8
Total		**25**

Examiner's comments

The case scenario for question 2 was on Sarbanes Oxley in the United States, and in particular the section 404 provisions on the external reporting of the adequacy of internal controls. This was a popular question for P1 candidates in the December 2013 exam and many candidates achieved good marks for the question.

Part (a) was mainly book work and should have been familiar material to any P1 candidate. It contained two tasks: to distinguish between rules and principles, and then to explain the disadvantages of a rules-based system. It was important to take these two tasks in turn as 'combined' answers were often confused and less clear than those that took each in turn. Most candidates were able to gain some marks in this requirement and it was one in which thorough revision was rewarded.

In part (b), candidates were required to define agency and then go on to discuss the benefits of maintaining a system of internal control over financial reporting in a rules-based jurisdiction. The first task in this requirement (to define agency) was evidently more straightforward than the second. Control over financial reporting was a key outcome of the Enron failure and a prominent issue within many corporate governance codes including Sarbanes Oxley. Many candidates produced weak answers on the benefits of internal controls over external reporting, although this is a central theme in sound corporate governance. It is not possible to produce reliable external reporting without the internal controls necessary to ensure the accuracy and robustness of the reporting.

Many candidates seemed to struggle with part (c) and some didn't answer it at all. The case scenario set out the situation with section 404 of Sarbanes Oxley and the requirement asked about how difficult it would be for smaller companies to comply with it. The point here is partly that the costs of compliance are proportionately higher than for larger companies, partly because of fixed costs that apply to all companies regardless of their size.

37   HWL (DEC 13)

Key answer tips

This question and in particular the first part of part a) was mainly bookwork and straightforward. The second part required thought and careful reading of both the question and scenario.

Part (b) required the advantages of diversity to be clearly linked to the situation in the case. Part (c) required an explanation of CSR and then the differences between CSR for a charity and "for profit" organisation. Some careful thought was required before attempting the second part of this requirement with the fundamental strategic purpose of each organisation being a good starting point.

(a)   **Roles of a nominations committee**

Nominations committees have five general roles, all of which are concerned with the recommendation of appointments to the board of directors. The first role is to establish the appropriate *balance between executive and non-executive* directors (NEDs). In some countries, this is influenced by regulation. In the UK, the UK corporate governance code specifies that a half of the whole board should be NEDs. The second role is to ensure that the *board contains the requisite skills, knowledge and experience* to effectively lead the company and provide leadership. Any identified gaps in these requirements should be filled by new appointments. Third, the nominations committee is concerned with the *continuity of required skills, the retention of directors and succession planning*. Fourth, it is responsible for determining the *most desirable board size* given the skill needs, cost constraints and strategies of the company. Finally, the committee is likely to be concerned with *issues of diversity* and to ensure that the company's board is adequately representative of the society in which it operates.

How to approach the task at HWL

In appointing new directors to the board of HWL, the challenge is finding directors who share the values of the charity and who are also prepared to serve at a market discount. The pressure from Marian Ngogo is to find competent people who match both of these criteria and this is likely to be a substantial challenge.

At HWL, the nominations committee could help in several ways with this.

The first is to use *personal recommendations* and business contacts of current or past executive and non-executive directors. In most industries, there is a network of people with similar interests and who are known to each other. These can be used and the recommendations of reliable people can be pursued as necessary.

It could *use search companies* and consultancies to find people likely to be willing to serve on the board. These may have databases of people serving on other charity boards or people who might be interested in working for a charity for a period of time in seeking to serve the wider public interest rather than just his or her own economic interests.

Third, the nominations committee could instruct the human resources function to *advertise for suitable persons*. This is likely to be the most common way of recruiting executives who may be required to have specific technical skills such as accounting or marketing. NEDs are less often recruited in this way.

(b) **Advantages of diversity**

Diversity policy aims to achieve a board which is demographically representative of the community in which it operates, such that no single demographic segment is over or under-represented. In the case of HWL, a diverse board of directors would provide several advantages.

First, it would make the board *more representative of the community* it is serving, including its donors and supporters. In doing so, HWL would increase its social legitimacy and enjoy a *stronger social contract* with its community and also with the service users. If the board were homogenous with a certain dominant demographic, it would be open to the charge of being aloof and with a weak connection to the local ethnic groups not represented on the board.

Second, diversity on the board will enable HWL to *meet the local government requirements for diversity* and thus to continue receiving that portion of its funding from the local government. With a large proportion of HWL's funding coming from the local government (40%), HWL is effectively required to comply with the diversity requirements as it would be difficult to replace such funding in the short term.

Third, diversity on a board allows the organisation to benefit from a *wider pool of talent* than would be the case with a less diverse board. Having a wide range of demographic segments represented should mean that a wider range of skills, abilities and competences are available. A demographically narrow board would exclude the talents possessed by those outside of the narrow representation and this would be against the board's best interests in seeking to be effective in its duties.

Fourth, a more diverse board would enable a *wider range of views* and opinions to be expressed. The dominant opinion of the majority and the phenomenon of 'group think' can lead to the adoption of positions and policies which can often be shown to be inappropriate in the longer term. So some contrary and challenging voices, especially from those speaking from the perspective of a demographic minority, can be important contributions in policy discussions.

Fifth, a diverse range of people on the board would provide a *greater understanding of the particular values and beliefs* of a wider range of people in HWL's catchment area. Given that HWL's work is most effective when the service providers share some of the values and beliefs of the clients, a board of directors able to understand as wide a range of beliefs as possible is a clear advantage.

Tutorial note

Some countries are beginning to regulate for diversity on boards. Allow this if placed in a particular national context.

(c) **Corporate social responsibility (CSR)**

CSR is a term used to include a series of measures concerned with an organisation's stance towards ethical issues. These include the organisation's social and environmental behaviour, the responsibility of its products and investments, its policies (over and above compliance with regulation) towards employees, its treatment of suppliers and buyers, its transparency and integrity, how it deals with stakeholder concerns and issues of giving and community relations.

Behaviour in all of these areas is largely discretionary and it is possible to adopt a range of approaches from being very concerned about some or all of them, to having no such concern at all.

CSR can be expressed and undertaken in several ways. It has been the case for some time that companies have exercised a social concern for employees (over and above regulatory compliance) and communities, but in more recent times, the idea has emerged that CSR can be integrated into an organisation's strategy. To be strategic about CSR is to undertake CSR initiatives which can have meaning for the organisation as well as those to whom the initiatives are directed. Ethical 'filters' and scrutiny procedures may be installed to ensure that the company acts in accordance with a set of agreed principles, perhaps expressed in a code of ethics. The organisation's ethical reputation may be viewed as a strategic asset and a key part of its competitive positioning.

CSR at HWL and in a commercial business

As a charity, HWL's *central strategic purpose is to be socially beneficial in nature*. The reason why any charity exists is to pursue a benevolent purpose. In the case of HWL, this is 'to help individuals and families with social problems and related issues.' It performs this service for no charge to the service users and seeks to maximise the quality of this service over other concerns of the organisation. A commercial business is likely to have a strategic purpose framed in terms of competitive or financial measures.

Second, HWL *measures its success in social outcome rather than in profits*. The case scenario says that HWL's strategic (i.e. most important) aim is to deliver its charitable services ('to help its service users') whereas a commercial business is more likely to measure success in financial terms such as returns on investment, net or gross margins, etc.

Third, HWL *supports its charitable purpose* through a number of operational measures. It asks those staff members working for it to *espouse certain values and beliefs* (consistent with those service users being helped). HWL also *asks its directors to forgo income* to work for it. Its attitude towards money was that it would rather spend what money it had on service provision than directors' pay. So asking people to accept a personal discount is perhaps made possible because those who help lead the charity (its directors) are more likely to share a belief in the value of what it does. Such an alignment of personal belief with company policy is rarely asked for in a business organisation and few would ask or expect directors to work for a level of remuneration below the market rate. Increasing personal incomes is often a strong concern of directors in commercial businesses, in contrast with the attitude asked for by Marian Ngogo at HWL.

ACCA marking scheme		Marks
(a)	1 mark for each role to a maximum of 5 marks. 1 mark for each approach for nomination to a maximum of 3 marks.	
	Maximum	8
(b)	2 marks for each advantage explained.	
	Maximum	8
(c)	3 marks for explanation of CSR. 2 marks for each relevant difference discussed. Half mark for identification only.	
	Maximum	9
Total		**25**

Examiner's comments

Part (a) asked about nomination committees and contained two tasks. The first task was mainly bookwork and required candidates to explain the roles of a nominations committee. Most candidates that attempted this question were able to do this task quite well. The second task was less well done. The task was to describe how HWL's nominations committee might actually go about appointing new directors and was more straightforward than some answers suggested. Some candidates saw clearly what this was asking and produced excellent answers whilst others produced confused and poorly-formed answers that seemed to misunderstand the meaning of the question.

Part (b) asked about the advantages of diversity on the board of HWL. Note that this, although touching on a general theme, requires careful analysis of the case because it is specifically about diversity on the board of HWL. So whilst a good knowledge of the importance of diversity in general was a good starting point, the high marks came with an explanation firmly linked to HWL's specific situation. A common weaker answer was to reproduce the advantages of board diversity with little or no linkage to the unique situation of HWL whilst the better answers realised, for example, that 40% of HWL's funding was dependent upon the charity demonstrating diversity on its board and that this funding might be threatened if HWL failed to comply.

Part (c) also contained two tasks, with the first being answered better than the second overall. The first task was to explain 'corporate social responsibility' and markers accepted a range of expressions of this explanation. Again, however, an explanation was required and a shorter 'definition' was less well rewarded in terms of marks. The second task was to discuss the ways in which CSR and ethical stances differ between a charity and a 'for profit' business. Of course the whole basis of their reasons to exist are completely different for these two types of organisation. Many answers were sketchy and incomplete on this, with some candidates writing very little

38   BADILSON

Key answer tips

This is a new question based on the syllabus change for December 2014. Be sure to be clear of the definitions in this syllabus area and in particular the differences in agency and stakeholder relationships and how accountability is monitored. Part c) and d) explore these differences

(a)   The term public sector refers to organisations that are, in some way, connected to, or deliver, public goods and services. This means that they help to, in some way, deliver goods and services that cannot be, or should not be, provided by 'for profit' businesses.

In most developed countries, the public sector is huge, within the UK, for example, the public sector accounting for around a quarter of all jobs, in many cases, thousands or even millions of people.

It is worth noting that public sector organisations are operated, at least in part, by the state. A state, not to be confused with a government, is a self-governing, autonomous region. A state is comprised of: the executive (or government), the legislature, the judiciary and the secretariat (or administration). In the UK for example, the head of state is the reigning monarch and the head of government is a different person (the prime minister).

The administration is the largest and is responsible for carrying out government policy and administering a large number of state functions such as education, health, local authority provision, central government, defence, foreign affairs, state pensions, tax collection and interior issues such as immigration, policing and prisons. This does however depend on the state. Organisations such as these are funded by revenues from the state (mainly taxes) and they exist to deliver public services that cannot, or – in the opinion of the government – should not be provided by the private sector.

(b) Public sector organisations emphasise different types of objectives to the private sector. Private companies focus on optimising their competitive positions, public sector organisations tend to be concerned with social purposes and delivering their services efficiently, effectively and with good value for money.

A common way of understanding the general objectives of public sector organisations is the three Es: economy, efficiency and effectiveness.

Economy represents value for money and delivering the required service on budget, on time and within other resource constraints.

Efficiency is concerned with getting an acceptable return on the money and resources invested in a service. Efficiency is defined as work output divided by work input and it is all about getting as much out as possible from the amount put into a system. It follows that an efficient organisation delivers more for a given level of resource input than an inefficient one

Effectiveness describes the extent to which the organisation delivers what it is intended to deliver

(c) One of the key concepts in corporate governance in the private sector is agency i.e. the people who manage a business do not own it, rather managing the business on behalf of their principals.

Management has an agency relationship with the principals in that they have a fiduciary duty to help the principals achieve the outcomes. In a private or public incorporated business organisation, the principals are shareholders and, in most cases, shareholders seek to maximise the long-term value of their shares. This is usually achieved by profitable trading and having strategies in place to enable the company to compete effectively in its competitive environment.

Public sector organisations differ in this context and whilst public sector workers are equally as diligent as their colleagues in the private sector and are set objectives that are just as well planned, clear and relevant the principals are different. Whereas private and public companies have shareholders, public sector organisations carry out their important roles on behalf of those that fund the activity (mainly taxpayers) and those that use the services (perhaps pupils in a school, patients in a hospital, etc).

The difficulty that often exists therefore is that the providers of funds are often not the same people who use those funds giving rise to disagreements on how much is spent and on what particular provisions. This is the fundamental part of political debate i.e. how much state funding should be allocated to which public sector organisation and how the money should be spent. It is, for example, a common theme in UK politics.

With no one single mechanism being appropriate to control and monitor the achievement of objectives, accountability is achieved, at least in part, by having a system of reporting and oversight. This entails those in charge of the service delivery to report to an external body of oversight which may be e.g. a board of governors or trustees.

The oversight body acts in the interest of the providers of finance, the taxpayer to ensure that the service is delivered on time and is for the benefit of the users. Members are drawn from all aspects of business life and can include executive and nonexecutive positions similar to those depicted within the private sector.

The roles of the oversight bodies are wide and varied. Typically they will include ensuring that the service complies with government rules, performance targets are met, oversee senior management performance appointments and removal of senior managers and ultimately to report to higher authorities on the above categories for the organisations being monitored.

(d)   Public sector organisations generally have more complex set of stakeholder relationships than some private sector businesses.

Because most public sector activities are funded through taxation, public sector bodies they have a complicated model of how they add value. For a private business, revenues predominantly come from customers who have willingly engaged with the business and gained some utility for themselves in the form of benefit from goods or services.

With a government, however, taxation is mandatory and may be paid against the wishes of the taxpayer. Citizens of a country might disagree with the levels of taxation taken by a government, especially when a taxpayer sees most of his or her tax being spent on causes or services that mainly benefit others (and not themselves) and with which they may disagree.

There exists a social contract between the government and those governed and the latter must feel like they are being fairly treated. The claims of different stakeholders are highly relevant here because, the stakeholder pressures on a government are often very difficult to understand.

Claims can be assessed separately and differently by different people. This means that some stakeholder claims are recognised by some but not by others, and this can make for a very complex situation. Some stakeholders have a very weak voice, while others have no effective voice at all when expressing their claim.

INTERNAL CONTROL AND REVIEW

39   DING (DEC 09)

Key answer tips

A common student error is not to apply knowledge to the scenario. This question offers you an opportunity to practice this application skill.

(a)   Part (a) has two tasks: to explain the content of a director's induction programme and to assess the advantages of an induction programme for Sam Mesentery, the new director who is the subject of the case.

(b)   Part (b) required a knowledge of unitary and two-tier boards in order to critically evaluate Annette Hora's belief. The task in part (b) was to provide arguments for and against this belief. This then was not just about the pros and cons of one type of board structure over another, but rather about their suitability in different environmental conditions: therefore this was an application question.

(c)   In part (c) it was necessary to know what the roles of a non-executive chairman are in order to compare Arif's views with those roles. The question was not asking what the roles of a non-executive chairman are. The most common error in answering this question was listing the roles of the chairman and failing to analyse what Arif had actually said.

(a)   **Director's induction programme**

The overall purpose of induction is to minimise the amount of time taken for the new director to become effective in his or her new job. There are four major aspects of a director's induction.

To convey to the new starter, the organisation's norms, values and culture. This is especially important when the new employee is from a different type of culture. Because Sam moved from a different country to join Ding Company, he had to adjust to a new national culture as well as a new corporate culture. There is evidence from the case that he misunderstood some of the cultural norms in that it was alleged that he made what he considered normal but what was perceived as an inappropriate remark to a young female employee. An induction programme including content on culture and norms may have prevented this situation from occurring.

To communicate practical procedural duties to the new director including company policies relevant to a new employee. In Sam's case this would involve his orientation with his place in the structure, his reporting lines (up and down), the way in which work is organised in the department and practical matters. In the case scenario, Sam made a simple error in the positioning of his office furniture. Again, this is an entirely avoidable situation had the induction programme provided him with appropriate content on company policy in this area.

To convey an understanding of the nature of the company, its operations, strategy, key stakeholders and external relationships. For a new director, an early understanding of strategy is essential and a sound knowledge of how the company 'works' will also ensure that he or she adapts more quickly to the new role. In the case of a financial controller such as Sam, key external relationships will be with the company's auditors and banks. If Sam is involved in reporting, the auditor relationship will be important and if he is involved in financing, the banks and other capital providers will be more important.

To establish and develop the new director's relationships with colleagues, especially those with whom he or she will interact on a regular basis. The importance of building good relationships early on in a director's job is very important as early misunderstandings can be costly in terms of the time needed to repair the relationship. It is likely that Sam and Annette will need to work together to repair an unfortunate start to their working relationship as it seems that one of her first dealings with him was to point out his early misunderstandings (which were arguably due to her failure to provide him with an appropriate induction programme).

(b) **Critically evaluate Annette's belief**

Tutorial note

Make sure the verb 'evaluate' is carefully considered. 'For' and 'against' needs to be discussed.

Countries differ in their employment of various types of board structure. Companies in the UK and US have tended towards unitary structures while Japanese companies and some European countries have preferred two–tier or even multi-tier boards. The distinction refers to the ways in which decision-making and responsibility is divided between directors. In a unitary structure, all of the directors have a nominally equal role in board discussions but they also jointly share responsibility (including legal responsibility) for the outcome of those discussions.

On a two tier board, the senior board acts as a 'kitchen cabinet' in which decisions are concentrated whilst other directors, typically departmental managers, will be on the 'operating board' and brought into board discussions where the senior (upper tier) board deem it appropriate.

There are some arguments in favour of the adoption of a two-tier structure in turbulent environments. As the case implies, turbulent and dynamic environments change often and strategic leadership is partly about continually adjusting strategy to optimise the company's fit with its environment. A smaller board can act quick and decisively in a way that larger and more cumbersome boards cannot. This is because meetings of larger numbers of people require excessive consultation, discussion and debate before a decision can be reached. When a decision needs to be taken quickly, this can be inconvenient. The meeting of a small number of people is therefore easier, cheaper and quicker to arrange because there are fewer diaries to match. As these arguments focus on both the efficiency and effectiveness of strategic decision-making, Annette has a strong case for supporting two-tier boards.

The arguments against two-tier boards are as follows. In any complex situation where finely balanced judgments are made, such as making strategic decisions in turbulent environmental conditions, input from more people is likely to provide more views upon which to make the decision. Where, say, technical, detailed financial or operational details would be of benefit to the decision then a larger board would be likely to provide more feedback into the decision making process. The second reason is that decisions taken by a corporate board with little or no consultation with the operating board may not enjoy the full support of those key departmental directors who will be required to implement the decision. This, in turn, may cause friction, discord and resentment that will hinder good relations and thus impede the implementation of the strategy. Additionally, without a full understanding of operations, an inappropriate decision may be taken by the corporate board and unworkable procedures implemented. Finally, Annette is quite an autocratic personality and the two-tier board may be little more than a device to grant her excessive powers over company strategies and activities.

(c) **Arif Zaman's understanding of his role**

The first observation to make is that over all, Arif Zaman has a poor understanding of his role as chairman and poorly represents the interests of Ding's shareholders.

He doesn't seem to understand his role as intended by Cadbury, Sarbanes Oxley and other influential codes on corporate governance.

It appears from the case that he cedes too much power to Annette. One of the purposes of having a separate chairman is to avoid allowing the chief executive to operate without recourse to the chairman. The chairman, along with the non-executive directors, should hold the chief executive to account.

Arif allowed Annette's views to take effect on matters such as board structure. Arif is legally head of the board and not Annette. Ding's shareholders have a reasonable expectation that Arif will personally ensure that the strategic oversight of the board will be a matter for the chairman who is, notionally at least, an independent non-executive director.

Being old friends with Annette threatens Arif's independence as chairman. Is he acting as a representative of the shareholders or as Annette's friend? He seems to be doing the job as a favour to Annette and seems to see no intrinsic value in his role in terms of acting to provide checks and balances on the activities of the executive board and the chief executive in particular.

Arif seems to view the chairing of board meetings as optional. He said that he saw his role as 'mainly ceremonial' and that he 'chaired some board meetings when he was available'. Both of these attitudes are inappropriate and demonstrate an underestimation of the importance of the chairman in leading the company and its strategy.

Marking scheme			Marks
(a)	1 mark for each relevant point recognised and explained. Half mark for identification only to a maximum of 2. 1 mark for development of point or assessment with regard to Sam in the case.		8
(b)	2 marks for evidence of understanding the meaning of 'unitary' and 'two-tier' boards (which could be in any part of the answer) 1 mark for each relevant point made in favour of Annette's belief to a maximum of 4. 1 mark for each relevant point made against Annette's belief to a maximum of 4.		8
(c)	1 mark for each relevant point of criticism recognised and 1 for development and application.		9
Total			25

40   TOMATO BANK (JUN 10)

Key answer tips

(a)   With a verb like 'criticise' careful analysis of the case is required to answer the question successfully. Ensure you read the scenario carefully.

(b)   The first part of this requirement, to describe components, was largely book work and should have posed no problem to well-prepared candidates. The second element is to apply this knowledge to Mr Woof's remuneration: this took a little further analysis.

(c)   This final requirement has a very open marking guide – one per relevant point – therefore allowing you to express your views in varying ways.

(a)   **Criticisms of remuneration committee**

The remuneration committee has demonstrated failures of duty in several areas.

There is evidence of a lack of independence in the roles of the non-executive directors (NEDs) who comprise the committee. One of the main purposes of NEDs is to bring independent perspectives within the committee structure and shareholders have the right to expect NEDs to not be influenced by executive pressure in decision-making (such as from the finance directors). Two of the NEDs on the remuneration committee were former colleagues of Mr Woof, creating a further conflict. The effect of this lack of independence was a factor in the creation of Mr Woof's unbalanced package. That, in turn, increased agency costs and made the agency problem worse.

There was a clear breach of good practice with the remuneration committee receiving and acting on the letter from Mr Woof and agreeing to the design of the remuneration package in such a hasty manner. Remuneration committees should not receive input from the executive structure and certainly not from directors or prospective directors lobbying for their own rewards. Mr Woof was presumptuous and arrogant in sending the letter but the committee was naive and irresponsible in receiving and acting upon it.

There is evidence that the remuneration was *influenced by the hype* surrounding the supposed favourable appointment in gaining the services of Mr Woof. In this regard it lacked objectivity. Whilst it was the remuneration committee's role to agree an attractive package that reflected Mr Woof's market value, the committee was seemingly *coerced by the finance director and others* and this is an abdication of their non-executive responsibility.

The committee *failed to build in adequate performance related components* into Mr Woof's package. Such was the euphoria in appointing Mr Woof that they were influenced by a clearly excitable finance director who was so keen to get Mr Woof's signature that he counselled against exercising proper judgement in this balance of benefits. Not only should the remuneration committee have not allowed representations from the FD, it should also have given a great deal more thought to the balance of benefits so that bonuses were better aligned to shareholder interests.

The committee *failed to make adequate pension and resignation arrangements* that represented value for the shareholders of Tomato Bank as well as for Mr Woof. Whilst pension arrangements are within the remit of the remuneration committee and a matter for consideration upon the appointment of a new chief executive, shareholder value would be better served if it was linked to the time served in the company and also if the overall contribution could be reconsidered were the CEO to be removed by shareholders for failure such as was the case at Tomato Bank.

Tutorial note

Candidates may express these and similar points in several ways.

(b)   **Components of a rewards package**

The components of a typical executive reward package include *basic salary,* which is paid regardless of performance; *short and long-term bonuses* and incentive plans which are payable based on pre-agreed performance targets being met; *share schemes,* which may be linked to other bonus schemes and provide options to the executive to purchase predetermined numbers of shares at a given favourable price; *pension and termination benefits* including a pre-agreed pension value after an agreed number of years' service and any 'golden parachute' benefits when leaving; plus any number of other *benefits in kind* such as cars, health insurance, use of company property, etc.

Balanced package is needed for the following reasons:

The overall purpose of a well-designed rewards package is to achieve a *reduction (minimisation) of agency costs.* These are the costs the principals incur in monitoring the actions of agents acting on their behalf.

The main way of doing this is to ensure that executive reward packages are *aligned with the interests of principals* (shareholders) so that directors are rewarded for meeting targets that further the interests of shareholders. A reward package that only rewards accomplishments in line with shareholder value substantially decreases agency costs and when a shareholder might own shares in many companies, *such a* 'self-policing' *agency mechanism is clearly of benefit.* Typically, such reward packages involve a bonus element based on specific financial targets in line with enhanced company (and hence shareholder) value.

Although Mr Woof came to Tomato Bank with a very good track record, *past performance is no guarantee of future success.* Accordingly, Mr Woof's reward package should have been subject to the same detailed design as with any other executive package. In hindsight, a pension value linked to performance and sensitive to the manner of leaving would have been a worthwhile matter for discussion and also the split between basic and incentive components. Although ambitious to design, it would have been helpful if the reward package could have been made reviewable by the remuneration committee so that a *discount for risk could be introduced* if, for example, the internal audit function were to signal a high level of exposure to an unreliable source of funding. As it stands, the worst that can happen to him is that he survives just two years in office, during which time he need not worry about the effects of excessive risk on the future of the company, as he has a generous pension to receive thereafter.

(c) **Ethical case for repaying part of pension**

Mr Woof was the *beneficiary of a poor appointments process* and his benefits package was designed *in haste and with some incompetence.* He *traded freely on his reputation* as a good banker and probably inflated his market value as a result. He then *clearly failed in his role* as a responsible steward of shareholders' investments and in his fiduciary duty to investors. In exposing the bank to financing risks that ultimately created issues with the bank's economic stability, it was *his strategies that were to blame* for the crisis created. The fact that he is receiving such a generous pension is *because of his own lobbying* and his *own assurance of good performance* places an obligation on him to accept responsibility for the approach he made to the remuneration committee five years earlier.

The debate is partly about legal entitlement and ethical responsibility. Although he is legally entitled to the full value of the pension, it is the perception of what is fair and reasonable that is at stake. It is evident that Mr Woof is being self-serving in his dealings and in this regard is operating at a *low level of Kohlberg's moral development* (probably level 1 in seeking maximum rewards and in considering only the statutory entitlement to these in his deliberations). A more developed sense of moral reasoning would enable him to see the wider range of issues and to act in conformity with a higher sense of fairness and justice, more akin to behaviour at Kohlberg's level 3.

Tutorial note

It is possible to express this case in a range of ways, therefore the examiner has given this requirement a very open 'one mark per relevant point' marking scheme.

Marking scheme		Marks
(a)	2 marks for each criticism identified and discussed (10 marks)	10
(b)	1 mark for each component identified and described (½ mark for identification only) to a maximum of 5 marks (5 marks)	
	mark for each relevant point of explanation of the benefits of a balanced package for Mr Woof to a maximum of 5	
		10
(c)	1 mark for each relevant point made	5
Total		**25**

41   ABC CO (PILOT 07) *Walk in the footsteps of a top tutor*

Key answer tips

This question is on a very examinable topic – remuneration. It is therefore important that you thoroughly understand the issues raised and the approach needed.

The highlighted words are key phrases that markers are looking for.

Tutor's top tips

Approach to the question

Look at the requirements carefully and from these you can establish the headings for your plan and also your answer. Every time you see the word 'and' you should consider introducing another heading into your answer structure.

Ensure that you are clear with the verb in the question, and what is required for that verb.

(a)   **Remunerations committees and cross directorships**

Tutor's top tips

Note that this requirement is actually split into two separate tasks:

1   Explain the four roles of a remuneration committee.

2   Explain and apply your knowledge of Cross Directorships.

Remunerations committees

Remunerations committees comprise an important part of the standard board committee structure of good corporate governance.

The major roles of a remuneration committee are as follows. Firstly, the committee is charged with determining remunerations policy on behalf of the board and the shareholders. In this regard, they are acting on behalf of shareholders but for the benefit of both shareholders and the other members of the board. Policies will typically concern the pay scales applied to directors' packages, the proportions of different types of reward within the overall package and the periods in which performance related elements become payable.

Secondly the committee ensures that each director is fairly but responsibly rewarded for their individual contribution in terms of levels of pay and the components of each director's package. It is likely that discussions of this type will take place for each individual director and will take into account issues including market conditions, retention needs, long-term strategy and market rates for a given job.

Third, the remunerations committee reports to the shareholders on the outcomes of their decisions, usually in the corporate governance section of the annual report (usually called Report of the Remunerations Committee). This report, which is auditor reviewed, contains a breakdown of each director's remuneration and a commentary on policies applied to executive and non-executive remuneration.

Finally, where appropriate and required by statute or voluntary code, the committee is required to be seen to be compliant with relevant laws or codes of best practice. This will mean that the remunerations committee will usually be made up of non-executive members of the board and will meet at regular intervals.

Cross directorships

Tutor's top tips

I would have drawn a diagram here showing how Frank Finn and Mr Ng have a cross directorial relationship.

	ABC	*DEF*
Exec	*Frank Finn*	*Mr Ng*
NED	*Mr Ng*	*Frank Finn*

Cross directorships represent a threat to the efficient working of remunerations committees. A cross directorship is said to exist when two (or more) directors sit on the boards of the other. In practice, such arrangements also involve some element of cross-shareholdings which further compromises the independence of the directors involved. In most cases, each director's 'second' board appointment is likely to be non-executive. Cross directorships undermine the roles of remunerations committees in that a director deciding the salary of a colleague who, in turn, may play a part in deciding his or her own salary, is a clear conflict of interests. Neither director involved in the arrangement is impartial and so a temptation would exist to act in a manner other than for the benefit of the shareholders of the company on whose remunerations committee they sit.

It is for this reason the cross directorships and cross shareholding arrangements are explicitly forbidden by many corporate governance codes of best practice.

(b)   **Mr Finn's remunerations package**

Different components of directors' rewards

Tutor's top tips

There are some easy book work marks here that a well-prepared student would have easily obtained. However, careful thought must be taken to ensure the whole requirement is answered. Therefore it is necessary to apply your knowledge to Mr Finn's specific remuneration package.

The components of a director's total rewards package may include any or all of the following in combination. The basic salary is not linked to performance in the short run but year-to-year changes in it may be linked to some performance measures. It is intended to recognise the basic market value of a director. A number of benefits in kind may be used which will vary by position and type of organisation, but typically include company cars, health insurance, use of health or leisure facilities, subsidised or free use of company products (if appropriate), etc. Pension contributions are paid by most responsible employers, but separate directors' schemes may be made available at higher contribution rates than other employees. Finally, various types of incentives and performance related components may be used. Short to medium term incentives such as performance-related annual bonuses will encourage a relatively short term approach to meeting agreed targets whilst long term incentives including share options can be used for longer term performance measures.

Mr Finn's remuneration package

The case mentions that, 'Mr Finn's remuneration package as a sales director was considered to be poorly aligned to Swanland's interests because it was too much weighted by basic pay and contained inadequate levels of incentive.'

The alignment of director and shareholder interests occurs through a careful design of the performance related components of a director's overall rewards. The strategic emphases of the business can be built into these targets and Mr Finn's position as a sales director makes this possible through incentives based on revenue or profit targets. If current priorities are for the maximisation of relatively short-run returns, annual, semi-annual or even monthly performance-related bonuses could be used. More likely at board level, however, will be a need for longer-term alignments for medium to long-term value maximisation. While Mr Finn may be given annual or even quarterly or monthly bonus payments against budget, longer-term performance can be underpinned through share options with a relevant maturity date or end-of-service payouts with agreed targets. The balance of short and longer-term performance bonuses should be carefully designed for each director with metrics within the control of the director in question.

(c) **Evaluation of the proposal from Hanoi House**

The dilemma over what action to take in the light of Mr Ng and Mr Finn's cross directorship is a typical problem when deciding how to address issues of conflicts of interest. Should the situation be 'put right' at minimum cost, or should the parties in the arrangement be punished in some way as Hanoi House suggested?

Swanland's more equivocal suggestion (that the remunerations committee reconsider Mr Finn's remuneration package without Mr Ng being present) may be more acceptable to some shareholders. This debate touches on the ethical issues of a pragmatic approach to some issues compared to a dogmatic approach.

For the proposal

Tutor's top tips

It is important here to see the use of the 'evaluate' verb meaning discuss the positives and negative aspects of the Hanoi House proposal.

Hanoi House's more radical proposal would have a number of potential advantages. Specifically, it could be argued that the resignation of both men from their respective NED positions would restore ABC shareholders' confidence in the remunerations committee. The appearance of probity is sometimes as important as the substance and resignations can sometimes serve to purge a problem to everybody's (except for the director in question's) benefit. The double resignation would signal a clean break in the apparently compromising relationship between Mr Finn and Mr Ng and, certainly as far as ABC was concerned, would resolve the problem decisively.

It would signal the importance that ABC placed on compliance with corporate governance best practice and this, in turn, would be of comfort to shareholders and analysts concerned with the threat to the independence of ABC's remunerations committee.

Against the proposal

Hanoi House's proposal was seen as too radical for Swanland. Among its concerns was the belief that only Mr Ng's resignation from ABC's remunerations committee would be strictly necessary to diffuse the situation. Clearly Swanland saw no problem with Mr Finn's position on the ABC board in his executive capacity. Furthermore, it took a pragmatic view of Mr Ng's position as NED on ABC's board. It considered Mr Ng's input to be valuable on the ABC board and pointed out that this input would be lost if Hanoi House's proposal was put into practice. Hanoi House may therefore have been mindful of the assumed deficit of talent at senior strategic level in corporate management and accordingly, wished to retain both Mr Finn's and Mr Ng's expertise if at all possible.

		Marking scheme	Marks
(a)	(i)	One mark for each valid point made for demonstrating an understanding of cross directorships	Up to 2
	(ii)	Award up to two marks for each valid point made on roles of remunerations committees	Up to 8
	(iii)	Award up to two marks for each valid point on undermining the roles	Up to 4
		Maximum	12
(b)		One mark for each component of a director's remuneration correctly identified	Up to 4
		One mark for each relevant point describing how Finn's remuneration might be more aligned to shareholders' interests	Up to 5
		Maximum	8
(c)		One mark for each point evaluating the proposal from Hanoi House:	
		Arguments in favour	Up to 3
		Arguments against	Up to 3
		Maximum	5
Total		**Maximum**	**25**

42   YAYA (DEC 12)

Key answer tips

This question asks about three key aspects of internal control and is progressive in that context.

Part (a) addresses why an internal control system might be ineffective; part (b) how deficiencies in the internal control system led to product failure and part (c) how would good information help address the internal control failures. The latter part should therefore address the information needs of the user and ideally these needs used as a structure for the answer.

In many respects this was a typical P1 question requiring both book knowledge and good levels of application to the scenario.

(a)   **Ineffective internal controls**

Well designed IC systems can be ineffective for a number of reasons.

Costs outweighing benefits. This is when an IC system provides poor value for money or it provides more assurance than is needed (i.e. the control is over-specified). In such a situation, the control will not be supported or trusted by those working alongside or within the control, and this will reduce its effectiveness.

Failures in human judgement when assessing a control, or fraud in measuring or reporting a control. Where a control relies upon human measurement, error is always a possibility either through lack of training, incompetence, wilful negligence or having a vested interest in control failure (such as with Jane Goo, who believed she could gain financially by a product failing to pass successfully through a quality control standard).

Collusion between employees, perhaps with a vested interest in misapplying or circumventing a control. The risk of this is greater when two or more people believe they may gain by it. It could be, for example, a sales team misquoting sales figures against a budget or directors misreporting accounting data to increase their bonuses or maintain a higher share price before exercising share options. The collusion between Jane Goo and John Zong (who received part of the payment) was one of the factors that may have led to the failure of QC controls being effective at Yaya.

Non-routine or *unforeseen events* can render controls ineffective if they are intended to monitor a specific process only. Most internal controls are unable to cope with extraordinary events and so need to be adapted or circumvented when such events occur.

Previous or existing controls *can become obsolete* because they are not updated to meet changed conditions. A control introduced to monitor a process or risk that has changed, reduced or been discontinued will no longer be effective. Changes to key risks, for example, need to modified if they are to continue to remain effective in controlling the risk.

(b)   **IC deficiencies at Yaya**

Jane Goo was *fraudulently entering compliance reports* with *no-one required to countersign* them or confirm her checks. The system did not require a second signature and no-one saw the product compliance reports after completion, so Jane had no one to review, confirm and assure that her QC measurements were true or accurate. She believed herself to be poorly paid and this may have increased the incentives for her to carry out the deceit. Additionally, it appears she was left to 'destroy' the goods that failed QC, allowing her to sell the goods externally. Segregating the disposal of the goods from the creation of the reports would also have helped prevent this fraud occurring.

Linked to this, there was *collusion between Jane Goo and John Zong,* who received part of the proceeds for his complicity in the fraud. This meant that the both of the people in the QC department were involved and the isolation of the laboratory made the discovery of their activities less likely.

There was *no control capable of automatically signalling to management* that the failure rate had increased. The fact that the rate rose gradually and not in a steep change seems to have made the change less visible, but a maximum acceptable failure rate with an appropriate measurement system would have triggered a signal to management that the rate had risen above it.

The way the QC department was viewed by the company meant that its activities would have received less scrutiny than other parts of the business. The QC department was *marginalised and located away from other activities* and the combination of these factors made it unlikely that they would often be disturbed. The fact that there was no automatic reporting link between QC and Mr Janoon was perhaps symptomatic of the marginalisation and this contributed to the problem.

The operations director Ben Janoon was *negligent as a manager and had little control* over the process. He rarely visited the QC lab, failed to monitor product failure rates, and failed to spot a fourfold increase in product failure rates. It was he that designed the system and with such a large number of weaknesses in the system, he must bear some of the responsibility for the lack of control, if not for the actual fraud itself.

(c) **General qualities of information specific measures**

Qualities of useful information to Mr Janoon

Useful information has a number of general qualities that distinguishes it from less-than-useful information. This is a very important element of an internal control system, as evidenced by a lack of information flow to Ben Janoon at Yaya Company. Information flowing to Mr Janoon should be relevant, reliable, timely, understandable and cost-beneficial.

Relevant means that anything that Jane Goo feels should be brought to Mr Janoon's attention should be included in the information. Any changes to the overall quality of finished goods should be voluntarily reported, for example, any issues that would prevent the QC lab performing its important function or any changes to product failure rates.

Reliable refers to the trustworthiness of the information and whether or not it is a faithful representation of what is being conveyed. It concerns the assumption that it is 'hard' information, that it is complete, correct, that it is impartial, unbiased, accurate and complete. Mr Janoon needs to know that the information he receives from Jane Goo is a true reflection of what is actually the case in the QC lab and that, for example, the reported failure rates are not understated for her personal gain.

Timely refers to the fact that information has a time value. Information that is late, for example, may be completely useless to the receiver. Information should arrive so that it can be processed effectively by the receiver and used for decision-making as it was intended.

Mr Janoon does not understand the science behind the QC processes and it is therefore important that any information from the QC lab is *understandable* by him. Because Jane Goo and John Zong had relevant scientific qualifications, it was important that information fed to Mr Janoon was free of jargon and in a form that is meaningful to him as a non-scientist.

Cost beneficial means that the cost incurred to generate the information does not outweigh its benefit. Simple reports on QC compliance at Yaya would probably be very cost-beneficial, for example, but in other situations, special reports can be expensive to produce and have little consequence to end users.

Tutorial note

Other approaches to this answer may also be taken.

Specific information-flow measures

Mr Janoon could receive *more frequent reports,* maybe weekly or monthly, on QC failure rates. The fact that two years went by without him noticing the increased failure indicated that he had no effective information flow on the problem. A reliable flow of key QC metrics would enable him to plot these metrics over time, thereby highlighting any changes over time. Providing a predetermined format for Jane Goo to complete would ensure that he obtained the necessary information and it would place the information flow in his hands rather than with Jane Goo.

The information he receives could be of a *higher quality,* with more detail and possibly 'drilled down' data on product compliance against specific metrics. The 'drilled down' data would have detected the fact that Jane Goo had failed products that should, according to the product specification, have passed, and this could also have detected the fraud earlier.

Regular *routine physical contact* with QC employees, especially the QC manager. The fraud was partly caused by the environment within Yaya that saw QC as marginal and inconvenient, and partly by Jane Goo, believing that her work was unaccountable and unmonitored. By moving the QC lab closer to the main operations or establishing a clearer formal reporting regime from the QC manager to the operations director, the quality of information flows would be improved, and opportunity for fraud diminished.

ACCA marking scheme		
		Marks
(a)	1 mark for an explanation of each relevant point. Half mark for identification only.	5
(b)	Up to 2 marks for each IC deficiency explained.	10
(c)	1·5 marks for each quality of information discussed in the context of the case, to a maximum of 6. Half mark for identification only. 2 marks for each relevant measure proposed to a maximum of 4 marks.	10
Total		**25**

Examiner's comments

The case in question 3 was about Yaya Company and a number of failures of internal control, mainly centred around the quality control laboratory. Part (a), on the typical reasons why internal control systems might be ineffective, was done quite well overall, partly because it was mainly bookwork. On a P1 paper containing so much need to analyse the case and engage with higher level cognitive verbs, it is very important that bookwork marks are obtained where available. This underlines the importance of revising the main 'lists', themes and concepts in the study guide and in study texts.

Part (b) was a typical P1 question and one that has been asked, in various forms, several times before. The task was to look carefully at the case and explain (not just list) the internal control deficiencies that led to the problems at Yaya. Well-prepared candidates were able to gain good marks on this requirement with the best approach being to carefully pick out the IC failures, one at a time, with a separate paragraph dedicated to each.

Part (c) was done less well. Weaker answers used a mnemonic to list the qualities of useful information (typically the 'ACCURATE' mnemonic) but the question specifically asked how they would be of benefit to Mr Janoon. Those that just listed the general qualities did not score highly as they failed to engage with the value to Mr Janoon. A second task was to recommend specific measures that would improve information flow from the QC lab to the case. Many answers given were general or vague whereas a good answer considered the specific information needs of Mr Janoon and was framed in that way.

43   SPQ

Key answer tips

This question provides a mix between theory (parts (a), (c) and part of (d)), and some application. The information on the computer system is not complete, so some speculation is needed in part (b) while much is made of the ethical issue for part (d). Be careful to allocate time in accordance with the mark allocation.

For part (a) it is insufficient to merely describe the terms – you are required to demonstrate an understanding of how internal audit is used in each of the internal control and risk management processes. This question can be answered in general terms, without regard to the scenario in the case.

In part (b) you need to focus specifically and solely on risks 'exposed by the review'. Control suggestions need to be practical and appropriate for this business. Part (c) requires an understanding of audit planning generally, with reference to any features specific to this scenario.

In part (d) you need to focus on the ethical principles relevant in <u>this</u> situation, so try to avoid a regurgitation of all five ethical principles – you will run out of time!

(a)   **Role regarding internal control**

Regarding internal control, internal auditors will review the system of internal control within an organisation. They will test the effectiveness of the controls as an independent third party and then provide a report on their work. Internal auditors do not establish the operational controls they test as this would impair the independence of their review.

Role regarding risk management

Regarding risk management, internal auditors will again review the system for identifying and responding to risks in an organisation. They will focus on high risk areas specifically, and, where controls are found to be weak, they will again prepare an appropriate report, making recommendations for control improvements.

To be clear, internal auditors are specialists in risk management and internal controls – but those risks are managed by individual line managers. Internal auditors ensure that risks have been identified, analysed and managed, giving advice on appropriate controls when asked.

Internal auditors may also advise the board of various internal controls and risk management, including areas such as:

- how to identify risks
- how to establish a culture to manage risks within an organisation
- reporting on how effective management are at managing risk in the organisation; and
- ensuring that appropriate legislation has been complied with.

(b)   **Risk: hacking and fraudulent access to computer systems**

SPQ's computer systems appear to have been accessed by unauthorised third parties with the aim of obtaining goods without paying for them. It is not clear how access occurred, although it is possible that other systems are also vulnerable.

Control recommendations

- Monitor access requests from 'customers' to identify where multiple requests are made from the same computer. Where this occurs, check transactions to ensure that they do not 'disappear'.
- Review firewall controls to ensure these are effective.
- Monitor system access from internal sources, using a control log, to identify whether staff in the IT department are placing fraudulent orders.

Risk: non-payment of deliveries

It appears that deliveries of goods have been made without the customer being invoiced for the goods or cash being received. The risk is that sales in SPQ are understated.

Control recommendation

Only despatch goods where payment has been received in full. This may require amendment to computer programs to ensure that this control is active.

Risk: transactions deleted from customer database

It is possible that the customer database is not complete given that transactions appear to have been deleted after delivery of goods. The risk is therefore that SPQ's accounting records are not being maintained correctly.

Control recommendations

Check the integrity of the details in the database using run-to-run totals or similar methods of reconciling transactions on a daily basis.

Monitor access to the database ensuring that all internal amendments are routed through the database administrator. Control logs can again be used for this purpose.

Risk: ineffective internal audit reports

There is a risk that internal audit reports do not identify the extent of risks identified in SPQ as managers are requesting that the report is modified. There is also the risk that the audit reports may not be actioned anyway as the internal auditor reports to the CEO rather than to a person independent of the operational running of the company.

Control recommendation

The internal auditor should report to an independent person, such as the chair of the audit committee. The latter will be able to ensure that all internal audit reports are actioned appropriately.

Tutorial note

Your answer should focus on risks that were specifically mentioned by the review carried out by the internal audit team. References to other risks will not be awarded marks!

(c) **Issues to be considered in planning an audit of activities**

Previous internal audit reports. These will identify the results of previous audits for each activity and therefore indicate the extent of work expected for the next audit.

Changes made to the system. Where significant changes have been made then the audit will take longer as amendments will have to be documented and tested. The level of testing will also increase as less reliance can be placed on the results of previous audits.

Review of the work carried out by external auditors. Where external auditors have audited a system and found no errors, then the internal audit department can take some confidence from these results and decrease the extent of its testing.

Discussion with local managers. This will help identify any concerns with the system and therefore affect the extent of work undertaken by the internal auditor.

Obtain information on known risks. In SPQ, the internal audit department was directed to audit the system by the chief accountant, who may have realised the risk of error. Identifying known risks will help internal audit focus work on those areas to determine the extent of risk and errors.

Confirm the audit objectives. Audit work should always be carried out with specific objectives in mind.

(d) **Ethical principles**

Integrity

The internal auditor should be straightforward and honest. He should not supply any information which is known to be misleading, false or deceptive. This means that the internal auditor should not give in to pressure to amend the report unless factual errors are identified in it.

Objectivity

This is a combination of impartiality, intellectual honesty and freedom from conflicts of interest. It means that the internal auditor should not allow the influence of others to override his decisions. Again this means that the report should not be amended, simply because managers suggest it will be unpopular.

Professional competence and duty of care

As a new appointee, the internal auditor will have confirmed that he has the appropriate skills and knowledge to perform his job and therefore that reporting will be carried out with reasonable skill and diligence. To amend the report would suggest that reasonable skill and care will not have been used, as the report would be inaccurate.

Professional behaviour

The internal auditor has to act in a manner which is consistent with the good reputation of the Institute. To amend a report would effectively involve being conservative with the truth, which an ACCA member should avoid.

Resolution of ethical conflict

Ethical conflicts should be resolved by:

- following the organisation's grievance procedures
- discussing the matter with a superior (unless that person is involved with the ethical situation), and then subsequent levels of management
- where necessary, discussing it with the member's professional body
- where the conflict has not been resolved, the member may have to consider resignation.

44   GLUCK AND GOODMAN (DEC 08)

Key answer tips

Part (a) covers two theoretical areas around control and audit hence should be straightforward marks. Note the verbs used are 'describe' and 'explain' which require more than bullet point lists.

In order to tackle part (b) you need to be clear as to what would be considered 'good' arrangements. By referring to what should have been there, as prescribed in accepted standards of good governance, you have a basis against which to compare and be critical of the company's arrangements.

Part (c) allows a couple of marks for a text-book definition before requiring you to apply this to the scenario.

(a)   (i)   **FIVE general objectives of internal control**

An internal control system comprises the whole network of systems established in an organisation to provide reasonable assurance that organisational objectives will be achieved.

Specifically, the general objectives of internal control are as follows.

To ensure the orderly and efficient conduct of business in respect of systems being in place and fully implemented. Controls mean that business processes and transactions take place without disruption with less risk or disturbance and this, in turn, adds value and creates shareholder value.

To safeguard the assets of the business. Assets include tangibles and intangibles, and controls are necessary to ensure they are optimally utilised and protected from misuse, fraud, misappropriation or theft.

To prevent and detect fraud. Controls are necessary to show up any operational or financial disagreements that might be the result of theft or fraud. This might include off-balance sheet financing or the use of unauthorised accounting policies, inventory controls, use of company property and similar.

To ensure the completeness and accuracy of accounting records. Ensuring that all accounting transactions are fully and accurately recorded, that assets and liabilities are correctly identified and valued, and that all costs and revenues can be fully accounted for.

To ensure the timely preparation of financial information which applies to statutory reporting (of year end accounts, for example) and also management accounts, if appropriate, for the facilitation of effective management decision-making.

Tutorial note

Candidates may address these general objectives using different wordings. Markers would allow latitude.

(ii) **Factors affecting the need for internal audit and controls**

(Based partly on Turnbull guidance)

The nature of operations within the organisation arising from its sector, strategic positioning and main activities.

The scale and size of operations including factors such as the number of employees. It is generally assumed that larger and more complex organisations have a greater need for internal controls and audit than smaller ones owing to the number of activities occurring that give rise to potential problems.

Cost/benefit considerations. Management must weigh the benefits of instituting internal control and audit systems against the costs of doing so. This is likely to be an issue for medium-sized companies or companies experiencing growth.

Internal or external changes affecting activities, structures or risks. Changes arising from new products or internal activities can change the need for internal audit and so can external changes such as PESTEL factors.

Problems with existing systems, products and/or procedures including any increase in unexplained events. Repeated or persistent problems can signify the need for internal control and audit.

The need to comply with external requirements from relevant stock market regulations or laws. This appears to be a relevant factor at Gluck & Goodman.

(b) **Criticisms**

The audit committee is chaired by an executive director. One of the most important roles of an audit committee is to review and monitor internal controls. An executive director is not an independent person and so having Mr Chester as chairman undermines the purpose of the committee as far as its role in governance is concerned.

Mr Chester, the audit committee chairman, considers only financial controls to be important. There is no recognition of other risks and there is a belief that management accounting can provide all necessary information. This viewpoint fails to recognise the importance of other control mechanisms such as technical and operational controls.

Mr Hardanger's performance was trusted without supporting evidence because of his reputation as a good manager. An audit committee must be blind to reputation and treat all parts of the business equally. All functions can be subject to monitor and review without 'fear or favour' and the complexity of the production facility makes it an obvious subject of frequent attention.

The audit committee does not enjoy the full support of the non-executive chairman, Mr Allejandra.

On the contrary in fact, he is sceptical about its value. In most situations, the audit committee reports to the chairman and so it is very important that the chairman protects the audit committee from criticism from executive colleagues, which is unlikely given the situation at Gluck and Goodman.

There is no internal auditor to report to the committee and hence no flow of information upon which to make control decisions. Internal auditors are the operational 'arms' of an audit committee and without them, the audit committee will have little or no relevant data upon which to monitor and review control systems in the company.

The ineffectiveness of the internal audit could increase the cost of the external audit. If external auditors view internal controls as weak they would be likely to require increased attention to audit trails, etc. that would, in turn, increase cost.

(c)   **Market risk**

Definition of market risk

Market risks are those arising from any of the markets that a company operates in. Most common examples are those risks from resource markets (inputs), product markets (outputs) or capital markets (finance).

Tutorial note

Markers would exercise latitude in allowing definitions of market risk. IFRS 7, for example, offers a technical definition: 'Market risk is the risk that the fair value or cash flows of a financial instrument will fluctuate due to changes in market prices. Market risk reflects interest rate risk, currency risk, and other price risks'.

Why non-compliance increases market risk

The lack of a fully compliant committee structure (such as having a non-compliant audit committee) erodes investor confidence in the general governance of a company. This will, over time, affect share price and hence company value. Low company value will threaten existing management (possibly with good cause in the case of Gluck and Goodman) and make the company a possible takeover target. It will also adversely affect price-earnings and hence market confidence in Gluck and Goodman's shares. This will make it more difficult to raise funds from the stock market.

Marking scheme

				Marks
(a)	(i)	Half mark for the identification of each objective. Half mark for brief description (Maximum of 1 mark per objective)		5
	(ii)	Half mark for the identification of each factor. Half mark for brief description (Maximum of 1 mark per factor)		5
			Maximum	10
(b)		1 mark for the identification of each criticism 1 mark for reason as to why identified behaviour is inappropriate (Maximum of 2 marks per criticism)		
			Maximum	10
(c)		Definition of market risk – 1 mark for each relevant point made		Up to 2
		No audit committee and risk – 1 mark for each relevant point made		Up to 3
			Maximum	5
Total				**25**

Examiner's comments

The case scenario for this question concerned a new NED joining a board and discovering a number of poor practices in relation to internal control and internal audit. Clearly then, these were the core themes in this question.

The first ten marks, **parts (a)(i) and (a)(ii)**, were both level 2 verbs asking about what should have been core knowledge for any well-prepared candidate. I draw attention to the level of the verb because it was on misjudging this that some otherwise well-prepared candidates failed to gain marks. As with Q2(a), it was insufficient to merely identify the content requested in Q3(a).

It was frustrating for markers, who always seek to award marks and give the benefit of the doubt where possible, to see an answer from a candidate clearly knew the answers to these parts but then failed to develop their answers according to the verb. Some candidates demonstrated their knowledge using a bullet list or a single paragraph. The following was an answer given by one candidates for Q3(a)(i):

The five objectives of internal control are safeguarding the assets, timely preparation of financial information, prevention and detection of fraud, accuracy and completeness of accounting records and the orderly and timely conduct of the business.

It is evident that this candidate knows what the objectives on internal control are as he or she has quite correctly identified them in their answer. Clearly though, this answer is an identification of the main objectives rather than a description. For five marks, a further sentence of description for each point was required.

Part (b) was the core of question 3 and employed the verb 'criticise'. In order to produce a criticism of something, the critic must know what good and bad practice is. Importantly, to criticise does not involve simply regurgitating the points in the case that were evidence of poor practice. That is only part of the answer. Candidates who merely listed the main negative points received only some of the available marks.

If I criticise a film I have just watched, I don't just make a list of the things I didn't like about it. To produce a critique, I have to discuss each point, perhaps in the context of other things (like reasonable expectations or, in the case of the exam scenario, regulations and code provisions) and why each point is important. It would be a poor criticism, for example, if I were to criticise a film by merely saying 'poor acting'. I would need to say much more about the acting other than my belief that it was 'poor' in order for it to be a useful critique.

One valid point of criticism in the case scenario, for example, was that the audit committee chairman considered only financial controls to be important. So the criticism begins with recognising that fact. In order to gain other marks, however, it is important to add why the criticism is valid. In this case, the audit committee chairman has failed to recognise the importance of other control mechanisms such as technical and operational controls.

Part (c) drew upon the 'types of risk' section of the study guide (C2b). It asked candidates to define market risk and then explain how an ineffective audit committee can increase market risk. I was surprised to see a lot of candidates unable to define market risk and I can offer no explanation for this as it is clearly listed in the study guide as an examinable area. This part of Q3 contained two verbs, one at level 1 (define) and one at level 2 (explain). It was obviously difficult for candidates to explain its importance if they were unable to produce a correct definition. I would remind candidates and tutors that any part of the study guide may be examined and that all of it should be taught, learned and revised prior to the exam.

45   YAHTY *Walk in the footsteps of a top tutor*

Key answer tips

This question looks at various aspects relating to internal control systems and the corporate governance principles surrounding them. Parts (a) and (b) require specific knowledge of the governance principles. Part (c) is not based on theory, but requires evaluation of the scenario provided.

The highlighted words are key phrases that markers are looking for.

Tutor's top tips

Approach to the question

*If, as always, you start by reading the **first paragraph only** the following can be determined:*

- *this organisation provides investment services*
- *it deals directly with many individual clients.*

*Now look at the requirements **before** reading the rest of the question. This will ensure that you*

- *read the question in the correct manner,*
- *do not need to read the question more than once,*
- *save time and can begin planning.*

*From the requirements you can establish the **headings** for your plan, and also your answer. Ensure that you are clear with the **verb in the question**, and what is required for that verb.*

Requirement

- *Prepare a report*

  *It is essential that your answer follows the **required presentation style**. Though, it is worth noting that there is no mention of professional marks being awarded for such a report style, so you may only get one mark for this format.*

- *Principles of a sound system of internal control*

  *This part is best tackled with reference to the **Turnbull Report's three criteria** for a sound system.*

- *Directors' responsibilities in relation to internal controls*

  *There are some specific responsibilities of directors regarding internal controls that are laid down in **corporate governance**.*

- *Evaluation of the organisation's internal control systems*

  *The verb 'evaluate' requires you to go into some depth in your answer. The requirement goes onto provide you with **sub-headings**:*

  - *weaknesses*
  - *effectiveness of controls over those weaknesses*
  - *improvements to the system of internal controls.*

Reading the question

*Now **actively** read the question i.e. as you read it you should add all relevant points to your planning page(s).*

The key issues to pick out from the question as are as follows:

- *the individual financial accountant has a lot of decision-making freedom*
- *additional investment advice is available*
- *payments over €100,000 require additional authorisation*
- *the list of investments is not linked to payment systems*
- *documentation is retained centrally*
- *full transaction histories may not be available to clients.*

Answering the question

Part (a) Principles of a sound system of internal control

Given that there are six marks available for three criteria for a sound system, the mark allocation is clearly two marks per criteria. Your answer should make clear what is required to satisfy the criteria, maybe providing an example to make your explanation clear.

Part (b) Directors' responsibilities in relation to internal controls

> *The main responsibilities of directors are:*
>
> - *to implement and maintain a sound system of internal control,*
> - *to ensure this is reviewed on a regular basis, and*
> - *to report to shareholders accordingly.*
>
> *These three points will need to be described fully for two marks each. Again, use of examples may assist in this description.*
>
> *Part (c) Evaluation of the organisation's internal control systems*
>
> *In this section there is no theory to assist. You are advised to tackle each aspect of the control systems evident in YAHTY separately. Each should be evaluated using the three sub-headings provided (and discussed above). All your comments need to be well-explained and evidenced from the scenario, with recommendations relevant to this type of business.*

REPORT

To: Board of YAHTY

From: An accountant

Subject: Internal control systems

Date: DD MM 200X

The purpose of this report is to discuss internal control systems and the responsibilities of directors towards these.

(a)   **Sound system of internal control**

[This answer is illustrated with references to the Turnbull guidance on Internal Control.]

The Turnbull guidance on Internal Control is provided in the UK Corporate Governance Code. There is no specific statement concerning what internal controls should be present in an organisation. Rather, organisations are encouraged to implement a sound system of internal control and risk management as part of a system of good corporate governance.

The guidance provides three specific suggestions:

- Internal control should be embedded within the processes of an organisation, enabling objectives to be pursued and met.
- The internal control system should remain relevant over time as the business environment changes.
- Each company must apply a system of internal control that takes account of its particular situation and circumstances, and allows for reporting of control failures and weaknesses.

The internal control system will therefore include:

- Control activities.
- Information and communication processes.
- Processes for monitoring the effectiveness of the internal control system.

In summary, the internal control system is provided to reduce risks in a company, not eliminate them completely. Elimination may not be cost effective, and it is by taking some risk that many companies obtain profits.

(b) **Duties of directors in relation to internal controls**

The UK Corporate Governance Code requires the board of directors to:

Maintain a sound system of internal control, which is embedded in the operations of the company and forms a part of its culture. The directors do not necessarily implement the control system; this action will be delegated to more junior managers.

At least once each year, carry out a review of the effectiveness of the system of internal control, and report to shareholders that they have done so in the company's annual report and accounts. This action shows that the directors are aware of their responsibilities and also should provide reassurance to investors that the company is being managed effectively. This annual review should cover all controls (financial, operational and compliance) and risk management.

Tutorial note

The key points to make here are those discussed above, since these are the explicit responsibilities of directors regarding internal controls. The discussion below about risk management is additional information.

The Turnbull Guidance comments that, in carrying out this review, the board should have a risk management policy to identify risks and take appropriate action in relation to each risk. Specifically that policy needs to identify:

- the nature and extent of the risks facing the company
- the extent and categories of risk which it regards as acceptable for the company to bear
- the likelihood that these risks will materialise
- the company's ability to reduce the frequency or incidence of any risks and to reduce the impact on the business of any risks that do materialise
- the costs of operating particular controls relative to the benefits obtained from managing the risk.

(c) **Comments on internal control system in YAHTY organisation**

Advice provided by investment accountants

Each investment accountant can provide/recommend the individual investment services for their clients. Whilst some accountants may be skilled and have appropriate knowledge, this may not be the case for all accountants. The internal control system appears to be weak in two respects:

- firstly, training of accountants, and
- secondly, ensuring funds are invested to produce a high return, not simply to meet the general investment requirements of clients.

The control of the senior accountant providing investment advice if required is ineffective for two reasons:

- Firstly, the span of control is excessive; with 35 investment accountants having 200 clients each, this could relate to over 7,000 different clients to provide advice to. Given a 200-day working year, this equates to about 12 minutes for each client pa. Control cannot be exercised on a timely basis.
- Secondly, there appears to be no necessity for any client account to be reviewed anyway. The senior accountant only acts on a request basis.

These control weaknesses could result in individual client accounts providing a financial performance well below optimum.

Controls that should be implemented include:

- decreasing the span of control by employing more senior accountants
- standard review of a percentage of client accounts each year
- more detailed investigations where any investment account shows poor investment decisions.

Payment authorisations

Each investment accountant is allowed to make fund transfers relating to investments for their clients. This is appropriate as the accountant will understand the specific client requests and therefore be able to ensure that investments are being made in the appropriate funds.

However, only transfers above €100,000 require a second signatory. This amount is potentially excessive, given that the average fund value is €500,000 and most transfers are below €50,000 anyway. The authorisation limit means that almost all transfers are not checked. Control weaknesses include:

- The investment accountant could make an inappropriate investment decision.
- Funds could be transferred to the investment accountant's own bank account. This could occur because the list of investments is not linked to the bank account – so the list can be manually amended by the accountant to exclude specific investments.

Controls that should be implemented include:

- Lowering the authorisation limit for second signatories to €25,000.
- Providing for a random check on other transactions to ensure they are valid and relate to appropriate funds.
- Linking the list of investments to the payment systems in the company. When a payment is made the list is updated, thus precluding manual updating by the accountant.

Storage of documents

YAHTY is quite correct to retain evidence of the funds transfers carried out by the investment accountants. This will be needed in case of dispute regarding the amount of transfer or the funds transferred to.

However, there is a control weakness in keeping the transfer documents in date order. While this assists initial filing, document retrieval may be extremely difficult. The normal method of searching for a document is likely to be by client name; the date of the transaction may not be immediately available. Working through all documents relating to one date will also be time consuming.

To improve the control, the ordering of the documents should be changed to storage by client name. Investment accountants may undertake this task if necessary as they will be raising the documents.

Alternatively, control would be improved by using pre-numbered documents and retaining the document number on individual client accounts on the computer system. Filing of documents by document number would then provide a quick and efficient filing and retrieval system.

Closing of client accounts

The closure of a client account provides the good control of a list of investments supported by the appropriate documentation. The weakness in the control is confirming the completeness of the list of funds being transferred. If a fund is omitted from the list, there does not appear to be any way to identify this omission. This is a similar issue to the manual updating of the list of investments already noted above.

The control of the senior accountant reviewing the list of investments and agreeing the source documents will be ineffective in identifying omissions. Similar controls are again required for the payment authorisations mentioned above.

Tutorial note

The last part of this answer is very long and includes more detail than you would be expected to provide to achieve a good mark. However even if you are not covering them in quite so much detail, you will need to identify the major areas of weakness which need to be addressed.

46 BLUP (JUN 13)

Key answer tips

The question requires candidates to consider key themes of the importance of internal audit, audit committees and effective internal controls in a highly regulated industry. As such it is important to apply the knowledge of these areas when answering the question.

Part (c) of this question in particular on the need for internal control to provide assurance on the integrity of financial reporting is a key theme in the increased significance of corporate governance regulation. This should have presented few problems.

(a) **Introduction to internal audit**

Internal audit is an independent appraisal function established within an organisation to examine and evaluate its activities as a service to that same organisation. The objective of internal audit is to assist members of the organisation in the effective discharge of their responsibilities. To this end, internal audit furnishes them with analyses, appraisals, recommendations, advice and information concerning the activities reviewed. The main functions of concern to internal audit are reviews of internal controls, risk management, compliance and value for money.

Tutorial note

Evidence of understanding of IA may be anywhere in answer.

Internal audit in regulated industries

Internal audit is generally considered to be more important in highly regulated industries (utilities, such as water or energy, and pharmaceuticals, defence equipment, etc) because there is a need, not only to deliver an internal service to aid organisational efficiency, but also to *ensure compliance* with externally-imposed requirements. These may involve a range of technical product compliance issues, product safety issues, hygiene issues, production facility issues or other, similar regulations. They may be legal in nature or may be enforced by an industry regulator at 'arm's length' from government.

Where requirements are imposed by external regulation, the company must usually provide compliance information to that external regulator. This involves the establishment of *systems for collecting and analysing* that data, and also producing *reports to demonstrate the levels of compliance*. Because compliance information may not always report 'good news', it is important that the auditor is independent of those being audited and, for this reason, a formal internal audit function is usually more necessary in such circumstances.

In regulated industries, the *assurance of compliance is a strategic asset* and is somewhat more important than (merely) a desirable outcome. Compliance failure may mean that the company loses its licence to operate, or it may be subjected to punitive fines. In either case, it could be unable to continue to conduct normal business and so internal audit's role is a key part of the company's strategic success.

(b)　(i)　**Criticisms of Blup Co's audit committee**

There are three ways in which Blup Co's audit committee fails against best practice criteria. First, it is likely that it is *not sufficiently independent* of the executive board, with its entire membership being retired executives. Some jurisdictions place a time limit (after retirement) before a former executive member can take up a non-executive director (NED) position. This is because of the likely lack of independence and objectivity that such a person would have.

Second, because the audit committee is required to monitor and review the company's accounts and internal controls, it is often required that *at least one member has recent, relevant financial experience* (in Singapore, this requirement is more stringent). In Blup Co, *all three members are water engineers*. Although clearly an important area to understand in the case of Blup, this does not appear to provide the level of financial literacy that the committee needs to perform its roles.

Third, the audit committee has allowed, and possibly encouraged, the *appointment and retention of an external auditor who appears to lack independence*. The fact that the head of the external audit practice was a member of the chairman's extended family could give the appearance of a lack of independence (even if not actually true) and is clearly a familiarity threat. Shareholders rely on external auditors to provide a rigorous and independent scrutiny of the company. The audit committee is responsible for recommending external auditor appointments to the board and in doing so, should ensure that there are no factors that might threaten their independence from the company being audited.

(ii) **Audit committee overseeing internal audit**

There are several reasons why internal audit is overseen by, and has a strong relationship with, the audit committee.

The first reason is to ensure that internal audit's remit *matches the compliance needs of the company*. The internal audit function's terms of reference are likely to be determined by strategic level objectives and the risks associated with them. The audit committee, being at the strategic level of the company, will frame these for implementation by the internal audit function.

Second, the audit committee will be able to ensure that the work of the internal audit function *supports the achievement of the strategic objectives of the company*. Whilst this applies to all functions of a business, the supervisory role that the audit committee has over the internal audit function means that this responsibility rests with the audit committee in the first instance.

Third, oversight by the audit committee *provides the necessary authority* for the internal audit function to operate effectively. This means that no-one in the company can refuse to co-operate with the internal audit function and that members of that function, whilst not being necessarily senior members of staff themselves, carry the delegated authority of the audit committee in undertaking their important work.

Fourth, by reporting to the audit committee, *internal auditors are structurally independent* from those being audited. Because they and their work is sanctioned and authorised by the audit committee, the IA function should have no material links with other departments of similar hierarchical level which might compromise independence.

(c) **Effective internal controls in assuring the integrity of financial reporting**

The integrity of financial reporting is an essential underpinning of sound corporate governance. Shareholders and others rely on this information for their own decision-making and in influencing their perceptions of the value of the company. Many corporate governance codes, in recognising this link, require the publication of a report on the effectiveness of controls over financial reporting. All of these can be made subject to internal audit review to ensure ongoing compliance. In some jurisdictions, the internal controls over reporting are made compulsory through such instruments as financial reporting standards.

Effective internal controls are necessary for several reasons. First, they are more likely to *create systems capable of generating accurate and reliable information*. A lack of IC systems may allow for subjective and 'best guess' figures to be fed into the reporting process, but a robust system of internal control, with specified ways of measuring and reporting, can minimise this. These systems also provide information systematically to include within financial reports.

Second, to *identify specific people and functions responsible* for operating a particular control. A robust IC system will not expect reporting information to 'just happen', but rather, a certain control and/or named person can be made accountable for the delivery of a specific input or set of inputs into the reporting process.

Third, to *make the process visible* and *amenable to scrutiny* by either internal or external auditors. By having a clear allocation of controls over each stage of the reporting process, an auditor can analyse the quality of control and the information it has produced, at any stage. Or, in the case of an error, the auditor can easily trace back to find how and where the error was introduced.

ACCA marking scheme		
		Marks
(a)	Up to 2 marks for explanation of internal audit anywhere in the answer. 2 marks for each point on regulated industry to a maximum of 6 marks.	
	Maximum	7
(b)	(i) 2 marks for each relevant criticism to a maximum of 6 marks. (ii) 2 marks for each relevant issue of AC and IA to a maximum of 6 marks.	
	Maximum	12
(c)	2 marks for each relevant discussion point.	
	Maximum	6
Total		**25**

Examiner's comments

The themes examined in question 2 were the importance of internal audit, audit committees, the internal audit function and the role of internal audit in providing assurance in the integrity of financial reporting. Overall, it was disappointing to sometimes see candidates resorting to memorised 'lists' rather than answering the questions set.

In part (a), for example, the question was not asking about the importance of internal audit per se, but rather to consider the importance of internal audit in responding to regulation in highly regulated industries (such as water in the case). This task required candidates to consider the roles of internal audit in a specific industry situation. Higher scores were awarded to those able to do this more successfully and this, again, underlines the importance of answering the question actually set rather than the one that candidates wish had been set. There were two requirements in 2(b) with both carrying equal marks (6 marks each). The first was to criticise the audit committee's performance in the case. This involved knowledge of best practice so as to assess how the audit committee has failed against that, and also, of course, a thorough reading of the case. Again, the question was not asking about the roles of an audit committee, and weaker answers wrote in general terms rather than analysing the content of the case.

The second task was to explain one particular aspect of an audit committee's work with regard to its oversight of the internal audit function. There is a difference between an audit committee and the internal audit function: the committee is a board level committee and the internal audit function is a department in an organisation responsible for monitoring compliance and other important internal audit outcomes. In many organisations, the internal audit function reports its findings to the audit committee and the question was asking why this arrangement is chosen in most cases. This means, 'why is the audit committee a suitable body to perform this function?'. Weaker answers, perhaps on seeing the words, 'internal audit function' produced a list of the purposes or functions of internal audit from COSO or similar. This was not the correct approach, and better answers considered the relationship in terms of internal audit helping to achieve the strategic aims of the company, remaining independent of those being audited, operating with the necessary board-level authority and meeting the compliance needs of the company as determined by the non-executive directors on the audit committee.

Part (c) was on the use of internal controls in assuring the integrity of financial reporting. It was disappointing to see this being poorly answered by many candidates, especially when the subject matter of the requirement was so important in corporate governance. It was a lack of confidence in financial reporting that led to the rise of corporate governance regulation in many countries of the world. It was the restatement of the financial reports of Enron in 2001/2 that was the first signal that its corporate governance systems were ineffective, and so the assumption that financial statements are true and fair is a very important assumption for investors to make. Strong internal controls are necessary to underpin this integrity of reporting. The most common answer to this was a brief discussion of the general importance of internal controls and this was clearly not what the question was asking.

47 FIS

Key answer tips

The first part of the question implies that there are inefficiencies in the information system, so a careful read through the scenario information will hopefully identify some of those inefficiencies.

However, having identified the inefficiencies, you also need to explain why they may cause problems for the fund managers. So again, relate your answer to the scenario to provide this information. For example, if information is only received every hour, state that this may be a problem and then show why the nature of the job may require more frequent information.

Finally, recommending a process for improving the situation means you need to explain how the MIS could be improved. These improvements may be related back to the scenario information – so check this information again. Alternatively, you may need to recommend enhancements to the system; in this case make sure that the enhancements are practical and not too expensive.

(1) **Inefficient processes for capturing knowledge**

The MIS appears to provide a very basic system for capturing basic information about each investment such as the shares held and their location etc. However, information that is of real use to the managers, including details of price movements on shares and other information which may affect the share price, is more difficult to obtain and is supplied by a variety of different systems. There is also no guarantee that all the data has been captured or that where similar information has been produced at different times information is not duplicated or even contradictory.

Information for fund managers needs to be amalgamated into one system, as proposed by the Board. This will remove the problems of timeliness and difficulty of comparing information from one source.

(2) **Failure to appropriate knowledge already available**

Additional knowledge may be available to the fund managers, but this is maintained in the new business section of the organisation. It is not clear whether information from this MIS will actually assist the fund managers, but given that the new business representatives are making similar decisions to assist potential clients, then the information is likely to be useful.

(3) **Difficulty of measuring intangible benefits**

The directors may well be correct in their assessment that the tangible benefits of the new system do not outweigh the costs. However, the CBA is incomplete because it does not take into account the intangible benefits that are likely to arise from the system. For example, better investment decisions may result in higher returns, or at least lower losses for client funds. However, these benefits do not actually affect FIS in tangible terms, and so will be excluded from the CBA. There are though distinct intangible benefits in terms of a higher return for clients and more favourable publicity by providing clients with a better service.

The CBA analysis for the new MIS needs to be expanded to include intangible benefits.

(4) **Information overload**

The fund managers may be making poor decisions that may be related not simply to the old system, but also to the problem of having to obtain and reconcile information from too many sources. Fund managers may be suffering from information overload, that is they are receiving too much information from too many sources making it difficult or impossible to identify important information from routine data.

This situation can be remedied by providing one comprehensive system for managers. This will remove the issue of having too many different sources of information, although care will also be necessary to ensure that the new MIS focuses on the information needed for investment decisions, rather than provide a lot of detail about the funds themselves, which may not help in making these decisions.

Tutorial note

The answer above provides examples of some of the suggestions that may be made to remove the inefficiencies in the situation of FIS Ltd. Other recommendations, that are practical and well-explained, will earn marks.

48   RG *Online question assistance*

Key answer tips

Part (a) of this question encourages you to read the scenario information to find weaknesses in the information provided to the directors. The three points provide the detail needed to make these comments – so think about what information the directors would like, and then see where the information provided does not meet these expectations. Other statements such as "without reference to past production data" also imply some weakness. In this example, think how a budget would normally be produced, and the weakness becomes apparent.

Improving the information in part (ii) then becomes relatively easy. There are two comments to make in this section; firstly to state how the weakness will be overcome, and secondly stating the other information that the directors may need. In other words the MIS does not provide all of the required outputs and so the missing information must be identified and commented on.

Part (b) is more theoretical; it doesn't really need the scenario to provide an answer. If you are short of ideas, consider what the MIS is doing; namely providing summary historical information to the directors. Therefore, the MIS is unlikely to be able to provide much information about the future, or changes in trends.

(a)   (i)   **Weaknesses in the information currently provided**

The directors want information which helps their strategic control of the business. Information used at the strategic level normally has the following characteristics:

- It is highly summarised.
- It does not need to be as accurate as operational information.
- It will often be used in making poorly-structured, non-programmable decisions.
- The information will often be forward-looking.
- Non-routine information and reports will often be required.
- It will contain a high amount of probabilistic information (estimates).

The output from the current system has the following weaknesses:

Summary business plan

This would appear to be an unreliable document as it has been prepared by an inexperienced person who seems to have ignored the information content of past production data. The plan is forward looking, though two years would be an absolute minimum for most strategic planning.

Because historical data is not shown on the report, it will be difficult for the directors to assess the assumptions lying behind the report. This is very important when dealing with future estimates where judgement will play a large part and will be especially important here where the author of the report is inexperienced.

Stock balances

This report is much too detailed for the directors and should be presented in a much more summarised form. As it stands, the report would be of use to people much further down the hierarchy in the firm who are making day-to-day operational decisions.

Changes in demand

This may be too detailed, but the directors may well want to have access to this information on demand. Five years is probably going back too far as there will have been many market changes over that time and early trends may no longer be relevant.

The report seems to be poorly presented being purely numerical and not allowing the directors to compare different sections.

(ii) **Improvements in information**

The information could be improved as follows:

Additional outputs

In addition to the existing reports the following could be useful in strategic planning:

- Financial model which allows the directors to see the effects of different inputs and assumptions.
- Summary accounting information. Though this is historical, future projections may depend on an analysis of past trends.
- Sales analyses by product, customer, type of customer, geographical area, sales rep.

Sales value, volume and gross profit percentages should be shown.

In addition, the existing reports could be improved as follows:

Summary business plan

This should:

- look further ahead
- show historical data
- show the assumptions on which the projections are based
- show income and expenditure on likely new product lines
- contain market and competitor information.

Stock balances

This should:

- be summarised much more
- highlight important data, such as large variances
- be arranged in ways which are of importance to the management of the business.

Summary of changes

- Information about all sections should be available on the same screen to allow comparisons to be made.
- Graphics would help the directors to identify important trends and significant events.
- It might be possible to omit data from over three years ago.
- Industry statistics, market growth and the changes in market share would be useful.

Tutorial note

You need to be very precise and specific in your suggestions in this part of the question, always ensuring that any improvements you suggest are cost-effective to implement.

(b)   **Strategic information unlikely to be provided by an MIS**

The MIS will predominantly use data which is generated internally by the organisation, though some external data, such as market growth and size can be entered.

The MIS system will be particularly poor at dealing with the following:

- Analysing strengths, weaknesses, opportunities and threats.
- Assessing customer satisfaction.
- Predicting changes in consumer taste.
- Predicting technological advances.
- Incorporating the effects of political, economic and social changes.
- Making use of information about competitors.

These limitations can be illustrated by considering the strategic decision about whether to expand abroad. It may be possible to look up some elementary data on a public database, but it is unlikely that such information will be incorporated into a formal MIS. Most of the work done on this decision will be once-only, ad hoc calculations. They may be performed on a spreadsheet, but they will be outside the routine reporting systems.

49   SUPERMARKET

Key answer tips

This question is focused on the area of internal control systems and how they can be reviewed. The COSO model of an effective internal control system is helpful in such questions, and could be used in either (but not both) parts of the question.

Ensure that any recommendations you make for improvements in part (a) are practical and cost-effective.

(a)   **Failures in internal control**

Failures in internal control can be categorised using a recognised formal framework. COSO is such a structure, recommended in the Sarbanes-Oxley Act and commonly used in the UK and elsewhere.

There are both systematic failures and human errors in judgement that have combined to create the problems faced by the organisation. COSO identifies a *control environment* as the ethical, structural and cultural foundation to a control system. In this respect failure would relate to the ethical policy of the organisation in pursuing profits to the detriment of quality and public safety. This is also a cultural and leadership issue that goes through the spine of the organisation to the board and the CEO. The CEO must accept that he has a personal responsibility for the failure and should act accordingly.

Control activities within the value chain are also a cause of failure. This COSO category investigates the practical controls that exist as part of operations and seeks to identify problematic areas. Suppler selection processes and criteria are one such failure. The criteria seem to be driven by price above all other issues and will, almost inevitably lead to ever increasing problems in quality. The lack of government control in the region should also have highlighted the potential risks involved in sourcing from this location.

Another control activity is the goods receipt process at the stores. This seems ill equipped to carry out any form of quality control except that of a cursory nature. Quality control without fully examining food stuffs will be inappropriate unless it relies on previous quality control carried out at some point higher in the value chain. Since this does not exist it suggests a system wide or systematic failure through the company.

Control reporting or *information and communication* is a third category in the COSO framework. There are two examples of failure in relation to this. Firstly, the failure of store managers to report upwards the problems they were finding with the foodstuffs delivered to them. This failure has continued for some time and so suggests senior management with the power to correct the fault were unaware of it. Secondly, the protracted failure of senior managers to take action down the chain for the last six months is clearly unacceptable and suggests another control environment or ethical failure.

The final category of COSO is *monitoring*. This relates to the audit function or the control over the control. Failure seems to relate to the local auditor who has possibly colluded with the factory managers in order to bypass hygiene regulation and standards. Independence of such individuals must be assured as part of future recommendations to the company.

Improvements

The most important improvement is the need to balance cost against control and risk reduction. This need must begin at the board level with a reassessment of objectives and standards for operations. The threat to the public health cannot be ignored on commercial and ethical grounds.

There may be no need to search for alternative suppliers if quality standards can be improved although it is more likely that current suppliers are tainted with the stain of the scandal and so really should be replaced. Supplier selection processes need to be tightened, using suitable board level non-executive (NED) expertise to assist. Experts within proposed countries of origin may also be employed to identify potential suppliers and assist in future local audits.

The seeming complacency of local store managers must be eradicated. Much more stringent control over quality must take place at each and every step in the supply chain ending with a detailed procedural check carried out by local store manager prior to food stuffs being paced in the shelves. The usual controls over sell by dates and stock rotation should be in place.

Lines of communication including the creation of whistleblower channels to the audit committee should be put in place in order to ensure the swift and effective communication of sensitive and commercially damaging data to the appropriate authorities.

Finally, it is important for this organisation to ensure that it is responsive to external stakeholder issues. There seems to be a failure to consider the needs of suppliers and certainly, through the store managers comment regarding the minor number of complaints, customer safety. Human life is of paramount importance and it is staggering that such comments are accepted by senior management as being appropriate. The reference to the environmental group and government action reinforces the need to consider all stakeholders that impact on the organisations part of a formal review of internal control.

The conclusion must relate to the responsibility of the board in implementing these changes swiftly and effectively.

Tutorial note

Your answer to this part of the question did not need to be based around the COSO model – you may have just chosen to talk of failures in internal control in general in this scenario, and made recommendations accordingly.

(b) **Review of internal control**

A formal staged process for the review of internal control might embrace the following.

1 *Identification*

This relates to the classification and examination of major risks faced by the organisation. It might centre on a stakeholder analysis to identify potential government action and customer response as well as on tangible risks such as the risk of quality failure in the supply chain.

2 *Estimation*

This relates to examining the likely impact of risk emergence or failures. The estimation might be a financial analysis of impact and the cost of problem rectification.

3   *Development*

Strategies to deal with a crisis of avert a crisis will be discussed and selected. Risk management might suggest the classic TARA (transfer, avoid, reduce, accept) classification of possible measures or a more specific company driven framework could be used.

4   *Evaluation*

The stakeholder impact and strategy costs should be matched before a final decision is made. Intangible estimates such as shareholder action or loss of good will may also form part of the decision making process.

5   *Implementation*

This could involve project planning and monitoring. Actual implementation is below board level but identification of reporting lines and how the board will monitor success will be important in any change process.

6   *Review*

This could include a number of elements in terms of the need to review the success of implemented strategies or the need to review the quality of the above process on a regular (annual) basis and the need to subsequently continually adapt and improve over time.

7   *Disclosure*

Good governance highlights the need to disclose the fact that such a process exists and its nature and content. This is a minimum standard expected of any large organisation such as the supermarket in the scenario.

Tutorial note

An alternative structure to part (b) would have been to use the COSO model of an effective internal control system (providing you had not already used it in part (a)) – this is very useful in questions requiring you to discuss reviews of controls.

50   TREADWAY (JUN 10)

Key answer tips

(a)   Part (a) contains two tasks: the first to distinguish between rules and principles-based approaches to internal controls, not to Corporate Governance in general; the second to discuss the benefits to an organisation of a principles-based approach.

(b)   Make sure this is not simply a 'bullet point' style list of all the good things about Internal controls and that you apply your knowledge to the question.

(c)   The first task on defining internal audit testing was rather straightforward. The second task required candidates to understand the broad role of internal audit.

(a)   **Distinguish between rules and principles**

This case refers to compliance with regard to internal control systems in particular but rules and principles are the two generic approaches to corporate governance and depend upon the nature of regulation.

Rules-based control is when behaviour is underpinned and prescribed by statute of the country's legislature. Compliance is therefore enforceable in law such that companies can face legal action if they fail to comply.

In a principles-based jurisdiction, compliance is required under stock market listing rules but non-compliance is allowed based on the premise of full disclosure of all areas of non-compliance. It is believed that the market mechanism is then capable of valuing the extent of non-compliance and signalling to the company when an unacceptable level of compliance is reached.

Benefits to an organisation

There are four main benefits to the organisation of a principles-based approach. First, it avoids the need for strict compliance with inflexible legislation which, typically, fails to account for differences in size and the risk profiles of specific companies or sectors. This means (second) that compliance is less burdensome in time and expenditure for the organisation as the minutiae of general legislation can be interpreted in context rather than obeyed in detail. Third, a principles-based approach allows companies to develop their own sector and situation-specific approaches to internal control challenges. These will typically depend upon each company's interpretation of its own internal control challenges. For example, physical controls over cash will be vital to some businesses and less relevant or not applicable to others. Fourthly, this, in turn, allows for flexibility and temporary periods of non-compliance with relevant external standards on the basis of 'comply or explain', a flexibility that would not be possible in a rules-based jurisdiction.

(b)   **Non-industry specific (i.e. general) advantages of internal controls**

The advantages and benefits of internal controls are partly as described in COSO's reasons. The case describes these benefits in terms of enjoying *'greater internal productivity and producing higher quality reporting'*. In addition, internal control underpins investor confidence, ensures compliance with internal and external control measures and facilitates the provision of management reports as needed.

Mr Rogalski is incorrect in his view that controls need to be industry sector specific to be effective. The effective and efficient performance of businesses of all kinds rests upon the observance of well-designed and tightly-monitored internal controls. Waste in the form of lost time, wasted resources, faults and other costs are avoided. Efficiency is increased by conformance to standards designed to support productivity. However, the types of controls in place and the systems supporting them will differ from sector to sector.

The information gained from compliance with internal control measures is used in the preparation of content for internal and external reporting. This is especially applicable to the external reporting on internal controls such as under Sarbanes Oxley s.404 which is mandatory in the USA. Other national codes have similar provisions.

Where compliance with agreed standards is an important part of the business, internal control data allows for this. This can be industry sector-specific but the general principles of effective control apply to all types of organisations: internal control data is needed to demonstrate compliance. Examples of sector specific internal controls (for managing sector-specific risks) include measures in financial services or those complying with certain ISO standards in their products or processes (e.g. ISO 14000).

Internal controls underpin and cultivate shareholder confidence which is relevant in any industry setting. Acceptable returns on shares rest upon conformity with systems to ensure adequate levels of efficiency, effectiveness, security, etc and the avoidance of waste and fraud.

Internal control systems enable the provision of reports and other information as needed by either external agencies or internal management. Whilst some industries are likely to have a need for external reporting (e.g. nuclear, oil and gas), internal report provision is necessary in any industry.

Tutorial note

The examiner will allow for other relevant points in answers. Some candidates may bring relevant content in from an earlier auditing paper.

'Unmonitored controls tend to deteriorate over time'

This statement refers to the need to establish which controls need to be monitored to support a sound system of internal controls and how to monitor those controls. Once a control system is designed and responsibilities for its management allocated, only those targets and controls that are made a part of someone's job or performance measurement will be monitored and thereby maintained. Any metrics that are not a part of this control regime will go unchecked and may not remain within compliance limits as circumstances change over time. The main roles of internal audit are to provide information to management on the relevance and effectiveness of internal control systems and to provide the evidence to demonstrate why those controls are effective or not. This requires the identification of which controls to monitor and developing effective ways of monitoring those controls.

The complexity of the control regime is also relevant. There is a balance between having a sufficient number of controls in place and having too many. In this context, 'too many' means that control systems must be actually useable. Over-complex controls are likely to deteriorate over time if their monitoring is not possible within reasonable cost limits and this could also cause operational inefficiencies.

Furthermore, an organisation is not static and so different controls will be needed over time. As activities change as a result of changes in organisational strategy, the controls that need to be monitored change and the tolerances of those controls may also change (they may become tighter or looser). Constant updating of controls is therefore necessary, especially in frequently changing business environments.

(c)   **Internal audit testing**

This is the *internal assessment of internal controls* using an internal auditor or internal audit function applying audit techniques to controls based on predetermined measures and outcomes. It is a management control over the other internal controls in an organisation and ensures the levels of compliance and conformity of the internal controls in an organisation.

Role of internal audit in ensuring effective internal controls

Internal audit underpins the effectiveness of internal controls by performing several key tasks.

Internal audit reviews and reports upon the controls put in place for the key risks that the company faces in its operations. This will involve ensuring that the control (i.e. mitigation measure) is capable of controlling the risk should it materialise. This is the traditional view of internal audit. A key part of this role is to review the design and effectiveness of internal controls. Many organisations also require internal audit staff to conduct follow-up visits to ensure that any weaknesses or failures have been addressed since their report was first submitted. This ensures that staff take the visit seriously and must implement the findings.

Internal audit may also involve an *examination of financial and operating information* to ensure its accuracy, timeliness and adequacy. In the production of internal management reports, for example, internal audit may be involved in ensuring that the information in the report is correctly measured and accurate. Internal audit needs to be aware of the implications of providing incomplete or partial information for decision-making.

It will typically *undertake reviews of operations for compliance against standards*. Standard performance measures will have an allowed variance or tolerance and internal audit will measure actual performance against this standard. Internal compliance is essential in all internal control systems. Examples might include safety performance, cost performance or the measurement of a key environmental emission against a target amount (which would then be used as part of a key internal environmental control).

Internal audit is used to review internal systems and controls for compliance with relevant regulations and externally-imposed targets. Often assumed to be of more importance in rules-based jurisdictions such as the United States, many industries have upper and lower limits on key indicators and it is the role of internal audit to measure against these and report as necessary. In financial services, banking, oil and gas, etc, legal compliance targets are often placed on companies and compliance data is required periodically by governments.

Tutorial note

Again the examiner will allow latitude when candidates introduce content from earlier papers, particularly 'F8 Audit and Assurance'.

Marking scheme			Marks
(a)	3 marks for distinguishing between rules and principles 1 mark for each relevant advantage/benefit of principles-based to a maximum of 4		
		Maximum	7
(b)	1 mark for recognition of each advantage and 1 for development of that point to a maximum of 8 marks 2 marks per point for explanation of the statement up to a maximum of 4 marks		
		Maximum	10
(c)	2 marks for definition of internal audit testing 2 marks for each internal role identified and explained to a maximum of 8		8
Total		Maximum	25

Examiner's comments

This case scenario drew on recent changes to the COSO guidance from 2009. It describes some of the contents of the guidance (it was not necessary to know about it prior to the exam) and then introduces a conversation between two journalists. Conversations have been used before in P1 scenarios and they are used to explore differences of opinion over certain issues which then may be asked about in the requirements.

Part (a) contained two tasks, the first, to distinguish between rules and principles-based approaches to internal controls. This was quite well answered overall although some became confused in their answers with rules and principles-based approaches to corporate governance in general. The second task was more challenging which was to discuss the benefits to an organisation of a principles-based approach. This 'to an organisation' was important as it placed a particular perspective on where the benefits were obtained.

In **part (b)** some less well-prepared candidates introduced a bullet list of 'purposes of internal control' from one or other of the study texts. This wasn't quite what the question was asking. In the context of the case, candidates were required, in response to Mr Rogalski's comment on industry specificity, to comment on the non-industry specific advantages (such as high quality reporting, efficient operations, compliance, etc.).

The COSO guidance used the term 'unmonitored controls tend to deteriorate over time' and the second part of (b) required candidates to explain what this meant. Most candidates who attempted this were able to provide something here but others seemed unprepared to explain a phrase that they had perhaps not encountered before despite it being an important theme in internal control.

Part (c) drew upon another part of the COSO advice. Again, the COSO advice was simply used to introduce a notion that should have been familiar to a well-prepared P1 candidate as it was on internal audit. The first task on defining internal audit testing was done well by many candidates but the second task less so.

51   FF CO (PILOT 07)

Key answer tips

This is an ideal practice question as it contains an important topic area – the three sections of the Turnbull guidance. These are highlighted in the answer, and offer a good approach to many internal control questions.

(a)   A two task requirement: (1) know your Turnbull and (2) apply it.

(b)   The definition of Reputation risk is a must learn and then to apply this to FF was necessary to gain good marks in this requirement.

(c)   Another important topic discussed here: the idea of professionalism.

Tutorial note

Key learning from this question is to ensure we see that a professional accountant has a duty not just to their employer and the shareholders of the company they work for, but we have a duty to act in the public's interest.

(a)   **FF Co and a 'sound' system of internal control**

Features of sound control systems

The Turnbull code employs the term 'sound' to indicate that it is insufficient to simply 'have' an internal control system. They can be effective and serve the aim of corporate governance or they can be ineffective and fail to support them. In order to reinforce 'soundness' or effectiveness, systems need to possess a number of features. The Turnbull guidance described three features of a 'sound' internal control system.

Firstly, the principles of internal control should be embedded within the organisation's structures, procedures and culture.

Internal control should not be seen as a stand-alone set of activities and by embedding it into the fabric of the organisation's infrastructure, awareness of internal control issues becomes everybody's business and this contributes to effectiveness.

Secondly, internal control systems should be capable of responding quickly to evolving risks to the business arising from factors within the company and to changes in the business environment. The speed of reaction is an important feature of almost all control systems (for example a servo system for vehicle brakes or the thermostat on a heating system). Any change in the risk profile or environment of the organisation will necessitate a change in the system and a failure or slowness to respond may increase the vulnerability to internal or external trauma.

Thirdly, sound internal control systems include procedures for reporting immediately to appropriate levels of management any significant control failings or weaknesses that are identified, together with details of corrective action being undertaken. Information flows to relevant levels of management capable and empowered to act on the information are essential in internal control systems. Any failure, frustration, distortion or obfuscation of information flows can compromise the system. For this reason, formal and relatively rigorous information channels are often instituted in organisations seeking to maximise the effectiveness of their internal control systems.

Shortcomings at FF Co

The case highlights a number of ways in which the internal control at FF fell short of that expected of a 'sound' internal control system. First, and most importantly, the case suggests that the culture of FF did not support good internal control. Miss Osula made reference to, 'culture of carelessness in FF' and said that the issue over the fire safety standards, 'was only one example of the way the company approached issues such as international fire safety standards.' While having systems in place to support sound internal control, it is also important to have a culture that also places a high priority on it. Second, there is evidence of a lack of internal control and reporting procedures at FF.

Not only was the incorrect fire-rating labelling not corrected by senior management, the attempt to bring the matter to the attention of management was also not well-received.

Third, there is evidence of structural/premeditated contravention of standards (and financial standards) at FF.

In addition to the fire safety issue, the case makes reference to a qualified audit statement over issues of compliance with financial standards. There is ample evidence for shareholders to question the competence of management's ability to manage the internal control systems at FF.

(b) **Reputation risk**

Defining reputation risk

Tutorial note

Reputation risk is a must learn definition.

Reputation risk is one of the categories of risk used in organisations. It was identified as a risk category by Turnbull and a number of events in various parts of the world have highlighted the importance of this risk.

Reputation risk concerns any kind of deterioration in the way in which the organisation is perceived, usually, but not exclusively, from the point of view of external stakeholders. The cause of such deterioration may be due to irregular behaviour, compliance failure or similar, but in any event, the effect is an aspect of corporate behaviour below that expected by one or more stakeholder. When the 'disappointed' stakeholder has contractual power over the organisation, the cost of the reputation risk may be material.

Effects of poor reputation on

There are several potential effects of reputation risk on an affected organisation. When more than one stakeholder group has reason to question the otherwise good reputation of an organisation, the effect can be a downward spiral leading to a general lack of confidence which, in turn, can have unfortunate financial effects. In particular, however, reputation risk is likely to affect one or more of the organisation's interactions with resource providers, product buyers, investors or auditors/regulators. Resource provision (linked to resource dependency theory) may affect recruitment, financing or the ability to obtain other inputs such as (in extremis) real estate, stock or intellectual capital. Within product markets, damage to reputation can reduce confidence among customers leading to reduced sales values and volumes and, in extreme cases, boycotts. Investor confidence is important in public companies where any reputation risk is likely to be reflected in market value. Finally, auditors, representing the interests of shareholders, would have reason to exercise increased scrutiny if, say, there are problems with issues of trust in a company. It would be a similar situation if the affected organisation were in an industry subject to high levels of regulation.

FF and reputation

At FF, the sources of the potential threat to its reputation arise from a failure to meet an external standard, an issue over product confidence and a qualified audit statement. The failure to meet an external standard concerned compliance with international fire safety standards. The issue over product confidence involved selling one product falsely rated higher than the reality. These would be likely to affect customer confidence and the attitude of any fire safety accrediting body. The qualified audit statement would be likely to intensify the attention to detail paid by auditors in subsequent years.

(c) **Ethical responsibilities of a professional accountant**

Tutorial note

Understanding and applying the role of a professional is a very common exam topic.

A professional accountant has two 'directions' of responsibility: one to his or her employer and another to the highest standards of professionalism.

Responsibilities to employer

An accountant's responsibilities to his or her employer extend to acting with diligence, probity and with the highest standards of care in all situations. In addition, however, an employer might reasonably expect the accountant to observe employee confidentiality as far as possible. In most situations, this will extend to absolute discretion of all sensitive matters both during and after the period of employment. The responsibilities also include the expectation that the accountant will act in shareholders' interests as far as possible and that he or she will show loyalty within the bounds of legal and ethical good practice.

Responsibilities as a professional

In addition to an accountant's responsibilities to his or her employer, there is a further set of expectations arising from his or her membership of the accounting profession. In the first instance, professional accountants are expected to observe the letter and spirit of the law in detail and of professional ethical codes where applicable (depending on country of residence, qualifying body, etc.). In any professional or ethical situation where codes do not clearly apply, a professional accountant should apply 'principles-based' ethical standards (such as integrity and probity) such that they would be happy to account for their behaviour if so required. Finally, and in common with members of other professions, accountants are required to act in the public interest that may, in extremis, involve reporting an errant employer to the relevant authorities. This may be the situation that an accountant may find him or herself in at FF. It would clearly be unacceptable to be involved in any form of deceit and it would be the accountant's duty to help to correct such malpractice if at all possible.

	Marking scheme	Marks
(a)	Description of 'sound' control systems – up to two marks for each valid point made	Up to 6
	Explanation of shortcomings at FF plc – one mark for each valid point	Up to 6
	Maximum	10
(b)	Definition of 'reputation risk' – one mark for each valid point made	Up to 3
	Explanation of the financial effects of poor reputation – one mark for each valid point made	Up to 4
	Recognition of the causes of FF's reputation problems – one mark for each valid point made	Up to 2
	Maximum	8
(c)	Responsibilities to employer – one mark for each valid point made	Up to 4
	Responsibilities to professionalism – one mark for each valid point made	Up to 4
	Maximum	7
Total		**25**

KAPLAN PUBLISHING

52   FRANKS AND FISHER (PILOT 07)

Key answer tips

Aspects of Internal audit will always be a well-examined area. Ensure you read the requirement carefully and in part (c) only argue for external appointment.

(a)   **Factors to consider**

There is an obvious cost involved in setting up internal audit in an organisation and so it is typical to ask what factors signify the need for internal audit before one is established. Several factors influence the need for internal audit:

The scale, diversity and complexity of the company's activities. The larger, the more diverse and the more complex a range of activities is, the more there is to monitor (and the more opportunity there is for certain things to go wrong).

The number of employees. As a proxy for size, the number of employees signifies that larger organisations are more likely to need internal audit to underpin investor confidence than smaller concerns.

Cost-benefit considerations. Management must be certain of the benefits that will result from establishing internal audit and it must obviously be seen to outweigh the costs of doing so.

Changes in the organisational structures, reporting processes or underlying information systems. Any internal (or external) change is capable of changing the complexity of operations and, accordingly, the risk.

Changes in key risks could be internal or external in nature. The introduction of a new product, entering a new market, a change in any of the PEST/PESTEL factors or changes in the industry might trigger the need for internal audit.

Problems with existing internal control systems. Any problems with existing systems clearly signify the need for a tightening of systems and increased monitoring.

An increased number of unexplained or unacceptable events. System failures or similar events are a clear demonstration of internal control weakness.

The case on Franks & Fisher highlights three factors that would underpin its need to establish internal audit. There has been growth in number of products, activities and (presumably) processes in recent times, thereby complicating the internal environment and introducing more opportunity for internal control failure. There have been problems with internal control systems (the line stoppage and Mr Kumas's comment that, 'problems with internal control in a number of areas').

Finally, there was an unacceptable event (the line stoppage) that was attributed to poor internal control. Mr Kumas confirmed this with his opinion about a 'great need' for internal audit.

(b)   **Benefits of external appointment**

In practice, a decision such as this one will depend on a number of factors including the supply of required skills in the internal and external job markets. In constructing the case for an external appointment, however, the following points can be made

Primarily, an external appointment would bring detachment and independence that would be less likely with an internal one.

Firstly, then, an external appointment would help with independence and objectivity (avoiding the possibility of auditor capture). He or she would owe no personal loyalties nor 'favours' from previous positions.

Similarly, he or she would have no personal grievances nor conflicts with other people from past disputes or arguments. Some benefit would be expected from the 'new broom' effect in that the appointment would see the company through fresh eyes. He or she would be unaware of vested interests.

He or she would be likely to come in with new ideas and expertise gained from other situations.

Finally, as with any external appointment, the possibility exists for the transfer of best practice in from outside – a net gain in knowledge for Franks & Fisher.

(c)   **Why Internal audit should not report to the Finance Director**

The first thing to say is that Mr Kumas's belief is inappropriate and it would be unacceptable for the internal auditor to report to a divisional director who might be the subject of an internal audit.

The reasons put forward in favour of his request are spurious. All of Mr Kumas's information and expertise would be available to the internal auditor in any event, with or without his oversight of the function. Reporting to Mr Kumas would be a clear threat to the independence of the internal auditor as he or she would not be objective in auditing the accounting and finance department.

The advice from relevant codes and guidelines would also strongly counsel against Mr Kumas's proposal. The Cadbury code is typical where, point (g) under the 'role of the internal audit committee' emphasised the independence of the internal audit function from management. Mr Kumas's request should be refused.

(d)   **Define 'objectivity'**

Objectivity is a state or quality that implies detachment, lack of bias, not influenced by personal feelings, prejudices or emotions.

It is a very important quality in corporate governance generally and especially important in all audit situations where, regardless of personal feeling, the auditor must carry out his or her task objectively and with the purpose of the audit uppermost in mind.

The IFAC Code of Ethics explains objectivity in the following terms (Introduction, clause 16): '... fair and should not allow prejudice or bias, conflict of interest or influence of others to override objectivity.'

Characteristics of objectivity

It thus follows that characteristics that might demonstrate an internal auditor's professional objectivity will include fairness and even-handedness, freedom from bias or prejudice and the avoidance of conflicts of interest (e.g. by accepting gifts, threats to independence, etc.).

The internal auditor should remember at all times that the purpose is to deliver a report on the systems being audited to his or her principal. In an external audit situation, the principal is ultimately the shareholder and in internal audit situations, it is the internal audit committee (and then ultimately, shareholders).

Marking scheme			
			Marks
(a)	1 mark for each factor identified and briefly discussed		Up to 7
	1 mark for each factor applicable to Franks & Fisher		Up to 3
		Maximum	10
(b)	1 mark for each relevant point identified and briefly described		Up to 6
		Maximum	6
(c)	1 mark for each relevant point made		Up to 4
		Maximum	4
(d)	2 marks for definition of objectivity		2
	1 mark per relevant characteristic identified and briefly described		Up to 3
		Maximum	5
Total			**25**

53   CC & J

Key answer tips

Ensure that you manage your time appropriately to answer all parts of this question. Parts (c) and (d) require more application than theory, so may require a little longer to tackle.

(a)   **Threats to auditor independence**

The threats to auditor independence may be categorised as self interest, self review, advocacy, familiarity and intimidation threats or considered through a practical reflection on the detail of the scenario.

The most obvious problem is the level of familiarity that existed between the auditor and Banco. The auditor has overstepped his professional relationship with the company and as such his ability to exclude personal considerations from professional decision making has been severely compromised.

His attendance at family gatherings affects his ability to deal with the executive and his inclusion in the shooting trip has a similarly detrimental effect on his relationship with other members of the audit committee, even if they are not effective in their position. Strict guidelines in relation to this area may have assisted had they been issued through head office.

A related point is how independence weakens over time. The relationship between the partner and the firm has existed for many years and this in itself suggests objective decision making may be compromised. The company should have a clear policy regarding auditor rotation, as required by governance regimes and auditing standards.

The contractual relationship between the two companies is another problematic area. Reliance due to size of revenues generated from single client is one area of concern. This can be coupled with the amount of non audit work carried out and the level of profits gained through this. Such financial interest reduces the ability of the auditor to operate without concern as to financial consequence. The limited size of the audit fee may in itself compromise the ability to carry out a full audit with the allowable budget. Fees should be set with reference to head office management and policy determined as to whether any non audit work can be carried out. It is well known that Sarbanes-Oxley specifically prohibits non audit work for financial auditors demonstrating the importance of the issue in global governance.

The existence of competitors and the strength of competition for lucrative work may affect the willingness of the auditor to make decisions that negatively affect client relationships. This is difficult to deal with except through reliance on the professionalism of the individual partner. It is clear in the case that such professionalism is in short supply at CC & J. This in turn brings into question the quality of recruitment and training practices at the firm. Head office cannot ignore their own culpability in what has happened. The seeming isolation of the individual involved and the lack of head office involvement in policy making is at the heart of the problems that have occurred.

(b) **Composition of audit committee**

The audit committee generally consists of three individuals as noted in the scenario. However, all three should be non-executives, independent of the executive and reporting directly to the chairman and shareholders.

Tutorial note

The above statement is the corporate governance principle that we are all familiar with in this area. The question requirement is, however, to "assess....using evidence within the scenario" so you will now need to go and see how this committee can be formed with the people present in CC&J.

This independence rules out the involvement of the CFO in any capacity since he cannot be at once the controller and the controlled. It is surprising, if not shocking, that the CFO has the role of chairman of the audit committee since this would not be accepted by any governance regime. Being a large company this should have come to the notice of the regulatory body and been dealt with immediately.

The independence of the audit committee does not mean complete separation from involvement in the company as is described here. They need to be separate and yet deeply involved, aware of financial position and accounting treatments. This suggests the need for financial expertise as a prerequisite to membership. In general guidance suggests that at least one member should be a financial professional, in reality all should have some understanding of audit issues and finance regulation.

Independence must be protected in the same way that auditor independence must be assured. This is not to suggest that the audit committee does not have any social involvement with officers of the company although their involvement in a company excursion seems to over step what would be considered to be appropriate. At the other end of the spectrum it is almost unbelievable that they do not meet regularly with the auditor and only consider company operations on an annual basis. If they were to be effective then a balance should have been struck and their role clearly defined.

The lack of an effective audit committee in itself threatens the independence of auditors and so could have been discussed in part a) of this question. Advice from relevant governance codes such as the Corporate Governance Code would have outlined their responsibilities including the need to operate as an interface between the auditor and the company (discussed next).

(c) **Audit committee operation as an interface**

The audit committee operates as an interface or point of connection between a variety of stakeholders, all involved in ensuring control exists and that the company continues to operate in shareholders' interests.

External auditors should report to the committee who in turn inform the board and shareholders of major issues arising from the audit. This creates an independent reporting line outside of communication directly to the CFO and so increases the likelihood of financial impropriety coming to light.

The same form of communication is available to internal auditors although the frequency of contact may be greater and the issues raised more diverse in line with the broad scope of internal auditors roles within the company. This form of interface can then extend to a direct channel of communication for all staff to use should ethical or professional dilemmas be unearthed. In this way the interface becomes a whistleblower channel for fast communication of important issues to those responsible in part for strategic control.

The audit committee reports to the board of directors regarding its own work and the work of those discussed above. This form of interface reduces the volume of issues identified for board consideration, filtering down workload to only major concerns.

Finally the audit committee through disclosure in the annual report operates as a direct interface between the company and its shareholders providing them with detail regarding the status of control and how risks are being managed.

(d) **Characteristics of good quality information required by audit committee**

In all of the above communication processes there is a need for good quality information in order to reduce redundancy and ensure clarity in reporting. Characteristics include the need for information to be limited to that which is relevant to the committee given its defined remit.

Reporting should be an accurate, factual account of the issue being raised especially in relation to financial matters. It should be concise with due consideration to clarity given the limitations of time and committee understanding of detailed financial concerns.

In addition, timeliness with respect to committee meetings and confidentiality, especially in relation to whistleblower issues, must be assured. Beyond this, consideration must be given to the cost of producing excessive data and the cost in terms of committee time in absorbing such information. Above all, reports must be useful and used to support their deliberations.

IDENTIFYING AND ASSESSING RISK

54 LANDMASS

Key answer tips

The syllabus does not specify which corporate governance codes you need to be familiar with. However if you do know the details of the UK's Corporate Governance Code this should give you an understanding of the typical requirements of such systems for part (b).

(a) Risks should be categorised by companies according to the circumstances in which the company operates and according to how it perceives its risks.

(i) A distinction might be made between business risks and governance risks. Business risks relate to the risks of failing to achieve objectives in business operations. Governance risks would relate to the risks of failing to comply with best practice in corporate governance, a failure of internal controls, or a failure to comply with legislation or regulations.

(ii) Broad categories of risk should be divided into sub-categories: for example, business risks might be categorised into strategy risks, competition risks and environmental risks (political risks, legislation risks, economic risks, technology risks, and so on).

(iii) If a company consists of several independent investment centres, each investment centre might be responsible for its own risk classification and risk management.

(iv) There might be established classifications of risk within a particular industry. For example, in banking, risks are classified for risk assessment and capital management purposes into credit risk, traded market risk, operational risk and other risks.

In most situations, however, companies should carry out regular assessments of the risks that they face, using risk categories that seem appropriate to their individual circumstances.

The risk categories that may be appropriate for Landmass are as follows:

(i) *Compliance risk.* Landmass is a planning to become listed company and hence will be subject to the listing rules of the stock exchange. These rules can change, and non-compliance met with penalties or, ultimately de-listing.

(ii) *Product risk.* A risk to any business is that the demand for its product may fall, or rise. With three different product lines, Landmass may hope to reduce this risk.

(iii) *Economic risk.* The property business is highly affected by the overall state of the economy, benefiting in times of boom, and suffering in times of recession. GDP, economic growth and unemployment will all be major risk factors for Landmass.

(iv) *Interest rate risk.* No information has been given of how Landmass finances its business, so it may or may not be directly affected by movements in interest rates. However, it is highly likely that its customers will be adversely affected if interest rates rise, and hence their demand for the property that Landmass offers could fall.

Tutorial note

The above categories are by no means the only risk categories that Landmass faces. To identify categories, it may have been helpful to brainstorm the risks facing the business, and then see which are major, or which can be grouped together under a single category heading.

(b) This answer assumes that the corporate governance guidelines which Landmass will be subject to are similar to those in the UK's Corporate Governance Code.

When Landmass becomes a listed company, it will be expected to comply with corporate governance guidelines. The board of directors will be required to carry out an annual review of the system of internal control and risk management, and report to the shareholders that they have done so.

In order to do this, a formal system of risk management should be put in place. An appropriate approach would be to establish one or more risk management committees. The risk management committee(s) should be responsible for the supervision of risk management within the company. The role of a risk management committee might be to:

- identify and assess risks regularly, and provide information to the board of directors and executive management

- formulate risk management policies, for submission to the board of directors for approval

- communicate with executive management, to ensure that risks are taken into consideration in decision-making.

Since many of the specific business risks and internal control risks will differ for each of the three business areas of Landmass, it might be appropriate to establish risk committees at a divisional level. However, other risks might apply to the group as a whole (for example, risks arising from changes in the value of land, or changes in legislation relating to property rights) and it might therefore be appropriate to have a risk committee at group level, to consider broader strategic risks facing the company.

The management of risk, and the implementation of risk controls, is the responsibility of the management who make decisions for the company. This responsibility might remain at board level (for example, in assessing strategic risk, or making decisions about acquisitions or major capital investments), or might be delegated to senior management.

A risk management committee should assess business risks and strategic risks, but there will also be a requirement to assess the system of internal control in the company. In the UK, guidelines for the review of internal control systems were provided in the Turnbull guidelines, which were based on the review structure proposed by COSO. It is recommended that the management and review of internal control should be based on five elements:

(i)   creating a suitable control culture and risk management environment within the organisation

(ii)   the regular review of risks, including procedures for identifying, assessing and prioritising risks

(iii)   selecting suitable internal controls to contain or prevent the risks

(iv)   communicating information about risks and risk controls throughout the organisation to the individuals affected by them

(v)   monitoring the effectiveness of controls, with a view to rectifying weaknesses in control that might be discovered.

This continual review of internal control could be made a responsibility of the risk management committee(s).

The board of directors should assess the adequacy of internal control and risk management systems each year. In addition, the company might be required to publish an operating and financial review (OFR) each year in which the significant risks facing the company are explained to the shareholders, together with information on how the company is managing these risks. The board of directors should therefore also consider a system for reporting on risks, based on the information provided by its risk committee(s).

It might also be appropriate to consider the role of an internal audit department within a risk management system. If a company has an internal audit department, the audit staff can provide a means of monitoring risks and controls, and reporting their findings to operational managers, possibly the finance director (or the person to whom the internal audit department reports) and the risk committee(s).

55 DUBLAND (JUN 13)

Key answer tips

The context of this question is the reduction of bank lending in Dubland – a popular topic and further emphasising the need for the well prepared candidate to read and keep up to date with current affairs.

Part (a) was an explanation of risk assessment and the need for constant update. This question has been asked before and should have been straightforward. Part (b) is more challenging requiring the candidate to consider several links within the syllabus and concentrating on the stakeholder/shareholder debate. Part c) required the consideration of embedding the assessment of financial risk in large organisations using a bank to illustrate. This should have presented few problems

(a)   **Explanation of risk assessment**

Risk assessment is the process of evaluating the importance of a risk by making an estimate of two variables: the probability of the risk event being realised and the impact that the risk would have if it were realised. Probability refers to the likelihood of the risk materialising and is expressed either as a percentage or as a proportion of one (e.g. a 0·5 risk is considered to be 50% likely). The impact refers to the value of the loss if the risk event were to materialise. The estimated values of these two variables can be plotted on a risk assessment 'map', where the two axes are impact and probability. Then, different risk management strategies can be assigned depending upon the area of the map the risk is plotted in.

Risks assessed at low probability and low impact can be accepted or tolerated, those with high impact but low probability are often transferred or shared, risks with low impact but high probability are typically reduced and those with high impact and high probability are typically avoided. Risks that are known to be more likely to occur in the near future ('proximate' risks) may be assessed as higher probability and have more urgent strategies applied for managing them.

Continuous and ongoing

The first reason why there needs to be a continuous and ongoing risk assessment is because of the strategic importance of many risks *and because of the dynamic nature* of those risks being assessed. Some risks reduce over time and others increase, depending upon changes in the business environment that organisations exist in. Accordingly, it should not be seen as a 'once and for all' activity. If there is a risk that companies who borrow money become less able to repay their loans than previously, this is a negative change in the business environment (thereby affecting liquidity risk). When business recovers and bank customers' ability to repay large loans improves, the liquidity risk for the banks is reduced.

Second, it is necessary to always have accurately assessed risks *because of the need to adjust risk management strategies* accordingly. The probabilities of risk occurring and the impacts involved can change over time as environmental changes take effect. In choosing, for example, between accepting or reducing a risk, how that risk is managed will be very important. In reducing their lending, the banks have apparently decided to reduce their exposure to liquidity risk. This strategy could change to an 'accept' strategy when the economy recovers.

For BigBank, changes in the economic environment of Dubland mean that liquidity risks have increased. As business confidence rises and falls in Dubland, the probabilities and impacts of different risks will change. In this case, BigBank has decided that a reduction in lending is a suitable response to mitigate its financial risks, but this measure is likely to change as business confidence improves and, indeed, the finance minister has asked the banks to consider this.

(b) **Fiduciary duty**

A fiduciary duty is an often onerous *duty of care and trust* that one party owes to another, mainly defined in terms of a financial duty of care in a business context. It can be either a legal duty or a moral duty (or both). In the case of a legal duty, it is legally required, for example, for a solicitor to act in the best interests of a client, or a nurse to act in the best interests of a patient. In other situations, the legal responsibilities are more blurred but an ethical duty may remain. Many would argue, for example, that people owe a fiduciary duty to certain ancient monuments or to the preservation of a unique landscape. The issue here is the fiduciary duty owed by Mr Ng, the chief executive of BigBank. In terms of his agency relationship with the BigBank shareholders, he is *legally correct in his belief* that he has a pre-eminent duty to the shareholders. The problem arises when the effects of his duty to the bank's shareholders is taken into account and this raises a number of potential issues.

Critical evaluation

In support of his belief about his 'only duty' being to shareholders (a pristine capitalist perspective) is the fact that as an agent of the shareholders, he is employed by them and *legally and morally bound to act primarily in their economic best interests*. It will often be the case that one strategy favours one constituency (e.g. the shareholders) whilst disadvantaging another, but this does not warrant him adopting a course of action that would increase the bank's risk exposure or reduce shareholders' returns. Such an action would be a *de facto theft of company value* and hence very unethical. If he were to weaken the bank's risk management in order to reduce the harmful effects on borrowers (and satisfy the finance minister's requirements), he would not be acting in the best interests of the shareholders, who have every right to expect him to *protect their interests* over all other claims upon the bank.

Arguments against his remark arise from the belief that he is being *naïve and shortsighted* by suggesting that his *only* duty is to the shareholders. There are both strategic and ethical reasons why, in this case, assuming a narrow and short-term focus on shareholder value is wrong. The finance minister mentioned the importance of banks in wider society and the fact that the lack of lending *has had negative effects on the Dubland economy*. Not only might this be *unfair to other businesses* and individuals unable to gain loan capital, but it might have a *longer term effect on BigBank itself*, and its shareholders, if the economy shrinks and there is less demand for lending when the economy recovers.

(c) **Financial risks**

Financial risks are those arising from a range of financial measures. The main impacts of financial risk are on either cash flow or cost of capital (or sometimes both). They are so important to a business because of the extent to which cash flows facilitate normal business operations. When cash flows are insufficient to meet cash needs, they can create difficulties including, ultimately, the failure of the business.

The most common financial risks are those arising from financial structure (gearing), interest rate risk, liquidity, credit, cash flow and currency risks. High gearing can be a source of financial risk, when, for example, monetary pressure in the economy increases interest payments and causes reduced cash flows from the income statement. This is similar to interest rate risk, which concerns the company's vulnerability to rising or falling interest rates (depending on whether the company relies on the interest rate from borrowings or from bank deposits). Liquidity risks concern the ability of the business to meet short-term financing challenges, credit risk is the risk of not being paid on time (or at all) and currency risks are risks arising from adverse movements in exchange rates that might devalue the value of cash held in a given currency, make imported goods more expensive or exported goods less competitive.

Embedding financial risk management

Risk management becomes most effective when it is embedded into the company. This means that it is not a 'stand alone' activity but becomes normal behaviour. The value of managing and controlling the risk becomes widely accepted and made a part of many people's roles, as a part of their normal behaviour. In particular, embedding financial risk management can be achieved in BigBank by the use of several measures.

First, because financial risks are technical in nature (concerned with risks that might affect the company's cash flow), it may be necessary to *inform and educate a wide range of employees* to understand and recognise risk factors. This may also involve advising on the importance of financial risks by discussing the impacts they can have and hence the necessity of managing them. The extent of this education and information will depend upon the specific structure of the company and the levels of the business that are deemed to 'need to know'.

Second, technical *accounting and monitoring systems need to be implemented* that measure and report (to management) on agreed targets, measures and compliance with those. These might involve regular reports against key targets (perhaps monthly) and 'alerts' if one or more of the measures strays out of its specified range.

Third, human resource systems can be designed to provide *incentives for monitoring and alerting* management about the risks. Rather than encouraging risk taking in BigBank, staff appraisals and the reward structures could be designed to reward behaviour more likely to control and mitigate the financial risks.

Fourth, awareness of financial risks, and those things that can increase them, can be *normalised as a part of BigBank's culture*. This would mean that it became a normal thing to discuss, tell stories about, create rituals around, etc. In the same way that health and safety risks have become a part of the culture in many organisations, financial risks could be more firmly embedded by achieving this.

ACCA marking scheme			
			Marks
(a)	1 mark for each relevant point on risk assessment to a maximum of 4 marks. 2 marks for each relevant point, in context, on the need for 'ongoing' to a maximum of 4 marks.		
		Maximum	8
(b)	2 marks for description of fiduciary duty plus 1 mark for context of case. 1 mark for each relevant argument in favour of Ron Ng's statement to a maximum of 2 marks. 1 mark for each relevant argument against Ron Ng's statement to a maximum of 2 marks.		
		Maximum	7
(c)	Up to 4 marks for explanation of financial risks. 2 marks for each point about embedding risk at BigBank discussed.		
		Maximum	10
Total			**25**

Examiner's comments

The case in question 3 was about a reduction in bank lending in Dubland, with one bank in particular, BigBank, being the subject of discussion. The requirements were about risk assessment, fiduciary duties and financial risk.

Part (a) began by asking candidates to explain the meaning of 'risk assessment'. This was a relatively straightforward requirement for many (with regard to the impacts and probability of identified risks). Weaker answers discussed the whole risk auditing process: identification, assessment, management, reporting, but this was not necessary. The question was only about risk assessment.

The second task in part (a) was to examine the case and to use that analysis to explain why risk assessment need to be 'continuous and ongoing'. Weaker answers forgot to attempt this task at all after discussing risk assessment but better answers showed how frequent and unpredictable environmental changes create changes to an organisation's risk profile.

Part (b) touched on the stakeholder/shareholder debate and asked candidates to critically evaluate a remark made by Mr Ng in the case. His remark that his 'only duty' was to the shareholders, was a 'pristine capitalist' type remark and the critical evaluation involved a consideration of both sides of the argument. Candidates who were able to see what this question was asking (the stakeholder/shareholder debate) often achieved good marks but weaker answers attempted to define 'fiduciary duty' but offered little discussion beyond that.

Part (c) was about embedding financial risks in large organisations using BigBank as an example. The requirement contained two tasks: to explain financial risk and then to discuss how financial risks can be embedded in BigBank. Weaker answers made an attempt to explain financial risk but then failed to develop the second task on embedding risk. Stronger answers were able to place the idea of embedding risk into the context of the case and with regard to BigBank's situation in particular.

56 ULTRA UBER (DEC 10)

Key answer tips

Embedding 'risk awareness' will always be a popular exam area, as it is very relevant to how in the 'real world' risk is controlled.

(a) **Liquidity risk**

Liquidity risk refers to the difficulties that can arise from an inability of the company to meet its short-term financing needs, i.e. its ratio of short-term assets to short-term liabilities. Specifically, this refers to the organisation's working capital and meeting short-term cash flow needs. The essential elements of managing liquidity risk are, therefore, the controls over receivables, payables, cash and inventories.

Manufacturing has historically had a greater challenge with the management of liquidity risk compared to some other sectors (especially low inventory businesses such as those in service industries like those that Bob Ndumo is NED for). In the case of UU, this is for three reasons.

Firstly, manufacturing usually requires higher working capital levels because it buys in and sells physical inventory, both on credit. This means that both payables and receivables are relatively high. It also, by definition, requires inventory in the form of raw materials, work-in-progress and finished goods, and therefore the management of inventory turnover is one of the most important management tasks in manufacturing management. In addition, wages are paid throughout the manufacturing process, although it will take some time before finished goods are ready for sale.

Secondly, manufacturing has complex management systems resulting from a more complex business model. Whilst other business models create their own liquidity problems, the variability and availability of inventory at different stages and the need to manage inventories at different levels of completion raises liquidity issues not present in many other types of business (such as service based business).

Thirdly, UU has a number of weaknesses that amplify its structural liquidity position as a manufacturer. Its ineffective credit control department and its voluntary 20 day supplier payment policy both increase the short-term cash pressure and thereby increase the likelihood of liquidity risks becoming realised.

(b) **Risk embeddedness**

Risk embeddedness refers to the way in which risk awareness and management are interwoven into the normality of systems and culture in an organisation. These two twin aspects (systems and culture) are both important because systems describe the way in which work is organised and undertaken, and culture describes the 'taken-for-grantedness' of risk awareness and risk management within the organisation.

The methods by which risk awareness and management can be embedded in organisations are as follows:

Aligning individual goals with those of the organisation and building these in as part of the culture. The need for alignment is important because risk awareness needs to be a part of the norms and unquestioned assumptions of the organisation. Training of staff at all levels is essential to ensure risk is embedded throughout the organisation.

Including risk responsibilities with job descriptions. This means that employees at all levels have their risk responsibilities clearly and unambiguously defined.

Establishing reward systems that recognise that risks have to be taken (thus avoiding a 'blame culture'). Those employees that are expected to take risks (such as those planning investments) should have the success of the projects included in their rewards.

Establishing metrics and performance indicators that monitor and feedback information on risks to management. This would ensure that accurate information is always available to the risk committee and/or board, and that there is no incentive to hide relevant information or fail to disclose risky behaviour or poor practice. A 'suggestion box' is one way of providing feedback to management.

Communicating risk awareness and risk management messages to staff and publishing success stories. Part of the dissemination of, and creating an incentive for, good practice, internal communications is important in developing culture and continually reminding staff of risk messages.

(c) **Obstacles to embedding liquidity risk management at UU Limited**

The case draws attention to three aspects of working capital management at UU Limited: payables, receivables and inventory. All of these are necessary issues in the management of liquidity and hence the reduction of liquidity risk. Specifically, however, it identifies four potential obstacles to embedding the management of liquidity risk. Primarily, however, the individual managers of the company are all acting in isolation and not working together for the good of the company.

The *sales* manager's *desire to have high levels of finished goods* for maximum customer choice. It is quite reasonable for a sales manager to support high levels of finished goods inventory but there is an inventory-holding cost associated with that which increases the amount of money tied up in working capital. A wider recognition of the overall liquidity pressures on the business would be a very helpful quality in the sales manager and this is a potential obstacle.

The same points apply to the *manufacturing* director's *desire to have high raw material levels.* Clearly, his effectiveness as head of manufacturing is partly measured by the extent to which the factory fulfils orders and avoids the disruptions to production that arise through inventory 'stock-outs'. He prefers having raw materials in stock rather than having to order them with a supplier's lead time but this, of course, leads to a greater exposure to liquidity risk.

The *ineffective credit control department.* According to the manufacturing director, the credit control department, responsible for the timely payment of receivables, is 'more of a social club than a serious way of getting receivables in on time'. The vulnerability to liquidity risk is clearly influenced by day's receivables and so an ineffective credit control department is a major obstacle.

Finally, the CEO's *desire to pay payables early* as part of the company's social responsibility efforts. Brian Mills is clearly of the view that offering a voluntary prompt payment of payables is an important component of the company's social responsibility and that is costing the company an average of 10 days payables on most accounts. Over the course of a year that will place a great deal of arguably unnecessary pressure on working capital. The fact that it is the CEO himself that holds this view might make it difficult to change.

(d) **Criticise the voluntary supplier payment policy**

Supplier payment disclosures have become increasingly popular in recent years in some countries as a signal of intent to suppliers that larger buyers will not exploit the economic advantage that they sometimes have over smaller suppliers. It is usual for these statements to announce that all payments will be made in line with the supplier's terms and so UU's intention to voluntarily pay within 20 days is more generous that would usually be expected.

In terms of criticism as a means of demonstrating social responsibility, the case says that the purpose of the policy is to 'publicly demonstrate our social responsibility'. A key limitation of the policy is, however, that the policy *only focuses on one stakeholder* (suppliers) and apparently ignores other groups. Given the information in the case, the social responsibility policy is apparently aimed at one single stakeholder which is an ineffective overall strategy.

Secondly, however, it is unlikely that this policy is the best use of resources *if the desire is to* 'publicly *demonstrate' social responsibility.* Measures aimed more at customers or more charitable causes would be likely to attract more publicity if that is the intention.

The policy is *very costly to UU in terms of cash flow. So* much so that the finance director has questioned whether it can actually be afforded, especially at times of a lack of short-term credit, particularly during the global economic recession. It is, of course, a matter of ethical debate as to how committed UU should be to its social responsibility in terms of resources.

Finally, the policy doesn't *enjoy the support of the other directors* and is thus hard to maintain as an ongoing commitment. This means it is vulnerable and susceptible to change if the CEO is the only person who really believes in it. As a part of the company's overall strategic positioning, the components of social responsibility must enjoy widespread support, especially among the senior officers in the company, and arguably most importantly, it must enjoy the support of the finance director.

	Marking scheme	Marks
(a)	2 marks for definition of liquidity risk. 1 mark for each explanation of manufacturing vulnerability to liquidity risk up to a maximum of 3 marks.	5
(b)	2 marks for definition of risk embeddedness. 1 mark for each method to a maximum of 5 marks.	7
(c)	2 marks for each obstacle identified and examined. 1 mark for identification only.	8
(d)	2 marks for each criticism made to a maximum of 5 marks. Maximum	5
Total		**25**

57 REGIONAL POLICE FORCE

Key answer tips

This question is completely focused on the area of risks and controls, but it has been placed in a non-listed company environment. The key to success here will be practical, precise suggestions entirely related to the information provided in the scenario.

(a) There are several significant risks to the achievement of the corporate objectives of the regional police force.

- The police force has several different stated objectives, which means that there will have to be some prioritisation of objectives, given limited resources to carry out the police work. For example, how should decisions be taken about allocating resources to tasks that reduce crime and those that promote community safety (such as road traffic safety or anti-terrorist measures).

- The objective of reducing crime and disorder is a very broad one, given that there are many different types of crime and lawlessness. Priorities will have to be assigned to the reduction in different types of crime, and efforts to deal with some types of crime will not receive adequate police resources.

- There might also be a temptation for the police force to divert resources away from 'normal' police work to money-earning activities such as policing football matches. There is a risk that money-earning activities will divert too many resources away from normal police work, and the amounts of money earned will be insufficient.

- Since the police force is a public body, there is a high risk of political interference. Political decisions are taken about specific priorities for dealing with crime, setting targets for achievement, and allocating money from taxation. Political decisions might increase or decrease the funds available to the police.

- There might be some conflict between the objectives of the police force. For example, if tough police measures are taken to reduce rates of crime or to deal with public disorder, public confidence in the police force might be adversely affected if the police tactics are too aggressive. Excessive violence in dealing with political demonstrations is a particular source of risk to public confidence.

- Risks to the achievement of the corporate objectives might also arise from a lack of public support. The police force are accountable to the general public as well as to politicians, and success in dealing with crime and improving community safety depends heavily on public support for the police – for example in reporting crimes and being willing to give evidence in criminal trials.

(b)   The risks in a regional structure for the police force are as follows:

- The regional management will want to set its own targets for the achievement of corporate objectives, but these might conflict with national targets set by government.

- A regional police authority might formulate its own strategies for dealing with crime that are different from the strategies adopted by other regional authorities. As a result, different crimes might be dealt with in completely different ways in different regions. The resulting lack of consistency in policing around the country could have an adverse effect on public opinion and public confidence in the police force.

- Crime is not restricted to regional boundaries, and regional forces rely on co-operation from other regional forces to carry out their work. Operational difficulties might arise that reduce the efficiency and effectiveness of inter-regional co-operation.

- Some crimes are of such potential importance, and operate on a national or international basis, that they need to be dealt with on a national or international basis, and not at regional level. Without national and international structures and organisation, much police work would be ineffective.

- Information will have to be shared between regions. There might be some risk that information held in one region might not be properly accessible to another region.

Tutorial note

In a question such as this it is acceptable to suggest risks that are not directly referred to in the scenario, but can be drawn from your experience of such a situation. However, ensure that your risks (and subsequent controls) are explained very clearly so that the marker can award you points for relevant suggestions.

(c)   In broad terms, the internal controls that should apply within a police force are similar to the internal controls that should operate in any large organisation. The aim of internal controls should be to ensure that the policies of the organisation are properly applied and that operations are conducted efficiently and effectively.

- There must be procedural controls, to ensure that activities are carried out in accordance with policy and legal requirements. Police work is subject to extensive procedural controls.

- There should be adequate management and supervisory controls. Supervisors should monitor the work of their subordinates, and should be accountable to their own superiors for the actions of the individuals in their charge.

- There should be controls over recruitment and training (personnel controls), to ensure that appropriate individuals are employed and that these individuals are given sufficient training to do their work properly.

- Organisational controls should ensure that there is sufficient accountability for police work that is carried out. Although there will be accountability through normal reporting lines in the organisational hierarchy, the work of a police force should also be subject to external assessment, for example from public or political bodies.

- There must be procedures for the authorisation and approval of police activity, including the commitment of expenditure to activities. Decisions to commit resources and spending to various activities should be taken at an appropriate level within the management hierarchy.

58   GHI GROUP

Key answer tips

The categories of risk used here in part (a) may include one or two which you have not specifically studied – however you should be able to use your general knowledge and information in the question to suggest examples.

The requirement to part (b) is precise in focusing solely on risks arising from the decision to sell all-inclusive deals. You will get no marks for including more general risks.

Ensure that you correctly identify the verb used in the question and the depth of answer required for it, since part (c) only requires a list of tasks. No further explanation of these is required, so no marks will be earned for it.

The highlighted words are key phrases that markers are looking for.

(a)   **Risks faced by GHI Group**

The following risks are faced by the GHI Group:

Financial risks

(i)   GHI is based in its home country, but organises holidays abroad. Its revenues will be in its home currency, but it will have to pay its suppliers of overseas accommodation and transport services in countries which do not use the Euro in their local currencies. The group is therefore exposed to currency risk given the mismatch of currencies between revenues and costs. It will be possible to charge customers in local currency for services they buy while on holiday (e.g. excursions, wines and spirits at meals, etc), so some matching of revenues and costs is possible, but there will still be a large mismatch. The risk is that, if the Euro depreciates against the foreign currencies, then more pounds will have to be paid to overseas suppliers, and the profitability of the holiday products may be undermined.

(ii)   There will be a cash flow *risk* arising from the uncertainty about how many people will actually take the holiday that they originally book. The traditional pattern is for holidaymakers to pay a modest deposit when they book a holiday, with the balance payable (say) a month before the departure date. The company must contractually book a room in a hotel once the initial booking is made, and will be liable to pay the hotel, but in practice a proportion of holidaymakers will be unable to take up their holiday due to illness, family bereavement, etc. They may forfeit the deposit they have paid, but the company must pay for the hotel rooms it has booked, and will lose the profits they had hoped to gain from selling excursions, etc. This uncertainty about the actual number of customers who will turn up leads to the cash flow risk of the company.

Political risks

(i)   The risk of terrorist acts in countries that are popular with GHI's customers may have a severe impact on sales. Overseas holidays are often a discretionary purchase so, if a bomb goes off in Egypt or Turkey or New York, then some holidaymakers will avoid that destination and choose either to holiday in their home country or perhaps just stay at home. It is difficult for a company such as GHI to predict when the next terrorist act will occur, but it is possible to buy insurance against the adverse effects that a major incident would cause the company.

(ii)   GHI is planning to buy two new hotels in the Eastern Mediterranean. The question does not state the countries in which these purchases are to be made, but there will be a discrimination risk that the local government authorities may disapprove of foreign owners of local assets and may make things difficult for the company. The nature of this risk may depend on the political relationship between the two governments.

Environmental risks

(i)   An increasing number of people are using the internet to book 'self-managed' holidays directly, rather than visiting a travel agent. This development in technology has created the risk to GHI that customers will no longer visit its retail travel outlets, and will no longer buy its packaged products. GHI must react quickly by offering its products on the internet at a competitive price, otherwise it will get left behind as the market develops.

(ii)   The growth in divorce rates and in people remaining single means that the traditional family 'bucket and spade' beach holiday with two parents and two children will become less of the norm. This social change means that GHI must offer products of interest to single people, older people and lone-parent families. The 'weekend break' trips to European cities are an example of products popular with the over 50s which will continue to grow in the future as the number of older people in society steadily increases.

Economic risks

(i)   GHI has decided to purchase two new hotels in the Eastern Mediterranean. These will be overseas assets whose cost is denominated in an overseas currency, therefore their translated value in the group's statement of financial position will fluctuate from year to year. This translation risk could mean that the statement of financial position appears weaker if the pound strengthens against the relevant overseas currency, which could have implications for the cost of borrowing charged by future providers of debt finance.

(ii)   GHI must decide on the currency in which it will pay its suppliers in overseas countries. It may be that anyone in the Americas or the Far East is happy to be paid in US dollars, while anyone in Europe or Africa can be paid in Euros. However, there is a currency selection risk in that, if GHI decides to pay African suppliers in Euros while its competitors pay their similar suppliers in dollars, say, then GHI's relative competitive position will depend on the dollar's performance against the Euro.

Tutorial note

The risks given here are by no means the only risks you could have identified. And, it is equally possible to put some risks under different category headings. So don't worry about this, just ensure that you are discussing your risks in plenty of detail to earn the full marks.

(b)   GHI has decided to move from offering traditional 'room-only' or 'bed and breakfast' holidays to offering 'all-inclusive' holidays where the customer pays a larger sum up-front but all food and drink, sports facilities, entertainments, and so on in the hotel are then free. The risk is that:

(i)   customers may not be willing to pay the higher price; and

(ii)   the costs of the additional items may exceed the incremental revenues, so that GHI is worse off after the decision.

The willingness of customers to pay more for a product depends on the elasticity of demand for the product. The demand for package holidays is price elastic, in the sense that higher prices will reduce demand, given the competitive nature of the market. GHI must therefore send a clear message in its marketing literature about the premium quality nature of the holidays it is offering. Services such as free magazines and drinks on aeroplanes are cheap to organise, but may differentiate GHI's offering from the competition.

The risk is that customers will compare the more expensive GHI holiday with a cheaper holiday offered by a competitor, and decide that the extras offered by GHI are not worth the premium price. GHI can combat this risk by describing long lists of facilities that are included in the price, e.g. use of the hotel gym, swimming pool, tennis courts, etc. In reality the likelihood of a customer using all these facilities is low, but they will impress the potential customer in demonstrating the added value in an all-inclusive holiday.

Keeping tight control of costs is also important. The risk is that customers and staff will not place any value on goods and services that are handed out for free in the all-inclusive environment. Customers might take several different desserts from a free buffet, eat the one that tastes best, and throw the others away. Portion control must be stressed to staff in their training: all portions of food and drink should be the minimum possible to dissuade customers from throwing large amounts away. A training and audit regime for hotel staff should be implemented to monitor and control all portions offered to customers.

A final method of monitoring the success of the all-inclusive packages is to ask customers to fill out questionnaires at the end of their holiday, asking for their feedback. After all, there is no point marketing a premium product that customers are not happy with. Their suggestions for improvements should be taken very seriously and fed back as inputs into the planning process for the future.

(c) The role of the internal audit department is to provide assurance to senior management and the board of directors that business risks are being managed properly and that internal controls are operating as effectively as they were designed to.

Thus, in the context of GHI's foreign property purchases, internal audit must first decide whether the controls over such property purchases are adequate, and secondly whether the controls have been carried out properly.

Relevant tasks for the internal audit department are as follows:

- Reviewing the procedures by which potential sites are identified. This could mean checking that a minimum number of overseas property agents were consulted (say, a minimum of three agents in each country), and ensuring that the agents' advice is communicated to the relevant people at GHI.

- Checking that company procedures are followed in respect of negotiation of prices to be paid for each hotel.

- Checking that professional advice is sought and followed in respect of the appropriate method of financing the purchase price, e.g. bank loans, share issue, etc. The treasury department at GHI head office should receive this advice and give their opinion on it.

- Checking that the treasury department paid the appropriate amount of foreign currency to the hotels' builders on time, and that foreign currency risks have been hedged in accordance with group policy.

- Checking that health and safety regulations are fully complied with, before customers are allowed in. This should include fire drills and the servicing of boilers, given the public's sensitivity to faulty boilers following a well-publicised tragedy in Corfu at the end of 2006.

- Creating a rolling timetable within the internal audit department to test all the operating sections of the new hotels over the next few months. The new hotels will then be fully integrated into all the other group assets that internal audit inspects.

Tutorial note

There are many other tasks that internal audit could carry out. The important thing here is to list out at least five items to reflect the five marks available.

CONTROLLING RISK

59   CHEN PRODUCTS (DEC 08)

Key answer tips

A brief scenario focusing on the area of risk management. There are some knowledge based requirements, such as part (a) and part (c) (i) which provide quick marks.

The four aspects of the TARA model provide the basis for your answer in part (b), though the key is to ensure that you explain **how** these strategies may be applied to the case.

Part (c) moves onto look at the membership of a risk management committee. This was the most challenging part of the question. General advantages and disadvantages of NEDS would not have scored high marks; answering the exact question was important.

(a)   **Typical roles of a risk management committee**

The typical roles of a risk management committee are as follows:

To agree and approve the risk management strategy and policies. The design of risk policy will take into account the environment, the strategic posture towards risk, the product type and a range of other relevant factors.

Receiving and reviewing risk reports from affected departments. Some departments will file regular reports on key risks (such as liquidity assessments from the accounting department, legal risks from the company secretariat or product risks from the sales manager).

Monitoring overall exposure and specific risks. If the risk policy places limits on the total risk exposure for a given risk then this role ensures that limits are adhered to. In the case of certain strategic risks, monitoring could occur on a very frequent basis whereas for more operational risks, monitoring will more typically occur to coincide with risk management committee meetings.

Assessing the effectiveness of risk management systems. This involves getting feedback from departments and the internal audit function on the workings of current management and risk mitigation systems.

Providing general and explicit guidance to the main board on emerging risks and to report on existing risks. This will involve preparing reports on apparent risks and assessing their probability of being realised and their potential impact if they do.

To work with the audit committee on designing and monitoring internal controls for the management and mitigation of risks. If the risk committee is part of the executive structure, it will likely have an advisory role in respect of its input into the audit committee. If it is non-executive, its input may be more directly influential.

Tutorial note

Other roles may be suggested that, if relevant, will be rewarded.

(b) **Risk management strategies and Chen Products**

Risk transference strategy

This would involve the company accepting a portion of the risk and seeking to transfer a part to a third party. Although an unlikely possibility given the state of existing claims, insurance against future claims would serve to limit Chen's potential losses and place a limit on its losses. Outsourcing manufacture may be a way of transferring risk if the outsourcee can be persuaded to accept some of the product liability.

Risk avoidance strategy

An avoidance strategy involves discontinuing the activity that is exposing the company to risk. In the case of Chen this would involve ceasing production of Product 2. This would be pursued if the impact (hazard) and probability of incurring an acceptable level of liability were both considered to be unacceptably high and there were no options for transference or reduction.

Risk reduction strategy

A risk reduction strategy involves seeking to retain a component of the risk (in order to enjoy the return assumed to be associated with that risk) but to reduce it and thereby limit its ability to create liability. Chen produces four products and it could reconfigure its production capacity to produce proportionately more of Products 1, 3 and 4 and proportionately less of Product 2. This would reduce Product 2 in the overall portfolio and therefore Chen's exposure to its risks. This would need to be associated with instructions to other departments (e.g. sales and marketing) to similarly reconfigure activities to sell more of the other products and less of Product 2.

Risk acceptance strategy

A risk acceptance strategy involves taking limited or no action to reduce the exposure to risk and would be taken if the returns expected from bearing the risk were expected to be greater than the potential liabilities. The case mentions that Product 2 is highly profitable and it may be that the returns attainable by maintaining and even increasing Product 2's sales are worth the liabilities incurred by compensation claims. This is a risk acceptance strategy.

(c) Risk committee members can be either executive on non-executive.

(i) **Distinguish between executive and non-executive directors**

Executive directors are full time members of staff, have management positions in the organisation, are part of the executive structure and typically have industry or activity-relevant knowledge or expertise, which is the basis of their value to the organisation.

Non-executive directors are engaged part time by the organisation, bring relevant independent, external input and scrutiny to the board, and typically occupy positions in the committee structure.

(ii) **Advantages and disadvantages of being non-executive rather than executive**

The UK Corporate Governance Code, for example, allows for risk committees to be made up of either executive or non-executive members.

Advantages of non-executive membership

Separation and detachment from the content being discussed is more likely to bring independent scrutiny.

Sensitive issues relating to one or more areas of executive oversight can be aired without vested interests being present.

Non-executive directors often bring specific expertise that will be more relevant to a risk problem than more operationally-minded executive directors will have.

Chen's four members, being from different backgrounds, are likely to bring a range of perspectives and suggested strategies which may enrich the options open to the committee when considering specific risks.

Disadvantages of non-executive membership (advantages of executive membership)

Direct input and relevant information would be available from executives working directly with the products, systems and procedures being discussed if they were on the committee. Non-executives are less likely to have specialist knowledge of products, systems and procedures being discussed and will therefore be less likely to be able to comment intelligently during meetings.

The membership, of four people, none of whom 'had direct experience of Chen's industry or products' could produce decisions taken without relevant information that an executive member could provide.

Non-executive directors will need to report their findings to the executive board. This reporting stage slows down the process, thus requiring more time before actions can be implemented, and introducing the possibility of some misunderstanding.

				Marks
		Marking scheme		
(a)		Half mark for each role identified Half mark for brief description of each role		6
				—
			Maximum	6
				—
(b)		Half mark for identification of each strategy		
		One mark for definition of each strategy		
		One mark for application of each strategy to Chen Products		
				—
			Maximum	10
				—
(c)	(i)	2 marks for distinguishing between executive and non-executive directors		2
	(ii)	1 mark for each relevant advantage		Up to 4
		1 mark for each relevant disadvantage		Up to 3
				—
			Maximum	9
				—
Total				**25**
				—

Examiner's comments

This question was attempted by the majority of candidates and was the best done in section B. It was centred around the risk sections of the study guide but also included elements on corporate governance, especially about non-executive roles.

The scenario gave some information about Chen Products. It was a company that made four products and one of them (Product 2) had some problems in that it had failed while being used by customers. The tasks contained a mixture of book work (which reward thorough revision) and application to the case.

Part (a) asked candidates to describe the typical roles of a risk management committee. Some candidates failed to observe the verb ('describe') and produced a list (more like 'identify') thereby failing to achieve full marks.

Others, perhaps misinterpreting the task, wrote about the purposes of risk management which is a slightly different thing. For five marks, the time budget of nine minutes should have been enough to write two or three sentences on each role by way of description. Again, I would remind candidates to obey the verb. If a question asks candidates to describe or explain, a bullet list of points in not an appropriate response.

Part (b) appeared to be straightforward but also required application to the case to gain maximum marks. The TARA framework of risk management options (transfer, avoid, reduce, accept) has appeared in a previous P1 paper and candidates gained some marks for correctly identifying and explaining each point. To gain the full 10 points, however, candidates had to consider how each option might be applied to Product 2 and this was where some failed to gain marks.

There were two sub-sections of **part (c)**. For two marks, candidates had to simply distinguish between executive and non-executive directors. This is a fundamental and core area of the P1 syllabus so it wasn't surprising that most candidates were able to do this. The more challenging task was part (c)(ii).

Part (c)(ii) asked candidates to 'evaluate the relative advantages and disadvantages of Chen's risk management committee being non-executive rather than executive in nature'. Clearly then, it was a question drawing on content from the exec/NED sections of the study guide. What some candidates missed, however, was its specific relevance to risk committees. It was not asking about the pros and cons of NEDs in general. Rather it was asking candidates to consider the pros and cons of the placement of NEDs on a particular committee (the risk management committee) and this raised slightly different issues than the general pros and cons covered elsewhere in the study guide. A typical approach taken by some candidates was to discuss the general advantages and disadvantages but to then fail to develop these into the more specific case of risk committees. Again, it is important to study what the question is really asking rather than assume that the sense of the task can be conveyed in a cursory glance at the key words in the question.

60   H&Z COMPANY (JUN 09)

Key answer tips

This is a challenging question, though it does have some straightforward theoretical elements to it. It would be helpful to plan your answer to avoid any potential for overlap between (a) (ii) and (b).

In tackling part (b) focus on the most popular risk assessment framework of an impact/ likelihood matrix. However, do not take this as the invitation to draw and describe the matrix in detail, since this will not earn you marks.

Some definition marks available in part (c) (i) and then onto more application. Note the mark allocation for part (c) (ii) of seven marks. So, ideally you will make seven points about the view of risk management. 'Critically evaluate' allows you to agree and disagree with the view stated, but fall on the side of overall disagreement.

(a)   (i)   **Roles of a risk manager**

Providing overall leadership, vision and direction, involving the establishment of risk management (RM) policies, establishing RM systems etc. Seeking opportunities for improvement or tightening of systems.

Developing and promoting RM competences, systems, culture, procedures, protocols and patterns of behaviour. It is important to understand that risk management is as much about instituting and embedding risk systems as much as issuing written procedure. The systems must be capable of accurate risk assessment which seems not to be the case at H&Z as he didn't account for variables other than impact/hazard.

Reporting on the above to management and risk committee as appropriate. Reporting information should be in a form able to be used for the generation of external reporting as necessary. John's issuing of 'advice' will usually be less useful than full reporting information containing all of the information necessary for management to decide on risk policy.

Ensuring compliance with relevant codes, regulations, statutes, etc. This may be at national level (e.g. Sarbanes Oxley) or it may be industry specific. Banks, oil, mining and some parts of the tourism industry, for example, all have internal risk rules that risk managers are required to comply with.

Tutorial note

Bullet lists would not be rewarded – the question says 'describe'.

(ii) **John Pentanol's understanding of his role**

John appears to misunderstand the role of a risk manager in four ways.

Whereas the establishment of RM policies is usually the most important first step in risk management, *John launched straight into detailed risk assessments* (as he saw it). It is much more important, initially, to gain an understanding of the business, its strategies, controls and risk exposures. The assessment comes once the policy has been put in place.

It is important for the risk manager to report fully on the risks in the organisation and John's *issuing of* 'advice' *will usually be less useful than full reporting* information. Full reporting would contain all of the information necessary for management to decide on risk policy.

He told Jane Xylene that his role as risk manager involved *eliminating* 'all *of the highest risks at H&Z* Company' *which is an incorrect view.* Jane Xylene was correct to say that entrepreneurial risk was important, for example.

The risk manager is an operational role in a company such as H&Z Company and it will usually be up to senior management to decide on important matters such as withdrawal from risky activities. *John was being presumptuous and overstepping his role* in issuing advice on withdrawal from Risk 3. It is his job to report on risks to senior management and for them to make such decisions based on the information he provides.

(b) **Criticise John's advice**

The advice is based on an incomplete and flawed risk assessment. Most simple risk assessment frameworks comprise at least two variables of which impact or hazard is only one. The other key variable is probability. Risk impact has to be *weighed against probability* and the fact that a risk has a high potential impact does not mean the risk should be avoided as long as the probability is within acceptable limits. It is the *weighted combination of hazard/impact and probability* that forms the basis for meaningful risk assessment.

John appears to be very certain of his impact assessments but the case does not tell us on what information the assessment is made. It is important to recognise that 'hard' *data is very difficult to obtain on both impact and probability.* Both measures are often made with a degree of assumption and absolute measures such as John's ranking of Risks 1, 2 and 3 are not as straightforward as he suggests.

John also overlooks a key strategic reason for H&Z bearing the risks in the first place, which is the *return achievable by the bearing of risk.* Every investment and business strategy carries a degree of risk and this must be *weighed against the financial return* that can be expected by the bearing of the risk.

(c)   (i)   **Define 'entrepreneurial risk'**

Entrepreneurial risk is the necessary risk associated with any new business venture or opportunity. It is most clearly seen in entrepreneurial business activity, hence its name. In 'Ansoff' terms, entrepreneurial risk is expressed in terms of the unknowns of the market/customer reception of a new venture or of product uncertainties, for example product design, construction, etc. There is also entrepreneurial risk in uncertainties concerning the competences and skills of the entrepreneurs themselves.

Entrepreneurial risk is necessary, as Jane Xylene suggested, because it is from taking these risks that business opportunities arise. The fact that the opportunity may not be as hoped does not mean it should not be pursued. Any new product, new market development or new activity is a potential source of entrepreneurial risk but these are also the sources of future revenue streams and hence growth in company value.

(ii)   **Critically evaluate Jane Xylene's view of risk management**

There are a number of arguments against risk management in general. These arguments apply against the totality of risk management and also of the employment of inappropriate risk measures.

There is *a cost* associated with all elements of risk management which must obviously be borne by the company. *Disruption* to normal organisational practices and procedures as risk systems are complied with.

Slowing (introducing friction to) the seizing of new business opportunities or the development of internal systems as they are scrutinised for risk.

'STOP' *errors* can occur as a result of risk management systems where a practice or opportunity has been stopped on the grounds of its risk when it should have been allowed to proceed. This may be the case with Risk 3 in the case. (Contrast with 'GO' errors which are the opposite of STOP errors.)

There are also arguments for risk management people and systems in H&Z.

The most obvious benefit is that an effective risk system *identifies those risks that could detract* from the achievements of the company's strategic objectives. In this respect, it can *prevent costly mistakes* by advising against those actions that may lose the company value. It also has the effect of *reassuring investors* and capital markets that the company is aware of and is in the process of managing its risks. Where relevant, risk management is *necessary for compliance* with codes, listing rules or statutory instruments.

		Marking scheme		
				Marks
(a)	(i)	1 mark for evidence of understanding in each type of role (half mark for identification and half for description)		Up to 4
	(ii)	1 mark for each relevant assessment comment on John's understanding of the role		Up to 4
			Maximum	8
(b)		2 marks for evidence of understanding of risk assessment (impact/hazard and probability)		2
		2 marks for recognition of uncertainties over impact and probability information and description		2
		2 marks for importance of return and recognition of lack of return/benefit information and description		2
			Maximum	6
(c)	(i)	2 marks for definition		2
		2 marks for explanation of its importance		2
	(ii)	1 mark for each relevant point made in the case for Jane Xylene's view (i.e. against risk management)		Up to 4
		1 mark for each relevant point made in the case against Jane Xylene's view (i.e. in favour of risk management)		Up to 3
			Maximum	11
Total				25

Examiner's comments

This was question based around themes of risk. Again, the parts based on bookwork were better responded to than those requiring higher levels of intellectual engagement.

Most candidates did well on describing the roles of a risk manager in **(a)(i)** but many then failed to see anything wrong with John Pentanol's understanding of his own job. In **part (b)**, candidates were presented with some advice from John Pentanol from the case and instructed to criticise the advice with reference to a risk assessment framework.

The most helpful risk assessment framework is the impact/likelihood (or hazard/ probability) framework and this was the one that candidates should have employed in this answer. The point was that John had only measured the impact of the risks (paragraph 2) and had completely ignored their probabilities. This was obviously a highly flawed risk assessment. Many candidates correctly described the risk assessment framework but then failed to note the flaw in John's analysis, thereby failing to gain high marks for this part.

Finally, **part (c)** invited candidates to consider some remarks made by company director Jane Xylene.

Part (c)(i) was about the necessity of accepting risk as a part of a successful strategy. Most candidates who attempted this question were able to define entrepreneurial risk but fewer were able to develop the theme of why it was important to accept it in business organisations.

Part (c)(ii) was a 'critically evaluate' question in which the answer should have contained arguments for and against Jane Xylene's view on risk management (she believed the risk manager's job was unnecessary and that risk management was 'very expensive for the benefits achieved'). There are a lot of comments that can be made in response to a belief such as this and the model answer includes some but probably not all of the possible responses. Markers allowed for a range of responses to this question but in each case were looking for evidence of evaluation of Jane's view (not mere repetition of her remarks, for example).

61 SALTOC (DEC 09)

Key answer tips

This is mainly a risk question:

(a)   To ensure good marks in this requirement it is important to refer to Saltoc.

(b)   Again this requirement requires application of the Turnbull Guidance on Embedding Risk into Culture to be applied. This is a 'how to implement' requirement style.

(c)   This requirement should have been relatively easy marks for the well prepared student, as this topic is raised in an examiner's article titled 'Risk and Environmental Auditing' dated March 2009.

(a)   **Embedding risk**

Good internal controls start with a full risk assessment and this control should be introduced and amended to respond to changes in the risk profile as appropriate on an ongoing basis. To have risk awareness and risk systems embedded implies a number of things. It means that risk management is *included within the control systems of an organisation*. The case refers to Saltoc's budgetary control system which will need to reflect the risk metrics in the embedded system.

When risk is embedded, the budgetary control and reward systems would recognise the need for risk awareness in them by including risk-related metrics. When embedded, risk is *interconnected with other systems* so that risks must be taken into account before other internal controls will work effectively. So a given job description, for example, might have a particular risk check included in it which is then assessed annually in the job-holder's appraisal. This would typically be a part of an operation manager's job description (Harry Ho at Saltoc) where, for example, the accident rate could be a metric built into his annual appraisal.

In an embedded risk system, risk is *not seen as a separate part of internal control but is 'woven in'* to other internal controls and is a *part of the organisation's culture*.

The cultural norms in the IT department, for example, would be an implicit understanding that sensitive data is not transferred to portable laptops and that laptops are not left in unattended cars. This is a part of the taken-for-grantedness of embedded risk systems when woven into culture.

Finally, the management of risk is *'normal' behaviour at all levels*. Behaviour concerned with risk management is never seen as 'odd' or 'interfering' but as much a part of the normal business activity as trading and adding shareholder value.

(b) **Saltoc's management culture and implementing embedded risk systems**

On the evidence of the case, the existing management culture at Saltoc would not be suitable for the introduction of embedded risk systems for four reasons.

There is evidence of a *lack of unity and some mutual distrust within the board*. Some of the members plainly dislike one another and the lack of trust in colleagues is likely to frustrate efforts to change systems and culture throughout the whole organisation. The fact that Peter believes Harry and Laura should be removed is ample evidence of the discord that exists.

Linked to this is the *blame culture*. Rather than seek to resolve the risk problems at Saltoc, the board's first instinct appears to have been to blame others for the problems. Peter blamed Harry and Laura whilst they blamed Peter for his budgetary allocations to their departments. There is no evidence of a consensus, or even a willingness to work together on new systems.

There is a *lack of leadership and understanding from CEO* Ken Tonno. He is clearly most concerned with short term financial measures and cash flow. The tone of his remarks is sceptical, referring as he did to 'even more' administration on risks and controls. It seems unlikely that he would personally lead an effort to redesign structures, systems and culture to embed risks at Saltoc.

The case makes reference to *problems with departmental leadership* among board members. Any change to systems or practice needs departmental directors to be able to lead their departments and this may not be possible if respect is lacking.

(c) **What external risk auditing contains and the case for an external risk audit at Saltoc Company**

External risk auditing is an *independent review and assessment of the risks*, controls and safeguards in an organisation by someone from outside the company. Internal risk auditing also occurs in many organisations. It involves an *identification of the risks* within given frames of reference (the whole company, a given area of activity, a given department or location) and *advice on managing those risks in terms of a risk assessment*.

The first argument in favour of an external risk audit at Saltoc Company is the *'fresh pair of eyes' effect* that applies to the use of any external consultant. It seems evident that the existing management is unaware of all of the risks faced by the company and a new person coming in might identify new risks.

An external person would *take responsibility away from the squabbling directors* who are unlikely to work together on it. There is obviously enough tension and discord among board members to threaten any audit where collaboration would be needed to provide information and implement any recommendations.

An external risk auditor would provide an *unbiased view of the causes of poor risk management* in Saltoc and hence be able to give advice on where things can be improved. This will be important when recommending changes to systems to account for risks as it may impact some departments more than others. If there is any validity to Peter's claims about Harry and Laura then their departments may be disproportionately affected and an independent auditor would be able to comment on this from an objective viewpoint.

In some countries, (i.e. under Sarbanes Oxley), an element of independent assessment is necessary for compliance. In any event, encouraging independent scrutiny is good practice and *reassures external stakeholders (such as shareholders)* in the same way that an external financial audit does. At a time when the effectiveness of internal risk controls have been questioned (such as recently after the fire and the laptop theft), investor confidence is especially important.

Saltoc needs to demonstrate a robust response to the incidents in order to *restore customer confidence*. They have already lost some customer confidence and so the implementation of risk systems following the risk audit, might assume strategic importance. The appointment of an external risk auditor would help in this regard.

	Marking scheme	Marks
(a)	1 mark for each relevant point describing embeddedness to a maximum of 3 marks.	
	1 mark for each relevant point of application to case to a maximum of 3 marks.	6
(b)	2 marks for each issue identified and discussed in context (1 for recognition only)	8
(c)	1 mark for each point of explanation of external risk auditing up to a maximum of 3.	
	2 marks for each relevant point in the construction of the argument (1 for recognition, 1 for development and application to the case).	11
Total		**25**

Examiner's comments

This question was mainly about risk and, like the other questions in section B, contained three requirements. The notion of 'embedding' risk in organisations is an important one in risk management and is examined in two requirements of this question. Part (a) asked candidates to describe what it is whilst part (b) required an analysis of the case study to assess how easy it would be to embed risk management into the company in the case (Saltoc).

Part (a) was not just asking for a description of embeddedness, however. The question specifically mentioned 'with reference to Saltoc Company'. This required the candidate to describe the term and then give examples of how it could be implemented in Saltoc. The first part was generally done quite well but many candidates failed to gain the application marks. I would again emphasise the importance of carefully reading the question. The 'with reference to Saltoc' indicated that some marks were reserved for this and so it was not possible to get a high mark in part (a) without this.

The case about Saltoc included some descriptions of key personnel and issues with the corporate culture. It was necessary to draw on these to answer **part (b)**. The requirement was to assess the ability of the Saltoc culture to implement embedded risk systems. In order to answer this, it was obviously necessary to study the culture using evidence from the case. Again, time spent studying and scrutinising the case usually resulted in better answers. It was not possible to gain a high mark without a careful study of the Saltoc culture based on the evidence of the case. Some candidates attempted a general discussion either about culture in general or about the importance of risk embeddedness but neither of these were well rewarded.

The third requirement **(part (c))** was worth 11 marks was about external risk auditing. I wrote an article about this in Student Accountant and so candidates should have been aware of the essentials. There were two tasks in Part (c): to explain what risk auditing contains and to construct the case for external (rather than internal) risk auditing at Saltoc. Many candidates were able to get the 'contains' marks but then did less well on making the case for risk auditing at Saltoc. Given that I had written an article on this, I was surprised and disappointed that some candidates were unable to recall the four stages in risk auditing.

But the level 3 intellectual level task in this requirement was to construct the case for an external risk audit. This meant that candidates had to study the case in order to place themselves in a position to make a convincing argument for external risk auditing. So, again, a detailed analysis of the case was necessary to gain the highest marks.

62 BTS COMPANY

Key answer tips

This is a question tackling a method of risk classification – strategic vs operational. Note that part (a) has actually got two parts to the requirement: to explain the importance of monitoring risks and to discuss problems if not done effectively. It is important that you always break out your question requirements into the separate elements to ensure that you cover them all in your answer.

Part (b) requires you to look for risks within the scenario and then to move onto discuss suitable controls. There is plenty of information in the scenario to work from in doing this.

(a)   **Risk monitoring**

Risks must be continually monitored to ensure that they do not adversely affect the organisation. Risk monitoring takes place on three levels:

Strategic level

This is the monitoring of risks affecting the organisation as a whole. For example, threats such as new competitors and new technologies must be identified on a timely basis and the risk management strategy updated to reflect these changes.

Lack of monitoring at best will result in the organisation starting to fall behind competitors in terms of functionality or design of products. At worst, lack of monitoring may threaten the ongoing existence of the organisation as the organisation may find that its products are no longer saleable e.g. due to technological obsolescence.

Tactical level

This is monitoring of risks which affect tactical managers. Risks in this category may affect individual divisions or units of the organisation, or individual departments depending on how the organisation is structured.

For a divisional structure, lack of monitoring may affect continuity of supply or availability of distribution channels. Not recognising that a supplier is in liquidation will result in delay in obtaining alternative sources of material.

Risks at this level also include the resignation of key staff which may result in key processes not being completed, e.g. customers invoiced for goods received. Staff motivation should be monitored to give early warning of staff leaving.

Operational level

Monitoring of risks at the operational level includes the basic day-to-day running of the organisation. Lack of monitoring is unlikely to be a specific threat to the organisation initially, but continued errors or risks will add to reputation risk over time. For example, lack of specific items to sell because sales patterns have not been monitored will result in customers choosing alternatives, or moving to other suppliers in the short-term. However, continued lack of key goods will increase customer dissatisfaction potentially resulting in significant and ongoing decreases in sales.

(b) **Risks affecting BTS Company**

Risks that the BTS company should be aware of include:

Strategic – IT failure

The company is heavily dependent on its IT systems. Failure in this area would mean that the company cannot sell its products via the website, or indeed process orders or make payments to suppliers.

To mitigate this risk, BTS needs to ensure that mirrored servers are available (so if one breaks then the second server starts processing immediately from exactly the same place) There is also the need to ensure that appropriate disaster planning and backup facilities are implemented.

Strategic – distribution systems

BTS is also heavily dependent on the reliability of its distribution system to maintain customer confidence in the company. Given the increasing number of customer complaints, it appears that confidence in the FastCour firm is decreasing. However, at present there is no evaluation of alternative couriers or systems to use.

To mitigate this risk, the board should investigate alternative delivery solutions e.g. use of a different courier firm or even purchase of their own vans for delivery. If the service from the existing couriers continues to fall then switching delivery methods should be seriously considered.

Tactical – key staff

Production of chairs and sofas is under the supervision of two key members of staff, Mr. Smith and Mr Jones. While it is essential to have skilled members of staff available to maintain production efficiently, there is the risk that one or both of these staff members could leave the company. If this happens the ability of BTS to continue production at current levels could be jeopardised.

To mitigate this risk, the knowledge of the production controllers should be codified into a production manual which means it will be possible for another staff member to take over production duties. Mr. Jones and Mr. Smith must be made aware that this step is being taken, not because they are not trusted, but simply so BTS has a full record of all its activities.

Tactical – suppliers

BTS is very dependent on the Woody company for supply of wood for its products. However, the relationship with the supplier appears to be inappropriate – late payment and lack of warning regarding future orders means that Woody cannot plan supplies to assist BTS and may not be inclined to help anyway given the late payment. If Woody decide to stop supplying BTS then production would be adversely affected while a new wood supplier is located.

To mitigate this risk, BTS should attempt to enter into more of a partnership with Woody. Providing future wood requirements and paying on time would help Woody to look on BTS more favourably and help BTS guarantee supply of wood.

Operational – lack of fabric

Occasionally, BTS is unable to sell a specific chair or sofa because the customer's choice of fabric is unavailable. Lack of fabric is caused primarily by human error at BTS – the procurement manager forgets to re-order fabric. While lack of fabric on an occasional basis is not threatening for BTS, an increase in errors would mean loss of more orders which will start to affect sales significantly.

To mitigate this threat, BTS should either implement a computerised re-ordering system or possibly try and ensure that the procurement manager is trained in memory techniques or implements some other system to identify low fabric stock levels.

Tutorial note

It may have been easier to tackle part (b) by brainstorming all risks that you can find tin the scenario and then returning to classify them as strategic/tactical/operational. In some cases the distinction between the classifications is blurred – just ensure that you have examples of all types of risk for your answer.

63   SOUTHERN CONTINENTS COMPANY (DEC 07)

 Walk in the footsteps of a top tutor

Key answer tips

The first two parts of this question focus on risk management with the last part drawing on the governance area of the syllabus. Parts (a) and (c) consist of some theory and some application to the scenario. Part (b) requires careful reading of the requirement and a precise answer.

The highlighted words are key phrases that markers are looking for.

Tutor's top tips

Look at the requirements carefully and from these you can establish the headings for your plan, and also your answer. Every time you see the word 'and' you should consider introducing another heading into your answer structure.

Ensure that you are clear with the verb in the question, and what is required for that verb.

Tutor's top tips

Hopefully you will quickly be able to remember the four strategies for risk management required for the first section of part (a) – the TARA acronym can help you here.

In answering the second section of part (a) you are required to address the risks that are stated in the case. These are all to be found in the first paragraph of information. References to risks other than these would not earn marks.

The key to earning good marks in this section is to ensure that you provide clear reasons for the strategy that you have selected, since a number of possible strategies would be acceptable.

(a)   **Risks at Southland and management strategies**

Risk management strategies

There are four strategies for managing risk and these can be undertaken in sequence. In the first instance, the organisation should ask whether the risk, once recognised, can be transferred or avoided.

Transference means passing the risk on to another party which, in practice means an insurer or a business partner in another part of the supply chain (such as a supplier or a customer).

Avoidance means asking whether or not the organisation needs to engage in the activity or area in which the risk is incurred.

If it is decided that the risk cannot be transferred nor avoided, it might be asked whether or not something can be done to *reduce* or mitigate the risk. This might mean, for example, reducing the expected return in order to diversify the risk or re-engineer a process to bring about the reduction.

Risk sharing involves finding a party that is willing to enter into a partnership so that the risks of a venture might be spread between the two parties. For example an investor might be found to provide partial funding for an overseas investment in exchange for a share of the returns.

Finally, an organisation might *accept* or *retain* the risk, believing there to be no other feasible option. Such retention should be accepted when the risk characteristics are clearly known (the possible hazard, the probability of the risk materialising and the return expected as a consequence of bearing the risk).

Tutorial note

You are only required to give four strategies here, so you can keep to those that fit into the TARA acronym.

Risks in the case and strategy

There are three risks to the Southland factory described in the case.

Risk to the *security of the factory* in Southland. This risk could be transferred. The transference of this risk would be through insurance where an insurance company will assume the potential liability on payment, by SCC, of an appropriate insurance premium.

Risk to the *supply of one of the key raw materials* that experienced fluctuations in world supply. This risk will probably have to be accepted although it may be possible, with redesigning processes, to reduce the risk.

If the raw material is strategically important (i.e. its use cannot be substituted or reduced), risk acceptance will be the only possible strategy. If products or process can be redesigned to substitute or replace its use in the factory, the supply risk can be reduced.

The *environmental risk* that concerned a possibility of a poisonous emission can be reduced by appropriate environmental controls in the factory. This may require some process changes such as inventory storage or amendments to internal systems to ensure that the sources of emissions can be carefully monitored.

Tutorial note

The strategies for the individual risks identified in the case are not the only appropriate responses and other strategies are equally valid providing they are supported with adequate explanation.

Tutorial note

It is acceptable to recommend acceptance for risks that are minor or hard to control. In the case of the possibility of poisonous emissions a recommendation of acceptance would be inappropriate – the business would not be allowed to continue with a possibility of harm to nearby residents.

Tutor's top tips

If you are unsure how to tackle part (b), a good starting point would be to explain the terms used in the question, such as 'risk awareness', 'embedded' and 'culture'.

Do not write all that you know about how to embed risk awareness since this is not quite what the question is asking for – it requires you to explain what the idea of embedding risk awareness in culture actually means. You may wish to draw a brief comparison between embedding awareness in systems as opposed to culture as part of your answer.

(b)   **Embedded risk**

Risk awareness is the knowledge of the nature, hazards and probabilities of risk in given situations. Whilst management will typically be more aware than others in the organisation of many risks, it is important to embed awareness at all levels so as to reduce the costs of risk to an organisation and its members (which might be measured in financial or non-financial terms). In practical terms, embedding means introducing a taken-for-grantedness of risk awareness into the culture of an organisation and its internal systems. Culture, defined in Handy's terms as 'the way we do things round here' underpins all risk management activity as it defines attitudes, actions and beliefs.

The embedding of risk awareness into culture and systems involves introducing risk controls into the process of work and the environment in which it takes place. Risk awareness and risk mitigation become as much a part of a process as the process itself so that people assume such measures to be non-negotiable components of their work experience. In such organisational cultures, risk management is unquestioned, taken for granted, built into the corporate mission and culture and may be used as part of the reward system.

Tutorial note

Other meaningful definitions of culture in an organisational context are equally acceptable.

Tutor's top tips

Part (c) is in two sections, so make sure that you tackle both parts to earn your marks. The first requires a theoretical explanation of the benefits of performance-related pay, which allows you to look at the agency issues and alignment of objectives.

The second part contains the verb 'critically evaluate' which will require you to consider good and bad points about the package offered here. Ensure that your answer to this section refers to specifics from the scenario provided.

(c) **Choo Wang's remuneration package**

Benefits of PRP

In general terms, performance-related pay serves to align directors' and shareholders' interests in that the performance-related element can be made to reflect those things held to be important to shareholders (such as financial targets). This, in turn, serves to *motivate directors*, especially if they are directly responsible for a cost or revenue/profit budget or centre. The possibility of additional income serves to motivate directors towards higher performance and this, in turn, can assist in *recruitment and retention*. Finally, performance-related pay can increase the board's *control over strategic planning and implementation* by aligning rewards against strategic objectives.

Critical evaluation of Choo Wang's package

Choo Wang's package appears to have a number of advantages and shortcomings. It was *strategically correct to include some element* of pay linked specifically to Southland success. This will increase Choo's motivation to make it successful and indeed, he has said as much – he appears to be highly motivated and aware that additional income rests upon its success. Against these advantages, it appears that the performance-related component does not take account of, or *discount in any way for, the risk* of the Southland investment. The bonus does not become payable on a sliding scale but only on a single payout basis when the factory reaches an 'ambitious' level of output. Accordingly, Choo has more incentive to be accepting of risk with decisions on the Southland investment than risk averse. This may be what was planned, but such a bias should be pointed out. Clearly, the company should accept some risk but recklessness should be discouraged. In conclusion, Choo's *PRP package could have been better designed*, especially if the Southland investment is seen as strategically risky.

	Marking scheme		
			Marks
(a)	Risk strategies:		
	Half mark for identification of each strategy		Up to 2
	1 mark for each strategy explained (Four from the five listed strategies needed to get maximum marks)		Up to 4
	Risks in case: 2 marks for each risk identified from case with an appropriate strategy identified and explained		Up to 6
		Maximum	12
(b)	1 mark for each relevant point made on 'embedding'		Up to 4
	Up to 2 marks for recognition of the importance of culture in embedding risk		Up to 2
		Maximum	5
(c)	1 mark for each relevant point made on benefits of PRP		Up to 5
	1 mark for each relevant critical comment made on Choo's reward package		Up to 5
		Maximum	8
Total			**25**

Examiner's comments

Introduction

Question 2 was a 'risk' question with elements of executive pay introduced in part (c). The case concerned the risk committee at Southern Continents Company (SCC) considering the risks associated with a new manufacturing investment it had made.

The case identified three risks and **part (a)** asked candidates to describe four risk strategies and then to identify an appropriate strategy from those four for the management of each of the three risks. The first part of this was well done by most candidates by identifying and describing the four 'TARA' strategies of transference, avoidance, reduction and acceptance. The second part, which required candidates to apply the strategies to the risks in the case, was less well answered overall and should act as a reminder that application of answers to the case will often be an important source of marks in professional level papers.

Part (b) addressed material from study guide section D2b but seemed to catch many candidates by surprise. The point here was to explain that embedding risk involved establishing risk awareness and management in a company's culture, systems, procedures, protocols, reward and human resource systems, training, etc. To have risk embedded is similar to having quality embedded in that the tone is set at the top and is then supported throughout using the cultural and systemic architecture of the whole organisation. Some candidates sought to use this answer to make recommendations to SCC of how to manage its risk with phrases such as 'SCC should...' or 'perhaps SCC might consider'. Others interpreted the question to be asking what 'risk awareness' meant.

Both of these approaches were incorrect. The question as it was set was to explain what embedding risk in culture meant (and nothing else).

Part (c) was a departure from the risk theme in an otherwise risk-based question and should serve to remind candidates that the questions in section B of paper P1 will often not be entirely located within a single area of the study guide. It took a particular theme from the case and asked candidates to explain the benefit of performance related pay and then to critically evaluate the pay package awarded to Choo Wang, the chief executive of SCC. This question therefore had two parts (based on the 'rule of and'): one based on what candidates will have learned from the course materials and one in which they were required to apply the learning to the scenario. Most candidates could explain some of the benefits of performance related pay but fewer were able to pass comment on Mr Wang's reward package.

64 TASS *Online question assistance*

Key answer tips

A good knowledge of a risk management process is helpful in many questions in this area of the syllabus. Sometimes you will be asked to describe the overall process, as is the case here. Other questions will focus on just one stage of the process.

Embedding risk (as discussed in part (c)), in either systems or culture, is a popular section of exam questions in this paper.

(a) **Risk management process**

COSO provides an enterprise risk management process to accompany its framework for internal control. The organisation could adopt this in order to ensure risks have been adequately considered and strategy devised prior to embarking on its expansion programme.

The organisation needs to firstly ensure its *control environment* is geared up to the new challenges. This would include defining roles such as that of the risk manager and those who will spearhead the campaign. The company's internal culture with its track record of success ensures it is well placed to deal with the problems ahead and a robust ethical stance will allow it to deal with the inevitable issues arising from interaction with local government and other stakeholders.

Formalisation of corporate objectives including financial and market based goals provides a necessary benchmark for determining the scale and thrust of strategy as well as providing performance indicators of success. Objectives should be decomposed to a national and stores level and the accumulated through to the strategic level.

Event identification is a *risk categorisation* process built on experience in their home markets, reflection of problems experienced by competitors in the new markets and independent assessment by internal experts such as the risk manager and outside new market consultants. Some of the risks have been identified such as the risk of competitor action, supply chain concerns and customer acceptance.

Risk assessment is a formal process of determining the strength, scope and depth of these risks. It might be the case that covert corruption has been overstated or that simple measures can negate these issues. It might be the case that existing home market quality control systems can be exported and used without undue cost escalation in the new markets.

Risk response relates to the determination of broad strategies in order to deal with risks. The TARA framework could be used to identify which risks can be transferred such as asking suppliers to take on logistical concerns, which can be avoided in terms of countries or regions, which can be reduced through control systems and which should be simply be accepted as part of any globalisation strategy. The latter may relate to the CEO's viewpoint that accepts a level of risk as part of the need to sustain or improve profitability. It is likely that shareholders will feel the same way.

Risk management moves from risk awareness through to the implementation of strategy. Control activities need to be hierarchically developed in order to reduce risks and ensure success. This means assigning responsibility at the strategic and operational level and developing systems both to execute operations and monitor their success. Quality control has been singled out as one such area for consideration.

Information and communication systems must be developed in order to deal with the geography of the venture. Technology allows a virtual presence in the new markets for executive and the development of management information systems to monitor performance. Investment will be large and project controls necessary to ensure success.

Monitoring the execution of strategy is through these information systems. It also relates to the role of internal auditors and risk auditors in formally evaluating the quality of system used and the level of control exacted over each new venture. Monitoring and reporting are essential to reduce risk by retaining control.

A final step might be one of *evaluation, reflection and adaptation*. This adaptation could include the rolling out of successful market development further into new markets allowing the company to rapidly gain a foot hold on different continents.

Tutorial note

A suitable alternative risk management process would have been to discuss the four stages of: risk identification, risk assessment, risk planning and risk monitoring.

(b)   **Role of a risk auditor**

The role of the risk auditor depends upon the existence of other risk related structures within the company. An organisation of this size will have a substantial finance function including internal auditors. This being the case the role of the risk auditor becomes more specialised and targeted.

If internal auditors are concerned with the back end of the risk management process in terms of monitoring the degree to which control systems are working effectively then the risk manager will concern herself with definition of risks and the development of systems and strategies to deal with those risk.

All of the stages relating to risk management shown above except possibly the monitoring process will therefore become the remit of the risk auditor. Her views in the scenario suggest that she has been active in risk identification and risk assessment although not so forthcoming in terms of risk strategies or solutions.

This definition of the role is only one interpretation of risk auditing. A separate view would be to liken the role to that of a risk manager. This would involve the risk identification, assessment and strategy determination issues as already identified.

It would also suggest a more senior role, possibly in a direct reporting line from internal auditors so as to cover all aspects of risk. This however seems unlikely.

A risk auditor is most likely to be a specialist internal auditor focused on monitoring compliance to detailed standards set by outside bodies. These would include ISO standards such as ISO9001 on quality management certification and ISO14001 on environmental management certification. Auditing and ensuring the maintenance of certification would form the main focus for their work.

Other standards might relate to health and safety, fire prevention or business ethics code maintenance. The concept of a risk auditor is flexible enough to involve anyone or all of these interpretations.

Risk audit is more commonly associated with the finance sector and banking where risk auditors consider the company's exposure to financial risk in the financial instruments it sells and uses. Hedging and portfolio management would be part of the work although this seems less of an issue for this retailer. The finance function would need to be quite sophisticated and diverse to warrant such a role in this capacity although it is not out of the question.

(c) **Embedding risk**

Turnbull and others talk of risk needing to be embedded in culture and embedded in systems. The latter relates to the need to take a proactive approach to risk management ensuring their threat is minimised within operations itself rather than relying on a reactive monitoring process that fails to deal with the threat materialising, rather seeking to understating why it has occurred and reduce its likelihood in the future.

Embedding risk in systems therefore relates to the design of systems, inclusive of the design of control systems but predominantly the design of the system used in the delivery of value adding services. Technology is often associated with this concept since the higher the level of automation the lower the level of human involvement and, arguably, the lower the likelihood of mistakes being made.

Embedding risk into systems in this organisation would include the need to develop sophisticated supply chain delivery and monitoring systems such as quality control, product production scheduling, transportation, refrigeration and warehousing systems. The scope of such an approach is as diverse as operations and the investment will be considerable. It is generally true that the quality of risk reduction is only as good as the weakest link in the value adding chain and so a comprehensive approach must be guaranteed.

65   YGT (JUN 11)

Key answer tips

A question included to examine new study guide material over four parts.

Part (a) needed awareness that risks are dynamic and subject to environmental change and an ability to criticise beliefs.

Part (b) straightforward application of the TARA matrix

Part (c) required an application of related and, in particular, "positive" related risk and how risks can rise and fall together.

Part (d) required careful though and the examiner comments reflected that candidates did not do well. The use of the verbs "explain" and "assess" are often underestimated by candidates.

(a)   **Criticise and explanation of dynamic**

Criticise Raz Dutta's beliefs

Raz Dutta is wrong in both of her assertions. The belief that risks do not change very much is only true in static environments. In reality, the changeability of risks depends upon the organisation's place on a continuum between highly dynamic and completely static. The case mentions changes in some of YGT's risks and this suggests that there is some dynamism in its environment. Clearly then, her belief is very difficult to defend.

Her belief that risks 'hardly ever' materialise may be historically true (but this is also unlikely) but the risk assessment highlighted at least two 'likely' risks which could well materialise. Risk D was assessed as 'highly likely' and Risk B was also likely with a high potential impact. Neither of these variables would be known were it not for intelligence gained as part of the risk assessment. Importantly, Risk B was a 'high/high' risk meaning that it is a likely risk with a high impact once it materialised. Being unaware of this could have caused great damage to the organisation.

Why risk assessment is dynamic

Risk assessment is a dynamic management activity because of changes in the organisational environment and because of changes in the activities and operations of the organisation which interact with that environment. At YGT, the case describes Risk C as arising from a change in the activity of the company: a new product launch. The new product has obviously introduced a new risk that was not present prior to the new product. It may be a potential liability from the use of the product or a potential loss from the materials used in its production, for example.

Changes in the environment might include changes in any of the PEST (political, economic, social, technological) or any industry level change such as a change in the competitive behaviour of suppliers, buyers or competitors. In either case, new risks can be introduced, existing ones can become more likely or have a higher impact, or the opposite (they may disappear or become less important). The case describes Risk D as arising from a change in legislation which is a change in the external environment.

(b)   **TARA**

The strategies for each risk assessment are as follows:

Risk A is accept. This means that the likelihood is low and the impact is low such that even if the risk materialised, it would not have a high severity. The case says that the activity giving rise to Risk A is capable of making good returns so given that both likelihood and severity are low, there is no obvious reason to pursue any of the other strategies with regard to this risk.

Risk B is avoid. When the likelihood and impact are high, it would be irrational to accept the risk and so the risk should be avoided. This may involve changing behaviour or discontinuing a certain activity. The case says that the activity giving rise to Risk B is capable of making good returns, but importantly, it is not strategically vital. Given this, and because the case information does not mention the possibility of viably transferring the risk, there is no reason to bear the risk unless the potential return is very large and the company has a high risk appetite.

Risk C is transfer. YGT says that the activity giving rise to the risk must not be discontinued (so avoidance is not an option) and specifies that it can be transferred ('alternative arrangements for bearing the risks are possible'). To transfer risk is to share it with another party. The most common way to do this is to insure against losses or to outsource or licence the activity to a third party thereby transferring that risk to that third party.

Risk D is reduce. The case emphasises that the risk cannot be transferred (by insurance or outsourcing) but that the activity that gives rise to the risk can be reduced. Reduction involves reducing the risk exposure by carrying out the activity in a different way, doing less of the activity that gives rise to the risk or adopting behaviour that, whilst still exposing the company to the risk, results in a lower impact if the risk is realised.

(c)   **Related and correlated**

Related risks are risks that vary because of the presence of another risk. This means they do not exist independently and they are likely to rise and fall in importance along with the related one. Risk correlation is a particular example of related risk.

Risks are positively correlated if the two risks are positively related in that one will fall with the reduction of the other and increase with the rise of the other. They would be negatively correlated if one rose as the other fell. In the case of environmental risks and reputation risk, they may be positively correlated for the following reasons.

Environmental risks involve exposure to losses arising from an organisation's consumption of resources or impacts through its emissions. Where an environmental risk affects a sensitive situation, (be it human, flora, fauna or other), this can cause negative publicity which can result in reputation damage. These two risks can have a shared cause, i.e. they can arise together and fall together because they depend upon the same activity. They are considered separate risks because losses can be incurred by either of both of the impacts (environmental or reputational).

Activities designed to reduce environmental risk, such as acquiring resources from less environmentally-sensitive sources or through the fitting of emission controls, will reduce the likelihood of the environmental risk being realised. This, in turn, will reduce the likelihood of the reputation risk being incurred. The opposite will also hold true: a reduction of attention to environmental risk will increase the likelihood of reputation loss.

(d) **Risk awareness**

Explanation

Risk awareness is *a capability of an organisation* to be able to recognise risks when they arise, from whatever source they may come. A culture of risk awareness suggests that this capability (or competence) is present throughout the organisation and is woven into the *normal routines, rituals, ways of thinking and is taken-for-granted* in all parts of the company and in all employees.

Assessment

Risks can arise in any part of the organisation and at any level. Not all risks are at the strategic level and can be captured by a risk assessment. A culture of risk awareness will help ensure that all employees are capable of identifying risks as and when they arise.

Risks are dynamic and rise and fall with changes in the business environment and with changes in the company's activities. With changes to the company's risk profile occurring all the time, it cannot be assumed that the risks present at the most recent risk assessment will remain the same. Being prepared to adapt to changes is a key advantage of a culture of risk awareness.

A lack of risk awareness is often *evidence of a lack of risk management strategy* in the organisation. This, in turn, can be dangerous as the company could be more exposed to risk than it need be because of the lack of attentiveness by staff. A lack of effectiveness of risk management strategy leaves the company vulnerable to unrecognised or wrongly assessed risks.

Tutorial note

Be careful with part d). The examiner uses the combination of "explain and assess" a lot. It tests the ability of a candidate to make a fact clear and then say how important it may be – all set in the context of the scenario. Question practice to prepare for this sort of requirement is important.

Examiner's comments

This question was mainly about risk. I used the question to examine some of the new study guide content on risk, namely the dynamic nature of risk and the idea of related risk. I cited six unspecified risks faced by YGT company and used letters A to F to identify them. Parts (a) and (c) were done quite well on the whole and parts (b) and (d) were very variable.

There were two tasks in part (a): to criticise Raz Dutta's beliefs (that risks 'didn't change much' and 'hardly ever materialised') and to explain why risks were dynamic. This question referred to new study guide section C1c and which I explained in the technical article I wrote on these study guide changes in May 2010. Many candidates were able to discuss the notion of risks arising as an organisation's environment changes but fewer were able to gain the 'criticise' marks which, in my view, were actually quite straightforward to get (see the published answer on the ACCA website).

Part (c) also drew on new study guide content: section C3h on related and correlated risk. I was pleased to see many candidates gaining the marks for explaining related risks, and many were also able to describe how risk E, an environmental risk, was positively correlated with risk F, a reputation risk. The point here was that in some cases, increased environmental losses can result in deterioration of a company's reputation (i.e. a rise in reputation risk) and because both risks rise and fall together, they can be said to be positively correlated as opposed to negatively correlated.

ACCA marking scheme		
		Marks
(a)	2 marks for each evaluation point made to a maximum of 4 marks 2 marks for each point identified and explained on dynamic to a maximum of 4 marks.	
	Total	8
(b)	Half mark for correct strategy selection for each risk. 1 mark for each risk strategy correctly explained and justified.	
	Total	6
(c)	2 marks for explanation of related and correlated risks. 2 marks for each description of why correlated to a maximum of 4 marks.	
	Total	5
(d)	2 marks for explanation. 2 marks for each relevant point for assessment.	
	Total	6
Total		**25**

Tutorial note

Other valid points regarding organisational size and risk strategy would be awarded marks. There is no definitive answer to this area, just various suggestions of the link between the factors.

---

66 DOCTORS' PRACTICE

Key answer tips

Part (a) implies that the risks require little explanation, the requirement word is identify, which is a low level requirement. An approach to this requirement would be to simply identify all the factors you can think of that would change and potentially create new risks as a result of the new facility.

In your answer to part (b) it is necessary to discuss embedding risk in both the systems and the culture of the organisation. Making this distinction will give you more to discuss in your answer, and hence it will be easier to gain high marks.

(a) **Business risk**

Business risk relates to the activities carried out within an organisation, including business interruption, errors or omissions by employees, loss of key staff, etc. In the context of the doctors' practice, business risks include:

- Loss of key staff; with only eight staff, one or two partners leaving may mean the surgery will have insufficient staff to operate.
- Lack of drugs for the new surgery due to loss of suppliers or delays in supply.
- Blood and samples being lost in transfer to the local hospital prior to testing.

Financial risk

Financial risk relates to the financial operation of the business, including credit risk through to interest rate and cash flow risk. In the context of the doctors' practice, financial risks include:

- Insufficient cash resources to pay for the new surgery.
- Practice income not increasing by the estimated 20% leading to cash flow problems after the surgery is operational.
- Increasing interest rates on loans taken out to pay for the surgery which are unforeseen or not sufficiently well hedged.

Environmental risk

Environmental risk relates to changes in the political, economic, social and financial environment within which the company operates. In the context of the doctors' practice, environmental risks include:

- Changes in legislation making the operation of a local surgery illegal – all surgery to be carried out in local hospitals.
- Other doctors' practices opening their own surgeries, taking customers away from this practice.
- Outbreaks of new diseases (e.g. bird flu) which the surgery has insufficient inventories of drugs to treat.

Reputation risk

Reputation risk is caused by the organisation failing to address some other risk. In the context of the doctors' practice, this could be a result of:

- The surgery providing poor or ineffective treatment due to lack of staff training.
- Doctors giving incorrect advice because blood samples were not tested correctly or results were mixed up between different patients.
- Doctors issuing prescriptions with incorrect dosage.
- Drugs becoming contaminated due to poor storage conditions.

Tutorial note

It is critical that you only discuss risks that are additional as a result of the new facility – risks inherent to a doctors' practice will not be rewarded.

It is not essential to classify your risks under headings, as has been done in this answer – marks will be rewarded for the risks themselves, not the categories.

(b) Embedding risk management is the process of ensuring that risk management becomes an integral part of the systems and culture of the organisation. In this way, risk management is no longer seen as a separate activity but part of the way in which the organisation does business.

Embedding risk in control systems

The aim of embedding risk management in the control systems of the organisation is to ensure that the processes required for risk management are incorporated in the everyday activities of the business. For example, in response to the risk of prescribing an incorrect dosage, a system could be put in place replacing all handwritten prescriptions and generating prescriptions from a computer system which only allows a selection of predefined dosages for a particular drug.

The process of embedding risk management within an organisation's systems and procedures involves:

- Identifying the controls that are already operating within the organisation.
- Identifying the controls required for risk management.
- Monitoring those controls to ensure that they work.
- Improving and refining the controls as required in order to incorporate risk management activities.
- Document evidence of monitoring and control operations.

In addition, the system needs to be:

- supported by the board and communicated to all managers and employees within the organisation
- supported by experts in risk management
- incorporated into the whole organisation, i.e. not part of a separate department seen as 'responsible' for risk

---

- linked to strategic and operational objectives
- supported by existing processes such as strategy reviews
- planning and budgeting, e.g. again not seen as an entirely separate process
- supported by existing committees, e.g. audit committee and board meetings rather than simply the remit of one 'risk management' committee
- given sufficient time by management to provide reports to the board.

Embedding risk in the culture of the organisation

Even if risk management controls are incorporated in the systems and activities of the organisation, risk management may still not be effective unless staff at all levels in the business recognise its importance and the need to carry out the activities required of them. This demands that risk management is embedded in the culture and values of the organisation so that it is seen as 'normal' for the organisation.

The first prerequisite for this is a high level of risk awareness. This means an understanding by all staff of the importance of risk and risk management, the way risks impact on the all aspects of the business and in particular on their department and activities, and their role in the management of risks faced by the organisation. It is essential for effective identification, assessment and monitoring of risks. A high level of risk awareness ensures that:

- All staff understand the risk management policy and processes and take responsibility for the management of risk in their particular area.
- Staff are able to identify risks, particularly at the operational level which senior managers are not aware of.
- The organisation identifies, assesses and monitors risks effectively across all functions and at all levels, strategic, technical and operational.
- The recognition and management of risk becomes part of the culture and everyday activities of the business.

Various cultural factors will affect the extent to which risk management can be embedded into an organisation:

- whether the culture is open or closed
- the overall commitment to risk management policies at all levels in the organisation
- the attitude to internal controls
- governance.

There are various methods of including risk management in culture, some of which also form part of the process of embedding risk in the systems:

- aligning individual goals with those of the organisation
- including risk management responsibilities within job descriptions
- establishing reward systems that recognise that risks have to be taken in practice
- establishing metrics and performance indicators
- publishing success stories.

PROFESSIONAL VALUES AND ETHICS

67 VAN BUREN (JUN 08)

Key answer tips

This question mixes the area of internal review with that of ethics, in both a theoretical sense (part (c)) and practical sense (part (b)). Part (a) should be largely revision from previous studies on F8.

Part (b) requires careful application of knowledge to this scenario. In deriving duties of an employee it is helpful to think of what your own employer expects of you. You will need to be precise and specific in your description of the ethical tensions to earn the full marks available here.

Knowledge of the theories of ethics is key to part (c) though you will still need to apply them in the given situation. Structuring your answer keeping each part of the question separate will produce a more professional result.

The highlighted words are key phrases that markers are looking for.

(a) **Importance of independence**

The auditor must be materially independent of the client for the following reasons:

To increase credibility and to underpin confidence in the process. In an external audit, this will primarily be for the benefit of the shareholders and in an internal audit, it will often be for the audit committee that is, in turn, the recipient of the internal audit report.

To ensure the reliability of the audit report. Any evidence of lack of independence (or 'capture') has the potential to undermine all or part of the audit report thus rendering the exercise flawed.

To ensure the effectiveness of the investigation of the process being audited. An audit, by definition, is only effective as a means of interrogation if the parties are independent of each other.

Three threats to independence

There are three threats to independence described in the case.

The same audit partner (Zachary) was assigned to Van Buren in eight consecutive years. This is an association threat and is a contravention of some corporate governance codes. Both Sarbanes-Oxley and the Smith Guidance (contained in the UK Corporate Governance Code), for example, specify auditor rotation to avoid association threat.

Fillmore Pierce provides more than one service to the same client. One of the threats to independence identified between Arthur Andersen and Enron after the Enron collapse was an over-dependence on Enron by Andersen arising from the provision of several services to the same client. Good practice is not to offer additional services to audit clients to avoid the appearance of compromised independence. Some corporate governance codes formally prohibit this.

The audit partner (Zachary) is an old friend of the financial director of Van Buren (Frank). This 'familiarity' threat should be declared to Fillmore Pierce at the outset and it may disqualify Zachary from acting as audit partner on the Van Buren account.

(b) (i) **Contrasting roles**

Joint professional and organisational roles are common to most professionals (medical professionals, for example). Although the roles are rarely in conflict, in most cases it is assumed that any professional's primary duty is to the public interest rather than the organisation.

Organisational role

As a member of the staff of Fillmore Pierce, Anne is a part of the hierarchy of an organisation and answerable to her seniors. This means that under normal circumstances, she should comply with the requirements of her seniors. As an employee, Anne is ultimately accountable to the principals of the organisation (the partners in an audit firm or the shareholders in a company), and, she is subject to the cultural norms and reasonable expectations of work-group membership. It is expected that her behaviour at work will conform to the social and cultural norms of the organisation and that she will be efficient and hard working in her job.

Professional role

As an accountant, Anne is obliged to maintain the high professional and ethical standards of her profession. If her profession is underpinned by an ethical or professional code, she will need to comply with that in full. She needs to manage herself and co-ordinate her activities so as to meet professional standards. In this, she needs to ensure that she informs herself in current developments in her field and undertakes continuing professional development as required by her professional accounting body. She is and will remain accountable to her professional body in terms of continued registration and professional behaviour. In many cases, this accountability will be more important than an accountability to a given employer as it is the membership of the professional body that validates Anne's professional skills.

Tutorial note

The requirement to 'compare and contrast' means to draw out similarities and differences between the two roles.

The answer can be structured under the headings 'similarities' and 'differences' or can be tackled as above under the headings of the two roles. If you went for the above approach it is essential that you discuss the actual similarities and differences, rather than simply describing the roles.

(ii)   **Tensions in roles**

On one hand, Anne needs to cultivate and manage her relationship with her manager (Zachary) who seems convinced that Van Buren, and Frank in particular, are incapable of bad practice. He shows evidence of poor judgment and compromised independence. Anne must decide how to deal with Zachary's poor judgment.

On the other hand, Anne has a duty to both the public interest and the shareholders of Van Buren to ensure that the accounts do contain a 'true and fair view'. Under a materiality test, she may ultimately decide that the payment in question need not hold up the audit signoff but the poor client explanation (from Frank) is also a matter of concern to Anne as a professional accountant.

(c)   **Absolutism and relativism**

Absolutism and relativism represent two extreme positions of ethical assumptions.

Definitions

An absolutist assumption is one that believes that there are 'eternal' rules that should guide all ethical and moral decision making in all situations. Accordingly, in any given situation, there is likely to be one right course of action regardless of the outcome. An absolutist believes that this should be chosen regardless of the consequences or the cost. A dogmatic approach to morality is an example of an absolutist approach to ethics. A dogmatic assumption is one that is accepted without discussion or debate.

Relativist assumptions are 'situational' in nature. Rather than arguing that there is a single right choice, a relativist will tend to adopt a pragmatic approach and decide, in the light of the situation being considered, which is the best outcome. This will involve a decision on what outcome is the most favourable and that is a matter of personal judgment.

Outcomes

If Anne were to adopt absolutist/dogmatic assumptions, she would be likely to decide that she would need to pursue what she perceives is the right course of action regardless of cost to herself or the relationship with the client or her manager. Given that she unearthed a suspect and unaccounted-for payment, and that she received an inadequate explanation from the client, she would probably recommend extension to the audit beyond the weekend.

If Ann were to adopt relativist or pragmatic assumptions, she would have a potentially much more complicated decision to make. She would have to decide whether it was more important, ethically, to yield to the pressure from Zachary in the interests of her short-term career interests or 'hold out' to protect the interests of the shareholders. Anne could recommend sign off and trust the FD's explanation but she is more likely to seek further evidence or assurance from the company before she does so.

		Marking scheme	*Marks*
(a)		1 mark for each relevant point on importance of independence made and briefly described. Half mark for mention only	Up to 3
		1 mark for each threat to independence identified	Up to 3
		1 mark for each threat briefly described	Up to 3
		Maximum	9
(b)	(i)	1 mark for each organisational duty identified and briefly described	Up to 3
		1 mark for each professional duty identified and briefly described	Up to 3
		1 mark for each contrast or comparison drawn	Up to 2
		Maximum	6
	(ii)	1 mark for each point made on inclination towards role as employee	Up to 2
		1 mark for each point made on inclination towards professional duty	Up to 2
		Maximum	4
(c)		4 marks for evidence of understanding the two positions (whether as a definition or in other parts of the answer)	4
		2 marks for explanation of how the positions affect the outcome	2
		Cross marks between these two to reflect adequacy of overall answer	
		Maximum	6
Total			25

Examiner's comments

Introduction

This was a popular question for candidates. It concerned an ethical dilemma facing a recently qualified accountant.

Part (a) asked candidates to explain the importance of auditor independence and then, using information from the case, to describe three threats to independence in the case. This task is a good example of the way that paper P1 links back to previous papers in the ACCA examination scheme, particularly F8. This task was performed well by many candidates.

Part (b) explored two themes related to professionalism and professional ethics. In the case, the recently qualified accountant faced a potential dilemma because both the client and her superior were putting pressure on her to ignore or overlook an irregular payment. Part (i) of part (b) was done reasonably well by many candidates but part (ii), which required candidates to explain the ethical tensions, was less well done.

All professionals, including professional accountants, face situations with ethical elements to them. Even when the decision has a regulatory or legal underpinning, as was the situation in the case, the professional still faces a choice to uphold the standards of the profession or to 'bend the rules' in the interests of an easier life in the short term. This was the nature of the ethical choice in this case.

Part (c) was challenging for some candidates. The terms absolutist/dogmatic and relativist/pragmatic are specifically highlighted in the study guide (section E1a) and so well-prepared candidates were fully aware of what the terms meant. In keeping with the nature of P1 questions, candidates were required to use and apply the theory rather than just repeat it. This is an important thing to note: candidates may be awarded some marks for explaining a theory but they will more often be expected to apply it to a case in some way (as in this case). Many candidates correctly recognised the links between absolutism and deontology and also between relativism and consequentialism.

68   DUNDAS (DEC 09)

Key answer tips

This is a very application-based question, needing you to grasp the fundamental 'issues' in the scenario. Parts (b) and (c) need careful consideration of the scenario.

However part (a) is a fairly straightforward five marks.

(a)   **Integrity**

The IFAC code of ethics (2005) s.110.1 explains integrity as follows:

Tutorial note

'Integrity' is one of the five ACCA fundamental principles and also one of the nine key concepts underpinning corporate Governance. It is therefore essential you can define it.

The principle of integrity imposes an obligation on all professional accountants to be straightforward and honest in professional and business relationships. Integrity also implies fair dealing and truthfulness.

Integrity is therefore a steadfast adherence to strict ethical standards despite any other pressures to act otherwise. Integrity describes the personal ethical position of the highest standards of professionalism and probity. It is an underlying and underpinning principle of corporate governance and it is required that all those representing shareholder interests in agency relationships both possess and exercise absolute integrity at all times.

In terms of professional relationships, integrity is important for the following reasons:

It provides assurance to colleagues of good intentions and truthfulness. It goes beyond any codes of professional behaviour and describes a set of character traits that mean a person of integrity can be trusted. For auditors such as Potto Sinter, integrity means not only observing the highest standards of professional behaviour but also maintaining the appearance of integrity to his own staff and also to the client.

It reduces time and energy spent in monitoring when integrity and openness can be assumed (the opposite of an audit situation where the professional scepticism should be exercised). Costs will be incurred by Miller Dundas if colleagues feel that Potto Sinter is untrustworthy.

It cultivates good working relationships in professional situations. It encourages a culture of mutual support that can have a beneficial effect on organisational effectiveness. John Wang's professional relationship with Potto is very important to Miller Dundas. It is important, therefore, that Potto has personal integrity.

Tutorial note

Other professional relationships may also be discussed.

(b) **Criticise Potto Sinter's ethical and professional behaviour**

The first criticism of Potto's behaviour in the case is that it gives rise to the *appearance of unprofessionalism and possibly of corruption.* $100,000 is a substantial amount but notwithstanding the amount, the allocation of company funds on what appears to be a home improvement on a director's house should be robustly challenged. It is possible that Potto is acting without integrity in this matter.

Potto's failure to act on the information strongly suggests that he has *failed in his duty to other shareholders of Mbabo and to tax and other state authorities.* The audit is for the benefit of several parties including shareholders and government/tax authorities and it is therefore vital that the information signed off is fairly presented ('true and fair' in the UK). Being fairly presented is normally evidenced by following all accounting standards. Other shareholders might be very intrigued to know why one director, even though a shareholder himself, has used company funds for his own private purposes.

The comment on the clearance document appears to be evidence that Potto *accepted a weak explanation from Mr Mbabo* or was prepared not to put any pressure on Mr Mbabo for other reasons (perhaps for reasons of an ethical threat such as familiarity, intimidation or self-interest threat or similar). Potto gave the appearance of a lack of objectivity in his actions, possibly as a result of the threats to independence. Auditors should be objective at all times.

Potto *failed to satisfy the queries of, and to work well alongside, other important members of the audit team.* Being able to be a leader of, and a member of, a team of people is an important part of professional behaviour and Potto's summary dismissal of Lisa's question after the sign-off was unprofessional and unhelpful.

As a senior member of the firm, Potto set a *poor example to junior colleagues*, such as Lisa, in his behaviour. Not only did he show evidence of poor audit practice but he also failed to satisfy Lisa's entirely justified curiosity over the matter.

Potto is complicit in a probable *breach of IAS 24/FRS 8 on related party transactions*. There is a disclosure requirement of all related party transactions regardless of value, and concealment of this is both unprofessional and technically irregular. Lack of disclosure should have led to a qualified opinion, a disagreement, on the audit report.

Tutorial note

Some candidates may refer to IAS 24/FRS 8 on related party transactions.

Candidates may refer to a disagreement leading to a qualified opinion on the audit report. It is possible to get full marks on this part without referring to IAS 24/FRS 8 but reward appropriate reference up to 2 marks.

Knowledge of IAS 24/FRS 8 is not necessary but is allowable.

(c)   **John Wang's ethical dilemma**

John Wang may attempt to resolve his ethical dilemma in the following two ways. The two alternatives are:

To *confront Potto* directly to see if the matter can be resolved in a professional manner between themselves. If Potto doesn't respond to this, John should take the matter higher up the organisation. John would be *complying with the professional behavioural standards* set out in the ACCA code of ethics and elsewhere, and, indirectly, insisting that Potto does the same.

To *take no further action and 'let it drop'*. He would decide that the information provided by Lisa should not go any further and that any knowledge he had gained from her and her achievement log should be kept confidential.

The evaluation should make reference to the following four issues that may be used to argue in either direction.

All professional accountants are required to *comply in detail with the highest professional and ethical standards*. In addition to the ACCA and other professional codes of ethics, most audit decisions are underpinned by regulation and, in some cases, legislation. There are also issues relating to quality control within Miller Dundas that need to be adhered to as best professional practice.

John Wang's *leadership position in his role as training manager, partner and professional accountant*. His decision would be an important signal to Lisa over the acceptability of Potto's behaviour in a professional situation and the importance placed on the complaints of junior staff such as herself.

Assuming that John recognised the non-compliance issue, this would also be a form of professional negligence on his part to ignore it.

His *confronting Potto would probably compromise their friendship and future professional relationship*. It may also have an impact on John's future career at Miller Dundas. These factors may conflict, in John's mind, with his duty of objectivity. It is important to develop harmonious relationships in professional situations as far as possible as they can be of benefit to both people involved and to the organisation itself but never at the expense of professional objectivity. Whistleblowers, whether internal or external, rarely have a stress free experience and John could possibly expect a certain amount of personal stress if he were to report Potto.

There is an issue over *how determined Lisa Xu is to take the matter further*. To confront Potto would *mitigate any risk that Lisa might take it further and compromise both Potto and John*. Lisa could, for example, approach the managing partner or even an outside body and implicate John as well as Potto: Potto for the unprofessional behaviour and John Wang for knowing about it but doing nothing.

Although there are two theoretical alternatives in this dilemma, John's required course of action is clear. He should confront Potto with the allegation and then pursue whatever course of action may ensue to satisfactorily resolve the situation.

Tutorial note

The pros and cons of each option can be used in evaluating either option depending on how the candidate approaches the question. Allow consultation with a third party, such as a professional body, as an alternative.

Marking scheme		Marks
(a)	2 marks for explanation and meaning.	
	1 mark for each explanation of importance up to a maximum of 3 marks.	5
(b)	1 mark for each criticism identified in the context of the case.	
	1 mark for development of the criticism with reference to practice or application.	10
(c)	1 mark for recognition of each option.	
	2 marks for each relevant argument for or against either alternative.	10
Total		**25**

Examiner's comments

This was a question about an irregular transfer of company funds for private use which gave rise to an ethical dilemma for John Wang, the training manager of the company's auditor. It raised issues of professional relationships, the role of auditors, and personal loyalties and friendships. The transfer of $100,000 for a security system of a company manager's holiday home was highly irregular and the behaviour of Potto Sinter, the engagement partner was wrong in several respects.

Part (a) should have been relatively straightforward. It asked for an explanation of 'integrity' and then an explanation of its importance in professional relationships. In context, this referred to the professional relationships between the actors in the scenario although explanations concerning other professional relationships were also rewarded by markers. Most candidates that attempted this question were able to define integrity but fewer were able to apply that knowledge to the case. Accordingly, some did not gain the marks for applying integrity to professional relationships.

Parts (b) and (c) were less well done overall. Both employed level three verbs and required a careful analysis of the case. In part (b), candidates were invited to criticise Potto Sinter's ethical and professional behaviour.

There were, in fact, five clear ethical and professional 'issues' in the case attributed to Mr Sinter and it should have been straightforward for candidates to pick these out. When I use 'criticise' in a P1 question, such as in Q3(b), the challenge is to carefully scrutinise the case, identify the behaviour which is wrong or inappropriate, and to discuss why the behaviour is wrong. Of course in order to do this, it is necessary to know what right and wrong behaviour is, hence the need to understand before the application of knowledge can be made. In this case, it should have been straightforward to identify Mr Sinter's shortcomings. This question was not done well overall, perhaps because candidates felt too time-pressured to spend time reading the case in detail and yet this was necessary to answer the question correctly. Where case analysis is essential for gaining marks, it is better to invest time studying the case to the required level rather than writing a long but unfocussed answer that fails to address the question.

The same point can be made in respect of part (c). It was necessary to know what John Wang's alternatives were before they can be evaluated. A dilemma, by definition, is a choice between two options (in the same way that a trilemma would have three choices) so there were two main options to be considered. In recognising that some other options were theoretically possible (such as consulting a third party for advice), markers allowed some latitude in the options that candidates discussed. Confronting Potto Sinter with his ethical and professional failures was the correct option in context and it was disappointing to note that some candidates failed to recognise this.

69 HAPPY AND HEALTHY (JUN 10)

Key answer tips

This question was quite broad scope requiring discussion on topics ranging from insider structures to ethics.

(a) A fairly straightforward requirement to a well-prepared student explaining the difference between an insider and an outsider structure.

(b) Within this requirement there are five marks for being able to describe the ACCA five fundamental principles. Again a well-prepared student should have been able to gain these marks easily.

(c) Within this requirement a considered, logical approach was necessary. Application to the scenario was the key to success.

(a) **Difference**

A family or insider-dominated business is one in which the *controlling shareholding is held by a small number of dominant individuals.* In many cases, these individuals will also work for the business making them owner-managers. When the insiders belong to a nuclear or extended family it is common to refer to the business as a family firm. In a listed company, *the shares are dispersed between many shareholders, the shares are publicly traded* and managers are unlikely to be substantial shareholders themselves (although they may own shares as a part of their reward packages).

Explore the governance issues

The *agency issues* are quite different in the two types of business. There are usually lower agency costs associated with insider-dominated businesses owing to there being fewer agency trust issues. Less monitoring is usually necessary because the owners are often also the managers. Principals (majority shareholders) are able to directly impose own values and principles (business or ethical) directly on the business without the mediating effect of a board. In the case of 'Healthy and happy', Ken and Steffi have been the majority owners for all of its 40 years and as long as they trust each other, director monitoring costs should be very low. This is complicated by the new knowledge that there are trustworthiness questions over Ivan.

Short and long-term decision-making issues and the pursuit of motives other than short-term profits. A smaller base of shareholders is more likely to be flexible over when profits are realised and so the expectations of the rates and timings of returns are likely to be longer. This gives management more strategic flexibility especially if, as is the case at 'Happy and healthy' the purpose of the business is simply to leave it in a good state to pass on to Ivan when Ken and Steffi retire. Ken and Steffi are motivated by factors other than the pursuit of short-term profit, such as promotion of healthy food, good service to customers, etc.

'Gene pool' and succession issues are common issues in family businesses. It is common for a business to be started off by a committed and talented entrepreneur but then to hand it on to progeny who are less equipped or less willing to develop the business as the founder did. When the insiders are unwilling or unable to buy in outside management talent then this issue is highlighted. There are clearly doubts over Ivan's commitment to the business if he has started up a competing business with his wife and this may mean an unfortunate outcome for 'Happy and healthy'. In addition, there are important differences in the formality of nominations, appointments and rewards. In larger companies these matters are dealt with by a formal committee structure whereas they are likely to be more informal in family businesses.

'Feuds' and conflict resolution can be major governance issues in an insider-dominated business. Whereas a larger bureaucratic business is capable of 'professionalising' conflict (including staff departures and disciplinary actions) this is less likely to be the case in insider-dominated businesses. Family relationships can suffer and this can intensify stress and ultimately lead to the deterioration of family relationships as well as business performance. Ivan's actions are likely to be relevant here as his transfer of inventory to Barong Company is likely to place a severe strain on the Potter family relationships.

Tutorial note

Allow for a range of relevant responses in the exploration of the idea of professionalism in society.

(b)   **Accountants as professionals**

Society accords professional status to those that both possess a high level of technical knowledge in a given area of expertise (accounting, engineering, law, dentistry, medicine) on the understanding that the expertise is used in the public interest. The body of knowledge is gained through passing examinations and gaining practical expertise over time. Acting in the public interest means that the professional always seeks to uphold the interests of society and the best interests of clients (subject to legal and ethical compliance).

Fundamental principles (responsibilities) as a professional

Society has reasonable expectations of all professionals. The major professional responsibilities of any professional are as follows:

Integrity. The highest levels of probity in all personal and professional dealings. Professionals should be straightforward and honest in all relationships. This has clear implications for Mr Shreeves in his dealings with Ken and Steffi.

Objectivity. Professionals should not allow bias, conflicts of interest or undue influence to cloud their judgements or professional decisions. In this case, Mr Shreeves should not allow his friendship with the Potters to affect his judgement as an auditor.

Professional competence and due care. Professionals have a duty to ensure that their skills and competences are continually being updated and developed to enable them to serve clients and the public interest. This includes continuing to study and scrutinise ethical guidance from Mr Shreeves's own professional accounting body and also IFAC.

Confidentiality. Professionals should, within normal legal constraints, respect the confidentiality of any information gained as a result of professional activity or entrusted to them by a client.

Professional behaviour. Professionals should comply fully with all relevant laws and regulations whilst at the same time avoiding anything that might discredit the profession or bring it into disrepute.

(c)   The normal behaviour for the auditor, regardless of the options available in this situation, would be to initially seek representations from Ivan to establish whether there is an explanation that has so far been overlooked or not known about. Following that, there are two options in Mr Shreeves's dilemma: to tell or not tell Ken and Steffi about Ivan's behaviour. In discussing these options, a number of issues are relevant.

Discussion of dilemma

Mr Shreeves is clearly in a difficult situation but he must be aware of his duty as a professional accountant which includes, in his role as auditor, a duty to the public interest

He has a *duty of due care and diligence* to society and government as well as the shareholders of a company being audited. Being complicit in Ivan's activity is clearly not an option as this would be incompatible with his duties to the shareholders and to society in his role as auditor. Furthermore, he has realised a disclosure of such transactions is required and it would be unprofessional not to discuss this with his clients.

He feels he owes a debt to the Potter family as a longstanding family friend and this has the potential to cloud his judgement as the company's auditor. The case says that the effect of Ken and Steffi finding out about Ivan's theft could be 'devastating' and this is bound to weigh heavily upon Mr Shreeves's mind. In getting too close to the family, Mr Shreeves has compromised his duty as auditor as he is probably less objective than he should be. He should probably have chosen between being a family friend or being the auditor some years ago and that would have made his resolution of the dilemma somewhat easier.

Ivan has been *unprofessional and has acted fraudulently* in his dealings with 'Happy and Healthy'. In such a situation, the auditor does not have latitude in how he or she deals with such a discovery. It is a very serious breach of trust by Ivan, regardless of whether he is the Potters' son or not, and it would be inexcusable to withhold this information from the owner-managers of the business.

Advise Mr Shreeves

Given that the auditor has a duty to the public interest and the company shareholders, he should *inform the majority shareholders (Ken and Steffi) what he has found during the audit.* To do anything other than this would be to act unprofessionally and irresponsibly towards the majority shareholders of the company. Family relationships or friendships must never be allowed to interfere with an auditor's professional duty and independence. This approach need not be in the form of a blunt confrontation, however, and it would *not be unprofessional to speak with Ivan before he spoke to his parents in order to convey to him the potential seriousness of his actions.*

Marking scheme		
		Marks
(a)	1 mark for each relevant point distinguishing between a family and listed business up to a maximum of 2 marks 2 marks for each relevant point of exploration identified and discussed up to a maximum of 8 marks	
	Maximum	10
(b)	1 mark per relevant point explained on accountants as professionals up to a maximum of 2 marks 1 mark for each relevant fundamental principle of professionalism described up to a maximum of 5. Half mark for mention only	
		7
(c)	2 marks for each relevant issue in the dilemma identified and discussed up to a maximum of 6 1 mark for each relevant point made of the 'advise' point up to a maximum of 2	
		8
Total		25

Examiner's comments

This question was on insider-dominated (family) businesses, professionalism and ethical behaviour. The case described a situation about a small but established family business, their auditor and the son of the couple whose business it was. There was evidence that the son, Ivan, had stolen inventory from his parents' business and the auditor, Mr Shreeves, had become aware of it.

Part (a) invited candidates to explain the differences between a family business and a public company. In particular, this was about governance. It drew on content that should have been familiar to candidates that had carefully studied the study texts and many candidates were able to gain some marks for this distinction.

There were two tasks in **part (b)**. The first was seemingly more challenging than the second. The second task was to describe the fundamental principles of professionalism and most well-prepared candidates were able to do this. Fewer were able to explain the position of professionals in society and the importance of the public interest to a professional like Mr Shreeves.

Part (c) was done poorly overall. As with Q2(c), this part required candidates to bring their ethical reasoning skills to bear on a problem. Mr Shreeves faced a dilemma on how to approach the issue of Ivan with Ken and Steffi Potter. There were a number of professional and ethical issues that were relevant to his decision and it was a discussion of these that was required. More detailed preparation for ethical reasoning tasks would have benefited candidates and this should represent a challenge to tutors and future P1 candidates.

70   PROFESSIONAL CODES OF ETHICS (PILOT 07)

Key answer tips

This pilot paper question was an indication of the topic areas the examiner was going to introduce into the Paper 1 exam in 2007. Here he signals his intention to ensure students learn:

- The importance of Professional ethics.

- The need to be able to apply the necessary depth of thought when asked to 'evaluate'.

- And to ensure that the deeper philosophical theory such as deontological are learnt.

(a)   **Professor Cheung's views on codes of professional ethics**

Professor Cheung adopts a sceptical stance with regard to codes of ethics. There are arguments both supporting and challenging his views.

Supporting Professor Cheung's opinion

Professional codes of ethics have a number of limitations, some of which Professor Cheung referred to. Because they contain descriptions of situations that accountants might encounter, they can convey the (false) impression that professional ethics can be reduced to a set of rules contained in a code (as pointed out by Professor Cheung).

This would be a mistaken impression, of course, as the need for personal integrity is also emphasised. Ethical codes do not and cannot capture all ethical circumstances and dilemmas that a professional accountant will encounter in his or her career and this reinforces the need for accountants to understand the underlying ethical principles of probity, integrity, openness, transparency and fairness. Although codes such as IFAC's are intended to apply to an international 'audience', some may argue that regional variations in cultural, social and ethical norms mean that such codes cannot capture important differences in emphasis in some parts of the world. The moral 'right' can be prescribed in every situation.

Finally, professional codes of ethics are not technically enforceable in any legal manner although sanctions exist for gross breach of the code in some jurisdictions. Individual observance of ethical codes is effectively voluntary in most circumstances.

Against Professor Cheung's opinion

There are a number of arguments for codes of professional ethics that challenge Professor Cheung's views. Firstly, professional codes of ethics signal the importance, to accountants, of ethics and acting in the public interest in the professional accounting environment. They are reminded, unambiguously and in 'black and white' for example, that as with other professions, accounting exists to serve the public good and public support for the profession is likely to exist only as long as the public interest is supported over and above competing interests. The major international codes (such as IFAC) underpin national and regional cultures with internationally expected standards that, the codes insist, supersede any national ethical nuances. The IFAC (2003) code states (in clause 4), 'the accountancy profession throughout the world operates in an environment with different cultures and regulatory requirements. The basic intent of the Code, however, should always be respected.' The codes prescribe minimum standards of behaviour expected in given situations and give specific examples of potentially problematic areas in accounting practice. In such situations, the codes make the preferred course of action unambiguous.

A number of codes of ethics exist for professional accountants. Prominent among these is the IFAC code. This places the public interest at the heart of the ethical conduct of accountants. The ACCA code discusses ethics from within a principles-based perspective. Other countries' own professional accounting bodies have issued their own codes of ethics in the belief that they may better describe the ethical situations in those countries.

(b)   **Integrity**

Meaning of 'integrity'

Tutorial note

To define 'integrity' also appeared in the December 2009 exam (see Question 57 Dundas).

Integrity is generally understood to describe a person of high moral virtue. A person of integrity is one who observes a steadfast adherence to a strict moral or ethical code notwithstanding any other pressures on him or her to act otherwise.

In professional life, integrity describes the personal ethical position of the highest standards of professionalism and probity.

It is an underlying and underpinning principle of corporate governance and it is required that all those representing shareholder interests in agency relationships both possess and exercise absolute integrity at all times. To fail to do so is a breach of the agency trust relationship.

Importance of integrity in corporate governance

Integrity is important in corporate governance for several reasons. Codes of ethics do not capture all ethical situations and the importance of the virtue of the actor rather than the ethics of the action is therefore emphasised. Any profession (such as accounting) relies upon a public perception of competence and integrity and in this regard, accounting can perhaps be compared with medicine. As an underlying principle, integrity provides a basic ethical framework to guide an accountant's professional and personal life. Finally, integrity underpins the relationships that an accountant has with his or her clients, auditors and other colleagues. Trust is vital in the normal conduct of these relationships and integrity underpins this.

(c)   **Deontology and consequentialism**

Deontological ethics

The deontological perspective can be broadly understood in terms of 'means' being more important than 'ends'. It is broadly based on Kantian (categorical imperative) ethics. The rightness of an action is judged by its intrinsic virtue and thus morality is seen as absolute and not situational. An action is right if it would, by its general adoption, be of net benefit to society. Lying, for example, is deemed to be ethically wrong because lying, if adopted in all situations, would lead to the deterioration of society.

Consequentialist ethics

The consequentialist or teleological perspective is based on utilitarian or egoist ethics meaning that the rightness of an action is judged by the quality of the outcome. From the egoist perspective, the quality of the outcome refers to the individual ('what is best for me?'). Utilitarianism measures the quality of outcome in terms of the greatest happiness of the greatest number ('what is best for the majority?'). Consequentialist ethics are therefore situational and contingent, and not absolute.

	Marking scheme		
			Marks
(a)	One mark for each valid point made supporting codes of professional ethics		Up to 6
	One mark for each valid point made on limitations of codes of professional ethics		Up to 6
	Up to two marks for using an actual code of ethics by way of example		Up to 2
			────
		Maximum	11
			────
(b)	Definition of integrity – one mark for each relevant point		Up to 4
	Importance of integrity – one mark for each relevant point		Up to 4
			────
		Maximum	7
			────
(c)	Explanation of deontology – one mark for each valid point		Up to 4
	Explanation of consequentialism – one mark for each valid point		Up to 4
			────
		Maximum	7
			────
Total			**25**
			────

71   PHARMA 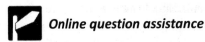 *Online question assistance*

> **Key answer tips**
>
> This question covers a range of areas within the Professional Values and Ethics section of the syllabus. Though the requirements for parts (a) – (c) do not specify reference to the scenario, you are advised to utilise the information provided to illustrate the points you are making in your answers.

(a)   **Definition of profession**

A profession is an occupation carried out by a privileged body of individuals. It is suggested that a profession has three characteristics.

The first is in the nature of training associated with the occupation. This should require a high level of formal qualification and be accompanied by the need to gain practical experience in the field. The nature of qualification may differ as will the balance between practical and academic rigor.

The second characteristic relates to the privilege bestowed on members of the profession. This may relate to the right given to doctors to prescribe medication or the right given to accountants to audit and prescribe change within the corporate body.

The final characteristic relates to the price of privilege. Any member of a profession must act in the interests of the society it is created to serve. This is known as acting in the public interest. As much as doctors work for the health of the social community so accountants work for the health of the business community.

Role of accountant in support of public interest

Within this distinction between doctors and accountants the role of the accountant and the problems in truly acting in the public interest can be examined.

In support of the business community the accountant has a valuable role to play. This includes monitoring companies and auditing accounts, reporting to regulatory bodies and providing market confidence in the well being of business entities. This general role assists fraudulent activities to be diagnosed and those perpetrating theft to be uncovered. The accountant becomes the watchdog of commerce ensuring rules are followed and regulation adhered too.

As an employee of a company the accountant has a related role to play extending into decision making and decision support of the executive through the provision of high quality information. The accountant is an advisor, a manger and a wealth creator through this process. He/she is also a communicator or agent for the owners in as much as it is a primary role to present accounting data in a form that is understandable to the business users. The accountant supports agency through transparency in disclosure and clarity in reporting.

Through the accountant's facilitation of commerce companies are able to raise funds, generate profits and pay taxes. These taxes support the wider community and so enable social functions to be funded for the benefit of all.

This final point is the only relationship the accountant has with the public in a general sense. The relationship is detached and dubious since a part of the accountant's role is to positively work against the payment of any monies to the wider community in the form of taxation.

This suggests that that focus for public interest is really restricted to the financial public meaning corporations and those that benefit through investment. Whilst it could be said that everyone's pension (assuming they will be entitled to one) benefits from the work of the business community the reality is that only a very small proportion of individuals gain from this form of output. The accountant working in the public interest seems limited in this sense.

Other issues seem to cloud the discussion further. People would not earn money to support themselves without business, economies would not grow and products demanded by customers would not exist. However, this strays from the question since it is not the existence of corporations or commerce that is called into question but rather the role of the accountant as a privileged member of society who does not actually work in the broader societal interest.

(b) **Support of value laden role in society**

The wider value laden role relates to an extension to the accountant's current role in order to embrace the remit of the wider society. This suggests an expansion to the stakeholders influencing the accountant's role away from corporate masters towards public health, societal needs, governments, environmentalist, disadvantaged communities and in general the ethical role of a corporate citizen.

To respond to the diverse and broader need to accountant will need to develop systems that monitor and report on broader issues such as environmental impact, quality of life, species extinction and resource usage. Some systems already exist including environmental management and sustainability monitoring systems in larger companies. These need to be used in order to bring environmentalism into the decision making reference framework used by executives when determining strategy.

The key question behind the wide value laden role is the extent to which accountants believe this is necessary or achievable. Whilst most appreciate the need for change the egoistical nature of ethical decision making ensure accountants suppress concern for the common good beneath their allegiance to the corporate flag. This seems appropriate since organisations generally pay their wages in one form or another.

Tutorial note

This is a challenging section so any answers that discuss the roles and influence of the accountant outside the traditional finance areas will be rewarded.

(c)   **Confidentiality**

Confidentiality relates to the need for secrecy. The scenario uses the word in association with the need to keep its research a secret from its competitors in order to ensure they do not steal the company's ideas.

Confidentiality is a key principle defined in the IFAC code of ethics and here the association is generally between audit client and audit firm maintaining the confidentiality of findings on examination of the body corporate. Confidentiality leads to confidence in ensuring that any problems identified can be discussed and resolved in a private arena without the issue being disclosed, discussed or acted upon by external groups.

The existence of confidentiality is also an element of the agency relationship. Shareholders expect a degree of confidentiality to be shown by managers ensuring that they are the first to know about any issues that relate to their investment and its returns. This is naturally extended to the relationship between the accountant as employee and the executive of the company.

The concept is not without its detractors. The issue of whistleblowers sits very uncomfortably with the need for confidentiality as shown in this scenario. The need for confidentiality must be weighed against the public good and when the latter is found to be dominant the accountant must act and not remain silent.

The CEO's use of the concept is entirely inappropriate in the scenario. He likens confidentiality to the need for trade secrets and yet the essence of the secret being kept is that the product may kill children. It is certain that competitors would like to know this but equally certain they would not want to copy the product which is the interpretation given by the ethically misguided executive.

(d)   **Courses of action in ethical dispute**

In a practical and personal way the Professor can be forgiven for taking no action. The sums of money involved and the effect on his personal career and therefore his family may be devastating if he decides to publish the report. It is worth bearing in mind that his findings may be flawed since the product would have been tested by government scientists prior to release.

If his report is correct, and he believes that it is, then despite the effect on his personal circumstances he may take a more utilitarian or egalitarian ethical stance where the needs of the many outweigh the needs of the one.

His first steps would be to seek advice from colleagues, both from an ethical perspective and to review the technical content of his findings. Professor Jones needs to be totally sure of his findings before publicising them.

If they are validated by colleagues then he would publish the document and accept the consequences that arise from that action.

72 DEONTOLOGICAL ETHICS

Key answer tips

This question requires a thorough understanding of the deontological (or non-consequentialist) approach to ethics. Part (a) allows you to earn marks for pure theory, explaining clearly the approach and the maxims. Part (b) moves onto applying this theory in the given scenario.

(a)   **Deontological approach to ethics**

This is a non-consequentialist theory. Whether an action can be deemed right or wrong depends on the motivation or principle for taking that action. Actions can only be deemed 'right' or 'wrong' when the motivation or reason for taking an action is also known.

The deontological approach is based on the theory of Immanuel Kant. Humans are regarded as rational actors who can decide right and wrong for themselves. This decision making then determines the actions they will take.

The theory introduces the concept of the 'categorical imperative', i.e. a framework that can be applied to every moral issue. Humans are deemed to work within this framework in deciding what actions they should take.

The framework provides three maxims that are tests for any action. An action can only be morally 'right' if it survives all three tests or maxims. The maxims are as follows:

Maxim 1

Act only according to that maxim by which you can at the same time will that it should become a universal law.

This is the principle of **Consistency**. An action can only be right if everyone can follow the same underlying principle. The act of murder is immoral because if this action were determined moral then human life could not exist; that is if everyone murdered everyone else then there would be no one left alive! Similarly lying is immoral because if lying were moral then there would be no concept of 'truth'.

Maxim 2

Act so that you treat humanity, whether in your own person or in that of another, always as an end and never as a means only.

This is the principle of **Human dignity**. Everybody uses other humans in some way, e.g. to take orders and bring food in restaurants, to receive/deal with requests in call centres. This does not mean that the other human should be seen simply as a provider of those goods or services although it is easy to do so, it is 'their fault' that something has gone wrong. According to this maxim, their own needs and expectations are important and this must always be remembered; they are also human beings.

Maxim 3

Act only so that the will through its maxims could regard itself at the same time as universally lawgiving.

This is the principle of **Universality**. The test is whether an action is deemed to be moral or suitable when viewed by others, not by the person undertaking that action. The basic test is that if a person would be uncomfortable if their actions were reported in the press (even if no other people were harmed and all humans could accept the principle) then the action is likely to be of doubtful moral status. In other words, actions must be acceptable to everyone in whatever situation.

(b) In this situation, toys have been produced in a country where the use of child labour is presumably either legal or accepted as part of the ethics of that society. Manufacturing is also carried out under poor working conditions, which appear to be the result of pressure to limit manufacturing costs. The result has been poor manufacturing quality and danger to health in the country where the toys were sold.

The use of child labour in one country must pass Kant's three categorical imperatives to be acceptable, both in the country of manufacture and in the country of sale.

The first principle is consistency. An action can only be right if everyone can follow the same underlying principle. In the country of sale the use of child labour is unacceptable; as child labour is unacceptable in one country then it is not possible to follow this principle in the manufacturing country. Both the toy re-seller and the purchaser of the toys are at fault. The re-seller should have insisted on the application of their ethics while the consumer could have not purchased the toys to indicate their disagreement with the use of child labour.

The second principle is human dignity. In other words, the needs and expectations of the child workers are important and this must always be remembered; they are also human beings. The use of child labour would appear to go against this principle. Children are being used to keep costs down in the manufacturing company, while being forced to work in poor working conditions. Presumably consumers in the country of sale would not like their children to work in these conditions as the needs of children in terms of security and expectations in terms of life expectancy are being compromised (do the child workers ever swallow magnets?). The use of child labour does not pass the second of Kant's tests.

The third principle is universality. The principle asks whether an action is deemed to be moral or suitable when viewed by others, not by the person undertaking that action. In other words, would the toy re-seller be comfortable with consumers knowing that child labour was used in the manufacture of the toys even though this was morally acceptable in the country of manufacture? The answer is presumably 'no' as consumers do not expect child labour to be used in their country. The fact that the re-seller kept this information secret also indicates that the use of child labour could be considered morally wrong.

From the view-point of the ethics in the country where the toys were sold, the use of child labour is wrong; it does not meet any of Kant's three maxims.

Tutorial note

Remember, you are not being asked for your own opinion on the matter of child labour. You are required to apply the theory to this concept, and reach a conclusion based on this ethical approach. By referring to the factors discussed in part (a) you should be able to reach a conclusion on the acceptability of child labour under a deontological perspective.

73   RDC (DEC 12)

Key answer tips

The question required the candidate to apply Tucker's model to a business decision and then consider the stakeholders affected and the claims that they had on the decision which needed to be taken. Similar questions had been asked in previous exam papers and articles written on the topics of "claim"

It is important to recognise that the mention of the word "stakeholder" does not automatically link with the Mendelow matrix. Careful reading of part b) was needed in this context.

Tuckers' 5 question model has proved popular in exams to date, so this question is good additional practice.

(a)   **Tucker and Route A**

Is the decision to choose Route A profitable?

Yes. This will be cheaper for the company (RDC) because it avoids the need to make the compulsory purchase of Mr Krul's farm. This will save the company $1 million and enable a profit to be made, over 10 years, of $5 million. The equivalent 10-year profit figure for Route B would, accordingly, be $4 million.

Is it legal?

The case says that both routes (A and B) had been given planning permission, so there is no difference between them on matters of legality. Route A is a legally allowable option as it has planning permission from the local government authority.

Is it right?

This depends upon the ethical perspective adopted. Route A would deliver a higher profitability for RDC and also preserve important local social and economic benefits by keeping Mr Krul's farm. The farm supports local jobs, perhaps has an important role in the local community and, being a farm, provides a source of local food. If these benefits are seen as more important than the future of the birds, then it is right to choose Route A. If the claim of the birds and their impact on the local ecosystem is more important than the profitability of the project and the benefits provided by the farm, then it was wrong to choose Route A.

Is it fair?

This depends upon how the legitimate and reasonable claim of Mr Krul to remain on his land is weighed against the claim of the colony of birds to survive. The choice of Route A ignores the claim of the birds' right to gain access to their feeding site and because the birds are endangered, it may threaten their future. It is fair to Mr Krul, but unfair to the colony of birds. Mr Krul, however, employs people who would otherwise lose their jobs, potentially having a negative impact on them and their families. In addition, the farm has been in Mr Krul's family for four generations and that may also be a relevant factor when considering the fairness of the decision.

Is it sustainable and/or environmentally acceptable?

Route A was probably the less environmentally-sustainable of the two options. Because Route A was chosen, it will mean destroying the important feeding site for the colony of threatened birds. This will threaten the population of these birds and the case suggests that this may represent a threat to the environmental sustainability of local ecosystems. The loss of the feeding ground and the birds may therefore have other unforeseen environmental consequences. Whichever route is chosen, an environmental benefit may accrue because of the replacement of car journeys with increased rail travel.

Summary

The company chose to prioritise cost-savings and the impact of the farm on the local community over the negative environmental impact that Route A entailed. This may have something to do with Eddie Krul having a louder 'voice' than the birds and so more able to express his claim than the voiceless birds (the pressure group did not speak up until after the decision was made). RDC essentially had two choices which would both have had negative effects on some of the stakeholders. It chose to take the decision that was less sustainable but more favourable to shareholders and the stakeholders in the farm.

(b) **Importance of recognising all stakeholders**

A decision such as the selection of a new route for a major construction project such as this is bound to create 'winners' and 'losers'. In any project such as this, it is important to identify and recognise the claims of all of the stakeholders for several reasons.

Stakeholder recognition is necessary to gain an understanding of the *sources of potential risk and disruption.* 'Save the Birds', for example, has threatened to disrupt the construction of Route A as it seeks to protect the birds' feeding ground. Mr Krul, similarly, threatened to bring legal action in the event that Route B was chosen.

Stakeholder recognition is important in terms of assessing *the sources of influence over the objectives and outcomes* for the project (such as identified in the Mendelow model). Stakeholder influence is assessed in terms of each stakeholder's power and interest, with higher power and higher interest combining to generate the highest influence. The local government authority, for example, had no view on which was chosen but as a high power stakeholder (capable of granting or withholding legal permission), it could have been very influential had it expressed a view either way.

Stakeholder recognition is necessary in order to identify *potential areas of* conflict *and tension* between stakeholders, especially relevant when it is likely that stakeholders of influence will be in disagreement over the outcomes. A survey of the stakeholders in a rail-building project such as this, once mapped in terms of influence, would signal which stakeholders are likely to cause delays and paralysis by disagreement and whose claims can then be studied for ways to reduce disagreement.

There is an *ethical and reputational case* for knowledge of how decisions affect stakeholders, both inside the organisation or external to it. Society can withdraw its support from organisations that it perceives as unethical or arrogant. This can affect organisational performance by reducing their reputations as employers and suppliers of future services. RDC may acquire a reputation for environmental damage and this could mean they lose public trust on future projects of this type. A 'deep green' perspective would take an unfavourable view of companies that failed to recognise some stakeholder claims.

(c) **Stakeholder claims**

Stakeholder claim

A stakeholder is any person or entity that can affect or be affected by the actions or policies of an organisation. In the case of RDC, two 'affected' stakeholders are Eddie Krul and the colony of endangered birds. The local government authority is both affected by the decision and can also have an influence over the decision. A claim is the outcome sought or the outcome that would most benefit or do least harm to a given stakeholder. It is what that particular stakeholder 'wants' or would want, if it were able to understand and voice its claim.

Assessment of the claims

Mr Krul was seeking to maintain his house and land by getting RDC to choose Route A. His claim is based partly on his family having been on the same land for four generations and that he employs a number of local people. As a 'vocal' critic, he is able to clearly articulate his views and lobby for his preferred option. He clearly understands what would happen to him if Route B was chosen and can clearly voice that concern to decision-makers.

The only concerns of the local government authority were making sure the investment went ahead with the benefits it believed would accrue to the local region. Its claim is to ensure that the investment and jobs are attracted and in pursuit of that, takes no view on the competing claims of Mr Krul and the colony of birds. It could be criticised for being passive in this decision and for assuming that RDC could evaluate such a decision adequately themselves, in both economic and ethical terms.

The colony of birds is ostensibly a voiceless stakeholder, although it does now have 'Save the Birds' claiming to speak on its behalf. The bird colony does not understand that its feeding ground is threatened but it will incur material loss when Route A is developed. Because it does not have an effective voice (other than the 'outrage' of 'Save the Birds' after the decision was taken), it was unable to contribute to the debate over the choice of route. The local government authority did not prioritise one stakeholder over the other when granting RDC permission to develop either route.

ACCA marking scheme			
			Marks
(a)	1 to 2 marks for a discussion of each point. Half mark for identification only.		10
	2 marks for a balanced summary.		
(b)	2 marks for each relevant point discussed. Half mark for identification only.		8
(c)	2 marks for an explanation of a stakeholder claim.		
	2 marks for an assessment of each claim.		
		Maximum	7
Total			**25**

Examiner's comments

This was a 'stakeholder' question in which a disputed route for a new railway set the scene. Both routes (A and B) had their pros and cons and eventually, Route A was chosen which would protect Mr Krul's farm but destroy the feeding ground for the colony of endangered birds. The Tucker 'five question' framework for assessing the decision to choose Route A (part A) was done well for the most part but some candidates merely listed the five questions with little attempt to engage with the case. The point here was that whilst the decision to choose Route A was profitable and legal, there were questions over its fairness, its rightness and its sustainability. The better answers were able to engage with these issues and show that the selection of Route A was not without its complexities.

Part (b) was done poorly overall. A similar version of this question was on a previous paper so it was disappointing to see that many candidates performed poorly. A common, and incorrect, response was to frame the answer around the Mendelow matrix. Perhaps the word 'stakeholder' in the question triggered an assumption that the answer must involve the Mendelow matrix – but this was not so, except to highlight that some stakeholders are more influential than others. The question specifically asked about the importance of recognising all of the stakeholders in a decision and therefore concerned stakeholders as sources of risk, disruption, conflict and reputation loss. A careful reading of the wording of the question was necessary to get the actual meaning of what was required.

Finally, part (c) asked about stakeholder 'claims' and then asked candidates to critically assess the claims of the three main stakeholders discussed in the case. I wrote a technical article about this in early 2008 and it was pleasing to see that most could explain the notion of a 'claim'. The second task, to critically assess the three claims was done less well, with weaker answers just repeating information from the case about each one.

74   POLICY SPEECH (JUN 09)

Key answer tips

Part (a) provides a good 'text-book' start to the question, though answers need to go into detail to earn the full five marks. Part (b)(i) is straightforward theory, with the ethical threats being a repeat of knowledge from paper F8. The application in part (ii) requires a bit more work – ensure that you are not just repeating the explanations you provided in part (i).

Part (c) is definitely the most challenging part of the question. You can earn initial marks by explaining the view of the social responsibility position.

(a)   **Explain 'the public interest'**

Public interest concerns the *overall welfare of society* as well as the sectional interest of the shareholders in a particular company. It is generally assumed, for example, that *all professional actions*, whether by medical, legal or accounting professionals, should be for the greater good rather than for sectional interest.

Accounting has a large potential impact and so the public interest 'test' is important. Mrs Yttria made specific reference to audit and assurance. In auditing and assurance, for example, the working of capital markets – and *hence the value of tax revenues, pensions and investment* – rests upon accountants' behaviour. In management accounting and financial management, the stability of business organisations – and *hence the security of jobs and the supply of important products* – also depends on the professional behaviour of accountants.

(b)   **Ethical threats**

In its 2005 code of professional ethics, the International Federation of Accountants (IFAC) identified five types of ethical threat (s.110.10). These are (quoted verbatim):

(a)   Self-interest threats, which may occur as a result of the financial or other interests of a professional accountant or of an immediate family member

(b)   Self-review threats, which may occur when a previous judgement needs to be re-evaluated by the professional accountant responsible for that judgement

(c)   Advocacy threats, which may occur when a professional accountant promotes a position or opinion to the point that subsequent objectivity may be compromised

(d)   Familiarity threats, which may occur when, because of a close relationship, a professional accountant becomes too sympathetic to the interests of others; and

(e)   Intimidation threats, which may occur when a professional accountant may be deterred from acting objectively by threats, actual or perceived.

There are obvious *familiarity threats* in supplying multiple services to the same client in that the firm will possibly be less likely to be rigorous in the audit and may tend to give the client the benefit of the doubt in marginal cases to avoid upsetting them and risk losing the other services. The potential lack of impartiality may give rise to *advocacy threats* in that whilst acting as 'referee' in audit and assurance work, the firm may be lobbying for the client on other areas of work. The high degree of dependence that the firm has on the client opens it up to the *threat of intimidation.* The more dependent the firm becomes on the client for its revenues and profits, the more tempting it may become for the client to seek favourable audit judgements from the firm with the implied threat that the firm could lose other business if it was too harsh. *A self-interest threat* therefore arises as senior members of the accounting firm give precedence to the protection of their own financial position over the wider public interest of having an auditor partially captured by a client.

(c) **Accounting profession and deep green (or deep ecologist) position**

Mr Nahum's remarks are similar to some of the positions espoused by deep green theorists, tending as they are, towards the anti-capitalist and the anti-corporatist political left.

Biased and value laden – the belief that accounting (and other professions) work within an unstated set of contestable values. The deep green position argues that accounting is captured by the minority interests of capitalism and acts as the 'servant' of capital.

Environmental degradation is a key charge made by deep greens against business in general and, by implication, against accountants. Accountants serve the interests of business (rather than the environment) and hence accountants are complicit in the creation of environmental damage by their unquestioning adherence (in the opinion of the deep greens) to a set of rules that supports capital.

Poverty and 'animal rights' are themes raised by deep greens as items that should be on accounting's agenda. One view among some deep greens is that humans have no more moral rights than animals and that activities perpetuating animal unfairness or human poverty should be challenged by accounting as a profession.

Inter and intra-generational 'social injustices' are often cited as problems with the 'unfettered' capitalist business model which, the deep greens argue, accounting supports and is therefore complicit in. Some business activities result in wealth disparities in this generation (intra-generational) and deprive future generations of resources (inter-generational injustice).

Tutorial note

Marks would be awarded to allow for other valid approaches to this answer.

Marking scheme			Marks
(a)	2 marks for definition/evidence of understanding of 'public interest' 3 marks for explanation of application to accounting		
		Maximum	5
(b)	(i) 1 mark for each type of ethical threat described (half for identification only)		Up to 5
	(ii) 2 marks for assessment of each ethical threat in the case highlighted by Mr Mordue		8
		Maximum	13
(c)	Up to 2 marks for each area of agreement identified and assessed		Up to 7
		Maximum	7
Total			25

Examiner's comments

This question was about public interest, ethical threats and one of Gray, Owen & Adams (1996) seven positions. The case itself was set in a ministerial policy speech after which, a discussion took place raising a number of issues on ethical threats as well as particular ideas on the nature of accounting.

The requirements contained a mixture of book work and case analysis. A sound knowledge of the P1 study guide would have enabled candidates to do well in **part (a)** on the public interest and (b)(i) on ethical threats.

The application marks were concentrated in parts (b)(ii) and (c). Mr Mordue was obviously a very experienced professional but his comments in paragraph 3 of the case raised a number of problems from professional and ethical perspectives. The five general ethical threats were asked for in **part (b)(i)** and where attempted, these were usually correct. Bullet lists of the threats were not well rewarded because they didn't respond to the verb 'describe'.

There was a wide range of responses to **part (b)(ii)** in which candidates had to 'assess' the ethical threats implied by Mr Mordue's beliefs (the ones he had expressed in paragraphs 2 and 3 of the case). Some candidates answered it by relisting the general threats and considering how Mr Mordue's beliefs might represent each threat. Others worked through Mr Mordue's beliefs and showed how each one was an ethical threat. Both approaches were rewarded by markers as long as they showed evidence of understanding of how some of Mr Mordue's beliefs were ethically wrong.

Part (c) on the deep green perspective was done poorly overall. Many candidates were able to say something about the deep green perspective (which is a common belief and a part of the international debate on how corporations should engage with environmental issues) but very few could show how Mr Nahum's remarks were deep green in nature. He was expressing anticapitalist and critical opinions which drew, in turn, from a general belief that accounting supports an economic system that degrades the environment and fails to address (in the words on the question) 'poverty, animal rights and other social injustices'. I would encourage candidates and their tutors to practice applying theories to cases as this tends to be how theory is tested in professional level exams such as P1.

75 INO COMPANY *Walk in the footsteps of a top tutor*

Key answer tips

This question is looking at corporate ethics and how a business can determine and use them. This is a popular topic in the business world these days, since many companies are implementing or promoting their codes of ethics. You may be able to find examples of these from a corporate website.

The highlighted words are key phrases that markers are looking for.

Tutor's top tips

Approach to the question

*If, as always, you start by reading the **first paragraph only** (of the body of the question, under part (b)) the following can be determined:*

- *this is a motor vehicle manufacturer*

- *the company has nine models in its product range*

- *it has a good reputation for safety.*

*Now look at the requirements **before** reading the rest of the question. This will ensure that you:*

- *read the question in the correct manner*

- *do not need to read the question more than once*

- *save time and can begin planning.*

*From the requirements you can establish the **headings** for your plan, and also your answer. Ensure that you are clear with the **verb in the question**, and what is required for that verb.*

Requirement

- *Corporate ethics, extent to which organisations must have corporate ethics and how they are reported*

  *There are actually **three things to cover** in this section, requiring some theoretical knowledge.*

  Note that the verbs used are 'explain' and 'discuss'. The latter requires you to go into some detail in your answer.

- *Issues relevant to the ethical stance of INO*

  *You will need to be looking for the **specific ethical issues** provided by the information in the question.*

  It would be advisable to use these issues as your headings for part (b).

  The requirement is to 'identify' which requires you to find the issues, and 'explain' which needs another sentence.

- Impact of ethical issues on the company and its stakeholders

  The verb here is 'discuss' which requires some **analysis** of whether the impact of the issue is significant or not, or of concern to INO or not.

  Note that the requirement mentions the company <u>and</u> its stakeholders – two **separate perspectives** that should be considered in your discussion.

- Recommend amendments to the corporate ethics of INO

  This does clearly state **'where appropriate'** so recommendations are not required for all issues previously discussed.

Reading the question

Now **actively** read the question i.e. as you read it you should add all relevant points to your planning page(s).

This process should enable you to identify the issues relevant to INO's ethical stance, for the first section of part (b). These are as follows:

- rectification of the N920

- tyre supplier's use of child labour

- charitable activities

- CSR reporting

- shareholders' preferences

- environmental impact of motor vehicles.

Answering the question

- Part (a) Corporate ethics, extent to which organisations must have corporate ethics and how they are reported

  There are six marks available here, and three things to cover in the requirement. Aim to write two to three sentences on each element, making two separate points under each sub-heading.

- Part (b) Issues relevant to the ethical stance of INO

  These have been identified from your review of the requirements. Use these as headings for part (b) and then go onto write a sentence explaining exactly what the issue is.

- Part (b) cont. Impact of ethical issues on the company and its stakeholders

  Try to think whether the issue will cause a big increase in, or loss of, business to INO. Remember the key facts about INO – particularly its reputation and trust of its customers.

  Also consider things from the perspective of any of the stakeholders – customers, suppliers, local community, employees or shareholders. You do not need to talk about the full range of stakeholders, but consideration of one of these most relevant to the issue under discussion would enhance your answer.

- Part (b) cont. Recommend amendments to the corporate ethics of INO

  If you can see that the company, or its stakeholders, could benefit from agreeing an ethical stance towards a particular factor, and stating this in its corporate ethics, then this is the place to make that suggestion.

  As always with recommendations, state your idea, explain it clearly and justify how this will assist the business.

(a)   **Corporate ethics**

Corporate ethics relates to the application of ethical values to business behaviour. In the same way that individuals have ethical values and are expected to follow those values, so organisations are now also expected to have ethical values.

Corporate ethics relates to many different areas of the organisation's activities. For example ethics is relevant to the overall strategy determination of the organisation through to the treatment of individual workers.

Again, as with individual ethics, corporate ethics goes beyond legal requirements indicating a higher moral standard than simply 'following the law'. There will be situations where an organisation follows the law, but ethical action means doing something more than this. This indicates that ethical actions are to some extent discretionary, in that the organisation does not have to take ethical action. However, expectations on the organisation from other sources (e.g. customers, suppliers and employees) also indicate that ethical action is normally expected of a company.

Organisations are encouraged to report their ethical approach in a corporate and social responsibility (CSR) report. In many jurisdictions, this report is again not required by law or accounting standards, but is indicative of best practice. Lack of standards mean that CSR reports are not necessarily comparable between organisations, limiting their usefulness. However, some organisations do provide comprehensive CSR reports (e.g. Marks & Spencer in the UK) providing detailed information on their ethical stance.

(b)   **Issues relevant to ethical stance**

Customers/goods produced

As with any other company, INO has a responsibility to produce quality goods and services for its customers at a reasonable price, allowing INO to make a reasonable profit for providing those goods and services. To this end, INO must attempt to build up customer trust and faith over time so customers will purchase and be satisfied with INO products.

The decision not to carry out rectification work on the N920 model may have little or no impact on INO as the risk of failure is extremely small. However, should failure occur and some cars overheat causing engine failure then the reputation of INO will be damaged (the company knew about the issue prior to failure) and faith in INO and its products will fall. Although there is no legal requirement to provide rectification, ethically INO must consider this to ensure customers are not injured driving INO vehicles.

INO should therefore provide for rectification work, even though the costs would appear to outweigh the benefits of this action.

Suppliers of tyres

Suppliers provide goods and services for a company. They will normally attempt to provide those goods and services to an appropriate quality in a timely fashion and in return expect to be paid on a timely basis.

INO does appear to pay its suppliers promptly, maintaining this element of any ethical contract. Similarly INO attempts to create partnership agreements with suppliers enabling both INO and the supplier to work to further their joint interests. However, the use of child labour in a foreign country by the UIN Company may not be seen as ethically correct. Not only is INO promoting potentially unethical (albeit legal) activities in that country, there is also an association risk. Most countries believe it is ethically incorrect to employ children and have enacted laws to confirm this view. INO may lose customers if information about the use of child labour appears in the public domain.

Given that INO and UIN do attempt to collaborate in the supply of tyres, INO should initially ask UIN whether the policy of using child labour can be amended. If this is not possible, then INO may consider choosing another supplier of tyres based on more ethical criteria.

Product development

INO produces motor vehicles. These products have a potentially damaging effect on the environment in terms of carbon and other emissions generated during their use. INO is therefore producing a product with a potentially damaging environmental effect.

However, INO does have an active R&D department which is researching into alternative fuels and other methods of decreasing the environmental impact of INO's products. These activities show appropriate environmental awareness on the part of INO.

To check the acceptability of the extent of R&D, INO can do two things:

- Firstly, INO can benchmark expenditure with other similar companies to ensure that the spend of €25 million is not a minimum amount.

- Secondly, a more judgmental view can be taken on the success of previous R&D projects and the effect increasing the R&D budget would have on the success of R&D and the timescales to project completion.

Just because INO is active in this area does not necessarily mean that sufficient is being done to reduce environmental damage from INO's products.

Shareholders

Shareholders are investors in the company. They will expect an appropriate and proper return on the money invested in INO. The board of INO will therefore be expected to provide information on the investment made by shareholders as well as a dividend showing the return on their investment. Good corporate governance principles would also indicate that shareholders will be involved in decision-making, especially where those shareholders are larger corporate investors.

The board of INO do not necessarily ascribe to all principles of good corporate governance so ethically they could be seen to be 'wanting' in this area. While dividends over the last few years have been above industry average, there has been no attempt to involve shareholders in decision making processes within INO. There could also be concern that dividends have been excessive, potentially jeopardising longer-term shareholder interests in favour of the short-term.

The board of INO need to take two actions:

- Firstly, find methods of involving shareholders more in the organisation, for example, by making an active part in the AGM.

- Secondly, providing more detailed profit and cash flow forecasts to determine whether larger dividend payments now limit opportunities for growth and investment in the future.

CSR reporting

The INO Company obviously works within society which implies some corporate and social responsibility to that society. Although not necessarily a legal requirement, many companies produce a Corporate and Social Responsibility report as a means of communicating this relationship to third parties.

At present, INO does not produce any CSR report which means the organisation is potentially missing out on positive publicity in this area. The ethical stance of the company is correct in carrying out CSR activities; it is the lack of reporting that is the issue here. However, the ability of INO to produce a CSR report is severely hindered by the lack of any CSR targets or reporting systems within the organisation. While INO does carry out some appropriate activities such as providing employees with a sports hall and ensuring that community projects are supported, there are no formal budgets for these activities or methods of evaluating the success of the investments.

INO therefore needs to set formal criteria for its CSR activities and then show in the CSR report how those targets have been met.

Tutorial note

There are many other points that could have been made for an acceptable answer in this part of the question. The above is an example of what could have been written.

76 IFAC

Key answer tips

Your knowledge of this code should assist you with part (a) of this question. Care was needed however when considering how gifts and hospitality are potentially exceptional circumstances

Part (b) required criticism of actions in the light of "public interest" and required you to know exactly what this is.

Part (c) was the first time that "insider trading" or "dealing" had been tested. Answers therefore varied considerably.

(a) **Ethical threats**

The five generally accepted types of ethical threat under the IFAC and ACCA codes of ethics and conduct are:

(i) Self-interest threats, which may occur as a result of the financial or other interests of a professional accountant or of an immediate family member

(ii) Self-review threats, which may occur when a previous judgement needs to be re-evaluated by the professional accountant responsible for that judgement

(iii) Advocacy threats, which may occur when a professional accountant promotes a position or opinion to the point that subsequent objectivity may be compromised

(iv) Familiarity threats, which may occur when, because of a close relationship, a professional accountant becomes too sympathetic to the interests of others; and

(v) Intimidation threats, which may occur when a professional accountant may be deterred from acting objectively by threats, actual or perceived.

The IFAC code highlights self-interest threats and intimidation threats as relevant in accepting gifts or hospitality.

260.1. 'Self-interest threats to objectivity may be created if a gift from a client is accepted; intimidation threats to objectivity may result from the possibility of such offers being made public.'

A self-interest threat is one in which a person's interests in him or herself obscures objectivity and the need to act with integrity. Clearly the promise of personal gain can be a threat to ethical behaviour, especially if, as in the case of Ann, it can be a large amount of money.

An intimidation threat can arise when the party who has given the inducement seeks to exercise power over the recipient in the belief that further advantage can be taken. In the case of a bribe, the recipient can be induced to take further unethical actions with the threat that their first bribe will be exposed if they do not comply. Ann may be induced to award other contracts to the contractor, for example, and this could act against the interests of the company, its shareholders and other contract providers.

There may also be an advocacy threat in addition to the self-interest and intimidation threats. An advocacy threat occurs when objectivity is impaired because of a person's advocacy for a certain interest (e.g. client, bidder, person, etc). In this case, the fact that Ann awarded the contract seemingly on the basis of a bribe, means she will have to defend (act as an advocate for) the successful bidder against her own management if the contract does not go well. In so doing, she may well be acting against the interests of her employer and the company's shareholders.

(b) **Criticise Ann Koo**

First, she did not allow the contract to be bid for by all competing parties equally. This is a failure of her duty to the public interest, to her employers and, as an accountant, to her professional body. Her employers and other stakeholders expect to gain the best value for money and this requires a fair tendering process giving all potential contractors an equal chance of winning the contract.

Second, she accepted a bribe to award the contract. This undermines the contract bidding system and offers poor value to the organisation's principals, which in the case of a public company are the shareholders.

Third, she exposed herself to ethical threats that may result in more unethical behaviour in the future. Safeguards are put in place to ensure that ethical threats are not incurred. Her family's personal financial misfortunes are of no direct concern to her employers and should have had no bearing on her management of the contract process.

Fourth, her belief that she deserves a 'higher personal return' suggests she is seeking more than just the career opportunities that come with being a qualified accountant. This belief or expectation may apply to most qualified professionals but acceptance of additional rewards in the manner that this case describes is totally unacceptable and is not a generalisable ethic in terms of Kant's deontological understanding of ethics. What if everybody sought to make a 'higher personal return' on their training through abusing their responsible position in this way?

Public interest

Ann Koo owes a duty to the public interest both as an accountant and as a company director. This means that it is her duty to behave in such a way as to maximise the public good and not act in terms of pursuing personal interests only. Accounting and other professionals are bound to recognise this duty and to comply with it regardless of the temptation or inducement to act otherwise.

(c)   **Insider trading**

Insider dealing/trading

Insider dealing (also called insider trading) is the buying or selling of company shares based on *knowledge not publicly available*. Directors are often in possession of market-sensitive information ahead of its publication and they would therefore *know if the current share price is under or over-valued* given what they know about forthcoming events. If, for example, they are made aware of a higher than expected performance, it would be classed as insider dealing to buy company shares before that information was published. Similarly, selling shares in advance of results publication indicating previous over-valuation, would also be considered as insider dealing.

Why is insider trading unethical and often illegal?

By accepting a directorship, each director agrees to act primarily in the interests of shareholders. This means that decisions taken must *always be for the best long-term value for shareholders*. If insider dealing is allowed, then it is *likely that some decisions would have a short-term effect* which would not be of the best long-term value for shareholders. For example, businesses which are about to be taken-over often see a significant rise in their share price. In this situation directors might purchase shares in their own companies, seek potential buyers for the company and recommend the sale to shareholders, in order to make a profit on their own share investments. For this reason, a blanket ban on insider dealing ensures that such short-term measures are not taken.

There is also the potential damage that insider trading does to the reputation and integrity of the capital markets in general which could put off investors who would have no such access to privileged information and who would perceive that such market distortions might increase the risk and variability of returns beyond what they should be.

ACCA marking scheme		
		Marks
(a)	1 mark for each threat identified and briefly described (half for identification only).	
	2 marks for each relevant ethical threat discussed to a maximum of 4 marks.	
	Total	9
(b)	2 marks for each criticism identified and developed to a maximum of 8 marks.	
	2 marks for evidence of understanding of public interests (in any part of the answer).	
	Total	10
(c)	3 marks for evidence of understanding of insider dealing/trading.	
	3 marks for explanation of why it is unethical.	
	Total	6
Total		**25**

Examiner's comments

This question was based around a discussion of the IFAC code of ethics (2009) and described the behaviour of an accountant, Ann Koo, who took a bribe when awarding supply contracts. It was not necessary to know about the IFAC code in advance as the case gave a quote from the code that was used as the basis for the requirements. The first part (part a) was about ethical threats, part (b) was a 'criticise' question and part (c) asked about insider dealing. In general, part (a) was done well and parts (b) and (c) were done less well.

The general ethical threats in part (a) were usually correctly identified and described. A second task in part (a) was to discuss how 'gifts' and 'hospitality' can give rise to specific ethical threats. This was less well done than the first task although most well-prepared candidates were able to show a connection between accepting gifts and one or more of the five ethical threats.

Tutorial note

When making recommendations for action it is useful to follow the same approach in all answers:

- *obtain detail and gather the facts*
- *follow established internal procedures (may include whistleblowing help-lines)*
- *consult with direct line management*
- *escalate issue to higher levels of management*
- *escalate to audit committee*
- *seek advice from professional institute*
- *finally, consider withdrawing from the engagement/situation.*

You will need to tailor these points to every situation since only some will be relevant in each case – but they provide a useful checklist to follow.

77 FIVE ETHICAL SITUATIONS

Key answer tips

A good answer to part (b) relies on clearly explaining why you think the situation is a specific type of threat, and providing sensible suggestions for safeguards. Don't expect the exam marker to 'work out' what you mean; make sure you explain things very clearly.

(a)   There are a number of possible threats to fundamental ethical principles which lead to conflicts of interest affecting accountants in their work. Professional codes of ethics aim to enable the accountant to understand how to resolve these conflicts of interest.

Conflicts of interest and their resolution are explained in the conceptual framework to the code of ethics. A framework is needed because it is impossible to define every situation where threats to fundamental principles may occur or the mitigating action required. Different assignments may also create different threats and mitigating actions – again it is not possible to detail all the assignments an accountant undertakes. The framework helps to identify threats – using the fundamental ethical principles as guidance. This approach is preferable to following a set of rules which may not be applicable in a particular case.

Once a material threat has been identified, mitigating activities will be performed to ensure that compliance with fundamental principles is not compromised.

Where conflicts arise in the application of fundamental principles, the code of ethics provides guidance on how to resolve the conflict.

The conceptual framework:

- provides an initial set of assumptions, values and definitions which are agreed upon and shared by all those subject to the framework
- is stated in relatively general terms so it is easy to understand and communicate
- recognises that ethical issues may have no 'correct' answer
- provides the generalised guidelines and principles to apply to any situation.

(b)   **Situation 1**

Ethical threat – dishonesty

Accountants need to be honest in stating their level of expertise – and not mislead employers by implying they have more expertise than they actually possess. In this situation, A is implying he was better at studying for his exams than his actual exam success rate. This may make the potential employer view A more favourably, or enable A to meet a recruitment criteria of 'first time passes only' for success in obtaining the job.

Ethical safeguards

It is difficult to stop provision of incorrect information in this instance. However, A should be following the fundamental ethical principle of integrity in applying for the job. Alternatively, the potential employer could ask all applicants to confirm that information provided is accurate as a condition of employment. Any errors or omissions found later could act as initial grounds for disciplinary action.

Situation 2

Ethical threat – overstatement of profits and salary

B's bonus is determined by the same accounts that B is working on. The threat is that B will overstate profits in some way to ensure that the bonus payable is as high as possible. Again, accountants should act with integrity and honestly, although these ideals conflict in this case with B's remuneration.

Ethical safeguards

The main safeguard will be to ensure that someone other than B determines the amount of B's bonus (and checks the accounts produced) – or that the bonus is not linked to the accounts that B is preparing. This removes the conflict of interest.

Situation 3

Ethical threat – receipt of bribes/gifts

D stands to gain 10% of a contract price by accepting the quote from F rather than another company. This means D's objectivity may be breached because he will be favourably impressed by the quote from F. There is also an issue of confidentiality because presumably D will want to keep the payment 'secret' from E Ltd so his employer does not know of the inducement.

Ethical safeguard

From D's point-of-view, the obvious ethical safeguard is not to accept the bribe. This removes the objectivity issue leaving D free to choose the best system rather than the one with the most financial advantage to him. Alternatively, D can inform the senior management and/or board of E Ltd, provide the relevant information on the three quotes, and let the board make the final decision. Should the board choose F then again D should not accept the bribe.

Situation 4

Ethical threat – Price fixing

In most situations, G would keep the affairs of his client confidential, and would be acting with integrity in taking this action. However, there is a conflict as H and I appear to have been acting illegally; increasing their profits at the expense of their customers. G can either choose to keep quiet about the situation or disclose the information to relevant third parties, effectively 'blowing the whistle' on H and I.

Ethical safeguards

G could report to the ethics committee or audit committee in H, should the company have either of these committees. As long as some appropriate action was taken, then this relieves G from external reporting obligations. External disclosure should only be made after taking into account various issues such as the gravity of the matter, the number of people affected and the likelihood of repetition. As many people are affected and repetition seems likely then external disclosure is likely to be appropriate.

Situation 5

Ethical threat – Incorrect financial information

Accountants need to be able to prepare information honestly and with objectivity. However, in this situation, J is being pressured into producing information which will be incorrect, simply to show K Ltd in a better light. The instruction provides a conflict with J's integrity because he wants to follow the instructions of L but may not be able to do so because this would be dishonest.

Ethical safeguards

J needs to consult with other people apart from L in an attempt to determine the correct course of action. J can consult with any committee charged with governance (e.g. the audit committee or ethics committee) or if necessary take advice from his professional body. If after these discussions, the situation cannot be resolved, J may have to consider resignation.

Tutorial note

Other suggestions for safeguards would have been acceptable and awarded marks.

78   HOGG PRODUCTS COMPANY (DEC 08)

Key answer tips

You could apply some common sense and gain marks for part (a) if you are unable to remember details of the content of a corporate code of ethics.

Part (b) has a bit of an overlap with the P3 syllabus, and is a difficult requirement but any good suggestions will be well rewarded.

Part (c) is the more familiar ground of deontological vs teleological arguments. The key here is to apply to the scenario, and to limit theoretical regurgitation.

(a)   **Purposes of codes of ethics**

- To convey the ethical values of the company to interested audiences including employees, customers, communities and shareholders.

- To control unethical practice within the organisation by placing limits on behaviour and prescribing behaviour in given situations.

- To be a stimulant to improved ethical behaviour in the organisation by insisting on full compliance with the code.

Tutorial note

Other purposes, if relevant, will be rewarded.

Contents of a corporate code of ethics

The typical contents of a corporate code of ethics are as follows.

Values of the company. This might include notes on the strategic purpose of the organisation and any underlying beliefs, values, assumptions or principles. Values may be expressed in terms of social and environmental perspectives, and expressions of intent regarding compliance with best practice, etc.

Shareholders and suppliers of finance. In particular, how the company views the importance of sources of finances, how it intends to communicate with them and any indications of how they will be treated in terms of transparency, truthfulness and honesty.

Employees. Policies towards employees, which might include equal opportunities policies, training and development, recruitment, retention and removal of staff. In the case of HPC, the policy on child labour will be covered by this part of the code of ethics.

Customers. How the company intends to treat its customers, typically in terms of policy of customer satisfaction, product mix, product quality, product information and complaints procedure.

Supply chain/suppliers. This is becoming an increasingly important part of ethical behaviour as stakeholders scrutinise where and how companies source their products (e.g. farming practice, GM foods, fair trade issues, etc.). Ethical policy on supply chain might include undertakings to buy from certain approved suppliers only, to buy only above a certain level of quality, to engage constructively with suppliers (e.g. for product development purposes) or not to buy from suppliers who do not meet with their own ethical standards.

Community and wider society. This section concerns the manner in which the company aims to relate to a range of stakeholders with whom it does not have a direct economic relationship (e.g. neighbours, opinion formers, pressure groups, etc.). It might include undertakings on consultation, 'listening', seeking consent, partnership arrangements (e.g. in community relationships with local schools) and similar.

Tutorial note

Up to six points to be identified and described but similar valid general contents are acceptable.

(b) **Code of ethics and strategic positioning**

Strategic positioning is about the way that a whole company is placed in its environment as opposed to the operational level, which considers the individual parts of the organisation.

Ethical reputation and practice can be a key part of environmental 'fit', along with other strategic issues such as generic strategy, quality and product range.

The 'fit' enables the company to more fully meet the expectations, needs and demands of its relevant stakeholders – in this case, European customers.

The 'quality' of the strategic 'fit' is one of the major determinants of business performance and so is vital to the success of the business.

HPC has carefully manoeuvred itself to have the strategic position of being the highest ethical performer locally and has won orders on that basis.

It sees its strategic position as being the ethical 'benchmark' in its industry locally and protects this position against its parent company seeking to impose a new code of ethics.

The ethical principles are highly internalised in Mr Hogg and in the company generally, which is essential for effective strategic implementation.

(c) **Mr Hogg's belief that employing child labour is 'always ethically wrong'**

Deontological perspective

Mr Hogg is demonstrating a deontological position on child labour by saying that it is 'always' wrong. He is adopting an absolutist rather than a relativist or situational stance. The deontological view is that an act is right or wrong in itself and does not depend upon any other considerations. If child labour is wrong in one situation, it follows that it is wrong in all situations because of the Kantian principle of generalisability (in the categorical imperative). Because child labour is wrong in some situations (exploitative) it must be assumed to be wrong in all situations. The fact that it may cause favourable outcomes in some situations does not make it ethically right.

Teleological perspective

An act is right or wrong depending on the favourableness of the outcome. Ethics is situational and not absolute. Therefore child labour is morally justified if the outcome is favourable (such as the provision of wages for family support). There is an ethical trade-off between the importance of the family income from child labour and the need to avoid exploitation and interfere with education. For HPC, child labour is likely to be cheaper than adult labour but will alienate European buyers and be in breach of its code of ethics. Child labour may be ethically acceptable if the negative consequences can be addressed and overcome.

Tutorial note

Other, equally relevant points made in evaluating Mr Hogg's opinion will be valid. The texts discuss teleology in terms of utilitarianism and egoism. Although this distinction is not relevant to the question, candidates should not be penalised for introducing the distinction if the other points raised are relevant.

	Marking scheme	*Marks*
(a)	For purposes of corporate codes of ethics – 1 mark for each relevant point made	Up to 3
	For contents – 1 mark for description of each identified content area	Up to 6
	Maximum	9
(b)	1½ marks for each relevant point made and explained	Up to 7
	Maximum	7
(c)	For deontological assessment, 1 mark for each relevant point made	Up to 5
	For teleological assessment, 1 mark for each relevant point made	Up to 5
	Maximum	9
Total		**25**

Examiner's comments

Question 4 was the least frequently attempted question on the paper and also the poorest done in terms of marks. It was firmly placed within the ethics area of the syllabus and concerned a range of ethical issues around a corporate code of ethics, child labour in some countries and the use of ethics as part of a company's strategic positioning. The poor quality of many answers to this question suggests that candidates may have some difficulty with this section of the syllabus and this should be a challenge for future candidates and their tutors.

Part (a) was about corporate codes of ethics, which, importantly, are different from codes of professional ethics. The content for this part is clearly covered in both approved texts so I was surprised that candidates overall did poorly on it. There were two tasks: to describe the purposes and also the typical contents of a corporate code of ethics. This was a 'bookwork' question and so should have been well done by any well-prepared candidate. Some candidates confused corporate with professional ethics and introduced the elements of professional ethical behaviour (integrity, etc.) in place of the contents of corporate codes of ethics (policies towards suppliers, customers, etc.).

Part (b) introduced the notion of 'strategic positioning'. The question defined the term briefly although most candidates will already be aware of it from other studies within the ACCA professional examination scheme (especially from F1 and P3).

Many candidates who attempted this part showed some misunderstanding of the term in question ('strategic positioning') despite it being briefly explained in the question itself. The question was referring to the ways in which some organisations use ethical behaviour and ethical reputation as a key part of the way they are perceived by their stakeholders. In the case scenario, a clear message that the company does not use child labour would be a key component of the supply chain ethics of the company itself and anybody who bought from it in Europe.

The final part, **part (c)**, covered the themes of deontology and consequentialism. The requirement was to 'assess' a particular belief (that employing child labour is 'always wrong') from deontological and teleological (consequentialist) ethical perspectives. It was therefore necessary to know what the two ethical perspectives were and also to be able to apply them to the particular belief.

It is fair to say that where candidates did attempt this question, many answers consisted of a page or so of notes containing semi-remembered definitions of the two terms. The fact that some candidates entered into definitions of consequentialism by detailing 'egoism' and 'utilitarianism' demonstrated that the question was either misunderstood or that those candidates were unprepared for this question. Again, I would like this to represent a general challenge to tutors and future candidates to increase the emphasis on the ethics parts of the study guide and the ethical reasoning capabilities in particular. Well-prepared candidates should not only be aware of the ethical theories but also to use them and apply them. It will not be sufficient to merely define: an ability to adapt and apply is also essential.

79 JH GRAPHICS (PILOT 07)

Key answer tips

This question firstly looks at the Donaldson and Preston model of stakeholder motivation and applies the model to the case. Clearly one protagonist is Normative the other Instrumental.

Also this pilot paper indicates to us the importance of Kohlberg's Cognitive Moral Development model – a model your examiner has incorporated into the 50 mark compulsory question on two separate occasions.

Tutorial note

A clear marking scheme here: four marks for normative and four for instrumental. Two marks to describe the model and two marks to apply.

(a)   **Normative and Instrumental**

The normative-instrumental distinction describes two different approaches or underlying ethical motivations. Often applied to the ways in which organisations behave towards stakeholders, it can be applied to any situation in which ethical motivations are relevant.

In the case, Jenny Harris is demonstrating a normative approach to adoption of the corporate code of ethics. It is evident from what she says that she is internally motivated. She described herself as personally driven by high ethical values and appears to see ethical behaviour as an end in itself. She tends not to take the business implications of the proposed code into account and thereby tends towards the altruistic rather than the strategic. Her attitude is informed primarily by internal motivation rather than the pursuit of external reward.

Alan, by contrast, demonstrates instrumental characteristics. He appears to be primarily motivated by business performance and sees the ethical code as a means to further other objectives (not as an end in itself). His attitude to the code of ethics is underpinned by questions about what can be gained, for the business, of the code's adoption. Accordingly, he is strategic rather than altruistic in his motivation.

(b) **Kohlberg's Cognitive Moral Development**

This question draws upon two of Kohlberg's three levels of moral development. In particular, it asks how the decision on possible apology for and withdrawal of the image would vary depending on whether Jenny, as the chief executive of JH Graphics, makes conventional and pre-conventional ethical assumptions.

The conventional ethical level views the moral 'right' according to whether it is compliant with the existing legal and regulatory frameworks and/or norms of the society or culture in which the decision is taking place. If the image was generally acceptable and offensive only to the religious group in question, it can probably be assumed that it was otherwise culturally inoffensive. It was certainly not illegal as no laws were broken. From the conventional level, therefore, there is no case for withdrawing the image.

The pre-conventional moral development level views the moral right as that which attracts the least punishment and the most reward. Whereas in the case of personal morality, such rewards and punishments are likely to be made at the personal level, the issues involved are more complex for organisations. Pre-conventional morality might ask, for example, whether the company is likely to be rewarded or punished by keeping or withdrawing the image. In this context, rewards or punishments are likely to be viewed in economic terms or in terms of boycotts or increased business arising from the publicity.

(c) **Factors to consider**

This is a complicated ethical situation and the board of JH Graphics will be considering several factors in attempting to come to a decision over what to do with the offending image.

One factor likely to be considered is the possible effects of the dispute on the reputation of company. It is not at all certain that the row will be damaging. In some industries, possibly including graphic design, to be seen to be capable of producing provocative and challenging imagery could be advantageous whereas in other situations it may be adverse.

The company will also be likely to take into account the level and direction of public/political opinion and support.

The case mentions that the controversy was a major news story and it would be necessary to find out whether the independent coverage of the issue was generally critical or generally favourable of JH Graphics. If the majority of public opinion was against JH Graphics and supportive of the religious critics, that may be influential in JH Graphics considering the withdrawal of the image.

Consideration should also be given to the economic importance of the advertisement/client to JH Graphics. The case says that the client is happy with the image (and presumably untroubled by the religious controversy) but from JH Graphics's point of view, the question concerns how much they could possibly lose if they unilaterally withdrew the rights to use the image and thereby upset the client.

The board would also be likely to consider the possible direct influence of offended religious groups on JH Graphics. The Mendelow map, which measures the influence of a stakeholder by considering its power and interest, may be helpful in determining how influential the religious group is likely to be on the wellbeing of JH Graphics. Is it, for example, large and potentially influential (e.g. in terms of mobilising opinion) or small and unlikely to have an effect?

The directors should also assess the value of all the unexpected publicity to JH Graphics? Mr Leroy is clearly of the view that is 'was bringing the company free publicity and that was good for the business'. Whilst such a profile raising controversy might be damaging to JH Graphics, it might also be advantageous, especially if being seen as being willing to 'push the boundaries' of taste and decency is a potential source of competitive advantage. The publicity received is obviously far more than the company could afford in terms of buying publicity but this needs to be weighed against whether the publicity is good for JH or adverse.

The national culture in which the decision is taking place could have an influence on the outcome. The intensity of the debate over the importance of not causing offence will vary depending upon the national culture, which can, in turn, be influenced and underpinned by historical and religious culture.

(d)   **Legitimacy of the religious group's claims**

This question touches on the debate over stakeholder recognition and the limits of corporate accountability and responsibility. It is in the nature of any stakeholder that they make a 'claim' upon the activities of the organisation. The debate is over whether that claim is recognised and whether, accordingly, the nature of the claim is taken into account in decision-making.

In this instance, it is relatively uncontroversial to recognise the religious group as a stakeholder (Freeman's definition defines a stakeholder as an entity that can 'affect or be affected by...'). The perceived legitimacy of the claim depends on where the limit of accountability is drawn and the reasonableness of the claim. There is a continuum of legitimacy with, perhaps, shareholders being 'entirely legitimate' in making a claim at one extreme and terrorists as 'entirely illegitimate' at the other. The legitimacy of the religious group's claim (they are unlikely to have a direct economic relationship with JH Graphics) depends upon where that line is drawn. It might also be pointed out that offence taken by a stakeholder doesn't necessarily imply a responsibility towards the stakeholder.

	Marking scheme		
			Marks
(a)	1 mark for each relevant point made on normative		Up to 4
	1 mark for each relevant point made on instrumental		Up to 4
			———
		Maximum	8
			———
(b)	1 mark for evidence of understanding the terms		Up to 2
	1 mark for application of each to case		Up to 2
			———
		Maximum	4
			———
(c)	2 marks for each relevant point made		Up to 10
			———
		Maximum	10
			———
(d)	1 mark for each relevant point made		Up to 3
			———
		Maximum	3
			———
Total			**25**
			———

80 CARPETS AND FLOOR COVERINGS

Key answer tips

To tackle part (a) you will need to start by defining the types of audit being discussed, and then draw out what is different about them. There will be no marks for explaining similarities.

Part (b) is straightforward requirement focusing on the specific type of audit and risks. Part (c) is more challenging since you will not be able to rely on text-book theory. Simply repeating ACCA's code of ethics will not be enough here – you need to think wider as to how they may assist in this situation.

(a) A value for money audit is an audit of economy, efficiency and effectiveness (the '3Es'). The audit investigates an aspect of operations, such as the work done in a particular department, or the work carried out to perform a particular activity (in more than one department). The aim of the audit is to establish the objective or objectives of the operations, and consider:

- whether the objectives are being successfully achieved, and if not what the reasons might be

- whether the operations are being performed in a cost-efficient manner, or whether there is unnecessary and wasteful spending on items of expense

- whether operations are being performed efficiently.

A value for money (VFM) audit of the accounts department might therefore look at issues such as:

- staffing levels in the department, and whether these are too high (resulting in low productivity)
- whether customers pay on time, or whether the debt collection staff give customers too much time to pay, and whether bad debt levels are high. (Poor debt collection procedures and high bad debts would indicate a lack of effectiveness)
- whether the department has spent too much on its computer equipment (resulting in poor economy).

A VFM audit might also investigate part of the accounts department that are not subject to an 'accounting audit', such as the management accounts and the capital expenditure appraisal procedures. For example, a VFM audit might assess the value that is provided by the current management accounting control system (in terms of what it achieves, and whether it does its work efficiently and economically), and whether the benefits justify the costs incurred.

In contrast, an audit of the accounting system would be concerned with the reliability of the accounting records and whether the assets of the company are being properly safeguarded. The audits will therefore consider the reliability of internal controls, and whether the auditors can rely on the effectiveness of those controls. The focus is therefore entirely different. An audit of the accounts is not particularly concerned with efficiency or economy.

(b)   An audit needs to be conducted against a clear set of standards or targets. Since the company intends to publish an annual Social and Environmental Report, it has to decide the criteria against which its performance and policies should be measured.

The key issues should be established. The board of directors should have some idea of what these issues are, but guidance can be obtained if necessary from the company's shareholders, or from external agencies that have been established to assist companies to prepare Social and Environmental Reports (or Sustainability Reports). These sources include the UN's Global Research Initiative sustainability reporting guidelines.

The aspects of social and environmental responsibility that might need to be covered by the report – and audited – include environmental issues (pollution, waste, sustainable supplies of raw materials) and work-related issues (human rights, working conditions, pay, employee education, avoiding discrimination at work, and so on).

A social and environmental audit should be planned within the framework of the company's policies for social and environmental matters and targets for achievement. An audit can then assess whether the policies are being applied and whether progress is being made towards the stated targets (which could be either quantitative or qualitative targets).

Tutorial note

Even if you are not too familiar with the detail of social and environmental audits you can still earn some marks by tackling this section from the perspective of planning any audit.

From the information available, two social and environmental risks are apparent. It is not clear how serious they are, but if they could affect the short-term or long-term value of the company, they should be disclosed in the Social and Environmental Report. (In the UK, listed companies may be required in the future to disclose significant risks, including risks relating to social and environmental issues, in their annual Operating and Financial Review.) The two issues that seem apparent are:

Environmental issues relating to the disposal of old carpets and floor covering. BK currently burns some old materials and disposes of the rest using methods that are not stated. There is an immediate risk that BK is in breach of the law by burning the materials (air pollution and possibly other pollution) and might also be in breach of the laws on disposals of materials. Checking on compliance with the laws should be an element of a social and environmental audit. The company might also be affected by further legal restrictions on disposals (and recycling) of used items.

There are also human rights issues in connection with the possible use of child labour or slave labour by suppliers. Although BK is not directly responsible for the labour policies of its suppliers, a socially responsible policy would be to influence suppliers to adopt different labour policies or switch to different suppliers. If BK is using suppliers who use child labour or slave labour, there will be a risk to the company's reputation. This could have an impact on sales of the company's services.

(c)   From the information available about the dispute, it is not clear whether or not the internal auditor acted ethically.

The ACCA Code of Ethics and Conduct states that an accountant should act with integrity, and should be honest and straightforward in carrying out his or her work. There is a suggestion that this might not have been the case. The executive director accused the auditor of being 'deceitful'. It would also appear that the auditor did not discuss his findings or his concerns with the director or anyone else in the department subject to audit. This would have been inappropriate behaviour, because it would have lacked integrity. An internal auditor is required to look for weaknesses in systems, management and controls, but should discuss issues with the individuals concerned and be straightforward in doing so.

The Code also requires an accountant to act with objectivity, and to be intellectually honest and fair. It is not clear whether the auditor acted in this way, or whether perhaps a personal dislike of the director might have affected his opinions and biased his judgements.

The Code of Ethics and Conduct requires an accountant to show professional competence and due care in his work. The director has accused the auditor of not being qualified for the work. Without further information, this cannot be assessed any further.

It is also possible that the internal auditor was subjected to strong pressure from the director and others in the department to give a favourable audit report, when a more critical report would be appropriate. If this was the situation and the auditor was under pressure from the director, he would have been the victim of an ethical conflict of interest. The ACCA guidelines recommend that in such circumstances, the accountant should report the problem to his superior. However, since the target of the auditor's criticism was a director of the company, it is quite possible that his superior also felt a conflict of interest and inability to stand up to such a senior person.

When an accountant is unable to resolve a conflict of interest by referring the problem to a superior (or the superior's boss), there may be no alternative to resignation. It is possible that this is what happened in this particular case.

In conclusion, from the limited information available, it is not clear who was 'at fault', the director or the accountant (or both of them). However, with more information, it would be possible to judge the matter by reference to the ACCA Code of Ethics and Conduct.

81 JOJO AUDITORS

Key answer tips

Your answer to part (a) will be assisted by any additional reading you have done into the area of the consequences of corruption or bad practice in industry.

Part (b) required candidates to note how the problem arose in the first place and then "describe" four possible safeguards against this happening again. The key here was to describe.

Part (c) required candidates to read the question carefully. This was about individual directors not boards of directors. Remember to justify any points made to ensure that the examiner can see your thought process in making those points.

(a) **Conflict of interest and discuss the consequences**

Conflict of interest

A conflict of interest occurs when a person's freedom of choice or action is constrained by a countervailing interest, which means that the most objectively correct course of action cannot be taken. The discretion to act correctly is fettered by the need to protect a related but contradictory interest. In the case of Jojo Auditors, Jack Hu experienced a conflict of interest between carrying out the agreed policy of dismissing all students assessed as 'poor' (such as Polly Shah) and his familiarity with the Shah family and his making a personal gain from the family in the form of free holidays.

Consequences

Mr Hu *acted against the best interests of the firm* including his fellow partners. In his role as managing partner, he owes it to the other partners, and to the employees and clients of the firm, to act responsibly and always in the best interests of the firm. His conflict of interest prevented this from happening.

In acting as he did, Mr Hu *compromised the other committee members and made them compromise their own professional values.* Both the training manager and the representative from human resources are engaged in order to maximise their benefit to Jojo and as managing partner, Mr Hu 'bullied' them into accepting his view. This decision undermined the training manager and thus circumvented the normal chain of command in matters of student assessment.

He knowingly allowed a technically weak student to be retained thereby potentially *compromising the quality and integrity of the audits* she would work on. He owes a professional duty to the shareholders of the companies that Jojo audits. Audits should be conducted diligently, and technical accuracy should underpin the application of auditing standards and in following procedures and protocols. A technical weakness (such as Polly's) would potentially weaken the effectiveness of the audit and hence be a failure of a duty of care to the client's shareholders.

In acting as he did, Mr Hu *gave the appearance of unfairness and a lack of objectivity.* The appearance of integrity and probity is important in leading organisations and even were it not true, Mr Hu allowed his integrity and objectivity to be seen as questionable. Once discovered to have made the decision he did, confidence in the assessment process at Jojo would have been lost and this could have the effect of damaging its reputation as a provider of training contracts, and therefore in the services provided by the firm.

(b) **Ethical safeguards**

Mr Hu could *undergo some instruction or continuous professional development (CPD)* on the fundamental principles of professionalism and the need to avoid conflicts of interest. As a professional accountant, he is bound in any case by the codes of ethics and/or rulebook of his professional body and the IFAC code. Most of these specifically warn against such conflicts, including the acceptance of gifts unless the value is trivial and inconsequential, and his professional body may provide such a course of instruction.

Enforce a requirement to *declare any* conflicts *of interest* at the beginning of each meeting to consider student assessments. This could be made a 'standing item' on the agenda so that it had to be considered before each time that assessments were considered. The declaration of conflicts of interests could also be made a part of the recruitment process for new partners where appropriate.

Rotate the partner who chairs the assessment committee. This would mean that the chance of Mr Hu being the partner considering Polly Shah's case would be reduced (in the case of Jojo) to one in five. Other partners without the conflict of interest would, in any given meeting, be more likely to be chairing.

Involve an additional partner in the review of student assessments, more able to confront Mr Hu than the training manager or HR manager, neither of whom are at partner level. Another partner would have the organisational 'weight' to confront Mr Hu in a way that the training manager or HR manager evidently did not.

The outcomes of the assessments could be *validated by an external party* (akin to the role that a non-executive director might play if Jojo were a public company). A retired partner could discharge such a role, for example, or a human resources consultant. The final decision on each student would not be made known until each had been 'signed off' by the external party.

Keep an internal HR file *formally recording the list of students by assessment category.* This would make the decision to retain Polly, in spite of her 'poor' assessment, much more visible to relevant business managers. This would apply greater consistency because it would be more transparent that Polly was retained even though her assessment was rated as 'poor'.

Tutorial note

Any reasonable safeguard that addresses the problem would also be allowed.

(c)　**Performance evaluation of partners.**

Criteria for individual performance measurement

The criteria used to measure the performance of directors and/or partners (in a partnership) vary according to the situation. Some criteria will be much more important than others, and highly context-specific criteria may apply in some organisations. In general terms, however, four typical criteria are helpful to consider.

The level of independence of the person (such as being free from external vested interests) and commitment to the public interest. This is especially important in accounting practices where serving the public interest is an important component of professional service.

Preparedness and fitness to practise including maintaining the relevance of skills and undertaking relevant continuing professional development. For the partners and Jojo, this would involve maintaining knowledge of current audit and reporting standards, for example.

Practice, including levels of participation in their allocated roles and their competence in those roles. Linked to this is the contribution made to the formulation and implementation of the organisational strategy.

Contribution to committee work and administrative duties as appropriate. Mr Hu's effectiveness in his role as member of the committee that evaluates student progress would fall within this area, for example.

Tutorial note

If other relevant criteria are included these can be allowed if they are appropriate and relevant to the question and scenario.

Difficulties of individual performance measurement at Jojo

As a privately-owned business, there is no external pressure for such a procedure. This is because, as an unincorporated business, there are no listing rules enforced by a stock exchange and no external shareholder pressures to be applied. There is no agency gap created by a separation of ownership and management.

There is unlikely to be an independent non-executive director (NED) structure in place to support and carry out the performance measurement. Because of the difficulties raised by full-time senior management appraising each other, NEDs take a role in this in listed companies. Without this element of external independent scrutiny, it would be very difficult to maintain independence and fairness in a performance measurement system.

The informality of relationships in a smaller partnership may make objective assessment impossible, especially if, as in a smaller practice, longstanding personal friendships may be a strong component of the culture. With the five partners being personal friends with each other, it would be very difficult for the partners to conduct objective performance appraisals on each other.

There is likely to be resistance from some partners, at least from Jack Hu, who, if appraised, would be likely to receive a poor assessment on some criteria. As the managing partner (the equivalent of a chief executive in a partnership), it would be difficult to arrive at a fair measurement process for Mr Hu without the involvement of external parties (such as NEDs).

ACCA marking scheme		Marks
(a)	2 marks for definition of conflict of interest. 2 marks for each consequence discussed to a maximum of 8 marks. Half a mark for identification only. <div align="right">Maximum</div>	 10
(b)	2 marks for each relevant safeguard identified and described. <div align="right">Maximum</div>	 8
(c)	1 mark for each relevant point on typical criteria to a maximum of 4 marks. 1 mark for each relevant point on implementation difficulty to a maximum of 4 marks. <div align="right">Maximum</div>	 7
Total		**25**

Examiner's comments

In question 3, the case was about the progression of student accountants in an audit practice. One of the students, Polly Shah, was given permission to continue despite being rated as 'poor' in her appraisal. This was against normal practice and it emerged that managing partner, Jack Hu, was a friend of Polly Shah's family.

Part (a) was, accordingly, on conflicts of interest. There were two tasks: to define the term, and then to assess the consequences of Jack Hu's behaviour. Most candidates were able to make an attempt at a definition, but the second task was less well done. Rather than considering the consequences, some candidates continued writing about how conflicts of interest can occur and this was clearly not what the question was asking. It is important to realise that corruption and malpractice in business have serious consequences for a range of people and this question sought to explore some of these consequences. Some of the consequences affected Jack Hu himself, showing that bad practices such as those he demonstrated, are often self-defeating as well as being a very bad example to others.

Part (b) was not well answered overall. It required candidates to consider the problems that had occurred at Jojo and then to describe four ethical safeguards that might prevent a recurrence of the events described. Candidates who reflected on how the events arose in the first place and how these might be addressed, received the best marks for this part. Again, short bullet points with little detail (i.e. no description), were not well rewarded.

The case raised issues about the performance of Jack Hu as a senior manager in the audit practice and these were examined in part (c). In a public company, shareholders are collectively responsible for deciding whether they are satisfied with each director's performance in the job. In the case of a smaller partnership, where partners need to appraise each other, these issues can be a little more complicated.

Again, there were two tasks in part (c): to explain the criteria used to measure the performance of individual directors (not of entire boards) and then to examine the particular circumstances at Jojo to discuss why individual performance measurement might be difficult there. This part was done poorly overall. Perhaps candidates had considered the performance of boards but not of individual directors of those boards.

82 MATTI

Key answer tips

Part (a) – requires knowledge of Kohlberg. As this is an application question to a theory with many different elements, a columnar form of answer is likely to be appropriate. The theory can then be seen clearly beside the application of that theory. Remember to state clearly your reasoning for the examples provided for each level of Kohlberg.

Part (b) – this is one of the 'classic' cases used to explain the Kohlberg theory – amended slightly for this question. It is important to show clearly which CMD level Z and M are working at and again give reasons for your decision.

(a)

CMD Level	Example from
1.1 Pre-conventional – Obedience and punishment Right and wrong is defined according to expected rewards and/or punishment from figures in authority.	The accountant will follow the advice of the senior accountant and not place the provision into the accounts. This unethical decision will be taken because the accountant believes that he will be punished in some way if the provision is made. Being new to MATTI, he may also be unsure on how to follow the recommendations of his superior.

CMD Level	Example from
1.2 Pre-conventional – Instrumental purpose and exchange Right is defined according to whether there is fairness in exchanges – individuals are concerned therefore with their own immediate interests.	The accountant will follow the advice of the senior accountant because he believes that in the future, the accountant will repay this favour in some way. For example, the accountant may believe that he can be late for work one day, or leave early and that the senior accountant will accept this behaviour.
2.1 Conventional – Interpersonal accord and conformity Actions are defined by what is expected of individuals by their peers and those close to them.	The accountant will follow the advice of the senior accountant because this is the way that all other staff acts within the department. Not to follow the suggestion would place peer pressure on the accountant to follow the senior accountant next time. Also, the accountant may not be accepted by his peers (this is a new company) and the accountant will not want to be 'rejected' by this group.
2.2 Conventional – Social accord and system maintenance The consideration of the expectations of others is broadened to social accord in general terms rather than to immediate peers.	The provision is unlikely to be made, but the accountant is verging towards insisting on one being made. The accountant will discuss the issue again with the senior accountant with an aim to understanding in more detail why a standard provision is not being made. He can suggest that in any other company the provision would be made.
3.1 Post-conventional – Social contract and individual rights Right and wrong are determined by reference to basic rights, values and contracts of society.	The accountant believes it is right to make the provision and seeks some method of doing this. For example, he may contact the audit committee and bring the matter to their attention, or even discuss the situation with the finance director. At this stage he will insist that the provision is made.
3.2 Post-conventional – Universal ethical principles Individuals make decisions based on self-chosen ethical principles which they believe everyone should follow.	The accountant believes it is correct to make the provision and activity seeks methods of doing this. If necessary, if the provision cannot be made then he may consider resignation rather than having his moral principles prejudiced by the ethical situation.

Tutorial note

The use of a tabular layout for your answer is acceptable on rare occasions in such a paper as this. It is important to ensure that you still write full sentences and explain your points clearly.

(b)   Z is clearly motivated by the need to improve his son's life. However, Z (presumably) also knows that stealing is wrong. Obtaining the drug without payment could be seen as unethical. In this situation, Z may also consider that it is a basic human right to have a good quality of life, and it is therefore incorrect for the health authority to deny the drug. The 'unethical' action of stealing is replaced by the need to justify his son's moral rights – it can be argued that Z is operating at level 3.1 of Kohlberg.

M is an employee of the hospital and therefore has to follow the rules and regulations of the hospital. If there really are insufficient funds to pay for the drug, then M must accept this, even though provision of the drug would improve the quality of life of Z's son. In this respect, M is following stage 1.2 or 2.1 of Kohlberg.

At stage 1.2 M is expecting an exchange from his employer, the hospital; following the hospital policy on drug provision means that he keeps his job.

At stage 2.1, M is acting in accordance with the expectations of his peers; all doctors presumably know that breaking hospital policy is not possible because the hospital will overspend on drug provision, putting jobs at risk as savings are made elsewhere.

83   BIGGO MANUFACTURING

Key answer tips

It is unlikely that you will be asked to explain all seven positions of social responsibility in a single question in the exam and, as indicated here, much more likely that you will be requested to explain aspects of these key components.

It was important here to read both the question and the case scenario very carefully.

(a)   **Rights and responsibilities**

The comment by Albert Doo identifies rights and responsibilities as being two essential characteristics of citizenship, be it human or organisational in nature. In the same way that individuals have rights and responsibilities in society, so do business organisations such as Biggo. The question asks about rights and responsibilities in the context of Biggo.

A right is an expectation of the benefits that Biggo can receive, by virtue of citizenship, from society. Biggo can expect the right to have the freedom to conduct business by engaging in resource and product markets, to enjoy the protection of the law and the goodwill of other members of society in supporting the right of the organisation to exist, to innovate and grow. Biggo had the right, for example, to expect fair treatment under law in respect of its planning application (and in fact received this permission).

A responsibility is a duty owed, by the citizen (in this case, Biggo), back to society as a quid pro quo for the extension of rights. These are owed by virtue of the citizen's membership of society. In most societies, responsibilities extend to compliance with all relevant laws and regulations, including the payment of taxes, and compliance with the behavioural norms of that society. Biggo, along with all other businesses, has a number of legal and ethical responsibilities but it is the extent to which the ethical responsibilities are recognised that is the subject of dispute along the Gray, Owen & Adams continuum.

Gray, Owen & Adams's perspectives

Gray, Owen & Adams described seven possible positions that can be adopted on a company's relations with its stakeholders. These concern the ethical assumptions of the roles of a business in society and are as follows: the pristine capitalist, the expedient, the social contractarian, the socialist, the social ecologist, the radical feminist and the deep green. The range of views along this continuum are primarily characterised by the ways in which they interpret the rights and responsibilities of business.

Broadly speaking, the nearer to the pristine capitalist end of the continuum, the greater the rights of shareholders and the fewer their responsibilities to a wider constituency. Conversely, the nearer the 'deep green' end of the continuum, the fewer the perceived rights and the greater the responsibilities of the company and its agents to a more widely defined group of stakeholders.

At the 'pristine capitalist' end of the continuum, rights and responsibilities are understood principally in terms of economic measures. The company has the right to pursue its legal business activity and to develop that business with the support of society and the governing authorities. In return, its responsibilities are limited to the profitable production of goods and services and, accordingly, the generation of profits that are entirely attributable to shareholders. It is not the responsibility of businesses to pursue any other social, environmental or benevolent end. In this context, it is clearly not the company's responsibility to use shareholders' money to contribute to the new children's play area.

At the socialist-to-green end of the continuum, it is argued that businesses like Biggo have fewer (and contestable) rights and much greater responsibilities. According to positions at the deep green end, Biggo, does not, for example, have the right to consume non-sustainable resources 'simply' for the purposes of wealth creation. They may not have the moral right, even if they have a legal right, to build on the community's play area. At the same time, Biggo has a wide responsibility to society and to the environment that might seriously constrain their behaviour and activities.

(b)   **The two comments**

Robert Tens is closest to the expedient position. The expedient position is one in which social responsibility is seen in terms of what return can be gained from social responsibility policies and actions. In other words, it may be expedient to adopt social responsibility actions but only if by doing so, it furthers its strategic interests. The expedient position does not recognise any implicit social responsibility as such and social policies are therefore only pursued if a clear strategic rationale can be identified for them.

His comment considers the actions towards the community in terms of cultivating current and future employees: it is an exercise of specific stakeholder management with the key stakeholder being the local community. By engaging in activities that give the appearance of being socially responsible, i.e. making the requested donation, other economically advantageous ends can be achieved. He highlighted three strategic benefits that might arise: it might 'cultivate the company's reputation' specifically in order 'help in future recruitment'. Third, it might 'help to reduce resistance to any future expansion the company might need to make.' He clearly sees the donation in instrumental terms.

Margaret Heggs's comment is closest to the pristine capitalist position. Her comment suggests that she believes that the social responsibilities of Biggo do not extend beyond the social benefits it already provides through employment and the provision of 'excellent products'. The purpose of Biggo is not to engage in costly social responsibility measures such as community donations, even if they can be shown to have a positive strategic benefit. That is not the purpose of a business. In accepting that the company had 'no further contractual or ethical duties to the local government nor to the local community', she was demonstrating a pristine capitalist perspective.

(c)   **SR and short/long term**

Social responsibility

This phrase refers to the belief that companies such as Biggo must act in the general public interest as well as in the specific interest of their shareholders. This can apply to the company's strategy and the way in which the company is governed, but Mr Doo is referring to the specific social footprint that the company has locally. It can also apply to the environmental footprint that a company has, i.e. the effect of company activities on resource consumption or the effect that emissions from operations have. It is possible to interpret this phrase narrowly, as Margaret Heggs has done, or more widely, as Albert Doo has.

Short and long-term perspectives

This question recognises that the attitude that a company may take towards a particular stakeholder claim can vary when a time perspective is introduced.

A short-term perspective is likely to consider a time period of days, months or perhaps up to a given financial year in terms of an action affecting short-term performance. A longer-term perspective, typically looking to years rather than months ahead, is likely to consider the legitimacy of a claim in terms of its effect on long-term shareholder value.

In the short term, Biggo may see the claim from Mr Doo, on behalf of the community, as a cost because a 'sizeable' contribution would have an effect on the profit for the year and hence the return to the shareholders. The case mentions that profits are likely to be low in the current year and so all costs should be carefully scrutinized for value for money and reduced or eliminated if possible. As Biggo is a public listed company, a short-term reduced profit can erode shareholder value because of reduced dividends and a potential reduction in share price.

In the longer term, Biggo can be seen to be cultivating two potentially key stakeholders (Mr Doo and the local community) and hence may create longer term value in terms of the advantages identified by Robert Tens (such as local employees and lower resistance to future factory enlargements). The case mentions the resistance from the local community and, given that the company will have to 'live with' the community for many years to come, it may be in Biggo's long-term strategic interest to do what it reasonably can to reduce any friction with this key stakeholder. There may, therefore, be a strategic case for making the contribution as requested.

ACCA marking scheme		
		Marks
(a)	1 mark each for an explanation of rights and responsibilities, and up to 3 marks each for explaining these in the context of Biggo, to a maximum of 6 marks.	
	Half a mark each for identification of the two ends of the continuum.	
	Half a mark each for explanation of terms (pristine capitalist and deep green).	
	Up to 2 marks each for descriptions of the pristine capital and deep green ends of the continuum.	
	Maximum	10
(b)	1 mark for correct identification of the position of each person to a maximum of 2 marks.	
	2 marks for justification for selecting the position of each person from the case information to a maximum of 4 marks.	
	Maximum	6
(c)	1 mark per relevant point on social responsibility to a maximum of 3 marks.	
	2 marks for recognition of short and long-term perspectives.	
	2 marks for discussion of short-term effects.	
	2 marks for discussion of long-term effects.	
	Maximum	9
Total		**25**

Examiner's comments

This was the least attempted question in section B of the paper. It covered the Gray, Owen and Adams continuum and the idea of social responsibility, both of which are important components of the ethics section of the P1 study guide. The case concerned Biggo Manufacturing, a company that was managing a number of stakeholder issues associated with the construction of a factory extension. It addressed issues similar to those examined in earlier papers where a certain project would have positive and negative impacts.

Part (a) began with what should have been a fairly straightforward requirement, which was to explain the meaning of rights and responsibilities. This is a key part of the citizenship of a business (from study guide section A7d) and is actually also a theme in earlier F-level ACCA papers. The more difficult task was to describe the ways in which rights and responsibilities are interpreted by pristine capitalists and deep greens, these being the two ends of the Gray, Owen and Adams continuum. A common mistake in this question was to list and describe the seven positions on the continuum. Again, a careful reading of the question should have avoided that error.

Part (a) is a good example of how theory (the Gray, Owen and Adams continuum) needs to be applied in a P1 question. It is not sufficient just to know what they are. To gain high marks, candidates also need to be able to use what they know to describe the two positions from a particular perspective, in this case, in terms of what the two positions say about rights and responsibilities.

Part (b) was done better than part (a) overall which was pleasing. In this case, two people were clearly described in the case, and candidates had to use the evidence from the case to identify and justify which of the seven positions best described the two people. Robert Tens was expedient and Margaret Heggs was a pristine capitalist. Where candidates sometimes went wrong was to get Margaret Heggs right but Robert Tens wrong, sometimes identifying him as a social contractarian. Again, a close and detailed reading of the case should have prevented such an error.

Part (c) was sometimes treated as a bit of an afterthought with some answers being very short, despite it being worth 9 marks. There were three tasks: to define social responsibility as used by Albert Doo in the case, and then to examine Biggo's decision about the play area from short and long term perspectives. Most who attempted it were able to gain some of the marks for defining social responsibility. The tasks about short and long term shareholder interests were often not done well. To achieve high marks, candidates had to engage with the case and to show how the decision would have different issues in the short term and, with the management of certain key stakeholders in the longer term.

84   JGP LTD (DEC 10)

Key answer tips

The Brundtland definition of 'sustainability' has been examined previously. Make sure you are able to effectively define and explain what sustainability is.

(a)   **Explain 'sustainability' and criticise the finance director's understanding of sustainability**

Sustainability is the ability of the business to continue to exist and conduct operations *with no effects on the environment that cannot be offset or made good in some other way.* The best working definition is that given by the Gro Harlem Brundtland, the former Norwegian prime minister in the Brundtland Report (1987) as activity that, 'meets *the needs of the present without compromising the ability of future generations to meet their own* needs.' Importantly, it refers to both the *inputs and outputs* of any organisational process. *Inputs (resources) must only be consumed at a rate* at which they can be reproduced, offset or in some other way not irreplaceably depleted. *Outputs (such as waste and products) must not pollute* the environment at a rate greater than can be cleared or offset. Recycling is one way to reduce the net impact of product impact on the environment. They should use strategies to neutralise these impacts by engaging in environmental practices that will replenish the used resources and eliminate harmful effects of pollution. A number of reporting frameworks have been developed to help in accounting for sustainability including the notion of triple-bottom-line accounting and the Global Reporting Initiative (GRI). Both of these attempts to measure the social and environmental impacts of a business in addition to its normal accounting.

The finance director has *completely misunderstood the meaning of the term sustainable.* He has *assumed that it refers to the sustainability of the business as a going concern* and not of the business's place in the environment. Clearly, if a business has lasted 50 years then the business model adopted is able to be sustained over time and a healthy balance sheet enabling future business to take place ensures this. But this has *no bearing at all on whether the* business's *environmental footprint is sustainable* which is what is meant by sustainability in the context of environmental reporting.

(b)   **Stages in an environmental audit and the issues that JGP will have in developing these stages**

Environmental auditing contains three stages.

The first stage is *agreeing and establishing the metrics* involved and deciding on what environmental measures will be included in the audit. This selection is important *because it will determine what will be measured against, how costly the audit will be and how likely it is that the company will be criticised for* 'window dressing' *or* 'greenwashing'. JGP needs to decide, for example, whether to include supply chain metrics as Professor Appo suggested which would be a much more challenging audit. Given that the *board's preference is to be as 'thorough as possible', it seems likely that JGP will include a wide range of measures* and set relatively ambitious targets against those measures.

The second stage is *measuring actual performance against the metrics* set in the first stage. The means of measurement will *usually depend upon the metric being measured.* Whilst many items will be capable of numerical and/or financial measurement (such as energy consumption or waste production), others, such as public perception of employee environmental awareness, will be less so. Given the board's stated aim of providing a robust audit and its need to demonstrate compliance, this stage is clearly of great importance. If JGP wants to demonstrate compliance, then measures must be established so that compliance against target can be clearly shown. This is likely to favour quantitative measures.

The third stage is *reporting the levels of compliance or variances.* The issue here is *how to report the information and how widely to distribute the report.* The board's stated aim is to *provide as much information as possible* 'in *the interests of transparency'.* This would tend to signal the publication of a public document (rather than just a report for the board) although there will be issues on how to produce the report and at what level to structure it. The information demands of local communities and investors may well differ in their appetite for detail and the items being disclosed. Given that it was the desire to issue an environmental report that underpinned the proposed environmental audit, it is likely that JGP will opt for a high level of disclosure to offset the concerns of the local community and the growing number of concerned investors.

(c) **Define 'environmental risk'. Distinguish between strategic and operational risks and explain why the environmental risks at JGP are strategic**

Define environmental risk

An environmental risk is an unrealised loss or liability arising from the effects on an organisation from the natural environment or the actions of that organisation upon the natural environment. Risk can thus arise from natural phenomena affecting the business such as the effects of climate change, adverse weather, resource depletion, and threats to water or energy supplies. Similarly, liabilities can result from emissions, pollution, and waste or product liability.

Strategic risks

These arise from the overall strategic positioning of the company in its environment. Some strategic positions give rise to greater risk exposures than others. Because strategic issues typically affect the whole of an organisation and not just one or more of its parts, strategic risks can potentially involve very high stakes – they can have very high hazards and high returns. Because of this, they are managed at board level in an organisation and form a key part of strategic management. Examples of strategic risks include those affecting products, markets, reputation, supply chain issues and other factors that can affect strategic positioning. In the case of JGP, reputation risk in particular is likely to be one of the most far-reaching risks, and hence one of the most strategic.

Operational risks

Operational risks refer to potential losses arising from the normal business operations. Accordingly, they affect the day-to-day running of operations and business systems in contrast to strategic risks that arise from the organisation's strategic positioning. Operational risks are managed at risk management level (not necessarily board level) and can be managed and mitigated by internal control systems. Examples include those risks that, whilst important and serious, affect one part of the organisation and not the whole, such as machinery breakdown, loss of some types of data, injuries at work and building/estates problems.

In the specific case of JGP, environmental risks are strategic for the following reasons.

First, environmental performance *affects the way in which the company is viewed by some of its key stakeholders.* The case mentions the local community (that supplies employees and other inputs) and investors. The threat of the withdrawal of support by the local community is clearly a *threat capable of affecting the strategic positioning* of JGP as its ability to attract a key resource input (labour) would be threatened. In addition, the case mentions that a 'growing group of investors' is concerned with environmental behaviour and so this could also have *potential market consequences.*

Second, *as a chemical company, Professor Appo said that JGP has a* 'structural *environmental* risk' which means that its membership of the chemical industry makes it have a higher level of environmental risk than members of other industries. This is because of the *unique nature of chemicals processing* which can, as JGP found, have a major impact on one or more stakeholders and threaten a key resource (labour supply). Environmental risk arises from the potential losses from such things as emissions and hazardous leaks, pollution and some resource consumption issues. CEO Keith Miasma referred to this risk in his statement about the threat to JGP's overall reputation. As a major source of potential reputation risk, environmental risk is usually a strategic risk for a chemical company such as JGP.

Marking scheme		
		Marks
(a)	4 marks for explanation of sustainability. 2 marks for criticism of the FD's understanding. Allow cross marking between the two tasks.	6
(b)	3 marks for each of the 3 stages of the audit (1 for explanation of the stage, 2 for exploration).	9
(c)	2 marks for definition of environmental risk. 4 marks for distinguishing between strategic and operational risks (2 for each). 2 marks for explanation of each reason why environmental risks are strategic at JGP to a maximum of 4 marks.	10
Total		**25**

85 BRIBERY

(a) A stakeholder analysis for ZZM's operations within Agriland would enable ZZM to identify the degree of interest and power possessed by each group or stakeholder. As an example, consider both the President of Agriland and a farm worker in one of the co-operatives. Both have an interest in ZZM's business but that of the President is very great whilst the farm workers' is much smaller. Similarly, the power to affect ZZM's business is very high in the case of the President but would be negligible in the case of the farm workers.

Having identified the stakeholders, it would be clear to ZZM whose support it will need in order to be successful. It will also identify any stakeholders who may have the power or potential power to disrupt its business.

Having categorised the stakeholders, ZZM then has guidance as to how it should manage these and their expectations in the future. Mendelow's suggested stances are:

- Minimal effort
- Keep informed
- Keep satisfied
- Must secure agreement – Key players

(b) **Social responsibility**

This phrase refers to the belief that companies such as ZZM must act in the general public interest as well as in the specific interests of their shareholders.

This can apply to the company's strategy and the way in which the company is governed, but in the case of ZZM it can refer to the specific social footprint that the company has within Agriland.

It can also apply to the environmental footprint that a company has, i.e. the effect of company activities on resource consumption or the effect that emissions from operations have.

Short and long-term perspectives

This question recognises that the attitude that a company may take towards a particular stakeholder claim can vary when a time perspective is introduced.

A short-term perspective is likely to consider a time period of days, months or perhaps up to a given financial year in terms of an action affecting short-term performance. A longer-term perspective, typically looking to years rather than months ahead, is likely to consider the legitimacy of a claim in terms of its effect on long-term shareholder value.

In the short term, ZZM may see the donation as advantageous to the company, as it may well help maintain the status quo of a profitable relationship between Agriland and ZZM.

On the other hand as ZZM is a public listed company, a short-term reduced profit, caused by this 'substantial' donation can erode shareholder value because of reduced dividends and a potential reduction in share price.

In the longer term, ZZM could be seen to be cultivating favours from political parties, and the relationship between ZZM and the reigning government could be seen to be improper, hence this may create longer term destruction of shareholder value as ZMM would be exposed to reputation risk.

The case mentions recent allegations of corruption made against the Government, ZZM would have to 'live with' the community for many years to come after the political party has lost power, it may be in ZZM's long-term strategic interest to remain independent, There may, therefore, be a strategic case to reject the request for a donation.

(c) **ZZM could agree to an extra tax on its Agriland operations. This could be used to increase the national minimum wage for farm workers.**

The effect of this tax may make ZZM's business in Agriland uneconomic. Although ZZM is an important part of Agriland's economy, it does not directly employ the agricultural workers. ZZM may consider that this proposal is unreasonable and, if agreed to, may create a bad precedent both within Agriland and also in other countries where ZZM trades.

ZZM should open an agricultural processes factory within Agriland to assist economic development.

The economic viability of this proposal needs to be examined. It could prove to be a realistic option and the contribution which it makes to the development of the economy of Agriland is important.

The President stated that his strategies were not mutually exclusive. He added that if ZZM was not able to help him then he would seriously consider nationalising ZZM operations without any compensation.

Of the three options proposed by the President only the last one seems to be potentially acceptable. The President's further comments suggest that he may be requiring that ZZM agrees to all three proposals and he has also threatened ZZM with nationalisation without compensation.

Taken as a whole, the President's views could lead ZZM to a strategy of its own; withdrawal from Agriland. This would have the disadvantages of the loss of profits from the business in Agriland and the effects upon the economy and people of Agriland. However, depending upon the results of the next general election, or even earlier depending upon the President's actions, ZZM may lose its business anyway.

(d) It is not obvious which option ZZM should follow. It will depend upon a number of factors, including an assessment of the likely results of the next general election and also how much the President's suggestions represent a bargaining stance and how much they are definite plans. ZZM also needs to evaluate changes in social conditions; the rise in militancy within the farm workers and the climate of corruption within Agriland. ZZM should also always have the interests of its shareholders in mind. Against these factors must be set the damage which will be incurred to ZZM's profits and also to the people and economy of Agriland should ZZM withdraw. Based on current information it is recommended that ZZM prepares to withdraw from doing business in Agriland.

86 GRINDLE

(a)   Integrated Reporting (<IR>) is seen by the International Integrated Reporting Council (IIRC) as the basis for a fundamental change in the way in which entity's are managed and report to stakeholders.

After a consultation process, the IIRC published the first version of its "International Integrated Reporting Framework" in December 2013. The <IR> Framework is intended as a guidance for all businesses producing integrated reports.

An integrated report is a concise communication about how an organisation's strategy, governance, performance and prospects, in the context of its external environment. Central to Integrated Reporting is the challenge facing organizations to create and sustain value in the short, medium and longer term. Investors need to understand how the strategy being pursued creates value over time.

Integrated reporting is a process founded on integrated thinking, resulting in a periodic integrated report by an organisation about value creation over short, medium and long term time periods. An Integrated Report should be a single report which is the organisation's primary report – in most jurisdictions the Annual Report or equivalent.

Integrated Reporting demonstrates the linkages between an organisation's strategy, governance and financial performance and the social, environmental and economic context within which it operates.   By reinforcing these connections, Integrated Reporting can help business to take more sustainable decisions and enable investors and other stakeholders to understand how an organization is really performing.

Social capital

This can be described as being concerned with the institutions that help us maintain and develop human capital in partnership with others; e.g. families, communities, businesses, trade unions, schools, and voluntary organisations. The institutions and relationships established within and between each community, group of stakeholders and other networks (and an ability to share information) to enhance individual and collective well-being.

Natural capital

This can be described as any stock or flow of energy and material within the environment that produces goods and services. It is the value that nature provides for us, the natural assets that society has and is therefore not only the basis of production but of life itself. It includes resources of renewable and non-renewable materials. For example:

*   Air, water, land, forests, materials, minerals, energy

*   Biodiversity and ecosystem health.

In addition related aspects include: climate regulation, climate change, emissions, effluents, and waste.

(b)   With the aim of supporting integrated thinking and decision making, <IR> can only be of benefit for the organisations wishing to adopt its principles. The adoption of these principles is conducive to the innovative approach to corporate reporting advocated by governance codes and indeed by Grindle plc and as such matches its reporting objectives.

Integrated thinking is described in the <IR> Framework as "the active consideration by an organization of the relationships between its various operating and functional units and the capitals that the organization uses or affects". This consideration of the relationships which will benefit the long term value of Grindle is compliant with the desire to maximise shareholder wealth and will therefore ease the pressure currently being exerted by the NED's and some of the institutional investors.

The capitals represent stores of value that can be built up, transformed or run down over time in the production of goods or services. Their availability, quality and affordability can affect the long term viability of an organisation's business model and, therefore, its ability to create value over time. The capitals must therefore be maintained and reported on if they are to continue to help organisations create value in the future.

The primary purpose of an integrated report is to explain to providers of financial capital how an entity creates value over time. An integrated report benefits all stakeholders interested in an entity's ability to create value over time, including employees, customers, suppliers, business partners, local communities, legislators, regulators, and policymakers.

With its focus on encouraging integrated thinking and behaviour within the business, Integrated Reporting <IR> leads to a better communication of value, a better relationship between the business and its providers of financial capital and, it is hoped, once it becomes wide spread, a more resilient global economy. <IR> leads to greater market-stability by promoting longer term investment. It leads to robust and resilient business and investment, identified as a major flaw in creating the financial crisis of 2008.

For example, a recent report from the Enhanced Disclosure Task Force of the Financial Stability Board highlighted the direct link between the investor's understanding of corporate strategy and business model, and the value of the business. The cost of capital may also be reduced if investors have visibility over the management's understanding of key risks and likely future performance and prospects.

The objectives for integrated reporting are convincing in their attempt to justify the adoption of this new initiative.

They include:

*   Improving the quality of information available to providers of financial capital to enable a more efficient and productive allocation of capital

*   A more cohesive and efficient approach to corporate reporting that draws on different reporting strands and communicates the full range of factors that materially affect the ability of an organisation to create value over time

*   Enhancing accountability and stewardship for the broad base of capitals (financial, manufactured, intellectual, human, social and relationship, and natural) promoting the understanding of the interdependencies between these capitals

*   Advocating integrated thinking, decision making and actions that focus on the creation of value over the short, medium and long term.

To make decisions over the short, medium and long term, providers of financial capital need to have an understanding of, and confidence in, the business model, as well as greater visibility, historic and future, over how the business creates value over time.

One key concern on behalf of the Grindle board is the potential that <IR> will only add to cost with little perceived benefit. The major cost to businesses from reporting is in the collection of information along with the systems and controls surrounding that process. Most businesses already collect the data that would be expected to be contained in an integrated report either as part of management information or because of disclosure requirements. Therefore, <IR> is unlikely to add to the costs of business.

In addition, it can be reasonably anticipated that, over time, <IR> will lead to greater efficiencies, as duplication is reduced or eliminated due to information "silos" being broken down within the business.

(c)   An integrated report should reference the <IR> Framework and should apply the key requirements as noted below.

These recommended guidelines should be followed unless the unavailability of reliable data, specific legal prohibitions or competitive harm results in an inability to disclose information for the organisation involved.

In addition, the integrated report should include a statement from those charged with governance that it meets particular requirements (e.g. acknowledgement of responsibility, opinion on whether the integrated report is presented in accordance with the <IR> Framework) – and if one is not included, disclosures about their role and steps taken to include a statement in future reports.

(NB a statement should be included no later than an entity's third integrated report referencing the <IR> Framework).

The <IR> Framework sets out several guiding principles and content elements that have to be considered when preparing an integrated report.

Guiding principles – underpin the preparation of an integrated report, informing the users as to the content of the report and how information is presented. These are:

- Strategic focus and future orientation – providing insight into the organisation's strategy, and how it relates to the organisation's ability to create value in the short, medium and long term and to its use of and effects on the capitals. For example, highlighting significant risks, opportunities and dependencies flowing from the organisation's market position and business model.

- Connectivity of information – showing a holistic picture of the combination, interrelatedness and dependencies between factors which affect the organisation's ability to create value over time e.g. economic conditions or technological change.

- Stakeholder relationships – providing insight into the nature and quality of the organisation's relationships with its key stakeholders. It does not mean that an integrated report should attempt to satisfy the information needs of all stakeholders. An integrated report enhances transparency and accountability, essential in building trust and resilience, by disclosing how key stakeholders' legitimate needs and interests are understood, taken into account and responded to.

- Materiality – An integrated report should disclose information about matters that substantively affect the organisation's ability to create value over the short, medium and long term. This is achieved by identifying relevant matters based on their ability to affect value creation, evaluating the importance of relevant matters in terms of their known or potential effect on value creation, prioritising the matters based on their relative importance and determining the information to disclose about such material matters (e.g. risks)

- Conciseness – An integrated report should be concise. It should give sufficient context to understand the organisation's strategy, governance and prospects without being burdened by less relevant information

- Reliability and completeness – An integrated report should include all material matters, both positive and negative, in a balanced way and without material error.

- Consistency and comparability – The information in an integrated report should be presented:

  - On a basis that is consistent over time

  - In a way that enables comparison with other organisations to the extent it is material to the organisation's own ability to create value over time.

Content elements – the key categories of information required to be included in an integrated report under the Framework, presented as a series of questions rather than a prescriptive list of disclosures. For example:

- Organisational overview and external environment – What does the organisation do and what are the circumstances under which it operates?

- Governance – How does an organisation's governance structure support its ability to create value in the short, medium and long term?

- Business model – What is the organisation's business model?

- Risks and opportunities – What are the specific risk and opportunities that affect the organisation's ability to create value over the short, medium and long term, and how is the organisation dealing with them?

(d) It is recommended that Grindle adopt the innovative <IR> approach to maintain its high reputation and objective in the communication and transparency of information to its stakeholders.

The key reasons for this recommendation are primarily related to the objective of integrated reporting i.e. to try to create a more holistic and balanced view of the company being reported upon, bringing together material aspects such as strategy, governance, performance and prospects in a way that reflects the commercial, social and environmental context within which it operates.

In addition, it is anticipated that, over time, <IR> will become the corporate reporting norm. Rather than organisations producing numerous, disconnected and static communications, delivered by the process of integrated thinking, and the application of principles such as connectivity of information.

Finally, integrated reporting is an emerging and evolving trend in corporate reporting, which in general aims primarily to offer an organization's providers of financial capital an integrated representation of the key factors that are material to its present and future value creation.

Professional Level – Essentials Module

Governance, Risk and Ethics

Wednesday 11 June 2014

Paper P1

Time allowed
Reading and planning: 15 minutes
Writing: 3 hours

This paper is divided into two sections:

Section A – This ONE question is compulsory and MUST be attempted

Section B – TWO questions ONLY to be attempted

Do NOT open this paper until instructed by the supervisor.
During reading and planning time only the question paper may
be annotated. You must NOT write in your answer booklet until
instructed by the supervisor.
This question paper must not be removed from the examination hall.

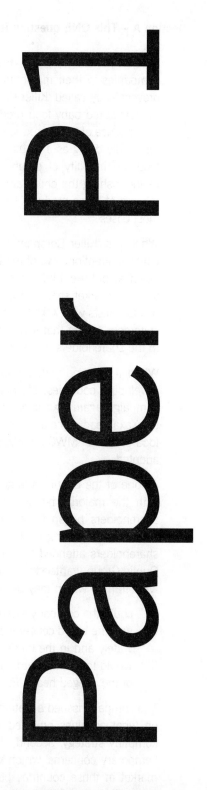

The Association of Chartered Certified Accountants

Section A – This ONE question is compulsory and MUST be attempted

1   Several years ago, World Justice, a well-known charity, published a report on the activities of three major food companies in their marketing of manufactured baby foods in some of the poorer developing countries. The report, provocatively called 'Killer Companies', said it had evidence that the three companies were 'aggressively mis-selling' manufactured baby food products in these poorer countries. It was argued in the report that several problems arose with the use of these products in poorer countries which negatively affected the health of the babies, with many babies reportedly dying as a result. These problems included the use of contaminated water in the preparation of the baby food, an inability of parents to read the instructions, making up product at insufficient concentrations (thereby malnourishing the child) and aggressive selling to health facilities in those countries. Doctors often advised against the use of these products for babies because natural feeding solutions were considered safer and more beneficial in most cases.

When the 'Killer Companies' report was published, it was widely reported upon and received a lot of social and political attention. Two of the three companies named in 'Killer Companies' immediately decided to withdraw from the business but the third company, Xaxa Company (Xaxa hereafter), recognised what it believed to be an opportunity to take the market share left by the other two. It set about increasing its production capacity accordingly. When asked by journalists why Xaxa had not also withdrawn from the criticised business activity, the chief executive issued a press statement saying that it was a profitable business opportunity and, as the steward of shareholder value, he owed it to the shareholders to maximise their returns.

When it became widely known that Xaxa had decided to expand and develop its baby food business in poorer developing countries, Mothers Who Care (MWC), a national charity concerned with infant nutrition, organised a campaign against Xaxa. Strongly believing in the natural feeding of infants, MWC initially organised protests outside the Xaxa head office and also encouraged the public to boycott a wide range of Xaxa products in addition to the baby food products. MWC members started to use the phrase, 'Xaxa kills babies' in the hope that it would become widely adopted.

As one of the country's largest companies and operating in many countries, Xaxa has a large issued share volume with the majority being held by institutional investors. Whilst the overall group profits remained strong, some shareholders began to feel concerned about the baby food issue. One prominent fund manager, Hugh Oublie, organised a meeting for institutional shareholders holding large volumes of Xaxa shares and 50 such institutional shareholders attended the meeting. The group became known as the 'Oublie Group'. Although all members of the Oublie Group wanted to retain their holdings in Xaxa because of the otherwise good returns, a number of questions were framed which they decided to put to the Xaxa management:

(i)   could the company explain the strategic logic of pursuing the baby food business in poorer developing countries?
(ii) was the board concerned about potential reputational damage with phrases such as 'Xaxa kills babies' being used widely and in the media?
(iii) would the Xaxa board consider withdrawing from the baby food business in poorer developing countries because of the alleged health impacts on children in those countries?

The company issued a statement through its investor relations department, replying that the strategic logic was based on what activities provided the most profit to shareholders regardless of the effects on other claims against the company strategy. Second, the board was not concerned with reputation risks because it believed that these were 'temporary concerns' which would soon be forgotten. Third, no, the board would not withdraw from the baby food market in those countries because, with the loss of two competitors, profit margins were likely to be higher and competition less. The Oublie Group expressed its dissatisfaction with this reply and said it might seek to influence the appointment of non-executive directors (NEDs) to the Xaxa board to increase the scrutiny of the executive members and their discussions on the subject.

Hugh Oublie appeared on television to say that he felt the board of Xaxa lacked balance. He said that, although profitable and a good employer in its home country, the non-executive scrutiny of company strategy had been poor for some time and the board had no meaningful sense of ethics at all. He believed that all of the executive board was dedicated to the mission to produce what he called 'profit at any social cost'. He further believed that none of the non-executive board members was strong enough to question the strategy and raise the problem of baby food as an ethical issue. It was this lack of non-executive scrutiny which Hugh Oublie believed was a major cause of Xaxa's unwillingness to reconsider its baby food activity. He said that he had been a long-serving observer and shareholder of Xaxa and he had noticed the company becoming more inward-looking and self-reliant in recent years. He believed this trend was very unhelpful. In addition, he expressed concerns, on behalf of the Oublie Group, about the strategic management of Xaxa and his belief that the board lacked concern for medium-term business risks brought about by the baby food marketing.

As World Justice and MWC continued their campaigns against Xaxa, some other groups became aware of the baby food situation in poorer developing countries. A television programme reported how Xaxa products were actually being used in some of the poorer countries. It claimed to confirm the problems highlighted in 'Killer Companies' and it highlighted a number of other Xaxa products which consumers might stop buying if they wanted to put pressure on Xaxa's management to change their policy on baby food.

Partly in response to these pressures, the Xaxa board decided to consider two new initiatives. The first of these was to consider introducing a corporate code of ethics. By carefully drafting this and placing it prominently on its website, the board believed that it could achieve a number of favourable outcomes including improving its reputation.

The second initiative was to consider instituting a full risk audit system in response to the negative publicity it had experienced, especially from MWC, whose members were considered to be natural customers of Xaxa's other products. Private research commissioned by Xaxa showed that the baby food business was damaging Xaxa's reputation and possibly the willingness of some talented people to apply for jobs with the company. Political support for other company plans had also suffered, such that a recent planning application to set up a new factory by Xaxa, in a business area with no connection with baby food, had received opposition. Protestors, mainly local activists and MWC members, opposed the application with placards saying 'Xaxa kills babies'. Because the idea of risk auditing was a new initiative for Xaxa, the board has asked a local consultancy to produce guidance on the benefits of risk audit and the benefits of an external, rather than an internal, risk audit.

Required:

(a) The underlying principles of corporate governance include transparency, judgement and reputation.

Explain these three terms and assess the Xaxa board's performance against each one. (9 marks)

(b) Explain the purposes of a corporate code of ethics and examine how the adoption of such a code might make Xaxa reconsider its marketing of baby food in poorer developing countries. (11 marks)

(c) Institutional investors are potentially influential stakeholders in a company such as Xaxa.

Required:

(i) Explain why institutional investors might attempt to intervene in the governance of a company.
(ii) Discuss the reasons why the Oublie Group should attempt to intervene in the governance of Xaxa following the events described in the case.

Note: The total marks will be split equally between each part. (10 marks)

(d) Produce notes from the consulting company for the Xaxa board in response to its need for guidance on risk audit. The notes should address the following:

(i) Discuss, in the context of Xaxa, the stages in a risk audit. (8 marks)

(ii) Distinguish between internal and external risk audit, and discuss the advantages for Xaxa of an external risk audit. (8 marks)

Professional marks will be awarded in part (d) for the clarity, logical flow, style and persuasiveness of the notes. (4 marks)

(50 marks)

2 Bob Wong was fortunate to inherit some money and decided he wanted to invest for the long term in one or more investments so he would have a higher income in retirement. He was not a specialist in accounting and had little understanding of how investments worked.

Bob studied an investment website which suggested that he needed to be aware of the level of risk in an investment and also that he needed to know what his basic attitude to risk would be. This meant he needed to decide what his risk appetite was and then select investments based on that.

When Bob studied share listings in newspapers, he noticed that they were subdivided into sectors (e.g. banks, pharmaceuticals, mining, retail). He noticed that some sectors seemed to make higher returns than others and he wanted to know why this was. One website suggested that risks also varied by sector and this was partly explained by the different business and financial risks which different sectors are exposed to.

One website said that if a potential investor wanted to know about any given company as a potential investment, the company's most recent annual report was a good place to start. This was because, it said, the annual report contained a lot of voluntary information, in addition to the financial statements. Bob could use this information to gain an understanding of the company's strategy and governance. The website suggested that the contents of the corporate governance section of the annual report would be particularly helpful in helping him decide whether or not to buy shares in a company.

Required:

(a) Explain 'risk appetite' and 'risk awareness', and discuss how Bob's risk appetite might affect his choice of investments. (8 marks)

(b) Explain 'business risk' and 'financial risk' and discuss why risks might vary by sector as the website indicated. (8 marks)

(c) Distinguish, with examples, between mandatory and voluntary disclosure in annual reports, and assess the usefulness of corporate governance disclosure to Bob in selecting his investments. (9 marks)

(25 marks)

3 Hum and Hoo is an established audit practice in Deetown and has a large share of the audit services market among local businesses. Because Deetown is a relatively isolated area, many clients rely on Hum and Hoo for accounting and technical advice over and above the annual audit. This has meant that, over time, Hum and Hoo has also developed expertise in compliance advice, tax, strategy consulting and other professional services.

Because non-audit work is important to Hum and Hoo, staff have 'business growth' criteria strongly linked with bonuses and promotion. This means that many of the professional accountants in the firm actively seek to increase sales of non-audit services to businesses in the Deetown area, including from audit clients. The culture of the firm is such that everybody is expected to help out with any project which needs to be done, and this sometimes means that staff help out on a range of both audit and non-audit tasks. The lines between audit and non-audit services are sometimes blurred and staff may work on either, as workload needs demand. Managing partner Cherry Hoo told staff that the non-audit revenue is now so important to the firm that staff should not do anything to threaten that source of income.

Cherry Hoo said that she was thinking of beginning to offer a number of other services including advice on environmental reporting and the provision of environmental auditing services. She said she had spoken to local companies which were looking to demonstrate their environmental sustainability and she believed that environmental reporting and auditing might be ways to help with this. She said she was confused by the nature of environmental reporting and so was not sure about what should be audited.

Required:

(a) Explain 'ethical threat' and 'ethical safeguard' in the context of external auditing, and discuss the benefits of effective ethical safeguards for Hum and Hoo. (8 marks)

(b) Explain 'environmental audit' and assess how environmental reporting and auditing might enable companies to 'demonstrate their environmental sustainability' as Cherry Hoo suggested. (8 marks)

(c) Some corporate governance codes prohibit audit firms such as Hum and Hoo from providing some non-audit services to audit clients without the prior approval of the client's audit committee. This is because it is sometimes believed to be against the public interest.

Required:

Explain 'public interest' in the context of accounting services and why a client's audit committee is a suitable body to advise on the purchase of non-audit services from Hum and Hoo. (9 marks)

(25 marks)

4 Mahmood is a junior employee of Tzo Company (a large, listed company). Tzo is a processor of food labelled as containing only high quality meat. The company enjoys the trust and confidence of its customers because of its reputation for high quality products. One day, when passing through one area of the plant, Mahmood noticed some inferior meat being mixed with the normal product. He felt this must be unauthorised so he informed his supervisor, the factory manager, who told Mahmood that this was in fact a necessary cost reduction measure because company profits had been declining in recent months. Mahmood later found out that all stages of the production process, from purchasing to final quality control, were adapted in order to make the use of the inferior meat possible.

The factory manager told Mahmood that the inferior meat was safe for humans to eat and its use was not illegal. However, he told Mahmood that if knowledge of the use of this meat was made public, it would mean that customers might stop buying the products. Many jobs could be lost, probably including Mahmood's own. The factory manager ordered Mahmood to say nothing about the inferior meat and to conduct his job as normal. Mahmood later discovered that the main board of Tzo was aware of the use of the inferior meat and supported its use in seeking to reduce costs and maintain profits. In covering up the use of the inferior meat, the factory produced a fraudulent quality control report to show that the product was purely based on high quality meat when the company knew that this was not so.

When Mahmood heard this, he was very angry and considered telling an external source, such as the local newspaper, about what he had seen and about how the company was being dishonest with its customers.

Required:

(a) **Explain how Mahmood might act, in each case, if he were to adopt either conventional or post-conventional ethical assumptions according to Kohlberg's definitions of these terms. Your answer should include an explanation of these two terms.**   (8 marks)

(b) **Construct an ethical case for Mahmood to take this matter directly to an external source such as a newspaper.**   (8 marks)

(c) Some jurisdictions have a compulsory regulatory requirement for an auditor-reviewed external report on the operation and effectiveness of internal controls (such as s.404 of Sarbanes Oxley).

Required:

Explain how such a requirement may have helped to prevent the undisclosed use of the inferior meat at Tzo Company.   (9 marks)

(25 marks)

End of Question Paper